I WAS WRONG

JIM BAKKER

with KEN ABRAHAM

I WAS
WRONG

THOMAS NELSON PUBLISHERS
NASHVILLE • ATLANTA • LONDON • VANCOUVER

Published in Nashville, Tennessee, by Thomas Nelson, Inc., and distributed in Canada by Word Communications, Ltd., Richmond, British Columbia, and in the United Kingdom by Word (UK), Ltd., Milton Keynes, England.

Unless otherwise noted, Scripture quotations are from THE NEW KING JAMES VERSION of the Bible. Copyright © 1979, 1980, 1982, Thomas Nelson, Inc., Publishers.

Scripture quotations noted KJV are from The Holy Bible, KING JAMES VERSION.

Scripture quotations noted NIV are from The Holy Bible: NEW INTERNATIONAL VERSION. Copyright © 1978 by the New York International Bible Society. Used by permission of Zondervan Bible Publishers.

Scripture quotations noted TLB are from THE LIVING BIBLE (Wheaton, Illinois: Tyndale House Publishers, 1971) and are used by permission.

Heritage USA photographs taken by PTL staff photographers. © Regent Carolina Corp. Used by permission.

ISBN 0-7852-7425-1

Printed in the United States of America

1 2 3 4 5 6 7 — 02 01 00 99 98 97 96

DEDICATION

To my two wonderful children,

Tammy Sue and Jamie Charles,

who never wavered in their love and support

and who gave me a reason to go on when

all hope was gone.

Contents

Acknowledgments

To Tammy Sue and Doug, for giving me the best gift a grandfather can receive—two wonderful grandchildren, my namesake, James Martin, and Jonathan Douglas Chapman.

To my mother and father, sister Donna and brother Norman, who never wavered in their love and support of me.

To my beloved Grandma Irwin, who gave me and taught me unconditional love.

To Dr. Ruth Westrick, a truly great lady and a compassionate, unsung hero of the prison system who fought to give me self-respect.

To all those faithful friends who wrote to me in prison and those who visited me.

To my PTL Partners, who prayed for and supported me throughout the years.

To Tammy Faye, for all she gave to me, especially our two fabulous children.

To all those I hurt and disappointed. Since I can't speak to each of you personally, please consider this my heartfelt apology.

To Dr. Dan Foster, who helped change my life and guided me through the valley of the shadow of death.

To my fellow inmates, who will always be my brothers.

To Paul Olson, Owen Carr, Dave Roever, C. M. Ward, Larry Wright, Bob Gass, and especially Pastor Phil Shaw, who went beyond the call of duty to keep me alive.

To Alan Dershowitz, for winning my appeal, and to the judges who granted it, and to Susan and Jim Toms, for never giving up!

To Professor Jim Albert, his students, and Ben Malcolm for their invaluable work on my case.

To the Honorable Judge Graham Mullen, for reducing my forty-five-year sentence to eight years. I will be eternally grateful.

To the entire Paulk family; and to Carlene Julian, Mike Young, and Bo Foutch; Molly and Bob D'Andrea; Tommy Barnett; and Mike and Heather Wall, for being an extended family to my son when I could not be there.

To all those God used in my life-changing journey, including the journalists, judges, prosecutors, lawyers, and those who testified in my trials.

To Roger, for teaching me so much, especially how to catch a ball.

To the kind guards, who helped make life a little better, and the unkind guards, who drove me closer to God.

To Shirley Fulbright, for all her hard work on this book and for standing with and helping our family for two decades.

To Sam Moore, Byron Williamson, Rolf Zettersten, Rick Nash, Ted Squires, Melanee Bandy, Bob Bubnis, and the team at Thomas Nelson Publishers, for believing in this book.

To Lonnie Hull Dupont, whose tenacious editorial skills were like those of a kind surgeon, wielded with charm, wit, and compassion.

To Doc, for teaching me how to clean toilets and for being a good friend when I needed one desperately.

To Billy and Ruth Graham, who demonstrated God's love to me, giving me dignity when my self-worth was zero.

To Franklin Graham, who risked so much to reach out and minister to me.

To the unknown guard.

To Ken Abraham, my patient, kind, long-suffering, gentle friend who used his skills to craft this book and tell my story.

Most of all, to my best friend, who never left me . . . Jesus!

Introduction

THE WORDS "I WAS WRONG" DO NOT COME EASILY TO ME.
For most of my life I believed that my understanding of God and
how He wants us to live was not only correct but worth exporting to
the world. One reason I have risked putting my heart into print is to
tell you that my previous philosophy of life, out of which my attitudes and actions flowed, was fundamentally flawed. God does not
promise that we will all be rich and prosperous, as I once preached.
When I really studied the Bible while in prison, it became clear to me
that not one man or woman—not even prophets of God—led a life
without pain. God does promise that He will never leave us or forsake us, no matter what trial or pain we must go through . . . whether
it be loss of reputation, loss of position or power, financial calamity,
addiction, separation, divorce, or imprisonment.

It is important to understand that some people who have played
key roles in my life have described events and circumstances discussed within these pages in radically different terms. Both friends
and foes have written books and given interviews to the media, and a
few have even given sworn testimony before judges. In doing so, they
have presented their stories from their perspectives. That is their prerogative. This book is written from my point of view and represents
how I saw events transpire that toppled me from the pinnacle of PTL
power and eventually put me in prison.

Admittedly, I would have been much happier to skip some of the
information within this book. I had no desire to relive many of these
experiences. Dredging up and facing for the first time many of the

things that were said and done during the pivotal days of PTL's demise was extremely difficult for me. Yet that was nothing compared to the torturous task of going back through the emotional breakdown during my trial and my first frightening experiences inside prison walls.

At several points during the writing of this book, I was ready to quit. I don't need to write a book. I do not have any axes to grind with anyone. What is in the past is over and done, and I am ready to move on with my life. Only the conviction that I owed this book to my family, friends, and the many dedicated former PTL staff members and PTL Partners, along with the confidence that God could use this volume for good, kept me going.

I hope that when you have finished reading these pages, you will have a better understanding of how and why I did things at PTL, in prison, and beyond prison's gates. More importantly, I hope that the lessons I have learned the hard way will be helpful to you. I trust too that my story will be preventive medicine for some. The mistakes I made are still being perpetuated in ministries, churches, businesses, marriages, and families. The temptation to have more, do more, earn more, build bigger, emphasize material things rather than spiritual, protect the image regardless of the cost, look the other way rather than confront wrong—these are just a few of the areas in which I have a new mindset, which I hope will be helpful to you.

I did not want to sugarcoat my story, but in some instances, with the help of the editorial team at Thomas Nelson Publishers, I have purposely sanitized certain parts of the account to avoid unnecessarily offending anyone. It is impossible to overemphasize the horror I felt when I was placed in an asylum after my collapse during my trial in 1989 or the dehumanization that I experienced in prison. Similarly, the lifelong impact and the fear of exposure I felt as a result of being molested as a child cannot be told too emphatically. While I have tried to stay within the realms of decency and discretion, please know that one's worst nightmares frequently become reality in prison, and I can give you only a shrouded glimpse into what I experienced.

To be sure, certain information in this book has been culled from other sources. Facts relating to my emotional breakdown, for example, obviously were supplied to me by the doctors, media personnel, and other witnesses. I was in no condition to chronicle anything, and to this day, many of the details remain hidden from me, embedded somewhere in the corners of my brain. Similarly, information regarding what happened at PTL after my resignation in 1987 was supplied to me in massive doses by friends, family members, and former employees. In all cases, any facts to which I could not personally attest veracity were corroborated by at least two credible sources, and usually three or more. My editorial team and I have meticulously researched any information that was not firsthand. This is an accurate story insofar as it can be told without destroying more lives. To prevent further pain, some names of people who are not public figures have been changed. In other cases, to shield the identities of real individuals, I have purposely created composite characters. Be assured, however, that these are stories of real people; the events recorded within these pages actually happened.

In many ways I have written this book with much trepidation, because in it I have attempted to tell the true story without violating the principles of forgiveness. It took nearly five years in prison for me to fully forgive others and to accept forgiveness for myself. I have no desire to uncover what God has laid to rest. Yet I have felt compelled to write this story to show you that, in the darkest moments of my life, God was there, even when I thought He had abandoned me. And I know that if God did not leave me in my time of trouble, He will not leave you when you walk through your deepest valleys.

I have been branded for life by the events you will read about in this book. Strangely, perhaps, I would not have it any other way. Through it all I have come to trust God more than ever before. By no means do I feel that because of my experiences I have arrived. On the contrary, I am in process; my restoration continues on an ongoing basis. I am a fellow struggler, living one day at a time, along with the millions of other people in the world whose lives have been decimated and who are now involved in the various stages of healing and rebuilding. For that reason, in this book I offer no simplistic solutions to difficult problems. Instead, what you will find is an irrepressible confidence that no matter how dark your day might be, you can make it, because God loves you. He really does.

1

Judgment Day

JUST BEFORE THREE O'CLOCK ON OCTOBER 24, 1989—THE day of my sentencing—Judge Robert Potter furrowed his brow and bowed his head slightly as he lowered his voice to a mumble. The crowd in the U.S. district courthouse in Charlotte, North Carolina, collectively leaned forward in an attempt to hear the judge's words. Judge Potter was known in the Carolina court system as "Maximum Bob," a nickname he had earned for his tendency to hand down the longest sentences allowed by law. Few in the courtroom that day expected him to deviate from his normal pattern.

It had already been a difficult afternoon. The sentencing procedures had begun promptly at 2:00 P.M., but by the time my lawyer, Harold Bender, and the Federal prosecutors, Deborah Smith and Jerry Miller, had completed their final presentations, it was 2:55 P.M. Now, after two and a half years of uncertainty concerning my future, it all came down to one man's opinion of what should be done with me.

It had been a tempestuous trial that received more pretrial publicity than any trial in Charlotte's history. Judge Potter had personally seated a jury for the case in one day. Once under way, one witness fell off the stand and was thought to have died. I collapsed the following day, and the judge shipped me off for psychiatric evaluation. When the trial resumed, it was interrupted again, this time by Hurricane Hugo, which ripped into the Atlantic coastline at Charleston, South Carolina, and struck nearly two

hundred miles inland, all the way to Charlotte, a rare meteorological phenomenon. The hurricane was one of the worst in history, devastating
thousands of homes and damaging millions of dollars' worth of property.
In Charlotte, my trial was postponed for several days.

I had been charged with fraud and conspiring to commit fraud for
allegedly receiving $158 million from 152,903 PTL Lifetime Partners dur-
ing my tenure as president of Heritage USA, a four-square-mile Christian
retreat center operated by Heritage Village Church and Missionary
Fellowship in Fort Mill, South Carolina. Heritage USA was intended to be
a modern version of the old-time camp-meeting grounds that had so profoundly shaped America's heritage during the eighteenth and nineteenth
centuries. The primary means of presenting the ministry and message of
Heritage USA to the world was our television program, variously known
as *The PTL Club, The Jim and Tammy Show,* and other names. From its
meager beginnings in a storefront studio in downtown Charlotte, *The PTL
Club* grew to become the flagship program of the Inspirational Television
Network, a satellite network which, at its peak, aired in more than fourteen million homes in the USA and around the world.

If *The PTL Club* was the inspirational mouthpiece of the ministry, the
PTL Lifetime Partners were the spiritual and financial backbone of Heritage
USA and the Inspirational Television Network. Nearly all the ministries at
PTL, including the television programs, were funded primarily by donations
from the viewers. Anyone who donated any gift at all to our nonprofit, tax-
exempt organization was known as a "partner" in ministry with us.
Absolutely no legal obligations or connotations were connected to the term
partner. It was simply our term for what another charitable organization
might call a financial donor or a contributor.

The PTL Lifetime Partners, however, were a group of people who
wanted to do more to support the ministry than send an occasional contribution. They wanted to be "partners" in our ministry for the remainder
of their lives; many of them wanted to come to Fort Mill and be on the
grounds to enjoy and become involved in the ministry, and they expressed
that desire in a tangible way.

Most of the PTL Lifetime Partners donated a one-time gift of one
thousand dollars to PTL. Those who did were offered lodging free of
charge for four days and three nights at the Heritage Grand Hotel, the gorgeous five-hundred-room luxury hotel constructed in 1984 on the
grounds of Heritage USA. It was this program (which I will explain in
greater detail later in this book) that eventually led to the government's

charges of fraud against me, and conspiracy to commit fraud along with one of my top executives.

The government purported that I had knowingly "overbooked" the lodging space at Heritage USA by continuing to encourage people to become Lifetime Partners beyond the point at which we were able to accommodate them. The government maintained that we were trying to dupe some of our most loyal financial supporters out of their money. Because I had promoted the program on television, I was charged with wire fraud. Because I had promoted the program through our brochures, newsletters, and other written materials that had been sent through the mail, I was charged with mail fraud. Since I had ostensibly done these things with the mutual consent and knowledge of my senior executive officer, he and I were charged with conspiracy to commit fraud.

Much of the case, however, revolved around my lifestyle. The government took three weeks to build their case against me, calling ninety-one witnesses, twenty-two of whom did not even speak to the issue of fraud, but who were apparently on the stand simply because I had made an "extravagant purchase" from them. When it was the defense's turn, however, Judge Potter complained, "It's getting ridiculous now," after two days of testimony on my behalf.

I felt that my lawyers did little to defend me against the government's charges. They spent most of their time trying to discredit the prosecution's witnesses, showing to the jury that the PTL Lifetime Partners trusted me. One juror later stated that throughout the trial, she kept waiting to hear my defense. It never came.

In a last-ditch effort I took the stand on my own behalf, hoping to convince the jury that just as I had said over the air and through the mail, we were in fact building enough facilities to house the Lifetime Partners. I had pinned most of my hope on a chart that I had made myself, which depicted the progressive growth of the Lifetime Partners program and facilities. I had planned to present the exhibit to the jury, but the judge ruled that I could not present it because substantiated facts and evidence must precede the introduction of a chart to the jury. I had submitted the required substantiating evidence, including PTL newspapers, magazines, blueprints, and promotional literature, which would have shown the progression of the Lifetime Partnership program and that the PTL Partners had been well informed concerning it. Unfortunately, my lawyers had simply placed the materials into evidence in a pile, without reading a shred of it to the jury during the trial. Therefore my chart depicting the information was inadmissible as an exhibit.

3

Judge Potter allowed me to place my chart out of the sight of the jurors, at my feet, so I could refer to it during my testimony, as long as the jurors could not see it. I presented the information, looking down at the chart, rather than at the jurors. My efforts to communicate were totally ineffective.

Ironically, my one last glimmer of hope was that the prosecutors would vigorously cross-examine me. I was ready for them. I knew what I had done and not done at PTL. But after only a few inquiries, the prosecutors announced, "No further questions."

My heart sank. I knew that I had not gotten my story across at all. At that moment, I felt certain I had lost the case. Few people were surprised when on October 6, 1989, the jury foreman announced "Guilty as charged" to all twenty-four counts.

Then, a mere nineteen days later, I was back in court to receive my sentence. Prior to pronouncing my sentence, Judge Potter commented on my character. I felt that he had shown contempt toward me throughout the trial, and in his concluding remarks, the judge said, "He had no thought whatever about his victims, and those of us who do have a religion are ridiculed as being saps from moneygrubbing preachers or priests." Although Judge Potter's comment would come back to haunt him later, at that moment, it sliced deeply into my heart and the hearts of my few friends and family members who were able to get into the courtroom that day. Looking back on that moment today and considering the information Judge Potter had before him, if I had been the judge, I would not have liked Jim Bakker either.

I was instructed to rise by my lawyer, and as I did, Harold Bender draped his arm around my shoulder. Terry Wilkinson, Harold's paralegal, placed her arm around the small of my back. It was as though my lawyers were trying to brace me for what was coming.

Judge Potter paused briefly, looked down from his elevated bench, and then in his usual muffled, gravel-toned voice began reading my sentence. The entire courtroom seemed to strain forward to hear what he was saying. Even standing only a few feet in front of the judge, I could not discern what he said.

The judge rattled off my sentences with machine-gun rapidity. "On counts One and Two, I sentence you to five years to be served concurrently. On counts Three and Four, I sentence you to five years to be served concurrently. Counts Five and Six, five years concurrent. Counts Seven and Eight, five years concurrent. Counts Nine through Eleven, five years concurrent. Counts Twelve through Fourteen, five years concurrent.

Counts Fifteen through Seventeen, five years concurrent. Counts Eighteen through Twenty-three, five years concurrent. Count Twenty-four, five years."

In a matter of seconds, it was done; the judge's words were on record, words that began my prison years . . . years that would bring the greatest pain, fear, and loneliness I have ever known.

Judge Potter stopped the proceedings long enough to allow reporters to exit the courtroom if they wanted to leave before he entertained any further motions. Thirty-eight of the forty-member press corps bolted out the door, racing to their cameras, microphones, and telephones. Hundreds of other members of the press, who were forced to wait outside due to the space limitations of the courthouse, screamed eagerly for scraps of information from the reporters tearing from the building. News desks around the world suddenly were trumpeting the news: *Bakker Gets Forty-five Years!*

Inside the courtroom, I still did not understand what had happened. I turned to my lawyer and asked what the judge's words meant.

My lawyer replied in what seemed to me a matter-of-fact manner. "Forty-five years."

Forty-five years! I was stunned. I felt as though a huge wrecking ball had dropped on top of me. Every bone in my body felt like it had been pulverized, yet I continued to stand expressionless before the judge. For a moment, I thought I might collapse right there in the front of the courtroom. The emotional pain was so intense, my body gradually slipped into a state of shock.

My daughter, Tammy Sue, was seated in the first row beyond a railing right behind me. I heard Tammy Sue gasp; she let out a loud cry and then began to sob uncontrollably.

Judge Potter rapped his gavel several times and called out, "Order in the court! If there is not silence in the courtroom, or if there are any more outbursts, I will have the entire courtroom cleared."

To avoid antagonizing Judge Potter further, Gene Kennett, a minister friend of mine sitting next to Tammy Sue, attempted to quell the sounds of her sobbing by pulling my daughter toward him so her face was buried in his shoulder. She continued to cry.

I wanted to hold her and tell her everything was going to be all right as I had done so many times when she was a little girl. But I had to let my daughter pour her grief onto the shoulder of a person she barely knew. I wished it were still earlier that day, when Tammy Sue had hugged me and told me she loved me as we walked into the courthouse together.

Tammy Faye, my wife of thirty years, was not in the courtroom during my sentencing; she was in Orlando trying to keep our fledgling ministry alive. The stress and strain of the past three years had taken a severe toll on Tammy Faye, and by this time, she was emotionally unable to handle much more. My thirteen-year-old son, Jamie Charles, now grown-up enough to wear my clothes when he had come to be with me during the trial, also stayed home to take care of his mother. We were all emotionally exhausted.

I had planned to stay in a Charlotte hotel room near the courthouse the night before my sentencing. Tammy Sue decided she didn't want me to spend the night alone, so she, her husband Doug, and their nine-month-old baby James—my grandson and namesake—all moved into my one room at the hotel near the courthouse. I was glad for their company.

Baby James especially helped me to keep my mind off the ensuing sentencing. I fed James his bottles throughout the night and took him from his crib and held him close to me all night long. My first grandchild was a bright spot in my rapidly darkening world.

The following morning I carried James in my arms as I stopped at my lawyer's office on my way to court. I was so attached to my grandbaby, I did not want to let go of him. I wanted to take him with Tammy Sue and me to the sentencing, but my lawyer said, "It would be very offensive to the court to have a baby in the courtroom."

On Tuesday afternoon, just after Tammy Sue and I entered the federal courthouse, a rainbow appeared in the sky. Journalists and the crowd of onlookers awaiting Judge Potter's sentence stared and pointed at the unusual sight. *The Charlotte Observer* later described the rainbow as "a multicolored halo—created by the refraction of sunlight through ice crystals in the wispy, cirrus clouds," forming a quarter of a circle around the sun.[1]

The rainbow remained in the sky from the time I went inside the courthouse until shortly after Judge Potter passed down my sentence. However, I never saw it.

Now the judge was ready to entertain further motions. Attorney Harold Bender immediately announced that we would be filing an appeal and asked Judge Potter to release me on bail, pending our appeal. Bender insisted that I was not a flight risk, that it would be highly unlikely that I would try to escape incarceration because I was so recognizable nationwide. Furthermore, the media reporters were already watching my home twenty-four hours a day. The essence of Harold's argument was, "Everybody knows who Jim Bakker is, so where can he hide?"

Throughout the trial, the prosecution, on the other hand, had painted a picture of me as a menace to society and to myself. The prosecution persisted in characterizing my friends and especially the PTL Partners, people who had supported PTL with their prayers and donations, as mindless, easily manipulated cult members who might attempt to spirit me out of the country. On the day my verdict had been read, Potter himself expressed an opinion that the supporters who had testified on my behalf in court were so zealous in my defense that they had what he described as a "Jim Jones mentality."

To counteract that impression, at the sentencing hearing, Harold Bender had called several character witnesses to speak on my behalf, including my brother Norman, who had attended nearly all six weeks of my trial. Norman and the others had spoken lovingly, making their case as to why I should be released on bail pending my appeal.

But Judge Potter would have none of it and abruptly broke off all further comments. I had been sitting at the defense table at the front of the courtroom, half-listening to the words of those speaking, and half-stunned by the realization that the forty-five-year sentence I had received, when added to my current age of forty-nine, was essentially a life sentence—but to me it felt more like a death sentence.

Now Judge Potter said, "Mr. Bakker, I order you to report to Federal prison immediately. Marshals, take the defendant to lockup until you can arrange to transport him."

It suddenly hit me: I was going to prison! Not someday, not next month after I had been allowed time to set my affairs in order, as is often permitted in white-collar cases. I was going to prison *today*. Right now!

I turned to reach out to the apple of my eye, to hug my little girl. Of course, Tammy Sue was no longer a little girl, but a grown, beautiful woman with her own husband and baby. But at this moment, she looked so fragile. Tammy Sue reached out to me and I embraced her with all my heart. Tears streamed down her delicate face, yet I felt helpless to take her pain away. The dad who was always able to make things happen was being pulled away by a Federal marshal and could do nothing to help his daughter.

I quickly removed my watch and placed it in Tammy Sue's hand. "I love you, Susie!" I whispered hoarsely. "I have to go now."

"I love you, Daddy." I could still hear her crying as the marshals led me from the courtroom.

The marshals escorted me down the hall, through several doorways, and finally into a room with a series of steel-barred cells. They unlocked a small, narrow cell with benches lining both sides. A strange looking exposed metal commode, with a sink atop the bowl where the water tank should have been, sat at the rear of the room. I walked inside the cell and sat down.

One of the marshals passed my travel clothes through the bars and instructed me to change. My attorney had warned me prior to my sentencing that there was a real possibility I could be going to prison and suggested I bring a change of comfortable clothing to court. Although I decided to heed his advice and pack an outfit of clothing, I never truly dreamed that I would need them. In my worst-case scenarios, I figured that even if the judge sentenced me to prison, he would surely allow me to return home to say good-bye to my family.

I had entered the courtroom on October 24 wearing one of my favorite, well-tailored suits. Little did I know that this would be the last day for years I would wear a fine suit of clothes.

As I reached through the bars of the tiny cell deep within the recesses of the Federal courthouse, I felt strange accepting the hanger holding my travel clothes. I took off my tie and coat and changed into my blue jeans and removed my white dress shirt and replaced it with a casual, deep blue shirt. I slipped on my favorite tennis shoes. Finally, I put on a bright royal blue corduroy jacket with squared shoulders. The jacket was one of my favorites. In selecting my wardrobe for that day, whether I believed I would wear the items or not, I had unconsciously chosen familiar, favorite clothing for a sense of security.

About that time the marshals came and unlocked my cell and took me across the hall to a small, closetlike room where I spent a few minutes talking to my lawyer, who could now only converse with me through a tiny opening from the other side of a glass window. The marshal gave Harold my wallet and clothes to give to my family for me.

Harold tried to be encouraging as best he could. "Don't worry, Jim," he spoke quietly. "We're going to appeal this. We'll get you out of there. You won't be gone for long. I'll come visit you soon and let you know how things are going."

I stared blankly back at Harold Bender. If I had any hope that his words were accurate, it was quickly slipping away.

"Good-bye, Jim," Harold said, showing little sign of emotion. Harold seemed to me as nonchalant as he might have been had I been going off on a brief vacation. But I was leaving to begin a forty-five-year prison sentence! Perhaps he was simply trying to cheer me up.

The officers then took me down to the end of the small cell block where there was a camera and equipment for fingerprinting. A marshal there took my hand and placed my fingers, one at a time, onto a black ink pad, and then rolled each finger onto the appropriate square on a card. He did the same with both of my palms.

Another marshal ordered me to stand against the wall to be photographed. I made a conscious commitment to smile in every picture anyone ever took of me in prison. Even though my heart was breaking, I was determined that I would smile for the record. And I did! While serving my sentence, I did time in ten separate prisons, jails, and holding units. Most of these facilities took pictures of me upon entering their institution. I smiled in every single picture. Occasionally I would hear an officer say, "Take a few extra shots." I'm not sure what they did with the extra copies, but I suspect they will show up someday.

The marshals at Charlotte Federal Courthouse took my photograph with the numbers that would accompany me everywhere I went within the prison system. In a matter of moments, I had ceased to be Jim Bakker; I was now Inmate 07407-058.

Little did I know that I was entering a whole new society, with its own hierarchy, rules, and even vocabulary. Nobody prepared me for what I was about to face in prison.

The marshals returned me to my cell where I sat for nearly two hours, numbly staring at the bars. Suddenly I could hear the sound of rattling chains.

They were for me.

An officer fastened the chains around my waist; my hands were handcuffed and fastened to the chain. My feet were cuffed with manacles and chained together. The marshals opened my cell and led me, shuffling as fast as I could move, down a corridor and out several doors until we stepped outside into the fresh air. The courthouse had at one time been a post office, with a large loading dock in the rear of the building. Whether it was standard procedure or to avoid publicity and commotion, the marshals had decided to take me out by way of the loading dock.

The word had already gotten out that the marshals would be bringing me out the back way. The area behind the courthouse was actually twenty-five to thirty feet below street level with sidewalks above surrounding the huge pit in the ground, creating a crude amphitheater-like setting. Our "getaway car" was parked at the bottom of the amphitheater, flanked in front and back by police cars.

As soon as I came out the door, I looked up and saw people standing all around the ledge above the amphitheater. Members of the press with their cameras crowded in next to the railings, trying to get one last picture of me in what appeared to be total defeat.

I recognized several faces as I scanned the crowd. I saw many curious onlookers, a few hostile faces, but mostly I saw friendly faces. Some of the people waved at me and called out words of encouragement. I tried to wave back, but my chains prevented me from doing so. I smiled and nodded at them; that was all I could do.

The marshals led me down the steps from the loading dock to the car and then guided me into the rear seat. As the marshals' car climbed the ramp to the street level, I caught a glimpse of one of my longtime employees, a dear, motherly sort of friend, who was standing by herself along the rail weeping. I tried to wave good-bye but could not stretch my chained hands to the window level. She was the last supportive human being I saw as I left Charlotte.

The police escorted us out to the interstate highway. The last time I had received a police escort in Charlotte, our PTL television program had just won a Dove Award from the Gospel Music Association in Nashville. Upon returning to Charlotte, the plane on which Tammy Faye and I were traveling was running late. We were trying to get to our live TV broadcast on time and the Charlotte police escorted us from the airport to our studio.

As the police escort led the way, I tried not to think about the painful parallels between the better days at PTL and what I was experiencing now. Hardly had I made that determination when I looked up and noticed that we were passing a road sign indicating the route to McAdenville, North Carolina.

McAdenville is a wonderful little town with a big Christmas spirit that had contributed to my inspiration to develop "Christmas City" at Heritage USA. Each year during the Christmas season, the people of McAdenville decorate their homes, stores, and trees with thousands of Christmas lights. This beautiful spectacle attracts thousands of appreciative sightseers and greatly enhances the Christmas spirit in the area.

As I passed the sign, I could not help recalling that about this time in previous years, our creative "Christmas City" staff at PTL would have been putting the finishing touches on our decorations. The trees throughout Heritage USA were adorned with 1,250,000 lights. Besides the celebration of lights, our staff created dramatic productions such as a "Living Nativity," featuring Mary and Joseph, the wise men, and baby Jesus, as well as dozens of live animals including sheep, goats, horses, and even three camels!

We also enjoyed "Angel Boulevard," an amazing display of angels depicted in lights all the way down the road behind the five-hundred-room Heritage Grand Hotel and the almost completed five-hundred-room Heritage Grand Tower. A huge lighted Christmas tree sat atop the twenty-one-story Tower. According to a national bus-tour association, Christmas City became one of the top Christmas attractions in the United States. The Heritage USA security department recorded over one million visitors during the 1986 Christmas season alone.

Memories of Christmas City only served to exacerbate the darkness that was enveloping my soul. As I peered out the window through the cage separating me from the marshals in the front seat of the car, everything within me wanted to scream.

All my life I had dreamed of building a center of inspiration that became PTL. Now, however, I honestly wondered if in fact it had not all been a colossal mirage. Was it real or had I merely imagined that I had once been the president of a worldwide ministry known as PTL? Maybe I had never implemented any ministry at all. Had I really been the host of a television program seen in all fifty states and many foreign countries? With the help of my dedicated staff and thousands of other people, had I truly spearheaded the building of a twenty-four-hour-a-day Inspirational Network?

Perhaps I had never received any divine inspiration to build anything at Heritage USA. And what of Fort Hope, a community designed to welcome homeless people; the more than nine hundred "People That Love" centers that fed hungry people every day in various parts of the world; and the Heritage House, a home for unwed mothers that provided a viable alternative to having an abortion; or the "Upper Room" prayer ministry, which had pastors available at any hour of the day or night to pray and counsel with hurting people? Maybe it was all an illusion. My brain continued to play tricks on me as I struggled in the back seat of a squad car to assemble the pieces of my broken heart, my dreams, and my now apparently meaningless life.

I had always believed that God loved me. He had literally granted me every desire of my heart, and I believed that His favor was upon me. Granted, anyone who knew my family and me also was well aware that we had gone through many personal problems and spiritual battles. Yet almost everything I had ever attempted to do in God's name prospered. Now I wasn't even sure where God was in my life, or if He loved me at all. I felt as though God had turned His back on me. Rejected and alone in the back seat of the squad car, questions ripped through my heart and mind. Was God punishing me for my sins? Was I really a "cancer upon the Body of Christ" as I had been labeled by one prominent Christian leader? Was I the

11

evil person that the prosecutors in my trial and the media had presented to the world? Did I deserve to go to prison? Did I deserve to live . . . or did I deserve to die?

Deeper and deeper I plummeted into my own pit of depression. No answers were forthcoming from heaven or from anywhere else. I heard no divine voice, only the sound of the police car's engine and the monotonous drone of tires on the pavement, taking me ever closer to prison.

How I did get into this mess?

2

Opening the Door to Destruction

THERE ARE MANY ANSWERS TO THE QUESTION "WHERE did things go wrong?" and one answer is my much-publicized encounter with Jessica Hahn. I knew I was wrong the moment I stepped through the door into room 538 at the Sheraton Sand Key Resort in Clearwater Beach, Florida, on December 6, 1980. I never dreamed, however, how much trouble opening that door would cause. Inside that room, I met for the first and only time in my life, a twenty-one-year-old woman named Jessica Hahn.

Earlier that afternoon, I had been relaxing on the beach with my ten-year-old-daughter, Tammy Sue, and my administrative assistant, David Taggart. We were in Clearwater, along with several other PTL television production people, to do a fund-raising telethon on our affiliate station, WCLF, Channel 22.

I glanced up and noticed John Wesley Fletcher, a frequent guest on our PTL programs, walking toward us. He was wearing street clothes and a broad smile. "Jim! I need to talk to you right away in private," he said, still smiling. "Why don't we take a little walk?"

I turned to Tammy Sue. "I'll be right back, honey." I got up, slipped on a pair of beach sandals, and followed John down the sidewalk toward the hotel. He had someone he wanted me to meet, he told me as we walked.

"My friend from Long Island that I was telling you about is here," he said. "I want you to come up and meet her."

"No, I am not comfortable with that," I replied.

"She really wants to meet you."

"Well, have her come down, and we can take a walk on the beach," I suggested.

"Oh, no! You can't do that! You're Jim Bakker. You can't be seen with a woman on the beach, unless it's your wife."

"Why not? I'm seen with people of all ages all the time. Everywhere I go, people come up to talk to me."

"Oh, just come up and see her. You don't have to do anything; just come up and say hello."

"I'm just not comfortable with that," I reiterated.

"Okay, I'm going to have her come out on the balcony and wave to you. That's the room, right up there," he said, pointing to a balcony of the hotel. Fletcher disappeared and in a few moments he and a young woman appeared on the balcony he had indicated. They both smiled and waved to me.

In a few minutes, John was back. "Now you've met her. Come on up. She really wants to meet you."

By 1977 the fire had begun to flicker and wane in Tammy Faye's and my marriage. Although we were candid about our problems, often discussing them on the set of our live television show, many viewers refused to accept that we were anything other than the ideal Christian couple with no more than a normal complement of marital woes. Many viewers actually took comfort in our troubles because they could identify with our problems. By admitting that we were struggling through various aspects of our marriage, Tammy Faye and I were giving the audience permission to acknowledge their own marital tensions. Few in our audience, or even among our staff members at PTL, really knew how close Tammy's and my marriage was to total dissolution.

Ironically, as PTL grew larger, so too did the rift in our relationship. Most of our arguments centered around my obsession to build Heritage USA. I felt that I had a vision and a commission from God to build PTL and eventually Heritage USA. Tammy Faye felt no such mandate. On the contrary, at times she even said she hated Heritage USA. She frequently referred to it, both privately and publicly, as my "mistress." Although Tammy loved being on television and genuinely loved the people who surrounded our lives as a result, she nonetheless resented the long hours I worked and the constant pressures of the ministry. I was home with her almost every night and lavished her with gifts and attention, but it was never enough. Our basic natures were very different. To Tammy, life was supposed to be fun, fun, fun, not work, work, work. She and I shared a passion since college to reach the world with the gospel message. We were convinced the means were through the medium of Christian television.

Tammy expressed her faith more comfortably through her music. Consequently, while I threw myself into building Heritage USA, she busily worked at recording Christian music, much of which we used on our *PTL* programs. I encouraged Tammy to develop and use her God-given talents; with Tammy's singing and my preaching, I had always thought we were a great one-two punch. About that same time, one of the guests on our show was a Nashville record producer named Gary S. Paxton. Gary's skills in the recording studio were legendary, dating back to his own pop records in the 1950s and '60s with songs such as "Cherry Pie," "Alley-Oop," and "Monster Mash." He had also produced hit records such as "Cherish" for a group known as The Association, and "Sweet Pea" for Tommy Roe. He had written country hits for Glen Campbell and Roy Clark, and one of his songs, "Woman, Sensuous Woman," recorded by Don Gibson, was a country classic.

In 1971, after a life of wild living, Gary S. Paxton became a Christian—and a gospel singer. He became an instant "Christian star," so it was only a matter of time before Paxton wound up on the set of our *PTL* television program.

Before long he was using his skills to produce music for us at *PTL*, including the *PTL* theme song, "Praise the Lord," which we used to open every program for several years. Gary also produced albums of my preaching and Tammy's music.

In the late seventies, Tammy began spending more and more time with Gary Paxton in his recording studio in Nashville. One of the reasons Paxton was such a successful music producer was his ability to bring the best out of people by providing just the right balance of encouragement and uplifting advice. It was the kind of positive feedback Tammy Faye longed for; Paxton encouraged Tammy and made her feel important.

In 1978, Paxton wrote the foreword for Tammy's book, *Run to the Roar*. About that same time, I embarked on a round-the-world trip to visit the growing number of mission projects sponsored by PTL, including numerous foreign versions of our *PTL* television program. Tammy Faye hated to fly, so she opted to stay at home to host the show while I was away. She invited Gary Paxton to cohost with her.

Any time that I traveled, I called home nearly every night. Usually Tammy wanted to talk, in her perky, chatty way telling me about everything from important issues to mundane matters. But now Tammy could hardly wait to get off the phone. I called from places all around the world, and she gave me the bum's rush, hastily concluding every conversation. Somehow or other, I could not bring myself to believe that she was merely being frugal. A man knows when his wife is brushing him off.

I sent Tammy Faye gifts from all over the world. Nothing seemed to make an impact. I knew we had not been communicating well lately, but I was nonetheless surprised and panic-stricken to sense my wife slipping into the arms of another man. My fears were not unfounded. Tammy Faye had indeed fallen in love with Gary Paxton. She later told me that she had not engaged in sexual intercourse with Gary, but they had spent long hours talking, hugging, and kissing. Consummated or not, in my mind, Tammy's and Gary's relationship amounted to an affair, even though both Tammy Faye and Gary insist to this day that they had "only" an "affair of the heart."

By summer of 1980, Gary and his wife would be getting divorced, and Tammy Faye and I would be close to it. Our marriage may not have survived the year had it not been for the outstanding help of a group of counselors at Palmdale Hospital, northwest of Los Angeles. The 123-bed hospital was owned and directed by Dr. Lester Nichols and his wife, June, both of whom were dedicated Christians. Many of the hospital staff members were Christians as well. In their professional counseling, the Palmdale team headed by Dr. Fred Gross, Palmdale's Chief of Psychology, used biblical principles and prayer along with psychological tests and psychiatric treatments. I had been extremely fascinated when I had interviewed Dr. Gross on *PTL* about his "psychospiritual" approach to counseling.

In 1980, I scheduled a physical examination at the Palmdale Hospital. During the course of my stay, I talked with Dr. Gross and told him that I felt sure Tammy was involved with another man. Dr. Gross was flabbergasted. He suggested that I send for Tammy immediately.

Tammy reluctantly flew from Charlotte to California—with the help of the tranquilizer Ativan to help calm her fear of flying. We spent the next two weeks meeting daily with Dr. Gross and his team of counselors. During that time, we laid some of our fears and frustrations with each other on the table for the first time. The counselors were extremely straightforward with both of us. They told me point-blank that I had better adjust my work schedule to allow more time to be with Tammy Faye.

As for Gary Paxton, when Tammy and I returned from Palmdale, I

16

called Gary in Nashville and angrily accused him of sleeping with Tammy Faye.

"No, Jim. I did not," Gary told me. "Just the opposite. I could have, but I didn't." Then Paxton attempted to turn the tables on me. "It's your fault, you know. You really should spend more time with your wife."

Gary S. Paxton never again appeared on any *PTL* television programs.

Tammy Faye and I returned to PTL, determined to patch up our marriage, though I was more enthusiastic about our reconciliation than was Tammy. I committed myself to spending more time with Tammy—no easy task, since we had just begun building the Barn, a $2 million, 2,000-seat auditorium and state-of-the-art television studio, from which we eventually began broadcasting our daily programs.

But before long, I was back to the regular grind, coming home exhausted after dark. For a while, it looked as though the Barn might not get built despite my best efforts. PTL simply did not have the money on hand. Construction at Heritage USA ground to a halt, and I lapsed into a deep depression as I saw my dreams beginning to disintegrate. Both the Barn and our headquarters building, the World Outreach Center, stood hollow and empty, monuments to defeat. For more than a year, the projects remained idle. Meanwhile, I sulked and despaired, trying desperately to find a way to get the projects moving again. During that time, I brought my problems home with me, so not surprisingly, Tammy saw me as a moody and discouraged man rather than as someone she wanted to run to for comfort and security.

In an effort to please Tammy Faye, I asked her to join me on the television set as the regular cohost of *The PTL Club*. The only problem was, I already had a cohost, our longtime friend and coworker, "Uncle" Henry Harrison. Although only fifty-two years of age as compared to my forty years, Uncle Henry evoked a grandfatherly image, parking his roly-poly paunch on the couch to my right, laughing boisterously, and fawning over my guests and me. I hoped Henry understood why I needed to replace him with Tammy Faye. He did remain on our show, but in a lesser role. Throughout the summer of 1980, Tammy's and my marriage remained strained. In an interview with *The Saturday Evening Post*, Tammy acknowledged our marital problems while giving the impression that our problems were in the past. "Thank God we've straightened them out," she told *The Saturday Evening Post*'s writer. "You've got to talk. Even if you're screaming at each other, you've got to get it out." Tammy attempted to encourage struggling marriage partners by saying that too many "see an easy way out and they take it. You've got to work at a marriage. If you don't, it will fail."[1]

To make matters worse, I was so obsessed with getting the construction projects at Heritage USA back on track that I moved our family from our home onto the grounds of Heritage USA. We lived in a small log cabin chalet, so I could more readily oversee the projects. I vowed that we would not move back home until the Barn auditorium was completed.

I worked feverishly trying to get the Barn open in time for our announced Fourth of July dedication. This was the first of many projects at PTL for which I would publicly declare an unrealistic completion date, making an already difficult job tougher than it had to be. In a way, setting such lofty goals caused all of us to expand our faith in God, and we completed projects in record time. Besides, like me, many of the young and idealistic staff members at PTL enjoyed a challenge. Just the thought that something couldn't be done was motivation enough for us. Although Tammy lent tacit public support to my efforts to build Heritage USA, inside she was unhappy about my growing obsession. Eventually, the projects were completed, but it would be years before the rift those buildings had created in our relationship could be healed.

Besides the toll my workaholic schedule took on my family and me, I remained suspicious of Tammy Faye. I was not convinced that she had broken off her relationship with Gary Paxton. By her actions and demeanor, I felt strongly that Tammy was still seeing him.

She wasn't.

There was someone else.

Despite our troubles, I loved Tammy Faye. She was my wife of nearly twenty years and she was the mother of my children. I realized that I was losing her, yet I refused to give up on her. I determined in my heart that I would do anything to get her back.

I tried more material gifts, but the presents had little impact on Tammy Faye. I took her, along with our two children, to Acapulco for a vacation. My secretary at the time, Ruth Egert, and her husband, Phil, accompanied us. Tammy Faye was still unhappy. We left Mexico and flew to Los Angeles. Tammy complained that I never took her anywhere without an entourage, our bodyguards, and other PTL staff members who were always available to help me handle the myriad responsibilities of PTL. I recognized that she was probably right about our never going anywhere alone, so I took her on vacation to the Bahamas—just the two of us. We enjoyed a brief respite from our day-to-day haggling, and for a few days, our love flourished.

Once back at Heritage USA, however, we quickly slipped back into our destructive patterns.

I was clueless, and I was exhausted. All my attempts to woo Tammy back from her mystery lover and make her happy proved futile. I did not know what else to do.

One day during a casual conversation with John Wesley Fletcher, I flippantly said that I ought to have an affair to make Tammy jealous. "I have tried everything else to win Tammy Faye back. Just think, I could say to Tammy Faye, 'I had an affair, too, Baby.' I'd be fighting fire with fire!"

"Really?" he asked. "Do you think that would help?"

"Well, you know how jealous Tammy Faye is. She would go nuts if she thought that I was even attracted to another woman."

"Hmmm," Fletcher answered thoughtfully.

Over the next few weeks, Fletcher and I occasionally joked about my having an affair to make Tammy Faye jealous.

I did not really want to have an affair. As a highly visible television personality, and as president of Heritage USA, had I desired to have a relationship with another woman, it would have been relatively easy to do so. But Tammy Faye was the only woman I wanted. She was the woman I loved.

Nevertheless, my foolish, male-ego-driven statement soon took on a life of its own, fueled by the hurt in my heart and by John's questionable motives.

I cannot say that I was surprised when John showed up in Florida with a woman in tow. I followed him inside the hotel, up the elevator, and down the hallway to room 538. I knew it was wrong; my conscience screamed at me every step of the way. But I stupidly determined to make my wife jealous and get back at her, and that is the truth. It was an adulterous act of the first degree. I stifled the screaming voice in my head and heart and stepped inside the room.

3

Crossing the Line

THE FIRST TIME I SAW JESSICA HAHN SHE WAS WEARING A plum-colored wraparound dress, which she quickly removed. Beneath the demure-looking dress she wore black lace. I had never before seen Jessica Hahn; nor had she been my secretary, as some people later mistakenly proclaimed, nor had she ever been employed at PTL.

Jessica Hahn, I learned seven years later, had grown up in Massapequa, New York, as a Catholic, but since the age of fourteen had been attending a Pentecostal church pastored by Eugene Profeta, a flamboyant, well-known, Brooklyn-born cleric. Immediately after graduating high school in 1977, Jessica Hahn went to work as Profeta's church secretary, a position she held the day I met her, and where she remained employed until 1987 when she resigned after becoming a household name.

Jessica Hahn and I never had a love affair. We had a fifteen- to twenty-minute tryst, a quick, furtive sexual encounter. We had no ongoing relationship, although our brief meeting intertwined our lives more than either one of us ever dreamed possible as we sized each other up that fateful afternoon.

We conversed very little. I may have uttered a total of six sentences to her. We did not drink wine, as was reported later. Nor did I imply that by having sex with me she was serving God somehow. Most of all, *I did not rape Jessica Hahn.* Foolish and sinful as it was, the sexual encounter for which we are both now infamous was completely consensual.

As I said, I knew I was wrong the moment I entered the hotel room. I should have run out of that place. Nobody forced me into the room or to stay once I was there. Yet I rationalized the situation: I was feeling rejected by my wife; I knew that Tammy Faye was seeing another man; I was wondering whether I was much of a man at all. Suddenly, I felt as though I were an adolescent boy who had to prove he was a man by having sex. I willfully crossed the line and went through with it.

At first, I was so nervous and afraid I could not even function sexually. I knew that what I was doing went directly against everything I believed as a Christian; I had never cheated on my wife in all our years of marriage. Jessica Hahn, however, seemed quite comfortable with the situation. When she recognized my problem, she aroused me to the point where I simply abandoned myself to the moment. We did not make love; we had sex.

When it was over, I quickly left the room, and in a daze, hurried to the elevator and pressed the button marking the eighth floor. The winter afternoon sun was already beginning to slide down on the horizon as I stepped inside my room.

I was horrified. *Oh, God! What have I done?* I had not considered the consequences of my absurd attempt to make Tammy Faye jealous. I had not even paused to think of the potential ramifications of my actions while I was giving in to the temptation of having sex with a woman other than my wife. I had simply reacted.

I had opened the door to attack on the ministry I headed, my family, and me personally. Worse yet, the devil had not made me do any of it; I had done it of my own stubborn will.

I disrobed and immediately stepped into the shower, turning the water on as hot as I could stand it. I never felt so dirty in all my life. *Maybe if I make the water hotter, it will wash it all away*, I thought.

Eventually I realized I had to get out of the shower and get dressed. It was almost time to go to the telethon at Channel 22, my reason for being in Florida in the first place. I thought seriously about canceling my appearance on the program that night. I felt that I had nothing to say to the audience, that I had somehow squandered away my credibility and my "right to be heard" as a result of my sexual sin that afternoon. On the other hand, I knew that my friends at the Clearwater affiliate were counting on me to help them meet their telethon goals. They were depending on my high profile to attract viewers and convince the audience to help support the very valid ministry of Channel 22. I went to the telethon and tried to put on a happy face, but it was a false face. I was anything but happy. I felt as if

21

the television cameras could see right through me, boring into my soul and exposing my sin to the world. I carried on, doing my duties as the special guest through sheer enthusiasm and religious hype. Inside, however, I felt dead; I knew that I was wrong.

That night following the telethon, I was in no mood for late-night dinners or conversations. I returned to my room around eleven o'clock and tumbled into bed. I felt exhausted in every way, yet sleep eluded me. I stared at the ceiling. I replayed the events of the day in my mind again and again. *How could I have been so foolish?* I asked myself a thousand times. *Why did I ever allow things to get to this point?* I tossed and turned all night long. Everything within me seemed to have come undone as a result of fifteen to twenty minutes of sexual "pleasure." If adultery is so pleasurable, why was I feeling so awful?

I arose at the first ray of sunshine. Although it was Sunday, I chose not to stay in Clearwater to attend morning worship services at a local church. I could not get away fast enough. By midmorning, Tammy Sue and I, along with several other members of our staff, were on our way back to Charlotte.

On Monday, I called for Dr. Fred Gross, the clinical psychologist from Palmdale Hospital who was at PTL that week conducting a series of marriage seminars. Dr. Gross had developed a Christian therapy program at PTL that had already helped hundreds of married couples renew and revive their marriage. In what has come to be relatively common practice nowadays, Dr. Gross was a pioneer in combining psychological principles with biblical precepts. I felt I could unburden my aching heart to Dr. Gross, and he would have both the spiritual and the psychological wisdom to help me find forgiveness.

If Dr. Gross was surprised that I called him to my office that Monday, he did not let on. He greeted me cheerfully but quickly realized that I was deeply troubled about something. We went back into the private dressing room next to my office and sat down. I wanted to tell Dr. Gross what was on my mind and heart, but the words seemed to get clogged in my throat. I didn't know where to start. Finally, I sat down and slowly began to tell him about my sin with Jessica Hahn the past weekend in Clearwater. As I spoke, I could feel my body beginning to quake. I was acutely aware of the enormity of my sin.

Dr. Gross did not attempt to counsel me. He did not allow me to rationalize that Tammy Faye was being unfaithful. Dr. Gross knew that the only way I would find emotional health and spiritual freedom was by seeking forgiveness from God, forgiveness from Jessica Hahn, and forgiveness from myself.

Together, Dr. Gross and I knelt down on the floor and began to pray. I cried out to God for forgiveness. I literally lay face-first on the floor, prostrate before God. Then, in a sense, Dr. Gross placed himself in the position of a priest to me and declared, "Now I tell you before God, Jim Bakker, that you have been forgiven of God."

That same day, I talked to Jessica Hahn by telephone and immediately asked her to forgive me. She invited me to meet her again in Long Island. I said, "We must not get together again. What we did was wrong, and we need to ask God for forgiveness." That was the last conversation I had with Jessica Hahn.

I did not and do not blame Jessica Hahn. If she has not already done so, I hope she will one day find it within her heart to forgive me. Before she and I ever met, she had been used and hurt by men who purported to represent God, but that does not lessen my responsibility or absolve me of the fact that I was wrong to have had sexual intercourse with her. To my dying day, I will always be grieved that I added more hurt to her already damaged heart.

At this point, I had sought and received the forgiveness of God, confessed to my spiritual "elder," Dr. Gross, and had attempted to seek forgiveness from the party I had offended. *Now I must tell Tammy Faye*, I thought.

No longer did I want to flaunt the fact that I'd had an affair too. Now, I genuinely wanted to confess to her and seek her forgiveness. I could only hope that she would be willing to forgive and give me another chance.

When I asked Dr. Gross about how I should break the news to Tammy Faye, he was adamant that I not tell her. "I am not sure Tammy Faye can handle this, Jim," Dr. Gross said to me. "News of your infidelity might devastate her."

"Do you mean that I should not tell Tammy Faye about this incident?" I asked, surprised.

"Absolutely not. The way your relationship with her has been floundering over the past few months, rather than making her jealous, as you originally intended, this will destroy any incentive Tammy Faye has for trying to work things out between the two of you. She is looking for any excuse to end the marriage already, and this news will just push her over the edge."

"I think she can handle it, Dr. Gross. Tammy Faye is a tough woman. She cries easily, but inside she has quite a bit of courage and stamina."

Dr. Gross remained unconvinced. "It's not worth the risk. Right now, from what I know and have seen of Tammy Faye, I don't think she could handle it. When the time is right to tell her about this incident, you'll know it, but in my professional opinion, that time is not now."

I was surprised that Dr. Gross would instruct me to keep my sexual sin a secret from my spouse. Nevertheless, I respected him immensely. He had been instrumental in helping hundreds of married couples restore their marriages, so I felt he knew what was best in this sort of situation.

In retrospect, I now believe that it would have been much easier—and the right thing to do—to have confessed to Tammy Faye right after it happened and accepted the consequences. I believe she could have handled it, and we would have been able to work through it. But I decided the doctor knew best. I kept quiet.

Over the next six years, as Tammy Faye and I tried to put our marriage back together, she often lamented her moral failures. Frequently, Tammy commented about how sorry she was and how guilty she felt about her own past. Usually, when she went on one of those guilt trips, I tried to console her by saying, "Honey, I am just as guilty as you are. I have failed you too." The burden of my guilt was almost more than I could bear.

But I never told Tammy Faye about Jessica Hahn . . . not until March 1987.

4

Strange Bedfellows

"TAM, I NEED TO TALK WITH YOU. PLEASE COME SIT DOWN with me," I said as I guided Tammy Faye toward the sitting area of our bedroom. "What's wrong?" Tammy asked, with a panic-stricken look. Tammy Faye could tell by the expression on my face that this was to be no ordinary conversation. Although the morning sunshine streamed through the windows, brightly lighting the Spanish architecture and natural desert wood of our home in Palm Springs, California, this was to be one of the darkest days of our lives.

"Jim, what's wrong?" Tammy asked once again as we had settled onto the sofa.

"I just talked to Reverend Dortch. He's coming out here tomorrow, and I need to tell you something before he gets here."

I had talked with my executive vice president, Richard Dortch, earlier that day, and he informed me that *The Charlotte Observer* had learned of my 1980 sexual encounter with Jessica Hahn. The paper was preparing to expose the matter to the world. Everyone involved recognized that the news of my moral failure could ruin me as a minister and possibly trigger the beginning of the end for PTL.

I had confessed to Dr. Fred Gross and had apologized to Jessica Hahn in 1980 the same weekend that the encounter had taken place. Dr. Gross assured me that since I had repented and sought forgiveness for the wrong that I had done, there was nothing more I could or should do. I went back to my work at PTL with a new vigor, thinking that the situation was over and done with.

I was wrong.

In December 1984, *The Charlotte Observer* and the executive offices at PTL both received a series of telephone calls from a distraught woman claiming I had raped her. Journalist Charles Shepard fielded the calls at the newspaper, and Richard Dortch handled the calls at our offices. Reverend Dortch maintains today that he did not believe the woman's story—he had received crank calls at PTL before—but he, along with Aimee Cortese, a PTL Board member and pastor in Brooklyn, arranged to meet with the woman in New York. There Richard Dortch met Jessica Hahn. Accompanied by a female paralegal, Jessica Hahn repeated her accusations to Reverend Dortch and Aimee Cortese. Hahn indicated that she had suffered emotional distress as a result of the encounter and needed money for medical bills and psychiatric help. At the close of their meeting, Reverend Dortch did what he now admits in his book was a tragic mistake—he gave the pastor two thousand dollars of his own money to give to Jessica Hahn to cover counseling or medical expenses.[1] Upon his return to PTL, Reverend Dortch felt that the matter had been resolved.

Reverend Dortch says he did not believe Jessica Hahn's story. Perhaps that's why in an almost offhand manner he said to me, "Oh, by the way, I have been dealing with a woman who says that you raped her."

No doubt Richard Dortch was not prepared for my response. I told him that I had never raped anyone, but I let him know that I had had a sexual encounter with Jessica Hahn. I suggested Reverend Dortch talk to Dr. Gross about what had transpired in Clearwater in 1980. Reverend Dortch talked first to Dr. Gross, and then at my invitation he returned to my office with Vi Azvedo, one of our top counselors and the head of the PTL pastoral staff. They asked me to tell them in exact detail what had happened between Jessica Hahn and me. I told them the truth and answered all of their questions.

I turned to my trusted advisors and asked, "What should I do now?"

They were all in agreement that I should have no further contact with Jessica Hahn, not even a telephone conversation. Richard Dortch assured me that he would handle the matter from that point. At that time, to our best knowledge, the issue was settled. Looking back, however, I now see what an untenable position in which I was placing Dortch.

According to Richard Dortch and others in our executive offices, at this point, Jessica Hahn began calling repeatedly. Then PTL received a legal-sounding letter, apparently written by Hahn's paralegal friend. The rambling letter, documented by both Richard Dortch and Charles Shepard in their books, again listed a number of accusations against me and stated, "We're giving you the opportunity to settle this matter justly and privately, according to what you perceive to be a rightful settlement. $100,000.00 (one hundred thousand dollars) is not excessive in view of what happened here."[2]

Had we been wise, we would have turned the matter over to the FBI at that point. But in an effort to avoid the negative publicity, and to protect the ministry and my reputation, Reverend Dortch decided on a wait-and-see course of action.

About the same time, Jessica Hahn began calling *The Charlotte Observer*. She repeated her story to Charles Shepard, referring to the same document her paralegal friend had sent to PTL, only skipping the part of the letter asking for $100,000 in return for her silence.[3] Charles Shepard smelled blood. He began chasing the story from coast to coast.

In January 1985 a package containing several legal-looking documents arrived at Richard Dortch's office. One, an eight-page document, was from Paul Roper, a California law student and a self-appointed watchdog of Christian ministries. Roper's watchdog group was known as Operation Anti-Christ.

Roper had enlisted the help of John Stewart, a fellow law student as well as a part-time pastor who eventually became a law professor and a popular Christian radio talk-show host. Nearing the completion of his law studies and preparing for his bar exam, Stewart found time to research and prepare a draft lawsuit—not an actual suit, but a formal complaint—outlining Jessica Hahn's charges against PTL and me and five other potential defendants. The complaint stated clearly that the potential "punitive damages" liability for me and the other defendants now totaled $12.3 million. The cover letter from Roper and Stewart, dated January 14, 1985, demanded a response by 8:00 A.M. on January 21, 1985—one week later—or "the documents would be sent to an attorney in an appropriate jurisdiction for possible litigation."[4] The letter included a phone number to call if a representative of PTL wanted to contact Roper before the matter became a bona fide "filed lawsuit and a public record."[5]

Richard Dortch met with Paul Roper in early February. According to Shepard and Stewart, Roper suggested a conciliation panel, made up of one person selected by Reverend Dortch, one person selected by Paul Roper, and one mutually acceptable person. The panel then could decide whether Jessica Hahn's claims and demands were valid and to what extent.

Richard Dortch took a different tack. He hired Los Angeles attorney Howard Weitzman to settle with Roper and Hahn out of court. By February 19, Weitzman and Roper had come to an agreement. A detailed document was drawn up and agreed to in the presence of now retired Superior Court Judge Charles Woodmansee on February 27, 1985. In addition to the judge, Jessica Hahn, Paul Roper, and Scott Furstman, Howard Weitzman's partner, signed the agreement. It was agreed before the judge that Jessica Hahn and her representatives should receive an immediate payment of $115,000, of which Jessica Hahn would receive $20,000. Paul Roper, the Christian watchdog, reportedly received $90,000, of which he paid John Stewart $15,000. Another $150,000 was placed in a trust fund for twenty years. In signing the document, Jessica Hahn agreed "not to discuss or otherwise disseminate to the public any information" regarding her claims. She also agreed not to contact or harass PTL or file further legal actions regarding this case. If she held true to her word, at the end of twenty years, the $150,000 was hers. In the meantime, she received the annual interest the trust fund accrued. If Hahn violated the agreement by going public, the trust fund was to return to PTL.[6]

Richard Dortch returned to Heritage USA with the task of coming up with $265,000.

Dortch considered who had the most to lose if there were any kind of reversal of PTL's growth. He determined it would be the contractor of the buildings, the developer of Heritage USA, Roe Messner.[7]

Roe put up the money to pay the Jessica Hahn out-of-court settlement. I did not know that at the time and didn't want to know. If the subject came up, and it rarely did, Reverend Dortch simply said that a concerned businessman had come to our aid.

Looking back, I now recognize that I should have handled the matter of my sin with Jessica Hahn differently in the first place. I should have admitted my moral failure to the presbyters of the Assemblies of God, my lifelong denominational affiliation. As a minister who committed adultery but who sought forgiveness and restoration, I could have defused the entire matter by submitting to my spiritual elders and accepting whatever discipline they decided to mete out. I knew the rules, however, and recognized that my admission of the tryst would most likely result in my ministerial credentials being rescinded for a two-year period. More disconcerting, I would probably be banned from the pulpit and from our television programs for at least a year. Moreover, if I had simply resigned my credentials with the Assemblies, it was likely that all of the Assemblies of God ministers on our PTL staff would have had to follow suit or give up their jobs at PTL.

In light of the staggering consequences, the possible ramifications in so many lives, I did not inform the Assemblies of God hierarchy of the matter. By March 1987, I felt that the Jessica Hahn matter had been adequately resolved by Richard Dortch in the best legal and spiritual manner possible, considering the awkward circumstances.

I was wrong.

Secret agreements rarely remain so for long. By late 1985, stories of my sexual indiscretion were already circulating in hushed tones. John Stewart, who had done the research for Paul Roper's original draft lawsuit, had contacted reporter Charles Shepard at *The Charlotte Observer*, seeking information that might satisfy his curiosity concerning where the Hahn settlement money had come from. In the process, he discovered that Shepard knew about Hahn, and Shepard found a willing source of information. The two remained in contact.

Nevertheless, Shepard had been unable to confirm enough of his allegations to satisfy his editor's concerns over accuracy and potential lawsuits. Charles Shepard may well have continued to stumble in the dark had he not found some allies in the Christian broadcasting ranks. In 1987, the National Religious Broadcasters' convention was held in Washington, D.C., the first week in February. It was there that John Stewart met John Ankerberg, and John Ankerberg met Jimmy Swaggart.

Both Ankerberg and Swaggart had television programs on our satellite network, the Inspirational Network that we had recently canceled. Ankerberg frequently attacked other ministries, organizations, and people by name, something the Board of Directors and I did not feel was appropriate. Rather than building up fellow Christians, I felt Ankerberg spent most of his program tearing the church world apart. After he met with Ankerberg at Heritage USA, Richard Dortch reported that Ankerberg's attitude was inconsistent with what we wanted to air on the Inspirational Network. The Board voted unanimously not to renew his contract. PTL was a ministry of other ministries; we had a wide variety of programs on our Inspirational Network, and we never told any of them what to preach or not to preach. We did not, however, want one program we aired to be firing bullets at another program or preacher on our network, Hatfield-and-McCoy-style.

In the mid-1980s Jimmy Swaggart was one of the most popular evangelists on television. His program aired fifteen times per week on the Inspirational Network. One of his time slots was 9:00 A.M., Monday through Friday. Tammy Faye's and my show, the flagship program of the

Inspirational Network, aired at eleven o'clock each morning. Swaggart had been publicly attacking PTL in writing through his magazine, *The Evangelist*, and on his television programs, which aired on our network! Jimmy Swaggart did not approve of much at PTL and he was extremely vocal about saying so. It seemed as though he did not like Christians having as much fun as we were having at Heritage USA. Nor did he like much of the music we aired, some of which was more contemporary than Swaggart's "down-home," gospel style. He was most critical of us having Hollywood celebrities on our program who came to give their Christian testimonies. Jimmy Swaggart was particularly opposed to Christian psychologists and Christian counseling in general, which we at PTL felt could be a valuable asset to many Christian families and individuals. At that time, Jimmy Swaggart had never stepped foot on the grounds of Heritage USA. Yet he spoke out loudly and often, denouncing almost everything we were doing at PTL. That was his prerogative as a Christian and his right as an American. But we did not have to provide him air time to do it!

In addition to PTL, Jimmy often castigated Roman Catholics and other denominations. When Swaggart and his guests started lambasting fellow ministers by name, such as Robert Schuller and Kenneth Copeland, men whom I respected and considered to be friends, he crossed a line. The PTL Board of Directors and I had a firm policy that nobody on our network could criticize another ministry by name. I asked Reverend Dortch to discuss this matter with Swaggart.

Richard Dortch made the decision to remove Swaggart's morning show from our network lineup. Our Board of Directors and I unanimously backed Reverend Dortch's decision. Initially, we continued to air Jimmy's program at other times of the day, but the morning show was his bread and butter.

Consequently, when John Stewart encountered Ankerberg and Swaggart at the 1987 NRB convention, he found two men who were extremely angry at PTL in general, and at me in particular. Not surprisingly, the three soon traded information back and forth, fanning the rumor flames even further. Ankerberg also discussed his "concerns" about me with Jerry Falwell, and before long a comradeship was formed between Ankerberg, Swaggart, and Falwell, with John Stewart serving as the willing liaison between the ministers and *The Charlotte Observer*.

On Thursday, March 12, 1987, Charles Shepard and John Stewart talked by telephone. In the course of their conversation, Shepard told Stewart that he had a story about Jessica Hahn, the money, and me almost ready to print.[8] Stewart immediately contacted Ankerberg, who asked the lawyer to write a letter to me on behalf of Ankerberg, Swaggart, and Falwell, ostensibly to confront me in the spirit of Matthew 18—Jesus' instructions for confronting a fellow believer—about the sexual episode with Jessica Hahn that had taken place seven years earlier. Stewart wrote the letter, but when Ankerberg faxed it to Swaggart and Falwell, the television preachers' response was less than enthusiastic. In a fax back to Ankerberg, a copy of which I have in my files to this day, Swaggart expressed his reservations about being associated with the letter. Falwell, too, shied away from the letter, saying he wanted to have his lawyer examine it before lending his name to it.

That same afternoon, Richard Dortch was in the Tampa Bay area when he received a call from his secretary, Leslie Jones. Leslie told Reverend Dortch that several members of Jerry Falwell's staff were trying to contact him. Reverend Dortch recognized the name of one of the men, Warren Marcus, who had once worked at the Christian Broadcasting Network. The other two men were Jerry Nims, a leader in Falwell's political action group, The Moral Majority, and Mark DeMoss, son of the famous philanthropist, Arthur DeMoss.

When Richard Dortch contacted Warren, the Falwell assistant told him, "We've learned there is a problem at PTL, and we want to help if we can."[9]

The Falwell representatives urged Reverend Dortch to meet them at the Tampa Airport executive aircraft area at eleven o'clock that very night! This was obviously serious.

When the men arrived on Jerry Falwell's jet, Jerry Nims got straight to the point. "John Ankerberg called us and told us he and Jimmy Swaggart know about the Jessica Hahn incident."[10] Nims showed Reverend Dortch the fax Jerry Falwell had received from John Ankerberg and a copy of the Swaggart reply.

Reverend Dortch had met with Jimmy Swaggart in a stormy meeting in Baton Rouge earlier in the year, but he was still shocked as he read Swaggart's response to Ankerberg.[11]

Swaggart's letter insinuated that it was only a matter of time before my sexual encounter with Jessica Hahn would be exposed, I would be brought down, and PTL would be vulnerable. He assured Ankerberg that *The Charlotte Obersver* would do its part, as would the Assemblies of God.

As Reverend Dortch read Swaggart's words, he immediately was reminded of the recurring rumors hinting that Jimmy Swaggart wanted to take over the PTL Inspirational Network. What Richard Dortch knew that the Falwell aides may not have known at that time was that I was the president of PTL for life. Written into our corporate bylaws was a stipulation that said if for any reason I could not serve as the president, the entire ministry was to be placed into the hands of the Assemblies of God. With me disgraced, Jimmy Swaggart could easily lay claim to PTL on the logical basis that he was the leading television preacher associated with the Assemblies of God denomination.

Consequently, the information that the Falwell aides provided about Swaggart rang true in Dortch's mind. It made sense, but Reverend Dortch remained reticent.

As a former presbyter in the Assemblies of God national office, Reverend Dortch recognized that the Falwell camp and the Bakker camp were poles apart on a theological spectrum. Falwell, a Baptist, preached a more traditional approach to Christianity. Those in "charismatic" circles such as PTL and the Assemblies of God believe that the "gifts of the Spirit"—such as speaking in tongues and prophecy—are still operative in the world today. Charismatics characteristically have a more upbeat, "God can work in the now" approach to life. Questions concerning spiritual gifts and how they are relevant to Christianity today often created a "Y" in the road when charismatic and noncharismatic Christians discussed these issues. It was highly unusual that Jerry Falwell and his staff, people who held such opposite views of the Christian life from ours, would rally to our assistance in what appeared to be a growing conflict between two charismatic ministries, Jimmy Swaggart and PTL. Consequently, Dortch's first questions to the aides were, "Why are you telling us these things? Why have you gotten involved in this matter?"

The Falwell aides were ready for Richard Dortch's questions. Jerry Nims answered, "Jerry Falwell is convinced, and we're convinced, that if Jimmy Swaggart brings you down, he would certainly bring us down, too. He's probably out to get us also. We need to stand with you to stop Jimmy Swaggart from trying to tear up your ministry."[12]

The Falwell aides went on to tell Richard Dortch that they had evidence that Jimmy Swaggart had obtained enough people to bring a class-action suit against PTL in regard to the PTL Lifetime Partnership program. Nims had suggested that such a case could put PTL into receivership and eventually shut down the ministry. (Ironically, the same ideas would surface less than a year later, only it would not be Jimmy Swaggart promoting the idea.) Nims also informed Richard Dortch that Jimmy Swaggart had a "plant, a spy, in your organization who keeps him informed of everything going on at PTL."[13] The idea seemed plausible to Reverend Dortch, especially in light of the fact that Nims accurately told him of a check written by PTL to a specific organization in recent weeks, a check that only some-one inside PTL's offices would know about.

Reverend Dortch and Jerry Falwell's men talked into the wee hours of the following morning. Throughout the conversation, it appeared to Dortch that two points were continually and emphatically made: Swaggart is out to get you, and Jerry Falwell can help you. Before the long meeting had concluded, Reverend Dortch had confirmed that certain parts of the Jessica Hahn story were true. He did not go into details at that time.

Jerry Nims reassured Reverend Dortch of Jerry Falwell's ability to assist in dealing with the negative fallout that was sure to come once the story became public. Nims told Reverend Dortch, "Dr. Falwell has helped others in this situation. There was a church in Maine whose pastor had a moral failure. Jerry Falwell took the church over for a period of time and helped them. Then he returned the church to its pastor."[14]

The obvious implication was that Jerry Falwell could and would do something similar for me. Reverend Dortch finally agreed to broach the subject of Jerry Falwell's help with me.

The meeting concluded around 2:00 A.M., after which Reverend Dortch immediately telephoned me in Palm Springs and gave me a full report. He faxed copies of the Swaggart letter and other materials the Falwell men had given to him. He told me that *The Charlotte Observer* was definitely planning to proceed with the story. It was not a matter of *if* the story would run, but *when* the story would hit.

As I listened to Reverend Dortch's fatigued voice on the phone, it was as though someone were punching me in the stomach with every word. I thought again and again, *This can't be happening!* But Reverend Dortch's report repeatedly assured me that it was happening and we needed to get ready for it. Falwell's men had advised him to call New York lawyer Norman Roy Grutman, a hard-boiled attorney who might be able to get the story stopped temporarily. Grutman had represented Jerry Falwell when Jerry had sued *Hustler* magazine for printing a derogatory parody of the preacher. Grutman won the case and a judgment of $200,000 for Falwell, although the case was later overturned by the U.S. Supreme Court.

Reverend Dortch said that the Falwell aides had suggested that the controversial lawyer might be able to stop the impending article and wran-gle us enough time to get our heads together. Reverend Dortch then con-tacted Jerry Nims about securing the services of Norman Roy Grutman.

As I hung up the phone, I sat quietly by myself, playing and replaying the possible scenarios in my mind. Even if Grutman could convince *The Charlotte Observer* to hold the article exposing the tryst with Jessica Hahn and the out-of-court settlement that had been arranged with her, Swaggart and Ankerberg now knew about it as well. Exposure was inevitable.

I worried, *What will our PTL partners think? How will the news affect the ministry? How will it affect the Church as a whole?* The press was always looking for a real-life Elmer Gantry-type story. Now, they were going to have one—me! I buried my face in my hands and grieved deeply. I kept thinking, *There are so many people who could be hurt by this—my staff and fellow ministers, my elderly mom and dad, and my children, seventeen-year-old Tammy Sue and ten-year-old Jamie Charles.*

And then there was Tammy Faye.

"Oh, God," I cried. "How am I going to explain this to Tammy Faye?"

5

Betty Ford

FRIDAY, MARCH 13, 1987, DAWNED ANOTHER GORGEOUS California day, but I did not want to open my eyes. I languished around the house in a deep depression. I did not want to go anywhere; I did not want to see anyone. I did not want to stray too far from a phone, because Richard Dortch had said that he would be calling to let me know about Grutman and Falwell's possible help.

Norman Roy Grutman was already at work. He contacted *The Charlotte Observer* and threatened the paper with a lawsuit if they ran the Hahn story that weekend. The paper pulled the story and we all thought Norman Roy Grutman was a hero. Actually, as I learned much later, the paper's editors had already decided to hold the story. Rich Oppel, editor of the paper, and in particular Mark Ethridge and the paper's legal counsel, Jon Buchan, felt Charles Shepard's story was not bulletproof. They had already killed the story for the weekend papers, the *Observer's* best-selling editions.[1]

Regardless, I was glad to know that the immediate pressure was off. Had I known, however, that the paper had pulled the story for lack of solid evidence, that Jessica Hahn had retracted much of her story, and that several key players had refused to be named publicly, it would have definitely influenced the way I responded to Jerry Falwell's overtures offering help and intervention. Thinking that Grutman had been influential in getting the paper to pull the plug on the article, I was open to accepting many other disingenuous Grutman moves in the following week.

When Richard Dortch asked me if I wanted to meet with Jerry Falwell, I told him that I would but that I did not want to leave Tammy Faye at that time. However, Falwell was welcome to come to Palm Springs.

Reverend Dortch forwarded that message to Jerry Nims and Mark DeMoss. They in turn took it to Jerry Falwell.

The reason Tammy Faye and I were in California in the first place was to get her well. While the tumultuous events were happening back east, Tammy Faye and I had been going through a twelve-step, Alcoholics Anonymous-type program at the Betty Ford Center to help Tammy overcome her addiction to over-the-counter drugs. Both of our children went to special classes for family members at Betty Ford.

The crisis began in the late fall of 1986. Tammy Faye was always medicating herself and had a dangerous habit of mixing over-the-counter and prescription drugs. She carried plenty of pills in her purse. It was a standard joke among many of our close friends that Tammy Faye's purse was like a mobile drugstore. If someone had a headache, Tammy was always quick to pipe up, "I have a pill for that." If someone had a sinus problem, Tammy had a pill for that. Arthritis pain? There was a pill in Tammy's purse for that too. Aspirin, nasal sprays, and allergy medications filled Tammy Faye's medicine chest at home and her purse and travel bags when we were on the road.

Tammy seemed to be getting sick before Christmas, and the many holiday activities we worked on at Heritage USA exacerbated her already weak condition. We had established a tradition of spending Christmas with the thousands of PTL partners who came to Heritage USA each year. We had special programs in the Heritage Grand, and our staff wrapped hundreds of presents for all of our guests. Christmas at Heritage USA was always the best of times and worst of times due to the huge crowds, the many Christmas parties, and other responsibilities of the season in addition to the usual pressures of doing a daily television program and keeping a huge ministry functioning. It was a festive but exhausting time.

As usual, we hosted a large Christmas party for the PTL management team. Tammy had not been feeling well but she was able to function enough to be a gracious and gregarious hostess to our guests. Upon entering our Tega Cay home, each person attending the party had his or her photograph taken with Tammy Faye and me. Despite being sick, Tammy Faye smiled happily in every picture.

The Christmas party was one of our best ever. PTL had enjoyed a wonderful time of growth and ministry during 1986. Our eighty-six services a week were instrumental in changing thousands of lives. Our Lifetime Partnership program was expanding as work continued on the Towers, and financially, PTL was enjoying its best year ever. PTL was clearly working. We had much for which to give thanks. We closed the party with prayer and our usual singing of Christmas carols.

Tammy struggled through the following week, but by the time we hosted our all-night gospel sing on New Year's Eve, she was extremely weak. As was our custom, we had planned our annual vacation after all the frenzied holiday activities—we usually needed a vacation simply to recover from Christmas week! We had purchased a getaway home in Palm Desert in 1984. Unfortunately, we rarely were able to spend much time there, so we had already decided to sell that home. We had purchased a new home in the mountains of Gatlinburg, Tennessee, which was much closer to Heritage USA and easily accessible by car from the Charlotte area. We decided to spend our vacation there this year.

Before departing for the mountains, however, on my forty-seventh birthday, January 2, I presided over the groundbreaking ceremonies for what I considered to be one of the most fabulous projects ever begun at Heritage USA—the construction of the Heritage Crystal Palace. The Crystal Palace Ministry Center was to be the largest church building in the world. Once completed, the auditorium was designed to seat as many as thirty thousand people, with electronic, moveable dividers that could be configured for a wide variety of smaller crowds. The Crystal Palace would house a five-thousand-seat television studio with state-of-the-art equipment. The huge structure would enclose 1.25 million square feet in glass and would have exhibition facilities large enough to accommodate large conventions such as the Christian Booksellers Association Convention. A unique and highly functional feature of the building was the planned underground loading dock in which the many tractor-trailer rigs used to service such conventions could unload their materials and have them hoisted by elevator directly to the exhibition floor.

I was convinced that the Crystal Palace would pay for itself by selling time-share units in the adjoining thirty-story Crystal Tower. Contrary to misinformation that would soon be widely propagated, our hotel space at the Heritage Grand was not used as time-share units, nor were the five hundred rooms in the nearly completed twenty-one-story Heritage Grand Tower. Those lodging facilities were included in our no-ownership, Lifetime Partnership program as well as open to the general public. The

Crystal Tower, however, would be built and paid for strictly with Partner-owned time-shares in mind.

With a special choir singing "The Hallelujah Chorus" from Handel's *Messiah* and a crowd of dignitaries looking on, I was ecstatic as the PTL Board of Directors and I pushed our shovels down into the soft ground and turned over the dirt. I looked up as the cameras flashed and said, "This is the best day of my life!"

I had envisioned the massive project for more than a year now, and I was thrilled to get started on it. My projected completion date was three years from groundbreaking. Little could I guess that the groundbreaking ceremony would be my last official, public act at Heritage USA. Nor could I have ever dreamed that I would not be celebrating my fiftieth birthday surrounded by friends and family in a glass superstructure, but instead surrounded by strangers, some of whom were dangerous, and confined by a razor-wire fence.

Tammy Faye, Jamie, and I left for Gatlinburg after the groundbreaking ceremonies. Tammy Sue stayed behind to visit with some of her friends. I was looking forward to a bit of rest and relaxation, but it was not to be.

Tammy Faye's condition worsened. She said, "My throat feels like razor blades are cutting it!" By our second week in Tennessee, she was so sick that she consented to go to a local doctor, a rare concession on her part. I drove Tammy Faye down the mountain, and up the road to the small town of Sevierville, where we were able to get an appointment with a doctor. The doctor prescribed some medicine for her flulike conditions, and I found a drugstore nearby where the medicine could be obtained.

With a prescription drug in her possession and her usual battery of over-the-counter medications at her disposal, Tammy Faye grew increasingly delusional and irrational. She eventually got to the point that she did not remember what medications she had taken or when. All she knew was that she was not feeling better, so she continued to take more and more.

On January 12, I was scheduled to present a long-term master plan of our vision for Heritage USA to the York County Commissioners, the local authority governing our growth and development. Although Heritage USA maintained its own facilities, roads, water towers and water lines, underground electric lines, and telephone system, the commissioners were still concerned about how our future expansion plans would fit in with the community. It was an important meeting and I dared not miss it.

At the same time, I felt that it would be unconscionable for me to leave Tammy Faye without an adult to help her, even though I planned to be gone for one day only. I asked Vi Azvedo to come from Heritage to

Gatlinburg (about a five-hour drive) to stay with Tammy Faye until I returned. I drove back to Heritage the day before my meeting with the local commissioners.

The meeting with the commissioners was held at Heritage USA. I gave them a tour of our current facilities, showed them the progress on the Towers, and showed them the site where we had just broken ground for the new Crystal Palace. After that, I took them back to the Heritage Grand for lunch and showed the commissioners the master plan and drawings for our future plans, including a retirement village, the re-creation of "Old Jerusalem," and numerous new hotels, camping areas, lakes, and the long-range development of our back acreage where we planned to construct a Christian theme park based on the lives of great characters and stories from the Bible.

The commissioners were more supportive than I could ever have expected. Heritage USA was the largest employer in the Fort Mill area, providing more than two thousand people with jobs. We were also one of the largest sources of local tax revenue. Our school taxes alone for one year were over $600,000, not to mention sales taxes from our shops and other property taxes paid by Heritage USA on those parts of the property not used directly in ministry purposes. Perhaps the commissioners hoped for even more tax revenue from our expansion plans.

While I was still with the commissioners, Vi Azvedo telephoned PTL from Gatlinburg with the news that Tammy Faye had gotten worse rather than better. The night before, Tammy had washed her hair and gone out into the snow on the deck. Vi brought her back inside and asked her not to do such things. Tammy went into the bathroom, locked the door, and washed her hair again. She was running a temperature of 103 degrees.

That night Vi slept on the couch in the living room, and ten-year-old Jamie slept in the same room with Tammy Faye. In the middle of the night, Tammy Faye awakened and started screaming. She yelled to Jamie, "There's a giant elephant in the room!"

Young Jamie had been around enough deliverance ministries that he felt he knew what to do. He called out in the direction where Tammy had indicated the elephant, "In the name of Jesus, get out of here!"

When Vi called and explained to me what was happening, I immediately asked her to contact our friend, Dr. Lester Nichols, a California physician, and the former owner of Palmdale Hospital. Dr. Nichols had treated Tammy previously, and I knew she would be more comfortable with him than a new doctor, especially under the circumstances. Vi called

Dr. Nichols, who answered the call from his car, where he driving on the freeway in Los Angeles. Vi urged him to come to Tennessee immediately.

"I have no clothes for a trip," the doctor said. "I will go home and pack and catch the first flight I can."

"No! No!" Vi protested. "There is no time. You must come now!"

"I'll be right there." Dr. Nichols changed his course, headed to the airport, and caught the first flight to Knoxville.

When Dr. Nichols arrived at our house in Gatlinburg, he was extremely concerned about Tammy's condition. He called me and told me she needed to get to a hospital—fast. We wasted no time in arranging to get Tammy into Eisenhower Medical Center, near our California home. Eisenhower was a top-quality hospital where our good friend Dr. Marvin Brooks served on the staff. Eisenhower was also accustomed to dealing with high-profile personalities who needed to have their privacy protected.

By that time, no commercial flights were available from the mountains of Tennessee to Los Angeles, and more importantly, Tammy Faye was in no physical condition to get onto an airplane with a crowd of strangers. Back at PTL, arrangements were made for a private aircraft to pick up Tammy Faye, Jamie, Vi, and Dr. Nichols and get them to California as fast as possible. Meanwhile, after completing my presentation to the county commissioners, I would catch a flight out of Charlotte the following day.

Before leaving the Gatlinburg house, Vi Azvedo went around the house and collected all the various medications Tammy was ingesting. She gathered enough medicine to fill half a grocery bag. Tammy had been taking megadoses of aspirin, so much that her hearing became temporarily impaired.

She also had been taking allergy medicine, Aspergum to soothe her sore throat, throat and nasal sprays, and the antibiotics the local doctor had prescribed. One container was conspicuously low—Tammy's supply of Ativan, a tranquilizer. The children and I could always tell when Tammy had taken the Ativan. Her system was on supercharged overdrive . . . for a day. Walking down the street or through a mall, it was difficult to keep stride with her. The following day, she moved in slow motion. The difference in her demeanor when she took the Ativan was like that of a strobe light one day, and a slow . . . slow . . . slow . . . neon flashing light the next.

Tammy's trip to California was a virtual nightmare for her and everybody with her. Dr. Nichols and Vi tried to make Tammy Faye comfortable, but it was a futile attempt. During the drive to the airport, Tammy talked nonsense. As the car passed a man standing in front of a small store, Tammy told Jamie, "Go tell that man, ashes to ashes, dust to dust; then he

40

will know that you are Jim and Tammy's son." Jamie had no idea what his mom was talking about. When they passed a fire hydrant, she said to Jamie, "Look at that cute little girl over there!"

On the plane, Tammy began hallucinating uncontrollably. She said she saw an orchestra playing outside on the airplane's wings and people dancing on the wings. She cried out to Jamie to get off the floor because he was covered with bugs. She also mistook the safety lights for giant bugs. She saw a cat sitting on the wing as the plane flew through the sky.

At one point, Tammy Faye tried to open the door to get out of the plane. Dr. Nichols and Vi had to restrain her to keep her from killing them all as the executive jet flying at high altitude and high speed whisked them across the country.

It was midnight by the time the plane landed on the West Coast. Dr. Marvin Brooks and a specialist in internal medicine met the group at the hospital. Tammy checked in under a pseudonym . . . or so everyone thought. The name may have been real to her just then.

Dr. Brooks and other doctors examined her immediately. The doctors were concerned that Tammy might go into shock at any moment. Their first task, they determined, was to get her off the medications she was on, but they had to bring her down slowly. To do so, they loaded her system with Valium. Valium had little effect on Tammy. They gave her more and more, and still she could not calm down enough to sleep. A doctor later said to me, "We gave her enough Valium to kill a truck driver." Dr. Nichols called me at 4:00 A.M. North Carolina time to let me know that they had finally succeeded in getting Tammy to sleep.

As I left Heritage USA the morning of January 13, 1987, little did I realize that it was the last time I would ever be there as president, C.E.O., and chairman of the board. I caught the first flight to California. By the time I arrived at Eisenhower hospital later that morning, Tammy Faye was resting comfortably. I was shown Tammy's X rays; she had pneumonia in her lungs. The doctors at Eisenhower also told me something I had feared to be true for some time—that Tammy Faye was addicted to drugs.

The combination of the pneumonia and the drugs could have permanently impaired Tammy Faye physically, the doctors told me, or possibly left her mentally incapacitated for life. More likely, one doctor told me, had we not gotten her into the hospital, within twenty-four hours, she would have been dead.

I listened in horror as the doctors described Tammy's condition. I knew she had been sick, and her moods ran the gamut from superplayful to almost dazed, but I never dreamed it was that serious!

41

The doctors explained to me that the drugs Tammy Faye had taken were not illegal—Tammy Faye never took illegal drugs—but she had unwittingly taken over-the-counter and prescription drugs that were in the same pharmaceutical family. This compounded their effects and created a powerful chemical dependency. The doctors attributed a major part of Tammy's day-to-day emotional instability to the fact that the drugs she took were not quite enough to give her a "high" such as one might get from heroin or cocaine, but because she took them so frequently, she lived a large part of her life in a constant state of withdrawal. Just as one medication was wearing off, she'd take another, prolonging the withdrawal symptoms, causing her to have extreme mood swings. The doctor's treatment plan was to slowly wean Tammy away from the drugs. They then recommended that when she was healthy enough to do so, she should go through the drug-dependency program at the Betty Ford Center, located right behind the Eisenhower hospital.

I agreed with the doctors and committed in my heart and mind that I would stick with Tammy Faye for the duration, whatever it took to help my wife get a fresh, clean start in life. In the past, I had not always been there for her when she needed me most. For instance, when Tammy was about to give birth to Jamie Charles, I took her to the hospital early in the morning, at the first sign of her contractions. When we got to the hospital, the doctor told us that, in all probability, Tammy would not be giving birth until much later that day. "Go ahead and do the television show, Jim," Tammy told me. "I'll be fine."

"Are you sure?" I asked. "I don't want to leave you, Tam."

"Yes, I'm sure. I'll be okay."

I left and did our television program, and while I was there, Tammy developed a complication of toxemia, which caused her blood pressure to skyrocket. Because Tammy Faye had experienced problems in giving birth to Tammy Sue, requiring a long labor period, the doctors decided not to take chances. For the sake of Tammy's life and that of the baby, they performed an immediate cesarean section. While I was still on the set of our live television broadcast, a staff member handed me a note, informing me that I was the father of a beautiful baby boy. We announced it on the air and made a big deal about it, and I was genuinely thrilled. Nevertheless, there was a deep regret in my heart because I had not been there with Tammy through that crisis time. Although I would not find out until 1980, when Tammy and I went through marriage counseling, she resented my not being there with her when Jamie Charles was born.

At Eisenhower it took three weeks for the doctors to detoxify Tammy

Faye. When they felt she was able to function without drugs, they released her from the hospital and immediately checked her in at the Betty Ford Center. On February 20, the first night she was there, staying in a room by herself, Tammy fell apart. She could not stand being cooped up. She screamed and cried throughout the night. In the early hours of the morning, she called and cried into the phone, "Jim, please come and get me out of this place!"

The next day, we arranged for Tammy to take the Betty Ford program as an outpatient. She made me a promise that if I would allow her to stay at home, she would do everything required by the Betty Ford program. And Tammy held true to her word. Days, we were free to rest, relax, shop. After dinner each evening, the Bakker family headed off to the Betty Ford Center. The doctors indicated that not only should Tammy be in the program but the entire family and those friends closest to her. Each evening, Tammy Faye stood by her chair in front of the others in her twelve-step group as she introduced herself, "My name is Tammy Faye, and I am addicted to over-the-counter drugs." About the same time, I was in a different group dealing with codependent issues.

Due to Tammy Faye's illness, we reconsidered our plan to leave the desert. We moved to a house in Palm Springs, a beautiful, old, Spanish-style house, once owned by the Florsheim family. The property included a large swimming pool and a guest cottage and was completely surrounded by citrus trees and a high privacy wall—which would soon come in handy.

That's where we were when I received Richard Dortch's phone call informing me that Jerry Falwell wanted to see me. Falwell would meet me in Palm Springs since I had made the decision that I would not go back to Heritage USA until Tammy was completely well. I could not possibly have imagined the full ramifications of that commitment.

CHAPTER

6

Beginning of the End

WHEN MY TELEPHONE RANG EARLY SUNDAY MORNING, IT was the call from Richard Dortch that I had been awaiting.

"The Hahn story did not run in today's paper," he told me. "Roy Grutman succeeded in stopping the story from running in *The Charlotte Observer*."

I breathed a huge sigh of relief.

"But. . . ." Reverend Dortch paused.

"But?" I asked nervously.

"But Grutman says that he can't hold them off much longer."

My heart sank. We were back where we started from, the story was going to run, and the world was going to learn about my sin in the worst possible light. I knew I had to tell Tammy soon.

"Jim, Jerry Falwell has offered to help us with damage control," said Reverend Dortch. "Falwell and his people have offered to fly out there to meet with you. I will come with them. We can be there as early as Monday night. Time is of the essence."

I didn't say a word.

"Jim, I think we should let them help us."

I spoke softly into the mouthpiece of the phone. "All right," I said reluctantly. "Tell them to come on."

I hung up the phone, and the plan that would change my life forever was set in motion. The next day Jerry Falwell and his aides flew out to see me. Mark DeMoss, Jerry Falwell's young spokesman, later explained to the press why Jerry Falwell came to Palm Springs without John Ankerberg and Jimmy Swaggart—who apparently were left out of the loop. Mark DeMoss said, "Dr. Falwell went to Palm Springs at Reverend Bakker's request, as a Christian brother and pastor."

Technically, I suppose that is true. I did indeed acquiesce to Richard Dortch's insistence that I allow Jerry Falwell to come meet with me . . . after Falwell's representatives had approached him and emphatically offered to do so.

Before the arrival of Falwell and his entourage, I sat down with Tammy Faye on the sofa in the sitting room of our bedroom at the Palm Springs house. I knew Tammy was a tough woman, much stronger than most people gave her credit for, but suddenly she looked so terribly fragile to me.

"Tam, I love you. You know that, don't you?"

"Of course, Jim. What's wrong? Just tell me. It can't be that bad after all we have been through. . . ."

How does one tell his wife that he has been unfaithful? And as a result, every facet of her existence is about to be blown apart, landing on newspapers, radios, and television screens around the world?

"Tam," I slowly started again, "I just got off the phone with Reverend Dortch. He's coming out to see us tomorrow."

"Why is he going to do that? Jim, tell me what is wrong!"

"Tam, *The Charlotte Observer* is going to print an article in the next few days and I want to tell you about it before it comes out." Tammy was listening intently. "Tam, the article is going to expose the fact that seven years ago, when we were going through a tough time in our marriage . . . remember?"

Tammy nodded but remained quiet.

"When we were going through a hard time in our marriage . . . the article is going to say . . . that I," I stopped and gulped hard. "It's going to say that I had an affair. . . ."

For a moment it looked as though Tammy was going to say something. After all, false accusations were nothing new in our life, so it would be easy for her to ignore them.

But I quickly said, "And it is true. I had an affair, if that is what you want to call it."

Tammy slumped against the back of the sofa as though somebody had just knocked the wind out of her. I guess somebody had. At first, the color drained from her face. Then just as quickly, her face flushed with color as she burst into tears.

She didn't yell. She didn't scream. She did not react violently. She just cried. And cried. And cried.

I tried to hold her in my arms but she would not let me. She continued to weep. I never felt so low in all my life.

I told Tammy exactly what I did, that I had had a one-time sexual encounter in Florida with a woman named Jessica Hahn. I emphasized that it had happened that one time only. I was not in love with the woman; I had been foolishly trying to make Tammy jealous. I told Tammy that Reverend Dortch and Reverend Jerry Falwell were coming the next day to help us figure out what to do next.

"Jerry Falwell?" Tammy asked as the tears streamed down her face. "What does he have to do with us?"

"I don't know, Tam," I replied. "All I know is that Reverend Dortch says that he has offered to help us deal with all of this. You know I trust Reverend Dortch completely."

Tammy nodded. She was taking this much better than I had expected. I now realize she was like someone whose house had burst into flames. It was time to put out the fire and assess blame later. For now, Falwell and Dortch were coming. We needed to get ready.

We spent most of the day in uneasy silence. Occasionally, Tammy would break out in tears. I was concerned for her emotional well-being. It had been a tough month already. Not only was Tammy Faye in recovery, about a week or so before Reverend Dortch's call, our seventeen-year-old daughter Tammy Sue had run away from home. Tammy Sue had hosted our television program, along with Richard Dortch and others, during the month of January. On the air one day, Tammy Sue introduced her boyfriend, Doug. A few weeks later, with no advance warning to her mother and me, they were engaged to be married. Tammy and I felt our daughter needed to give the relationship some time, so we had Don Hardister, our chief of security, bring Tammy Sue to California to stay with us. Tammy Sue was not happy. When she ran off in March, we had a fairly good idea of where she might be going. Within a month, she and Doug were husband and wife. The untimely marriage ripped our hearts out, as it would most parents who dreamed of a glorious wedding for their son or daughter and a life of happiness and fulfillment. But our relationship with our daughter would not be the only thing wrenched away from us this week.

Monday afternoon, March 16, Richard Dortch flew to Lynchburg,

Virginia, to meet Roy Grutman and Jerry Falwell. Dortch had met Falwell previously but was meeting Grutman for the first time. Together the men, along with Falwell aides Jerry Nims and Mark DeMoss, boarded Falwell's private jet and took off for Palm Springs.

Jerry Falwell had first met Norman Roy Grutman as his adversary in a courtroom. At that time, Grutman was representing Robert Guccione, publisher of *Penthouse* magazine, and Falwell was suing *Penthouse* for printing what he claimed was a bogus interview. So impressed was Falwell by Grutman that after the trial he said, "Counselor, if I ever get in serious trouble, be assured I will call you first." Mr. Grutman replied, "It will be my great honor to represent you, Doctor."[1]

Even before the plane took flight, Jerry Falwell began questioning Reverend Dortch regarding the Jessica Hahn matter and the overall operating structure of PTL. Reverend Dortch answered Falwell's questions cautiously, avoiding any discussion of the details concerning PTL's out-of-court settlement with Jessica Hahn.

After dinner, Reverend Dortch asked Roy Grutman to go to the front of the plane so he could speak privately to the lawyer. The previous Friday, during a phone conversation between the two men, Grutman had agreed to represent PTL. "I will be your lawyer," he promised Reverend Dortch.

Now, aboard Jerry Falwell's jet, Reverend Dortch asked Roy Grutman, "Can I tell you some things confidentially?"

Grutman assured Dortch that he could speak openly, with complete lawyer-client confidentiality. At that point, Reverend Dortch told Roy Grutman everything he knew concerning the out-of-court settlement, the money that was paid to Jessica Hahn, and how it was paid. Before the plane landed in Palm Springs on Monday afternoon, Grutman was privy to all the intimate details of my sexual indiscretion.[2]

I have often wondered how much of that Dortch-Grutman conversation was known to Jerry Falwell on Tuesday, March 17. Although I did not know it at the time, PTL had already paid Roy Grutman a fifty thousand dollar retainer to represent us. Besides violating Richard Dortch's confidentiality, Roy Grutman conveniently ignored this conversation—and the retainer—when a month later Jerry Falwell appointed a committee to investigate the financial settlement with Jessica Hahn. The committee was comprised of two new PTL board members . . . and Roy Grutman.[3]

Reverend Dortch and the Lynchburg group were met by Vi Azvedo's husband, Eddie. En route to the hotel, the group's discussion centered completely around the upcoming presidential election and Vice President

Bush's campaign. The Falwell troupe checked in at Maxim's Hotel in Palm Springs and Reverend Dortch came straight to see Tammy and me.

I was glad to see Richard Dortch. I had known Richard since 1977, when he had already earned a reputation within our denomination as a pastor to pastors. At the time of his first appearance on our *PTL* program, Reverend Dortch was serving as the Illinois state superintendent of the Assemblies of God and as one of our denomination's thirteen national presbyters. In 1978, as PTL was beginning to grow exponentially, I sensed the need for a strong, pastoral influence on our Board of Directors. I asked Richard Dortch to consider the position, and he accepted.

By the fall of 1983, PTL had taken on a life of its own. We had a huge budget, hundreds of employees, and an exhausting schedule of television productions and growing ministries. I knew I was in over my head trying to run an organization this large. Although I had read many business, customer-service, and people-management books in an attempt to be a good manager, I had no formal business training. I was an ideas person; I could look at a lot covered by weeds, rocks, and trees, and see a vision of a Grand Hotel. But when it came to poring over financial statements or confronting staff members, I was gladly willing to let other people handle that.

Nevertheless, I was the president of our organization and it was my responsibility to find good people to deal with the myriad details of taking care of the business and personnel matters. That is how I came to hire Richard Dortch. Not only was he a trusted PTL board member, but I figured that anyone who knew how to manage hundreds of ministers and churches, plus the Illinois state office staff and radio stations, could handle the financial and personnel pressures at PTL. Richard came on staff full-time as our senior executive vice president, corporate executive director, and my copastor of Heritage Village and Missionary Fellowship Church.

I basically hired Richard Dortch to be my general manager, to be the executive at PTL that I was not. I was the visionary, the dreamer, the builder. Let Richard handle the details. Unfortunately, television is heady work.

Richard Dortch put it this way:

> The fascinating aura surrounding television can suck you in like quicksand if you let it. Almost every time I went to PTL for a board meeting, I made a television appearance. It didn't take long for me to be captivated and enchanted by the experience. Surrounded by cameramen and sound people who focused on my every word and movement, I enjoyed the exposure and attention of television—not realizing its dangers.[4]

Reverend Dortch's admitted fascination with the spotlight of television and his intense desire to protect and maintain the ministry of PTL most likely colored some of his decisions and advice that third week in March. I will never know.

I do know that when Reverend Dortch visited with Tammy and me on Monday evening, March 16, there was no man in the world I trusted more than him. He gave me a glowing report of PTL's progress during the first few months of 1987 and then reluctantly told me that he had slowed construction on our building projects almost to a standstill until more money came in. I was not happy to hear that, and Reverend Dortch knew it. But that was not the reason he was in Palm Springs.

Speaking quietly but emphatically, he told Tammy and me the same information he had given me by phone. Reverend Dortch seemed convinced that Jerry Falwell's help was the only way to stave off an attempt by Jimmy Swaggart to destroy our ministry. Beyond that, Falwell was a highly visible, credible television preacher himself, and his vast influence would help us defray some of the certain fallout if and when *The Charlotte Observer* story went to press.

It seemed to make sense.

The next day Tammy Faye and I again met Richard Dortch at his hotel room around 8:30 A.M. on Tuesday, March 17. We talked briefly and then prayed before going to meet Jerry Falwell and his group in a suite at Maxim's Hotel around 9:00 A.M. When we arrived, Jerry Nims, Mark DeMoss, and Norman Roy Grutman met us there. After introductions, Jerry Falwell invited Tammy and me into an adjoining room in the suite. He closed the door and came over to where we were standing. He stepped between Tammy and me and put his big arms around us, forming a small huddle.

"Jim and Tammy, I want to help you," he said, sounding like a compassionate father. "I love you and I want to help you," he repeated. "First of all, I need to know the facts. I want you to tell me everything that happened seven years ago in Florida with the Hahn woman."

Still huddled together with Falwell like a big bear holding his cubs, I told Jerry the story in specific detail, right in front of Tammy, emphasizing that it was not an ongoing affair, but a foolish, fifteen- to twenty-minute sexual encounter, and that I definitely did not rape the woman. Next we talked briefly about the potential Swaggart attack on PTL. Then Falwell encouraged Tammy to go back home. He and I would remain to discuss how things should best be handled. As Tammy left the room, Jerry called after her, telling her that he would be praying for her. Tammy did not answer.

Once Tammy was gone, Jerry closed the door, and he and I sat down and began to discuss the attempts of Jimmy Swaggart to take over the ministry of PTL. We discussed Jimmy Swaggart's letter to John Ankerberg, indicating that *The Charlotte Observer* would do its part, and the Assemblies of God would do its part to excoriate me. Jerry implied that he felt it was a conspiracy to bring me down. He also made it sound as though his motives for getting involved were not totally altruistic, but that he was concerned about Swaggart's designs on his own ministry. "Jim, if we don't stop Swaggart at your place, he will eventually be at our door."

My suspicions of Jerry Falwell's motives for wanting to help us began to break down. I wanted to believe the man, and the fact that he seemed so open and sincere about wanting to protect his own interests rather than trying to convince me that he was concerned about mine lent credibility to what he was saying. I had been suspicious of Jerry because it was common knowledge that he regarded charismatics as doctrinally unsound. He had often joked that charismatics were people who had eaten too much pizza and thus their propensity to speak in tongues. But because Jerry was expressing his own self-interest and his concern for self-preservation, he came across to me as believable.

Falwell indicated that he could help me fend off Swaggart's attempts and deal with the Hahn fallout. He was willing.

"But you must ask me to help you, Jim," Jerry said.

"Well, of course, I'd be glad for your help," I replied.

Jerry was extremely specific and emphatic. "I want to help you, Jim, but you must ask me."

I thought it rather strange that Jerry was stressing the point that I had to ask him, but I thought it might be necessary because his denominational affiliation was so different from my own.

Again he said, "You must ask me, Jim."

"Okay, I'm asking you," I said. "Will you please help me?"

Jerry Falwell smiled broadly. "Why certainly, I will help you, Jim. Let me tell you what we need to do. . . ."

For the next hour, Jerry Falwell outlined how I should resign from all three of my positions at PTL, as president, chairman of the board, and pastor of the church. After thirty to ninety days, when the furor over the Hahn disclosure would have dissipated, I could then return to my positions. He told me how he had once helped a church in Bangor, Maine, when its pastor committed adultery. Jerry told me that he had stepped in and "helped," and now the church and pastor were both doing fine. He felt in his heart, he said, that we could see similar results at PTL.

Jerry then suggested that we should have the current board members resign as an act of good faith, humility, and a willingness to show that PTL was making a fresh start. We could replace them with a new Board, all friends of mine whom I respected and trusted—pastors and people such as Pat Boone and Dale Evans Rogers. We agreed that Richard Dortch would serve as the new president in the interim and as host of the television program.

"You stay here in Palm Springs and take care of getting Tammy Faye completely well," Falwell said. "You'll still be in charge of the ministry. We'll work to protect you and save PTL from Jimmy Swaggart." He then outlined how he would take a group of leaders, including Billy Graham, to meet with Jimmy Swaggart and try to persuade him to back off from his destructive plan for the Body of Christ's sake. That idea sounded good to me, but I was still hesitant to resign from the organization to which I had given birth.

"Is this okay with you, Jim?" Jerry asked.

"Well, I don't know. . . . I guess as long as Richard Dortch is the president and the host of the show . . . and as long as I choose any new board members. . . . "

"You must make up your mind, Jim. We don't have much time. Do you want my help?"

"Yes, I do."

"Okay, I'll have Roy Grutman come in and explain how we can do all of this. Excuse me just a minute," Jerry Falwell said. He stepped outside the conference room and I buried my head in my hands at the table.

Jerry Falwell closed the door. He spoke to Grutman within the hearing of the others. "Roy, Jim wants to talk to you."

Falwell then walked over to where Richard Dortch was sitting. He looked down at Reverend Dortch and according to Dortch spoke firmly, "Jim has just turned the PTL ministry over to me, provided that you are the president and the host of the show. I've agreed to that. So you and I need to get to work to decide who we want on the new board of directors, because Jim wants to approve who the new board will be."[5] Falwell went on to tell Dortch that "within six months to a year, we'll give the ministry back to Jim."[6]

I was shell-shocked. Perhaps because of that, I violated several of my own personal principles during my meeting with Jerry Falwell. For one thing, in all my business dealings, I made it a practice never to meet with anyone alone. I always wanted someone else as a witness for all my dealings. I wanted to avoid the "my word against your word" syndrome. But for some reason, possibly because I knew that we would be discussing the sensitive matter of Jessica Hahn, I did not invite Richard Dortch or anyone else into the conference room that day. That was a mistake. Once Tammy was gone, I had nobody to corroborate what was said in the meeting that morning. To this day, Jerry Falwell and I recall the words and intent of that meeting differently.

Roy Grutman came in and talked to me, and while Falwell talked to Dortch, Grutman kept reiterating, "This is like a play, Jim. You have to play dead for a while. If you don't, Swaggart is going to destroy you. You'll only have to play dead for thirty to ninety days and you will be back at PTL."

I was concerned about how Tammy was going to take all this and I told Grutman so. I wanted to trust Norman Roy Grutman, and his authoritative eloquence engendered my confidence; he said that he would represent me and I believed him. Grutman suggested that he and I go over to my house and tell Tammy what was going on so he and the other members of Falwell's group could get back east as soon as possible to put the plan into action. Compliantly, I agreed.

My head was in a whirl as Grutman and I walked out of that room. But I was still surprised when I heard the bombastic lawyer announce to the other men, "Jim and I are going over to the Bakkers' house to tell Tammy about the decision to turn the ministry over to Jerry Falwell."

I had not turned the ministry over to Jerry Falwell. I *never* turned the ministry over to Jerry Falwell! I had agreed to turn my presidency and television responsibilities over to Richard Dortch for a period of thirty to ninety days, after which I would return to my own posts. Richard Dortch was already the general manager of PTL, so I felt safe in doing so. Jerry Falwell had assured me that he himself would remain in the background as one of the men working to save the ministry. "Jim, I'll never even go to PTL!" he told me.

Norman Roy Grutman and I drove back to my home to tell Tammy. It was one of the longest drives of my life. Along the way, Grutman continued to emphasize that my resignation was the only way to defuse the powder keg that was about to explode with *The Charlotte Observer*'s disclosure of my sin with Jessica Hahn. Grutman implied that the best way to take the attention away from that story was to make a bigger headline with my resignation. He also spoke in threatening terms of how Ankerberg and Swaggart in their efforts to take over PTL might instigate the PTL Partners to initiate a class-action lawsuit in an effort to take over PTL. Grutman seemed fond of using the term "hostile takeover" to describe what he said Jimmy Swaggart was trying to do. I was aware of some of the articles Jimmy had written in his magazines concerning certain ministries that had theme parks (I wonder whom he meant!) and some of the comments he had made concerning me in recent meetings with Assemblies of God leaders. According to the reports I received, Jimmy's words about me, as well as his actions and attitude, were virulent. Consequently, Grutman's constant warnings of a "hostile takeover" attempt seemed plausible.

By the time we arrived at my home in Palm Springs, my stomach was tied up in what felt like a million knots. Tammy was not happy to see me coming through the door with Roy Grutman in tow.

"Tam, we need to talk to you," I told her. Grutman took it from there. He told Tammy in detail the reasons why I had to resign. We walked outside in our garden as Grutman laid out the scenario. "Jim needs to appoint this blue-ribbon panel to the board to lead the ministry for thirty to ninety days and get you well while you finish your outpatient program at Betty Ford. We'll take care of everything. Richard Dortch will be president and, of course, Reverend Falwell will help. You and Jim can choose the board of directors."

Tammy smelled a rat. She distrusted Jerry Falwell's motives and she was not buying Grutman's story at all. She was especially reluctant to have me resign my position on the board. She could almost handle why I might have to stay off the air for a while; that wasn't a major change since I had not been hosting our show for almost three months anyhow. She could also understand the need for me to stay out of the pulpit for a while. Tammy was aware of how the Assemblies of God normally handle moral failures. But she could not see why I had to step down from the PTL Board of Directors.

Outside in our yard, she adamantly insisted that I not resign. Grutman seemed to sense that although he was the master orator, Tammy Faye's instinctive intuition was swaying my position.

"Look, Mrs. Bakker, if it makes you feel any better, we will have each member of the new board, including Reverend Falwell, sign resignations before they even come on." Grutman looked squarely at me as he continued speaking. "We will place those signed resignations in your hands, and that way, any time you are ready to return, you just turn in those resignations of the new board, and you can bring back your old board members or do as you please. It will be your prerogative."

I looked at Tammy. In my nervous, embarrassed condition, the arrangement was sounding better to me, but I could tell by Tammy's facial expression she was unconvinced.

"I don't feel good about this," Tammy said.

"Oh, everything will be fine," Grutman assured her. "You have been through quite a lot lately. You need to just relax and take your mind off this situation. We'll take care of everything. Go relax and read a book."

Later that day, Grutman sent a thick romance novel to Tammy. Tammy Faye may have been through a lot, but she was beginning to resurface stronger than ever. Our marriage was flourishing despite the recent revelations of my infidelity. Tammy had forgiven me, and we were starting to fall in love all over again. We had nearly completed our aftercare program at Betty Ford, and would have, in all probability, returned to PTL within weeks had not these new developments occurred. Tammy was ready for a fight, but I was not. She saw through the sham that was being perpetrated in the name of God; I did not. She felt that my resigning was an inappropriate way to handle the situation. As the events unfolded in the weeks to come, it became increasingly clear that she was right and I was wrong.

Grutman seemed in a big hurry to get going. "We must make haste and get back to the plane," he kept saying. "We must hurry."

I have often been asked since that day, "Why didn't you take some time to think things over before making such an important decision?"

That is exactly what I should have done, but I did not, and I was wrong. Years before, when I was just starting out as a young preacher, the words of another speaker at a charismatic Lutheran conference in Minneapolis left an indelible impression upon my heart and mind. He said, "Beware voices of haste."

It was excellent advice that unfortunately I disregarded. Both Falwell and Grutman, as well as the others in their group, emphasized that I must make up my mind quickly. We had to act quickly to stave off the "hostile takeover." We had to act quickly to thwart the impact of *The Charlotte Observer*'s ensuing article. Everything had to happen now. Fast. Hurry.

In retrospect, I firmly believe that had I taken just twenty-four hours to think about the Falwell-Grutman proposal I would have rejected it out of hand. If I were going to implement any part of what they had suggested, I would have done it under the careful watch of men with whom I had worked over the years and trusted to have the ministry's and my best interests at heart. Unfortunately, I did not take time even to consult the usual battery of PTL lawyers and financial advisors concerning Jerry Falwell's offer. Had I simply stopped long enough to think, to seek God's direction, to surround myself with a group of wise counselors as the Bible instructs,

I would not have allowed a group of men, many of whom I barely knew, to take the reins of PTL. Unfortunately, because of my concern for Tammy's recovery, the impending Hahn article, and my own fears and foolishness, I allowed Heritage USA to be stolen from the PTL Partners and me while I looked on. Because of my haste, within twenty-four hours I lost my ministry, my life's work, and my will to live. Overnight, I went from having a worldwide ministry with several thousand employees to having no ministry at all and being an unemployed pariah.

Back home on Tuesday night, our houseguests, Doug and Laura Lee Oldham, assured me that I could trust Jerry Falwell. Doug had worked in ministry with Jerry for many years, long before he ever came to PTL. When I confided to Doug some of the details of the day's meeting, my friend repeated again and again, "Jim, Jerry Falwell would never hurt you."

7

The Hostile Takeover

ON WEDNESDAY, MARCH 18, RICHARD DORTCH CALLED A special emergency meeting of the PTL Board of Directors. The board convened in the boardroom of the PTL World Outreach Center about 9:00 P.M. After a brief explanation of the purpose of the meeting by Reverend Dortch, Roy Grutman informed the board members that they were being asked to resign. Grutman took special care to emphasize that there could be legal and financial problems for the members if they did not comply with Jerry Falwell's request. Several of the board members later told me that they felt they were being threatened.

Before the board resigned, however, they annulled the official board resolution of December 10, 1980, which had placed PTL in the hands of the Assemblies of God if for any reason I could no longer serve as president of PTL. Thus, in one fell swoop, all threats that Jimmy Swaggart could legally exercise a "hostile takeover" of PTL through the Assemblies of God were removed. Nobody on our board had yet figured out that the hostile takeover was not being orchestrated in Swaggart's office.

Grutman had arranged for me to talk to the board over a speakerphone. Dejected and extremely embarrassed that I had failed my faithful friends and coworkers on the PTL board, I sat at a desk in an enclosed outer veranda of our home, waiting for Grutman's call. When it rang at about 7:00 P.M. Pacific time, I stared momentarily at the phone as if it were a snake before I finally picked it up. With his usual loquacious flair,

Grutman took us on a meandering journey of words before turning the phone over to me. In a simple, brief statement, I resigned as president of PTL, as the chief executive officer, and as chairman of the board. The heartbreaking gesture took very little time. I did not invite any questions and none were asked. The dedicated board members all promised that they would be praying for me. One of the most crushing events of my life to date had taken only a few minutes. It was over. I hung up the phone and went back to the couch in our living room, lay down, curled up in a ball, and hoped the world would go away. I just wanted to die.

Back at PTL, Jerry Falwell, who was also connected to the meeting by phone was elected as the new chairman of the board. He accepted the position over the phone, and then continued to listen as one by one, the board members stepped down and were replaced with selections made by Jerry Falwell and his aides. Pat Boone, Dale Evans Rogers, and most of the other well-known charismatic leaders whom I had chosen to serve on the new board were not asked. Nor was I given opportunity to approve those who were asked to serve on the new board, one of the fundamental aspects of Jerry Falwell's and my discussion little more than thirty-six hours earlier.

In addition to Richard Dortch, two men of charismatic persuasion were elected to the new Falwell board: James Watt, former U.S. Secretary of the Interior, and Rex Humbard, pastor of the Cathedral of Tomorrow, near Akron, Ohio, and a frequent guest on our programs. The remainder of the new board were noncharismatics: Jerry Nims, one of Falwell's close associates; Ben Armstrong, executive director of the National Religious Broadcasters; and Sam Moore, president of Thomas Nelson Publishers. Pastor Charles Stanley of First Baptist Church, Atlanta, was extended an invitation to serve on the new Falwell board, but he declined the offer. Bailey Smith, former president of the Southern Baptist Convention, eventually received that seat around the table.

Grutman never produced the signed resignations of the new board members. I had informed my former executive secretary, Shirley Fulbright, of Grutman's promise before the board meeting. When Shirley raised the question of the whereabouts of the missing signed resignations, she was told by Reverend Dortch to keep quiet. The subject never came up in any official meeting ever again.

On Thursday afternoon, March 19, at about 2:30 P.M., in a conference call arranged by Norman Roy Grutman, I went on the phone line to do the interview Grutman had promised *The Charlotte Observer* the weekend before if they would hold the Hahn article, which they had already decided to kill. Other than Grutman's call, little had changed since last week as far as the paper was concerned. Because of the potential for lawsuits, it is highly debatable that the editors would have run the story the next week, or ever, had it not been for us providing them with a scoop better than they dreamed.

Earlier that day, I called several of my key staff members and told them what was about to happen. I did not go into detail; I just wanted them to know before the rest of the world knew. I told them that I planned to be back within thirty to ninety days, and I pleaded with them to do their best to hold PTL together. Reverend Dortch had already scheduled a staff meeting for later that day when he and Norman Roy Grutman could break the news of my resignation to the rest of the staff.

The editors of the local paper were not sure what to expect when they learned that I would be talking to them from my home in Palm Springs. Grutman had promised them a front-page scoop, though, so they knew something big was in the air. *The Charlotte Observer*'s editorial offices, I later learned, looked like a war room that day, with tape recorders set to record my interview, reporters ready to write the story, and the paper's top brass and lawyer ready to call any shots necessary.

In the presidential lounge of the Heritage Grand Hotel, the scene was similar, as Richard Dortch, Roy Grutman, Neil Eskelin (PTL's public relations officer), Roe Messner (PTL's builder), and David Taggart sat together expectantly. Shirley Fulbright prepared to record the conversation as well.

The newspaper people must have been shocked when they learned that our "interview" would not be an interview so much as a statement by me. Norman Roy Grutman had written every word of my formal resignation, taking kernels of the truth and twisting them together with his own interpretations. He faxed it to me at my home in Palm Springs shortly before I was to read it publicly. As I read it over—the resignation sounded much more like Grutman than me—I thought back to a question I had asked Richard Dortch when I had come out of my meeting with Falwell. Looking him straight in the eyes, I asked Reverend Dortch, "Is this what I should do?"

Dortch looked back at me and said, "There are no other alternatives. This is what must be done."

I had no other option. I had to resign. I fumbled nervously with the fax in front of me. I didn't want to read it. Tammy Faye would not even listen. *But I have no alternatives*, I thought.

Grutman asked the reporters to allow me to read my statement without interruption, and they agreed. I began to speak.

Thank you. As you know, for many years, Tammy Faye and I and our ministries have been subjected to constant harassment and pressures by various groups and forces whose objective has been to undermine and to destroy us. I cannot deny that the personal toll that these pressures have exerted on me and my wife and family have been more than we can bear.

In fact, as our friends are all too well aware, my and Tammy's physical and emotional resources have been so overwhelmed that we are presently under full-time therapy at a treatment center in California. We want to express our gratitude for the support and encouragement we've received from so many of our friends and partners. I have decided that for the good of my family, the church, and of all of our related ministries that I should resign and step down immediately from PTL.

I have also today resigned from the Assemblies of God. I am not able to muster the resources needed to combat a new wave of attack that I have learned is about to be launched against us by *The Charlotte Observer*, which has attacked us incessantly for the past twelve years.

Although I did not mention Hahn's name, I went on to admit that I had been guilty of adultery. Grutman wrote it more ambiguously:

I am appalled at the baseness of this present campaign to defame and vilify me.

I categorically deny that I've ever sexually assaulted or harassed anyone. I sorrowfully acknowledge that seven years ago, in an isolated incident, I was wickedly manipulated by treacherous former friends and then colleagues who victimized me with the aid of a female confederate. They conspired to betray me into a sexual encounter at a time of great stress in my marital life. Vulnerable as I was at the time, I was set up as part of a scheme to co-opt me and obtain some advantage for themselves over me in connection with their hope for position in the ministry.

I have sought and gratefully received the loving forgiveness of our Savior who forgives us of our sins. I have told Tammy everything and Tammy, of course, has forgiven me, and our love for each other is greater and stronger than it has ever been.

59

Now, seven years later, this one time mistake is seized upon by my enemies to humiliate and degrade me to gratify their envious and selfish motives. They have falsified, distorted, and exaggerated the facts so as to make the occurrence appear many times worse than it ever was. Anyone who knows Jim Bakker knows that I never physically assaulted anyone in my life.

In retrospect, it was poor judgment to have succumbed to blackmail. But when extortionist overtures were made, I was concerned to protect and spare the ministry and my family. Unfortunately, money was paid in order to avoid further suffering or hurt to anyone, to appease these persons who were determined to destroy this ministry.

I now, in hindsight, realize payment should have been resisted, and we ought to have exposed the blackmailers to the penalties of the law. I'm truly sorry for all this that has happened in the past or any harm that may have occurred.

I bear no malice to anyone. I forgive those who have borne false witness against me.

I cannot undo the past, but must now address the future. I have no doubt God has a redemptive plan for PTL and for Jim and Tammy.

I fervently pray for the future of PTL and Heritage USA. It is my life to preserve, to protect those cherished values which it embodies.

I had the most difficulty reading the next section of the resignation letter. First of all, Grutman had intimated that Jerry Falwell and I were friends, which could only have been said in the loosest sense of the word. Prior to our Tuesday morning meeting, I could remember exchanging only a few words with Jerry in my entire life, usually encountering him at Christian Bookseller Association conventions or National Religious Broadcasting functions. Anyone who knew me well also knew that Jerry and I were not "friends."

I've asked my friend, Jerry Falwell, to help me in my crisis. The PTL board of directors has accepted my resignation, and appointed Jerry Falwell as chairman of our board of directors, requesting him to designate a new board of directors. He has done this and the old board has accordingly resigned.

> I ask the prayerful support of our friends and foes for the
> preservation and advancement of God's work and the future of
> PTL.
>
> > God bless you and good-bye.[1]

Like a zombie I had read the whole thing just as it had been written, saying things I knew were not true. How foolish! I was lying. I was not really resigning. It was a "play act," Grutman had said. I knew things were not happening the way Falwell, Grutman, and I had discussed. Most importantly, Jerry Falwell had selected a new board, without consulting me. Nevertheless, I went along with the play, thinking I was saving the PTL ministry and everything I held dear.

I was wrong to do so. Lying never justifies the cause; the end does not justify the means. Not only was I wrong, I was a fool ever to go along with such a hoax.

According to Grutman's instructions, I quickly hung up the phone to avoid answering any questions. In the presidential lounge, my assistant, Shirley Fulbright, burst into tears.

Grutman continued the interview and answered *The Charlotte Observer*'s questions. He then introduced Jerry Falwell, who came on the line from Lynchburg. Falwell's comments were telling: "They [the new board members] all have promised to continue in prayer for the complete healing and restoration of Jim and Tammy Bakker and with the prayer that God somewhere down the road has another fruitful and effective ministry in store for them somewhere."[2]

The editors at *The Charlotte Observer* were skeptical. The paper and I had had a running battle for years, and they could not imagine that I would give up so easily. In an attempt to allay their suspicions, Grutman lied to the reporters and emphasized to them that my resignation was for real. "There are no conditions," he said. "It is not a sham, word is that he has resigned and stepped down. Period. End of report." As Falwell closed out the interview he remarked, "It's my intention in the next thirty days *The Charlotte Observer* and PTL are going to be friends."[3]

The Charlotte Observer's reporters rushed the story to press. So, too, did most major news outlets. Almost immediately, our Palm Springs home came under a media siege with reporters and satellite trucks up and down the street everywhere.

The Charlotte Observer sold more papers the next day than at any other time except the death of Elvis Presley. They had to restart their presses three times on Friday to keep newspapers in the racks.

Within hours of my resignation becoming public, my telephone began ringing constantly. One of the first people to call was Dr. Billy Graham. I was shocked to hear his voice. Dr. Graham let me know that he and his family cared and were praying for me. Bill Bright, president of Campus Crusade for Christ, called soon after. So did Oral Roberts.

One of the most unsettling early calls I received was from Dr. Robert Schuller. First, Dr. Schuller assured me of his love and prayers. As we talked longer, however, Dr. Schuller's tone turned ominous. Dr. Schuller warned me not to resign hastily.

I cringed. "It's too late," I said quietly. "It's already been done."

A few days later, as the media uproar about a "holy war" began to explode, Robert Schuller called again, offering Tammy and me his ministerial retreat center in Hawaii if we wanted to escape the crowds for a while. Again Dr. Schuller reiterated the concerns he had expressed in his previous call. I thanked Robert for his kind offer but felt that I needed to stay in Palm Springs and finish Tammy's aftercare program in spite of everything that was happening around us.

Several people whom I had never expected to respond to our hurt called almost immediately, offering everything from financial help to invitations to spend time in the privacy of their homes. Richard Simmons, the fitness guru who had appeared with Tammy Faye on her show, called within hours, offering to help. According to one of my former aides, singer Elton John, whom I had never met, invited us to his home. But I wasn't sure if the call was real or a hoax. I appreciated their kindness, but I felt as though I had just been hit by a speeding automobile. I did not want to do much of anything. I wanted to die.

For the next few days, I could barely function as a human being. Again and again, I simply curled up on the couch and shut my eyes. I stayed like that for hours on end, thinking, thinking, racking my brain over what I had done, wondering, *Could I have handled it differently? What could I yet do to improve the situation?* I drew blanks every way I turned.

One night on television I watched an interviewer ask both Jimmy Swaggart and Jerry Falwell about rumors of a "hostile takeover" of PTL. Swaggart denied having designs on PTL and called me "a cancer that needed to be excised from the Body of Christ." When the interviewer pressed Falwell on the question of a hostile takeover of PTL, Jerry Falwell looked straight into the camera and said, "I do not know anything about a hostile takeover."[4]

At that moment, I knew I had been deceived. Jerry Falwell was the man who had informed *me* of the hostile takeover threat!

He later reiterated his on-air comment. "I . . . at this moment, do not feel anyone attempted a hostile takeover." He covered himself by adding, "I did not say the Reverend Bakker did not think that. . . . He may have hard evidence to prove that."[5]

A letter was sent out to the PTL Partners in addition to my regular monthly communiqué to them. The second letter was not written by me but went out under my name saying that I was resigning, but PTL would be going on to higher heights than ever before, and the partners could trust this group of good men!

A week or so after my resignation, Tammy and I taped a video segment from our home in California that was to be run on PTL. The purpose of the segment was to give our side of the story to our PTL audience and partners. I apologized for my sins and the hurt I had caused the Body of Christ. Tammy, too, expressed the fact that she had forgiven me and was willing and ready to move on with our lives. As I concluded my remarks, I told our viewers, "The sun will shine again." Tammy Faye then sang a song, "The Sun Will Shine Again," from the porch of our guest house.

When I saw the way the tape had been edited, I was appalled. The format sheets—the written record of what was said and done on tape and how it was edited—looked as though it had been shot through by a machine gun. Specific, crucial details had been edited. For example, on the original tape, I confessed to our audience that I had had a fifteen- to twenty-minute affair seven years ago. The words "fifteen- to twenty-minute" were deleted, making my statement, "I had an affair seven years ago," implying an ongoing relationship.

Despite the edits, something connected with the audience at PTL that day. The studio audience spontaneously responded to the videotape with a standing ovation. According to Neil Eskelin, our public relations officer, the PTL phone lines lit up with callers saying, "We love Jim and Tammy. We want them to return."

For my part, I was ready and willing to return, but the Falwell troupe firmly resisted that idea and even some of my closest coworkers, Richard Dortch, David Taggart, and Shirley Fulbright, assured me that everything was working out as planned. I telephoned my friends repeatedly, saying, "Something is not right. I think we have been had!" They in turn went to Jerry Falwell with my concerns. Jerry said, "Oh, no. We're right on schedule."

David Taggart said, "Falwell assures us he is going to give it up; just be patient."

I called Jerry Falwell and expressed my concerns to him personally.

Again Jerry replied, "Oh, no, Jim. We're right on schedule. The plan is working perfectly. Just stay calm. This is like a play. You have to play dead or PTL will be destroyed."

Within hours, Jerry Falwell sent David Taggart and Shirley Fulbright to Palm Springs on a private jet to allay any of my concerns and to assure me that everything was going according to plan. "Just stay calm and lie low," they told me. "Jerry Falwell is taking care of everything."

Over the next few weeks, even Richard Dortch slowly began to change his tone. I told him, "Reverend Dortch, I have to come back to PTL." Reverend Dortch was aware of the plan for me to return from the beginning of my discussions with Falwell and Grutman. Nevertheless he replied, "Oh, no, Jim! You can't come back. The Assemblies of God rehabilitation program requires that you must be gone for a year or two." Ironically, both Richard Dortch and I had resigned from the Assemblies of God when my sin became news.

I never went back to my office at PTL again. I was not even given the opportunity to clean out my desk or gather my personal possessions and pictures in the room. It was suddenly as though I had never existed.

I spent much of those early days in seclusion behind the walls of our home. When I wasn't curled in a ball on the couch, I occasionally went out to our swimming pool, dodging the helicopters that hovered over our house and the reporters attempting to get photos over the walls. It got to be almost like a game. Every time a helicopter came by, I'd jump up from where I was sitting and run back under the large eaves of our house to avoid detection. One day I was sitting on a chaise lounge at our pool. Scott Ross, with whom I had worked at CBN, and Tammy Faye were in the water, only inches away. Next to me, Scott's wife Nedra was stretched out on another chaise. We were engaged in conversation with our friends whom we had not seen in years. Unknown to us, a full block away a photographer was perched atop a local hospital and, with a high-powered lens, was shooting pictures of us. The following day, a photo of Nedra and me appeared with Scott and Tammy Faye cropped out of the frame. The picture ran in papers across America. The caption blared: *Jim Bakker and Unidentified Woman!*

Tammy and I completed our aftercare program at Betty Ford. After that, when we attempted to go out for dinner, we were always followed by a parade of press cars and vans. Often the only way we could lose the media for a while was to go through a gated community where some friends of ours lived. The press was not permitted to follow onto the private property. If we did manage to get to a restaurant, we usually made our way out through the kitchen to avoid the hoard of press that would gather by the time we ate our meal.

It was due to Tammy's urgings that we went out to eat at all; had it been up to me, I would have been happy to eat peanut butter and jelly sandwiches at home to avoid the press. Not so with Tammy; she wasn't reticent about our going out. We dined mostly at Sonny Bono's restaurant in Palm Springs. Sonny was kind enough to arrange a table behind some plants in an alcove. During those early days, with our names and photos splattered all over the world, Sonny often came and talked with Tammy and me about his own hurt when his former wife Cher left him. He told me how he had felt that his world had fallen apart and how it had taken time to pick up the pieces. He told us step by step how he rebuilt his life, family, and business. Sonny was encouraging us not to give up when some of our closest friends were no longer calling. Unwittingly, in his own way, Sonny Bono ministered to Tammy and me and helped us through some of the most difficult days of our lives.

By Wednesday, April 22, Jerry Falwell and others seemed extremely concerned that I was going to make a bid to return to Heritage USA. They were not far wrong, but I knew that the first step toward my eventual return, pastoral rehabilitation, and restoration must be to get PTL back into the hands of a group of leaders who might be sensitive to those issues. By telephone, I dictated a letter to Shirley Fulbright. When Shirley completed the letter, she walked to the fax machine and inserted the letter.

"What are you doing?" Shirley heard Richard Dortch's voice behind her.

"I am sending this letter from Reverend Bakker to Reverend Falwell," she replied in her best formal executive assistant's voice.

"You can't do that!"

"Oh, yes I can." Shirley hit the button and the letter curled through the fax machine, over the phone lines, and into the office of Jerry Falwell.

The letter read:

Tammy and I have tried many times to reach you by telephone so I decided to send you this message.

Due to the unrest in the Charismatic world and also among the Charismatic leadership, I feel that it is time now for you to turn the PTL Ministry over to Charismatics, appointing James Watt as Chairman of the board, with Rex Humbard and Richard Dortch remaining. Others will be added.

I am recommending that a strong COO [Chief Operating Officer] be appointed by this Charismatic board.

As you committed to me at our meeting in Palm Springs when you brought me the information that you believed that Jimmy Swaggart was plotting a hostile takeover of PTL, promising to save the Ministry from this hostile takeover, you were going to hold the Ministry and, when I asked, you would turn it back. I am asking that you turn it over to this group of Charismatics. I am going to submit to a large group of elders in the Charismatic church world and I will return to PTL when they feel it is God's time.

I have been in touch with major leaders of the Charismatic world. Jerry, I will not fight you if you ignore my wishes but I must let you know that what you are embarking on will truly start what the press has labeled a "holy war." Please let brotherly love continue and control what we do, and let us not allow the world to have any more opportunity to wag their tongues at the cause of Christ. Let us get back to our first love and calling, winning souls for the Kingdom.

There is great unrest among Charismatic leadership, which I am meeting with in a few hours.

I have given to one of the most outstanding Christian journalists in the world all the documentation on what is being done on both sides of this issue and I have also given the documentation to a journalist in the secular media. I have sworn them to secrecy unless something happens. No matter what happens to me, they will write the true, documented story of this unprecedented event in the history of Christianity.

In warmest Christian love,
Jim Bakker[6]

I received no response from Jerry Falwell concerning my letter. Or, maybe I did. . . .

That same day, Jerry Falwell and Jerry Nims met in a Nashville hotel with John Ankerberg and four men who claimed to have damaging information about me in regard to alleged homosexual actions. Ankerberg declared that he was going to accuse me of homosexuality on the talk show *Larry King Live*, airing on CNN later that week.[7]

When Ankerberg's interview aired, I was at Little Bear Lake, not far from Palm Springs, with my son Jamie and our longtime security guard, Don Hardister. Unknown to me, Don had shifted his allegiance from me to Jerry Falwell. In fairness to Don, he had been told by the new leaders at PTL that if he wanted to keep his job, he must keep a close watch on me and keep my family and me away from Heritage USA. Consequently, even on a trip for Jamie and me to have some father-and-son time together, Don came along. I had taken Jamie to the mountain lake area to protect him from the awful things that were swirling around us, the constant siege by the press outside our door, and what he was hearing said about Tammy and me every day on television. We had been gone only a day or so when Hardister called home. Tammy Faye told Don to have me call her right away.

Don brought the message to me just as Jamie and I were about to go fishing. The fishing would have to wait. I went to a pay phone and dialed our number. When Tammy came on the line, she was furious. She informed me of Ankerberg's accusations of homosexuality not only on Larry King's program, but repeated that same night on ABC's *Nightline* with Ted Koppel as well.

My heart sank. When I learned what Ankerberg had said about me on national television, I was devastated. His words struck deeply into my soul. Like Ankerberg and Falwell, I knew well that an accusation of homosexual conduct was one of the most damaging charges that could be leveled at an evangelical minister. That is why of all the things said about me during the weeks and months following my pseudoresignation from PTL, John Ankerberg's accusations were the most painful. Not only were they the death knell of my reputation, they signaled the end of my ministry, I felt sure.

I tried always to avoid even the appearance of evil, so much so that in my early evangelistic years I would not even lay my hands on a woman to pray for her. When praying for a woman, I had Tammy put her hands on the woman, and I put my hands on Tammy's. Consequently, I would not hire a female masseuse for the same reason. Nor would I ever go to a massage parlor, which I had been accused of. All of the massages I received were given by a male masseur. I never considered this type of contact as a homosexual act.

The nightmare of everything that was happening wrapped itself more tightly around my neck. I drew deeper and deeper into a comalike existence. For the first time in my life, I seriously contemplated suicide. Fortunately, Jamie and Don Hardister were with me, or I might not have returned from the lake. Thoughts of suicide became a regular part of my mental contemplation nearly every hour, every day, for several months to come. In a strange way, thoughts of suicide kept me alive. I had lost all other control over my life; I had lost my position, my possessions, my ministry, and now my reputation. The only thing I felt that I could control was my existence—that I could kill myself and escape if the pain got too bad. I even believed my family would be better off without me. Only thoughts of hell and eternal damnation kept me from killing myself—those, and the hand of God.

On a day when I had actually planned out how, when, and where I was going to commit suicide, Pastor Ty and Jeannette Beeson and some friends drove all the way from the Palmdale area, about three hours away, to our home at Palm Springs. They said, "We feel God sent us here to minister to you." They literally helped pack our clothes and insisted that Tammy and I go with them to church and stay with them for the weekend.

I have often wondered whether I would have followed through on my suicide plans had not those friends shown up. I would like to think that I might have resisted the urge for spiritual reasons or out of respect for my family, not wanting them to live with that sort of albatross around their necks. Yet my depression was so deep, only God knows what I might have done. Thanks to some friends who were sensitive to the Lord and who loved Tammy and me, I never had to make that choice.

Many people wondered aloud how and why Jerry Falwell, an avowed anticharismatic, could become involved in PTL, a leading charismatic-oriented ministry. Certainly supporters of PTL were confused, but Falwell's friends were equally frustrated in their attempts to make sense of Falwell's actions. One pastor who was extremely upset was Dr. Bob Gray, a close friend of Jerry Falwell's, pastor of Trinity Baptist Church and president of Trinity Bible College in Jacksonville, Florida. Dr. Gray could not understand what Falwell was doing. Addressing this issue with his congregation in a regularly scheduled service, Dr. Gray first emphasized his close affinity to Jerry Falwell:

While I was in Germany for the month of March doing missionary work, the news broke on the immorality of the sponsor and emcee of the PTL television club. When I got back, I tried to read as much I could on the news magazines and the papers to find out exactly what happened. It's a tragic mess, and of course, the thing that perhaps shocks you and shocked me the most was that Dr. Jerry Falwell, who is a very dear personal friend and has been a friend of our church down through the years, took over this ministry and became the chairman of its board. . . .

Let me say, first of all, that Dr. Falwell has been a friend to [our] ministry like few other preachers of our acquaintance. We love him; we thank God for him. . . .

However, when I learned that he had taken over the chairmanship of [PTL's] board, I was, frankly, shocked. I could not comprehend what was going on. . . . So, I got one of the letters that he sent out to everybody on his mailing list, asking for money to save the PTL Club.

Several of you had told me that you had seen a televised news conference where he was answering questions from the press. I did not see it, but I take your word for it. You said that on that news conference he said that there would be no change in the format of the PTL Club, which meant that the charismatic influence and program would go right on. Well, that shocked me also. So then when I got this letter pleading for money, I felt like that was just absolutely as far as I could go without making an inquiry. I flew to Lynchburg on Thursday. Dr. Falwell gave me an appointment, and I met with him, and I will give you the essence of our conversation. . . .

I said, "Realize that I am only saying this as your friend, I'm not trying to tell you what to do, and I'm not trying to tell you how to conduct your ministry, but as your friend, I think you've made the biggest mistake you've ever made in your life and your ministry by identifying favorably with the PTL format." I said, "I know that you're not charismatic, and unless you've changed since the last time we've talked, in your doctrine, I know that you certainly have not changed to embrace the charismatic position."

He said, "You're absolutely right. I haven't changed one iota. I've always been against it, and I still am. Let me explain to you what my motive is and where I am going.

"When I received word that this was about to happen, I determined that if at all possible I would try to get the PTL network for *The Old Time Gospel Hour,* and this is the only way that I felt like I could do it."

I said, "Well, I personally don't agree with your methods, and I don't agree with your philosophy. But that's between you and the Lord. But I do feel that it was wrong for you to identify with this movement."

He said, "My whole purpose—I don't care what happens to the country club down at Charlotte and all of the jamboree stuff that goes on there. I'm only interested in the PTL cable network. It's the largest Christian cable network in the nation, and I'd like to get that for *The Old Time Gospel Hour.*"

I said, "Well, I feel that you have placed your friends in an indefensible position, and I'm one of them. I am 100 percent opposed to PTL, and when I got your letter asking for money to save it, my first reaction was, why not go ahead and bury it, and everybody would be a lot better off. I've never felt that God was in it from the beginning. If that offends you, I'm sorry, but that's my honest conviction. I think it's been the biggest charade on television that's ever been telecast, and I've been 100 percent against the charismatic movement. . . . "

Then he said, "I think that you would also like to know that this coming Tuesday I'm having a press conference, and at that time we plan to expose Jim Bakker, not only for immorality with a woman, but homosexual immorality. Not only him, but Dortch, and all of those in a leadership position on PTL. I plan to fire 1,600 workers on Tuesday, and probably it will be in bankruptcy before too long, and the sooner the better. All I want out of it is the cable network for the Lord."

I said, "Well, that's between you and the Lord, but again, I do not agree with your philosophy of getting it. I do not agree with what you had to do to get it. Millions of people across this nation are confused and wonder what in the world is going on, and why would you suddenly identify with a movement that you've always been in opposition to." And he has. For example, on the application blanks for Liberty University, this question is clearly asked: "Do you believe in speaking in tongues, and have you ever spoken in tongues?" And if a person says "yes" they don't get enrolled in Liberty University. That's how strong of a stand he's taken in the past. And that stand, he says, will continue.

He also said that he thinks the sooner the organization goes bankrupt, the better off it will be because the assets will then be auctioned and disposed and the network will then be free for purchase, and they hope to purchase it and go on from there. . . .[8]

Events leading to the demise of PTL proceeded rapidly after Ankerberg's television appearances. Whether there was a direct correlation between them or not, I can only guess. On April 28, amidst rumors that he might resign, Jerry Falwell announced at a PTL board meeting that he was staying on "for the duration."

He then turned to Roy Grutman, who accused Reverend Dortch of using PTL funds to pay off Jessica Hahn. He also asserted that Reverend Dortch knew that the Lifetime Partners programs were actually time-shares, which they were not. Mr. Grutman apparently conveniently forgot that he represented Reverend Dortch, PTL, and me. Instead, he suddenly turned coats and became the ministry's antagonist. Ironically, within little more than a month after Reverend Dortch and I first met Norman Roy Grutman, he was paid a half million dollars from PTL funds for his role in decimating the ministry, almost half as much as I had been paid the entire year before to build it! Just then, Bailey Smith moved that Richard Dortch be terminated or allowed to resign as president of PTL. The motion was seconded and Falwell called for a vote.

Rex Humbard would have no part of it. He stood up and announced, "I will not be a part of what is taking place here." He walked out of the room and off the board.

Sam Moore, Ben Armstrong, and James Watt voted against the motion to fire Reverend Dortch. The Lynchburg group voted to dismiss Dortch or allow him to resign.

Overnight, PTL became something out of a George Orwell novel. Armed Pinkerton guards took control of the PTL headquarters building. The guards permitted no one to leave the building without being searched. Women's purses especially were searched for documents and other PTL materials. Firings of employees were taking place hourly. Weeping could be heard all over the building as faithful employees, many of whom had come to PTL to fulfill what they felt was God's call upon their lives, were summarily terminated. Those who remained employed were required to sign a loyalty oath to Jerry Falwell.

One senior executive who stayed on until he was fired said that suddenly a piece of Christian paradise was turned into somthing like a totalitarian government. Each level of middle-management employees was made to fire the level below them. Then the next level fired the managers who had just been responsible for terminating the jobs of the people on the level below them. Whoever perpetrated the plan must have studied the Nazis.

Toward the end of May, Jerry Falwell sent Roe Messner to visit Tammy and me and to deliver a curious message: "Jerry Falwell announced that he wants to continue your salary at or about the same level you were receiving when you resigned. He wants you to have a house, a car, a maid, and a secretary as well."

From the beginning Falwell had said publicly, "PTL would not be here without Jim and Tammy Bakker. It would be less than Christian to terminate and cut off the life supply for the persons responsible for this ministry."[9] Then during the press conference following the termination of Reverend Dortch, Falwell announced that PTL would no longer offer lifetime partnerships to be sold (they were never *sold* in the first place!), and that Tammy and I would no longer be paid. The Bakkers' "ministry here has ceased," he told 270 members of the press.[10]

Now nearly two months later, Falwell had suddenly taken an interest in paying us. Roe seemed pleased that Falwell had apparently had a change of heart. As Tammy, Roe, and I sat in our living room, Roe reported that Jerry Falwell had instructed us to make up a list of what we needed to continue life as we normally would if we were at PTL. "Don't be afraid to make it a little extravagant," Roe told us that Falwell had said. "These are simply negotiating points, and we will establish the final package from here."

Tammy Faye wrote an exaggerated "wishlist" on her stationery of things we thought we might need to maintain life as it had been. It was not a formal request or a presentation of any kind. Roe took the wrinkled piece of Tammy Faye's stationery, just as it was, back to Jerry Falwell.

Imagine our horror and embarrassment when at a news conference on May 27, 1987, Jerry held up the list, written on Tammy Faye's personal stationery, and declared, "I don't see any repentance there. I don't see any concern for the welfare of this ministry in that kind of request. I see the greed. I see the self-centeredness. I see the avarice that brought them down."[11] I could not believe my ears! We had done exactly what Jerry had asked us to do, and most of the things on the list were items he had suggested we should have. Roe Messner and I had been merely business associates and coworkers before that incident, but after Roe saw that news conference we became close friends.

Tammy and I were scheduled to appear live on ABC's *Nightline* that night. How coincidental that Jerry would hold up the "wishlist" that very afternoon.

Tammy's and my appearance on *Nightline* was historic, not for us, but for ABC. The show that night received the highest ratings in its history. As of this writing, the Nielsen record set that night still stands.

The interview with Ted Koppel went well, so well in fact that Tammy and I decided to go back to PTL for a visit to explore return possibilities. We also had to pack up all our things from the Tega Cay house, since we had been ordered to get our possessions out of there. The house was owned by the ministry; we had no choice but to comply. On June 10, 1987, we returned to the Carolinas. When we visited Heritage USA a few days later, we were greeted by a crowd. We weren't sure initially whether the throng was friendly or hostile. As we pulled up right in front of the Heritage Grand, people mobbed our car. Don Hardister bolted from the car, leaving us at the mercy of the clamoring crowd. Don had once told me, "Jim, I would take a bullet for you if I had to." Now that his job was to keep me away from PTL, he did not want to be seen with me. Years later, Don apologized for his actions.

Fortunately, the crowd was, for the most part, excited to see us back. They started clapping their hands, shouting, "Jim and Tammy, we love you! Welcome back!"

Tammy and I got out of the car and greeted the people and basked in the warm reception. We walked into the hotel and down "Main Street," sweeping down the street and back out to our car. A few days later we were invited to a reception at "Kevin's House," the home we had built for handicapped children. Hundreds of people began taking PTL trams to cover the distance a quarter mile or so away. They formed lines snaking down the driveway. When the trams stopped running suddenly, the people literally walked through a muddy field to get to where Tammy and I were greeting and hugging everyone we met. It was a reception I will never forget.

Later I was told by several people that the reception sent shivers through the Falwell ranks. That same week, Jerry Falwell and his board of PTL directors voted to seek bankruptcy protection.

Things moved quickly from that point. After months of badgering by insiders of the new PTL regime, a federal grand jury was convened in Charlotte on September 21, 1987, to investigate PTL in general, and me in particular. South Carolina officials, where Heritage USA's offices were located, had refused to get involved in the case, so the pressure was shifted to a North Carolina jurisdiction because technically some of Heritage USA was located across the border. Somebody had given the government the impression that our Lifetime Partnership program had been illegally operated with the PTL Partners not receiving the benefits they had been promised. Interestingly, the first witness called was Jessica Hahn.

The government spent hundreds of hours and thousands of dollars over the next sixteen months going through a mountain of materials, including personal letters and private files that had been flung wide open and made available by the Falwell team to the press and to government investigators. Grand-jury members heard testimony from everyone who had anything negative to say about PTL, whether they were credible witnesses or not.

On October 8, 1987, after a judge refused Jerry Falwell's reorganization plan for PTL and allowed the PTL Partners and creditors to present a separate plan, Jerry Falwell abruptly resigned. Adapting a line from Jimmy Swaggart, Falwell referred to me as "probably the greatest scab and cancer on the face of Christianity in two thousand years of church history."[12] I felt that PTL had been placed in bankruptcy for one main reason—to keep me from coming back. I would have given anything to try to save PTL and to pay back our creditors. By placing PTL and Heritage USA into bankruptcy it was now in the hands and complete control of the government.

Little did I know that I would have such a long time to think about it. On December 5, 1988, I was indicted by a federal grand jury. The judge said that if I was convicted I might be going to prison for as many as 120 years.

CHAPTER

8

The Collapse

NOW, LESS THAN A YEAR LATER, I HAD BEEN TRIED, CONVICTED, and sentenced to forty-five years in prison. The marshals' car carrying me closer to incarceration sped south along Interstate 85 toward Atlanta on our way to Talladega, a small town approximately sixty miles away from Birmingham, Alabama. The trip was almost 350 miles long and would take about six hours. The marshals accompanying me were kind and occasionally spoke to me, but for the most part, I sat silently in the back seat, watching the daylight slowly fade to blackness. Along with thoughts of my past, impressions of what prison life might be like began to pummel their way into my brain. Fearful images of scenes from old Jimmy Cagney prison movies, of prison riots, rapes, and murders filled my mind. I felt stark terror.

Although I had visited prisons many times as a minister, my only other knowledge of what incarceration might be like related to a horrifying experience I had recently undergone during my trial. The trial began in mid-August 1989. Approximately two weeks into the ordeal, on Wednesday, August 30, Steve Nelson, a former PTL employee, was testifying as a government witness against me. As I sat listening to Steve's testimony, I was deeply hurt. I believed that some of the information he was relaying to the court was inaccurate.

During his cross-examination of Steve, my lawyer rigorously grilled him on the details he was purporting to be true. Steve answered haltingly, and his face turned ashen in color. It soon became obvious that he was in trouble. Steve suddenly keeled over and literally fell off the witness stand!

Pandemonium swept through the courtroom. Judge Potter sprang to his feet and peered down at the body sprawled on the floor to his right. Marshals quickly converged on the courtroom floor. Nobody knew whether Steve Nelson was dead or alive. My lawyer, Harold Bender, was extremely distraught, fearing he had verbally bludgeoned Steve to the point of death. Harold stood in the middle of the front court area, looking on in abject fear, at the same time trying to maintain some remnant of courtroom protocol.

In the midst of the confusion, one of the jurors, a nurse, left the jury box, ran to Steve Nelson, and began attending to him. Her actions severely violated a cardinal courtroom rule, that a jury member is not to have any contact with a witness, but at that point nobody seemed too concerned about it. She quickly took Nelson's pulse and announced, "This man has fainted!"

Steve Nelson had been a part of my staff for several years, so naturally I was deeply concerned for his well-being despite the fact that he had been testifying against me. As Steve's former boss and former pastor, my first inclination at the sight of him lying on the floor was to pray for him. My lawyers asked Judge Potter for permission for me to pray for my former employee. The judge reluctantly granted the request.

Torn between my deep desire to pray for Steve and my unwillingness to get too close to an obviously awkward situation, I stepped up to Steve, knelt down near him, and placed my hands on his foot as I prayed and asked God to touch him and heal him. Almost immediately, he revived. Nelson's fortuitous revival prompted some people to later proclaim that I had raised the man from the dead, which, of course, I had not.

An ambulance crew had arrived by then, and Steve Nelson was placed on a gurney and taken to a local hospital for examination. His collapse was later blamed on a case of the flu and the fact that he had not eaten breakfast that morning.

Back in the courtroom, Judge Potter regained order just long enough to announce a recess until the following day.

A marshal noticed that I too looked as though I was close to collapsing. He quickly approached me and offered to help me escape the onslaught of questions from people in the courtroom by exiting through a side door. I nodded my head and whispered, "Yes, please. I would appreciate that."

Following the marshal's lead, I made my way out of the courtroom through the side door and into a conference room across the hall. The cumulative emotional strain of the case was overwhelming me. The pressure of almost three years of unprecedented publicity and public disgrace, the loss of my life's work, and the deep pain my family and friends were going through were more than I could bear. I could no longer hold back the tears. I slumped into a chair and simply began to weep. I wept and wept and could not stop.

Someone sent for my father, who had been in attendance at the trial that day. Dad came into the room and attempted to console me. I appreciated Dad's kind words, but I still could not contain my emotions.

That afternoon, one of my lawyers called Dr. Basil Jackson, a good friend and highly respected psychiatrist from Milwaukee who had made several appearances on our television shows and had helped many of my ministerial friends. Dr. Jackson had been trained as a psychiatrist by a variety of academic institutions, including the Menninger Clinic in Topeka, Kansas. He now directed a psychiatric clinic with a large staff at Milwaukee's St. Francis Hospital.

When Dr. Jackson learned of my condition, he dropped everything he was doing and caught the first flight to Charlotte. He arrived the evening of Nelson's courtroom collapse and my emotional upheaval. He came directly to the apartment where I was staying during the trial. As soon as he saw me, he knew I was in bad shape.

Dr. Jackson examined me thoroughly and we talked well into the night about the extreme stress I had been experiencing. I told the doctor that I anticipated that I was going to have a difficult time sleeping that night. He gave me a small dose of a popular antianxiety medication known as Xanax, which he said would calm my nerves and help me sleep, yet allow me to function normally. He assured me that the dosage of the drug he was giving me was extremely small, less than half of the lowest dose he normally prescribed for most of his patients. The usual dosage of Xanax prescribed by most doctors is one to two milligrams. The tablet I was prescribed was only .125 milligrams, and Dr. Jackson suggested that I begin by taking only half of that amount. The doctor said Xanax would be "good medicine" for me.

"Try taking this dosage every four hours," my doctor ordered me. Since he was prescribing such a low dosage, Dr. Jackson suggested that if I had trouble sleeping, I could take the medicine more frequently.

What the doctor did not tell me, however, was that Xanax is a tranquilizer. Unfortunately, in my deeply distraught state, I failed to inform the doctor that my body reacts violently to tranquilizers of any kind. While they produce a calming effect in most people, for some reason tranquilizers produce the opposite effect in me. Tranquilizers make me hyper and powerfully affect my nervous system. They cause me to feel like I'm out of touch with reality.

Certain that my good friend, Dr. Jackson, would never knowingly give me any medication that would be harmful to me, I followed his instructions. Every few hours the night of August 30, I swallowed another Xanax.

On Thursday, August 31, I got up early and dressed in a new suit that my sister Donna had recently bought for me. I had gained weight since leaving Heritage USA in 1987, and the emotional stress I had endured in 1989 caused me to be less diligent about maintaining a healthy diet. Few of the clothes I had worn prior to the fall of '89 would now fit me. Despite publicized reports to the contrary, my financial resources had already been depleted. Consequently, my sister Donna, who had always looked after me when I was a child, went out and bought me a new outfit.

I had already taken several Xanax tablets throughout the night, but I gobbled down another before Herb Moore, the elderly friend with whom I was staying, and I set out for Harold Bender's law office, located downtown near the courthouse. Considering Herb's feeble physical condition and my drug-induced lethargy, it is a miracle either of us could drive the car. To this day, I am not sure who actually sat behind the wheel that morning.

By the time Herb and I arrived at my lawyer's office, I could hardly move, let alone walk. My entire system was on autopilot. We parked our car in the adjoining parking lot and walked up the stairs of the beautifully renovated Victorian-style home that served as Harold Bender's office. We walked across the spacious wraparound porch to the front door and on into the reception area. Straight ahead, the former dining room, which now served as the conference room, was stacked with boxes of files concerning my case. Herb and I turned to the left and walked past several desks where Harold's paralegals were busily at work. The room was buzzing with activity, just as it was every morning of my trial. Like two drunks, Herb and I weaved our way through the clatter and entered Harold's private inner office.

Harold took one look at me and knew immediately that something was wrong. My body had become bloated, I had a dazed look on my face, my speech was slurred, and I was making ridiculous, erratic statements. It was as though my body was saying, "You cannot take anymore. I'm shutting you down."

In addition to Harold Bender, Dr. Jackson had already arrived at the office. The doctor was extremely concerned about my emotional state, and he quizzed me thoroughly about how I was feeling. Early on, he recognized that I was distraught and anxious. As the hour wore on, and the time approached for us to head for the courtroom, Dr. Jackson noticed that I was becoming increasingly agitated.

Also in the office that morning was my other lead lawyer, George Davis, a feisty eighty-four-year-old criminal law specialist who had earned his reputation by winning numerous murder trials on the basis of establishing reasonable doubt in the minds of jury members. I had secured George's services through the help of Herb Moore.

Although I had been indicted by a federal grand jury on December 5, 1988, I felt that my legal representation was not the most important issue in my case. I totally underestimated the seriousness of the charges against me. I knew in my heart that I was not guilty of trying to defraud anyone, and I was confident that any lawyer who had passed the bar exam could convince a jury of my peers. Besides that, I often told my friends, "I would rather trust God than the best lawyers in the world!"

Herb Moore, a former PTL executive and a longtime friend and confidant, was not so passive about my legal representation. Herb kept prodding me, "Jim, you better hire a lawyer."

Finally, I said, "Okay, do you have any idea who is good at this sort of thing?"

"No, I don't," Herb replied, "but I know someone who does." Herb called a good friend of his, well-known prison minister "Chaplain Ray" Hoekstra. "If anyone knows criminal lawyers, Chaplain Ray does," Herb assured me. Chaplain Ray suggested that we contact George Davis, one of the most famous trial lawyers of his time.

I hired George, and George hired Harold Bender, and my legal team was in place. Because of his age and reputation, George pulled no punches with anyone, least of all me. The morning of August 31, George's word was law. He said straightforwardly, "Jim, you are in no condition to go to court today."

"I agree," said Harold quickly.

"I have to go," I answered.

"You will never make it!" George railed.

"I have to go!" I replied desperately. Even though I had lost control of many of my mental faculties, I nonetheless knew that the last thing I wanted to do was to make the judge and jury angry at me. Already during the trial, I had been publicly castigated, mocked, and derided as everything from a pampered emperor to a self-aggrandizing, manipulating madman. I did not care to give people any more ammunition they could use against me.

I could feel that I was losing touch with reality, so while everyone else moved to the outer office in preparation to leave, I slipped into Harold's private office to pray. I knelt down at a couch with my knees on the floor and my elbows on the sofa cushions and literally began to cry out to God. At some point—I have no recollection when—my nervous system collapsed. Harold told me later that when he came looking for me in his office, he found me hiding beneath his camelback sofa with my face on the floor and my knees tucked up against my chin. The sofa stood on arched wooden legs, providing an open space of less than twenty inches between the floor and the bottom of the cushion area. Dressed in my new suit, I somehow had managed to crawl into the narrow cavern . . . and I had no intention of ever coming out. I lay there sobbing and babbling unintelligibly.

Harold immediately ran out of the office to get Dr. Jackson. When the doctor entered the room, he took one look and got right down beside me on the floor. Dr. Jackson spoke to me very softly and compassionately. He quickly determined that I was "decompensating," a fancy psychological term for "flaking out." I had no clue as to what was going on. Dr. Jackson saw that I had regressed to the point that I was curled up like a baby in a fetal position and that my nasal secretions were running down my face.

With great anxiety and trepidation, I began to tell Dr. Jackson about the giant bugs that were coming at me. He soon realized that the "bugs" to which I was referring were stimulated by the thick maze of television cameras, microphones, aerials, and antennae through which I had to tread a path each day on my way into the courtroom. He concluded that in some way, I was experiencing the media equipment as fearful menaces. How ironic that the same technology that had helped make my face familiar to millions of people now struck terror into my heart and mind.

Dr. Jackson attempted to calm my fears and reassure me. "Jim, you are not feeling well. You do not need to go to the courthouse today. Your lawyers can take care of it. They can explain to the judge what has happened and I will go with them to vouch for your medical condition. You just need to rest." He then left the room to speak to Harold Bender. The doctor emphatically told Harold that I was totally incapable of attending the court proceedings that day. Harold certainly was already convinced of that.

Dr. Jackson wanted to have me hospitalized as soon as possible, but he knew that because I was on trial, to have me admitted he would need a second professional medical opinion. He immediately set about the task of telephoning other psychiatrists and mental health services, hoping to find someone who could corroborate his opinion. Finally, he called Charter Psychiatric Hospital in Charlotte. The resident doctor on duty that day was Dr. Kevin M. Denny.

Dr. Jackson placed a telephone call to Dr. Denny—whom I had never met—and asked him if he would come to Harold's office to provide a second opinion regarding my inability to continue with the trial at this time and to arrange for my hospitalization if necessary. Dr. Denny agreed to come that morning.

Once Denny arrived, Dr. Jackson went with my lawyers to inform the court concerning my condition. The doctor testified to the court that I was in a severe state of panic, precipitated by the stress under which I was living at that point. Unfortunately, Judge Potter refused to accept my friend's word or his highly regarded professional opinion that I required immediate hospitalization. The judge gave little credence to Dr. Jackson's emphatic appeals that my mental state was so precarious and that I was in such desperate need of psychiatric evaluation and treatment that I should be admitted to a private psychiatric facility that very morning.

Judge Potter wouldn't hear of it. Instead he ordered me to be sent to Butner Federal Penitentiary for evaluation to see if I was mentally competent to continue standing trial.

Dr. Jackson warned that I might never recover if the judge ordered me to be committed to a prison psychiatric hospital. "I believe that to commit him to a state hospital at this time would produce a definite aggravation in his psychiatric condition," he told Judge Potter.

The judge disregarded Dr. Jackson's testimony and ordered the marshals to go to Harold Bender's office to get me. It was about 10:30 A.M.

Frustrated and worried, Dr. Jackson left the courthouse to return to check on me at Bender's office. On the way to the car, a film crew from CNN stopped Dr. Jackson and questioned him about my condition. The doctor replied, "Mr. Bakker is completely broken because of the tremendous stress to which he has been subjected."[1] Some of the reporters followed the doctor back to my lawyer's office and set up their cameras on the front yard.

When Dr. Jackson got back inside Bender's office, he quickly closed and locked the door. He knew a plethora of reporters could not be far behind him.

Dr. Denny had spent the past hour with me and confirmed Dr. Jackson's diagnosis completely. I had talked with the new doctor freely from my secure place under the sofa, but I have virtually no recall of what I said to him. Eventually, he too left the room, but I remained where I was, lying under the sofa in a fetal position.

Dr. Jackson rightly assumed that he did not have much time to get me ready to leave for the federal prison facility. He finally coaxed me out from beneath the sofa and had me lie down on it instead. He tried to gently break the news to me that the marshals would soon be coming to take me to a facility for evaluation. My mind was so agitated, however, that my friend could not get through to me.

Soon five grim federal marshals arrived at Harold's office in a taupe Chevrolet Caprice at about 11:00 A.M., less than ten minutes after Harold and George had returned. In seconds, the marshals bounded out of the automobile and were pounding on the front door of Harold's law office. The door was still locked and the marshals demanded that it be opened immediately.

"Just wait a minute; just wait a minute," Dr. Jackson called through the door. He then came back to the inner office to get me. As he and Harold Bender slowly walked me to the front door, he again tried to explain what was happening.

I kept asking him, "Where am I? What's going on? Where are they taking me?" Again and again, I repeated the same questions, but Harold's and Dr. Jackson's answers never sank into my brain.

When Harold opened the front door, the marshals burst into the office foyer and quickly placed shackles on my hands and feet. It became obvious that one of the other marshals was upset. Dr. Jackson later found out that the marshal was a kind Christian gentleman who despised placing me in custody in my condition.

The marshals escorted me out the door and onto the porch, with Dr. Jackson slightly behind me, helping to support me by holding onto my left elbow. My body was bloated; my hair and clothes were disheveled. One of the marshals placed my new suit coat over my cuffed hands as we slowly made our way toward their car. I was disoriented and weeping uncontrollably. My nose was dripping profusely, but since my hands were shackled, I had no way to wipe it.

As we shuffled down the porch stairs, I grimaced with every step. I cried out, "Please, don't do this to me! Please don't do this to me!" But the marshals continued to drag me toward their car.

Adding to my humiliation were the incessant questions being hurled at me by the throng of reporters as well as the much quieter but far more debilitating sounds for me of clicking cameras and rolling videotape. One of the most humiliating moments of my life was splattered across television screens and newspapers around the world. To this day, it is indelibly impressed in many people's memories as the worst scene in my highly publicized "fall from grace."

Both Dr. Jackson and Dr. Denny later said that I was the first and only patient ever seized from their hands in the midst of treatment. Moreover, Dr. Denny later commented in the press that what was done to me sent mental health care back to the Dark Ages.[2]

In no way do I blame the marshals for what happened to me. They were only doing their job. To a man, they were always kind, polite, and professional in carrying out their orders. In the years since that day, many people have told me they thought the marshals were being cruel when they pushed my head down to get me into the car. Actually, they were being kind. If I had tried to get into the police car while handcuffed and shackled, I would have smashed my head against the door frame of the car as I fell into the back seat.

Even with the marshals' help, I still fell over when they placed me in the car that day. I didn't care. It was almost a relief simply to be away from the prying eyes of the cameras. I had landed on my side; my hands were raised up toward my head as far as the chains would allow, and my knees were drawn up toward my chest.

The marshals drove me to the courthouse, a short distance from Harold's downtown office. They pulled me out of the car and helped me walk past another crowd of reporters and photographers and into the courthouse. Once inside, I was taken to a holding cell, where I waited in silence for the next two and a half hours while a decision was being made about where I would be taken. Finally the federal marshals came and got me. They led me out a rear door and down the steps of the loading dock. Again they helped me get into the back seat of the car. I sat upright for a few moments, and then slumped across the seat as the car drove off. I stayed in that same fetal position for the next three hours as I was driven to a place I thought I heard the marshals refer to as *Butler*. In my foggy state of mind, the name reminded me of the animal hospital where, in better days, my family and I had often taken our pets.

Surely they are not taking me to an animal hospital! I thought. I had no idea where I was going. All the tops of trees and telephone poles looked alike from my vantage point. I lost track of time. After what seemed like several hours had passed, my kidneys felt as though they were going to explode. I was in real pain, needing to use the rest room, but I refused to ask the marshals to stop. I was in a nightmare, like a caged animal being transported to a zoo.

At last, the car stopped. I tried to raise my head to look around.

Oh, God; where am I?

CHAPTER

9

The Asylum

IT WAS LATE AFTERNOON, ALMOST 4:00 P.M., BY THE TIME we arrived in Butner, North Carolina, a small town thirteen miles north- east of the city of Durham. I had not moved or spoken during the entire three-hour trip. Looking up from my position on the back seat, I could see an ominous, massive complex of buildings looming largely in front of me. At first I thought it might be a hospital, but I soon learned that Butner was no hospital—it was a federal psychiatric penitentiary.

Butner Correctional Institute is a medium-security prison, located on 769 acres of land. It is considered one of the two top psychiatric prison facilities in the United States. The large facility had been opened in 1976, but it still looked relatively modern. It was completely surrounded by chain-link fence with razor barbed wire scrolled across the top.

The marshals opened the car door. I had not moved an inch from where they had placed me several hours earlier. My nose was still running, but I could do nothing about it. Wet mucus smeared on my face as the marshals carefully pulled me from the vehicle. I felt as though I were watching a dream sequence in a B movie . . . everything seemed shrouded in darkness. The lights had all been turned down. My world was literally getting darker and darker.

Six years later, Dr. Basil Jackson would explain to me that I had, in fact, suffered a nervous breakdown that morning. The darkness was my brain's way of "dissociating," a process in which the brain begins to blot out aspects of one's consciousness that are too difficult for that person to handle, shutting down as a means of emotional and physical self-preservation. When a person's body can take no more, the brain says, "Switch off." Dr. Jackson had often seen the same sort of reaction when he served as director of a U.S. Veterans Administration Psychiatric Hospital during the Vietnam War. Some Vietnam veterans' dissociation shattered them so completely, they literally went insane. For many others, their minds are unable to fully return to reality. When they try to recall the acutely stressful conditions they went through, their minds fade to blackness. That was what I was experiencing.

Although my mind was enveloped in darkness as the marshals helped me from the car, my body was instantly awash in brilliant light. Members of the media had beaten us to Butner and were already entrenched on both sides of a sidewalk leading from the parking lot to the building, camera flashes blazing, videotape rolling, and microphones stretched toward me all the way down the sidewalk to the door. I now understand that these people were simply doing their very difficult jobs, but at the time, they were the last people on earth I wanted to see. To my eyes squinting through the glare, the parallel rows of reporters reminded me of a royal honor guard pointing their swords high above their heads, the microphone boom extensions forming a peak above the center of the sidewalk. But this was no honor guard—quite the opposite; to me they were the *dishonor* guard. They stood ready to record every detail of my dehumanizing circumstances. My blurred mind marveled, *The photographers aim and shoot, but I do not die.* I wished I could have.

Unaccustomed to moving in manacles, I had difficulty walking. Furthermore, my legs had remained motionless for several hours and now they did not want to function. Consequently, the two marshals held me, one on each arm, and helped me walk, virtually having to drag me each step of the way. I walked like a staggering drunk; my appearance was atrocious. My beautiful new suit, my sister's sacrificial gift to me, now looked wrinkled and sloppy, as though I had rolled it into a ball, tossed it into a clothes hamper, and then put it on again the next day. I still wore the white shirt and tie that I wore when I left the apartment that morning. My hair looked as though I had been sleeping in the streets for months. And the interminable snot hung grossly from my nose. I felt that I was no longer a human being.

Inching along in my shackles, the sidewalk leading to the building seemed to be at least half a block long. As the marshals patiently dragged my limp body down the sidewalk, I felt as though I were being pulled into a long, dark tunnel. Each step doused a little more light from my eyes. Every inch of the way, the tunnel's sides constricted, getting tighter and tighter as I approached the door. One of the marshals reached out to open the door . . . and suddenly everything went black. The protective pain shield had closed over my brain.

The next thing I remember is being in a small dismal-looking room about the size of a large elevator. I was seated on a backless bench in the middle of the room, staring blankly ahead. The cubicle seemed to be filled with people, most of whom appeared to be doing nothing other than watching me.

One man, whom I had never before seen, was sitting on the bench to my left and was meticulously rifling through my wallet. He took out my money and counted it. He took out my credit cards and pictures, examining each one carefully. I saw him flip past the picture in my wallet of baby James. Something stirred within me.

"Please!" I cried, reaching toward the man. I suddenly realized that my hands had been unshackled, a sign, I later came to understand, that I was now deep within the bowels of prison with no chance of escape. Instinctively, I knew the man was going to take my treasure away. "Please, let me keep a picture of my grandson, baby James," I pleaded.

The man looked in my direction for the first time. He stared at me hard, then down at the picture of James, then back at me. "I'll see about it," he finally replied with cool detachment.

My compassionate Charlotte marshals had been replaced. No doubt they were well on their way back to Charlotte to enjoy a nice evening at home with their families. In the marshals' place now stood brusque prison officials.

The officers ordered me to take off all my clothes, including my underwear. They offered no reason for their demand, nor did they give me any hint as to what they were going to do to me. But their order was obviously nonnegotiable.

Slowly I began to strip. I fumbled with my expensive tie that I had so carefully knotted that morning, which now seemed like a lifetime ago. Eventually I got the tie off and laid it neatly on the bench behind me. I began unbuttoning my shirt.

"Hurry it up!" someone growled.

Nervous beyond description, I could barely force my fingers to push the buttons through the buttonholes. At last the shirt fell open and I struggled to pull it off my back. My body ached and even the slight stretching to remove my shirt caused every muscle in my back and shoulders to wail in protest.

I laid my shirt next to the tie, removed my shoes, then began pulling at the belt on my trousers. My captors never took their eyes off me. I have always been a shy person off camera or away from the pulpit, so the idea of pulling my pants down in the middle of a room full of strangers made me extremely uncomfortable. I hesitated. . . .

"Come on, let's go, Bakker," a coarse voice commanded.

I reluctantly allowed my suit trousers to slide down to my ankles. I stepped out of my pants, took off my socks, and hesitated once again. I glanced around the room at my captors. There was no point in prolonging this exercise. I removed my underwear and placed it in the pile on the bench. For a long moment, I simply stood there. I didn't know what else to do. I was stark naked in a room filled with people, and everybody was looking at me.

Every corpuscle in my body was crying out, *My God! What is happening to me?*

I could not understand how my dear friend, Dr. Jackson, and my lawyers, Harold and George, could possibly have allowed these people to do these things to me! I felt betrayed by my friends. I was not a convicted criminal! This was happening in the middle of my trial—the trial in which I had been confident some portion of my integrity would be restored. Whatever happened to the concept of "innocent until proven guilty"? Not only were these people treating me as a criminal, they were treating me as though I were some sort of carnival freak to be gawked at.

Was I not an American citizen? Did I not have rights guaranteed by the Constitution? Or, was I now in some Communist country? I had grown up hearing horror stories from behind the Iron Curtain, tales of how the Communist secret police had stormed in on an unsuspecting citizen and hauled him or her off to prison with not so much as a chance to say good-bye to loved ones, let alone a bona fide trial. No United States citizen should have to be subjected to such inhumane treatment as I was being given, I thought. My mind, sluggish as it was, flashed such thoughts on and off, much like a slow-blinking strobe light. *How could they violate me so unabashedly?* and *What does it matter? I am nothing. My life is over.*

It got worse.

An officer handed me an orange prison jumpsuit and a pair of underpants. "Put them on," he ordered. I took the jumpsuit and hastily climbed into it.

The guards led me out of the small room into another slightly larger room. It appeared to be some sort of clinic.

"Take off your clothes," commanded a man wearing a white medical smock.

It seemed useless to remind the man that I had just put on the prison clothes. Besides, by this point, I was moving in a daze. I had no will to argue or resist in any way. Whatever they wanted me to do, I'd do it. I slowly peeled off the jumpsuit and underwear and stood before them, nude once again.

Two or more individuals inspected every cavity of my body—they felt or looked inside my mouth, ears, navel, rectum, under my arms, between my legs, everywhere. Perhaps they were doctors; I had no idea what they were looking for, but whatever it was, the men were not subtle about trying to find it. I simply complied with their orders. Finally, they were finished. "Put it back on," a prison official said as he nodded in the direction of the jumpsuit.

After I had put my jumpsuit back on, another faceless guard—in my condition they all looked faceless—escorted me out into the prison compound. The heat of the late summer evening hit me as I came out into the open air. The guard started leading me across the empty prison yard when suddenly from someplace high and to the right of me, I heard a voice shouting my name.

"Jim! Jim! Don't let them break you!"

I turned and looked up, but all I could see were large buildings with narrow horizontal slits for windows.

There it was again! "Jim, don't let them break you!"

I heard it more distinctly this time, but was not coherent enough to get a fix on which window hid my secret encourager. In a weird way, I appreciated the compassion being expressed by the prisoner, but I wondered, *What does he mean? What do the men in this prison know about this place that causes them to issue such a warning?* Whatever it was, my benefactor was too late. I was already broken.

The guard hurriedly steered me across the prison yard and into a room in another building. More guards awaited me there. Again, I was told to take off my clothes. As I dutifully began shedding my clothes for the third time in less than an hour, one of the officers took out a Polaroid-type camera. They were going to photograph me in the nude, but a man who must have been a senior official called out, "Let him leave his underpants on!"

The officers took several pictures of me standing in my underwear. No explanation was offered why the photos were necessary. At that point, I didn't much care. When the photo session was completed, the guards ordered me to get dressed again. They led me into another room and gave the pictures to two ladies, a white woman and a black woman, who were seated at a large, heavy, wooden table outside of an office. I later learned that the white woman was Dr. Sally Johnson, the chief of psychiatric services at that prison. The women were cordial and asked me to sit down while they filled out some forms. They asked me a multitude of questions, but I have no idea what they asked or what I answered.

Following my interrogation by the two women, the guards began leading me toward my cell. I say "began" because paranoia had so completely taken over in my body, I was too fearful to take normal-sized steps. I had to take baby steps as if walking on eggshells, slowly, tentatively, with my eyes glued to the ground. The guards had to drag me along, step by step. In my mind, I felt as though I were picking my way along a rugged, steep cliff, and the guards were trying to pull me over the edge. I didn't dare get too close to the precipice because I knew if I fell over the edge, I would tumble into a huge gorge, hundreds of times the depth of the Grand Canyon. I was tiptoeing along the very edge of the earth, and I was scared to death.

For the next six years I would live with the fear that became instilled in my mind during that initial trip down the Butner prison corridor. I awakened every single morning terrorized by the image of the guards coming to pull me out of my bed, fearing that I would crack my head on the cement, my skull would split open, and my blood would gush out. Apart from God's power to heal my memories, I may never totally get over those first moments in prison.

I was completely unprepared for what happened next. I had never been in prison before except as a visitor, but as the guards led me into the cell block, even though my mind was terror-stricken and numb, I immediately recognized that I was in no ordinary jail. This was a high-security facility! Worse still, as I tiptoed past rows of cells, I could feel eyes staring at me. Everywhere I looked, I saw wild eyes peering through the slots in the solid steel doors where the prisoners' food is passed into the cells. The slots were only about four inches high and eighteen inches wide—just large enough to get a tray of food and small cup or carton of milk through—and were positioned in the doors about thirty inches up from the floor. For a person to see out those slots, he would have to sit or kneel down next to the door and place his head up against the open food slot. Only the eyes could be seen to passersby.

As I proceeded into the cell block, the guards nudged me to make a right turn down a corridor. Just as we were about to make the turn, I was able to see, because of the way my head was cocked, straight into a food slot on a corner cell. As I passed by, I caught a glimpse of the man's eyes, not merely empty, hopeless eyes; these were the eyes of a man possessed, the most demonic, crazed eyes I had ever seen. I was already stepping precariously close to the edge of insanity, but seeing the eyes of that man and the others I passed nearly sealed my doom.

The place was a madhouse. Some prisoners were screaming incessantly at the tops of their lungs. Others were talking gibberish. Many were groaning or whining. If a person was not mentally ill upon entering this cell block at Butner Federal Prison, the sheer cacophony of the place was enough to drive him insane.

When the guards pulled me past the next-to-last cell on the right, I heard a man singing—if that is what you could call it. He sounded like an old 45 rpm phonograph recording on which the needle had gotten stuck and was continually skipping back to the same notes. He sang three notes over and over: la . . . la . . . la; LA . . . LA . . . LA; *LA . . . LA . . . LA!*

As I reached the end of the corridor, the guard indicated that I was to enter the last cell on the right. Just as I turned into the cell, I paused long enough to look back up the row. The awful sights, sounds, and smells struck my senses full force. I suddenly realized that I was not simply in prison—I was in an insane asylum!

The guards led me into the cell next to the man who was singing the nonstop, three-note concert. The man seemed never to stop singing the entire time I was there.

Looking into my tiny cell from the doorway, I could see that on the right-hand side of the back wall was a hard slab with a one-inch-thick plastic pad on which to sleep. No pillow was allowed. I later learned that pillows were not permitted in this solitary confinement cell due to the potential suicide risk to prisoners who might use the pillow to smother themselves. Above the middle of the slab, a narrow, vertical window about as wide as a book provided my view—a bird's-eye view of another cement block wall of an adjacent building. Only inches from the front of the bed, along the right wall, sat a commode and a sink. Toward the back left corner was an exposed shower, with no curtain. The door, with its slot, was on the left side of the front wall of my cell. To the right of the door was an observation window, approximately three square feet in size. I stepped across the threshold of my cell, and the guard slammed the door behind me. I will never forget the terrible thud that door made as it closed. The

91

sound sealed my tomb, sucking away the last remnant of what little freedom I felt.

Right outside my cell was a guard's station, a desk that was occupied at all times by a guard, who could view me through the observation window in my cell. I was to be watched twenty-four hours a day. The guards had plenty of help, though. At night, every time I glanced at the narrow window above my bed, I saw the reflection of another set of eyes peering in at me through the observation window. Every employee of that prison must have come to look at me that night. I was the highly publicized, new animal on display. Everyone wanted to see Jim Bakker. I imagined their conversation:

"Oh, look! He moved."

"What's he doing now?"

"Nothing much, just lying there in a fetal position, staring at the wall."

"Listen! What was that sound? Did he say something?"

The curious onlookers kept coming all night long, and every new set of eyes I saw reflected in my window magnified the fear that continued to build in my mind.

I slept very little that night. I tried, but the sleep simply would not come. Then in what seemed liked the middle of the night—I could not yet see any daylight through the window in the wall above my bed—prison medics came and injected me with needle after needle. Apparently they were drawing vials of blood, but in my darkness, I had no way to be sure. My blurry mind wondered if they were drawing blood out of me or putting something into me.

Why did the government want me so badly? I asked myself again and again throughout the night. *And if they did want me, surely there must be a better way, an easier way.*

It was during those early hours in Butner that I learned to fear the sound of rattling keys. Most prison workers wear large rings of keys on their belts. The keys jingle when the guards walk. I quickly learned that the sound of the keys coming in my direction meant they were coming to stick me with more hypodermic needles. Like Pavlov's dogs, I responded reflexively to the sound. My stomach began churning every time I heard the prison keys.

At some point during that first night, my picture of baby James was returned to me. The guard must have thought he had given me a million dollars; in fact, he had given me much more. He had given me a reason to survive. I curled up on my bunk, faced the wall, and held that picture close to my face.

I tried to block out the surreal world around me, but it was impossible. The inmate in the next cell continued singing his three-note song over and over. Periodically the guards pushed food through the door slot to me. They never opened the door to bring in a tray of food. It was always pushed through the slot. *Feed the animal, but be careful you don't get too close.*

It didn't matter to me; I was not hungry anyway. Any appetite I might have had was obliterated by the obscene conditions in which I was expected to eat. For meals, I had to sit on the edge of the slab and place my food tray on the bed, right next to the commode. Consequently, if I attempted to eat, I had to do so while gazing directly into the toilet.

The "singer's" commode must have been on the other side of the wall where my commode was located. In any case, his toilet's plumbing was connected to mine. The poor man not only sang incessantly, but he was desperately sick. He could keep nothing inside him for long; anything he ate landed in the commode either as vomit or diarrhea.

Besides the awful sounds emanating from the cell next to mine, it did not take me long to discover that the plumbing system at Butner was not functioning properly. When my sick neighbor flushed his commode, it came up in my toilet. Often, the singer would flush while I was sitting on my slab, staring into the commode, with a tray of food on my lap or on the bunk, as I was trying to eat. Overeating at Butner was not a problem for me.

I wanted to make a phone call to let my family and lawyers know what the doctors were doing to me. Every time the guard started to bring a phone to me, the doctors would show up, saying it was time for more testing. I felt isolated and rejected, as though no one knew what was happening to me, or nobody cared. The constant, horrendous din of the place was driving me over the edge. Again and again, I wondered, *Is this a nightmare or have I gone completely mad?*

I finally got to the place where I could take no more. I decided to allow myself to go insane. I dropped to the floor in the corner of the cell, close to the door. It was the one spot in the room where no eyes could see me. Just as I was letting go of my will to go on, a voice called out my name.

"Jim . . . God loves you!"

I stopped short, like a deer caught in an automobile's headlights. I thought, *Surely my mind is playing more tricks on me. Now I am hearing things.* Then I heard the voice again.

"Jim . . . God loves you!"

"But I think I'm going crazy," I responded aloud.

The voice answered, "No! No, you are not. God loves you!"

Had God sent an angel? I looked up and saw two eyes filled with compassion looking at me through the slot in the door. The voice belonged to the guard who was on duty. He spoke again, this time much more quietly, and he offered to pray with me. I wasn't sure I could pray; I was confused and close to being convinced that the God I thought I knew had abandoned me, but I gladly accepted the guard's offer. He began to pray with me, he on one side of the steel door, and me huddled on the floor on the other side. The guard prayed quietly but fervently, with incredible faith in his voice. When he finished praying, I knew there was a God in prison, even if I could not sense His presence in my own life just then.

After he prayed, the guard talked quietly with me for a few more minutes. He told me that he was a lay pastor in his church. Nevertheless, he asked me not to tell anyone about our time of prayer; if anyone found out he had prayed with me, he could be fired.

I shall never forget that servant of God who risked his livelihood to save my life, for whether he knew it or not, that is exactly what he did. Years later, Dr. Basil Jackson confirmed to me that I was indeed at the point of willing myself into either insanity or death. It was over for me. All hope was gone. But at the ebb tide of my existence, a courageous prison guard allowed himself to be a vehicle through whom the Lord could reach out to me with His message of love and hope. Like the Good Samaritan in the Bible, he decided to cross the line to reach a dying man. It would have been much easier, and far less risky, for the guard to have looked the other way. But if he had, I might not have lived to tell you this story. I will be eternally grateful to my nameless "angel." I hope God lets me meet him here on earth someday. If not, I know I will meet him one day in heaven.

Days blended into nights at Butner. All frameworks of time lost their meaning for me, so it is difficult to know on what days certain events took place. I knew time was passing, however, because of the sunrises and sunsets. My days were consumed by batteries of psychological tests, including the Minnesota Multiphasic Personality Inventory, the Wechsler intelligence test, and a Rorschach test. I looked at ink blots until my vision blurred. Square pegs did not fit in round holes, no matter how many times the psychologists asked me to try to assemble them.

Interestingly, many of the questions I was asked had religious connotations. The questions subtly implied that anyone who talked with God, believed that Jesus would return, had spiritual dreams or visions, or had experienced any sort of ecstatic religious phenomena must be considered suspect. Of course, I qualified.

My head was still in a fog, but I was becoming increasingly aware of my environment. I could hardly believe the way I was being treated at that facility. No one from the outside world was allowed into my cell, and I could get no personal messages out, so I decided to draw a picture of what my cell looked like. I hoped to give it to Tammy Faye when she came to visit me. But I had nothing with which to write. I sat down on the floor and spoke into the slot in the door and asked if I could have paper and a pencil.

The guard on duty said he would try to get them for me. A short time later, through the slot in the door, several sheets of paper and a pencil were slipped into my cell. To prevent it from being a potential weapon, the pencil was ground down to a meager two inches long, but I was glad to get it, nonetheless. My grade-school art course on perspective came in handy as I set about drawing my cell.

Tammy Faye first heard about my collapse from the news media. During the early part of my trial, Tammy had stayed behind in Orlando, Florida. On Thursday afternoon, a gaggle of reporters was encamped around our home. Within minutes after news of my dilemma hit the wire, reporters were banging on the doors for an interview. When Tammy learned the news, her first concern was for thirteen-year-old Jamie Charles, who was expected home from school shortly. Tammy did not want Jamie subjected to another media blitz. She decided to make a deal with the press.

She went outside our house and was immediately inundated with shouts from reporters. Tammy boldly told members of the media that she would agree to talk with them, if, and only if, the reporters would leave before Jamie got home. The members of the media agreed to abide by Tammy Faye's conditions—which they did, for the most part.

Tammy Faye gave a brief but emotionally charged statement about what had happened to me, outlining the details as best she could considering she had been nowhere near Charlotte at the time and was relying completely on secondhand information. She then answered the reporters' questions. She concluded her statement by saying, "If you came to see me cry, you got your wish."

Tammy Sue was living in Fort Mill, South Carolina, near Heritage USA, when she heard about my collapse. She watched the newscasts of me being brought out of Harold Bender's office in chains and cuffs. It was devastating to my daughter.

Tammy Sue called her mother, who confirmed the details as much as she knew them. Tammy Faye said that she was going to leave for Butner in the morning. "What you need to do," she told Tammy Sue, "is bring baby James, and you and Doug and I will go see Daddy tomorrow." Tammy Sue agreed and they continued talking briefly about meeting in Butner on Friday.

On Friday evening, the officers said that I should get ready for a visit. My wife was coming to see me! She had been driving all day to North Carolina from Orlando. My sister Donna and our good friend Fran Moore accompanied her. Tammy Sue arrived earlier and waited at a nearby motel along with Shirley Fulbright.

The women were extremely tired after traveling all day. Tammy Faye had not been given specific directions how to find the prison, nor had she been informed about standard prison protocol concerning visitation procedures. No information had been given to her concerning my condition. Not knowing what to expect made every mile of the trip seem interminable. When the women finally arrived at the prison, Tammy was shocked to learn that the facility she was coming to visit was not a hospital, but a prison.

Inside the facility, I hastily attempted to make myself presentable for my wife. I asked the guard for a razor with which to shave, and then I stepped into the shower in my cell. While I was showering in ice-cold water, Tammy Faye was getting an even colder reception at the entrance to the prison. Thinking that she could simply identify herself to the supervisor and she would be swept in to see me, she was surprised to discover that she, too, in some ways, was at the mercy of the prison officials.

The prison officials asked Tammy Faye for two pieces of identification, one of which needed to be a photo ID. Such irony! On that day in history, Tammy Faye's face was one of the most familiar in the world, yet the prison officials demanded formal identification. Another of the requirements for entering the prison was that every visitor must register, which included listing each person's Social Security number. Tammy Faye was at a loss. She could not remember her Social Security number! Neither could she find her Social Security card.

The prison officials refused to allow Tammy to enter the prison without registering. She was becoming more unnerved by the minute. Through a series of phone calls, Tammy was finally able to track down her number and after completing numerous forms she was ready to come see me.

Back in my cell, I was still having an extremely difficult time walking. I felt the same sort of fear that I had experienced on Thursday evening when the guards first accompanied me to my cell. Again, I was like a man walking on the edge of a high cliff, totally possessed with fear. Slowly picking my way up the same corridor I had entered, I tentatively made my way to my waiting loved ones. As I shuffled along, the guards informed me of the rules governing my visit. For instance, I was allowed to hug my wife when I greeted her, and we were allowed one kiss. After that, no touching was permitted until the visitors were ready to leave, when we could repeat the routine. No gifts or food were allowed.

The guards pointed the way into a narrow, makeshift visiting room, which looked as though it could also be used as a clinic area. A guard sat inside the entrance. Entering the doorway, I had to turn to my right to walk past a partition that hid a commode and sink against the wall behind it. Inside the room were several institutional-type chairs.

When I walked into the room, I hugged and kissed my wife, and sister. I was overjoyed to see my family members. To them I looked frightened.

We sat down in the chairs facing the guard. Tammy attempted to comfort me. She assured me that God would use even this for good.

I had no sooner sat down when I started pouring out my story to Tammy and Donna. I was agitated and nervous as I told the women about the barbaric conditions in which I had been living. I spoke softly, not daring to let the guard hear me talking about the prison, yet emphatically telling my wife and sister all the gruesome details my semiblurred mind allowed my lips to blurt. Concerned that I was so upset, Donna attempted to rub my neck, in hopes of relaxing me and easing my pain. I jumped back in stark terror.

"Prison rules say 'no touching whatsoever in the visiting room'!" I shrieked. Donna recoiled as though she had been snakebitten. After a while, Donna left the room to allow Tammy Faye and me a few minutes of privacy. I talked and talked, faster and faster, knowing that our visit could end at any moment or at the whim of the guards. But the more I talked, the more upset Tammy Faye became. I wanted to hold her and express my love for her, but of course that was not possible.

All too soon, the guard indicated to me that it was time for our visit to end. That was hard enough. Worse yet, it was time to go back to my cage.

I had hoped that Tammy Faye might be able to tell somebody about my awful conditions at Butner. She didn't let me down. From the moment Tammy Faye and the other two women had pulled into the prison parking lot several hours earlier, members of the press were after them every minute. Tammy tried to avoid answering their questions as best she could.

After visiting with me, however, despite her fatigue, Tammy wanted to talk to the media. I'm sure I had not yet reached my cell before an emotional Tammy Faye was outside the prison talking with the reporters who were awaiting her exit.

It was nearly 9:00 P.M. when she told reporters, "I'm really upset tonight. As I walked in, I didn't realize that I would be coming to a prison." From there, Tammy went on to describe the way I had been treated. She was especially irate that I had been strip-searched. Little did she know that even as she spoke, the guards were strip-searching me again, which was standard procedure after a visit.

I slept very little, if any, that night. I simply lay on the hard slab with my face to the wall, listening to the three-note song of the demented soul in the next cell. At every sound of jangling keys, my heart jumped with fear.

The next morning, I took more tests. Then in the afternoon, a guard informed me that my mother, my father, Tammy Faye, Donna, Tammy Sue, and my brother Norm were all coming to see me. I was glad to see them.

After I had been in Butner for several days, one of the staff members gave me an encouraging word. "Tomorrow," the counselor said, "if all goes well, you may be able to go outside for some exercise."

I was so excited! Outside! Exercise, fresh air, being able to move around without restraint! I could hardly wait. To me, being allowed to go outside was a ray of hope that my captivity was coming to a close, that perhaps I would be released soon.

True to the counselor's word, the next day, I was allowed to go outside for some exercise. A guard came to my cell door and, speaking through the slot, he ordered me to turn around with my back to the door, then stick my hands through the slot. I obeyed his command precisely. As soon as I put my hands through the slot, he slapped a pair of heavy steel handcuffs on my wrists. "Now, pull your hands back through the slot," he instructed me.

When I had my cuffed hands back inside the cell, the guard opened the door and allowed me to come out. "Come on, you get to go outside today," he told me. He led me through the corridors and out a side door.

I was outside! Fresh air! A small sense of freedom began to grow inside me.

"You will be over here," the guard informed me. With my hands behind my back he led me to a chain-link cage a few feet away from the building. The cage was about the size of a small office; it was not much larger than my cell inside. The guard instructed me to step inside the cage, after which he closed and locked the cage behind me. The officer told me to stand with my back to the slot in the cage door and stick my hands out through it. I did as I was told, once again. As I obeyed, he removed the handcuffs, and I was free to move my hands. The guard stayed there and watched me.

I couldn't believe it! So this was my reward. I had anticipated being able to walk outside in a grassy area, perhaps even in a parklike setting with trees and benches. Instead, I was permitted to come outside and pace around in a cage like a wild animal. Some exercise. Some freedom. I went over and stood in a corner of the cage. When added to all the demeaning treatment I had received at the hands of my captors, this insult was totally dehumanizing. I had not even been convicted of a crime, yet I was being treated as an animal. I would not have treated a stray dog that way!

After about five minutes of standing in the corner, I told the guard that I had finished "exercising." He recuffed me and took me back to my cell inside. Although I later learned that the cage is standard procedure for prisoners who are in solitary confinement, the false hope of increased freedom only served to plunge me deeper into depression.

My being taken to Butner Correctional Institute raised serious concerns about whether I would be able to return to stand trial. Many trial observers predicted that Judge Potter might even declare a mistrial because of the series of events leading up to my incarceration at Butner. It is highly unlikely that the judge ever considered that possibility. On the other hand, he seemed quite interested in getting me back into court as soon as possible.

When I was first admitted to Butner, Dr. Sally Johnson, chief of psychiatric services at the facility, told reporters that normally evaluations such as mine take at least thirty days and sometimes run as long as forty-five days and longer. No wonder the world was surprised to learn that instead of four to six weeks, I was ordered to return to court after six days at Butner. Believe me, I was not complaining! I was thrilled to be getting out of that place.

It is interesting to note, however, that when the assistant to the warden was asked whether he was pressured to expedite my evaluations, he would not comment except to say, "A judge has to request . . . an accelerated study."[1]

Dr. Johnson's team determined that I had indeed suffered from a stress-induced panic attack. (I could have told them that much!) "He is not going crazy," she said. "Our evaluation did not find Mr. Bakker was suffering a severe mental disease or defect. He does not have a psychotic disorder. He is in the midst of a serious trial and a life-changing circumstance. That is the source of the stress that got him to our doorstep."[2] Johnson's report was a mixed blessing; it got me out of Butner, but it sent me right back to court.

The guards awakened me early on Wednesday morning, September 7; it was moving day. At 6:15 A.M. the marshals from Charlotte, acting under Judge Potter's direct orders, arrived at Butner Correctional Institute to take me back to court for a competency hearing later that same morning. I left Butner wearing a pair of gray prison work pants and a bright, open-necked prison shirt. Two and a half hours later, I arrived at the federal courthouse much the way I had left six days previously—rumpled and unkempt, manacled and handcuffed, and lying prone in the back seat of a marshal's car. The marshals wasted no time; they whisked me into the courthouse, past the usual throng of reporters who were shouting questions at me.

In front of the courthouse that morning, local deejays Billy James and John Boy Isley of WRFX-FM did their irreverent radio show on location from a couch. They offered a special feature: Anyone who wanted an album by Tammy Faye Bakker could have one for free. All a person had to do to get a free album was drop by the boys' show and stick his or her head under the couch.

Street vendors were hawking food, drinks, pictures, pins, bumper stickers, T-shirts, and all sorts of paraphernalia. A young woman and man dressed in white were trying to sell belts with small Bibles on them. One man who looked to be in his twenties was doing brisk business selling cassette tapes of songs making fun of Heritage USA, our PTL television program, and of course, Tammy Faye and me. It was a circus, and I was their clown.

The marshals escorted me to a holding cell, took off my shackles, and told me I needed to get ready to go back into the courtroom as soon as Judge Potter called for me. Tammy Faye arrived at the courthouse about twenty minutes after I did. She brought a clean gray suit, a white shirt, black shoes and socks, a blue tie, and a shaving kit. By the time the competency hearing began later that morning, I was beginning to look like a human being again, but it would be years before I felt whole again.

Judge Potter must have anticipated the outcome of my competency hearing before it began. He had already instructed the jury to return at 2:00

P.M. The hearing itself lasted two and a half hours. For most of it, I sat slumped in my seat, holding my head with my right hand, my eyes looking at the table. I never heard most of the speakers.

I did hear Judge Potter, however, when he asked me if I thought I could understand the charges against me and assist in my own defense.

I answered slowly, "I am very tired, but I believe I can, sir." As for understanding the charges, I never quite understood the charges in the first place. How could nearly a week in Butner's snake pit change that? Five weeks later, when Judge Potter sentenced me to forty-five years in prison, I still did not understand how I could possibly be on trial.

A car horn honked and brought me back to my present fears. The trial was now over, and I was a convicted criminal in the back seat of a marshal's car on my way to Talladega Federal Prison to begin serving a forty-five-year sentence. The horrors of Butner Correctional Institute, fresh in my mind, colored every thought as I contemplated what new terrors I might encounter at Talladega. I was about to enter the shadowy, unknown world of prison where, without the grace of God, I would most likely die.

10

Talladega

AS THE CAR I WAS IN MOVED CLOSER AND CLOSER TO Talladega, I was moving deeper and deeper into my personal twilight zone. We drove about an hour and a half east of Atlanta through the heart of Alabama. Approximately sixty miles away from Birmingham, the marshal driving the car turned off Interstate 20 and pointed the vehicle southwest down State Road 21, a desolate two-lane stretch of road. Darkness had fallen several hours ago, but at least up to this point in our trip there had been lights along the roadside indicating signs of life. Now, however, we were moving into a rural section of Alabama where nothing but darkness lined both sides of the road. Only occasionally did the headlights of a passing car pierce the darkness. I sat upright on the back seat, staring out into blackness.

I kept thinking, *How can this be? I am in chains on my way to spending the rest of my life in prison. I must be having a nightmare. This can't really be happening!*

But it was.

The marshals in the front seat were talking on their police radio with officers at Talladega Federal Prison, making preparations for my arrival. I knew we must be getting close.

In the distance, I could see a glow of light. I wondered if the lights emanated from my new abode. As we drew closer to the glow, I saw an old, country-style general store with gas pumps out in front of it. A few other buildings hugged the intersection, and that was the extent of the town. The entire area seemed to be bathed in an ethereal, amber light. The few people I saw seemed eerily untouchable, as though if I reached out to them, they would disappear, or if I called out to them, they would not have answered. The scene reminded me of a movie I had seen many years ago in which aliens had landed on earth and taken over a small town. Although I was afraid, I was nonetheless straining to see anything that might give me a clue as to what my new prison environment was going to look like.

I was still dressed in the same clothes I was wearing when I had left the federal courthouse in Charlotte—my casual shirt, jeans, tennis shoes, and my bright blue jacket. The marshals had offered to stop at a McDonald's along the way so that I could get something to eat. I declined. I was tired and hungry, but my stomach was churning too much to put anything into it. The marshals spoke kindly to me, but I cannot recall carrying on any conversation with them. When I tried to talk, the words would not come out.

I remembered several years earlier when actor Burt Reynolds had invited Tammy Faye and me to attend a rehearsal of a play Burt was producing. The play was written by Bill C. Davis and starred Charles Durning. The full cast was in rehearsal at Burt's private rehearsal hall on his estate in Florida. The plot was a religious topic, so Burt was interested in our opinion.

The play included a powerful scene of a dedicated young priest in training who was presenting one of his first sermons. The young man told of a day when he had awakened to find all his beautiful, tropical fish floating on the top of the water in their tank. Apparently, the thermostat had malfunctioned and the water had gotten hotter and hotter, killing every fish in the aquarium.

The young priest wondered if his fish had begun to scream—a scream nobody could hear—as the tank got hotter and hotter. The priest paused and said, "I wish I had ears that could hear fish scream, I wanted to save them so much." Then he drove home his point, that many people are hurting and lonely, and similar to his fish, these people are screaming a silent scream, and no one hears them.

I felt like one of those fish. Every cell in my body was in pain, my entire being was screaming for help, but no one could hear me.

As we pulled into the Talladega prison, my brain began to close down just as it had when I had entered Butner prison. I was still suffering the effects of the nervous breakdown and my brain could not accept the painful reality of this moment.

At the front of the prison, the marshals helped me out of the car, and we began shuffling toward a two-story, cement-block building about a half a city block away. There the marshals turned me over to the prison authorities, and I was escorted into a narrow cell with benches all around the walls. More benches lined the middle of the room. A television hung near the ceiling at the far corner of the room. Approximately twenty-five to thirty men were crammed into the cell, and most of them were talking loudly, all at the same time. The cell grew quiet as I entered. After a few seconds, the noise level increased again, and I was sure the men were talking about me.

For years I had heard of the crowded living conditions in prisons, and since this was the first time I was being checked in as an inmate, a convicted felon, I could only assume that this room so chock full of flesh was to be my "home" for the rest of my life. I was horrified!

Still wearing my bright blue jacket, I sat down on a bench against the left wall. Cowering and trying to be inconspicuous—as if I would not stand out in that room!—I slumped my shoulders forward slightly and kept my gaze on the floor. I was scared to death. Once I dared a furtive glance at a couple of tough-looking men and immediately the thought hit me, *Bakker, you are a dead man.* Horror stories I had heard about prison violence and rapes flooded my mind.

A guard entered and gave me a health form to fill out; everyone in the room was either completing a similar form or was holding the finished form, waiting to be further processed. The questionnaire asked whether I had ever had any communicable diseases, such as chicken pox, polio, hepatitis, venereal diseases, or HIV.

I became aware that the room was buzzing with whispers of my name. Finally someone asked me, "Hey, are you Jim Bakker?" I hesitated for a moment. I was not happy to be Jim Bakker just then. Of course, it never crossed my mind to deny my identity, and it would have been futile anyhow. My picture had been all over the television newscasts throughout the day, and most prisoners watch a lot of TV. Probably everyone in the room knew who I was the moment they saw me. Besides that, prison rumor mills are constantly churning out the latest information about what is happening inside those walls. When there is a highly publicized trial, speculation runs rampant among the prison population that the convicted person will land in their particular prison. Because of the laserlike speed of the prison grapevine, most of the inmates at Talladega probably knew I was coming there before I did.

I bashfully acknowledged, "Yes, I'm Jim Bakker."

"Alriiiiighhht," I heard someone say.

A number of the men tried to talk to me, but I was not very talkative. I certainly did not want to offend anyone during my first encounter as an inmate, but I answered so briefly and quietly the men soon left me alone and moved on to other subjects in their conversations.

We waited for what seemed like over an hour before a guard came in and barked out our processing orders. "Step this way," he said, pointing to the door exiting the room, "and line up in a straight line outside in the cell block. Let's move it."

The men began moving toward the door. Several guards awaited us outside the room and helped herd us along into a single file. I stepped out into the cavernous cell block and caught a good look at it for the first time. It was a huge, open space, two stories high, with cells on upper and lower levels. A single, open, steel staircase connected the two stories in the middle of the cell block. Each cell was a self-contained, walled-in room made from cement blocks, with cement floors and a heavy metal door. The entire cell block was painted stark white. Each cell door had a small window, approximately twelve inches square, with wire mesh inside double-paned glass. All sounds in the room seemed to have a half-life longer than that of nuclear waste. As the sounds reverberated from one cement wall off another and continued to echo throughout this man-made cavern, it was as if no sound ever truly died.

At one end of the cell block was a recreation area housing a number of Ping-Pong tables and small card tables. At the opposite end of the cell block was a shower and toilet area, behind opaque glass.

"No talking, and keep the line tight!" I heard a guard bellow like a Marine drill sergeant. He pointed to a row of metal folding chairs lined up outside the processing room. "Move as far down the line as you can and sit down on a chair. Keep the line tight, no empty chairs. Let's go, keep it moving, all the way down."

When the line of chairs was completely filled, one of the guards began going man to man, passing out small brown bags to each new inmate.

"Thank you," I said as he handed me a bag.

The guard did not reply. He simply looked at me as though I had just dropped into the prison from another planet.

I opened my brown bag and found a cheese sandwich and an apple in it. Although I had not eaten since early that morning, I did not feel hungry. My stomach was swirling and I simply had no appetite for food.

The other guard kept yelling, "Tighten up that line. Come on, tighten it up now!"

As I looked up the row of men jammed against each other, I felt as if we were a line of cattle on our way to a slaughterhouse. Although it was late at night, and the prisoners who lived at Talladega were all locked down until morning, I noticed that many of the inmates were peering out their small windows at the line of men with which I was sitting.

"Fresh meat," someone said.

The men nearest the processing room were ordered to remove their street clothes and hand them to the guard inside the door. "You cannot have any article that you brought in here with you," the guard informed us. When each man neared the processing room door, he stripped naked out in the open cell block.

The line stretched down the cell block, where five or six men at the end of the line stood naked waiting to enter the processing room. As one man entered, the man on the last chair got up, took off his clothes, and took his place standing, while all the rest of us slid down the line from chair to chair.

"Keep the line tight!" a guard repeatedly barked.

When at last it was my turn to enter the processing room, I stepped inside, not knowing what to expect. I gave the guard my name and number, and he wrote the information on a bag and tossed my personal clothing items into it. I reluctantly watched as the man stuffed my favorite blue jacket into the bag. He then tossed the bag into a large canvas cart. The processing guard assured me that my street clothes would be sent back to my home address.

Bereft of our clothing, about fifteen men at a time stood in line inside the room for a superficial medical examination. Then the prison medical personnel conducted a strip search. "Hold your hands up in the air. Okay, turn your hands back and forth, palms in, palms out. Let's have a look behind your ears. Pull your ears down. Rub your hands through your hair. Open your mouth, please. Lift up your tongue. Pull up your privates. Turn around. Bend over and pull your buns apart. Okay, fine. You're done. Move down the line. Next!"

Grateful that the indignities of my physical exam were over, I stepped into the next room where I was issued something to wear—prison underwear, socks, shoes, and a bright orange jumpsuit. I had started out the day of October 24, 1989, wearing a fine-tailored suit, changed into jeans and a casual shirt after being sentenced, and now I was finishing the day dressed in a much-too-big, wrinkled, orange jumpsuit.

Just before I walked out of the processing room, a guard handed me a set of sheets and a blanket for my bunk. I exited the processing room and took my place on the first vacant chair at the other end of the constantly moving line.

"Keep the line tight!" I heard again.

When we had all been processed, one by one, the men at the end of the line were escorted to their cells. As the line got shorter and shorter, and I knew my time was approaching, I became increasingly nervous.

What will my cell be like? I wondered. My only reference point was the cell in which I had been confined at Butner. *Oh, God, please don't let it be like that!* I begged. *Would I have a cellmate? If so, what kind of person would he be?* I thought back to the tough-looking group of men I had initially encountered. *Which of them would be confined with me in a small room?* The more I thought about it, the more anxious I became.

"Bakker, let's go," a disinterested voice broke in on my thoughts.

Moving like a robot, I stood to my feet and began to follow the guard. We walked to the cells on the opposite wall, facing the processing room. A little more than midway down the row of doors, the guard stopped. He fumbled with his large ring of keys and finally picked out a single key and inserted it into a cell door. The door swung open, and the guard stepped aside for me to enter.

As the big, steel door closed behind me, I heard the guard turn down the lock. I was in my cell . . . I knew not for how long. My eyes panned the room to see my living quarters. This was my "home away from home" for the next forty-five years, as far as I knew.

In the dim light, I saw a man move. An inmate was already in my cell. He looked as though he was waiting for me.

11

The Colombian Connection

"HI, I'M DAVID SINGLETON," MY NEW CELLMATE SAID amiably. He held out his hand as he spoke.

"Hello, I'm Jim Bakker," I replied, cautiously reaching out to shake hands with the man. My eyes were becoming more accustomed to the light by now, and I saw that the stranger standing before me looked nothing like a stereotypical convict. David looked like a clean-cut, successful, young businessman. I guessed him to be somewhere in his late thirties or early forties.

"Come on in. Welcome to our home; have a seat," David said as though he were welcoming me to a visit at a posh country home.

He described himself as a former attorney and a jet pilot, who had flown numerous missions during the Vietnam War. David was among the last group of Americans to leave Southeast Asia at the end of the fighting. He fascinated me with his many war stories, but the most astounding story he told me that night had to do with me. David said that he had been airborne, transported in a prison jet, to a prison camp at Eglin Air Force Base, near Pensacola, Florida. In midair, a prison official sat down in the seat next to him and asked David if he would be willing to be my cellmate for a while and help orient me to prison life.

In many ways, what the official was asking David to do was a sacrificial thing. Besides housing the regular prisoners, Talladega was a transfer prison, where all sorts of prisoners were housed for short periods of time as they were being moved from one location within the U.S. federal prison system to another. The population at Talladega included hard-core criminals as well as those convicted of lesser crimes. One of the inmates later told me that murderers, bank robbers, rapists, and repeat offenders brushed shoulders with tax evaders and mail-fraud felons.

On the other hand, Eglin, the prison to which David Singleton was en route when he was approached about being my cellmate, was a minimum-security prison camp. Most of the people incarcerated there were either on their last stop on the way out of the prison system or were imprisoned for less serious crimes. Although there is no such thing as a "safe" prison, the degrees of risk at Talladega and Eglin were like night and day. For David to willingly choose to put himself into jeopardy merely to help me become acclimated to prison life was a tremendous act of kindness. I was genuinely surprised at what David told me. Throughout my trial, psychological evaluation, and sentencing, the government seemingly had not been concerned about me. "Why would the government go to such lengths on my behalf now?" I asked David.

"I can't say for sure, but I would guess that they do not want anything nasty to happen to you in prison while the world press is looking over their shoulders."

David told me that part of the reason he accepted the assignment of helping me adapt to prison life was because of the culture shock he had experienced when he was first processed as a prisoner. Due to David's crime and the circumstances surrounding it, he, like many people in prison nowadays, had been allowed to return home for a few weeks following his sentencing. He then had to report on a specific day to begin serving his sentence. For him the shock of going from the life of a successful attorney to prison life was nearly overwhelming.

"I made a comfortable living, Jim," he told me, "and the night before I went to prison, I was eating a delicious dinner off fine china and drinking from crystal stemware. The next night, I was in prison, eating prison hash with a plastic fork and spoon. One night I slept in a soft, warm bed with my wife; the next night, I was sleeping alone, on a steel bunk bed in the hell of a prison cell."

As an act of kindness—or perhaps it was a concession to my age— David allowed me to have the bottom bunk. As I made the bed, David sat on the edge of an old, wooden desk next to the wall and began to explain some basics of prison survival. He emphasized that prison was a dangerous place that had its own code of ethics. The residents would not be patient with me while I learned the ropes, and one major mistake could be fatal. "I am not trying to frighten you, but you must understand these things."

In a straightforward manner David informed me, "Trouble often takes place in the TV rooms in prison. Guys have gotten into serious fights over something as simple as changing the channel on the set. My advice is to stay out of the TV room as much as possible."

"TV room?" I asked. "Where's the TV room?" If I was to avoid going to the TV room, I wanted to know where it was.

David burst out laughing. "Why, you were in it, Jim!"

"I was? When?"

"The first room they brought you into tonight, up the corridor, near the processing room. That is the TV room."

"It is? I had thought that was going to be my cell," I replied sheepishly.

David convulsed in laughter again. "No way, man! Next to the chow hall, that's the most popular room in the place." Then David turned serious again. "It is also one of the most dangerous."

I nodded as David continued. "Don't ever get involved in an argument or a fight in the chow hall. If you do, the prison officials will not take it lightly. They will give you a major 'shot'—a dose of punishment. All prison offenses are given a number indicating the severity of the offense and the shot that you will receive as punishment in return. For example, you can slug someone in your cell, and that might be considered a lesser offense. But if you slug the same guy in the chow hall, they consider it inciting a riot. The prison officials will give you a major shot—a long stay in the 'hole,' solitary confinement with no privileges. Or, if you accumulate a certain number of demerits, they'll put you in the hole."

I had finished making my bed, so I sat down and listened intently as David went on. "Snitches and child molesters are hated in prison. Don't ever snitch on anyone, if you know what is good for you. Obey all the prison rules, whether or not you think they are fair. Make your bed by 7:30 A.M. every day or you will get a shot."

"When can I call my wife?" I asked.

"Rules regarding telephone privileges vary from prison to prison. For instance, if you want to use the telephone in this facility, you have to get out of your cell first thing in the morning and sign up for a fifteen-minute time slot on the call sheet, which is out in the cell block near the window where you get your clean sheets and clean clothes. If there are any other time slots left open, you might be able to get a second calling time."

David yawned—it was getting late. "Tomorrow, I'll fill you in on some more important details of prison life," he promised as he climbed into the top bunk. "Right now, you better get some sleep. You've had a long day."

I took off my orange jumpsuit and put it over the bed's cross board, part of the bed frame at the foot of my bunk, as I noticed my cellmate had done with his jumpsuit. I rolled into the bottom bunk and stared at the bottom of the bunk above me. My body craved sleep, but I was too nervous to shut my eyes. Worse still, as I lay there thinking about the events of the day, the denial process began to pound away at my brain again. *This can't be happening to me*, I thought.

But I *was* in prison, and a quick glance around the sparsely furnished cell, with the open commode and sink next to the wall, the desk, and a small storage cabinet, confirmed my whereabouts. After a while I allowed my eyes to close and I tried to sleep.

Clang! Crash! Clank! A loud metallic sound scared me half to death and I bounded out of bed and stumbled toward the door in the dark. I heard loud voices outside my cell door, so I stepped up to the door and looked out the window into the main cell block. To my surprise, I saw dozens of inmates, all handcuffed and shackled, coming into the prison cell block to be processed. Big guys, little guys, black, white, and all ethnicities in between. I watched as they went through the same entry routine I had experienced several hours earlier, with one exception—their chains. A guard was unlocking each man's cuffs, shackles, and chains as he went through the line. The chains were thrown onto the cement floor, where another guard came along and tossed them into a bag made of strong, heavy material. The noise from the chains clanging and banging on the floor and against each other as they landed in the bags was ear piercing. A clock on the wall above the door to the processing room showed that it was near 2:00 A.M.

I pressed my face up against the window and watched the scene repeated again and again. I watched men come in, have their chains removed, sit down on the chairs, eat their bagged lunch, strip before entering the processing room, and emerge dressed in bright-orange jumpsuits. Around 4:00 A.M., just about the time one group of men had been completely processed and taken to their cells, another group of prisoners was brought in and the entire routine started over. Clang! Crash! Clank! And on and on.

I stood at my cell-door window most of the night, watching human beings herded around like animals. Finally, when I could stay awake no longer, I tumbled into my bunk and fell into a troubled sleep for a few hours.

I awakened just as the guards were opening our cells; I looked around and wondered, *Where am I?* My next thought was, *I can't be in prison. Why in the world would I be in prison?* Before long, reality began to set in and I recalled what had happened yesterday. Utter despair engulfed me as I realized that not only was I in prison, I was going to be in prison for the remainder of my life. I wanted to roll over, shut my eyes, go to sleep, and never wake up.

David, however, was already up, dressed, and was making up his bunk. "Come on, Jim," he said kindly, but firmly. "It's time to get up. You must have your bunk made up by 7:30 A.M."

Reluctantly I rolled out of bed, put on my jumpsuit, and walked over to the sink. I brushed my teeth and shaved. My top priority for the morning was to get my name on that telephone registration list so I could call Tammy Faye. I wanted to run right out to find the list, but I was extremely afraid of doing something wrong and getting into trouble either with other inmates or with the prison officials. I decided I better stick with David.

The noise of the awakening prison population was staggering. As I stepped out of our cell into the open cell block, the din was nearly deafening. It seemed to be growing louder every minute as more men poured out of their cells into the cell block. I had never heard such a roar. It seemed that everyone in the prison was talking at once. As more men struggled to be heard, everyone tried to talk louder than the next person until the decibel level in the white echo chamber was so high I thought my eardrums were going to explode. I quickly realized that the leader in this environment was the man who could talk the loudest. He may not have been the strongest or the brightest, but that was irrelevant so long as he was loud.

I wanted to find the telephone sign-up sheet, but David said it would be out after breakfast; right now I should follow him closely. This was my first experience in a prison chow line, and I was not prepared for the cattle-call atmosphere. Almost all of the inmates were already lined up by the door, so David and I got in the back of the line and awaited our cell block's turn to go eat breakfast. Talladega Federal Prison houses hundreds of prisoners, so only some of the inmates can eat at one time. Prisoners from each separate cell block must eat together, then leave the chow hall "mainline," as it is known in prison, as a group.

As we exited our building, the guards were yelling at us repeatedly, "Keep in double lines and don't move out of formation." We were marched outside to the edge of the sidewalk and told to halt until we were given further orders. As I stood there in the light of day, getting my first real look at the huge prison compound, I noticed a large group of inmates to my left. Their hands and feet were cuffed and manacled, and the men were chained together in a line. I had never before seen human beings treated like this, and the sight was nearly overwhelming for me. I fought back the tears, knowing that I dared not cry in front of my fellow inmates.

Someone gave the signal that it was our cell block's time to eat. We were marched across the compound to the chow hall. We entered the building just as the men from the previous building exited. Once inside, the men spread out, filing through the several lines in which inmates were dishing out the food military style. I was still in the back of the line. I didn't really mind. Breakfast had never been my favorite meal, and besides, the grits, eggs, and other food being dished out of giant rectangular pans did not look very appetizing.

Nevertheless, I did not want to stick out of the crowd, so I went through the chow-line routine, picking up my plastic spoon and fork and a plastic plate full of food just as everyone else did. As I went through the line I could hear guys whispering my name. Many men openly stared at me, making no effort to divert their gaze if I happened to see them. I hastily took my tray and tried to find a seat.

I had no sooner sat down than the guard said, "Let's go! Time's up. Breakfast is over." I couldn't believe it. I had not even taken a bite, and the guard was saying it was time to get out of the chow hall. The next group was already lined outside in front of their cell block, waiting for their signal to get into the chow hall. I dumped my food in the garbage and put my tray on the rack to be cleaned for the next group of inmates to use. We marched back to our cell block, which some of the inmates told me was a transfer unit, a holding unit for men who were in transit to somewhere else. That was my first hint that I may not be staying at Talladega for the rest of my life. Once inside the cell block, the men scattered in all directions. Some went to the showers; some gathered around the Ping-Pong tables; many started playing dominoes. I never dreamed that dominoes could make so much noise as they were slapped down onto the tables. Other men went to the laundry lineup to get fresh clothes to wear or clean sheets for their bunks.

By far the most popular place in our cell block was the phone sign-up line. The line of men waiting to use the phone was already long by the time I got there. I waited my turn to place my name on that important sheet of paper. I had to talk to my precious wife. I scheduled my fifteen-minute segment for that afternoon. Later that day, I was also able to secure another fifteen-minute block for that evening.

I turned to go back to my cell, and as I did, I saw a man approaching

113

me. He was headed right for me. I stopped cold, paralyzed with fear, not knowing what to expect in my first one-to-one encounter with an inmate other than David Singleton. As the man got closer, he stuck out his hand and broke into a broad smile. He introduced himself to me as John and told me that he had been in prison most of his adult life. John said that he knew his way around in the prison system, and he offered to advise me on prison "etiquette."

I started to thank him and to let him know that I was already receiving some helpful instructions, but before I had a chance to get out a sentence, we were suddenly surrounded by guys coming from everywhere. A group of men gathered around me and began asking me all sorts of questions. They were not belligerent; they seemed honestly interested in me, Heritage USA, my trial, and what had happened to me.

One man was particularly interested in the "million-dollar, air-conditioned doghouse" he had read so much about in the papers, flaunted as proof of my extravagant life at PTL. The men all laughed when I told them the doghouse had cost me about four hundred dollars and that it was nothing more than a big shed built out of rough lumber. My family loved animals, so the shed was large enough to provide shelter for all six of our dogs.

"Six dogs!" one of the men behind me exclaimed.

Before I knew it, I started telling my fellow inmates the entire story. "Yes, six dogs," I repeated. "Tammy Faye loves dogs. I used to tease her, saying that she loved animals more than people."

The inmates roared in laughter at that. "I'll say!" one of them chipped in. "You can trust them a lot more!"

The guys all cracked up again.

"Well, we were out of town back in the winter of 1986 when a bad cold spell hit the Carolinas. Tammy Faye was worried that our pets would freeze to death, so I called our security department at Heritage USA and asked them to find one of the old window-mounted air-conditioner units that would also blow heat and put it into the doghouse to keep the animals from freezing. Our chief of security at PTL couldn't find a unit in the warehouse, so he took an air conditioner out of our little backyard cottage. He cut a hole in the side of the dog shed to fit the air conditioner inside so it would blow heat and keep the dogs warm. The dogs never used the shed, but it made Tammy Faye feel better.

"After I left PTL, the new managers had a truckload of men go over to our home and lift up the doghouse to take it back to PTL to be sold at an auction. You may have seen the picture in the national magazines of a bunch of guys carrying that shed. The people who bought the doghouse at the auction took it around to shopping centers, hoping the public would pay money to see it. But people who saw our 'luxurious' doghouse were so angry they wanted their money back from the people who were putting it on display. They were disappointed that it was nothing more than a shed. So that's it. That's the real story about the famous doghouse."

Again, the inmates seemed to truly enjoy getting the inside story on something they had seen on TV or had read about in the papers and magazines.

"Well, let me tell you the real story 'bout this place," one of the men said. "We're mighty glad you were sent here."

"Really?" I asked.

"Yep. From the moment everyone found out 'bout you coming to Talladega, our food has gotten ten times better."

"Yeah," another man piped up, "and they pulled a lot of the men out of here, so we aren't sleeping on mats on the floor anymore. 'Fore you got here, Jim, we were sleeping two guys on bunks and one on a mattress on the floor in just about every cell."

I had noticed some mats under the beds in some of the cells, but I had not guessed that men were sleeping on them on the floor.

"And you prob'ly noticed the paint job they done. Did it in one day. They painted the whole place here. Guess the government boys wanted everything to look pretty for the cameras that might be followin' you around."

"Now that you mention it, I did notice the paint smell in the air," I said. "I just thought somebody was painting something somewhere."

"They were!" one man said to the laughter of all the others. "See all this clean, white paint around here? You didn't think these walls looked like that last week, did ya?" The men roared with laughter once again.

"Well, I . . . I don't know. . . ."

"Hey, Jim, it's all right. We're glad you came. Best cleanup job we've had 'round here in a long time." I wasn't sure whether the men were exaggerating or not, but they made me feel like a hero rather than a heel.

A number of the fellows came up to me and began asking me for autographs. Many wanted me to sign things for their moms or their grandmothers.

After a few minutes, my new friend John, the seasoned inmate, invited me to come down to his cell, which was two cells down from mine. I said, "Sure," and we walked under the steel staircase together toward his cell. Several of the men followed us.

When I got outside John's cell and looked in, I was surprised to see that John had a game table and some chairs in his cell. No other cell that I had seen so far had such a table or chairs. John obviously had connections. We talked some more, with John and the other men offering me their best advice on how to survive in prison. Then John pulled out what looked to be his personal address and phone book, the kind I now know are sold at most prison commissaries.

"I'd like you to sign my book," John requested with a laugh. "But I want you to sign it, 'To John, my best road dog.'" By then John's cell was filled with inmates and they all burst out laughing when John told me how he wanted me to sign his book.

I had no idea what John meant by *road dog*. I was so paranoid after my trial, I did not want to be signing my name to anything that I did not understand.

I said, "John, I'll be glad to sign your book, but I can't sign it that way because I don't know what that means."

"Oh, go on. Just sign it," John said, and the other men broke out laughing again.

I looked around at the other men in the room. They were obviously having a good time at the expense of my ignorance, but they did not look mean spirited. They were just having fun. I asked in a lighthearted way, "Are you guys sure that it's not something dirty, or something wrong?"

Gales of laughter filled the room again.

I felt that I better not take a chance. I signed John's phone book, but I did not sign "To my road dog."

Later, someone informed me that the term "road dog" was actually quite a compliment, especially in the culture from which John had come. A dog is your good friend. A road dog is one who travels the same road with you, who "hangs out" with you. Basically, what John was asking me to do was to sign, "To John, from your best friend, Jim Bakker." John was a bit disappointed with a simple signature and "God bless you," but he remained my good friend while I was at Talladega.

Suddenly a guard showed up in the doorway and announced, "You have too many men in that cell!" The officer then walked on down the cell block.

I was petrified that I was breaking a prison rule, something David had told me never to do, so I made a move toward the door to leave.

"Sit down, Jim," John said with a laugh. "If that cop was really concerned, he would have moved us out of here right now." I marveled at

John's prison savvy. The guy even knew when the guards were serious and when they were not.

Although I was still shell-shocked as a result of all I had experienced in the past two and a half years (especially the past thirty-six hours), I was beginning to feel a strange sense of acceptance and camaraderie in my new environment. At Talladega we had men from diverse racial and ethnic backgrounds. One of the fellows who was laughing with us in John's cell was from the country of Colombia. His name was Carlos and he was built like stone, with strong, muscular legs and arms on a finely chiseled, athletic body.

As we were all laughing in John's cell, someone said that it was almost time to line up for recreation time. In front of all the other men, Carlos looked straight at me and, in a thick Latin-American accent, said, "Hey, Mr. Jim. We are playing soccer today. You come. Be on our team."

I paused a long time before answering. This was the first time in my life I could remember anyone asking me to be on a sports team. As a child, I was extremely small and shy. Nobody ever picked Jim Bakker to be on their team. Consequently, I had never played sports. I had no clue how to play soccer. Nevertheless, to my surprise, I heard myself answering Carlos, "Yes, I'll play. But I don't know how to play soccer."

Without a moment of hesitation, Carlos replied, "No problem. Just stick with me; just do what I do. I won't let you get hurt."

Actually, at that moment, I felt it would be a blessing if I were to get killed on the soccer field. I had no fear of dying, although I *was* a bit concerned about making a fool of myself. But then I realized that I no longer had any reputation to protect. I thought, *What do I have to lose?*

Carlos left to remind his fellow Colombian inmates about the big soccer game coming up at rec time. Meanwhile, David guided me to where the guys were lining up in double columns waiting for the guards to march us out to the recreational fields, a distance of about a city block.

When we arrived at the rec area, the men fanned out to various activity areas such as the basketball courts and the running track. Some of the older men simply sat at picnic tables and philosophized. Some of the younger men—jailhouse lawyers—sat around debating their cases. I fell in step with a group of men headed toward the running track and the soccer field beyond that. I wasn't convinced Carlos wanted me to play. But as I neared the end of the track, Carlos came running up to me and shouted, "Come on, Jim. We're ready to go."

"Okay," I replied nervously, as though I were heading for my execution.

Carlos positioned me right next to him and ran interference for me. Occasionally he would feed the ball to me so I got an opportunity to kick it. I knew immediately that these men were not amateurs. They were skilled soccer players. They played with passion and a strong competitive spirit. Most of the men were in their twenties and in excellent physical condition. I later learned that many of these players were in fact semiprofessional soccer players. Even those who were not semipros were highly skilled. Soccer was their national pastime.

Carlos and his Colombian inmates treated me like a guest star rather than a disgraced minister. They deferred to me, spoke respectfully to me, and protected me, attempting to make sure that I was not kicked unnecessarily. I was surprised. This was not the perception of hardened inmates that I had imagined prior to entering prison.

During a break in the action, Carlos told me it was my turn to play goalie. From being brought up in Michigan, I was vaguely familiar with ice hockey. I knew the goalie position was a highly important spot on the team. I was scared stiff! Besides the possibility of getting smeared, these boys took their soccer seriously. I did not want to make any mistakes that might cost our team the game.

As it turned out, I was goalie in name only because Carlos always stayed a few feet in front of me, deflecting most of the shots that came near the goal. God knows I tried! When the game was over, in my heart I knew I had not contributed much to our team, but all of my teammates acted as though I had. Several of them told me that they were going to write to their family members to tell them that they had played soccer with Jim Bakker.

I honestly do not remember who won the soccer game that day, but I know I came away from it feeling like a winner. For the first time in a long while, I felt a part of a team. I had felt acceptance, concern, and compassion from my Colombian soccer players that caused me to remember that I was still a human being.

It was almost time for my phone call home. I could hardly wait to talk to Tammy Faye. When I arrived back at my cell block, I was dirty, hot, and sweaty. A guard told me that my lawyer had come to visit, so I hurriedly picked up my soap and towel and went down to the end of the cell block where the showers were located. The shower stall was made of opaque glass and had a door that could be shut, providing some semblance of privacy, even though the guards and others could see someone in the stall. I hastily showered and informed the guard that I was ready to receive my visitor.

One of the guards escorted me to the room where Harold Bender was waiting for me. When Harold had arrived, he could not believe that he had to wait because his client was out playing soccer with the Colombians. Harold probably had expected to see me depressed and cowering in the corner of a dark cell. Actually, I was extremely depressed, but the active prison community in which I was now living allowed little time for introspection. . . . That time would come later.

Harold informed me that he had filed an appeal concerning my case. He also told me something about a "Rule 35" by which I could have my sentence reconsidered and possibly reduced. I listened to Harold rattle off his legalese, but I had little faith left in the justice system and even less confidence in lawyers. Harold's visit brought me face-to-face again with the harsh reality that I was facing forty-five years in prison. Any euphoria I had been feeling after surviving my soccer experience was squelched by my lawyer's offers of what I considered to be false hope. It was easy for Harold to speak optimistically about the time it might take for the appeal process. He wasn't living in a prison cell.

I ended my meeting with Harold abruptly when I noticed the time on his wristwatch. "I have to go, Harold. It's almost time for my phone call." I did not want to miss a chance to call Tammy Faye.

The guard escorted me back to the cell block and I made a beeline for the telephone. The phone was located about shoulder high in the open cell block, next to the laundry room. An industrial-sized clock hung directly above the phone, so there could be no mistaking when a prisoner's allotted time began and ended. There was no phone booth to provide privacy for sweet nothings to loved ones or legal specifics to lawyers. Anyone nearby could eavesdrop on anyone's phone conversation if he wanted to do so. Many did.

When I arrived at the telephone, several men were standing in line, hoping someone would give up his time. Another man was on the phone, finishing his call. He actually ran a bit over his time, but I was reluctant to say anything. Finally it was my turn.

All calls by inmates had to be placed collect. Tammy Faye had been anxiously waiting to hear from me, so she could hardly wait to accept the charges.

"Yes, yes, yes!" she said before the operator had even completed her spiel. We had not talked to each other directly since before my sentencing. I told her how much I loved her and tried to inform her about everything that had happened in the past forty-eight hours. It was difficult to squeeze all the details into a fifteen-minute phone call.

Tammy Faye was worried sick. She had no idea where the authorities had taken me until she had seen it on television. She told me that she was going to do everything in her power to get me out of prison. I was glad to hear that but even more excited because my wife said she would be coming to visit me. Tammy said she would leave for Talladega first thing in the morning. I told her to be sure to give my love to Jamie and Tammy Sue. Tammy Faye said Jamie was taking everything very hard. He had been mocked in school because of me. Although Jamie has always been extremely polite and well-mannered, he would not stand by and let kids say horrible things about his dad. Jamie nearly slugged one boy who had made a cruel, demeaning remark, but Jamie's friends grabbed his arms until the boy could escape.

The clock on the wall alerted me that our time was almost up. Not only that, a man in the line behind me was noisily letting me know that if I went a second past my time, I would regret it.

I hated to hang up, but I quickly said, "I love you, Baby. I have to go. My fifteen minutes are up and the other guys are waiting."

"I love you, Jim. Don't worry, honey. We've made it through other things. We'll make it through this too."

I had barely hung the receiver in the phone's cradle when another man had it up to his ear and was already dialing a number.

Just as she promised, Tammy Faye was at the prison the following evening in time for the beginning of visiting hours. She, Donna, and Fran Moore had driven from Orlando to Talladega. My brother Norman also drove from Charlotte. That evening I heard my name called out by a prison guard, using my new title for the first time:

"*Inmate Bakker*! You have a visitor."

A guard accompanied me to the visitation building, where Tammy Faye was waiting for me. I had been briefed on prison policy of one hug and one kiss upon meeting, so when I saw Tammy Faye I gave her an extra long hug before I kissed her. It was as though I was trying to absorb her warmth, her scent, and her vibrant energy. Tears filled our eyes, tears of joy at seeing one another and tears of sadness at our circumstances. I was nervous and physically depleted, but just having Tammy Faye in my presence lifted my spirits. We had quite a reunion that night. I told them, in as much detail as I could remember, what had happened to me since I had last been seen publicly in Judge Potter's courtroom.

My family stayed for several days and visited me every night. Tammy Faye, Donna, and Fran checked into a motel near the prison. They were constantly hounded by reporters wanting to interview them. Reporters booked rooms on both sides of theirs and watched for the women to come out so they could interview them. Some reporters stooped to hiding in the shrubbery near the motel, trying to get candid photographs of the women when they came out of their room. One evening, the reporters from a tabloid paper followed the women to their room, where one man stuck his foot in their door and absolutely insisted that Tammy Faye talk to him. Donna fought the man off, then hurried to call the front desk for help. The person answering the call said that there was nothing that could be done.

The next day, while my family members were visiting me in the prison visiting room, a warm, friendly family introduced themselves to us. The father and mother were there visiting their son at the time. The family members asked if they could have a photo taken with Tammy Faye and me. We wanted to be cordial, so we agreed. The photograph later turned up in a tabloid newspaper. I hated to see Saturday come. Tammy Faye had to return to Orlando to be at the church where we had been pastoring prior to my incarceration. For our final visit together, an inmate who had become a friend did a special favor for me—a fresh, clean, *blue* jumpsuit from the laundry room where he worked. It felt so good to be wearing something other than an orange prison jumpsuit.

Tammy Faye and I ate our usual prison-visit lunch consisting of stale vending-machine sandwiches. We talked as long as the guards would allow and had an emotional visit. And then it was time for her to go.

"Wrap it up. Visiting time is over," the guard announced.

Tammy Faye and I hugged and kissed our legal limit. I held her in my arms, not wanting to let her go.

"I'll see you next week, Jim," she said as cheerily as possible.

Little did we know that by this time next week, I would be thousands of miles away.

12

Crying in the Chapel

ONLY ONE GUARD WALKED BACK WITH ME FROM MY VISIT with Tammy Faye. As we passed the building on the right next to my cell block, the guard began to tell me about the inmates in it. "Everyone living in that building is from Cuba," he said.

My guard told me that the ceilings and walls inside the Cubans' cell block were steel plated, because the Cubans were so adept at tunneling through the cement blocks, making passageways from cell to cell with no tools other than their own fingers. Even the lighting fixtures in that cell block were recessed into the ceiling and covered with steel mesh.

When I got back to my cell block, I immediately went to see John. "Tell me about that mystery building next door to us," I asked. John told me that most of the men in that cell block had never been convicted of a crime in the United States before they were imprisoned. They were boat people, political prisoners who had escaped Fidel Castro's oppression, or people Castro wanted to be rid of, such as criminals and the insane. John went on to say that the Cubans lived in a constant state of lockdown and were not even permitted on the recreation fields.

From then on, every time I went past that building, I prayed, "Oh, God, please help these men somehow." I was beginning to realize that there were many people in prison living in far worse circumstances than I was.

The next day I was in the chow hall, going through the line as usual. I was too bashful to push my way to the front of the line, but I had learned by now that if I wanted to eat enough food to maintain minimum health, I must start eating while still going through the line. Otherwise it would be time to go back to my cell block before I got a chance to eat. As I picked up my tray and started searching for a table, I saw the vaguely familiar face of a man outside looking in the window. To my amazement, the man was waving at me. I looked around quickly to see if he had been trying to get someone else's attention. He waved at me again.

I raised my hand and hesitantly waved back at the man.

The man was mouthing words to me through the window. "Blackwood," he seemed to be saying.

Blackwood? The only Blackwoods I knew were singers who used to appear on my television program at PTL.

The man held a Bible up in the window. Then suddenly, he was gone. I went on eating my food, unaware of the drama that began unfolding outside the window. A guard outside had seen Ron Blackwood looking into the chow-hall window and waving a Bible. The officer was one of the toughest guards on the compound. He had a reputation for sending prisoners to the hole, even for minor infractions.

The guard yelled at the prisoner, "Blackwood, what are you doing?"

"I'm trying to get this Bible to Jim Bakker," Ron replied.

The guard began cursing at Blackwood. The guard was a huge man and Ron is about my size. The guard got right in Ron's face and screamed at him, "What are you trying to do?"

Ignoring his fear, Ron looked back at the man and said, "Sir, let me tell you something. I may go into the hole over this, but you have a chance to do something for God. That man needs this Bible because it is a comfort to him. It won't cost you a thing to give it to him."

The guard stared back at Ron Blackwood and didn't say a word for the longest time. Finally, the guard reached down and grabbed the Bible out of Ron's hand. He took it, brought it into the chow hall, and gave it to one of the officers on duty. When an officer gave me the Bible, it was like someone had given me the greatest gift in the world. I opened it carefully. Inside, I found Ron's name and prison number written on a page near the front of the Bible.

One day a prisoner who had been to the chapel told me that Ron Blackwood, the chapel choir director, had invited me to attend the chapel service on Sunday. Finally, I recognized Ron's name! Ron's dad was one of the original Blackwood Brothers and had died in a plane crash. Ron and his famous family of singers had appeared on the *PTL* television show. His uncle, James Blackwood, was a good friend of mine and had also appeared on our show along with Cecil Blackwood and the world-renowned Blackwood Brothers Quartet. All of the Blackwoods continued to support Tammy Faye and me long after we had departed PTL and had started a new ministry in Florida. Although our outreach and audience were far less than the satellite network on which we had appeared while at Heritage USA, the Blackwoods were not too proud to appear on our programs. I will always be indebted to the Blackwood family.

I was surprised, however, to learn that Ron was in prison. Apparently, he had gotten in trouble over a tax problem. I was excited to see him nonetheless. I made up my mind that although it might be awkward, I would go to chapel on Sunday morning.

Chapel was held at 10:00 A.M. on Sunday morning in a small room in a concrete multipurpose building. The chapel could comfortably seat about fifty or sixty inmates. To the left was a room where a Muslim group met. A guard escorted me to chapel and sat down behind me.

As we walked into the room, the service was just beginning. I tried to ascertain whether I was welcome there. After all, the media blitz that had made my name a household name in America had also made my name infamous. I felt that many religious leaders might not be happy to have me in their services. To this day, I still check ahead of time with a local pastor to see if it is permissible to attend a service in his or her church.

I walked into the room and sat down about halfway back on a seat next to the aisle. I no sooner sat down when the prison chapel choir began singing "You Can Make It," a song written by Mike Murdock and popularized by Tammy Faye, who sang it on our *PTL* television program. I was overwhelmed! This was the theme song of my television ministry for years, sung almost every day by my wife. Hearing it in prison, at first, was cutting rather than comforting. It was almost like an indictment. My own words were being thrown back into my face. It was like a voice from the past reminding me of a message I had given to millions of people at the close of almost every television program, but had by now forgotten myself. All my hope was gone.

When I saw Ron Blackwood up close in the chapel, I recognized him immediately. He had aged a bit since coming to prison, but he was still vibrant. An inmate informed me that prior to my arrival at chapel, the prison chaplain had instructed the other prisoners to stay away from me, not to communicate with me in any way, not even to talk with me at chapel. He said that I was coming to chapel to worship like everyone else and that I should be left alone. Ron Blackwood, however, had arranged to sit next to me, and Ron talked with me throughout the service. Ron talked so much that I feared the guards were going to get angry. Ron told me that he had been at Talladega for over a year. He wanted to encourage me; he could tell that I was a beaten, traumatized human being.

Ironically, most of the songs Ron taught the members of his choir were songs he had first heard sung on the *PTL* television program. What they did not know about music they made up for with enthusiasm. The morning I attended chapel, about twenty-five men were singing in Ron's choir.

Later in the service, Ron got up to introduce the choir's next song, "Don't Give Up on the Brink of a Miracle." He looked directly at me and said, "Jim, I want to dedicate this song to you this morning. This is your song."

As soon as Ron and the choir began singing the song, tears began to flow from my eyes. The song's message said "don't give up," yet I knew that I had already given up. I wrapped my arms around myself, trying to contain my feelings, but it was no use. Tears surged down my face. I sat in the seat and actually shook with raw, pulsating emotion.

Ron cried all the way through the song as well. When Ron returned to sit back down with me, I leaned over and told him that "Don't Give Up on the Brink of a Miracle" had been written for Tammy Faye and me by Mike Adkins, another frequent guest on our program. Ron said that was the reason he had selected that particular song for the choir to sing that morning. He said that as soon as he saw me, he could tell that I was extremely distraught. He wanted to do all he could to help lift my spirits. The chapel piano player gave a short testimony that morning, and Chaplain Paul Kennedy, a man who I could tell really cared about the inmates, brought a fine morning message. It would be many years before I was able to fully realize the miracle of that morning. As I looked back, only God could have arranged for a prison choir to sing on the first Sunday I was incarcerated two of my favorite songs written by two of my best friends, directed by a member of a family I respected and loved, a man who risked all to get a Bible to me.

It would be years before a mutual friend would tell me about the high price Ron Blackwood had paid to get that Bible to me. About a month after I left Talladega, three officers approached Ron Blackwood on the prison compound. One of the men was holding the Bible Ron had given to me. I had been afraid to take it with me for fear of breaking prison rules. He asked Ron, "Is this yours?"

Ron hesitated. "Does it have my name in it?" he asked.

"Yes," the guard replied.

"Well, then I guess it's mine."

"All right, come along with us," the guard answered. They put Ron Blackwood in the hole for thirty days. His offense? Giving me a Bible. The guards said that Ron had given me contraband, that prisoners were not allowed to give each other personal items, even though the Bible Ron had given to me was one that he had gotten from the prison's government-issue supply.

Every day during my first week at Talladega, I met with a prison counselor. He had an amiable personality and seemed genuinely interested in knowing how I was doing and how I was acclimating to prison life. I assumed because of my collapse during the trial, the counselor wanted to keep a close watch on my condition.

One day, as I began to talk to the counselor, he told me that I would not be staying in Talladega for much longer. Fear gripped me all over again. I had made up my mind to serve my time with as much quiet dignity as I could muster. I did not want any more attention; on the contrary, I wanted to drop off the face of the earth. I begged the counselor to please keep me from being exposed to the media and to more public ridicule. I knew I was breaking a vow I had made to myself that I would never ask for any special treatment while I was in prison, but I found myself shaking over the mere thought of more public humiliation.

A few days later, I was called back to the counselor's office. He informed me that within a few hours, probably early the next morning, I would be transferred to Rochester, Minnesota, where I would be incarcerated at the Rochester Federal Prison, known officially as the Rochester Federal Medical Center. I was just starting to become familiar with my surroundings at Talladega and beginning to make friends. Now the fear of the unknown came back with all its fury as I faced going to the far northern part of the United States while most of my family was living and working in Florida. I felt the prison system was conspiring to separate me as far from my family as possible. Actually, I learned later, they were putting me in a place where I could receive immediate attention if I were to suffer another nervous breakdown.

My friend David Singleton had already been transferred to Eglin. I now had a new cellmate whom I hadn't really gotten to know yet, so I wasn't sure if I could confide in him. Consequently, when I went back to the cell block, I told my friend John that I was being shipped out and where I was going. John was surprised. He said, "Inmates are never told when and where they're going." John explained the prison system kept such information secret to avoid security risks and possible escape assistance.

"Stay here," John said. "I'll be right back." He stepped out of his cell for a few minutes. When he returned, he was smiling broadly. Once back inside the cell, John produced a black, hardbound book written by a lawyer who had been in prison. It was like an unofficial "guide to prisons."

"Do you want to see where you're going?" John asked. "Look it up."

I looked up Rochester Prison in the directory and discovered that the prison there was a former mental institution near the famous Mayo Clinic. I had images of an old stone monastery with some interesting castle-like architecture. In fact, it was comprised mostly of standard, ugly, institutional architecture from the mid-thirties and forties.

I was baffled as to why I had been told of my imminent departure and my destination. Perhaps my counselor felt it was safe to tell me since I was to travel along with several other prisoners aboard a small jet rather than a large plane or bus with masses of men. Maybe the prison officials felt that in my fragile state of mind, I needed to know. Regardless, I appreciated the opportunity to telephone Tammy Faye and let her know that I was being transferred. She had already planned another trip to Talladega for that week. Had she shown up and I'd been gone, she would have been frantic.

I went through the usual exit process. Take off your clothes. Strip search. Chains. I was given khaki travel clothes to wear with dark blue canvas shoes. No jacket. Driven in a van to an airport, I was surprised to find that I would be traveling to Minnesota in a Lear jet. One of the marshals told me that this plane had been confiscated from a drug smuggler.

I sat down in the plush leather seat on the back right side of the plane next to a telephone. I had flown in many private jets over the years. At one time, our ministry had owned a jet with almost the exact same cabin configuration, and I had always sat in exactly the same spot to which I was assigned today. Here I was sitting in the multimillion-dollar Lear aircraft wearing handcuffs, chains, and shackles. The irony was not lost on me.

As the Lear jet whisked us across the country, I lay my head back on the seat and closed my eyes. What sort of place was Rochester Prison going to be? I wondered.

I was about to find out.

13

F. M. C. Rochester

IT WAS SNOWING WHEN I ARRIVED IN ROCHESTER, Minnesota. Since I was sitting in the back of the plane, I was the last person to exit. When I popped my head out the door, the snow fell on my hair and on my face; several snowflakes lingered on my eyebrows before melting. With my hands cuffed and chained, it was impossible to brush the chilly flakes away.

The first thing that struck me in Minnesota was how awfully cold it was! I had been living in Florida prior to returning to Charlotte for my trial from August to October. The weather at that time had been quite warm. Following my sentencing, I had spent my first days in prison in Alabama, where it was still pleasant, shirtsleeves weather. I left Talladega wearing my lightweight prison clothes, a collarless pullover shirt with a scooped neck and short sleeves, and lightweight khaki prison pants, held up by only a thin piece of elastic. The entire outfit looked similar to what a doctor might wear in an operating room.

Now, here I was in Minnesota—a beautiful state, especially if you are a fan of winter—and where any temperature above zero from October to April is considered a heat wave! My teeth were chattering, and I was shivering and feeling nervous about entering another prison. In addition, I was not looking forward to another dose of the dehumanizing prison entry process, which seemed designed to strip a person of all dignity and self-worth. My personal pride and self-esteem had long since been reduced to rubble. Prison exacerbated my sense of devastation.

I stepped off the plane. I could see no signs of Minnesota's lush, green parks and its pristine lakes. I had attended Bible school many years before in Minneapolis—it was where I had met Tammy Faye—so I knew the state. But on this day, the place looked gray and barren. I felt like I had come to the end of the world.

Inside the prison, the men were watching my arrival on television. Both local and national news teams had assembled at the airport to cover my arrival. Fortunately for me, as standard policy, prison officials refuse to allow the press to get too close to a runway when prisoners are being transferred. The cameramen had to use telephoto lenses and shoot from a distance at least a city block away to even capture my photo. The lenses so magnified the snow that one reporter stated that I had arrived in the midst of a bad blizzard. In fact, it was merely a light snow.

Guards stood on the runway with automatic rifles at the ready as the other prisoners and I clambered out of the plane. We were herded toward a prison van the moment our feet touched the pavement.

When the van pulled out and we made our way from the tiny airport toward the town of Rochester, daylight was waning. I was still able to make out the images of drab, squat homes—houses built to take the weather. I would wonder for years what downtown Rochester looked like.

We approached the front gate of the prison. I saw an electric fence with three-foot-high spirals of razor wire at the top, enclosing the entire perimeter of the prison. Another electric fence with the identical type of razor wire enclosed the inside perimeter. About fifteen feet separated the two fences. Two white pickups carrying armed guards perpetually patrolled the no-man's-land outside the two fences. One of the inmates told me that the fence had sensors all over it, so if a person even touched the fence with his hand, an alarm went off and a sensor in the monitoring room showed exactly where the infraction took place. "No escaping over that fence," the inmate lamented. "It will cut you to shreds." Me, I wasn't planning any attempted escapes; I was simply hoping to survive, and I wasn't real certain about that.

The van pulled into the prison parking lot and up to the gatehouse. Even the gatehouse had rolls of razor wire spiraling across its roof. Every person who entered Rochester prison—guards, doctors, visitors, and prisoners—all had to pass this way. We got out of the van and walked into the gatehouse. Again, guards with guns watched our every move. Once inside, sliding bars opened in front of us. We stepped inside a small space where a guard sat behind a window, checking everyone in or out. Then another set of bars opened and we entered the main part of prison compound. We turned right, escorted by officers, and walked a distance of about two hundred feet into "R & D"—Receiving and Discharge.

The guards took my cuffs, chains, and shackles off, and I was free to move. I was processed by myself. I was photographed and fingerprinted. I completed more health forms. The Rochester officials appeared slightly keyed up about me being there and acted as though they were in a hurry to get me settled. It was similar to checking into a hotel in which the bellhop could not wait to get you and your bags dumped off into your room—only in this case, I had no bags. I had nothing but the clothes on my back and they were about to come off again. And this surely was no hotel!

It was time for my reentry strip search. Any time a prisoner leaves or enters a prison, every cavity of his body is inspected for drugs, concealed weapons, or other contraband he might be trying to smuggle into the prison. I didn't think I would ever grow accustomed to the strip searches. I gave a physician's assistant the same medical information I had given the medical staff a few days earlier at Talladega.

After the search, I was given a fresh set of clothes, better and warmer clothes than those in which I had traveled. They resembled military clothing without the epaulets. I was learning that fresh clothes are also standard procedure when entering a prison. A prisoner is never permitted to enter a prison compound in the clothing he was wearing outside the prison compound, even if he just came from another prison. Again, it is a precaution against the smuggling of contraband into the prison. For some reason, however, the guards checking me in allowed me to keep my blue travel shoes. I soon discovered that it was highly unusual for the guards to have allowed me to enter the prison in the same shoes I had worn on the plane. I later wished that the guards would have taken those shoes away from me right then and there.

Rochester Federal Prison was comprised of many large buildings inside the razor-wire fences. Building One was the mental hospital, housing inmates who were mentally ill or those being evaluated for the courts, as I was at Butner. Building Two housed the general prison population. In addition, many inmates were confined to the hospital and the outpatient facilities, which were also inside the prison compound.

A team of guards escorted me to Building One. We went upstairs and turned left into an office. The office was warm and homey, with plants in the windows and family pictures on the desk. Indian art pieces decorated

130

the walls. Other pieces of art—made by inmates, I later learned—were placed around the room.

A sophisticated-looking woman sat behind a desk. She exuded a commanding strength yet had a frail, almost grandmotherly quality that reminded me of my Grandmother Bakker who had died when I was a little boy.

The woman rose to meet me, extended her hand, and said, in a crisp, aristocratic tone, "Hello, Mr. Bakker. I am Dr. Westrick." Despite my stupor, I could not help wondering what such a charming and dignified woman was doing in this place. Dr. Westrick turned toward a tall man standing off to the side of her desk. "And this is Dr. Foster," she said. Dr. Foster stepped forward and smiled broadly. He leaned over toward me like a towering oak bending in the wind and stretched his hand toward me. He said in a deep but gentle voice, "Hello, Jim. I'm glad to meet you. Have a seat." Dr. Foster exuded confidence and compassion as he spoke to me and motioned toward a chair. I gratefully sensed that there was something different about this man.

I sat down and stared at Dr. Westrick through my puffy eyes. She picked up the conversation from there. She welcomed me to the medical center and told me of their commitment to treating me—and all people— with dignity and to protecting my privacy and well-being in the best way they could. She assured me of her and Dr. Foster's support. She also explained that it was their policy not to judge me because I was incarcerated but to assist me in any way they could to sustain a healthy quality of life and my personal integrity. Dr. Westrick and Dr. Foster then asked some basic questions concerning my mental health. The prison at Butner had already sent them a large report on my test results there, my I.Q., and my mental competency, so Dr. Westrick and Dr. Foster already knew a great deal about me. But it was obvious that they were probing for something that was not in the written file. Finally, I realized, by the tenor of their questions, they were trying to assess whether or not I was suicidal.

After a short while, Dr. Westrick stood up and extended her hand again. "I have asked Dr. Foster to make himself available to you. I will be seeing you again soon," she said. I wasn't sure if that was good or bad, but by the way she spoke to me, I felt a tinge of personal human dignity.

Dr. Foster rose as well and nodded toward the door. "Right this way, Jim." Dr. Foster escorted me to his office where he continued to talk quietly to me. I was surprised when Dr. Foster began listing the names of numerous people we knew in common. Although I did not know it at the time, Dr. Daniel V. Foster was one of many "coincidences" that I would experience in prison. Educated at Willamette University in Salem, Oregon, Dr. Foster did his graduate work at Oregon and received his doctorate in clinical psychology from Baylor University in Texas. He had been serving in the Federal Bureau of Prisons for over a decade when I was sent to prison. At the Federal Medical Center, he was the chief of psychological services.

What made Dr. Foster such a gift to me was that in addition to his outstanding academic qualifications, he also had an understanding of my religious background. Dr. Foster had been raised in the same church denomination as I had been. He had worked with the well-known Christian counselor, Dr. Richard Dobbins. He had spent many years counseling ministers, missionaries, and their families. Dr. Foster was uniquely qualified to understand where I was coming from, the road I had traveled thus far, and how I could best adjust to spending the rest of my life in prison.

My initial interviews with Dr. Westrick and Dr. Foster were relatively short but extremely important moments in my life. Although I did not know it at the time, besides getting acquainted and making small talk, the doctors also had to decide if I was mentally competent to live in the general prison population. Had they assessed me as suicidal or mentally unstable, I would have been placed in Unit One, a unit where inmates with mental problems were incarcerated.

I was taken to Building Two, which was a large, two-story structure that housed the general prison population. The brick on Building Two, like all the other buildings in the prison compound, was a yellow color probably considered contemporary when it was built. This building, along with the others at Rochester Federal Medical Center, had been abandoned for a number of years and water had frozen in the bricks along the flat rooftops. Before the buildings could be used again, the broken bricks had to be replaced, creating a chaotic, zigzag look to the masonry. The government had spent a lot of money to reopen this facility.

Once inside Building Two, my new home, I was escorted up a stairwell to the second floor. As soon as we opened the door at the top of the stairs, I saw a guard station. The officials led me down the corridor to what I would come to know as "my wing."

The prison official ushered me into the office of a man named Sam Houston, the unit manager, the ultimate authority in Building Two. He was the man in charge and was responsible for everything that happened there. Mr. Houston was a big man who wore glasses and smiled easily, but despite his jovial demeanor, it was clear that he was tough and not a man to be tangled with. Mr. Houston greeted me warmly and then in a businesslike manner said, "Sit down, Jim. I want to talk to you." Sam Houston then proceeded to give me a talk concerning survival at Rochester. His advice was as close to being a fatherly lecture as one ever gets in prison. Sam seemed to have a genuine concern and compassion for the men living under his control. Yet he was not a "do-gooder" idealist. Houston had been through several prison riots and had received commendations from the Bureau of Prisons for his handling of the conflicts. He was a tough, seasoned professional. He was used to being cautious about convicts; Mr. Houston had been conned by the best of the cons. He knew that the prison world could be an extremely dangerous place for someone so naive and lacking in "street sense" as I was. In addition to the same cautions that David Singleton had expressed at Talladega, Houston instructed me to beware of predatory individuals in prison. "There are people here who will try to take advantage of you in every way imaginable," he warned.

Mr. Houston also added some rules about vices I had not even thought about. "Avoid gambling," he said. "Stay away from 'hooch,' beer, wine, or whiskey made by prisoners." Prisoners, I was discovering, can be quite creative when it comes to making or securing contraband items. Sam was wisely instructing me to be on my guard.

I could tell by talking to Sam Houston that he was a man who went strictly by the rules, but he also let me know that if I played by the rules, he would protect me as he would any man in his unit. I appreciated Sam's wisdom and advice, but I was still in a traumatized state and not functioning normally, so I simply sat silently in his office, my shoulders hunched over, awaiting my next order.

Finally, Mr. Houston said, "Come on, Jim. I'll introduce you to your cellmates." Mr. Houston had already selected my cell, across from the shower and right around the corner from his office. We walked out of Sam's office and turned the corner. Just then, we nearly banged into an inmate who was hurrying up the hall in the opposite direction. The man was wearing shorts, T-shirt, and tennis shoes. He looked like an athlete on his way to a game. In one lithe movement, he steered his body out of the path of Sam Houston and me. "Excuse me, sir," he said in Houston's general direction. But he was looking at me as he spoke. "Hi!" he called enthusiastically.

I raised my gaze from the floor long enough to return his greeting. "Hi," I replied solemnly.

"That is Tom Brandon," Houston explained. "I'll introduce you to him more formally tomorrow. It might be good for the two of you to get to know one another."

Sam Houston continued walking toward my cell. The cell was a small, narrow room about the size of my walk-in closet at home. It was originally designed to house one human being, but now four men were living in that small space. In addition to the two sets of bunk beds, it had a small desk, a commode, and a tall, narrow clothes closet with room enough for two or three outfits per person. The cell was so small that if all four men in the cell stood up at once, they would bump heads. Sam Houston explained to me that all new arrivals at Rochester are placed in a four-man cell. Through good behavior, in two years, an inmate could earn the privilege of being in a two-man cell.

Houston introduced me to my "cellies"—my three new cellmates. One of the men, Bob Grayson, was a pharmacist and owned a drugstore. He looked to be about my age. He told me that his pharmacy was still open and his wife was struggling to keep things going until he got out of prison.

One of the fellows, Shawn, was a "good ole boy," just a down-home, country fellow in his early twenties. The third man, Billy B., was a young, heavy-set, good-natured fellow. He looked like a kid to me. They were a friendly bunch of guys.

When I first entered the room, we immediately began making small talk, just getting to know one another. One of the men was from Minnesota, so I said, "Well, do you know where International Falls is? That's where my wife, Tammy Faye, was born and grew up."

The man replied, "Oh, yeah, of course I know where International Falls is. I grew up not far from there. International Falls is the icebox of the nation. It gets to forty below zero there in the winter."

I told him, "I know what you mean. Once I pulled Tammy Faye on a sled and almost burned my lungs out from sucking in the frigid air." The guys laughed good-naturedly.

The farm boy talked about Minnesota's short growing season. "My dad always said, 'Summer comes on the Fourth of July; it also leaves on the Fourth of July.'"

I told the men, "When I used to introduce Tammy Faye in churches I told the congregations that the reason Tammy Faye was so short was because they had such a short growing season in International Falls!" The guys really cracked up at that.

"Hey, Bakker," one of the guys called. "I saw you on TV tonight. I watched you get out of the plane."

"Oh, really? I didn't see any cameras."

"Yep. They were there. It looked like they must have been bouncing around a lot."

"They must have been shooting from far away." I explained, "When you use a telephoto lens from a distance, it is hard to hold the camera still enough because the distance magnifies even the slightest move of the camera."

"It must be nice to have all that attention," the younger fellow piped up. "I'd like to get on TV."

"Not me," I mumbled, as the pain of my public ridicule came pouring back. I thought, *This kid doesn't know what he's asking for.*

"Yeah, we were kinda expecting you," the heavy-set kid said. "Matter of fact, we knew even before you were found guilty that you were coming here!" The room erupted in laughter at that.

All three of my cellmates smoked in our cell. I had been assigned an upper bunk, and as I lay in my bed that night, cigarette smoke curled up all around me. My head began to pound from the smell. I have never used tobacco products, and my system is extremely sensitive to smoke. It irritates my eyes and makes breathing more difficult. Yet I didn't want to complain. I understood that I was in a far different environment than the one with which I was accustomed. For the most part Heritage USA was a smoke-free environment. Now it was extremely difficult for me to breathe in a room that looked as though it had been socked in by a dense London fog.

Even more irritating than the smoke surrounding me was the language that permeated the prison air. Almost every other word I heard was obscene. I am not implying that the language was merely offensive—it was a cesspool. I had never in my life heard such talk. The most crushing curses were those that incorporated the name of Jesus Christ. Growing up in a Christian family as I did, my dad once literally washed my mouth out with Palmolive soap for saying "Gee whiz." Dad always said that "Gee" was a short way of saying "Jesus," and we should never use the name of Jesus without respect.

In prison, hearing the Lord's name used as a curse word bruised my soul. I could hardly stand it. Any time I heard someone use the Lord's name in a derogatory manner, I silently prayed, "Oh, Jesus. Please forgive us."

Even in the sluggish mental condition in which I was living, the name of Jesus retained all its beauty, majesty, and power. Although I was emotionally bruised and battered to the point that I had begun doubting God's love for me, somewhere deep in my heart I still believed that Jesus was as good as His word. He had promised never to leave me or forsake me, and I knew Jesus was not above going into prison to be with me.

Most of my life I had been surrounded by people who did not use profane language. Rarely did I hear anyone using Jesus' name as a curse, or using vile terms for excrement, sexual intercourse, or disparaging comments about someone's parentage.

The men in prison were not purposely being crude. Many of them spoke respectfully around me, and those who frequented our cell often apologized when they swore in front of me, especially if they used the name of Christ. For many prisoners, using vulgar language was not a conscious choice; profanity was simply the vocabulary of prison and the streets from which many prisoners had come.

Nevertheless, as I lay on my bunk that first night in Rochester prison with the swirling smoke enveloping me and the sludge of language inundating me, I thought, *I must be in hell.*

I had been traveling all day and was feeling all sweaty and soiled—not to mention smoke saturated—so I decided to take a shower. I hopped down from my bunk, removed my clothes, and wrapped a towel around my waist. I started walking barefoot across the hallway toward the shower room when suddenly a huge black man roared at me, "Stop! Stop! You can't do that!"

I whirled around in terror, thinking, *Oh, no! What did I do wrong?*

The man walked up to me and pointed at my feet. "You can't take a shower in your bare feet."

"Why not?"

"You'll get the worst case of athlete's feet you've ever seen, and who knows what else!"

"I don't have any shower shoes." All I had were the clothes that were given to me when I checked into the prison and the blue canvas shoes.

"Wait a minute. I have an extra pair." Before I had time to point out the obvious disparity between our shoe sizes, the man bounded down the hallway toward his cell. He returned in a minute or so, carrying a pair of used shower shoes . . . size humongous! I ordinarily wear a size seven-and-a-half shoe. This man must have worn at least a size fourteen!

"Here, give these a try," he said. "They're a little big, but they'll keep you from getting some sort of disease. You can keep them."

A little big? I slipped my foot onto the flip-flop and slid my toes up toward the thong. I still had room for another person's foot on the back of the flip-flop!

I was deeply grateful for the man's kindness, though, and I told him so, as I flipped and flopped toward the shower stalls, my feet sounding like a seal.

The Minnesota prison had private shower stalls with white rubber curtains that could be pulled shut in each stall. The stalls allowed more privacy than those I had used in Talladega. I stepped inside the stall and turned the water on full blast, as hot as I could stand it. It was as though I somehow felt I could wash the "prison" off me if I could only get the water hot enough. I stood for a long time in the stall. I did not want to get out.

After my shower, I walked back to my cell. Bob the pharmacist was reading a book and smoking. Billy B. was lying on his bunk, listening to some music on a radio with a headset in his ears. Federal prison rules did not allow cassette or CD players, phonographs, televisions, personal computers, or any other electronic equipment. The only link to the outside world we were allowed to have in our cells was a small, battery-operated radio like the one Billy B. was using. There were no blaring boom boxes in the prison. The radios could only be used with headsets.

"Where did you get that?" I asked Billy, wondering if it was legal.

"In the commissary," Billy B. answered loudly since he had not removed his headset. I determined that I wanted to get one of those radios as soon as possible.

"But I have no money," I yelled so Billy could hear me.

"Get it from your old lady!" Billy replied.

"Can we have money in here?"

Billy lifted the headset off one ear, still listening to the music as he spoke to me. "No, but you can have it sent to your commissary account."

"I didn't know I had a commissary account."

Billy B. explained: "You need to go get your picture taken over at R & D, and they'll give you a card that looks like a credit card. You can't even buy a candy bar around here without that card. Then you have to get a commissary slip that will list what items you are able to buy. You turn that in at the commissary window and they'll deduct your purchases from your account. You can shop at the commissary once a week on your assigned day. If you miss your time, you won't be able to get anything until the next week."

"Thanks, Billy. It sure seems like a lot of trouble just to buy a radio."

Billy nodded, already lost again in his music.

Later that evening Tom Brandon, the man I had nearly bumped into in the hall with Sam Houston earlier that day, stopped by to see me in my cell. "How do you like the place so far?" he quipped, with a sparkle in his eye.

"I'm not sure," I answered glumly. "My head feels like I'm in a fog."

"Yeah, we've all known that feeling," Tom tried to reassure me. "Anything you need?" Tom glanced around the room. "Well, let me put it this way, is there anything you *don't* need?"

I liked Tom instantly. His upbeat attitude and his sardonic sense of humor piqued my interest. I would never have guessed that he was a former medical doctor and a recovering alcoholic who had lost his practice and wound up in prison in one fell swoop.

"Well, I could use some stamps. But I don't have any money. Is there anywhere I can get some stamps around here?"

"I don't think so. Not without money," Tom laughed. "They don't give you anything here. You have to earn it. But don't worry. I think I have some stamps in my cell. I'll be right back."

Tom returned a few minutes later with a book of stamps. "I'll loan you these till you get some," he said with a smile. "Here, take these too." Tom handed me a pair of blue tennis shorts. "I noticed that you don't have any clothes yet. Have you called home and told your little sweetie to send you two outfits? Otherwise you'll be wearing prison khakis day and night. During the day, the prison requires us to wear khakis, but they let us wear our own clothes at night around here. Anyhow, you can have these shorts to get you started. Wear 'em with a T-shirt and you will be right in style."

I went to bed early that night and every night during the early weeks of my prison life. I wanted to anesthetize myself, maybe sleep away my troubles. Our room was in such an active area of the wing, though, it was difficult to get any sleep. Right outside my door, guys were running numbers and devising sports pools. Not wanting to get into trouble, I soon learned to block out any overheard conversations. I did not want to guess who was doing what when it came to illegal activities. Nor did I try to match voices heard in the hall with those I heard elsewhere. I just wanted to ignore anything or anybody that might be a potential "con." Sam Houston's lecture had taken well with me.

Sometimes it was impossible to avoid hearing about covert activities. Once when I was trying to get some rest, I overheard a conversation several guys were having about new bank alarms and supposedly burglar-proof systems. They had already figured how to circumvent the complicated wiring and tripping devices in the alarms. One man sounded as though he could easily have been a college professor as he instructed the others how to defeat the supposedly fail-safe alarm systems. I had always heard that prisons were "schools of crime," and now I understood why.

I hated to do it, but I knew I needed to call Tammy Faye for some money. I needed to buy stamps, toiletries, pens, paper, food items, and shower shoes . . . and I definitely wanted one of those radios like Billy's. I was extremely embarrassed, though, to ask my wife for money. This was the first time in thirty years of marriage that I had been forced to ask Tammy to help me financially. The last time I had asked Tammy for money was when I had borrowed the money from her to make the down payment on her engagement ring.

Now as I contemplated calling and asking her to send money when she had so little to support herself, our struggling ministry, and our son, I really despised myself. I thought, *Jim Bakker, you have really sunk a long way.*

I called Tammy Faye the next day and told her where I was and what it was like at the Rochester prison. I explained to her why I needed some money right away. I asked her to send my blue jeans and my favorite blue-and-white-striped jeans shirt, a pair of black slacks, a pair of black dress shoes, my tennis shoes, a sweat suit, and the shirt and sweater that Fran and Herb Moore had given me. That was the limit of personal clothing allowed by the prison. Tammy assured me that she would send the clothes and the money for my commissary account as soon as she received the necessary paperwork from the prison.

From then on, we talked by telephone every day for about an hour throughout the first two years of my prison experience. Tammy Faye's love, prayers, and optimistic attitude helped carry me through the tough transition period. She was always upbeat and cheerful when she talked to me, even when she was exhausted and emotionally drained, as she was during that first phone call from Rochester when I told her I needed money.

Fortunately, that was the only time in my entire prison experience that I had to ask Tammy Faye, or anyone else, for money. I would soon have a job inside the prison. My starting pay would be eleven cents an hour. It was not an accident, I now believe, that the job would involve Tom Brandon.

Sam Houston called me into his office. We talked briefly about how I was adapting to my new surroundings. Then he called Tom Brandon into his office.

"Doc," he said, "I want you to teach Jim Bakker how to clean toilets."

Officially, Sam Houston assigned me the job of being an orderly, a part

139

of the support staff who helped keep the entire medical and prison facility functioning. Specifically, Tom's and my duties were to clean all the public toilets, sinks, and showers on our wing of the second floor of Building Two. Tom did not really have to teach me much about toilet cleaning. It is not exactly rocket science, after all. Moreover, I had been an orderly while working at North Central Bible College when I had been a student there. Cleaning the bathrooms in the dormitory was part of my job.

I did not have to clean any toilets in inmates' cells. Those were the responsibility of the inmates living in their cells. But the bathrooms and showers that we all used in common were my responsibility. And I went after it with a vengeance. In Tom's inimitable way, he bragged, "Why, our toilets are so clean you could eat a Caesar's salad out of them!"

Word leaked out quickly that Jim Bakker, former president of PTL, was now cleaning toilets in prison. Many people took strange delight in the image of me doing one of the most demeaning jobs on the face of the earth.

Actually, I didn't really mind cleaning toilets. To me, it was not a degrading job—messy maybe, but not degrading. Someone had to do it. Beyond that, there was at least one valuable fringe benefit. Every morning after the men on our floor left for their various work duties—every prisoner who can physically function works in prison—I could do my job well and still have plenty of time for reading, writing, or doing whatever I wanted before the rest of the guys returned after lunch. Besides, Tom Brandon and I often joked that we were not simply toilet cleaners, we were "porcelain experts"!

Having a friend like Tom really helped. I was beginning to settle into my new environment—nobody ever gets used to prison—but I was still waking up every morning in despair and denial. I simply could not understand what I was doing in prison. Beyond that, I was living in constant apprehension, never knowing whom I could trust. Who were the "good guys" and who were the "bad guys" in this place? I was about to meet one of the bad guys . . . and he was not an inmate.

CHAPTER

14

Miracle in the Airwaves

I COULD HARDLY WAIT TO GET TO THE OFFICER'S STATION to get my commissary slips. Securing a radio similar to Billy's had become almost an obsession. My clothes, shoes, and money from home had not arrived yet, but I wanted to be ready to go to the commissary as soon as I could. After all, Billy B. had said if I missed my assigned time, I would have to wait another week to get the items I needed.

It was after work hours, so I had changed out of my khakis into a white prison T-shirt and socks, the blue tennis shorts that Tom had given me, and my blue canvas shoes. I was dressed as well as I could be.

I had gotten my commissary slips and was excitedly walking down the hall back toward my cell when I heard a guard's booming voice. "Bakker! Come here!"

We were not allowed to run in prison but I came close to it as I scurried back to the officer's station.

"What are you doing with those shoes on?" he screamed at me.

"Well, they gave them to me. . . . "

"You're not allowed to have those shoes in here," he bellowed. "Those are travel shoes."

"Well," I stammered, "they gave them to me at Talla—"

"Give me your shoes," he demanded. Another guard seated next to the one talking smirked as though he was trying to keep from laughing.

I took off my shoes and held them in my hand.

"Throw them here," the guard ordered, pointing at a low table near his desk. I tossed the shoes onto the table.

The guard crossed his arms over his chest as he glowered at me standing there in my socks. Finally he said, "Don't you have any other shoes?"

"Yes, sir. I have a pair of black, high-top, work shoes." The steel-toed high-tops were given to me on my first day of work duty. Hardly anybody wore his work shoes around the prison after work duty was done.

But the guard started yelling loud enough to be heard all up and down the corridor. "Go put them on," he ordered. "Put these shoes back on, go get your work shoes, and bring these blue ones back to me."

I was petrified! I was doing my best to obey all the rules in prison—many of which you do not know about until you have broken them—and I was committed to being a model prisoner. I did not want to get into trouble about anything. This was prison, after all, a strange, hostile environment in which I had already been stripped of my sense of self-worth and personal security. I was scared stiff that the guards would put me in the hole, and memories of Butner still gave me nightmares.

I hurried back to my cell, put on my black work shoes, and returned to the officer's station carrying my blue canvas shoes. The officers were laughing when I reached their desk. They quickly wiped the smiles off their faces as the belligerent guard turned to talk to me again.

"Throw the blue shoes right over here," he nodded toward the table, curling his lip as he spoke. I tossed the shoes onto the table. "Now get out of here," he roared.

Looking back on it today, I am still hard pressed to explain why I was so deeply traumatized by this incident. To some people it may seem to have been an insignificant event, but to me, in a fragile condition, having just undergone a nervous breakdown a few weeks before, and now facing forty-five years of prison, the officer's head game could easily have sent me over the brink.

I walked back to my cell, literally shaking. I climbed into my bunk, pulled the covers over my head, and turned my face toward the wall. I could not help thinking that just a few years ago I had employed almost three thousand people and had an annual budget of well over $150 million, and now I was being humiliated by a prison guard over a pair of cheap shoes. I began to realize that this episode had little to do with wearing the wrong shoes. It was all about power. A prison counselor with whom I later confidentially shared this incident told me, "Jim, there are some sick guards in here. Just as there are good guys and bad guys outside these gates, there are good guards and bad guards here. Officer Jerry Ensley, the man you have been telling me about, fits into the latter category. If I don't miss my guess, you will be having more encounters with Jerry Ensley. It's part of his nature."

"But I didn't do anything to him!"

"It's because you were once successful and famous," the counselor told me. "The bad guards love to pull rank with you; they love to make you grovel. It just gives them a charge. That's how they get their jollies."

The counselor was right. Officer Ensley personified the worst aspects of prison life. He became my personal bogeyman, popping up in my life and always intent on messing with my mind. One day, for instance, I was moving from one cell to another and had a pile of books and other possessions stacked on a cart used for such purposes. Officer Ensley was not even the guard on duty in our wing but happened to walk by just as I was pushing the cart out of my cell.

"Hold it!" he shouted. "Bakker has too many personal belongings there. You better do an inventory count on him," he called to the guard on duty. Ensley glowered at me.

I knew that I did not have too many personal belongings, but there was no use in protesting. No doubt Officer Ensley would have been delighted to find an excuse to throw me in the hole. When the guard on duty arrived, he bowed to Ensley's bluster and consented to do an inventory of my belongings. As soon as Officer Ensley went on his way, the guard on duty turned to me and whispered, "Forget it, Bakker." I quickly moved my belongings to my new cell.

Another day, I was walking back to my cell and I saw Officer Ensley and a work cadre of four or five inmates working in the hallway. I tried to walk by inconspicuously, but Ensley spied me. "Bakker!" he bellowed. "Come over here and clean these panels." I stopped dead in my tracks, turned around, and walked back to where the officer was standing. He was pointing to a stack of stainless-steel panels that had been removed from the interior of the prison phone booths in our hallway and were now spread out on the floor. The backsides of the panels looked as though they had not been cleaned in decades.

The prison phone booths represented one of the few areas of semiprivacy in prison, and it was known that inmates often masturbated in the booths during phone calls with their wives or girlfriends. Although the outsides of the panels were cleaned regularly, the inside panels were covered with filth and grime, spittle, and dried semen that had apparently caked on them for years. I nearly gagged. Nevertheless, I maintained my composure, went over to my mop closet, gathered my cleaning materials, and put on a pair of rubber gloves.

I took the panels into the tiled bathroom and started scrubbing. I used every kind of disinfectant and cleaning product available. I made a conscious effort to accept this grotesque, demeaning job and do it as unto the Lord. I forced myself to concentrate on Christ rather than Officer Ensley. I scrubbed and scrubbed. And when I was done, the stainless-steel panels shone like mirrors. I took the panels back to Officer Ensley and lined them up against the wall.

Ensley stared at the shining panels in disbelief. Then he looked back at me and said gruffly, "Bakker, that's all."

From that day on, anytime I saw Officer Ensley walking across the prison compound, I turned away and went in the opposite direction if at all possible.

"Jim. Jim! Come on, little buddy. It's time to get up. I can't clean these toilets without you." I rolled over and pulled the covers higher over my face. I hated it when Tom Brandon called me "little buddy."

"Let's go, little buddy. We're going to be late," Tom called again as he pulled the covers off me. I reluctantly rolled off my bunk. "Come on," said Tom. "If we can get our work done quickly enough, we can go over to the recreation building to see if your money has come in yet. The commissary is in the rec building, and there is a machine in the hall outside the commissary door. You can put your commissary card into the machine and it will tell you how much you have in your account. Even though the commissary is closed right now, the machine will tell you if something has come into your account. I've been wanting to show you around over there anyhow. The rec building has a workout room, a library, a place to do leather crafts and ceramics. You can sign up for college courses, all sorts of things."

Tom and I hurried through our toilet-cleaning responsibilities and got to the commissary by midmorning. I ran my card through the scanner, and to my delight, my account showed that I had one hundred dollars in it!

Tom showed me around the rec building. When I saw the prison ceramics room, I looked in and saw the beautiful pieces of art the men had made. I thought, *Tammy Faye would love some of those for Christmas!* I knew I would have no ability to buy Christmas presents this year, so I signed up for the ceramics class right then.

Later that evening, I skipped going to mainline for chow because I was so excited about getting my radio at the commissary. I thought I would be first in line, but by the time I got there, the line snaked out of the room into the hall. At least fifty men were already waiting ahead of me.

The commissary was like a small grocery store. It stocked toiletries, postage stamps, socks, tennis shoes, T-shirts and running shorts, tobacco products, inexpensive watches, cans of tuna fish, rice, picante sauce, corn chips and potato chips, fruit, powdered milk, oatmeal, soft drinks, cookies, and a wide variety of other products. One of the best things about the commissary was that it provided the prisoners with the opportunity to make choices, while most other aspects of prison life did not.

The commissary had queue lines that reminded me of the way Disney World lines people up to get into the attractions. Back and forth, back and forth, until you finally got on the ride. The commissary was noisy and chaotic, but everybody seemed to be in a good mood.

As I got closer to the entrance, I began to notice something quite unusual about the commissary. A large window separated the inmates from the products that were for sale. The inmates turned in their grocery lists by inserting them through a narrow slot. Inmates working inside the commissary retrieved the lists and then filled the orders, which were delivered out a chute where each prisoner bagged his own groceries with his own bag, usually his laundry bag. We were allowed to "buy" one roll of quarters, one roll of dimes, and one roll of nickels to be used in the vending machines on our wing and in the visiting room. The entire bill was deducted from our commissary accounts.

On my first visit to the commissary, I purchased some stamps, enough for myself and enough to repay Tom. I also bought a pair of shower shoes in my size, some oatmeal, food snacks, and the main object of my shopping spree—the battery-operated radio, batteries sold separately.

I couldn't wait to try it out. As soon as I got the radio back to my cell, I put the batteries in it, placed the headset in my ears, and turned it on. I was stunned! Suddenly my ears were filled with rapturous sound! On the one hand, hearing the music made me realize how bleak my existence had become in such a short time. On the other hand, it was like finding a rose garden in the midst of hell.

When I took the headset off, however, the music stopped. I was not in a rose garden; I was in a crowded, four-man cell, confined in a federal prison. The contrast nearly overwhelmed me. Outside the razor-wire fences was a world filled with a symphony of beautiful sounds expressing the freedom of the human spirit. Inside the fences, everyone played the same sour note, the music of prison life, the sound of the living dead.

That night, as required by prison rules, one of my cellmates turned the ceiling lights out at ten o'clock as usual. I climbed up onto my top bunk and awaited the ten o'clock count, one of the five daily, mandatory, counts of inmates conducted by prison personnel to make sure all prisoners were still present. Other counts took place at midnight, 2:00 A.M., 5:00 A.M., and 4:00 P.M.

At the Rochester prison, there was no official time when prisoners had to go to bed. An inmate could stay up all night if he so desired, as long as he was in his cell for the counts. But for many inmates the workday began at 7:30 A.M., so as soon as the main lights went down at ten o'clock, it was a signal for many prisoners that it was time to start getting ready for bed, especially since for the ten o'clock count, it was not necessary to stand, or even to be awake.

On the other hand, at four o'clock each day, every prisoner in the federal prison system across the United States must stand up next to his or her bed to be counted. The four o'clock "holy count" is the only one of the five counts for which all prisoners must be in their cells, awake, and standing. At least once a day, the federal prison system wants to know that all of the men and women confined within its walls are still alive.

Although the overhead lights were out, my three cellmates had small gooseneck reading lights attached to their beds so they could continue reading without disturbing their cellies. The reading lights were legal and available in the commissary, but I had been so interested in securing my radio, I hadn't given a thought to how I was going to see it in the dark. Now alone with my thoughts, I lay on my side, faced the wall, and cupped the tiny radio in my hands as though it were a priceless treasure.

The man in the bunk below me was smoking and scouring a newspaper, looking for sports scores. The pale glow of his reading light and the rising smoke shrouded my bunk.

Soon a guard checked to see that my cellmates and I were still there, all prisoners present and accounted for. The heavy cell door made a *whooosh!* sound as the guard closed it behind him. I hated that sound. It was as though all the air was being sucked out of the closet-sized room.

The closed door had become a symbol of my life. As I lay there that night, I felt as though all the life had been drained out of me. I didn't know if God cared about me anymore; I could not feel His presence in my life. I wondered if He had written me off, if He had simply said good-bye to me. At my lowest times, I even doubted that God existed.

Oh, sure, somewhere deep within the recesses of my heart and mind, I knew that God was still alive and well. But wherever He was, I could not find Him. Whatever He was saying, if anything at all, I could not hear His voice. I honestly did not know where God was.

I began to think, *Maybe one of the things that have been said about me are true. Maybe the well-known preacher was right when he had proclaimed, "Jim Bakker is through. He will never preach again."*

In the semidarkness of the room—which seemed bright when compared to the complete darkness of my soul—I fumbled with the dial to my transistorized treasure chest. I put on the headset and began turning the dial back and forth, scanning the frequencies. The little radio was emitting nothing but static. I began to wonder if perhaps the radio was defective when suddenly the static cleared and I heard a familiar tune. And then I heard a familiar voice!

It was the voice of my wife, Tammy Faye! And she was singing the song we had used as our theme song at PTL, the same song that Ron Blackwood and the prison choir had sung in the Talladega Prison chapel service—"You Can Make It."

In stunned silence, I lay on my prison bunk bed and listened as my wife sang these words:

> You may face some of life's toughest trials.
> You may walk some long, lonely miles,
> But trav'lin' with you, you will find a friend,
> And there won't be a battle you and God can't win.
>
> If there's someone who has crushed your dreams,
> The things you want may never seem to happen, it seems.
> Every single doubt your Father will dispel.
> You're His child, there's no way He'll let you fail.
>
> You can make it. You can make it.
> This trial you're going through,
> God's gonna show ya just what to do.
> You can make it. You can make it.
> I don't care what's going wrong.
> God won't let it last too long.
> You're not in this thing alone;
> You can make it.[1]

Amazingly, as the last refrain of the song finished, the radio station faded out. I tried my best to tune it in again—I wanted to know where this

147

music was coming from—but to no avail. For the remainder of the night, I heard nothing but static at that location on the radio dial.

To some people, this event might seem to have been mere coincidence. To me it was a miracle. I had experienced many miracles over the years. I used to laughingly say that I needed a miracle every day just to keep the PTL television ministry alive. But since the loss of PTL and Heritage USA, it seemed that all miracles in my life had ceased and God had turned His back on me. Looking back, I now realize that hearing Tammy Faye's song on the radio was one of the more significant miracles in my life.

Few if any radio stations were playing Tammy Faye's albums at that time. She and I were outcasts on the religious airwaves and the subjects of ridicule on secular broadcasting systems. It had been more than two and a half years since our departure from PTL, and most of Tammy's records had long since been confiscated by the new "caretakers" of the ministry. And "You Can Make It" was not exactly on heavy rotation at most radio stations.

Yet out of the static, all the way from a station I later discovered was located somewhere in Georgia, as I lay in my prison bunk in Rochester, Minnesota, I heard the message, "You can make it." To me, it was as though God was saying, "You are going to make it, Jim. I will never leave you or forsake you. And here's a little miracle to help remind you." Sadly, in my emotional pain and devastation, I did not perceive the full impact of this miracle until nearly six years later.

I could hardly believe what I had heard. I sat up in bed and excitedly told my cellmates, "I just heard my wife singing on the radio!"

"Oh, yeah? That's great," one of the men replied. The men responded politely but indifferently. Their lack of enthusiasm doused my excitement over hearing Tammy Faye singing the song. Hearing Tammy Faye's voice so clearly in my headset reminded me that I was not at home in our bed with Tammy with our children sleeping down the hall. I was in a smoke-filled prison cell with three other inmates. I had little hope of ever spending another night at home with my family. I was no longer a man of faith and power; I was a man of utter despair and hopelessness. At that moment, I felt like a scared little boy.

But things were about to change.

15

Surprises

I SPENT MUCH OF THE MONTH OF NOVEMBER 1989 getting acclimated to my new surroundings and lifestyle at the Rochester Federal Medical Center. Each day my routine was basically the same—up early, skip breakfast or eat something purchased from the commissary, then clean the rest rooms shortly after 7:30 A.M. when the 192 men who lived on our floor left for their work assignments. Once I completed my chore of cleaning up after the men had used the rest rooms and showers, I was on call to the guard on duty to do whatever jobs needed done on our floor.

During those first evenings, I did a lot of talking with inmates who dropped by my cell. Many of my visitors had some sort of spiritual background and some were genuine Christians. Some men wanted to know about my experiences at PTL. Others wanted to talk theology. Even in my shell-shocked state, I tried to enter into the conversations as wholeheartedly as possible. These were, after all, my new neighbors, and I did not want to be rude or give the impression in any way that I felt I was above talking to them about any subject.

Contrary to popular public perceptions, throughout my life I have always been an extremely shy, private person. Because people saw me on television, they assumed that I was a gregarious, outgoing, spontaneous personality. Nothing could be further from the truth. In prison, my shyness, coupled with my extremely low self-esteem, often caused men to think that I was aloof and unfriendly.

Many men tried their best to involve me in the warp and woof of prison life. Tom Brandon kept telling me that the guys really wanted to be my friends. I could not believe anyone wanted to associate with Jim Bakker, the man they had read and heard so many negative things about, a man even church leaders had castigated and declared as no good.

One of the big pastimes in prison is playing cards, and several of the guys constantly wanted me to play. I was reluctant because I was virtually ignorant of most card games. I knew how to play a few children's card games such as "Old Maid," not exactly a prison staple, and I knew how to play "Rook" but beyond that I was lost around a card table. Nevertheless, in an attempt to be friendly, and at the insistence of a young, former drug dealer, I tried to learn, and the guys patiently tried to teach me. With my strict upbringing, however, I never felt comfortable playing cards, and once I became more involved in various prison activities, I had no time for card playing anyhow. Nevertheless, I will always be grateful to the guys who reached out to me in friendship and with an offer to include me in their favorite pastime.

The highlight of my day was my daily telephone conversation with Tammy Faye. I would usually call her in the morning after I had finished my work. We often talked for well over an hour. Tammy Faye always answered my collect phone calls in her perky voice no matter what sort of difficulty she was encountering herself. She was a tremendous encouragement to me during those days, and in many ways, she carried me through them.

We were not only marriage partners, we were best friends, so we talked about all sorts of things. Every day I described for her in as much detail as I could all the things that I was doing, the new men I had met, and the concerns I had. She told me about the church and her responsibilities as the pastor of the congregation in Orlando. Frequently she would tell me what she was planning to speak about in church on Sunday and we would discuss the sermon ahead of time on the phone. It probably helped Tammy Faye to clarify her message in her mind by talking it through with me, and the spiritual insights we shared were a source of inspiration to me at that time.

Tammy Faye would always tell me how Jamie Charles was doing in school. She also informed me about the latest bargains she had found while shopping and the new restaurants she had recently discovered. As she described them to me in detail over the telephone, I would dream of going there with her someday. I remember she once told me about a restaurant called "The Bubble Room," where the desserts were gigantic. Tammy Faye had a way of making the most mundane and routine things sound exciting. Even though I knew she was hurting deeply, Tammy Faye's voice on the phone was always filled with life and hope.

In one of our many telephone conversations, I asked Tammy Faye to send what I called my "Crisis Bible," the one I had used in the two years after I had lost PTL up to the time I had gone to prison. It was my favorite Bible and the one in which I had written many personal study notes. I had marked hundreds of verses that had helped me during those difficult years. Unfortunately, in the flurry of activity surrounding my hasty departure from the federal courthouse in Charlotte, the Bible had been misplaced, and Tammy Faye could not find it. She promised to send me a *PTL Parallel Bible*, a dual translation Bible, the same as those we had sent out to many of our supporters during our best days at Heritage.

In order to receive anything from the outside, I had to have permission from the prison authorities, just as all prisoners at Rochester were required to do. I went to Sam Houston and asked him what I needed to do to have a Bible sent in by my wife.

"You must have a written permission form signed by the chaplain," Mr. Houston informed me.

The next day during my free time, I went to visit the chaplain. He was a kind man with graying hair and beard who looked to be in his early sixties. We talked briefly and I told him my desire to have a Bible sent in from home. He readily agreed to sign the form, granting permission for me to receive the Bible. He explained that the Bible had to be sent through the prison chapel but he would do everything he could to see that I received it. In the meantime, he gave me a prison Bible to use until mine arrived.

We talked a bit further, and he stammered uneasily and kept saying things such as, "I'm always here if you need me, Jim." Slowly but surely, it began to sink in to me that the man did not want me to attend the chapel services. "It would be better if you did not come around the chapel," he suggested. He did not come right out and tell me not to attend chapel, but I got the message.

The chaplain was not a cruel man; in fact, he was a good man, but he was also a man under orders. Several years later, I learned that he had been given specific orders by his superiors to make sure that Jim Bakker did not do any preaching in prison. He was afraid that if I became involved in the chapel program, eventually I might take advantage of an opportunity to speak, and then both of us would be in trouble. The best way he knew how

151

to avoid the problem was to keep me as far away from the chapel as possible.

In my current state of depression, I was not all that enthused about attending chapel services anyhow. I still loved the Lord, and my heart was tender toward God, but I felt that because some ministers had worked so hard to discredit me and others had even pressed to put me in prison, I really wanted no part of organized religion.

After my conversation with the chaplain, whenever any of the Christian men asked me to attend chapel services with them, I tried to avoid the subject. If they were close friends and they continued to press me on the issue, I would eventually let them know, "I have been asked not to attend chapel services. But don't worry about it," I cautioned. "It's fine. It's okay with me." I did not want any of my Christian brothers to get upset because I could not attend chapel and begin to make trouble. I did not want to make any waves in prison.

True to his word, the chaplain received my Bible from Tammy Faye and made sure I got it. He called me to his office, and there on his desk was the *PTL Parallel Bible*. It was like being reunited with a dear, old friend. That Bible became my "prison Bible." I marked key verses; I filled every page with notes and underlined numerous passages in multiple colors. I also wrote prayer requests in the margins of the text, next to verses that had special meaning to me or passages in which God promises to answer prayer. That prison Bible remains with me to this day and is my most prized earthly possession.

In 1989, the American public was becoming much more concerned and aware of the health hazards associated with using tobacco products. Restaurants began offering no-smoking sections. Airlines began restricting smoking on flights of less than two hours. And many government agencies pressed for restrictions on smoking in all federally operated buildings, including federal prisons. In many ways, the Federal Medical Center at Rochester was ahead of its time when it came to allowing prisoners to live in a nonsmoking environment if space was available for the inmates to do so.

Since my arrival at Rochester, I had been living with three cellmates who smoked almost constantly. I never complained about the putrid smell or the stifling haze that perpetually filled our cell, but it bothered me, and my friend Tom Brandon knew it. "We have to get you out of that cell before you choke to death," Doc often said, only half-joking.

One evening as I was resting in my smoke-filled cell, Tom came rushing in to see me. "I need you outside in the hall right away." It was not unusual for Tom to need me to help him clean up a mess somewhere on our floor, so my cellmates probably did not even give it a second thought when I followed Tom out the door.

Once out in the hall and away from my cell, Tom began talking excitedly. "We have just found out that there is going to be an open bunk in our cell. One of my cellies is getting transferred tomorrow. As soon as he is out the door, you need to be in Sam Houston's office, requesting a transfer to a room with nonsmokers, our room to be exact."

"Can I do that?" I asked Tom in amazement.

"Sure you can," Tom replied. "It's the new nonsmoking rule coming down out of Washington. Prison policies are going to be changing and the prison officials know it. If you request to be put in a room with nonsmokers, the prison will be happy to comply if it is possible. Tomorrow it will be possible. But you will have to act quickly. If you do not get your room-transfer request into Mr. Houston's office, the prison will simply assign another inmate to our cell. These bunks do not stay open for long."

"Okay, I'll do it," I promised Tom.

The next day, as soon as Tom's former cellie had vacated the room, I was knocking on Mr. Houston's office door. Sam Houston was happy to transfer me to Dr. Brandon's cell. From my first day at the prison, Mr. Houston had encouraged my friendship with Tom. By the end of the day, I was out of my "smoking room" and bunking with Tom and two other nonsmokers.

One of the first inmates to welcome me to my new smoke-free environment was a jolly, rotund man named Gleason West. Gleason looked like a combination of the Pillsbury Doughboy and the Michelin Tire man, with a mischievous twinkle in his eye. Gleason worked in the prison kitchen so it was no surprise that his cell was mysteriously filled with food and goodies. A few days later, Gleason's huge body waddled down the hall hiding a large, restaurant-sized can of tomato sauce.

Tom tried to warn me that Gleason was the epitome of a prison con man. Affable, extremely likable, he was always working a deal somewhere. Dr. Brandon joked that Gleason was so crooked that when he died, he would have to be screwed into the ground.

Gleason stopped by our cell almost every day. He was always asking me to sign things for him, pictures, news articles about me that he had salvaged from newspapers and magazines, or anything else that was loosely associated with me. Gleason was especially fond of bringing me the more

153

outlandish tabloid papers that often contained fabricated articles about me. I had to refuse some of Gleason's requests to sign the tabloids. I made it a policy never to sign anything I did not read, and most of the "rag mag" articles were so preposterous, I refused to read them.

Some of the stories, although they were total fabrications, still hurt. For instance, from the first day I went to prison, the tabloids ran stories "reporting" that Tammy and I were divorcing. We were not. I loved Tammy Faye and we talked by phone every day.

One article said that my mother and dad had no place to live and were out begging in the streets because of me. In reality, Tammy's mother and my parents were living in homes that we had purchased for them while we were still at Heritage USA. When our world fell apart, Tammy Faye and I sold our home and paid off our parents' places so they would not have to suffer because of our problems.

Another article defamed my dear daughter by "reporting" that to help finance my legal appeal, Tammy Sue had agreed to pose nude in *Playboy*. Anyone who knows my daughter knows that she would never consent to such a thing regardless of the reason or the amount of money offered.

Other articles were simply ludicrous. One purported that during my trial I had eaten peanut butter and vitamin sandwiches and clucked like a chicken while watching X-rated movies in my hotel room.

In a strange sort of way, while the tabloid papers and magazines ravaged what little remaining reputation I had in public, inside the prison the rags actually tended to give me more credibility with the inmates. In many cases, the men read the articles and knew for a fact that what they were reading were out-and-out lies. For instance, one popular tabloid ran headlines: "Jim Bakker Escape Plot Foiled." In a two-page spread, the article purported that a Colombian drug cartel had attempted a daring escape plot that had helicopters landing at the Rochester prison in hopes of sweeping me off into the sunset. The article included sketches of the prison walls, complete with gun turrets at each end.

When the inmates read that story, they howled with laughter. Not only did they know that no such helicopter raid had ever taken place, they were quick to point out that the Rochester prison does not even have gun turrets.

Another article that got a big response declared that Jim Bakker was standing on his bunk, preaching to inmates. Considering that I had the top bunk and the ceiling was only three or four feet above my head, that would have been quite an accomplishment! Again, however, the sheer lunacy of the report caused my friends to respect me more. They often commented that the Jim Bakker they had read about in the rag mags was not the same man they knew and who was living with them.

Most of the inmates at Rochester tried to protect me from such inane articles. They often hid the tabloids when I was around or tried to keep me from seeing them. They recognized that even though I knew the articles were ridiculous, they often sent me into prolonged states of depression. I would curl up in my bed and try to forget that I had seen my picture with another deprecating headline smeared across another paper or magazine.

In contrast to most of the inmates who attempted to shield me from the rag mags, Gleason would bring them to my cell and want me to sign them! I signed some of the articles and pictures he brought—no doubt they will turn up again somewhere—but I refused to sign the more salacious articles. Nor would I sign the *Playboy* photos of Jessica Hahn that Gleason and other men brought to my cell for me to sign.

Besides his mischievous streak, Gleason was also a constant source of accurate current information. He seemed to know precisely what was happening or going to happen at the prison. He had an inside line to the prison grapevine. At times I thought Gleason *was* the grapevine!

It was Gleason who introduced me to one of the true "delicacies" of prison life—prison pizza. Actually it is not a delicacy, nor is it really pizza. It is more like deluxe nachos, and while the recipe may vary from prison to prison, some basic ingredients are usually included.

The pizza was prepared in a cardboard box—the biggest box that would fit inside the microwave oven. The base of the pizza was a layer of tortilla chips spread all across the bottom of the box. On top of that we spread a wide variety of ingredients, whatever was available from the prison commissary at the time—tomatoes, green peppers, and any sort of meat we could obtain. Occasionally we were able to get actual pepperoni, making the pizza taste almost normal. For the weight conscious, I often made my prison pizza with pieces of canned chicken. We doused the entire conglomeration with picante sauce.

Atop the growing mountain of ingredients, we placed plenty of cheese, whatever type was available from the commissary. String cheese was our favorite because it could be pulled apart in strips and melted down over the other ingredients. We often used jalapeno cheese, much to the delight of my Latino friends.

Once all the ingredients were included, another row of chips was added and the process began again. More tomatoes, more peppers, more cheese, and whatever personal favorites anyone cared to add to the recipe. The prison pizza recipe was constantly in flux; it changed with the resources that could be obtained by the person making the concoction. Once the mountain of ingredients was near the top of the box—the size of the box and therefore the size of a person's pizza was only limited by the capacity of the microwave oven—a final layer of cheese was spread across the top.

The pizza was then inserted into the microwave and usually took about twenty minutes to cook. On a busy Friday or Saturday night, a line formed early at the microwave. While one pizza was cooking, the next guy in line placed his pizza on the top of the oven.

A much quicker, though less tasty, way of producing a prison pizza was to throw all the ingredients into a large plastic garbage bag. We then melted gobs of cheese in the microwave oven, and simply poured the hot cheese into the sack and shook it. Voila! Instant prison pizza!

Each guy then scooped some of the pizza out of the bag and into a small plastic bowl. Sometimes we would eat out of each other's bowls, rinsing them off in the bathroom sink. My mother, who emphasized fastidious standards of cleanliness as I was growing up, would have been appalled. At first, I too cringed a bit at the thought of eating from the unsanitized bowls. After a while, though, I got to the point where I no longer worried about it.

Much of the weekend "social life" of prison as well as any special celebrations or going-away parties revolved around prison pizza. Just as people outside of prison might have a dinner party and invite some friends over for a gourmet meal, inmates invited their friends over to their cells for a pizza party. Gleason's pizzas were the rave of the prison, because he had access to ingredients the rest of us only dreamed about.

To my surprise, soon after my arrival at Rochester, I began to receive an unusually large amount of mail. Some of the cards and letters I received were merely addressed to "Jim Bakker, Minnesota." One letter was addressed "Jim Bakker, Federal Pen." The most amazing delivery was a letter addressed simply to "Jim Bakker." The postal system obviously knew where to find me. Daily mail call was at 4:30 P.M.

"Mail call; mail call!" a guard would call out over the intercom system. The guards always said everything twice.

As the guard retrieved a piece of mail from the trays, he called out the prisoner's name to whom it was addressed. Technically, the guard was required to hand each prisoner's mail to that individual; nobody could pick up someone else's mail. In the beginning of my time at Rochester, the officers simply called out my mail with all the rest of the men's mail. After a while, however, because I was receiving so much mail, especially toward the Christmas holidays, it began to get a little embarrassing. I was receiving over five hundred cards and letters some days, while some of my friends hardly got any at all.

One man who was a longtime prisoner told me that he had not received a letter in over twenty years. Once he even asked me if he could have one of my letters. I felt so sorry for the man; I wanted to share my mail with him, but it would not have been fair to the people who were writing to me. I was committed to answering every piece of mail I received. One day, the man actually received some mail. He was so excited! But when he opened the envelope, he discovered that it was nothing more than a government form, not even a form letter. I will never forget the dejected expression on the man's face.

Later when I told Tammy Faye about the poor man's disappointment, she was so touched that she began to rally members of our church and friends of our ministry to become pen pals to prisoners. Many responded to Tammy Faye's call. Tammy Sue continues that ministry to this day.

It was not necessary to open our mail. The prison staff had already done so, searching for contraband and removing any money that might have been sent to us. When I received a greeting card or letter that had included money, the prison staff took the money out, deposited it in my commissary account, and issued me a yellow slip, notifying me that the deposit had been made. Prisoners were never allowed to receive directly any checks, paper money, or coins.

Newspapers and magazines were handed out last at mail call. The hallway then emptied in seconds as the men scurried back to their cells to read their mail in semiprivacy. Immediately after mail call, I went to my cell, climbed into my bunk, and began to read my mail. Even though we talked on the phone every day, I always found a familiar pink, Estee Lauder-perfume-scented envelope from Tammy Faye. I saved my wife's letters to read last, sometimes tucking them under my pillow to read later when things were quiet.

Many of the letters I received were kind and encouraging, but I also received a few vile letters. The hate mail jolted me, especially during my first few weeks in prison. I had thought that my enemies would be satisfied that I would probably die in prison. I could not fathom why anyone would want to send such letters to me now that I was out of the public arena. Perhaps some people felt they could say anything they wanted to a convicted prisoner who was locked away for life.

More than one person wrote to me: "I hope you die in prison."

One wrote, "I hope you get raped by the biggest black man in prison."

Some of the oddest mail I received came from individuals who felt compelled to shred me into tiny pieces and then sign their letters "In Christian love."

The cruelest mail I received came from the same person. This person wrote such vulgar filth in his letters to me, I dare not attempt to describe them. The letters continued throughout my entire stay in prison.

Even though the hate mail was not even 1 percent of the total mail I was receiving, it left the most indelible impression. No matter how many beautiful rabbits you may have, one skunk can leave a lasting impression. Beyond that, those nasty letters did nothing to help my ever-declining self-worth.

In stark contrast to the hate mail were the hundreds of letters of encouragement and support I began to receive. Many people said they were praying for me. Some even went so far as to express their faith that through some miracle I might be released from prison and restored to Christian ministry. At that point, my correspondents had much more faith that I had.

During my phone conversations with Tammy Faye throughout the month of November, she expressed her intention to come to visit me for Thanksgiving. I was elated, but I was also concerned. The media blitz that had surrounded us for the past three years had not yet diminished. For a while it seemed as though I had to report to the warden's office nearly every day to respond to interview requests from around the world. I refused every interview opportunity. I knew, however, that if Tammy Faye showed up at Rochester, the media would follow her every move.

More disconcerting than that, she would be alone, far from home, with no friends or family nearby. I worried about Tammy Faye's safety as well as the simple logistics about where she would stay and how she would get around. But from inside the prison there was little I could do to help.

About that time I received a letter from Phil Shaw, a local pastor with the Assemblies of God. The pastor had seen my arrival at Rochester Federal Medical Center on television. I had never met the man in my life and his only contact with me had been from watching our television programs. Nevertheless, Pastor Shaw wrote kindly and compassionately, "Dear Jim, I am a brother in the Lord. How can I help you?" Pastor Shaw added, "I am an Assemblies of God pastor," and he included his phone number.

Pastor Shaw later recalled his concern that I might mistake his motives for writing the letter. He told me he thought I might think he was a flake or a publicity hound.

I was extremely reticent about talking to anyone outside my immediate family circle. My emotional bruises were so raw, I did not trust anyone and my recent experiences with "men of God" caused me to be even more cautious. Yet as I lay awake in my prison bunk, pondering how I could possibly handle all the details pertaining to Tammy's upcoming visit at Thanksgiving, feelings of helplessness continued to plague my mind. With my consummate concern for details, I had always taken care of everything for Tammy and my family. I paid our household bills and I arranged for all our basic, daily needs to be cared for. If I couldn't do it myself, I hired someone else to do whatever needed to be done around our home. But now I was unable to help my family at all.

I didn't know where they could stay. I didn't know the city of Rochester—I didn't know the streets, the good side of town or the bad, I didn't know the airport or the transportation systems, the hotels, or the restaurants, and I certainly didn't have an enclave of friends or family in the area upon which I could call. I did know that everywhere Tammy and the children had gone in recent months, an onslaught of press people soon followed, surrounding them at their hotel rooms, badgering them for interviews and photographs.

As I pondered how I could provide some semblance of protection and privacy for my family, my mind kept turning back to Phil Shaw's letter. Pastor Shaw had offered to help me, but he had also offered to help my family. I wondered if he really meant it. For several days, I mulled the pastor's offer over in my mind, and finally, in desperation on a Sunday night about a week before Tammy's planned visit, I decided to call Pastor Shaw. Telephoning the pastor was a terribly humiliating act in itself since I had to place the call collect because of prison regulations. Reluctantly, I dialed the operator.

The number I gave the operator was Pastor Shaw's church phone number, and one of the pastor's staff members answered the call. Pastor Shaw was not in the church office but out in the church somewhere, the staff member told me. I nearly hung up. *Maybe this isn't such a good idea*, I thought. But the person who had answered the phone had already gone to locate the pastor, so I remained on the line.

When Pastor Shaw finally spoke into the phone, his voice took me by surprise. He did not sound like a bombastic preacher; he was soft-spoken, articulate, and most of all, extremely kind. In comparison, my voice was frail and pain filled. I immediately began apologizing to Pastor Shaw for calling him collect. I apologized for bothering him, especially on a Sunday night, after a busy day of church services.

"Oh, Jim, call anytime; don't worry about calling collect."

I told the pastor I was calling in response to his letter. I must have sounded like a scared rabbit, because several times in our conversation, Pastor Shaw encouraged me, "Don't hang up on me, Jim. What can I do for you?"

I told him that Tammy was planning to come to Rochester to visit me at Thanksgiving, and I expressed my concern about how she would deal with the media mayhem, where she should stay, how she would get through the airport and into the hotel, and a host of other details.

Pastor Shaw instantly replied, "Don't worry about a thing. I will take care of it."

"Well, if you are too busy, if you could just point me in the right direction. . . ."

"No, no! Don't hang up, Jim. I'll take care of everything. How can I get in touch with your family?"

"Well, I don't want you to feel obligated or anything. . . . "

"No, no. I wouldn't have it any other way. You just relax and let me help you."

We talked briefly. Pastor Shaw was so humble and kind. He did not at all sound as though he was trying to make a name for himself or had any false motives. Nor did he sound the least bit judgmental. Many pastors, some of them quite famous who used to appear regularly on the PTL television network, did not dare to associate with me now that I was a convicted felon. Many of my closest associates and peers had not spoken to me since the day I had lost the PTL television ministry. I felt like I was a zero in their eyes. But Pastor Shaw seemed genuinely interested in helping my family and me, no strings attached. I sensed that the pastor truly had a servant's heart.

I gave Phil Shaw a phone number where he could reach Tammy Faye, and I thanked him for his time. The pastor assured me that he would call Tammy the following day and make any necessary arrangements, which he did.

Phil arranged for Tammy to stay at the Kahler Hotel, a fine, stately hotel right across from the Mayo Clinic. He visited with the hotel security personnel prior to Tammy's arrival and made special arrangements to get Tammy Faye into her room safely without having to deal with a deluge of media.

A few days before Tammy's visit, another weekly tabloid paper boasted headlines announcing Tammy's and my divorce. "There is no truth whatsoever to it," Tammy responded when reporters in Florida asked her about the article.

Pastor Shaw recruited a group of friends from his church to accompany him in a van to pick up Tammy at the airport. The pastor thought he might need assistance to whisk Tammy through the throng of reporters who he felt would inevitably be at the airport upon her arrival. Pastor Shaw was right. When Tammy Faye showed up accompanied by Jamie and my sister Donna, the media were already waiting for them at the airport. Tammy responded graciously to the press, then Pastor Shaw and his friends quickly ushered my family members into the van and drove them to the hotel. Tammy Faye, Donna, and Jamie stayed in the same room at the Kahler to save money, but also to be able to present a united front to the press if necessary.

On Thursday, November 23, 1989, Phil Shaw drove Tammy Faye, Jamie, and Donna to the prison around 8:30 A.M. Pastor Shaw had been to many prisons over the years of his ministry, but he had never been at this federal facility. He was surprised at the intense screening process required of visitors.

Prison regulations required that I submit a list of names of individuals whom I wished to come visit me. Anyone whose name was excluded from that list could not visit me without special clearance from prison officials. Pastor Shaw assumed that the prison system ran background checks on all visitors.

The visitors were searched upon their arrival. The visiting room itself was about forty feet long and about twenty-five feet wide, constructed of cold, yellow-glazed brick, with windows on each side. The room had all the warmth of the mental institution for which it once served. The floor was covered with indoor-outdoor carpet. Video cameras concealed in the ceiling behind dark glass recorded every image and every move anyone made in the room. Approximately twenty low Formica tables lined the room. Four to six white plastic chairs surrounded each table. Inmates and visitors were not permitted to put their feet on the table, even though there was an incredible temptation to do so. If an inmate or visitor forgot and rested his or her foot on the table, a guard would quickly reprimand that person.

Adjoining the main visiting room was another visiting room about the same size, this one with tile floors. Vending machines lined one wall. Candy, potato chips, soda pop, microwave popcorn, ham-and-cheese sandwiches, hot dogs, turkey sandwiches, and occasionally small, personal-size pizzas were available from the vending machines. We soon learned that if we wanted anything from the vending area, we had to get our food early in the day and hold on to it until we were ready to eat. Otherwise the vending machines would sell out before visitation time was over.

A microwave oven for heating our vending-machine delicacies and a water fountain sat along the wall opposite the machines. A television was mounted high in the corner at the front of the room. In the far back right corner was a cubicle with a large window so the guards could see inside it. This room was used for legal visits in which inmates and their lawyers could have some measure of privacy within the visitation area. The room was locked unless a guard opened it for a legal visit. It was not to be used as an area in which a husband and wife could have privacy.

Outside the two visiting rooms was a paved walking area for inmates and visitors. The walking "yard" was about the same size as the main visiting room and enclosed by a high wooden fence. Smoking was not allowed in the visitation rooms, so inmates and their visitors congregated outside in the walking area to smoke.

Once inside the visitation room, Tammy Faye, Jamie, and Donna found seats around one of the low tables, where they waited for me to arrive.

The night before Tammy Faye's visit, I pressed my clothes with extra care. I wanted to look my best for my wife and family members. The last time I had seen Tammy Faye had been at Talladega Prison, several weeks earlier. I could hardly wait to see her again. I was excited to see Jamie and Donna as well.

When I walked through the door, I spotted my family members immediately. I wanted to race to them and embrace them, but I knew I had to check in with a guard first. I walked over to his desk and said, "Inmate Bakker, sir: 07407-058."

He wrote my name and number on a list on his clipboard and nodded. I quickly walked toward the table where Tammy Faye, Jamie, and Donna were waiting for me. They rose to their feet as I approached and we met and embraced in the aisle. It felt so wonderful to kiss and hold my wife. It seemed like an eternity had passed since we had last been together. Other than that, no touching was allowed during visits. When inmates or their family members dared to violate the rules, a guard was quick to remind them that if they wanted to continue to have the privilege of visitation, they had better abide by the regulations. Of course, for the inmates themselves, the threat of "the hole" always loomed large in their minds as a preventive measure against breaking the rules.

My family members and I spent the next six hours together talking. Tammy Faye was upset, yet she was upbeat. She tried hard to encourage me. "We're going to lick this thing," she kept saying. We were not able to have a traditional Thanksgiving dinner because no food was allowed to be brought into the prison, and visitors were not permitted in the chow hall. Instead, our Thanksgiving dinner consisted of food purchased from the vending machines in the visitation room.

Throughout our visit the room was constantly buzzing around us as family members of other inmates approached us to ask for autographs. Often someone would say to me, "Would you please sign this for my grandmother? She just loves you." At that point, it was nice to be loved by *somebody*. Tammy Faye and I signed numerous autographs. I felt rather strange doing it, but most of the people were extremely nice, so I complied. At times, family members of inmates wanted to talk further with Tammy and me, but the guards hastily broke up our conversations after only a few minutes. They reminded us that it was against the rules to talk with anyone not on my own visitor list.

Tammy often broke into tears during our visit. She cried over our situation, but she just as readily burst into tears when she saw other inmates and their families grieving together. Watching other inmates and their family members leaving each other at the end of visitation time was the toughest part of the ordeal. Besides exacerbating our own pain, it was awful to see little children being pulled away from their daddies as the guards impatiently waited for the inmates and family members to say good-bye. "Wrap it up!" the guards called callously.

Our Thanksgiving visit was the first of many heartrending marathon visits by Tammy Faye and other family members and friends. Visitation days were usually allowed over a four-day period, which in our case was helpful in view of the distance my family members had to travel to get there. I was always glad to see them come, but after a few hours together with nothing to do but talk, with no place to go, and no privacy, the visits often were as draining as they were refreshing. I would challenge any husband and wife or parent and child to turn off the television set for a weekend, and do nothing but stay in the same room with each other and talk for six straight hours, three straight days!

Tammy Faye managed to make friends with some of the other inmates' wives in the visitation room. Her vivacious personality was an encouragement to everyone with whom she talked. She stayed through the

163

Thanksgiving weekend before heading back to Orlando. The moment she stepped outside of the prison, reporters were waiting for her. "How is your husband doing?" one reporter asked.

Tammy Faye replied in her usual upbeat tone, "As well as can be expected. He's a tough man."

I wasn't feeling so tough just then. While Tammy Faye was talking to the media, a guard had ordered me into a small room between the hall and the visiting room. The room had a movable partition and on the other side of the partition a guard was running another inmate through the normal strip-search routine.

"Take your clothes off, Bakker," the guard said to me. I peeled off my stiffly pressed khakis and tossed them onto a chair as I prepared for yet another dehumanizing strip search.

It would be Christmas before I would see Tammy Faye again.

16

The First Christmas

"INMATE BAKKER! COME TO THE OFFICERS' STATION," I heard a guard command.

I immediately dropped my cleaning materials and briskly walked up the hall to where the guard was waiting.

"Decorate this Christmas tree here in the sitting area," he ordered as he pointed to a shabby box containing an artificial Christmas tree and shoved a box of ornaments in my direction. Although I did not say a word and would not have disobeyed his command, I must have shown my reluctance. The guard noticed my pained expression and mellowed just a little. "Do the best you can," he said quietly.

I looked at the box of ornaments—a few colored lights, one short straggly garland, and beat-up ornaments that most people would have given up on years before and put in the garbage. These ornaments were worse than ragtag—they were the ragtag ends of nothing.

The scrawny artificial Christmas tree was worse yet. It was actually an assortment of parts from two separate trees. I began working on it, carefully removing the dilapidated branches from the box and laying them out on the floor, trying to determine where each one went on the tree. It was like putting together a puzzle in which a large number of the pieces were either broken or missing. I assembled the three-legged base, forced the warped pole into the hole, and screwed the pieces together as tightly as I could. The tree was truly pitiful.

I started to string the Christmas lights around the tree. Some of the lights were burnt out, but being the new style lights, the others continued to work. As I wrapped the tree in the shabby lights, I could not help thinking, *God, are You trying to beat me up? Is this some kind of trick You are playing on me? Is this rubbing it in, God?*

The point was not lost on me that our Christmas decorations at Heritage USA had been spectacular. We had won great acclaim and had been listed as one of the top Christmas destinations in America. I remembered the hundreds of trees and their more than a million lights all across the property. The Grand Tree in the lobby of the Grand Hotel was nearly three stories tall. The tree on Main Street had been decorated with elaborate, moving characters.

Now, here I was trying to decorate this poor excuse for a tree with these pathetic lights, many of which did not work. It was like a sadistic joke was being played on me.

The guard ordered another inmate to help me decorate the tree. While I was trying my best to make something decent of the miserable tree, my helper was totally unconcerned about it. He could not understand why I kept trying to find a place where our one garland would look the best. He just wanted to slap the few decorations on the tree and be done with it as soon as possible, but I continued moving the ornaments around, hoping to create a better look, repositioning the bulbs, stretching the garland as far as it would go.

Several of the inmates passed by and cursed. "What are you doin', Bakker, puttin' that tree up like that?" several asked bitterly. More than a few told me in no uncertain terms where I should shove that tree. I was shocked! I could not understand why the men would not welcome any semblance of the joy of Christmas in prison.

I was a person who had always loved everything about Christmas, but suddenly I was confronted with the darker side of my favorite holiday. Of course I was aware that the Thanksgiving and Christmas seasons were hard times for some families and individuals, but in prison I began to realize in a profound way that for many people, the season was not one of rejoicing but one of despair.

Not long after I arrived at Rochester, I received a letter from a woman whose boyfriend was serving a life sentence in prison for committing murder. In an effort to familiarize Tammy Faye and me with the prison mindset, the woman predicted that we would soon start telling the time by Christmases instead of months, days, or years. She was correct. If you were to ask a prisoner who had been incarcerated for fifteen years, "How long have you been in here?" most likely he would respond, "Fifteen Christmases."

For this reason and others, many of the inmates hated that tree and all that it symbolized. They didn't want it there and would have preferred that it be tossed out. Many long-term prisoners have not received a gift or a Christmas card from the outside in years. Others remember their wives and children and what used to be, and they do not want to be reminded of Christmases past. They would prefer to ignore Christmas altogether, which, of course, is impossible, even in prison. The men see and hear Christmas advertisements on the television and radio or see ads in the newspapers and magazines. They cannot escape Christmas, yet for many it is too painful to celebrate the holiday.

I was about to find out why.

I was so excited on Christmas Eve! My new friend Phil Shaw had picked up my family members at the airport and they were planning to visit me on Christmas Day. It was one of the few times Tammy Sue, her husband Doug, and little baby James could come all the way to Minnesota to see me. I had not seen Tammy Sue and her family since I had been escorted out of the federal courthouse in Charlotte. It seemed like ages ago when I had last held baby James in my arms. Ironically, I felt a bit nervous at seeing my family members; it was almost like going on a date when I was a teenager.

Christmas Eve had always been a special time at the Bakker home, but in prison it was just another night. I made it special by preparing for my family's much-anticipated Christmas Day visit. I went to the guard station and exchanged my commissary card for the privilege of borrowing one of the two irons and ironing boards available to the men on our floor. I took the ironing board and iron back to my cell, where I meticulously pressed every wrinkle out of my clothes and ironed creases in my pants and shirt. After I returned the ironing equipment, I went back to my cell and began shining my high-top boots. I wanted to look my best when I "hosted" my family for Christmas dinner tomorrow.

Tammy Faye, Donna, and our children were staying at the beautiful Kahler Hotel, the same place where they had stayed during their Thanksgiving visit. By now, our funds had been thoroughly depleted and Tammy was concerned that the fine hotel was out of her price range. She approached the front desk and asked to speak to the manager. "Do you have any fifty-dollar rooms?" she ventured.

The manager recognized Tammy and smiled kindly. "Well, er . . . let me see what we can do." The manager began punching up something on his computer screen at the registration desk. He scowled momentarily, pushed some more keys, and a broad smile spread across his face. "Yes, this will be just right," he said aloud.

He turned back to Tammy Faye and handed her a key to a large room with two double beds and a roll-away bed for Jamie. "You are welcome here anytime, Mrs. Bakker, at this same rate."

"Oh, thank you very much," Tammy Faye gushed. "God bless you!" From then on, every time Tammy and our family members came to visit me in Rochester, they stayed at the Kahler . . . at the greatly reduced rate.

By the time my family members got into their rooms at the Kahler on Christmas Eve, all the stores were closed. Only the Webber and Judd drugstore in the lobby of the hotel remained open. My family members went to the drugstore late at night and purchased small presents for each other. The drugstore manager gave them some leftover gift wrap and they went back upstairs to wrap their presents. A friend of our family had sent a basket of flowers to their room, so they placed their presents around the basket as though it were a Christmas tree. Tammy Sue made a tray from a box, covered it with a bath towel, and arranged it with cookies and candies. Then my wife, my children, and my sister opened their simple presents to each other. It was a far cry from the many wonderful Christmas Eves we had known together with presents strewn around our gorgeously decorated tree in our home in South Carolina.

I awakened early on Christmas morning. I couldn't wait to see my family, but other than the childlike excitement I was feeling, it was difficult to tell that it was Christmas. No music filled the air. Nobody was hurrying to get the last present wrapped before the children awakened. No warm sounds and smells of Christmas breakfast; only the everyday sameness of prison life could be seen and heard. The only distinction this day had over any other was that the inmates did not have to go to work.

Around 6:00 A.M. on Christmas morning, Pastor Phil Shaw drove my family members to the prison gates. Phil said that he would be back to pick them up at the end of visiting hours, later that day.

Then came the long waiting game. Inside my cell, I waited to be called to the visiting room, while my family members stood outside in the cold, waiting for the gatehouse doors to open at around 8:30 A.M. Once inside the gates, they endured the arduous process of getting into the prison visiting area.

After the visitors went through the x-ray machine, the guards searched everything—even Tammy Sue's tube of lipstick and baby James's diaper bag.

Finally, the call came for me. "Inmate Bakker to the visiting room."

I hurried across the compound from Building Two. As soon as I stepped inside the doors, I spotted my family members through the crowd. I quickly made my way to them and kissed and hugged each one. Tammy Sue hugged me for so long I was afraid the guards were going to reprimand us.

I was so happy to see everyone. Our emotions were running at a high pitch, and we were all on the verge of tears. We spent several hours visiting together in the hot and stuffy room packed with visitors. It was difficult to hear one another, and we were unable to express our feelings well, but we were together as a family.

Eventually, the visitation room became so crowded the guards announced that they were going to move us to the basement of the chapel, where we could continue our visit until it was time for Christmas dinner. The prisoners were moved to the chapel basement first, and then the family members were escorted across the compound. Soon we were reunited in the chapel basement in a large multipurpose room that could seat about one hundred people at round tables. The crowd of people in the room quickly swelled to the point where people were crammed in back-to-back. My family and I stayed in the noisy basement for several more hours.

The crowd of prisoners and their families was too large for everyone to eat Christmas dinner together, so we had to eat in shifts. Somehow my family and I were assigned to the last group to enter the chow hall. My family went through the chow-hall lines with me, just as though it was any other day. On this day, however, we had a wide variety of foods to select from—ham, turkey, all sorts of vegetables, and pumpkin pie. We even had a visit from Santa Claus, one of the inmates dressed in a Santa's outfit.

It was getting near three o'clock and the guards had already warned our group that we were not going to have much time to eat together. It was imperative that all inmates be back in their cells in time for the four o'clock count, even on Christmas Day.

We quickly placed some food on our trays and hurried to a table where we could all sit together. It was the Bakker family Christmas dinner, prison style. Tammy Faye and I sat on one side of the table, and Jamie, Tammy Sue, Doug, and baby James sat across from us. I prayed a hasty prayer, thanking God for the food and for our special time together. We had barely begun to eat when a prison official announced coldly, "Wrap it up. It's time to wrap it up."

Sadly, we took our trays to the garbage area, dumped most of our Christmas dinner in the trash, and stacked our trays, dishes, and utensils on the counter of the dish room. It was not the lack of food that wrenched our stomachs, it was the total loss of our freedom to celebrate anything sacred, holy, or personal about Christmas. We were not able to read the Christmas story or exchange gifts. We sang no carols about the true meaning of Christmas.

"Wrap it up," the prison official again said matter-of-factly.

My family and I looked at each other in disbelief and disappointment. This was to be the extent of our long-awaited Christmas dinner. It was over before it had really gotten started, and now it was time for my family to leave. It was almost impossible to hold back the tears. We all hugged and kissed one more time. As Jamie, who had just turned fourteen, hugged and said good-bye to me, he started to sob. Everyone had been trying so desperately to remain stoic and strong throughout the exasperating day, but now the emotion was more than Jamie and Tammy Sue could contain. Susie burst out crying. Tammy Faye followed suit. She pulled us closely together as a family and put her arms around us. Standing right there in the chow hall of a federal prison with other prisoners and their family members looking on, we experienced one of the worst moments in our family history. It was a moment none of us will ever forget, no matter how hard we try.

Then it was time for Tammy Faye and the children to go. Once again, our family was being torn apart.

A guard's voice sheared us away from each other. "Come, let's go."

I was not allowed to accompany my family outside, so I remained in the chow hall, watching out a window as my family followed the guards out the door and started walking across the prison yard. It was a cold, dreary, Minnesota winter afternoon. The skies had already started to darken. Just as my family began to walk across the compound, it was as though a cloud exploded and the snow came pouring down. It was the sort of snow songwriters and poets write about, and people dream about when they think of a white Christmas—large, soft flakes falling to the ground. But who cared?

My entire family was crying openly by now. They did not speak to each other; they walked, Jamie and Doug supporting Tammy Sue and the baby, and they cried. Only Susie looked back and waved. Tammy Faye later told me that she was crying too hard to look back.

I pressed my hands and face against the cold glass, the hot tears streaming down my face and mixing with the condensation on the window. I was

170

straining for every last, longing look as my family trudged through the blizzard and then disappeared inside the gatehouse.

I had never felt so utterly alone in all my life. I stood there staring out that window as the snow quickly covered the tracks of my family. In a few minutes, it would be hard to tell that they had ever been there.

"Merry Christmas," I said sarcastically to myself.

The Christmas dinner had run late. It was almost 4:00, so rather than strip-searching us in private, all the prisoners in the last group through the chow line were herded into an open room and made to strip off our clothes. Like a bunch of naked cattle, we stood there in a row. We were quickly examined for drugs or other contraband.

"Open up your mouths, men," one of the guards commanded. "Hurry up. We don't have much time. Run your fingers through your hair. Pull your ears down. Lift up your privates. All right, turn around, lift up your feet. Bend over and spread 'em."

I kept thinking that since it was Christmas, the guards would be kinder and more compassionate in their search. No such luck. I should not have been surprised. Nor could I blame the guards. They had an unpleasant job to get done in a hurry, as the sacred four o'clock count was looming. No one dared violate the four o'clock count, not even for Christmas.

Finally we were ordered to reclothe and were hurriedly marched to our cell block. As I made my way back to my cell, passing numerous men already in their cells, I sadly realized that the majority of the inmates had not had any Christmas visitors. I could tell by the reaction of my fellow inmates that many of them envied me. I knew that I was blessed to have my family visit, but the pain of the day had blurred the reality of the blessing.

I arrived back at my cell just in time for the count. I stood at my bed until the guard passed by and I heard the words, "Count clear!" Afterward, I climbed up into my bunk and collapsed. I thought, *My family needs me now more than ever, and there is nothing I can do to help them.* I felt helpless, worthless, and emotionally exhausted. I lay there for the longest time, wondering, *Are we going to have to go through this sort of emotional devastation every Christmas for the next forty-five years? How long can my family stand the gut-wrenching trauma of being pulled apart like this? Will this nightmare ever end?*

In a deep depression, I fell asleep, hoping against hope that the new year would somehow be better than the past year.

17

God, Where Are You?

I DIDN'T FEEL MUCH LIKE CELEBRATING ON NEW YEAR'S EVE. My family had gone back home, and since I didn't have to work on the holiday, I spent most of New Year's Day in bed. Nor did I feel like facing my fiftieth birthday on January 2. I spent most of that day, as well, hunkering down in my bunk. My depression was so deep I did not even bother to eat. I felt that life had come to an end. My appeal to a higher court was stalled and seemed to be going nowhere, so I was rapidly losing hope of any sort of action concerning my sentence.

Around seven o' clock, my perpetually jovial friend, Gleason, stopped by my cell to see me and to ask me to sign a clipping of a press report about Tammy Faye's recent visit to Rochester. Because it was a legitimate news article, I signed it for him. "Be sure to date it," Gleason reminded me. Gleason was convinced his collection of signed memorabilia would be more valuable one day if it was dated. We talked briefly, and Gleason recognized that I was having a rough time dealing with things, so he said, "Jim, come on down to my cell. I just made a big pizza and you look as though you could use some food. Come help me eat it."

"No thanks, Gleason," I replied.

"Oh, come on, Jim," Gleason chided me as he started gently urging me toward the door.

"No, thank you, Gleason, I think I'll just stay here."

But Gleason would not take no for an answer.

"Oh, all right," I finally acquiesced. "But only for a few minutes."

As we walked down the hall closer to Gleason's cell, I began to notice a number of men hanging around outside his door. We weaved our way through the crowded hallway and stepped inside Gleason's cell. The ceiling light was out, but the desk lights were on, creating a warm and inviting look.

To my surprise, the cell was filled with men, some of whom I knew, many of whom I did not. Huge trays of food, all sorts of food—crackers with tuna fish, chicken salad, cheese, hors d'oeuvres, and, of course, prison pizza—were spread all over the bunks. A mop bucket lined with a plastic bag was full of cans of soda pop packed in ice.

"Happy Birthday, Jim!" the men called out to me.

I could not believe it. As I stood there in the doorway, I was so emotionally moved I almost burst into tears. I was absolutely amazed that these men would do something like this for me!

The fellows broke into a discordant but enthusiastic rendition of "Happy Birthday." It wasn't the most melodious version of the song I had ever heard, but it was one of the best. Over the years, I had experienced some wonderful birthday parties. Especially during my years at PTL, my birthday became an occasion on which my staff loved to play "Can You Top This?" They outdid themselves every year in pulling off a birthday party that verged on an extravaganza. We sometimes planned special events around my birthday party. On my last birthday at PTL, for example, we broke ground for the Crystal Palace Church and Conference Center.

I was always deeply appreciative of the friends and family members who made my birthday parties so special at Heritage USA. But I had never experienced a more meaningful party than the one these prisoners had worked to put together from nothing. At a time when I was feeling totally worthless and not caring whether I lived another day, the inmates reminded me that every day of life is special. Even the day you turn fifty.

Throughout the early part of 1990 I continued to ride an emotional roller-coaster, occasionally having an up day and then plunging headlong into another stomach-wrenching period of despair.

Often when I was alone in my cell, I would lie with my head against the wall, groaning from deep within. It was more than a physical or emotional pain; it was a soul pain. "Oh, God, where are You?" I cried. "Have I offended You so badly that You will not even speak to me anymore?" I feared, *I must have done something terrible that God would turn His back on me.* I thought God must be punishing me for every sin I ever committed.

173

Beyond my own troubles, Tammy Faye told me that my eighty-four-year-old mother, who still lived at Heritage USA, was in the hospital again. Mother had been devastated by my departure from PTL and her emotional hurt was taking a physical toll as well. She had fainted one day at home, so Daddy and my brother Norm picked her up off the floor and rushed her to the hospital. She was hemorrhaging by the time they got there. The doctors discovered the problem was related to my mother's kidneys not functioning properly. Her condition was exacerbated by the fact that she had injured her spine as a young girl, and by now she could hardly straighten up enough to walk.

I felt awful that my mother was in the hospital, yet it was impossible for me to do anything to help her. Since all prisoners were required to call collect, and I could not reverse the charges when calling the hospital, I asked for, and received, special permission to call my mom from a prison office. I tried my best to encourage her. Mother appreciated my call, but she was sharp enough to recognize that there was a hollowness to my words that had never been there before.

Back in Florida, Tammy Faye was having problems of her own. Lacking sufficient financial support, she had reluctantly stopped doing our television show altogether. The show had never really regained its popularity after we left PTL, but it aired on more than two dozen television and cable stations around the country and was a sort of lifeline to us and our friends. Now, that too was gone. Tammy concentrated her efforts on trying desperately to hold our church together.

Prior to my imprisonment, our church fellowship, New Covenant Church, had been meeting in a large shopping plaza near what is now Universal Studios in Orlando. The land on which the church was located is now a vacant lot, overgrown with weeds and mangroves. Only a billboard stands on the grounds, advertising "ValuJet—Now with 20 Destinations."

I had high hopes for the property. Besides providing plenty of meeting space, offices, and potential television studios, the plaza could also be occupied by Christian-oriented businesses and shops. I had actually received verbal commitments from numerous shop owners who were ready to move their businesses to our new location. But because the former owners of the shopping plaza had gone bankrupt, our plans were delayed. Looking back, it was probably providential that we were not able to complete our plans rapidly. We had been having difficulty raising enough money to rent the shopping plaza even before I went to prison.

Once I was out of the picture, the plaza became an albatross around the neck of the church.

Early in 1990, while trying to get into a permanent church building, and in an attempt to reduce costs, Tammy Faye and the congregation moved out of the shopping plaza. The church began meeting in a piano store, which the owner, Dale Griner, allowed the congregation to use free of charge. Before each service, members of the congregation had to move the pianos out of the way for the people to be seated!

On a family level, we had recently discovered that our son Jamie suffered from dyslexia, an impairment in the brain that made written communication difficult for him. In one sense, we were thankful to find out the cause of Jamie's learning difficulties. We knew he was an extremely intelligent boy, yet he continually had trouble with his subjects at school. No wonder! The pressure on Tammy during this time was immense and, although she tried to be encouraging to me during our conversations on the phone, I could hear the stress beginning to gnaw at her stamina. I wondered how long she could take it.

Tammy Sue and her family had moved back to South Carolina, where they were now living in a mobile home not far from Heritage USA. Susie and her husband, Doug, were struggling financially, like most young couples with a new baby. Their phone had been disconnected and the electric company was threatening to turn off their power. They had been having yard sales, selling their possessions in an attempt to pay their bills. When Tammy Sue dared to venture from her home into the community, she was often accosted by people who felt compelled to make snide and often lewd remarks about me. The caustic comments seared my daughter's sensitive heart.

Tammy Sue plunged into a severe depression. For about six months she refused to come out of the house unless absolutely necessary. She became so reclusive she was almost as much a prisoner as I was. Being the daughter of Jim Bakker was not exactly a plus for Susie at that point.

Night after night, as I turned my face against the wall next to my bunk, I could not escape the thought, *My entire family is in some sort of turmoil because of me, and I am buried alive in prison unable to help. Oh, God, where are You?*

To make matters worse, about this same time the NBC television network began to produce a movie about my family, PTL, and me. The movie starred Bernadette Peters as Tammy Faye and Kevin Spacey as me. The inmates in prison scoffed up every tidbit of news about the movie and brought it to my attention. I didn't want to see the articles, and I didn't really want to talk about the movie. To my new friends in prison, it was a big deal that somebody they knew was the subject of a movie. But to me it was just more dredging up slime and slapping it onto a caricature of parts of my life.

Besides, I had already read the script.

A scriptwriter for the project, Ken Trevey, and an NBC researcher had spent four days interviewing Tammy and me in early 1988. Tammy and I answered their questions as thoroughly as possible. When the writers left our home, we felt that we might have a shot at seeing a fair representation of what happened at PTL come to the screen. Later when the original script was shown to us, we still believed the same. We should have known better.

Before the movie went into production, the script was rewritten and revised several times. Referring to the new script, Trevey said he wrote what he called "a newer, tougher one that was more balanced and dramatic".[1] When Tammy and I read the new script, the one the network decided to use, we were very unhappy. The script only vaguely represented the information we had shared with our interviewers.

Not surprisingly, throughout the filming of the movie, crew members made fun of things Tammy and I held sacred. Filming took place in Pasadena in a Presbyterian church. On February 28, 1990, an earthquake hit Pasadena—right in the middle of Bernadette Peters's rendition of one of Tammy's songs. The "gospel choir" backing up the singer quickly scampered off a cross-shaped portable stage, and crew members immediately scurried out of the church. I honestly have to say that I was tickled by this report.

In prison, I was longing to hear Tammy Faye sing again. Each night as I went to sleep, I turned on my battery operated radio and scanned the dial, searching for the gospel station from Georgia that had played Tammy during my first week in Rochester. One night, when I was in a deep depression, I was sure I had found it. A station was broadcasting gospel music, but I could not get a clear signal. The sound kept fading in and out. Finally, I fell asleep with my radio headphones still on.

I don't know how long I slept, but suddenly I awakened. Strangely, I didn't know where I was. I thought for a moment, *Maybe I have died and gone to heaven!* A wonderful peace filled the prison cell. That's when I noticed the sound in my ears. I was still wearing my radio headset. I strained to hear the sound again. The radio signal cleared of static, and I could hear plainly the voice of Tammy Faye singing:

Don't give up on the brink of a miracle,
Don't give in, God is still on the throne;
Don't give up on the brink of a miracle,
Don't give up, remember you're not alone.

When Satan would have you look at the trials of life that surround you
And he tries to appear and brings doubt and fear all around you.
Don't look with the eye, or listen with your ear,
Just cry out to God, He is always near;
In your darkest hour, your miracle is here.

The devil is a thief and he sends those troubles to confound you
And he lies and says, This time there's no way you can find to make it
    through.
Remember God's true Word, the battle is the Lord's,
Don't give in to fear, think on things that are pure.
And praise the Lord, your miracle is here.[2]

I could hardly believe my ears! Twice now, right at a time when I was
feeling totally overwhelmed by my own circumstances and the problems
others I loved were facing largely because of me, God sent this special message to me over the airwaves. As before, it was not just any song; it was a
song written by Mike Adkins, a dear friend of Tammy's and mine, who
had appeared on our television programs many times. Nor was it just any
voice; it was Tammy Faye singing a message that reached directly into my
heart. Although my spiritual senses were numb and my emotional system
was running on overload to the point that I walked around the prison compound most of the time looking like a scared rabbit, I could not escape the
fact that God was showing me something. But what? What did it all mean?
Surely God must have some concern for me. Otherwise, why would He
set up such an unusual set of circumstances? Yet if I had any value to God,
why would He allow me to be publicly disgraced, humiliated, and dumped
into this prison in the first place?

The next day I could hardly wait to tell Tammy about hearing her
singing "Don't Give Up On the Brink of a Miracle" on my radio. Tammy
was excited and believed that God was showing me that He was going to
do something really special.

In at least one sense, Tammy was absolutely right. God was about to
perform a series of miracles in my life, but I was not ready to receive them
yet.

18

Clubs in the Fed

IN AN EFFORT TO DULL THE ACHE IN MY HEART, I HURLED myself into keeping busy inside the prison. In addition to my daily responsibilities cleaning the rest rooms, showers, laundry areas, and hallways on my floor, I joined any organization in the prison that expressed an interest in having me become a part. The prison authorities prohibited me from preaching, and I was not in any spiritual condition to stand behind a pulpit anyhow, so the effort I might have expended in religious activities I poured into prison service organizations.

One of the first groups with which I became involved was the prison Jaycees. I had been tremendously impressed with the Jaycees during my first few days at Rochester. Tony, the president of the Jaycees, had invited me to the organization's annual banquet and awards presentation, an event for which the members work all year. The banquet was held in the multipurpose room in the basement of the chapel. Calling the event a banquet was certainly a misnomer since we were served the exact same food as was being served in the chow hall that night. But the inmates did their best to make the evening special. Awards were presented to various men for their outstanding work within the prison during the previous year. A band comprised of inmates provided the musical entertainment, then a guest speaker gave a motivating and humorous message. As I sat there eating our regular chow-line fare served at our table by inmates from another prison club who had volunteered to help the Jaycees, for a few precious minutes, it was almost possible to pretend that I was not in prison. Tony and his fellow Jaycees had done everything possible to transform the chapel basement into a fine restaurant, although it still required quite a stretch of one's imagination.

The Jaycees' primary fund-raiser and service within the prison was taking prisoners' photographs, which the inmates could send home. Other than pictures taken in the visiting room, all photos were required to be taken in one location, in the recreational building in front of a prison-supplied wall mural depicting a picturesque Minnesota lake and river rippling through a lushly forested area. The photos taken in front of the mural had that "Having a great time. Wish you were here!" look to them. The prison did not allow us to take a camera anywhere on the compound, or to take shots of the tiny, crowded cubicles in which we really lived.

In the early part of 1990, I spent a great deal of time working with the Jaycees, so much so that I became the executive secretary of the group. Much of our work had to do with the Jaycees' photo program. Each week, the inmates could purchase tickets from the commissary to be given to the Jaycees as payment to have their pictures taken. The tickets were then redeemed by the Jaycees to purchase more film and used to pay for special events, such as the annual Inmate Family Christmas Dinner, including gifts for inmates' children who visited at Christmas time, and the Fourth of July Inmate Family Picnic. The Jaycees also paid for pay-per-view sports events and movies in the television room and many other worthwhile programs.

When I first arrived at Rochester, the prison officials let me know that they did not want me to have my picture taken with other inmates. At the same time, the officials said that since they planned to treat me the same as every other inmate, they would not prohibit me from having my photo taken, but they advised against it. No doubt they were concerned about photos of me being shipped out of the prison. Consequently, when guys asked me to have my picture taken with them by the Jaycees, I refused. I'd say, "I'm sorry, but I have been asked not to do that." Inevitably, the look in the eyes of inmates with whom I refused to be photographed told me they felt rejected personally. They weren't asking for much, just a few minutes of my time to pose with them for a picture. They were asking for the one thing I had plenty of—time.

Prison was bad enough. Why should I inflict insults, real or imagined, upon anyone inside these walls? I began to think, *I don't have anything to lose. My reputation is gone. What is everyone so worried about, anyway? I am not going to turn down the photo requests anymore.* After a while, when men asked me to have a photo taken with them I agreed to it. Of course, once I agreed to one picture, I had to agree to them all. Some days I would spend several hours in the rec building just having my picture taken with other inmates. Once, when it was thought that I might be transferred out of Rochester, I posed for 125 pictures in one day! Over the course of my imprisonment, I probably posed for literally thousands of Jaycees' pictures. Most of them were sent home to inmates' family members; a few showed up in tabloid newspapers.

I also joined the Growth Awareness & Development Association (GADA), a club that had replaced the NAACP club in the prison. All of the members of GADA were black except for two—Lyndon LaRouche, the Libertarian Party presidential candidate, and me. I had met Lyndon in the visiting room prior to joining GADA. He was always warm and cordial to me and to my family members and friends. Lyndon was the epitome of charm in the visiting room. He was a brilliant man, even if he was perhaps a bit eccentric, and an articulate spokesmen for all sorts of causes. It was no surprise to see his white face in a group dedicated to promoting issues relating to black people. Little did I know that this controversial man would soon be my cellmate.

The guys in GADA voted me in as the religious coordinator of the club. My job was to arrange for guest speakers at our meetings. One of the highlights on GADA's schedule was the Martin Luther King Day celebration. It was an entire day of special speakers, music, and seminars. Ironically, the day honoring Dr. King's spiritual impact upon our nation was the occasion for another brush with prison authorities for me.

The members of GADA asked me to pray the opening prayer of the day's events. Knowing how sensitive the prison officials were about me being involved in any kind of public, organized religious service inside prison, I said, "I'll be glad to do the prayer, but we better get permission first."

Our club sponsor, an employee of the Bureau of Prisons, agreed to take the issue up the ladder of authority to the warden's office if necessary. The answer came back a categorical "No! Jim Bakker is not to lead any religious activities in prison. And that includes prayer!" The members of GADA were upset by this decision. I assured them that it was no problem to me and I did all that I could to defuse the situation.

Another group I joined in my efforts to fill the void in my life was the Vietnam Veterans. I had never even been in the military, let alone been a Vietnam vet! But the Vietnam Veterans sold greeting cards in the prison, and I was one of the group's best customers. I received an avalanche of mail, and I tried to answer as many of the cards and letters I received as possible. To do so, I would often send a nice greeting card in response. The Hallmark company donated thousands of first-rate greeting cards to the federal prison system, cards that were in perfect condition and quite beautiful but for one reason or another had not been sold. Rather than simply destroying the cards or selling them at greatly reduced prices, the company donated them to the Bureau of Prisons. A certain number of these cards were available to each prison and were given to the chapel for distribution to any inmate who wanted them, free of charge.

Each week after I had exhausted my allotment of Hallmark cards, I still needed many more to answer my mail. I spent a portion of my commissary money on cards I purchased from the Vietnam Veterans. One day, one of the vets invited me to join the organization. "But I'm not even a veteran," I said.

"That's okay," the vet said. "Our organization is open to anyone. If you have a concern for the Vietnam vets, you are welcome."

I was concerned for the vets. But beyond that, I was so surprised and overwhelmed that men would actually want me as part of their groups—especially in light of the public humiliation and rejection I had recently experienced—that when anyone in prison invited me to join anything, I always accepted if possible. I was simply thrilled that they wanted me! I readily accepted the invitation to join the Vietnam Veterans. Before long, the guys asked me to be the chaplain of the group.

I developed a deep empathy for the soldiers who had served in Southeast Asia. And I learned a lot too. One of our guest speakers said that more Vietnam veterans have committed suicide than any other group of soldiers, and that more Vietnam vets have committed suicide since the war than the number of American soldiers who died in the war. Another statistic he presented startled me as well: Of all the single-auto accidents in America, the highest percentage of drivers have been Vietnam veterans. One of the best things I was able to do as part of this group was to help get Dave Roever to come in to the prison to speak. Dave is a Vietnam vet whose face was nearly blown off by a hand grenade during the war. No matter what you are going through or have gone through, it's tough to feel sorry for yourself when you look at Dave and hear his heart-wrenching but inspiring story.

Later in my prison experience, I also joined the Toastmasters, a group designed to encourage a person to speak in public. Ironically, as a man once accustomed to speaking to millions of people on television and to thousands of people at our regular church services at Heritage USA, now I was having trouble talking to a small group of inmates and our sponsors. Nevertheless, I served in almost every Toastmaster position, including table chairman, the guy who was supposed to keep the talk going and encourage the other members of the group to speak in public.

My joining various groups was not lost on Dr. Westrick and Dr. Foster. Dr. Ruth Westrick, the psychiatrist who was assistant warden in charge of mental health at the Federal Medical Center in Rochester, also served on the board of directors at the Mayo Clinic. At five feet, four inches tall, Dr. Westrick was anything but diminutive. She was on a first-name basis with numerous heads of state. A bright woman of German descent who looked to be in her early sixties, Dr. Westrick was the "Mother Teresa" of the Department of Prisons. I found her to be a deeply caring and compassionate woman who was dedicated to helping humanity. Dr. Westrick was one of the truly bright lights of the prison system. She oversaw the mental health status of inmates as well as the Chemical Dependency Program at the Rochester prison. Dr. Westrick always found the time to listen to an inmate's problems. She had checked on me at regular intervals since my arrival in Rochester and kept, through Dr. Foster, close tabs on my mental condition.

More than anyone else, Dr. Westrick and Dr. Foster realized how far I had fallen in a short period of time. Beyond losing my position at PTL, my reputation, my friends, and most of my material possessions of any value, I was feeling as though I had been abandoned by God. Consequently, I was burying myself in busywork. Good work. Helpful to others and to myself, but nonetheless, a poor solution for the awful sense of loneliness and loss I felt deep within my soul.

Every night all inmates checked the following day's "call-out" sheet, a long list of various appointments inmates were required to attend the next day. Each Thursday night I was on the list, requested by Dr. Foster to meet with him in his office. Although Dr. Foster had told me from our first meeting that it was not mandatory that I counsel with him, the guards checked the call-out sheet every day to make sure the inmates working for them were where they were supposed to be. If Dr. Foster had my name on this list, I did not hesitate to attend my one-hour counseling session with him. Many days I did not feel like seeing anyone, but I would go to Dr. Foster's office and sit with my heavy, army surplus coat pulled up high around my neck, like a turtle hiding in his protective shell. I didn't trust anyone anymore.

Dr. Westrick and Dr. Foster noticed my silent cry for a reason to live.

In January 1990 Dr. Westrick broached an idea to my cellmate Tom Brandon. "Jim has fallen so far, he needs a challenge in his life that going to a club meeting once a week is not going to satisfy." Because of new federal regulations coming to the prison system in the years ahead concerning smoking in a government-run facility, Dr. Westrick wanted Tom and me to create and teach a smoking cessation class to any inmates who wanted to break the smoking habit. A program had been tried several years earlier, but of fifty men who had attended, only two stopped smoking permanently. Dr. Westrick was hoping Tom and I could devise a program that would be more successful.

When Tom told me about Dr. Westrick's ideas, I was excited yet reticent. After all, trying to convince inmates to stop smoking is a formidable task. At the time more than 80 percent of the prison population smoked. Many of the inmates incarcerated at Rochester were serving long-term prison sentences. To prolong their lives meant only that they would spend that much more time in prison, even if the quality of their lives improved. What a challenge! Then, too, can you imagine telling a bank robber, a professional hit man, or a Mafia kingpin that he can stop smoking and that you can help him to do it? The program better work!   Dr. Westrick called Tom and me to her office to discuss the details of the program. She was convinced we were the perfect combination to develop and teach a program that would be effective. With Tom's medical background, plus his own battle with alcoholism, and my background in motivating people to work toward a cause, she felt certain we could succeed where others had failed. I wasn't so sure, but I was willing to try. In addition to the other clubs and organizations with which I had become involved, I threw myself into the job of gathering resource material Tom and I could use in our smoking cessation class.

Tom waxed downright philosophical about our serendipitous selection. "What are the odds of two men with our backgrounds and specialized skills ending up as roommates in the federal prison system and getting the chance to teach a smoking cessation program to the most difficult group of nicotine addicts imaginable—federal prisoners? Probably less than one in ten million!"

Best of all, because the smoking cessation class would be taught as an all-day seminar for a month, Dr. Westrick had hinted that Tom and I might get out of cleaning toilets for a while. "Just think, maybe I can even start biting my fingernails again!" Tom quipped.

Of all the groups I joined in my attempts to bury myself in work, the one that grabbed my heart the most was my work as a hospice volunteer. A number of my friends in prison were volunteers in the hospice program, and when they told me about it, something jumped within me at the chance to help someone hurting. The men with whom the hospice volunteers were working, however, were not merely hurting—they were dying. As a hospice volunteer, my job would be to sit with a dying man at the prison hospital and help him to express his feelings, overcome his loneliness, realize that his life was not lived in vain, maintain some degree of control over his last dying days, and basically come to grips with death. Hospice workers provided companionship and emotional support to the dying man as well as help with any light housekeeping and recreation that the person required. Hospice workers often stayed and sat with their companions into the wee hours of the morning, then got up and went to their regular prison jobs at daybreak.

Although I was already keeping extremely busy, I could not pass an opportunity to be involved in such a program. The first patient to whom I was assigned was a heavy-set man named Cecil. Cecil was dying of cancer. I never saw Cecil walk; he was always in bed. In the early days, I was able to move Cecil, with the help of several other orderlies and nurses. We used a board to slide him onto a gurney so another hospice worker and I could take him to various special events around the compound. As the cancer progressed in his body, the doctors no longer permitted me to take Cecil out of his room.

Cecil told me that while serving time in another prison, he had developed a pain in his hip. He reported the malady to the prison officials, but they thought Cecil was simply a chronic complainer and they ignored his requests for help. The pain in Cecil's hip grew worse to the point that he could not even get out of bed to go to chow. Eventually, the prison officials sent Cecil to have surgery in Florida. The doctors there operated on him and released him after saying that he should have no further problems with the hip.

The pain in Cecil's hip persisted. His condition worsened to the point that he could no longer move. That's when the prison system sent Cecil to the Federal Medical Center in Rochester. When the doctors at F.M.C. examined Cecil's hip, they discovered that he had a cancerous tumor that had been punctured during his previous surgery. Like a leaking water pipe, the cancer had slowly but surely leaked from that tumor, spreading to various parts of Cecil's body.

By the time I met Cecil, the cancer had advanced extensively. Little could be done for him medically. He was going to die. All I could do for

Cecil was to be there for him. I sat by his bedside every day for several hours. Cecil told me that he was a former biker, so I took him motorcycle magazines to read. Many of my Vietnam vet buddies were also bikers, so I borrowed some of their magazines; others I picked out at the library and took to Cecil. He enjoyed reading the material about motorcycles, but most of all, Cecil wanted me to read to him about heaven.

I searched the Bible and found every Scripture about heaven that I could, and I read those Scriptures again and again to Cecil. He loved to hear the Scriptures describing how God would one day wipe away all our tears and that there would be no more pain. He especially enjoyed the passages at the end of the book of Revelation, describing heaven's streets of gold, gates of pearl, and walls of jasper, and how Jesus is the light of that city. Eventually, I introduced Cecil to Jesus Christ. Cecil put his trust completely in the Lord and became a bona fide born-again Christian. Although he was dying, maybe because he was dying, he quickly developed a love for the things of God.

Cecil did not have a Bible of his own, so when I talked by telephone to Tammy Faye, I asked her to send Cecil one of our *PTL Parallel Bibles*, because it included both the King James Version of the Bible and the modern-day paraphrase, *The Living Bible*. Tammy was delighted to send the Bible to Cecil. She wrote him regularly after that, sending him words of encouragement and special Scriptures to help him grow stronger in his newfound faith. Cecil often called Tammy Faye on the telephone. She always had a way of lifting his spirits. He even asked Tammy Faye to call his mother and encourage her, which Tammy was glad to do. Cecil loved and appreciated Tammy Faye so much that even though he had never met her, he wanted her to sing and speak at his funeral.

When Cecil's Bible arrived, he could hardly wait to show me. He was so excited! I arrived for my regular daily visit and was enjoying Cecil's exuberance over receiving his new Bible when suddenly into Cecil's room barged Officer Ensley, the guard from whom I had received such a scathing rebuke for wearing the wrong shoes during my first few days in prison. Prison policy required the guards to shift to a new location within the compound every ninety days. Not long after I had signed on as a hospice volunteer and had begun to strike up a friendship with Cecil, Officer Ensley was transferred to the hospital, on the same floor where Cecil was located.

When Officer Ensley saw Cecil's Bible, he came over to Cecil's bed and ripped the Bible out of Cecil's hands. "You can't have that!" Officer Ensley roared.

185

Cecil's elation instantly turned to pain. Officer Ensley glared at me as though I had done something terribly wrong. He turned on his heels and stalked out of the room, taking Cecil's new Bible with him.

I could not fathom why the prison would allow such a cruel man to be on duty around men who were already suffering cruel deaths. Many of the men and women who worked in the prison hospital genuinely cared for the well-being of the inmates. The nurses and doctors who served on that death ward were dedicated "angels of mercy." Officer Ensley was not one of those caring people. On the contrary, he was literally mean to dying prisoners. Often upon completing my hospice service, I returned to my cell and climbed into my bunk, my heart aching over how that officer treated another human being under his control. This unhappy man treated all inmates as if we were the scum of the earth. In all my life, I had never seen such a vicious person.

Fortunately, the chaplain must have gotten wind of what happened because Cecil's Bible mysteriously reappeared the following day.

Officer Ensley's desk was located near the nurses' station in an area enclosed by glass, right inside the door through which I entered every day when I came in to see Cecil. Prior to Officer Ensley's arrival on the ward, I had always walked up the stairs onto the hospital's intensive-care floor and down the hallway past the guard station. With all the other guards, I merely waved as I walked by the glass enclosed area. I was a registered hospice volunteer, approved through proper procedures to be there, so when the guards saw me they simply put my name on the list and waved me on.

Not so with Officer Ensley. He demanded that the hospice workers go inside the enclosed area and stand in front of his desk to report to him. It was almost as if he wanted the prisoners to pay homage to him. Each day, I had to say, "I am Inmate Bakker, 07407-058, checking in to the hospice unit." This was not optional with Ensley. He demanded it.

One day, as I was reporting for hospice service, I was thinking about Cecil and not concentrating completely on my check-in routine. I simply stood in front of Officer Ensley's desk and said, "I'm Mr. Bakker, checking in."

I had seen many faces gawking and glowering at me during my trial and sentencing. Yet never in my life had another human being looked at me with the disdain that Officer Ensley did just then. He curled his lip and snarled, "You mean *Inmate* Bakker?"

I bowed my head and said, "Yes, Inmate Bakker, 07407-058."

In a single sentence, Officer Ensley destroyed all the dignity and respect that Dr. Westrick and Dr. Foster were trying to rebuild in me. I felt like an ant being crushed beneath a jack boot.

Ensley waved me away with a flip of his hand. I went on to see Cecil, but I had little inside to give to him.

One day when I arrived for my hospice service, I was surprised to see Cecil extremely angry. I asked, "Cecil, what's wrong? Why are you so upset?"

"Oh," he said, "I'm just so mad at God. I thought for sure that God would take me home last night. But He didn't. I didn't die."

I said, "Cecil! You're my friend. Do you mean you want to leave me?"

"I just want to die," he repeated.

In his final days, I helped Cecil plan his funeral. I helped him say good-bye to friends and family members. I helped him write to an old girl-friend; he just wanted his friends to know that he cared.

Cecil had two wishes that dominated his thoughts during his last days. He wanted to be buried next to his father back home in the family ceme-tery plot rather than in a nondescript prison cemetery plot without even a headstone. His second wish was to initiate a lawsuit against the federal government for the "wrongful" death he was suffering, which he believed was due to the ineptitude of the doctors who performed his original oper-ation. He hoped to help others avoid the terrible suffering he was going through so his death would not be in vain. Obviously, I could not do any-thing about Cecil's second request, but I was able to help contact his mother and sister who arranged to have his body sent back home for buri-al. By the time Cecil was losing his grip on life, the chaplain and Cecil's family had made all the funeral arrangements.

One of the common prison rumors concerning terminal patients struck fear into Cecil's heart, as it did most other inmates and patients. Although prison officials denied it, orderlies who worked in the prison hospital claimed that the corpses of inmates who had died of AIDS and other debilitating diseases were cuffed and shackled for their transport to the morgue. To inmates, this was the ultimate insult and degradation of their personhood.

One night when I went to see Cecil, I could tell he would not be with us much longer. The cancer had been working its way through his body, eating through his internal organs. The nurses gave Cecil as much painkiller as they were allowed, but it wasn't enough to completely dead-en his pain. He could no longer talk. He merely made gestures. I could do little for him other than sit and talk to him and read Scriptures. Long after Cecil nodded off to sleep, I continued to sit there in the dark with him.

After a while, I got ready to go back to my cell for ten o'clock count. Before I left his room, I leaned over Cecil, took his hand, and prayed. Then I said softly, "Cecil, I'll see you tomorrow."

Cecil roused slightly and shook his head no.

The next morning when I went back to see Cecil, his room was empty. All his things had been removed and his room had been cleaned. Cecil was gone, and it was as though he had never existed.

But I knew he existed. And I know he is in heaven waiting for me. Over the years, well-intentioned people had lavished praise on me for the huge number of people I had led to have a relationship with Jesus. I wasn't sure anymore how many people I had actually helped get to heaven. Only eternity will reveal the truth about that. But I know I led at least one person to heaven, because I walked him right to the gate.

A few days later I received a note from Cecil's sister: "Cecil was buried on Wednesday morning aside his father at Pleasant Lawn. . . ."

After Cecil died, I slid deeper into my pit of depression. I was not healed of my own emotional trauma, but by taking my eyes off myself and pouring my life into Cecil's, I had been able to rise above my despair for a while. I knew that Cecil was going to die from the first day I met him, yet I had allowed him to become a part of my life. Now he was gone. I was not ready to jump quickly into another hospice relationship.

For the next few weeks, I simply stopped doing anything that was not necessary. Yet Tom and I had promised Dr. Westrick that we would prepare the smoking cessation class, so I did not want to let them down. I still had a weekly appointment with Dr. Foster every Friday, and I still had to clean toilets every morning. Life goes on, even when we wish it would not. Good thing; otherwise, I might have simply crawled up into my bunk and slept . . . and slept . . . and slept. The inmates call it "doing hard time."

CHAPTER

19

Tega Cay

EARLY IN 1990, FOR MY NEWEST DIVERSION, I BECAME immersed in ceramics and painting. Although the great artists of the world were in no danger of competition from me, I had some innate drawing ability, and I had a fair sense of how colors could be used. More importantly, I enjoyed it, and it kept my mind busy. Often, I would stay up for hours at night, painting pictures for my family and friends.

For Tammy Faye's birthday on March 7, I stayed up until midnight painting a watercolor picture of her beloved little Yorkshire terrier, Tuppins. Actually, my painting was of Tuppins II. Tammy's first Yorky had been a faithful companion to her all the way through the frenzied, emotion-packed days following our departure from PTL. Then in 1988 Tuppins died of a brain disease. The veterinarian said that by rights, Tuppins should have died months earlier, and the only reason Tuppins stayed alive was because the dog sensed that Tammy Faye needed her.

I desperately wanted to get Tammy Faye another dog when Tuppins died, but by this time, our financial resources were gone. We had sold nearly everything except our furniture and clothing. We had even sold our car to make ends meet, so "Doc" Boyd, a dear friend who owned the Chrysler dealership near Heritage USA, loaned us a new car to drive. We certainly did not have any extra money for an expensive little puppy.

Nevertheless, I knew how much Tuppins had meant to Tammy Faye and I found a way to get her another dog.

When I got back home, Tammy Faye was asleep. I tiptoed into the bed-room and turned on the lamp next to the bed. I leaned over Tammy Faye and said softly, "Honey, I have a present for you."

Tammy opened her eyes. I unzipped my jacket to reveal the puppy nestled inside. I gently placed the little puff of fur on the bed near Tammy Faye, and the dog ran right over to her and began licking Tammy's face. It was love at first sight.

"I love you, baby," I said.

"Oh, honey! Thank you. You shouldn't have done it, but I love her so much."

Tammy dubbed the new Yorky Tuppins as well, and before long, it was as though the first Tuppins had never died. When I went to prison in 1989, Tuppins II became Tammy's constant companion.

A prisoner has precious little he can give as a gift, so I wanted to paint the picture of Tuppins for Tammy's birthday. To express to Tammy how I was feeling about missing her birthday, I painted in two tears falling from Tuppins's eye. On the back of the painting, I wrote:

This is how I feel tonight. I miss being with you. It's the first birthday of yours I missed in 29 years. I will make it up to you someday. Hope you like the picture. It is watercolor; they do not allow oil paints in the prison.

Happy Birthday! Love, Jim

Tammy Faye wrote back:

I love the little Tuppins picture, only it makes me cry when I look at it. Someday you will be able to paint over that tear! I know that "great joy" is ahead for you and me and our family.

Our attorney Mr. Bender called today. Attorney Allen Dershowitz is anxious to meet with you, but he is very busy right now on Leona Helmsly's case. I'm glad that he is going to take part in your appeal. He assured Harold Bender that he will meet with you soon. Harold has great confidence in him.

Yesterday I got a sideways look at Jamie standing out by the car with a bunch of kids and I thought it was YOU! He looks more like you everyday. Everyone says so. It's unbelievable!

I *never* stop thinking about you. From the minute I get up in the morning, until I go to bed at night. You are always on my mind!

This nightmare will be over one of these days, Honey. Hold on, be strong!

Love, Tam

On Friday, March 9, I had just begun another painting, this one for Tammy Sue. I had become so absorbed with the painting that I suddenly realized I would have to hurry to make it through the chow line.

I rushed to the chow hall. I had just picked up my tray when a young inmate came up behind me and said with a heavy foreign accent, "Jim, I hear your home at Teka Bay just burned down!"

I nearly dropped my tray. "What?" I said. "What are you talking about?" I asked.

"Yes, it's true. I see on the television. Jim Bakker. Teka Bay. It's burned. All burned down."

The inmate was mispronouncing Tega Cay, the location of my family's former home. More than any other place my family and I had ever lived, the Tega Cay house was the place that instantly came to mind when we thought of "home." We had lived there for nearly a decade while we were at PTL. It was where Tammy and I had raised our children.

I hurriedly gulped down my food and headed back to my building. I had heard so many false reports about me and had been told so many rumors about my former staff and family members, I refused to believe anything I could not verify.

When I returned to my cell, however, I received a message from the guard on duty to report to the warden's office. The warden confirmed the shocking news. Our former home at Tega Cay had been gutted by fire. Only remnants of the structure remained standing.

As I walked back to my building again, my immediate thoughts were for Tammy Faye and the children. I was concerned about how they would take the news. As soon as I was able, I called Tammy Faye. Yes, she had seen the newscast and had seen our home in flames. So had Jamie and Tammy Sue. I started to cry right there on the telephone. I had never before cried over losing a material possession. But this was different. My heart was broken over that house. Though my family and I had been forced to vacate the property when I resigned as president of PTL in 1987, I had secretly hoped to buy the house back someday and restore it to my family.

To the world, it was simply another news story, another page in the saga of Jim and Tammy Bakker. But to me the house represented so much more. It was the house where we put our marriage back together. . . .

In the late 1970s it was no secret around PTL that Tammy Faye and I were having serious marriage problems. Nor was it a secret to our viewers, for that matter. Anyone who watched our program for long could witness Tammy and me airing our dirty laundry on television. Not that we would tattle on each other or be indiscreet, but as we went through our problems, rather than trying to hide them and pretend that we weren't having marital stresses, we talked about them on our programs, often bringing a guest on the show who could address the issues. At times watching our program was like watching a soap opera in which the audience could vicariously experience someone else's problems through the television. Actually many marriages were helped as people realized that they weren't the only ones who had trouble spots that needed fixing in their relationships. Although our show was thriving on the chaos of our lives, our own marriage was falling apart.

As I said before, after Gary Paxton I suspected there was another man in Tammy Faye's life, and by 1980 I was sure of it. In December, we took our television show to Hawaii to do a series of programs from Waikiki. We also held our international conference at this time, so we brought in our hosts from the various *PTL* programs around the world. At that time we were on the air in fifty-two nations so we had a French-speaking *PTL*, Italian *PTL*, Spanish *PTL*, Thai *PTL*, Japanese *PTL*, the list went on and on.

Every show from Hawaii was spectacular. With Diamond Head in the background, bouquets of beautiful Hawaiian flowers on the set, and the help of graceful Hawaiian dancers and singers, we probably did some of our most beautiful programs ever. Tammy and I dressed in Hawaiian outfits; our children were with us so Tammy Faye and Tammy Sue dressed in matching clothes and Jamie and I did the same. All week long, every time we were on camera or with our friends, we were the picture of an ideal, loving family, even if we did look a bit hokey in our Hawaiian muumuus and shirt jackets.

Our friends and television audiences did not know, however, that Tammy Faye and I had agreed to separate at the end of that week. During one of our first days in Hawaii, before the shows began airing, Tammy and I were walking along Waikiki beach when she suddenly turned to me and said, "Jim, I don't love you anymore."

I was devastated. Her words confirmed my worst fears. I felt strongly that Tammy had been seeing someone else, but I didn't know who the person was. I would later be shocked to discover that I had paid for him to accompany us to Hawaii as part of our PTL staff!

I smiled through every show that week despite knowing that when we were done, Tammy Faye was going to fly off to California where she planned to get a job and eventually fulfill her lifelong ambition to go into nursing. At the conclusion of the week of shows and our international convention, we held a traditional Hawaiian luau. On the way to the luau, Tammy and I argued; she refused to get out of the car when we arrived. She said she didn't feel well enough to sing that night and went back to the hotel.

At the close of the luau, as I stood alone on the stage to thank the people for coming and to say good-bye, I began to weep uncontrollably. Most of the crowd thought I was just overcome with emotion at saying good-bye. In a way, they were right. I had held up well through all the shows and all the convention meetings, but now the thought of Tammy leaving was overwhelming to me. I walked away from the microphone, across the stage, and sat down on the back steps to the stage. I sat there for the longest time, sobbing and sobbing.

The following day, Tammy Faye boarded a plane to California, and Tammy Sue, Jamie, and I boarded a plane and flew back to Charlotte. When we got home, the kids and I moved out of our home in downtown Charlotte near South Park and put it up for sale. We moved into a double-wide mobile home next to the church, which would eventually be known as "The Barn" on the property of Heritage USA. The double-wide trailer had previously been used as a makeshift dressing room and extra office space as the PTL ministry began to expand.

I continued to do the television show without Tammy, which was not unusual during those days. Tammy had often been absent from the show. She had been sick frequently, so nobody gave it much thought that she did not show up after the shows from Hawaii. "Uncle" Henry Harrison, my faithful cohost, was there, and between Henry and our many guests, the show perked right along, without missing a beat.

But I missed Tammy horribly. So did Tammy Sue and Jamie. I would have done anything to get her back home with us. Although Tammy Sue was only ten years old, she seemed to be keenly aware of the void in my life. Every time she saw me throughout the day, she said, "Daddy, I love you." Her love helped carry me through those difficult days.

One night our good friend Joyce Caudle and her daughter Kelly, Tammy Sue's best friend, asked Tammy Sue to go to the circus with them.

Tammy Sue had always loved going to the circus since the time she was a little girl. Joyce later told me that Tammy Sue had accepted the invitation, but then called her back and declined. She said she couldn't go because "Daddy would have to eat supper all by himself."

Since Jamie Charles was too young to go to school, I took him with me everywhere I went, even to the office. Jamie loved it. One day, however, Jamie crawled into a cardboard box in my outer office and was saying over and over, "I hate my mommy, and my mommy hates me. I hate my mommy, and my mommy hates me!" One of our staff members heard Jamie's lament and called Tammy Faye in California. Tammy Faye later told me that this incident pierced her heart like an arrow. Jamie Charles was the apple of her eye. He loved his mother; he just couldn't understand why she had gone away and left him.

My children needed their mother, and I wanted my wife back. We loved her dearly. I prayed, "God, You have to show me what this is all about."

I sensed the Lord urging me to go out to our house at River Hills. This was a small house we were trying to sell on the lake at River Hills, about fifteen miles out of Charlotte. Before we had gone to Hawaii, Tammy Faye had been spending a lot of time there, but I had not been to the property in several months. Nevertheless, I felt strongly that God was guiding me to go there.

I got in the car and made the twenty-minute drive by myself. When I arrived at the house, it was deserted but well kept. I went inside and began to look around, not really knowing what I was looking for.

Again I felt impressed by God. As strange as it seemed, I felt certain that the Lord was directing me to look in the garbage can. The kitchen garbage can was full, so I dumped the contents of the can onto the floor. Then I saw it. At the bottom of the garbage were some shreds of paper with writing on them . . . Tammy Faye's handwriting.

The shreds seemed to be some sort of letter. I began slowly putting the paper shreds together on the dining-room table. I found a small roll of tape and I began taping the puzzle together, one piece at a time. My heart was pounding as I assembled and read each line and began to realize that I was reading a letter from Tammy Faye to her lover. Tammy had apparently decided not to mail it and had instead ripped it up and thrown it in the garbage, never imagining that I would be visiting the River Hills property.

It took me hours to piece that letter together—it was several pages long. I ran out of tape long before I got the final pieces in place. Without the benefit of tape, my shaking hands made it almost impossible to lay the tiny pieces together. But I kept at it. Not until I had reassembled the last pieces of the letter did the shreds reveal the identity of the person to whom it was addressed. Shocked, hurt, and disappointed, I slumped over, held my head in my hands, and stared out the window in disbelief. The person to whom Tammy's letter was written was one of my most trusted associates.

I drove back to Heritage USA in a daze. At that point in the history of PTL, I rarely did any of the hiring of personnel, so I was not in the habit of personally firing anyone, either. But in this case, I decided to make an exception. Normally I am a good-natured person, willing to forgive anyone of anything; I'd go the second, third, or umpteenth mile with anyone. Over the years, we had a number of men and women in our employment at Heritage USA who could attest to the fact that we were willing to give them a second chance when it was discovered that they had been guilty of a moral indiscretion, whether it was adultery, drunkenness, or whatever.

But I did have a limit to my leniency. And the one unwritten policy I would not violate was: "You cannot fool around with my wife and stay on my payroll!"

I confronted Tammy's lover—and my coworker . . . and fired him.

I still loved Tammy and was committed to trying to win her back. I began courting her as though we were two high school kids who had just started dating. At the same time, however, I had to do a live daily television program. How could I woo Tammy and keep the show going at the same time?

A local businessman came to the rescue. He had an airplane that he was willing to rent. It was a small jet aircraft, and the businessman allowed me to take out some of the seats so I could lie down in the plane. Back and forth across the United States I flew, spending a few precious hours with Tammy on the West Coast, then flying back all night to be on the East Coast in time to do the morning television program. I maintained this routine for several weeks.

When Tammy and I were together, away from the pressures of PTL and building Heritage USA, it was like old times. We went out for quiet dinners. We talked. We laughed. We had fun together. We went to church.

One Sunday we went to church together in Van Nuys, California, at The Church on the Way, pastored by Dr. Jack Hayford. The church had several morning worship services, and Jack was not preaching at the service we attended, but at that time his assistants always preached on the same subjects that he did. That way the various members of their large congregation would receive the same teaching, no matter which of the services they attended.

The sermon that morning sounded as though it had been prepared with Tammy and me in mind. The message hit us right between the eyes and discussed in detail many of the problem areas Tammy and I were experiencing in our marriage.

The following week, Tammy began to seek God in earnest. She opened her Bible and it seemed as though God was speaking directly to her. She told the Lord that she was willing to go back home to the children and to me. Within ten minutes of Tammy's prayer, I called her on the telephone. Tammy agreed to come back home. My heart leaped for joy!

The first public appearance Tammy Faye and I made after our reconciliation was in Washington, D.C., at the inauguration of President Reagan in 1981. We were invited to numerous inauguration festivities, including the Reagans' candlelight dinner, the parade, the Inaugural Ball, and the official inauguration church service, at which I was to pray the dedicatory prayer. When I entered the church and took my seat on the platform, to my utter chagrin, I saw seated two rows behind Tammy Faye the very man whom I had fired only a few days before!

Tammy Faye looked stunning at every event we attended. At the candlelight dinner held at the John F. Kennedy Center for the Performing Arts, we were seated next to a charming, although rather rotund, gentleman. After we had enjoyed a dinner of striped bass, medallions of veal morel, and raspberry bettina florentine, the gentleman politely asked Tammy to dance.

"I don't know how to dance," Tammy replied truthfully. She had never danced in her life. Tammy grew up in an extremely strict home and her family's church believed dancing was sinful.

"You don't know how?" the gentleman asked in disbelief.

"No," Tammy answered.

"Why, you must dance at the president's inauguration," the man insisted. "It is tradition. You will speak of these events to your grandchildren."

"But I don't know how!"

"Come along, dear. Just step on my shoes."

"What?"

"Just place your feet on mine," the man instructed her.

Tammy got up and stepped onto his shoes, placing the entire weight of her four-foot, ten-inch body, high heels and all, on the huge man's feet.

The tuxedo-clad man whisked Tammy around the dance floor one time, standing atop his shoes, before returning breathlessly to our table.

"Oh," exclaimed Tammy. "I could have danced all night!"

That same week, Tammy Sue, Tammy Faye, and I attended the star-studded Inaugural Ball. As we walked in, we were greeted by the reigning Miss America. We were ushered to our private box alongside the dance floor. After the Osmond Brothers and their sister Marie Osmond performed, the family invited Tammy and me backstage to visit. By all outward appearances, "Jim and Tammy" were back on top of the world.

By the time Tammy Faye and I returned to South Carolina, our house in Charlotte had sold and the new occupants were ready to move in within thirty days. The children and I had been living in the double-wide trailer, so as soon as Tammy Faye came back, we began house hunting . . . again.

We looked all around the area within a reasonable distance from Heritage USA and nothing seemed suitable or within our price range. We were about to give up when one day we were out house hunting along with our friends Paul and Loretta Mays. As a last resort, I suggested that we look at Tega Cay, a then problem-riddled subdivision on Lake Wylie, about a fifteen- to twenty-minute drive away from Heritage USA. Along the way, our children led us in singing a takeoff of the song, "This Is the Day (That the Lord Has Made)." "This is the way; this is the way to Tega Cay! We will rejoice; we will rejoice at Tega Cay!" We all sang at the top of our voices, and then we laughed uproariously. It felt so good to be back together again as a family.

When we arrived at the subdivision, we went to the real-estate office on the property. The man there showed us around the development, but nothing seemed to be right. We were about to leave when the real-estate agent said, "Well, you know, there is a doctor living here and his house is not up for sale, but he has told us that he might be interested in selling his house sometime soon."

Tammy Faye and I looked at each other. We knew we had to find a house soon. With our former home already sold, we needed a place to store our furniture if nothing else. Beyond that, we were trying to put our marriage back together. We shrugged our shoulders and said, "Sure, let's go look at it."

We drove around the lake and as soon as we turned the corner, I saw the house perched on the cliff overlooking the edge of the lake. It was a strange but marvelous-looking Polynesian cedar wood house with pagoda roofs. It looked a bit old and run down, but the moment I saw it, I said, "This is it! This is it!" We hadn't even seen inside the house, and we were not sure whether it was for sale. The doctor and his wife who owned the home were not there at the time, so we made an appointment to return.

I couldn't wait! Once I stepped inside the house, I knew we were home. The living room was two stories high with dry, unvarnished mahogany paneling. It had a large fireplace and plenty of room for all our needs. Out back was a kidney-shaped swimming pool visible from the windows on the side of the house facing the lake. I noticed a number of places where the roof had obviously been leaking, but I figured it would be a minor repair job to take care of that. All in all, the big, sprawling, split-level house was a one-of-a-kind dream house to me.

We decided to make the owners an offer. The odds were stacked against their accepting it. First of all, we did not make an exorbitant offer of money, but worse yet, we told the couple we had to be in the house within thirty days! Amazingly, the couple accepted our offer and within thirty days, we were living at Tega Cay.

Immediately Tammy Faye and I set about remodeling the house. I had noticed that some of the happiest times in our marriage had been when we were working on putting a house together, so I attacked the house at Tega Cay with every bit of energy I could muster.

Over the years that we lived at Tega Cay we practically remodeled the entire dwelling. Upstairs I had a large dressing room built for Tammy Faye, complete with counters and closets, a dressing room fit for a queen.

When Tammy Sue was old enough, she chose her own wallpapers and furnishings for her bedroom, as we allowed her to create her own sanctuary in her room. I had a wonderful time taking my daughter from store to store and watching her as she picked out all her furnishings with tender, loving care. I was pleasantly surprised to learn what exquisite taste and flare my little girl had for decorating.

Her room included an old bathroom that was small and ugly. To give the room a fresh, feminine look, Susie decorated the tub area with a canopy and drape she designed herself. She decorated the entire room for around five hundred dollars. In 1989, during my trial, one of the examples of our lavish living was Susie's so-called five-hundred-dollar shower curtain. It was not the shower curtain only for which we had spent that money, but also the canopy and the draperies for her bathroom.

Downstairs, we remodeled the guest bedroom, which was often occupied by friends. We also redid the kitchen of the house. We had to rebuild the kitchen floor when the boards rotted out beneath the refrigerator, almost allowing the refrigerator to fall through the floor. We enlarged our dining room by putting in a large, rounded greenhouse-type window to give it an unobstructed view of the lake. Tammy Faye designed the room to look like a cafe, with several square tables that could be used separately or placed together to make one long dining table. The room was filled with green ficus trees and plants with white twinkle lights in them. It was a beautiful setting where Tammy and I frequently entertained our PTL staff and guests. My office and Tammy Faye's and Tammy Sue's music room were on the ground level, so we could look out toward the lake as we worked. The house was big to start with, but by the time we would leave in 1987, it would grow to over ten thousand square feet.

The house was more than a piece of property; it was a haven, a place of respite in our frenetic lives. It was a place where we could relax, let our hair down, and just be a family rather than television personalities. Beyond that, to Tammy and me, the house was a symbol of our marriage. We took an existing structure, removed what was decayed or rotten, rebuilt on what was good and salvageable, and replaced what was not with airy new rooms. We were doing something similar in our relationship.

But the best thing about the house is that it was where Jamie Charles and Tammy Sue grew up. Our next-door neighbors, Judy and Dr. Blair Bycura, had two sons, Ryan and Darren, who were close to our children's ages. The Bycura boys and the Bakker children became best buddies and played together constantly. Dr. Bycura took an approach to fatherhood similar to my own. Because we were both so busy with our work, when we were home and could play with our children, we went all out. For instance, our kids wanted us to build them a tree house, so we weren't satisfied to build just any old tree house. Dr. Bycura and I built a two-story tree house for our children. The kids loved it. They often spent the night in it and had many real and imaginary adventures there.

One hot summer Saturday morning, our children were out back playing between the Bycuras' house and our house. The kids had brought home a long sheet of plastic and were pouring water on it with a hose, then sliding down the plastic. Before long, Dr. Bycura and I were right in there with the kids, pouring water on the plastic and sliding down the hillside toward the lake.

Suddenly I got an idea. *If it is such great fun to simply slide a few feet down the hill in the water, what would it be like to slide all the way down the hill to the lake?* We were all soaking wet and covered with mud anyhow, so we started digging out a trench down the hill toward the lake. As we did, we lined the trench with plastic, ran water down it and slid our way down the hill

199

toward the water. Once as I slid down the makeshift waterslide, I hit my ankle on a tree root that was sticking out of the ground and ripped open a gash. But I didn't care. We were having a ball!

Call it the builder in me, but later, after we had all cleaned up and dried off, I began to talk with Dr. Bycura about building a real waterslide in our backyard down the hill to the lake. After all, we had the trench practically dug! Excitedly, we made plans. We ordered pipe and began construction of our backyard waterslide, but a neighbor in our subdivision complained. Soon inspectors came to see our project, and they refused to allow us to continue. They said, "You can't build something like that in a residential community. We reluctantly abandoned our idea, but I never forgot the sound of our children squealing in delight as they slid down that muddy hillside. *Someday*, I thought.

Perhaps more than anything, the Tega Cay house established some semblance of stability in the life of our family. From the time Tammy and I married on April 1, 1961, to the day we moved in at Tega Cay, we had lived in over twenty homes. In the early years, Tammy and I had ministered as traveling evangelists, so we were always moving around. Even after our children were born, we continued to move quite frequently. At one point during the mid-seventies, Tammy and I moved several times in a single year. It was almost as though every time we had another problem in our marriage, we moved to a new house and started fixing it up. Working together on those houses brought us together in a common cause.

When we finally settled at Tega Cay, my children, my wife, and I had a place we could call home.

The news commentator's detached voice brought me back to my present reality in prison. I had made my way to one of the television rooms at the end of the hall where some of the older inmates gathered to watch the news. Most of the televisions in prison are tuned in to "escape from reality" types of shows, but there is usually one set that is kept on a news channel throughout the day. Because I rarely went near the TV room during my first months in prison, I had to search to find the room where the news was on. In the TV room closest to my cell, the inmates had on CNN's *Headline News*. I didn't have to wait long.

The newscaster described the details of how sometime around 2:00 A.M. on Friday, March 9, the house had caught fire. I watched in horror as the screen filled with flaming images of our former home. The house was a virtual inferno, with flames twenty to thirty feet high.

I cried out loud, "Oh, my God, no!" Some of the guys who were standing around in the room stopped and stared at me. I didn't care.

The newscaster was talking about gold faucets and a black marble fireplace, although the fireplace was made of man-made stone and the faucets were actually made of brass. At that point, however, I could have cared less about misrepresentation of the facts. There was one incontestable truth right there on the screen—our family home was engulfed in flames and burning to ashes. The reporter went on to say that the fire seemed to have a suspicious origin, and investigators were already on the scene.

I later learned that it had taken fifty firefighters nearly two hours to extinguish the blaze. The house was completely gutted; the entire rear of the home collapsed, leaving only the entryway, part of the garage, and part of a chimney still standing. An agent with the South Carolina Arson Investigation unit commented wryly, "We're looking at all possibilities and talking with everyone who knows anything. But one thing's for sure—Bakker's alibi is solid."[1]

Sitting in that prison TV room watching my former home crumble in flames was one of the most traumatic times of my life. The house was a part of me. It was a tangible expression of my love for my family. Now it was gone. It was the end of an era. Although it was impractical and improbable, I had always dreamed that someday we could go back there. Now there was nothing left to go back to. Prison or no prison, I could not hold back the tears.

The inmates watched in respectful silence as I got up and walked back to my cell. I climbed into my bunk and shut my eyes. *Oh, God!* I thought. *Why did You allow this to happen? What are You doing to me? I have already lost everything I owned. My ministry is gone. My reputation is gone. I am locked up, facing a forty-five-year sentence, and I can't get out, and I sit here in prison and watch my family home burn down! God, is this some sort of cruel trick? God, where are You? What are You doing to me?*

20

Love at First Sight

PEOPLE DEAL WITH TRAGEDIES IN DIFFERENT WAYS. THE night I watched our family's former home at Tega Cay burning on television, I went back to my cell and began to paint. I was overwhelmed with emotion, and with every stroke, my heart was bleeding through the tip of the brush.

I painted furiously, as though I were a man on a mission. I stopped neither for food nor sleep. *I must rebuild our home at Tega Cay*, I thought, *at least, on paper.* As I reconstructed with paints the rear view of our family's home, each section I painted brought back special memories. I painted the pagoda rooftops, the extended dining room where we had entertained so many friends, my office windows, and the outdoor grill where I had cooked so many meals for our family and our constant flow of visitors. I painted the pool area, with the curved oriental garden bridge that arched over it. With less than an hour or so before dawn, I finally finished the painting. When it dried, I wrote the date on the back of it, along with this message to Tammy:

Tam,

I painted this the night the house burned down. I was so very sad; it was like an old friend had died. For a few hours, I relived the happy times we had in this house. I painted until 4:00 A.M. Will our pain ever end?

This house was a symbol of my love for you and Tammy Sue and Jamie. Now all I can give you is this picture of what used to be and my love.

I love you!
Jim

Tammy's response was characteristically upbeat:

Hi Honey,

I miss you so much tonight. Some nights get so bad that at times I can hardly stand it without you. Sometimes I want to strike out at the whole world! But, I think a quiet trust in the Lord will eventually pay off for you and me.

I love the paintings (the one of Tuppins and the one of the house). They both make me cry! We had so many wonderful times there, raising our kids. But I guess God wants us to move ahead, and the house would have been awfully big with the kids grown up and married.

Besides Tammy Faye's letters, I also received a constant flow of encouraging mail from Tammy Sue. Tammy Faye's letters always resonated with love and hope, no matter how difficult things were for her personally. On the other hand, each of Susie's letters was bittersweet. I loved reading about my grandson's first steps, his first words, his first experience playing in the sandbox, the first time he went to the park, and the day he ate his first orange. Yet with every "first" that Tammy Sue shared with me, it drove home the truths that I was missing the joy of watching my grandbaby grow up and that James himself would be my present age before I had served the complete forty-five-year prison term to which Judge Potter had sentenced me.

One of the most poignant cards I received in prison came from my son Jamie. More than ever before, I now understood how difficult it was for him to write to me because of his dyslexia. Yet Jamie picked out a special card. On the front of it was a sort of red rubber blob with white eyes and a large mouth. The blob was funny looking in one sense and sad in another. Jamie had written on the front of the card around the blob, "Hi, Dad. We will get you home." Then around the remainder of the blob, he wrote, "This is my latest picture (with an arrow pointing at the red face), Your son, Me." On the inside of the card he had written, "I miss you and I want to see you. So try to have fun. I know you will be home soon. I love you Dad. Jamie."

Another letter I received about this time was a mixed blessing. It was from Roe Messner, the man who owned the construction company that had built several of our larger building projects at Heritage USA. When I went to prison, PTL still owed Roe's company millions of dollars for work he had done or was in the process of doing at the time of my departure. When the leaders who replaced me at PTL chose to take the ministry into bankruptcy, PTL's collapse directly affected Roe and his business. Ironically, during my imprisonment, Roe Messner, the man who personally lost more money at PTL's demise than any other person in the world, became one of my best friends. In a letter dated March 8, 1990, he wrote:

> I want to encourage you to keep a good, positive attitude and keep believing God for a miracle. You have tens of thousands of people praying for you. . . . I want to make you aware of a recent development in my situation. I filed Chapter 11 Monday, March 5, 1990, to protect my personal assets until the PTL bankruptcy is finalized. I know the Lord has a purpose in all this and will work it out for His glory. . . . Is there anything I can do to help Tammy or Jamie?

Tammy Faye continued to write faithfully every day, even though we talked by phone each day. In 1990 she wrote, "I look forward so much to your calls each day. I have to be really careful that I don't build my whole life around them. All I want to do is stay home and wait for your calls." Some days, her letters informed me about events in our children's lives. For instance, "Saw Sissy on *Oprah*. You would be so proud of her. She's a great little gal! She can hold her own just fine. She sure does love her daddy!"

As the weeks and months wore on, although Tammy Faye always tried to present a positive impression, the loneliness began to show through her letters. She wrote:

> I can hardly look up at the moon. I always think, "That same moon is shining on Jim." I get so terribly lonely for you. I remember how good it felt to just lean against you on our last visit. For a few moments I felt secure again—whole again. I'm just *nothing* without you, baby!

Another day Tammy Faye expressed:

I miss you an extra lot today. Some days are so much worse than others. Today is one of those "worse" days. I need your hugs so *bad*! I need you to take care of me. I'm not very good by myself. Sometimes I miss you so bad that I get physically sick. I guess I'm going to have to come see you soon. But then that's worse than ever!

I sent a card to Tammy Faye every day. In each one I conveyed my love to her and feelings of hope for a future together, although I knew it would not be soon: "I want to spend the rest of my life with you! The hurt inside of me, from being away from you, will not go away."

Tammy replied: "I love the cards you send me! I look at them and read them over and over again. They make me feel close to you. I miss not being with you. I miss your hugs—our talks—I miss you lying next to me in our bed. I'm so terribly lonely for you. . . ."

It was April 1, 1990—our twenty-ninth wedding anniversary—before Tammy Faye was able to return to see me in Minnesota. She, Jamie Charles, my sister Donna, and our friend Vivian Keller drove ten hours a day for three days to get from Orlando to Rochester. Our good friend Fran Moore flew in to meet the group. We had not seen each other since Christmas. That three-month period of time was the longest we had ever been apart since we had met thirty years earlier.

I first met Tammy Faye when we were both students at North Central Bible College in Minneapolis, Minnesota, where we had gone to study for the ministry. It was love at first sight on my part. The first time I saw her, Tammy Faye LaValley was wearing a lavender argyle sweater, and a deep purple, pleated skirt, with white tennis shoes and white bobby socks. She had the brightest blue eyes and wore no makeup. Her hair was long, and at four feet, ten inches, she was the cutest girl I had ever seen. Unfortunately, Tammy Faye was engaged to be married that Christmas to the son of the pastor of her hometown church.

Midway through our first term, Tammy Faye broke up with her fiancé. That was exciting news to me!

I worked as the night door monitor—sort of an amateur security guard—at the front entrance to the dormitory in which Tammy lived. My job was to keep the riffraff out and to sign out the students when they went out at night and to check them back in as they returned to the dorm. Tammy Faye had to pass right by me on her way out and back into the dorm every night. I may not have noticed when all of the students left and returned, but I certainly knew when Tammy came by. Once, she teasingly gave me a little bell that had fallen off one of her ice skates. I put that bell in my pocket and carried it with me everywhere I went.

One night after Tammy had broken up with her boyfriend back home, she went out bowling with a group of about ten guys, all Bible college students. To Tammy, hanging out with ten guys seemed quite natural, since she was one of eight children in her family. To Tammy Faye, the college students were all simply "brothers and sisters in the Lord." I didn't see it that way, but then, I was interested in dating Tammy myself.

That night, when Tammy Faye walked into the dorm and up to my desk to sign in, I looked up at her and said, "Little girl, you are going to ruin your reputation if you keep going out with all those guys." Tammy looked back at me as if she had no idea what I was talking about—which, I later discovered, she did not. A few days later, I worked up my courage and asked Tammy Faye to go out with me—just me, not as part of a group. She turned me down flat. She wasn't comfortable with the idea of dating solo so soon after breaking an engagement, but at the time, I simply thought she didn't like me. I decided then and there that I would never ask her again . . . at least not before the next week!

I had already fallen head over heels in love with Tammy. A few days later, I asked Peggy, a mutual friend of Tammy's and mine, to go upstairs to Tammy's dorm room and ask Tammy if she might be interested in going out with me sometime. I anxiously watched and waited for Peggy's return like Noah anticipating the return of the dove he had sent out from the ark. Finally Peggy came back, and to my delight, she was carrying a message of peace. Tammy Faye really did like me and was interested in going out with me.

I worked up my nerve and asked Tammy to go to church with me. This time she accepted. For our first date, one cold winter evening we went to church at Minneapolis Evangelistic Auditorium, located at Nicholette and 14th Street, and pastored by Pastor Russell and Fern Olson. I did not own a car in those days, so we had to walk from the Bible College to the church, a distance of more than a mile.

On the way back, I suddenly stopped and said, "Tammy, I can't see you anymore."

Tammy was stunned. We had been having a great time together. "But, Jim, why? What have I done?" she asked.

"Nothing," I replied. "It's just that I am falling in love with you." I knew that North Central did not permit students to get married during the school year, and I knew that what I was feeling for Tammy Faye was more than a high school crush.

I was mulling things over as we walked on a bit farther in the cold.

Suddenly, I made up my mind. "Tammy, kiss me!" I said in hopes that she would take me seriously.

For some reason, she did. Although Tammy later told me that she had never before kissed a fellow on the first date, she did kiss me.

On our second date, I asked Tammy Faye to go steady with me. On our third date, I asked her to marry me. Three months later, on April 1, 1961, we were married after a church service at Minneapolis Evangelistic Auditorium in the prayer room. We did not have the money to have a big wedding. We did not even have enough money for a wedding gown and tuxedo, so Tammy wore a mint-green dress and I wore my favorite black blazer and gray slacks. Pastor Olson conducted the ceremony as his wife Fern looked on. My college roommate and my sister Donna were the only other people to attend our wedding. My mother and father were opposed to Tammy and me getting married while we were in college. Tammy Faye's mom gave us her reluctant blessing the night before the wedding.

Tammy and I held hands throughout the ceremony, with Tammy Faye giggling and me looking stoically ahead. Tammy had just turned eighteen years old and I was twenty-one. We had no money or time for a formal honeymoon, and for nearly three decades I would try to make up that deficiency to Tammy.

Because of the Bible school's policy prohibiting students from marrying during the academic year, and since we were unwilling to wait any longer, we had to drop out of North Central Bible College. We were in love! To us that was all that mattered. Tammy Faye had a job at Woolworth's department store, and I worked as a busboy in the beautiful Fountain Room Restaurant at Rothchild's Young-Quinlin, a famous, old, aristocratic department store in downtown Minneapolis. We volunteered our spare time at Pastor Olson's church and worked with the youth group. I learned to preach my first sermons to this youth group.

One of the guest speakers visiting in our church was Pastor Aubrey Sara from Burlington, North Carolina. He took an interest in Tammy and me and invited us to hold a series of meetings in his church in which Tammy sang and I preached. We had never preached a revival before, but Pastor Sara had so much confidence in us, he convinced us we could do it. When we concluded the meetings at Pastor Sara's church, with his continued guidance and support, we struck out on our own as traveling evangelists. Tammy Faye sang and played the piano and accordion, and I did the preaching.

While I awaited the call on the morning of our twenty-ninth wedding anniversary, my mind again went back to the early days of our marriage. I thought of our little, third-floor, walk-up apartment in which we lived when we had first gotten married in Minnesota. We bought our furniture at the Salvation Army store. We decorated the apartment ourselves . . . and it definitely needed redecorating! Some fellows had lived there before us, and the apartment looked like a pigpen. The bathroom decor was bright red with pictures of naked women hung on the walls.

We bought a few rolls of wallpaper and wallpapered the kitchen. I had never before wallpapered anything, but we had fun figuring it out and working together. Tammy Faye loved lavender, so I painted the bathroom lavender, and she put little white drapes around the old claw-footed bathtub. A friend gave us a well-used dresser with a big mirror on it. We took the mirror off and hung it on the wall, then cut the dresser apart to make two end tables, one for each side of our bed. Lena Williams, my boss at Rothchild's, gave us some chipped dishes and some of the bent silverware from the Fountain Room. We scrimped and saved and used anything we could find to transform that first tiny apartment into a home. Even though we had little in terms of material possessions, we were richer than at any other time in our lives. Years later, when we had money in the bank and lovely possessions in our homes, I often longed to return to those days when our poverty drove us to creativity and each other.

Although Tammy Faye and I were not able to go on a honeymoon, we were passionate young lovers and "honeymooned" most every day. Tammy's and my walk-up apartment truly became a "love nest" in every sense of the term.

Throughout our first twenty-nine years of marriage, although we were stressed and strained in many ways, our physical expressions of love for each other remained an intense, integral part of our relationship. When reporters insinuated that Tammy's and my love life was cold or nonexistent because of my obsession with building Heritage USA, at first we flinched, and then we had to laugh. Nothing could have been farther from the truth. In the best of times and in the worst of times, Tammy and I made love. We always took time with each other. We did not merely have sex; we made love.

Now, on our anniversary, as I waited and waited to hear my name over the prison intercom, the memories of anniversaries past caused desire for my wife to build within me. In expectation of Tammy Faye's visit, I had gotten new prison khakis. Because of my twenty-eight-inch waist and five-foot, eight-inch height, I practically swam in my prison garb so an inmate who worked in the laundry room had altered my clothes so they would fit

I'm sitting on my father's lap next to my mother in this early 40s family photo. My brother Norman is on the far left, my older brother Bob is in the middle, and my sister Donna is standing next to my mother.

Lucky was my best friend for 12 years.

This picture was taken in 1961 on a train trip to introduce Tammy Faye to my parents. A few months later we left Bible College to get married.

Oh, to be nineteen again!

Tammy and I pictured in the mid-Sixties on the first set that I built by hand for our fledgling children's TV program. It was produced at Pat Robertson's Channel 27 at Portsmouth, VA, and as far as I know, it was the first live daily Christian programming specifically for children in America.

Our daughter Tammy Sue was almost born on television; she was raised in front of the camera. She's pictured here on the last and more sophisticated set built for "The Jim and Tammy Show" in the early 70s.

Our puppet family. During the early 1960s Tammy and I felt our ministry was reaching out to everyone except children, so we created this family of puppets called the "Susie Moppet" family. The puppets were the original reason Pat Robertson invited us to join CBN, his pioneering Christian television ministry.

Tammy Faye and I were invited to appear with Paul Harvey at the Hampton Roads Coliseum during our years at CBN. This appearance almost three decades later would be the theme of one of Paul Harvey's "Rest of the Story" segments.

After leaving CBN, Tammy and I journeyed to Southern California, where we helped pioneer the Trinity Broadcasting Network with my former youth pastors, Paul and Jan Crouch. I'm pictured hosting one of the first PTL programs from the original studio in Santa Ana, CA.

Jamie Charles, Tammy Faye, and I clowning around in happier days.

In the mid-Seventies, I resigned my presidency at TBN and moved to Charlotte, NC, where Tammy and I began the PTL Television Network in an abandoned furniture store. Here we are presenting our newborn son Jamie Charles to our television audience.

This is one of the pictures of my son, Jamie, that I had on my prison bulletin board.

Three generations of Bakkers. My father, Jamie, and I in a rare, quiet moment backstage at the PTL studio located at Heritage USA.

Both of our children grew up on the sets of our television programs, and often cameramen and directors became their best friends. Here's Jamie Charles on the set of PTL while we were on location at Gerald Derstine's Christian Retreat in Bradenton, FL.

Tammy Faye pictured with her beloved Grandmother Fairchild, her mother Rachel Grover, and our daughter Tammy Sue in the early 70s.

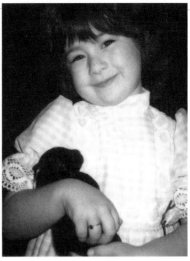

Tammy Sue, the sweetest little girl who ever lived, pictured with her new pet.

Tammy Sue, on an archaeological expedition we had sponsored in Jerusalem. Times like these, spent with my children, were some of my happiest.

Tammy Sue at her "Sweet Sixteen" party at our home in Palm Desert, CA. She had just released her first singing album, simply called "Sixteen."

I always tried to do something unusual for Tammy Sue's birthday. One time we even celebrated in a sultan's tent I had erected in our driveway. This time we celebrated in our playroom at the Tega Cay home.

Our family on the set of PTL.

Our family "on location" with Uncle Henry in Hawaii

Philip D. Egert

Our family posing for a Christmas card picture.

Our family pictured with Patti and Gavin MacLeod at our Palm Desert home. I think the kids were in the swimming pool.

This is my favorite picture taken of Tammy Faye in the office I had built for her next to mine. This picture was taken without any artificial light, just the ambient light coming in her office.

Tammy Faye pictured with her little dog Tuppins II which I purchased after the death of her beloved dog Tuppins I.

Tammy Faye not only hosted her own program, Tammy Faye's House Party, *she also co-hosted and often hosted our* PTL *program. Pictured here, she's interviewing Mickey Rooney and his wife Jan.*

Art Linkletter dominated the television scene during my formative years, and it was always a thrill to have him on TV with me. Here I am introducing him to my son.

Every time Tammy and I visited Israel, Prime Minister Menachem Begin took time from his busy schedule to meet with us. He always gave me a carte blanche letter giving full access to all archaeological sites, including those under the Temple Mount.

Over the years, I had the privilege of visiting with Ronald Reagan in his home, at his Beverly Hills office, and several times in the White House. The most treasured moments came when we were able to spend hours just sitting around in our shirt sleeves, discussing his beliefs with a small group of friends.

One of the greatest, true Christian gentlemen to ever occupy the White House in my estimation was Jimmy Carter. I had the privilege of not only having breakfast with him in the White House and receiving a dual humanitarian award presented to his wife and me, but I also had the privilege of flying and praying with him on Air Force One.

I felt honored when George Bush asked for me to have lunch and meet with him privately and discuss his deep faith and belief in the fact that Jesus Christ was and is the Son of God.

The original sign marking the entrance to Heritage USA.

Heritage USA was just a rugged landscape when construction began. Pictured above, staff member Bob Daniel and I discuss plans for the first stage of the development of Heritage USA.

When we opened the first phase of Heritage USA, which included the Fort Heritage Campground, instead of cutting a ribbon, I used a chain saw and cut a log.

One of the biggest undertakings of my life was the building of the Heritage Grand Partner and Ministry Center, consisting of 500 lodging rooms, shops, restaurants, and beautiful meeting facilities.

This is one of the 500 beautiful guest rooms utilized by PTL and lifetime partners. This shows a standard room in the Heritage Grand.

In Phase 2 of the lifetime partnership program, I added the beautiful facilities of the Heritage Inn.

Fort Heritage Campground at Heritage USA featured almost 500 campsites.

One of the most popular places at Heritage USA was the fellowship lobby. Surveys showed that the number one reason people came to Heritage USA was for Christian fellowship.

The exciting Main Street Heritage USA located in the beautiful Heritage Grand Partner Center housed a variety of shops, restaurants, and activities with well-appointed hotel suites and rooms located above the shops.

The Heritage Island was the nation's only inspirational water park, which provided water fun, recreation, live Christian music, Bible teaching on the beach, refreshments, and fellowship in a wholesome family atmosphere.

me better, then pressed them in crisp military-style pleats. I was the epitome of a well-dressed prisoner.

When the call finally came—"Inmate Bakker, report to the visiting room"—I raced across the compound as fast as I could go without running. I hurried to the guard station, and the guard unlocked the door and escorted me to the strip-search room, where he patted me down. Inside that room, I also had to complete an inventory form, listing each of the personal belongings I was bringing with me—my belt, glasses, wedding ring, money for the vending machines, or anything else on my person that was not prison issued. When I was finally able to enter the visitation room, I was so excited to see Tammy Faye that I forgot to sign in. I spotted her immediately and walked straight to her. I embraced her hungrily, holding her in my arms, and kissing her much longer than prison rules deemed appropriate.

"Happy anniversary, honey," I whispered in her ear. "Thank you so much for coming! I have missed you so badly."

I had not been intimate with Tammy Faye in over six months. I desperately missed the closeness we had always shared in our marriage. Through even the worst of times, we were always great romantic lovers. Now I slept alone in a narrow bunk, aching to be with the woman I loved so deeply.

It was so wonderful to be able to hold her close to me for an extended moment—which ended abruptly when the guard yelled, "Bakker! You haven't checked in yet!"

I quickly let go of Tammy and hurried to the officer's desk. The guard gave me a "You know better than that!" sort of look.

I checked in and then returned to greet Jamie. "Hey, Dad!" he called to me as I approached him with outstretched arms. Jamie and I hugged each other, and I was surprised at how much he had grown since the last time I had seen him. He was almost as tall as I was. I greeted my sister Donna and our dear family friend Fran, and we all pulled our plastic chairs around the tiny table and wiped the tears from our eyes. It was wonderful to see everybody! We got some food from the vending machines and sat for hours, catching up on what was going on in each other's lives.

After a while, I wanted to spend some time "alone" with my wife on our anniversary. While the others remained at the table, I offered to show Tammy Faye the recreation field. I guided her toward the back visitation room, to the window near the end of the line of vending machines. From that vantage point, I stood behind Tammy Faye, reaching around her and pointing out the various areas on the recreation area.

"And over there is the softball field," I said, pointing past her shoulder. "And there's the volleyball court and the boccie ball court."

Tammy Faye leaned over slightly to look out the window and as she did, I could feel the warmth of her body next to mine.

"And there's the track that we walk around," I said, trying to sound nonchalant.

"Yes, I see it," Tammy said as she backed closer to me.

"That's the area we use for ice skating," I went on.

"Uh-huh," she said as though she was fascinated by my tour-guide spiel. "Yes, I understand."

I stepped forward slightly, reaching around Tammy Faye and pointing to the right side of the recreation area ostensibly to show her the area where the workout equipment was kept. When I did, our bodies pressed fully against each other for a few seconds. It was like electricity shot through me. I wanted to be a husband to my wife in a complete sense, to hold her, touch her, caress her, to express physically the love I felt for her, as I had thousands of times before, and to experience one more of those intimate times that seemed to temporarily heal so many of our hurts. Tammy Faye's hand brushed my leg. We were a married couple, celebrating our twenty-ninth year of marriage on this day, yet we furtively concealed our touch like two teenagers stealing a kiss outside the front door.

We were jolted back to reality by a heavyset man who loudly asked, "Hey, Jim and Tammy! How about an autograph?" Our intimate moment was over. A sense of fear swept through me as I thought of the guards glaring at us and the ever-present overhead cameras recording our every move. I knew that even a slight indiscretion could send me to the hole. Almost instinctively Tammy Faye and I stepped away from each other as I reached out to sign an autograph on the man's paper. The man thanked me and handed the paper to Tammy for her signature. I tried not to resent his unwitting intrusion into the first intimate moment Tammy and I had been able to share in over half a year.

"Wrap it up!" The guard's order signifying the end of visitation time came all too soon on our anniversary. "Inmates to the front, visitors to the back. Everybody sign out."

"I love you, Dad," I heard Jamie's nervous voice saying as he hugged me good-bye.

"Don't give up, honey," Tammy Faye said as we kissed good-bye in a much more perfunctory embrace than our previous kiss that day. "We can make it," she said. The room was clearing and I knew the guards were going to be calling for me at any moment if I didn't get going. As I waved good-bye and started toward the strip-search room, I heard Tammy Faye say to Jamie, "Don't look back." None of us wanted to let go of each other, yet none of us wanted the pain of that last look before going out our respective doors—my family going out the door to freedom, and me going through the door to be strip-searched once again.

As I began peeling off my clothes in front of the guard, I thought of my family on their way back to Florida. The old saying was right: "You don't know what you have until it's gone."

21

Dying Embers

"DADDY, I THINK I'M PREGNANT."

When I first read the words in Tammy Sue's letter, my heart leaped for joy at the thought of another grandchild. Then the reality of the situation set in. I realized how difficult it would be for her and Doug to have a new baby at this time. Susie and Doug were struggling to make it financially. Doug was out of work, and the family had no health insurance. Beyond that, Tammy Sue was still dealing with her own depression. She and Doug were not in an ideal condition to bring another baby into the world.

Tammy Sue sounded almost apologetic in her letter. I knew that she would be a great mom to her baby, just as she already was to baby James. Nevertheless, I worried about her prenatal care. Where was she going to get the money for proper nutrition, for herself and for the new life growing within her? Would she find a doctor who would take adequate care of her? How would she ever pay a hospital bill? These and a thousand other questions tossed about in my mind. Again, my inability to help my family in their time of need smacked me right in the face.

Concern over Tammy Sue's pregnancy, combined with the sense of loss I was feeling since Tammy Faye's anniversary visit and the still-smoldering memories of the Tega Cay house fire sent me spiraling downward into my own trough of despair.

During the week following Tammy's visit, in my ceramics class I had made a vase. I kiln fired the vase on April 7, 1990. Again, as part of my futile attempt to re-create the burned-out house, I painted a picture of the Tega Cay house on the vase. I fired it in the kiln again. The vase came out beautifully. I was going to send it to Tammy Faye, but then I discovered something.

At Dr. Westrick's request, Dr. Tom Brandon and I had been preparing for several months now to teach our smoking cessation class. We were receiving a deluge of information from a wide variety of sources, as part of our research for the class. While studying and making notes, I came across some interesting comparisons between giving up smoking and other losses people experience, such as the death of a loved one, divorce, loss of property, or the loss of position or prestige. As one of the first major steps toward healing, my research purported, one had to quit living in denial and stop pretending that nothing has happened. Accept it, begin to deal with it, and get on with your life.

The awful pictures I had seen on television of our home engulfed in flames still haunted me at night. But I knew the house was nothing more than rubble by now. It was time to accept that fact and move on.

In an almost tangible expression of what I was learning as I studied for the smoking cessation course, I grabbed the vase on which I had painted a lovely rendering of our house at Tega Cay, the same vase that I was planning to send to Tammy Faye. I spattered black and red paint all over the vase in an attempt to portray the house on fire. When the paint dried, I placed the vase in the kiln again. The intense heat did its work. When the vase cooled, and I removed it from the kiln, I was flabbergasted. The black and red ceramics paint had spread over the house, creating an eerie sense of fire, smoke, and darkness. The vase portrayed the emotions I was feeling. In a real way, seeing the vase with the house on fire helped me to come out of denial, to admit that the house was gone, and to accept the fact that I must move on with my life. Before any other inmates benefited from the smoking cessation class, I already had.

Because Tom had been a medical doctor, he still received more than twenty medical publications each month. He had also joined the American Society of Addiction Medicine before I had moved into his cell. Consequently, Tom received a wealth of current medical information on an almost daily basis. He scanned every medical publication for material pertaining to smoking and nicotine addiction. He wrote to every drug company he could find requesting any information they might have concerning smoking and health topics. Over several months, Tom contacted seventy-five private organizations and government agencies in an attempt to gather as much information as possible concerning nicotine addictions and the multiple health consequences.

The information poured in; it was as though a floodgate had been opened. At the same time, Tom and I scoured newspapers, magazines, and religious periodicals for information we could use in teaching our class. Tom handled the medical aspect of the material, and I prepared the motivational material.

I devoured dozens of books on the psychology of motivation, self-worth, and a positive mental attitude. I read books by authors such as Zig Ziglar, Og Mandino, Robert Schuller, and a host of other spiritually based authors. Additionally, I studied information from the Hazelden Addiction Center. I wrote to some good friends, Dr. Marvin Brooks and his wife, Sally, who were active in the American Cancer Society. They sent more materials for us.

I had one big problem. How was I to stand in front of a group of inmates and help motivate them to stop smoking without referring to God, the Bible, or my faith (weak as it was at this point)? The prison administrative officials were adamant that I not be involved in anything that gave me access to a pulpit. Moreover, the warden and his assistants did not want me in a position of leadership. It was only through Dr. Westrick's significant influence that I was allowed to do anything other than clean toilets.

"I can see the headlines in the tabloids now," Tom quipped. "Bakker Faith-Healing Inmate Smokers!"

No doubt the prison officials were concerned that if the press learned of my involvement with the smoking cessation class, it would be blown out of proportion and distorted. As it turned out, they were not far wrong. Nor was Tom, for that matter.

I was informed that I was not permitted to do any preaching in the smoking cessation class. I could talk about a "higher power" but references to Jesus Christ, the Bible, or to prayer all had to be avoided. The prison had used a smoking cessation program once before, and the material that was used in that course was approved for my use. I was required to confine any Scripture references or spiritual information to the material that had already passed government censorship. To my delight, when I examined some of the material that had been used previously, I found that the accepted program was the "Breathe Free Plan to Stop Smoking," which included some of the most effective materials in the world for dealing with addictions, and was prepared by the Seventh-Day Adventists, a group that based their instruction on biblical principles. The best materials, films, and devices for demonstrating cessation techniques all came from the Adventist material, so Tom and I used their ideas as the foundation for our course.

Throughout the first four months of 1990, Tom and I collected materials and prepared our course. The desk in my cell was constantly stacked high with books and materials, so much so that the guards often said, "Bakker, too many books. Too many books!" Since inmates were only permitted a certain number of books at any one time, I would read the books quickly, make notes on them, then give them away to other inmates or donate them to the prison chapel library. Still the guards complained, "Too many books on your desk."

Finally, we believed we were ready for our first class. Tom and I personally put up posters all around the prison compound, announcing the class. One of our favorite posters included a vivid, full-color picture of the human lung of a smoker. The lung looked like a burned pot roast. We had trouble keeping the posters on the walls. Inmates kept tearing them down! Many inmates did not want to stop smoking, and they certainly did not want to see what smoking was doing to their bodies. Inmates who had no intention of giving up smoking found our posters offensive.

Another poster we used was a skeleton with a lighted cigarette in its hand. One of our most successful slogans we used to attract inmates to the class was: "Sign up now for our next class and give yourself eighteen bonus years of life." We promised that certificates were to be awarded to all inmates who completed the class. Most enticing of all, participants were excused from work detail to attend our seminars between 8:00 and 10:30 A.M. for eight straight mornings, followed by aftercare to be conducted over the next two weeks, with two sessions per week.

Tom and I didn't know what to expect when we stood before a roomful of inmates for our first session. Twenty-four men had enrolled in our first course. We had obtained permission to have our first session in the "Blue Room," one of the nicer meeting rooms in the same building as the chapel. The Blue Room had carpet on the floor and tables and chairs around which the men could sit.

We had also arranged for a special mixture of orange and grapefruit juice to be available to the men who enrolled in our class. The juices actually change the acid content in the person's body who is trying to quit cigarettes "cold turkey." It decreases the rate of nicotine excretion and lessens the withdrawal effects.

Sunflower seeds were distributed to the inmates to munch on during class. Part of the cessation process involved keeping the addicted person's hands occupied. We had discovered that handling the cigarette was part of the total addiction. Tom and I ordered enough sunflower seeds to make the late Euell Gibbons proud of us. For our first class, the prison supplied most of our juices and seeds. After that, Tom and I purchased the seeds with our commissary funds.

I was extremely nervous. I was a relatively new resident in the prison and didn't know if the men in the room that first morning were hardened criminals or former bank presidents. Besides, I hadn't spoken in front of a group in a long time. My own feelings of worthlessness only exacerbated my insecurity. As I looked into the faces of the men attending that first session, I thought, *This has to be the toughest audience I have ever seen!* Dr. Westrick introduced the program and told the men that this class was one of the most important that any inmate who smoked could take. She added some complimentary statements about Tom and me, and then she left. Her confidence in us was astounding.

Tom began the first session by giving the men a brief history of smoking in America, going back all the way to Christopher Columbus, who first saw tobacco used by the Indians, to John Rolfe who introduced it to the Jamestown Colony in 1612, and on up to the present day when major tobacco companies roll out ten thousand cigarettes per minute. Then Tom gave the men some of the hard-hitting facts about smoking. He told them, "Smokers die (on the average) eighteen years sooner than nonsmokers." He went on to say, "Each year smoking kills over four hundred thousand people in the U.S. There are more deaths than the number of people who died in World War I, World War II, the Korean Conflict, the Vietnam War, and all the deaths related to cocaine and heroin use combined."

With the passion of a country doctor, he proclaimed, "If smoking continues in its current popularity, according to the World Health Organization, over five hundred million people will die smoking-related deaths within the next twenty-five years."

Then Tom said something that really hit home with me. "According to the Surgeon General of the U.S., at the current rate of increased smoking activity, five million teenagers who are alive today will die of smoking-related diseases. Over a billion packs of cigarettes are sold annually to children under eighteen years of age."

As I listened to Tom's lecture, I became angry at how our children were being duped into becoming addicted to cigarettes. My own son, Jamie, had recently been suspended from the Christian school he attended when he had been caught smoking. Here I was in prison, about to teach a course in smoking cessation, and my son was out there learning how to kill himself with cigarettes!

Tom went on to provide the inmates with a wealth of current, accurate medical information concerning the damaging effects of smoking. One of Tom's caustic one-liners about smoking was: "Once you get lung cancer, you might as well send your shirts to the laundry one at a time."

The inmates laughed but Tom's message hit home.

Tom then outlined the reasons why this program would work for the inmates and why they should quit smoking immediately. He emphasized the fact that he and I did not think we were know-it-alls, but that we had done our homework and the men could be confident that the methods and techniques we were going to teach them had worked for fourteen million other people who had used the "Breathe Free" program to quit smoking. A major key to success, he said, was to find a friend in this program to whom you could be accountable and whom you could help too. Tom reviewed the reasons why most of the guys had started smoking and helped them realize that cigarettes did not deliver what their advertisers had promised. In each morning session, Tom, as a medical doctor, delivered a litany of information to the class concerning the dangers of smoking and how they could quit. Sometimes Tom's information was so technical I could not understand it all, but his material could be summed up in two words: Smoking kills.

When it was my turn to speak, my first session was on the subject "You Are Valuable." I started by telling one of my favorite stories about the Queen of Holland. The queen wanted to honor the farmers and the agricultural people of Holland because they had done a tremendous job during a time of dire straits in the country. She decided to throw a state dinner for the farmers. The queen's adviser protested vehemently. "Your Majesty, these are farmers!" he said. "They won't know how to eat in a fine dining room. They'll embarrass you." The queen could not be swayed. The dinner was planned.

At the state banquet, the table was set with the queen's finest china and silverware, with all the fine cups and glasses, including finger bowls. Everything was going along well until one of the farmers began to drink from his finger bowl. The queen's more sophisticated guests chortled in amusement as they watched the uncouth farmer fulfilling the prediction of the queen's adviser. When the queen noticed the man drinking from the finger bowl, she immediately raised her finger bowl to her lips and began to drink from it. All the other guests followed suit and began drinking from their finger bowls.

"This woman recognized the value of the human spirit," I told the inmates. "She was truly a great person who would not allow another human being to be embarrassed. She saw the value of the common farmer to the nation." The men to whom I was speaking sat in rapt attention. I knew that most of them had been embarrassed through the process of coming to prison. They had all been in court. They had all been "prisonized." They had grown accustomed to strip searches and the many other ways the prison experience degraded them as people. They could relate to the farmer in the story. I knew that if I was going to help these men kick the nicotine habit, they must be convinced of their value as people.

"You are incredibly valuable," I said. "According to calculations by Professor Harold Morowitz of Yale University, your body is worth $245.54 per gram of dry weight. This means that a 168-pound man is worth $6 million in chemicals alone.

"Your body is not just biochemical compounds; it is made up of high-tech tools. Think of your eyes, for example. How many of you would sell your eyes for a million dollars?

Not one of the men put up his hand.

"Who would sell your ears for $5 million?"

No takers.

I asked how many of the fellows knew who Betty Grable was. Only a few of the older men raised their hands. I guess you know how that made me feel! I quickly continued, "Betty Grable's legs were insured for a million dollars! What are your legs worth? See? When you start adding up your value, you are a billion-dollar person."

I then gave the Judeo-Christian background to the idea that the men had value. I was able to quote the Bible at this point because the previously approved program had done so. I told the men, "I believe in God; you may not." I explained to them that they had the right in our program to believe in God or not to believe, and they could take from the program what helped them and leave the rest. I reminded the guys, however, that the most successful addiction cessation programs had a "faith factor." Such groups as Alcoholics Anonymous, Teen Challenge, and D.A.R.E. all had at their core a firm belief in the power of faith in God. "Addiction is bigger than the individual," I said, "so it takes something bigger than the individual to cure it."

I reminded the men of Eleanor Roosevelt's statement, "No one on earth can make you feel inferior without your permission." Then I began to zero in on the real issues behind many people's habit. I said, "People sometimes continue smoking because they are not convinced they deserve freedom from destructive habits. You must decide whether to stop smoking or not."

I told the men about Booker T. Washington, founder of Tuskegee Institute, a school known primarily for its education of black men and women. "In the middle of awful racial prejudice, Washington said, 'I will permit no man to narrow and degrade my soul by making me hate him.'"

I also mentioned the experience of Natan Sharansky, who was imprisoned by the K.G.B. in the former Soviet Union. Sharansky said of his captors, "They cannot humiliate me; I alone can humiliate myself."

As I spoke, it was becoming clear to the men attending our first class that this message was about much more than merely learning how to quit smoking. It was about learning how to develop an entirely new mind-set about life, particularly life inside a prison.

I closed my session that morning by telling the men, "Stop looking at what you see, and start looking at what you can have. Believe you are worth it. Believe you are a valuable human being, accept yourself as a worthwhile person. Be nice to yourself. You are the best 'you' in existence."

Outside, as we were leaving the chapel building, an inmate who had attended the sessions that morning walked up to me and nervously said, "Thank you for your speech. It was really good." He paused and looked me in the eye, and said, "You are the first person who ever told me that I am worth anything."

Ironically, the message I was presenting to the men that morning was one I desperately needed to hear myself.

Although I did not realize it at the time, looking back now I can see that every lesson I taught the men, God wanted me to learn. To teach the smoking cessation class, I had to pore over mounds of material, study it, distill it, absorb it, and apply it in ways that I otherwise would have never considered while in prison. In each session, the lessons I prepared for the inmates who wanted to be free from smoking were the exact truths I needed to know if I was ever to climb out of my own pit of depression and despair.

For instance, my second session was on the subject of "Your Self-Image." I was standing up teaching the men how to raise their self-esteem when my own self-esteem was nonexistent. I felt lower than a worm.

Yet I told the men, "Your self-image controls you. Everything you do—your actions, feelings, and behavior patterns—is consistent with the image you hold of yourself. If you think you are shy, you will act shy. If you see yourself as a smoker, you will be a smoker. Your life will always move in the direction of your strongest thoughts."

I went on to say, "Don't let others paint a bad self-image for you. Label a man a loser, and he will start acting like a loser." I did not recognize it then, but that was exactly what I was doing to myself. I was allowing the words of men who had engineered my departure from PTL to influence the way I was thinking about myself. I knew better, but I kept thinking, *Well, maybe they're right.*

Even when I turned the message around in a positive sense, I still did not yet see it as applying to myself. I told the men, "Your self-image is not permanent. You can change. You don't have to keep playing the old broken record of the past. You don't have to wallow in self-pity. You can design your own mental blueprint. You can hold a good picture in your mind, and your outward behavior will fall into line."

I quoted my friend Mike Murdock, who says, "What happens in the mind, will happen in time." I heard myself saying, "If you think about negative things, they will destroy you." And yet most of the time in prison when I was not actively studying for this course, I had been dwelling on all the awful things that had happened over the past three years! I closed my session that day by encouraging the men, "You can only move away from a bad thought by deliberately moving toward a good one."

It was strange that I would be teaching the inmates about how to improve their self-image when my own self-image was so horrible, but I now see it as God's way of reaching me through the mental, emotional, and spiritual fog in which I had been living. The very messages that I needed somebody to tell me, I was telling myself as I prepared to teach someone else.

The process continued with my third session, which was on "Positive Mental Attitude." I started by comparing a positive mental attitude to what I called a "prison mental attitude."

As an example, I said, "Some inmates say all prison food is bad, even when it isn't, even when the food is good. That is a prison mental attitude.

"Others say to me, 'Hey, man! Why are you working so hard cleaning toilets? You're just working for the guards.' I always answer, 'The guards don't use these toilets. You use them and I use them.'"

I went on to say, "Whenever you do a job less than you are capable of doing, you are cheating yourself. You are stealing from yourself. The biggest thief steals your dreams. Sometimes your best friend can be your enemy." I gave the men a biblical definition of an enemy: "Anyone who keeps you from doing your best for Jehovah." I knew that many of the guys' friends would make fun of them for trying to stop smoking. Often the friends of the person who was trying to quit felt guilty when their buddy stopped smoking.

"Who got you into drugs?" I asked. "Who got you into crime? Many times your best friends were partially responsible for you being here in prison. But don't let them hold you back. Other people can stop you temporarily; only you can stop yourself permanently."

I told the men, "God is on your side," and I quoted several Scripture verses (that were listed in the approved prison program) to prove it. "It says in 1 John 1:9 that if we confess our sins, He is faithful and just to forgive us our sins. We can be guilt-free," I told the guys. "Furthermore, God does not condemn you!" I gave another Scripture, John 3:17, "For God sent His Son into the world not to condemn the world, but that the world through Him might be saved."

I concluded this session by saying, "God's love and forgiveness are the bridge we can cross from low self-esteem to high self-esteem. You can make it!" Again, the message was as much for me as for any of the inmates who wanted to quit smoking—maybe more.

At the end of our third day's seminar, we had a special ceremony. On day one, we had encouraged those who were serious about breaking their addiction to save their cigarette butts, matches, open packs, and any other tobacco-related items and bring them all to class on the third day. At the close of the third day's sessions, we had the men bring all their smoking paraphernalia to the front of the room and drop it into a coffin of wood and cardboard that had been made for the occasion by the prison's woodworking shop. It was nicknamed the "Coughin' Coffin." All twenty-four of the men who signed up for our first class threw away their smoking materials as an outward expression of their inner commitment to stop smoking.

On day four, Tom continued to hammer away at the medical, psychological, and social reasons to stop smoking, and how to handle the cravings and urges that accompany a cessation of smoking. That same day, I dealt with "Rationalizations," the excuses we often use to explain our foolish acts, beliefs, and self-deceptions.

"A lot of people say, 'Well, I could give up smoking. I've done it many times!'" I joked with the men. I then listed some of the rationalizations many people use for continuing to smoke, even though they know it's killing them. One of the rationalizations I mentioned was that of fatalism, the idea that says, "I'm going to die when I'm supposed to die anyway. . . ."

I said, "This rationalization sounds almost spiritual! But that is a lie.

Fatalism is not spiritual," I heard myself speaking to the men, and to myself. "Sure, we're all going to die sometime, but you don't have to die prematurely or from a painful disease such as lung cancer or emphysema. You can change. Even God changes His mind, sometimes." I told the men the story of Jonah, and how God used the man to warn Ninevah that it was doomed. But when the people of Ninevah repented and changed their ways of thinking and acting, God abandoned His plan to destroy them.

On day five of our eight-day crash course, I taught the men about the stages of loss or grief, using the pattern established by Dr. Elisabeth Kübler-Ross, and showing how smokers who give up their nicotine go through similar emotional stages as a person who has lost a loved one, a job, a friend, or has lost a spouse through divorce. Research done by a group in Minnesota discovered that smokers consider their cigarette a "buddy," but "it is a buddy that will always let you down," I told the men. When that buddy is gone, the grieving process sets in.

"Although there is no orderly flow to the grieving process, the first stage is often denial," I told the class. "Denial is a psychological buffer that protects us from feelings we are not yet ready to deal with mentally, emotionally, or spiritually. Many smokers live in denial, denying that they are addicted, denying that they can't quit, or trying to deny the validity of information concerning smoking-related diseases and deaths."

Although I didn't realize it at the time, part of the reason I had painted the Tega Cay house and reproduced it on the vase was an effort to deny in my mind that it had been destroyed. I did not want to accept the fact that it was gone, that a precious portion of my life was obliterated forever. Moreover, for the first few years after losing PTL I lived in denial. I had lost so much, not simply materially or in terms of personal power and prestige, but in terms of emotional and spiritual losses as well. I did not want to admit to myself that it was gone.

Now here I was trying to help other inmates, and by digging out the materials to teach the men, I was finding the tools I needed to dig out of my own quagmire.

"The second stage of grieving is usually anger," I taught the fellows. "Anger comes when you have lost something dear to you."

I was going through these same emotional processes myself! I was angry at the prosecutors, the judge, some of my friends, angry at those who had become obsessed with bringing me down, and most of all, angry at myself for letting it all happen. The question *How did I get in this mess, anyway?* haunted me day and night.

"Anger can be extremely destructive unless it is expressed in healthy ways," I said. "Instead of beating up your cellmate, pound your pillow. Or go work out, play handball, run, do something physical to express your anger in a positive, safe way. Because if you don't," I warned the men, "your anger will lead to depression. Depression is anger turned inward."

I could hardly believe my ears! I was living in depression. I was telling the other guys exactly what I was doing myself. I felt like a total hypocrite. Consequently, I determined that I was going to start working out, that I would begin to practice the very things I heard myself teaching others.

The same process began to unfold in my life as I taught the men about sorrow, despair, depression, bargaining, and finally, acceptance. It was not until I went back and painted in the fire and smoke on the vase of the Tega Cay house that I came to accept the fact that it had burned and was gone.

My day-six lecture was on the subject "A Mind to Win." Much of the session involved attitude, what we think and say to ourselves. The men readily agreed that bad attitudes were running at epidemic levels in prison. Many guys were living in prison with chips on their shoulders. And I had to admit that my attitude was bad too. As I taught this program, God began to change my attitude about many things. Almost imperceptibly at first, God began to whittle away at the chip on my shoulder.

I spent part of this session teaching the men how to speak positively rather than negatively to other people and more importantly, to themselves. I quoted studies to show how our minds go to work trying to fulfill our words. "So we need to be careful what we say to ourselves," I told the class. "Even comments such as, 'I really want to quit smoking' or 'I am going to quit smoking,' are counterproductive. You are reinforcing that you are a smoker. Instead," I suggested to the guys, "say something such as 'I really love being free from smoking.' Or, 'I am enjoying tasting food, and it is so delicious.' Or, 'My cough is gone!'"

I continued along the same lines on the seventh day of classes, showing the inmates how to develop the characteristics of a winner. "Winners work at it," I said. "Getting started is 50 percent of success. Winners keep their minds on their goals," I told the men. "Never give up! Don't even think about failure. Avoid tempting situations by spending time with other nonsmokers. Winners want complete victory. You can make it! God is on your side."

On the eighth and last day of classes, my session was on the subject of "Reciprocal Dependence." Again the message was for me as much as anyone else. I told the class a story about a little boy who was mad at his mother and ran outside and shouted, "I hate you!" His words echoed back to him from the valley, "I hate you!"

Terrified, the boy ran back inside the house and cried, "Mother, there is a mean boy in the valley! He said he hates me!" His mother wisely took the boy back outside, and instructed him to shout, "I love you!"

"I love you!" the little boy shouted at the top of his lungs.

"I love you!" came the voice from the valley.

I told the inmates, "Life is similar to that echo. What you send out comes back to you. By helping others, you help yourself. As my friend Mike Murdock says, 'What you make happen for others will happen to you.' Others need your motivation. Find a need and fill it. If you really want to stop smoking, one of the keys is to find a buddy and help him stop smoking. If you help others break free from smoking, you will not slip back yourself. What you sow you will reap. All successful people help people."

Tom and I taught the smoking cessation class seven times during 1990 and early 1991. Including the several months it took us to prepare our course, I was immersed in these lessons for over a year. Every time I taught the course, I was teaching myself the survival techniques I needed to know.

What an amazing, wonderful trick God played on me! Until I wrote this book, I truly never realized that as I was teaching others how to escape the stranglehold of their addiction, I was in fact learning what I needed to know for the rest of my life. Not only was God going to use this material to help pull me out of my own doldrums, He was also preparing me for the tough days ahead.

22

Through the Valley of Loneliness

IF GOD WAS TRYING TO GET MY ATTENTION, HE HAD succeeded. God got my attention in a way I would have least expected— not by striking me with a lightning bolt as punishment for my sins, but He spoke to me instead through the valley of loneliness and the silence of solitude.

It is possible to be surrounded by people, to be immersed in activity, and still be unbearably lonely. I lived in a building with nearly three hundred other men, surrounded by a constant cacophony of men talking, laughing, and cursing. The blaring TV was rarely quieted. Noise is not enough to drive away loneliness.

I had been making new friends. Though some of them were of dubious backgrounds, I had discovered an unusually high level of friendship, compassion, and camaraderie in prison. I had also been hearing from friends I never knew I had. One day, for example, I received a warm letter from U.S. Senator Mark Hatfield of Oregon. The highly esteemed senator sent me a devotional book he thought might be of help to me. He wrote:

> The enclosed came to me from a friend and, in turn, I am sending it to you with the thought that perhaps it will serve to comfort and inspire

you. While I am sure that the past months have been difficult, I hope that your faith in God has sustained you and I wanted you to know that. . . . You are in my prayers each day.

Sincerely,

Mark Hatfield

I greatly appreciated Senator Hatfield's note, and the book he sent to me was helpful. More than that, I appreciated his support and prayers.

About that time, a friend sent me a beautiful little card with a picture of the ocean on the front. The artist had painted the scene so it appeared as though the tide was beginning to go out. Printed across the inside of the greeting card were these words: "A friend is one who comes in when the whole world has gone out."

As I looked at the picture on the front of the card, the ebbing tide became a mental picture of people walking away from me by the thousands. Some could not get away too quickly. I didn't hold it against them; I understood that the tide was going out. Yet awful, almost palpable loneliness enveloped me as I stood on that shore, looking out after the fleeing masses, the words sticking in my throat, "Come back! Please, come back. It's me. I'm still the same person."

Then I saw a form moving in my direction, a familiar face coming toward me, struggling against the ebb tide. It seemed to be the image of one of my dear friends, who, as he emerged out of the water, ran toward me, his arms outstretched. How wonderful it was to see him!

As I gazed at the greeting card, I thought, *Thank God, real friends don't go out with the tide of public opinion.*

Roe Messner was that kind of true friend to me. Roe wrote to me regularly while I was in prison. The man who had lost so much money because of my demise at PTL still cared enough and trusted me enough to go to bat for me. By the spring of 1990, Tammy Faye and I could not afford to hire a dream team of lawyers to handle the appeal of my case. Our funds were depleted to the point we could barely afford a nightmare team of lawyers. Even though his own business was being dragged into bankruptcy largely because of us, Roe had become personally involved in the negotiations with appeals attorney Alan Dershowitz of Harvard Law School, hoping to secure the services of the famous lawyer to help make my case. Finally, Roe's efforts bore fruit. On May 31, 1990, Roe sent me a copy of a letter he had sent to Dr. Dershowitz:

Dear Dr. Dershowitz:

It was a pleasure to talk with you today on the telephone. I want to thank you for taking Rev. Bakker's case. Jim and I have great confidence in your ability to help him. Please coordinate everything with Mr. Harold Bender and begin working immediately. Enclosed you will find our check. Tammy is sending another check under a separate cover. This will total your retainer.

I am willing to help in any way I can. Our firm designed and built the buildings at PTL for Rev. Bakker. I do not believe he is guilty of overselling the hotels or other charges they have accused him of.

Sincerely,
Roe Messner

Roe's willingness to help was overwhelming to me. Certainly, as our primary builder, Roe's company had profited greatly by working for PTL. On the other hand, here was the one man who had lost more "real" money than any other person when PTL fell apart, yet he remained willing to put up still more of his own money in the effort to get me out of prison.

Another friend who surfaced quickly when the tide was rolling out was Bob Gass, a popular pastor and evangelist. With his quick wit and charming Irish brogue, Bob endeared himself to our PTL television audiences and appeared on numerous programs over the years. Early in my prison experience, Bob wrote me a powerful letter. In it he said:

In the past week I talked with . . . Malcolm Smith and Jamie Buckingham. They all said the same thing . . . that you are going to come out of there a new man, with a message you have never had before, to touch people you could never identify with. Those people are not a tiny stream, but rather a raging river of human need, disillusionment, emptiness, and bondage.

Bob went on to remind me of his own experience. For five years, Bob and his wife had traveled the evangelistic circuit. After that, they settled in Bangor, Maine, with a desperate need for identity, self-worth, and success. He found it by building the biggest church in northern New England. But it wasn't enough. His letter continued:

My self-worth was based on the acceptance I got from a crowd. That meant they were my jailer. Since they gave me self-worth, if I disap-

227

pointed them, they would take that self-worth away from me. They would also take away my living, my financial security, my future. I had to hide . . . whatever my issues were, they could never be known! I almost bled to death in secret. I marvel in retrospect at the things God brought me through.

Jim, even though you may not be able to believe what I'm going to say—all of your hurting emotions will move against the words I'm going to speak; even your surroundings will mock the truth of them—I want to tell you: not only are you going to come out of prison, but God's going to restore you to a ministry that will touch multitudes . . . but not at the performance level. Out of your own pain will come lessons that you will never forget. Knowledge is forged in the fires of affliction, and from it you will pour healing oil into the wounds of people that the church has passed by.

Waiting time will not be wasted time! I am praying out of the love I have for you, that God during these hours of darkness, pain, and pressure, will help you to turn to Him with all your heart and find in Him new insights, new understanding, new truth, that will first change your own life, then the lives of others.

I will always love you and be grateful to God for the blessings you brought into my life. For that reason, I will always be your friend, and I will always be there for you.

Friends because of Him,
Bob Gass

As I read Bob's letter, I was deeply touched by his concern for me, but I did not understand then how deeply I would be affected by the truths he shared with me—that out of my deep sense of loneliness I would learn things that would change my life and the lives of many others.

Pastor Karl Strader and his wife, Joyce, of Carpenter's Home Church in Lakeland, Florida, wrote to me every week. They always lifted my spirits and let me know that they were praying for my release from prison.

Another dear friend who wrote early and often was C. M. Ward. C. M. was a pioneer in Christian broadcasting, the inimitable voice of *Revivaltime*, the official worldwide radio program of the Assemblies of God denomination. In more than thirty years on the air, C. M. Ward never repeated a sermon.

Although C. M. and his wife Dorothy were already close to eighty years of age and in poor health when I entered prison, C. M. wrote to me faithfully. "Make no mistake about it," he said in one of his early letters,

"Dorothy and I remain your friends. To me 'steadfastness' is the essence of the Gospel." C. M. Ward never failed to include a gift in the form of a money order to help me pay for stamps, cards, and other commissary items.

One of the first friends to come visit me in prison was Kenneth Copeland, the renowned faith teacher. Kenneth has always demonstrated his faith by his works, so it was not surprising that he would be among the first to find his way to Rochester to see me. He did not simply stop in to say hello. Kenneth stayed with me for five hours and ministered to me amid the noise and confusion of the prison visitation room, sharing biblical insights with me.

Kenneth told me that his Native American heritage taught him the power of an earthly blood covenant. If a man is an Indian blood brother to another man, he would dedicate his life to the defense and protection of the other. The brothers would die for one another. How much more should we as Christians stand together in covenant, Kenneth encouraged me. When I lost PTL many of my longtime friends and employees switched loyalties faster than I could keep up with them. I realized then that for some, PTL had been little more than a paycheck. We had few covenant relationships.

On the other hand, in the midst of the 1987 scandal revelations, Kenneth and Gloria Copeland had invited Tammy Faye and me to their Believers Conference in Los Angeles, California. At a time when our names were being besmirched in every conceivable way, the Copelands put us up in a lovely hotel and arranged for us to sit right on the front row during the services. They knew Tammy and I were hurting, so they invited the ministers at the conference to come to our hotel room to pray for us privately. I will always be indebted to Kenneth and Gloria Copeland for their kindness and compassion at a time when the tide had gone out in our lives.

Others who visited me during the early days of my imprisonment included Reverend Owen Carr, the founder of the first full-powered Christian television station in Chicago. Owen wrote numerous letters to me and constantly attempted to lift my spirits by giving me scriptural words of encouragement. Owen almost made me cry when in one of his early letters he wrote, "I was your friend before you went to prison. I am your friend while you are in prison. I will be your friend after you leave prison." Like C. M. Ward, Owen always added a bit of what he called "practical encouragement" in every letter—a twenty-five-dollar money order I could use to purchase items from the commissary.

Paul Olson was also a regular visitor in the early days of my incarceration at Rochester. Paul is the son of Pastor Russell Olson, the pastor of the church Tammy and I attended before we were married. Paul is now a powerful evangelist in his own right, crisscrossing the world in his travels, yet he always found time in his busy schedule to stop long enough to see me. In almost all of Paul's services around the world, he asked his audience to pray for me.

Herb and Fran Moore, faithful friends who stood by my family and me through the deepest travail of my trial in 1989, were also frequent visitors, traveling all the way across the nation to spend a few hours with me in the visiting room. Singer, songwriter, and speaker Mike Murdock often rerouted his travel plans through Minnesota to see me as well.

And of course, Pastor Phil Shaw and his wife, Faith, for whom visiting me and ministering to my family and me had become something of a mission, were regular guests in the F.M.C. visiting room. Sometimes Phil and Faith came to see me together; at other times Phil visited me alone. Regardless, they always made me feel so special. Phil often spent all day with me, sometimes talking theology or current events, at other times sitting for hours in relative silence, just being there with me, as the awful reality of my forty-five-year sentence began to set in. Frequently Phil came to see me on his day off, so he would not be taking too much time away from his own congregation to minister to me. Phil was such a humble man, with a strong but gentle servant's heart. I was humbled just being around him. Phil was more than a friend; he was like a spiritual shepherd. He listened calmly to me when I ranted and raved. He encouraged me to keep my eyes on Jesus when I reviewed the various personalities involved with my demise at PTL and subsequent imprisonment. Phil never put me down. He never judged me; he just loved me as a brother.

Sam Houston, the unit manager of Building Two, where I was housed, and Mr. Greg Kropp, the correctional counselor, through whom all individuals who wished to visit me were screened, insisted that I be treated the same as any other inmate. Nevertheless, no other inmate that I knew of at F.M.C. had nearly as many pastoral visits as I did. Although strict procedures were followed for my friends to receive permission to visit me, I appreciated the prison officials' willingness to allow them to come. Later when Tom Peterson took over the job of correctional counselor, he too was extremely kind and helpful when it came to facilitating my visitors.

Despite the many cards, letters, and visits I received during those early days, a gnawing loneliness continued to eat at my soul. It wasn't a loneliness for people; it was a loneliness for God. I simply did not know where He was. Worse yet, I felt that He had forgotten my address. I attempted to keep busy by pouring myself into the various clubs I had joined and by preparing and teaching the motivational material I used in the smoking cessation course. I needed the activity and the interaction with people that the clubs provided, and I needed to absorb the motivational principles I was teaching. But all the positive principles I was espousing could not satisfy the deepest needs of my soul.

I believed in the motivational message. When I had been at PTL, I had often simply taken a "positive thinking" type of message and put a Scripture to it and labeled it "positive confession." Now, I was beginning to understand how severely I had cheated my listeners. Although the positive message was true and was helpful, it was not enough. It was similar to going to a banquet and eating only the appetizer, ignoring the more nutritious food.

I was learning that although it was marvelous to be motivated and it was an important piece in the puzzle, mere positive thinking did not meet my needs when I was lying in my bunk by myself. I was still alone. I was still lonely. I still woke up in prison every morning, wondering, *What in the world am I doing here? Is this a dream?*

The mail continued to pour in, and along with it came the usual assortment of encouraging letters as well as the hate mail. Several of the photographs for which I had posed with people in the visiting room were now showing up in tabloid newspapers, accompanied by the wildest of headlines and stories. One of the signed photos of my family and me appeared in a tabloid under the headline, "Jim Bakker Cowers in Cell—Terrified He'll Be Raped by Fellow Inmates." The story went on to describe how I never went anywhere in prison without my protective cellmate known as "Big Doc." Tom Brandon got quite a charge out of that one! It was a made-up story. *No one would try to rape me in this prison, would they?* I thought. I had been told that one of the reasons I had been placed in F.M.C. Rochester was for my own protection. The human species has an incredible ability to adapt. Although I was still on edge, I was beginning to relax and feel a little more secure. That, I was soon to discover, was a major mistake.

Another scandal sheet ran a color photo of Tom and me presenting a certificate to one of the inmates who had completed our smoking cessation course. The headline? "Jailbird Jim Bakker Is Back on Top—With a New Flock Behind Bars."

I also received numerous books, magazines, and articles from people around the world. Many of the materials I tried to prevent the other inmates, especially the new Christians, from seeing. The materials were just too divisive. One book pounded away at what is wrong with the Pentecostals; another castigated all the Catholics; one book that was receiving a lot of attention described everything that was wrong with television evangelists. Many of the Christian magazines were not much better than the tabloids, going on regular excursions into "yellow journalism" in their attempt to uncover the latest scandal in the church.

Of course, I also received many wonderful, uplifting books in the mail. One such book, *Through the Wilderness of Loneliness*, by Tim Hansel, was literally life-changing to me.

Tim Hansel is the founder of Summit Expedition, a wilderness survival school and ministry. Often in his work, Tim led groups of mountain climbers and hikers, youth and adults, on exciting trips and retreats throughout the western ranges of the U.S. In the mid-1970s, as Tim was guiding an expedition up the side of a mountain, he was unaware that the bottom of his climbing shoes had iced over. Tim lost his footing and literally fell off the side of the mountain. He dropped a distance the height of a five-story building, landing on his back at the bottom of a crevasse.

It was a miracle that Tim Hansel did not die on the spot. Amazingly, he survived, but unfortunately, his life was never the same. From that day to now, Tim has lived with chronic pain racking his body. It never goes away. The pain is there when he goes to bed at night; it is there when he awakens in the morning. It is Tim's constant companion.

Tim Hansel knows what it's like to be on a mountaintop. He also knows the desolate feeling of having to slog through a hot, dry wilderness experience—both in a physical sense, and in the spiritual. I had never met Tim, but Sue Williams, a woman in East Hampton, New York, who had sent me many other books as part of her church's prison ministry, saw Tim's book on a book table, was intrigued by the title, and thought it might interest me. The book came at the exact moment I needed it.

As I read the book, I immediately began to identify with Tim's experience of falling off the side of a mountain and living in the valley of loneliness as a result. More than that, however, I began to find clues as to how to endure the chronic pain that followed and how to survive in that valley after the fall. In the early pages of his book, Tim quotes Elisabeth Elliot, a woman familiar with valley walking. Elisabeth says, "That's where faith begins . . . in the wilderness, when you are all alone and afraid, when things don't make any sense."[1]

Tim refers to Clifton Burke, who says, "There is no shortcut to wholeness: if you want to reach the Promised Land you must first go through the wilderness."[2] Tim went on to emphasize that there is no avoiding life when you are going through the wilderness experience.

Tim told of a time when he had been speaking to a large crowd. They had clapped their hands and cheered him as a great and entertaining speaker. But when the auditorium was empty, Tim walked out alone and drove back to his hotel room, where he had intentionally left the lights on so the room would not seem so dark and lonely when he returned.

The light didn't help.

The pain he had been able to put out of his mind for a short time while he was speaking to the group came back with a vengeance. He tried to sleep but could not because of the pain, yet he was too tired and emotionally drained to do much else. Exhausted, Tim closed his eyes and hoped and prayed morning would come quickly. It didn't. Tim tried to write. Just then, at one of his weakest moments, Tim Hansel wrote in his journal words that God used to begin prying open the ever-thickening shell I was building around my heart. Tim wrote, "The loneliness was so bad tonight that it sucked all the oxygen out of the room. It was so intense it felt like it could peel the paint off the walls."[3]

Whoooom! Tim's words exactly described what I had been feeling since coming to prison. I was amazed that another person had put into words my exact emotions.

Tim continued, "Lately I have experienced a loneliness so deep that I feel as though I need a second heart to contain all the pain."[4]

Yes! I wanted to shout. *That's how I have been feeling.* My heart had been so badly bruised over the past three years, I had pulled into myself and I did not want to be hurt anymore.

I read Tim's book. And reread it. I underlined things that spoke to my heart and mind. And then I read it again. Tim wrote:

Loneliness does not always come from emptiness. Sometimes it is because we are too full . . . full of ourselves. Full of activity. Full of distractions. Paradoxically, if I want to heal the loneliness in my life, I've got to get away . . . to be alone with God.[5]

Tim suggested that part of the reason God allows us to walk through the valleys in our lives is so we will learn to depend on Him in new ways.

But I can't even hear God's voice anymore! I talked back to the pages. *I feel like God has abandoned me.*

No, Tim wrote, "Loneliness is not a time of abandonment . . . it just feels that way. It's actually a time of encounter at new levels with the only One who can fill that empty place in our hearts."[6]

I had been reading Aleksandr Solzhenitsyn's books about the same time as I had received Tim's. I had even written in the front of my Bible one of the statements the brilliant Russian writer had penned while in prison: "When you have robbed a man of everything, he is no longer in your power. He is free again." I felt like I had lost everything, but I in no way felt free . . . yet.

Through the combined impact of Hansel's and Solzhenitsyn's books, I caught the first dim glimpse of what God might be doing in my life. Tim drove home the message:

> Perhaps one of the main reasons we fall into loneliness and despair is
> that we are so preoccupied with ourselves, so invested in our own egos.
> We're so concerned with how we are doing that we can't seem to get a
> clear focus on what God is doing in us and around us.[7]

Could it be? I wondered. *Could it possibly be true that I was in prison by the very design of God? Was there really a larger purpose behind my imprisonment, as some of my friends had implied?*

I didn't know where God was, but I was not about to attribute my loneliness to God's plan for my life. That thought did not fit into my theology very well, so I tossed it aside.

Still, Hansel's words (and the Spirit of God through them) were insistent.

> We cannot overcome loneliness by trying to escape it. We must lean
> into it, and thereby transform it into solitude. We must not just keep
> trying to avoid the loneliness by constant distraction. He is here. He is
> here. He is here. We must push through the loneliness to joy.[8]

Tim Hansel taught me how to turn my loneliness into solitude with God. What a difference! "Loneliness," says Tim, "parches our lips for the living God, makes us hungry for His presence."[9] I learned that

Loneliness is feeling alone. Solitude is being alone. Loneliness feels frantic. Solitude is still and focused. Loneliness focuses on external circumstances. Solitude focuses on the inner adventure. Loneliness relies on what others think and say about you. Solitude relies on what God says about you and to you.[10]

At this point in my life *Through the Wilderness of Loneliness* impacted me second only to the Bible. No other book has been more useful to me. The transformation did not come quickly or easily for me. I still felt as though I had not heard from God in several years.

In early 1980, I had sinned seriously, but when I repented and sought God's forgiveness, I knew He was there. I knew He forgave me, whether other people chose to believe that or not, or whether they chose to forgive me or not. God continued to use my life and seemed to bless everything I set out to do in His name. The ministry kept getting bigger and bigger. Then, after the disclosure of my sin and my subsequent departure from PTL, nothing I tried to do in God's name bore any fruit. Nothing worked. I tried to start another television program in Charlotte. It didn't work. I tried to begin again in Florida; that also soon fell apart. Everything I tried turned to dung.

What do you do when God doesn't hear you? Where does a person go who feels that God doesn't want him anymore?

Even though God had blessed me so much in the past, I began to think, *Is there no hope for me? Were my detractors correct?* I relived the words of my accusers almost every day. I thought, *Well, maybe my sins were too awful. Maybe I hurt other people and the kingdom of God so badly that my sins were beyond God's willingness to forgive me.*

The words Tammy and I had said so many times at the close of our television programs, "God loves you; He really does!" now taunted me.

Finally, as I read Hansel's book, I felt that there might be hope. I renewed my cries to God. "God, please talk to me! Show me something, anything, just please let me know that You care, and that You haven't given up on me."

Then one night, I had a dream. It was unlike any dream I had ever experienced before. The colors in the dream were so vivid; it was like dreaming in blazing Technicolor! In this dream, I was sitting next to Jesus. He was dressed in white and blue and He seemed to have a brilliance and depth like diamonds—yet like nothing I had ever seen in my life!

As I was sitting there, Jesus reached up and pulled out a slice of His own eye. It looked like a contact lens. He reached over and gently put the thin slice of His eye into mine and said, "I want you to see everything and everyone through My eyes."

Then, just as suddenly as the dream began, it was over and I woke up. I knew that something supernatural had happened. And I felt it was the first time in several years that God was speaking to me in an overt way again. But what did it mean?

I began to ask, as much myself as God, "How can I see everything and everybody through the eyes of Jesus?"

The answer, whether from God or my conscience or my own mind, was crystal clear: *I must read every word Jesus said, because if I know Him and His words, then I can see everything through His eyes.*

Instead of reading my usual two motivational or inspirational books each day, I began reading the Gospels every day. I read Matthew, Mark, Luke, and John. I didn't bounce from one book in the Bible to another; I studied every spoken word of Jesus recorded in the Bible. I got a red-letter edition of the Bible from the chapel library, the words written in red indicating the words of Jesus. I literally wrote down every word Christ spoke as recorded in the Scriptures. Then I wrote a condensed version of the verses to help me remember them. For instance, "Love your neighbor." "Love God." "Do not sin." As I studied the Scripture, I began to see things in the Bible that I had never seen before. I made up my mind then that I was going to ask God all the difficult questions I'd skirted over in my busy years. The first question I asked God was, "Why are there so many dying people here, and why can't I help them? I'm not allowed to preach. I don't even feel welcome at chapel. What can I do?"

I was surprised at the answer I heard from God: "You are arrogant. You think that you are the only person I have in this prison. I have many others here. I am God."

And then God said to me, "I did not bring you to prison to minister. I brought you here to get to know Me."

CHAPTER

23

Power Plays

FROM THE MOMENT MY LAWYERS REALIZED I WAS
going to be convicted and possibly sentenced to prison in the fall of 1989,
they began talking about an appeal of my case. I paid little attention to their
legal wranglings. I was numb.

In recent years, many people have asked me, "Why didn't you hire a
'dream team' of lawyers?" Quite simply, we could not afford it. As I mentioned previously, between 1987 and 1989, Tammy Faye's and my financial
resources had been depleted except for the salary we received from New
Covenant Church in Orlando, so we had little money to go lawyer shopping. Most of our salable possessions were long gone, sold in our futile
attempts to keep the television ministry solvent and to make ends meet.

Even my retirement funds were gone. PTL had established a retirement fund for Tammy and me through my denomination, the Assemblies
of God. By the time I went to trial in 1989, our retirement fund had grown
to nearly $1 million. Shortly after I went to prison, our retirement savings
were divided by the Internal Revenue Service and my lawyers as payment
for their legal representation in the original charges brought against me. It
was only through the kindness of people who had generously contributed
to a legal defense fund we had established that we were able to mount any
defense at all. Yet despite the sacrificial gifts of many friends and family,
when it came time to hire lawyers who would appeal my case, our options
were few. Roger McDuff, a singer who had appeared on our PTL television

programs, recommended to Tammy a legal team within our price range headed by an attorney from Houston, Texas. Although he had done none of the work on our original case and was virtually ignorant about the massive amount of material involved, we hired him anyway. Not long after that, we were able to secure the services of Harvard law professor Dr. Alan Dershowitz to handle a part of our appeal as well.

Professor Dershowitz is known as one of the leading appeals lawyers in the world. With his bespectacled, freckled face and wiry red hair, Alan Dershowitz looked like a soft-spoken, unassuming professor. But once in a courtroom or in front of a camera, Dershowitz turned into a bulldog. He was a full professor at Harvard by age twenty-eight. He was a frequent guest on television shows, including *Nightline*, *60 Minutes*, and most of the popular talk shows. His clients had included millionaire Claus von Bulow, who had been accused of trying to murder his wife; kidnapped newspaper heiress Patty Hearst; New York hotel owner Leona Helmsley; and Wall Street's Michael Milken. The fact that Alan Dershowitz would even take my case gave me a ray of hope for the first time. He was convinced that my appeal had validity since several points of law had been violated in my trial. I wanted to believe Dershowitz's optimistic outlook, but I kept remembering the prison adage, "You ain't got nothin' comin'."

The appeal process was scheduled to begin on May 25, 1990, but was delayed while the courts prepared the transcripts of my trial. For several months prior to this date, my lawyers had been requesting transcripts of the original trial so they could be used in preparing my appeal. The transcripts were not completed, they were told, but they would be forthcoming. When they finally came, they did not come cheaply; it cost in excess of fifteen thousand dollars simply to obtain the written record of my trial. On June 15, 1990, my written appeal was filed before the Fourth Circuit Court of Appeals in Richmond, Virginia. The prosecutors then had time to file their legal briefs reasoning why the trial had been fair and why I should spend the rest of my sentence in prison. Throughout the summer of 1990, the process ground along.

Back in Florida, Tammy Faye was fighting an appeal of a different sort. After finally finding a new location for our church, a former Tupperware training center in an industrial section of south Orlando, Tammy Faye and members of the congregation had conducted only one service at the new location before they were closed down by the county zoning board. Ironically, the board said it was okay to have our ministry offices there, and it was even permissible to broadcast worship services on television from the location, but it was not legal to conduct worship services in the building.

Traffic and parking problems were the reasons cited. Although the former occupants of the building had conducted seminars with nearly five hundred people in attendance, it was deemed illegal for people to gather to worship at the same location.

The zoning board allowed in that area of Orlando everything from a restaurant to a bank. One official had quipped that the location could be used as a nuclear waste dump under the current zoning codes, but not for church services.

Tammy Faye and the congregation cried, "Foul!" For six weeks they made their case, appealing to the Orange County commissioners. Interestingly, even the American Civil Liberties Union got involved in the fracas . . . on the side of the church! Eventually, the zoning adjustment board ruled that the church posed no potential problems to safety, parking, or traffic, and the church was allowed to open for services once again. Even though Tammy was elated at the church's victory, handling this situation and the many other details involved in leading a congregation by herself was beginning to take a heavy toll on her. "I need you home, Jim," she said to me repeatedly.

The NBC-TV movie *Fall from Grace*, the supposed "balanced and dramatic" portrayal of Jim and Tammy Bakker and PTL, aired early in May. The movie riveted prisoners to the set in the TV room. I had no desire to see it, so I went back to my cell and crawled into my bunk. One inmate after another called into my cell, "Come on, Jim! Don't you want to see yourself in a movie?" No, I did not. I could hardly remember who the real Jim Bakker was. In my counseling sessions with prison psychologist Dr. Daniel Foster, we were trying to work back through my life to separate the real me from the images of me as "Jim Bakker, television personality" and to discover what God expected of me. At that moment I was not interested in seeing a Hollywood caricature of myself.

I kept busy throughout the spring and summer of 1990 by immersing myself in teaching the smoking cessation course, even though at times I was so depressed I did not want to get out of bed. Often my only motivation to do anything at all was the knowledge that Tom and I had committed ourselves to helping the inmates who attended our classes kick the smoking habit. The class provided me with a sense of being needed.

The highlight of the summer came when the prison Jaycees hosted the annual Fourth of July Inmates' Family Picnic. This was one of two times each year when the inmates and family members could actually eat together outside of the visiting area. The other occasion, the Christmas dinner, was also sponsored by the Jaycees. At the Fourth of July picnic, inmates and their family members were permitted to sit on the lawn in a roped-off area in full view of the razor-wire fence or at picnic tables that had been collected from all over the compound and brought inside the ropes for this special occasion. Apart from the ominous fence looming nearby and the guards patrolling the area, we were able to have a seminormal picnic, including hot dogs, hamburgers, baked beans, fried chicken, potato salad, watermelon, the works. For a few hours, Tammy Faye, Jamie, Tammy Sue, baby James, and I were almost able to forget that I was in prison. We were simply a family enjoying a picnic in the Minnesota sunshine. But when it was over, I went back to a cell, and my family members went back to their hotel room, and then back across the country.

Each week, my meetings with Dr. Foster were becoming more and more helpful in acclimating me to prison life. I had just begun an upturn on my emotional roller-coaster ride when I learned that a deal had been accepted by U.S. Bankruptcy Judge Thurmond Bishop to sell Heritage USA to California-based evangelist Morris Cerullo for $52 million, about ten cents on the dollar of what the total ministry was worth at the time I resigned as president of PTL. Morris had been a guest on our television program and hosted his own TV show as well. At the time the judge accepted Cerullo's offer, the evangelist placed $7 million in an escrow account to secure the purchase of the Inspirational Satellite Network, the prize plum at Heritage USA. Morris had until November 2, 1990, to come up with the other $45 million.

Of course Morris Cerullo was certainly not the first to have designs on Heritage USA and the powerful satellite network the PTL supporters and I had assembled there. Jerry Falwell (and others) claimed that Jimmy Swaggart wanted it, a rumor Swaggart vehemently denies to this day. Jerry Falwell took control of it and eventually realized that he had to get away from it. Within a few months after Jerry had encouraged my resignation, he and his associates took Heritage USA and the Inspirational Satellite Network into bankruptcy.

After Jerry Falwell and his friends left Heritage USA, Dr. David Clark, an employee of the Christian Broadcasting Network, became the trustee of PTL. David Clark remained in control of PTL from late 1987 though the summer of 1988. Sam Johnson, a former employee of mine, who had been appointed by Jerry Falwell as pastor of Heritage Church, did his best to spearhead a reorganizational plan to save Heritage USA and the television ministry, but his plan never got off the ground. At a 1988 meeting with James Robison serving as a neutral party between us, I pleaded with

Sam to allow me to return to help pull the ministry back together, but he said that because I was under disciplinary action by the Assemblies of God, he felt that as a minister in that denomination he could not allow me to come back.

I had offered to meet with Reverend Roland Blount, the district superintendent of the South Carolina Assemblies of God, under whose jurisdiction the church now functioned. Reverend Blount, a personable and caring man, had agreed without reservation to a meeting with his district board and me concerning my possible restoration. But then I received a letter from him stating that I had already had plenty of opportunity to appear before the North Carolina presbytery, the district with which I was ordained and under which the church had originally been established at Heritage Village in Charlotte. Therefore, my request for a meeting to discuss reconciliation was denied. The possibility of my returning to Heritage USA with any sort of blessing from my denomination was a dead issue. Along with the letter, the South Carolina presbytery sent me copies of a batch of letters.

As I looked at the letters, I could hardly believe my eyes. They were letters that had been sent to me via registered mail at PTL, requesting me to appear before the North Carolina Board of Presbyters. These letters were from North Carolina District Superintendent Charles Cookman, and they were warm and kind and held out the possibility of pursuing a restoration process. But because I had not responded to the letters, the Assemblies of God leadership had assumed that I was not interested in working with them any longer.

Not only had I not received the original letters, I did not recognize the name of a single person who had signed for the registered mail. As I looked at the dates I began to piece together what had happened. The letters had been sent to PTL while I was still in California in the months immediately after the news of my resignation had been made public. They were clearly addressed to me personally, but not a single one of the original letters was ever forwarded to me following my ouster from PTL. I would never have known the letters existed had not the copies been sent to me by Reverend Blount more than a year later.

In September 1988, I had hoped to buy Heritage USA and return it to the PTL Partners—whom I considered to be the rightful owners—but I was unable to obtain the necessary funds. That same month, Stephen Mernick, a Jewish real-estate investor from Toronto, backed out of his $65 million offer. By late 1989 a number of people, including billionaire David Murdock, owner of Cannon Village in Kannapolis, South Carolina, and the Christian Broadcasting Network's founder, and my former boss, Pat Robertson, had their sights set on PTL assets. According to the *Charlotte Observer*, Pat and CBN actually submitted a bid to purchase the PTL satellite network.[1]

My friend and the chief building contractor of PTL, Roe Messner, also let it be known that he intended to offer over $50 million for Heritage USA. George Shinn, owner of the NBA basketball team the Charlotte Hornets, and Cy Bahakel, owner of a group of television stations including one in Charlotte, also expressed an interest in the property. Oral Roberts and his son Richard announced their intentions to purchase the television network in July of 1990.

But by August 5, 1990, the top bidder was Morris Cerullo, thanks to the financial backing of a group of Malaysian Christian businessmen. Cerullo's offer was accepted by the bankruptcy judge.

Cerullo emphasized to the press that Tammy Faye and I would not be offered roles in his new ministry, which he dubbed "New Heritage USA" and the "New Inspirational Satellite Network." He did say that we were welcome to visit whenever we might like. Concerning Tammy and me, Cerullo said, "We're not looking for their endorsement. We're not looking for them to have any role. They'll be welcome on the property, just as anyone would be welcome on the property."

From my vantage point, it seemed doubtful that I would be visiting Heritage USA anytime soon.

In prison, I learned of the proceedings at PTL with mixed emotions. I wanted it to survive, yet in watching the various bidders fighting over it, I felt as though people were fighting over my own child. Although I had always known Heritage USA belonged to the PTL Partners and ultimately to God Himself, the Lord had used me in many ways to give birth to the place. At the 1979 groundbreaking for Heritage USA, when we had dedicated the property to God, I prayed a prayer like I had never prayed before. I said, "God, I dedicate this property, Heritage USA, to You today. If it ever be used for anything other than the gospel of Jesus Christ, let it be accursed."

At the time I spoke those words, I did not even realize what I had said. Years later, someone showed me a transcript of the dedication ceremony, and I was shocked to see my prayer in print. I had never before prayed a curse on anything or anybody, nor have I since.

Now, as I watched the legal scrapping to gain control of Heritage USA, all I could do was hope and pray that it would fall into the hands of a group who would use the property for its intended purpose. The sellout was heartrending to read about or talk about, so I rarely did.

I had numerous visitors during the spring and summer of 1990, including Jimmy Blackwood of the famous Blackwood Brothers Quartet and Jimmy's wife, Mona. Jerry and Sandy Barnard visited from San Diego where Jerry was pastoring at the time. Herman Rohde, an executive with the Minnesota Assemblies of God, also visited. My cousin, Marge Klages, sort of the matriarch of my family, visited shortly after I learned of the sale of Heritage USA. Marge and her sister Beverly Halgren greatly lifted my spirits by talking about our childhood days, growing up in Muskegon, Michigan. Marge had experienced some tough times with the death of her husband and her beloved son, and I thought, *If she can keep trusting God after all that she has been through, so can I.*

Other visitors that summer included Don Argue, president of North Central Bible College and now president of the National Association of Evangelicals. My faithful friends, Mike Murdock, Paul Olson, and Phil and Faith Shaw also came to see me regularly.

The month of September was a big month at F.M.C. Rochester. It was the time when inmates who had completed their Adult Basic Education, GED, or any other educational program went through formal graduation ceremonies, complete with cap and gown. The warden and other prison officials handed out the diplomas as the inmates filed by in the chapel. The diplomas were then placed in the prisoners' permanent record files. Besides the recognition that accompanied graduation, the graduates were allowed to stuff themselves with good food and all the cookies they could eat following the ceremonies. That in itself made graduation a big deal.

Dr. Westrick insisted that all the men who had completed Tom's and my smoking cessation course be honored along with the other graduates by going through the formal ceremonies. That was fine with Tom and me; it meant we could go to the ceremony and eat some good food too! It was rewarding, however, to watch our course participants traipsing across the platform to receive their "Nonsmoking" certificates from the warden.

Our course, which had begun in May, was beginning to be an effective deterrent to smoking in the prison. Although a large percentage of the men in prison smoked, about 60 percent of the inmates who had taken our course remained smoke-free four months after completing the course. We recognized that our results required long-term data to substantiate them, but usually if a person can beat a habit, even an addictive habit, for six to eight weeks, the person has the potential to remain free of the addiction.

Our outstanding success rate soon caught the attention of the staff at Mayo Clinic, probably with the help of Dr. Westrick. The famous medical center was also involved with a smoking cessation program. Mayo's Dr. David S. Colville, of the hospital's division of hypertension and internal medicine, sat in on one of our classes and afterward talked at length with Tom and me about our program. Dr. Colville expressed surprise at our high rate of success, even though our course participants had not been tracked for a long period of time. Dr. Colville told us that Mayo's success rate was one of the highest in the world, in the 20 percent range. Most other smoking cessation programs averaged a success rate of only around 6 percent. Over 60 percent of our graduates were still walking around smoke-free after four months, despite living in an extremely smoke-saturated environment!

In September my family lost a dear little friend; her name was Tinkerbell. When Jamie Charles and Tammy Sue were just young children, Tammy Sue and I were shopping at the mall one day. Before long, we were looking in the window of the pet shop, watching a litter of kittens. The store clerk asked if we would like to have a free kitten.

You can imagine how long it took for Tammy Sue to answer that question. We picked out a pure-white ball of fluffy fur and took it home with us. We named the kitten Tinkerbell, and for the next thirteen, almost fourteen years, she was queen of the house. She grew fat and lazy but always seemed to sense when a family member was not feeling well. Then she would lie on the bed with the sick person until he or she was well.

When Jamie was three years old, Tinkerbell had kittens. Jamie wanted to show the kittens to everyone on television, so we allowed him to bring the basket of kittens onto the set at PTL. As Jamie walked onto the set, somehow he dropped the basket, and suddenly, on live television, we had kittens running every which way! As Jamie, Tammy Faye, and I scurried around the set trying to gather the kittens, the audience roared with delight.

When our world fell apart and we were forced to move away from Heritage USA, Tinkerbell moved with us. She snuggled close to Tammy Faye, especially after I went to prison. Then in September, after almost fourteen years with our family, Tinkerbell died . . . and I was not there. Jamie and Tammy Sue wept as though they had lost a sibling.

To some people, the passing of an animal may seem insignificant. But any pet owner understands how that animal grows to become a member of the family. For me, Tinkerbell was yet another loss.

Our family mourning was turned to celebration, however, when on September 24, 1990, Tammy Sue gave birth to a six-pound, ten-ounce baby boy, Jonathan Douglas. Tammy Faye drove up from Orlando to visit her new grandbaby for a few days, and each night during her stay, I called from prison to talk to members of the family. Tammy Faye said it was almost like we were a family again . . . except that I was not there in person. I remembered so clearly Tammy Sue's giving birth to our first grandbaby, my namesake, James. Our entire family rode with Tammy Sue to the hospital. As Tammy Sue was giving birth, our family paced the hallway along with her husband, Doug, and his mother. Just seconds after James was born, we were allowed to peek inside the door to look at him wearing his tiny little tossle hat to keep his head warm.

As I talked to the family members by phone in the days following Jonathan's birth, I knew I was missing so much. I couldn't wait to see my new grandson, Jonathan, but he would be more than a year old before I ever saw him face-to-face.

Near the end of September, I learned of a difficult development in the life of someone I had once considered to be one of my best friends, Doug Wead. Doug had been a frequent guest on our television programs in the mid-1970s and early 1980s. He was a tremendous inspirational speaker and was a favorite among our audiences. In the mid-1980s Doug made a decision that would have profound ramifications on both our lives. He backed George Bush early in the vice president's quest for the presidency in 1988. Doug left the ranks of professional motivational speaking and writing, where he had carved a comfortable niche, and threw himself headlong into the Bush campaign organization. His desire to see George Bush in the White House became an obsession. For several years, Doug worked full-time for the campaign; in the process he lost a lot of money and a lot of friends.

Another friend who had become politically involved in the mid-1980s was Pat Robertson, host of *The 700 Club*. His political clout and his campaign war chest were growing on an almost daily basis.

In 1986, Pat came to visit me at Heritage USA. I had not talked with him personally about his political aspirations—actually, I had not talked to Pat about much of anything. Tammy and I had hosted many daily programs on CBN and after almost eight years had resigned. Pat and I were never close after that. Nevertheless, I was delighted when I learned that he wanted to stop by Heritage USA, and I welcomed him with open arms. Following our visit, a guest on my television show brought up the subject of politics and a Christian's role in the political arena. Without endorsing Pat or any other candidate, I emphatically supported Pat's right to run for president of the United States. Just because Pat was a Christian minister, I contended, he should not be excluded from our nation's political process or automatically denied an opportunity to seek a role of political leadership if he were elected to it. I made a generic statement supporting Pat's right to run; I could have just as easily made the statement about a member of the ACLU or a Buddhist or any other citizen. I believed in the American Constitution that provides this freedom for all.

Since the late 1970s, it was obvious that PTL was growing. As the host of a daily talk show seen by millions of people, I wielded some measure of influence, and I had been courted by politicians of all sorts. I had been to the White House on several occasions and had flown in *Air Force One*, the presidential airplane, with Jimmy Carter. I had been a guest of President and Mrs. Reagan at the White House as well as at their home in California. During one of my visits to Washington, while the Reagans were in office, I met then Vice President George Bush. On another visit, Barbara Bush even invited Tammy Faye to her upstairs sitting room at the vice presidential residence to look at some of her needlepoint. I was not an enemy of the Bush presidential campaign.

Nor, however, was I a card-carrying member of the Moral Majority in the 1970s and 1980s. I have always been opposed to preachers publicly throwing their spiritual influence after a political candidate, regardless of the person's party affiliation. I have felt that as a private citizen, preachers have a responsibility to vote and to be involved in the political process as well as to help their congregations recognize their responsibility as citizens to do the same. But beyond that, it always seemed like a step down for a preacher to publicly endorse a particular person for political office. More important, I felt a minister should not alienate any group, but be able to minister to "whosoever will." My policy had always been if the president or any other leader called for prayer or spiritual help whether he be Democrat, Republican, or Independent, I would be there. I felt that was my spiritual responsibility as a minister of the gospel.

When George Bush came to Charlotte for a speech in 1986, I received an invitation to have lunch with the vice president privately in his downtown Charlotte hotel room. I gladly accepted. By this time, Doug Wead had become one of George Bush's closest advisers, especially in regard to religious issues and specifically those concerns of the Christian community that made up a large voting bloc in our nation.

Consequently, I was not surprised when, shortly after our lunch began, the vice president brought up the subject of Christianity. I quickly realized that the future presidential candidate was interested in how he might make inroads with the evangelical Christian voters. In the presence of only his personal aide and my assistant, George Bush probed, "Jim, I believe in God, but I am just not comfortable with the term 'born again.' That is not a term we use in our church tradition."

"Well, do you believe the Bible is the inspired Word of God?" I asked.

"Yes, I do."

"Do you believe that Jesus Christ is the Son of God, that He was born of a virgin, and that He died on the cross for our sins? Do you accept Him as your Lord and Savior?" I asked the vice president.

"Yes, yes, I do," George Bush replied.

"Well, that's what being born again is all about."

The vice president and I went on to talk about prayer, and he emphatically declared that a day never went by when he did not ask for God's help and wisdom in dealing with his responsibilities.

Perhaps one reason the vice president asked me to lunch was so that I would support his efforts to become president and use my influence in any way I could to that end. But because of my past association with Pat Robertson and my recent support of his right to run for president, some members of the vice president's staff were not sure whose side I would be on in the coming primary elections. One of those people was my good friend Doug Wead.

By the time the election campaigns had begun in earnest in 1987, my problems had already become national news. Doug was a key player in the Bush campaign, still advising the vice president as to how he could best win the hearts and votes of the Christian voters. That is why, no doubt, Doug advised George Bush at this point to stay away from me. Doug later confessed to me that in the midst of my troubles, before I was ever even brought before a grand jury, much less indicted for a crime, George Bush asked Doug, "Should I intervene to help Jim Bakker?"

Doug replied, "Don't get involved. It could hurt you politically."

Doug Wead rode the Bush political bandwagon all the way to the top. He helped coalesce the evangelical community behind George Bush and in 1988 even wrote Bush's biography, *George Bush: Man of Integrity*, in an effort to convince conservative evangelicals that the candidate was "one of them." As a result, George Bush received a higher percentage of the evangelical vote in the 1988 election than he did any other single voting bloc. Once in the White House, Doug continued to serve as President Bush's liaison to the conservative religious community, which included Catholics and evangelical Protestant denominations.

Doug's demise came in July of 1990 after President Bush's staff members began inviting liberal and left-wing leaders to White House events. Among the groups invited to various bill signings and other events in the spring and summer of 1990 were representatives from The National Gay & Lesbian Task Force, the ACLU, *Playboy* magazine, and the gay newspaper *The Washington Blade*. Conservative groups criticized the president. In an effort at damage control, Doug Wead wrote a letter that strongly reaffirmed the president's commitment to traditional family values. Doug further stated that the president's staff had not served him well by inviting such groups. Within weeks, on Friday, July 13, Doug Wead was fired. As often happens in the political arena, when a problem occurs, a scapegoat must be found and fired. Doug Wead became such a political sacrifice.

Tammy Faye sent me a news article describing Doug Wead's undoing. The man reflected in the article was not the man I knew, a man whose children had grown up with mine.

I never knew Doug to be intolerant; in fact, I felt he was often liberal in his dealings with others. Furthermore it struck me as extremely ironic that Doug would be dismissed from a conservative White House for being intolerant to homosexual groups. His own brother, whom he loved dearly, lived an openly homosexual lifestyle and died of AIDS.

As I read of Doug's termination, I was reminded afresh of the fickleness of politics and the corrupting influence of power. But if I thought being in prison would shield me from political intrigues, I was greatly mistaken. I was about to encounter a political figure unlike any I had ever known.

24

Lyndon LaRouche

AS I WALKED TOWARD MY CELL ONE AFTERNOON IN October 1990, I could not help noticing the large, imposing figure standing next to a pushcart in front of the cell. The cart was loaded with books, a few personal items, and a drab wardrobe of prison-issued khaki clothing. The disheveled man turned his head slightly, and I immediately recognized him as Lyndon LaRouche. I had first met Lyndon months before and had often talked with him briefly in the visitation room, when I introduced him to some of my guests, but I really did not know the man. Now, as I got closer to my cell, I realized Lyndon LaRouche was moving into my cell!

Lyndon was a political extremist and a five-time presidential candidate, although even the best political analysts could not pinpoint his positions on most issues. At various times LaRouche had been labeled as being on the extreme left, and sometimes the extreme right.

When I first met him, Lyndon was approaching seventy years of age and had deteriorating health. The menial work duties assigned to Lyndon by the prison officials—often jobs that required him to stand on his feet all day in a hot, sweaty environment—did not do anything to help his physical condition. Eventually (according to the prison grapevine), Dr. Westrick was able to have Lyndon assigned to less draining work duty.

Despite his failing health, Lyndon's mind was still sharp. Lyndon's greatest pleasure came from engaging in combatant dialogues with any inmate who dared match wits with him. Most of Lyndon's dialogues quickly slid into diatribes, with Lyndon exercising his masterful grasp of the English language.

When one of our cellmates was transferred, the prison officials decided to house Lyndon with Tom and me since we were older and supposedly more stable inmates.

"This fellow is a real live wire," Dr. Tom Brandon said about Lyndon. "He is running on 440 voltage." Tom thought it was extremely interesting that the prison now had two of its more notorious inmates—Lyndon LaRouche and Jim Bakker—living together in the same cell, something most press reports incidentally said would never happen when I was first incarcerated.

I actually enjoyed living with Lyndon—he certainly made prison life more interesting. The man was brilliant in many ways; he was conversant on almost any issue I could name. Sometimes I tested Lyndon's knowledge just for the fun of it. As I lay on my bunk below Lyndon's, I would open my Bible dictionary or some other theological book and pick out the most remote word or subject I could find, something I knew little about. Then I would call up to Lyndon, "Hey, Lyndon, tell me about this subject." Lyndon would launch into an explanation of the subject that often matched the material in the book almost word for word.

Besides being an expert on every topic from virology to classical music, Lyndon knew every subject from its inception. Tom was convinced that Lyndon could not give a guy directions how to get to the rest room without going back to the time of Rome to explain it. Lyndon loved to quote the classics, and he could rattle off more names and sources than the Library of Congress!

Although Lyndon had never been elected to any office that I knew of, the man was well connected to high-level information sources. While most inmates were still struggling to be fully awake each morning at 6:00 A.M., Lyndon received a daily news briefing by phone that kept him up to date on world issues. He also received daily, lengthy, computer-generated intelligence reports through the mail. I was amazed that at times Lyndon's intelligence reports told of major news events halfway around the world several days in advance of their happening! Tom and I would often listen in awe as Lyndon would ramble on, speaking in German, on his long-distance phone calls. We couldn't understand a word the man said, but he sure sounded impressive! Of course, many inmates said that about Lyndon when he was speaking in English.

I soon learned a little-known fact about LaRouche: The guy is really funny. He was always upbeat, even when other inmates made fun of him, which they often did. And he always had plenty of jokes to tell. The only problem with his humor was that he was the only one who could understand most of his jokes. But I laughed along with him, because Lyndon's telling of the story was hilarious, regardless of whether the punch line made any sense to me.

To say that Lyndon was slightly paranoid would be like saying the Titanic had a bit of a leak. He was convinced that our cell was bugged by the prison officials. I never saw any evidence of it. But my friend Gleason introduced me to another inmate who worked on electronic systems for the prison. The inmate reported that the prison had recently received a shipment of small electronic listening devices. The electronic worker said that he had actually installed the bugs, but not usually in prisoners' cells. He had been ordered to install the bugs in locations where the prison officials could listen in on one another. That was all Lyndon needed to hear. He was convinced we were living in a virtual recording studio.

During the Gulf War, Lyndon's intelligence reports increased in frequency. Fascinated, I read some of the reports and then went to the television room (by now I had overcome my fear of the place) to watch the war reports on TV. Again and again, what I had read in Lyndon's reports was reflected on the screen . . . sometimes as much as a day or two later.

Perhaps because Tom and Lyndon were constantly haggling over some political issue or current event, Tom approached Dr. Westrick with the suggestion that it might be a good idea to have a weekly current-affairs group at which inmates who were "thinkers" could gather to discuss issues of the day. The idea was to provide a setting in which inmates who were interested in such things could express their thoughts and opinions in a give-and-take atmosphere without fear of reprisal. Lyndon especially loved the idea. Dr. Westrick approved, and we initiated a Friday night meeting in one of the conference rooms in Building One. The group included several Wall Street stockbrokers, bankers, lawyers, Dr. Tom Brandon, me, and of course, Lyndon.

In no time at all, our current-affairs discussion group turned into *The Lyndon LaRouche Hour*. It was interesting just to watch Lyndon "wow" the unsuspecting listeners who did not know him as he attempted to explain the current Persian Gulf crisis by reviewing history as far back as the ancient Roman Empire. Newcomers to the group did not want to appear ignorant, so they often simply sat there nodding their heads in agreement as they listened to Lyndon ramble on, even though they didn't have a clue what the man was talking about.

Fortunately, a former mayor of Syracuse soon joined our group and we immediately selected him as moderator of the discussions. "Mr. Mayor," an articulate man himself, was a strong enough personality to rein in Lyndon's loquacious verbosity.

One Friday night we had a new member attend our discussion group. The newcomer was a bald, young, black man, about six feet tall with a muscular physique, wearing dark sunglasses. As was our custom, the moderator invited the newcomer to introduce himself and tell the group a little about his background.

"I am the Messiah," he announced threateningly, "and I have come to save the world from Ronald Reagan and George Bush."

Something told me that this might not be the time to mention my dinners at the White House!

Most of the members in our discussion group stared at one another in disbelief. Then, not wanting to burst out laughing or cause the young man to become angry, we looked down at our shoes, at our hands, or anywhere except at each other or at the young man. All of us except Lyndon, that is. Lyndon was delighted to meet the fellow and quickly engaged him in conversation. Lyndon looked as if he finally had discovered someone in this prison who really understood him!

We later learned that the young man had been a law student at Berkeley and had actually broken into President Reagan's house in California, hoping to confront the president about how he was running the country. He had gotten as far as the Reagans' front door before Secret Service agents apprehended him. The young man had a history of serious drug abuse, which is how he ended up being incarcerated at F.M.C. Rochester. Fortunately, the fellow did not attend our discussion group often; I'm not sure we could have handled the volatile mixture of Lyndon LaRouche and "the Messiah" in the same room for long.

Lyndon never left the political arena, not even while he was in prison. For instance, he ran for Congress in the 1990 Virginia elections . . . while he was still in prison! As part of his campaign, Lyndon's backers plastered the Virginia area with billboards and placards denouncing the president of the United States, not exactly a wise thing to do when you are in prison, awaiting an appeal of your case. Of course, Lyndon said he would have won that race had the election officials not tampered with the voting machines.

Some of Lyndon's ideas were quite interesting, especially his theories concerning the best ways to solve world hunger. His economic theories were fascinating too, as were some of his proposals to eliminate the national debt, but his ideas about colonizing Mars seemed a bit far-fetched to me. I never really knew whether Lyndon was serious about that one or not.

I was always respectful of Lyndon. I appreciated his quick wit and brilliant mind, even if I could not always understand him. However, many of the men who stopped by our room did not see Lyndon in the same light. One fellow who riled Lyndon was Rod Netherton, a wiry, extremely strong, karate expert. Rod was an airplane pilot, a sky diver, and a major marijuana smuggler.

Rod and Lyndon argued constantly. Regardless of the issue, we could be sure that Rod and Lyndon would be on opposite sides. Eventually Rod's incessant needling of Lyndon would be one of the major factors causing Lyndon to leave us and move down the hall to another cell, where he could have his own desk and a bottom bunk. Lyndon said he moved because of the constant parade of people coming to our cell. Tom said Lyndon moved because he needed the writing space from which he could mount his next presidential campaign.

Tom and I missed the daily intelligence reports and Lyndon's animated presence in our cell. Most of all we missed his colorful commentaries on everything from world events to what sort of efficiency measures should be instituted in the chow hall. Lyndon certainly livened things up. Fortunately, we still had the opportunity to enjoy his oratory at our weekly current-affairs meetings.

CHAPTER

25

Buckingham, Colson, and Dershowitz

TOWARD THE END OF OCTOBER 1990, I RECEIVED A LETTER from Jamie Buckingham, one of the foremost Christian journalists of our day. At the time, Jamie, a pastor, was editor in chief of *Ministries* magazine, a columnist for *Charisma* (a leading Christian magazine), and had written more than forty books.

In 1987, shortly after I had lost PTL and the ensuing scandal had become public knowledge, Jamie had come to visit Tammy Faye and me at our home in Palm Springs. Jamie Buckingham was the first person in the media to whom I had bared my soul concerning how it all had happened. I trusted Jamie and hoped that as a journalist who understood my mission at Heritage USA, he would be able to sift through the rumors, innuendoes, and outright lies swirling around recent events and get to the truth. Jamie and I talked at great length, and I answered every one of his questions as completely and honestly as possible, but he never printed the story. I never learned why the story was squelched. I knew that because of the media hype and the hysteria surrounding Heritage USA it would be difficult to hear a single voice speaking the truth, but I had hoped that Jamie could be an unbiased historian, looking at all sides, and recording the facts accurately for posterity's sake.

I had not heard from Jamie for some time and when I opened his letter in prison, I began to understand why. In June of 1990, Jamie found out that he had cancer of the kidney, which had spread to his lymph glands and was said to be inoperable. Jamie and his wife, Jackie, immediately entered a time of intense prayer. In July of that year, amazingly, the doctors were able to remove the cancer and Jamie's lymph glands were clear as well.

Enclosed with Jamie's letter to me was an article entitled "Praying for the Forgotten," which he was sending to me in advance of its publication in the December issue of *Charisma*. As I read Jamie's article, I was stunned by his bluntness and also by his kindness. A young evangelist had written to Jamie saying that he had been praying for me. The letter touched the heart of Jamie Buckingham and prompted him to write:

> I prayed for Jim while he was under attack by the press. I prayed for him during his trial. I lamented his sentence. Judge Robert Potter was harsh beyond reason. To sentence a nonviolent offender—of any kind— to 45 years in prison is not justice. In Jim's case it was cruelty, motivat- ed, it seems, by vengeance against all enthusiastic Christians.
>
> The man who raped a 14-year-old girl, then hacked off her arms with an ax and left her staggering, naked and armless, along a dark road, received only seven years in prison. He now has resumed his normal life in a free world. . . . It is not right to give Jim Bakker a sentence seven times as severe as that given Al Capone. Bakker has been punished enough. He should be released.[1]

Jamie then went on to encourage his readers to pray for me and to write to me. I was deeply moved when I read the article. It was the first positive article I had seen about me or anyone associated with me in over three years.

About the same time, I received a visit from Chuck Colson, former President Richard Nixon's famed "hatchet man" lawyer and special coun- sel who went to prison for obstruction of justice as a result of his role in Watergate. Shortly before going to prison, Chuck had become a Christian. Upon his release, he had founded Prison Fellowship Ministries, the largest prison ministry of its kind in America. Since then, Chuck had risen to become one of Christianity's most articulate spokesmen. Perhaps that's why the one question I was asked more than any other in the mail I received in prison was, "Has Chuck Colson come to see you?"

When Chuck wrote to ask permission to visit me at F.M.C. Rochester, I was pleasantly surprised. On the day that Chuck was scheduled to arrive at Rochester, I invited my friend Pastor Phil Shaw to schedule a visit also.

Chuck came to F.M.C. with an entourage. Even the prison chaplain came along. Chuck and I greeted each other in the visiting room, then sat down at the table to talk.

Chuck told me of his prison experience. He had served seven months in a federal prison for his role in Watergate. Many had said at the time that the prison in which he had been incarcerated was a "country club" prison, but as Chuck emphatically stated, "If you were locked up at the Waldorf-Astoria, it would still be prison, because of your loss of freedom and being away from the ones you love."

Chuck went on to tell me stories of Solzhenitsyn and Pasternak and Dostoyevsky, authors whose prison works I was already reading.

Since reading their works and Tim Hansel's book, I had begun to see prison as part of God's plan for me to learn how to experience solitude with God as a badge of honor rather than dishonor. This helped me take Chuck Colson's words to heart. Unquestionably, had Chuck Colson come to visit me earlier, I would not have been ready or able to receive his encouragement.

"It really is true," Colson commented, "that as long as we continue to try to defend our past or cling to our innocence, we are still being held hostage by prior events."

He went on to tell me about a conversation he had with Richard Halverson, chaplain to the U.S. Senate, while Chuck was serving time in prison. "Dick Halverson called me and told me to rejoice because God must have something very great in store for me, that He was chastening me and that it was all in preparation for the future. At the time, I really resented the call," Chuck said.

"I thought to myself," he went on, "'*That's okay for Dick Halverson, but I'm the one in prison doing the time.*' I now realize, of course, that what he told me was absolutely right and that because of prison, God has been able to do things in my life that He never could have done otherwise."

Chuck continued by encouraging me to fight my case through the appeals system, but to detach myself from it emotionally. "Take it one step at a time," he said. "I know that you'll be able at some point to look back on this and see God's sovereign hand."

Chuck gave me a copy of his book *Loving God*, and assured me that he and his staff were available to help me any way possible while I was in prison. It seemed that they had just arrived and I was already waving good-bye to them as they were accompanied by the guards out the visiting room door.

I had been in prison for more than a year when, on October 30, 1990, my appeal was finally to be heard before the Fourth U.S. Circuit Court of Appeals in Richmond, Virginia. My team of attorneys presented part of my case, and Professor Alan Dershowitz presented the remainder to a panel of three judges, Judge Harvie Wilkinson III; Judge Dickson Phillips Jr., and Judge John Butzner Jr. I was not required or permitted to attend the proceedings.

My lawyers contended that the trial judge failed to ensure that an impartial jury, untainted by publicity, heard the case. They also challenged Judge Potter's decision to disallow a five- to six-day break in the trial after I was released from my psychological evaluation at Butner Federal Prison. Also called into question by my lawyers were the judge's instructions to the jury before their deliberating my case, which said that they could convict me if they felt I had deceived people in raising money for PTL projects.

When it came to my sentencing, Alan Dershowitz hammered home the point that U.S. District Judge Robert Potter made an "incredible departure" from federal guidelines in sentencing me to forty-five years in prison. Alan argued that if my conviction was not overturned completely, at the very least I should be resentenced by another judge. Most important of all, however, was Alan Dershowitz's argument that Judge Potter had been biased by his own religious beliefs in sentencing me.

Dershowitz reminded the appeals judges that moments before imposing the forty-five-year sentence, Judge Potter had said that "[Bakker] had no thought whatever about his victims, and those of us who do have a religion are ridiculed as being saps [by] money-grubbing preachers or priests."[2]

Deborah Smith, one of the U.S. Justice Department lawyers who had prosecuted the case, replied that Judge Potter's comment merely reflected overall testimony. "I don't think it at all reflects a personal bias on the part of the judge, but rather a reflection of what went on in that courtroom," Smith said.[3]

Alan Dershowitz did an outstanding job highlighting the errors in my case and in my sentencing. The same could not be said, however, of my Texas attorneys' attempt to contest the merits of the case. Their arguments were confusing and unconvincing. At one point they implied to the judges that I had not intended to defraud the PTL Partners, merely deceive them. "You can intend to deceive but not intend to defraud," my lawyer said. "It is not against the law in this context to deceive."[4] Of course, I had intended to do no such thing—defraud or deceive the PTL Partners! That was the last day the Texas firm worked as part of our legal team.

Now came the waiting game. This was not Judge Wapner making an arbitrary decision in a few moments of time after listening to the arguments on both sides. The appeals judges were permitted by law to take as long as necessary before rendering a decision and putting it in writing. Most appeals courts for involved cases such as mine usually took between four to six months before presenting their verdict.

In rendering their decision, the judges could decide in several possible ways: They could declare my trial a mistrial and throw out the case altogether; they could demand a new trial; they could reduce my sentence from the forty-five years to something less; or they could reduce my sentence to "time already served," and I would be free.

Tammy Faye rallied our friends to pray and petition lawmakers on my behalf. In a letter to me, she sounded almost exuberant,

> *Everyone* is praying for the appeal! I feel that God must move in our behalf. We have been faithful to Him during this thing, and I know He will not let us down. I believe, Jim, that we are on the brink of a miracle. So hold on a little longer, honey. This too shall pass. I love you! I miss you!
>
> Tam

As for me, I was encouraged by the report that Alan Dershowitz had done well but discouraged that the remainder of the issues surrounding my trial were still blurred and distorted. I had lost hope that I would ever find justice in a courtroom.

I resigned myself to the attitude Chuck Colson suggested I adopt. The week following his visit, Chuck wrote to me and said, "Not only did I spend a little time in prison, but I have been in and out of prisons ever since. I've only discovered two kinds of inmates: . . . those who are still fighting their case and are miserable and . . . those who have accepted their lot, understand God has a purpose for their life and therefore are at peace and free."

I was beginning to understand what Chuck meant. I did not feel free, but I was at peace.

26

I Won't Be Home for Christmas

NOW THAT MY APPEAL HAD BEEN MADE AND WAS IN THE hands of the judges, I could do nothing but wait . . . and pray. I had been study-ing the words of Jesus now for several months, trying to see the world through His eyes, as I felt He had instructed me in a dream. I was coming to grips with the truth that God had impressed upon me—that I had not come to prison to minister to other inmates; God had allowed me to come to prison to get to know Him.

During this time I heard from a Florida man, Dr. Richard Arno, pres-ident of the National Christian Counselors Association. Dr. Arno felt compelled to send me information concerning their counseling course and the Temperament Analysis Profile, a psychological testing tool used in helping an individual understand his or her temperament.

The course cost well over $1,500, but Dr. Arno offered to send it to me for free if I was interested. I was intrigued, and I wrote back to Dr. Arno, telling him I would indeed be interested.

I was fascinated when I began to study the course. From Dr. Arno's material I learned that temperament is the inborn part of a person that determines how he or she reacts to people, places, or things. Temperament pinpoints a person's perception of himself, determines how that person deals with the stresses and pressures of life, and shows a person's weaknesses and strengths.

Most temperament tests define four categories: Melancholy, Sanguine, Choleric, and Phlegmatic. Dr. Arno's test included a fifth category: Supine. Most people are a combination of temperaments rather than exclusively one or the other. Nevertheless, we usually lean toward one or two areas, and the characteristics that are dominant in that area will show up sooner or later in our lives. People who have a melancholy temperament often exhibit great intellectual abilities and are self-motivated, but they may also be extremely withdrawn, moody, and living with a constant fear of rejection.

Sanguine temperaments are usually people oriented, upbeat, open, and friendly individuals, but they may also be self-indulgent, rude, and superficial.

Cholerics tend to be well-organized people motivators who require a great deal of recognition, but they can also be dictatorial and controlling.

People with a phlegmatic temperament are often slow paced, calm, easygoing peacemakers, but they may also be self-contained, stubborn, uninvolved, and lacking in emotional response.

A supine is often a person who has a gentle spirit, is servant oriented and a people pleaser, but may also suffer from lack of self-esteem, loneliness, fear of rejection, and a victim mentality.

Like many people who study temperaments for the first time, I began to see myself, as well as my family members and friends, in the various characteristics. My temperament, I found, is a mixture of melancholy and supine.

Beyond the temperament material Dr. Arno's course provided valuable information about how to counsel people suffering all sorts of psychological and spiritual maladies, especially those suffering depression. Again, as I studied in preparation to help someone else, God was providing me with the precise information I would need to face what was happening and about to happen in my own life.

Thanksgiving time was rapidly approaching, and Tammy Faye and Jamie were making plans to come to Rochester to visit me. Tammy Faye wrote: "Can't wait to see you! I am so excited about coming. I would give anything in the world if I could bring you back home with me. One day that will happen. Jamie is so excited about seeing you!"

My family's second Thanksgiving in prison was tough to handle, but at least we knew what to expect. Pastor Phil Shaw was once again the great facilitator, picking them up at the airport, taking them to their hotel, and transporting them to the prison. It was wonderful to see my family members again. I could hardly believe how big Jamie was getting. I was so proud of my son.

Our good friends Faye and Ray LaForce from Canada had flown to Florida to accompany Tammy and Jamie to Minnesota. We discussed my appeal and the possibility of getting out of prison, helping people, and even the possibility of building or buying another retreat center where we could invite all the PTL Lifetime Partners to come and receive the benefits of the partnership they had anticipated at Heritage USA. Despite my own financial indebtedness and my emotional depression, one of the things I regularly dreamed about in prison was how I could somehow restore to the PTL Lifetime Partners that which they had lost when PTL collapsed.

Following our Thanksgiving Day visit, which included our vending-machine dinner, Phil Shaw and his wife Faith invited my family members and the LaForces home for a real Thanksgiving dinner. I longed to go with them, but as they headed for turkey and stuffing, I headed to the strip-search room.

The following day, we were joined in the visitation room by our dear friends Dr. Basil Jackson and his wife Leila from Milwaukee and Dr. David Lewis and his wife from Springfield, Missouri. What a thrill it was for me to see these family friends who gave up time with their own families to spend part of their Thanksgiving weekend with my family and me in prison.

The last time Dr. Jackson had seen me for any length of time, I had talked with him from a fetal position beneath the couch in Harold Bender's Charlotte law office. Dr. Jackson was delighted to see me adapting relatively well to prison life. I probably wasn't as together as the good doctor thought, but at least I was standing upright—that was some improvement! The psychiatrist later expressed concern, however, that my imprisonment was beginning to take a heavy toll on Tammy and especially on Jamie.

As Tammy Faye and my other guests prepared to leave, my emotions began to get the better of me. We hugged and kissed and then waved good-bye. "Honey, I love you. Keep singing!" I called after Tammy Faye. My words sounded hollow as they echoed across the noisy visiting room.

Tammy Faye called back, "I love you too. See you in a few weeks for Christmas!"

Christmas, I thought. *Oh, no. Not again.* I was not looking forward to my second Christmas in prison.

Throughout the fall, I kept busy teaching the smoking cessation class. Each month, Tom and I started all over again with a new batch of inmates who wanted to quit smoking. We were just finishing our November class when the unit manager, Mr. Houston, called us into his office for a conference. We assumed that the guards had been complaining to him again about our books. Over and over, Tom and I had heard the guards say, "Too many books," as they looked at the desks in our cell. It was perfectly fine for inmates to stuff their desk drawers and cabinets with pornography, but because Tom and I had our desks stacked with reference books, the guards would write us up. Being written up on the daily inspection sheets by the guards was a warning that could lead to serious disciplinary action if not corrected.

However, Mr. Houston told us that some of the inmates were complaining that Tom and I were not working hard enough since we had begun teaching the smoking cessation course. They were threatening to file discrimination charges, Mr. Houston said. As a result, the unit manager informed us that if we wanted to continue to teach the class, that was fine, but we would also have to clean toilets on the weekends. Tom and I were assigned to toilets again.

The first week in December, I received some good news: My friend Franklin Graham, son of the Reverend Billy Graham, was coming to see me. Franklin and I had known each other for a number of years and had worked together on several projects dating back to the early 1980s. In 1980, Franklin joined Samaritan's Purse, a Christian relief and evangelism ministry that spreads the gospel by meeting the physical and spiritual needs of victims of war, famine, disease, and natural disasters. In 1982, Franklin was organizing an effort to help build an additional wing to Tenwek Hospital in western Kenya. The hospital was seriously overcrowded, often filled to 200 percent occupancy, with many patients sleeping on the floor.

When Franklin came on *PTL*, we talked very little about his famous family; instead we talked at length about his work with Samaritan's Purse. Our interview was nearly over when I asked Franklin about his most recent project. Franklin began to tell me about the hospital in Tenwek and its over 200 percent occupancy.

"How does that work?" I asked. "One hundred percent is full. What does it mean to have a 200 percent-plus occupancy?"

"It means they have more than two patients to a bed." Franklin handed me a photograph that had not two people in one hospital bed, but three. My heart broke for those people. I held the photo up so the cameras could get a shot to show the viewers, and I turned to Franklin and asked, "Franklin, what can I do to help?"

"Well, they need a new ward, and I'm trying to raise some money to have it built," Franklin replied.

"How much is it going to cost?" I asked. No doubt members of our staff were gripping their chairs in terror. I had a habit of committing PTL and myself to helping other ministries on the spur of the moment. My spontaneity often sent the staff into spasms of "Oh, no. How are we going to do that?"

Franklin Graham answered, "They think it's going to cost about four hundred thousand dollars."

I turned to the camera and said, "Everybody watching right now, I want you to send Franklin Graham one dollar. Send more if you want, but send him at least one dollar. Don't send it to me. Don't send it to PTL. Send it to Franklin Graham. Can we put Franklin's address on the screen?" I asked our technicians in the control room. Almost immediately, the address showed up near the bottom of millions of television screens. "Everybody, please send one dollar to help build this hospital wing." I knew that many would not stop at giving only one dollar but would give much more.

I turned to our studio audience. "All of you in the audience—we're going to take an offering, and I want each of you to put in one dollar or more."

Again our staff was probably going bonkers. "An offering? Where does it say anything on our production cue sheets about an offering?"

But within minutes ushers were assembled and buckets were found to collect the offering.

Before we knew what was happening, the buckets began to fill up. Every dollar went to Franklin Graham and Samaritan's Purse to help build the wing on that hospital in Kenya.

Two months after our spontaneous offering, I invited Franklin to return to *PTL* to give us a progress report.

"Money has come in from all over the country," Franklin told our viewers. "We received more than fifty-six thousand letters." Franklin reminded me that the hospital had needed four hundred thousand dollars to add the new wing. "And Jim, God provided through you and your partners more than we needed." Then Franklin Graham did something that nobody had ever done before on *PTL*. He reached into his pocket, pulled out a check, and handed it to me as he said, "We received a total of $409,000. Here is a check for $9,000. We want to give this back to PTL."

In the years since then, Franklin often reminded me that the interview on *PTL* had not only been the springboard to launch the new wing of the hospital, but it also made many people aware of Samaritan's Purse for the first time. Many of those became fast friends of Franklin's ministry. Moreover, he said that many of the people who sent in that first dollar have been some of the most faithful and generous benefactors of Samaritan's Purse over the years.

Franklin Graham was coming to see me, and it was not on the comfortable television set of *PTL*; it was in prison. I had not seen Franklin in a long time, and I wasn't sure how he would react to me, but I could hardly wait to see my friend.

Franklin also agreed to speak in the prison chapel that evening. Tom Brandon and I were in the chapel early to help arrange the room when Franklin arrived with singers Dennis and Danny Agajanian. We walked toward each other and embraced. Franklin greeted me warmly, and all my fears concerning his acceptance of me melted away instantly. Franklin Graham had been my friend before I went to prison and he was still my friend now. Dennis and Danny Agajanian greeted me with huge bear hugs. Dennis and Danny are extremely talented musicians who can play almost any instrument put before them. The brothers are both huge, rugged looking guys. I knew the inmates would love the Agajanians, and they did.

The brothers performed a blend of gospel, country, and bluegrass music, including a rip-roaring guitar rendition of "Dueling Banjos." The prisoners roared their approval. Following the Agajanians' music, Franklin Graham stood before the men and told them of his rebellion against being Billy and Ruth Graham's son and more importantly, his rebellion against God. The prison officials had informed Franklin prior to his visit that he was welcome to come on two conditions: that he did not acknowledge that he knew Jim Bakker and that he not have an invitation to accept Christ at the close of his talk. Franklin disregarded both conditions. From the podium, he publicly referred to me as his friend as he told the inmates how we met. Then at the close of his talk, he invited the inmates to commit their lives to Jesus Christ. Many of them did. Even my cellmate, Dr. Tom Brandon, said the night with Franklin Graham and the Agajanians was one of the best times of his life.

As Franklin and the Agajanians prepared to leave, I thanked them profusely for coming. "You will never know what your coming here means to these men . . . and especially to me."

Franklin Graham laid his big hand on my shoulder and said, "Jim, you stood with me when I was just starting out. I have not forgotten that. You were my friend then and you are now. Anything you need, you can count on me."

No gift Franklin could have given me was greater than his affirming friendship.

That night, long after Franklin was gone, I began to realize what a gutsy thing he had done by identifying himself with me, a disgraced television evangelist as far as the world was concerned, and a convicted felon. Of all the people whom I might have expected to allow their names to be linked with mine, I would never have thought that Franklin would have risked the Graham name. He had nothing to gain and everything to lose by identifying with me, but he did it. I had been in prison for over a year now and had not heard a word from many of the people who were regularly seen on our television programs. But Franklin Graham demonstrated risky, genuine Christian love.

Not that I did not receive many wonderful cards and letters through the Thanksgiving and Christmas season. I did, indeed. Many friends wrote to me during the holidays, friends such as the great gospel singers Nancy Harmon and Vestal Goodman. Ralph Wilkerson, founding pastor of Melodyland Christian Center in Anaheim, California, wrote, as did Dr. C. S. Lovett, who sent me gospel tracts that I could give away to other inmates.

Another letter that meant much to me came from Pastor Marvin Gorman. Marvin had been the pastor of a large church in Louisiana when he was accused by Jimmy Swaggart of being involved in an adulterous affair. Marvin's life and ministry collapsed around him, although his precious wife, Virginia, and his children Beverly, Randy, and Mark remained committed to him. Marvin understood some of the hurt I was experiencing. Interestingly, Marvin mentioned in his letter a visit he had recently received from our mutual friends, Owen and Priscilla Carr:

> Owen told me of the wonderful visits he has been privileged to have with you. He was greatly inspired by your attitude and outlook upon the total situation that the Lord has you in for this period of time. Jim, I'm sure that I don't have to tell you this, but Owen Carr is a true friend. He has stayed in touch with us throughout this ordeal and has edified and inspired us through every contact.

Marvin was right. Owen Carr—as straight and upright a preacher of the gospel as I had ever met—was more concerned about ministering to Marvin and to me than he was his own reputation. That very week, I received another letter from Owen: "We eagerly await word of the outcome of your appeal. I don't see how they can do anything but reduce that horrible sentence. Certainly there is nothing of justice in what you are enduring."

Nevertheless, Owen seemed to recognize that I was not in prison by accident, without God being cognizant of my whereabouts and circumstances. It was as though Owen had sensed what God was beginning to teach me. "I have confidence in you, Jim, that you will walk near to the heart of God, and that you will let Him bring peace and quiet to your heart, and keep victory in your soul."

More and more, I understood why the Christmas season is one of the toughest times of the year for people in prison, so I especially appreciated the many kind cards and letters I received. I read and saved every one and sent them home in big boxes. I did not want to throw away one bit of love expressed in those cards and letters. I also received kind letters during the holiday season from a black pastor, Reverend Larry Allen, a faithful friend who reminded me that some people still referred to him as "the black Jim Bakker," because he was on television and always in some new building project.

I also received a number of letters from people I had never met before. One such letter came from John Hagee, pastor of Cornerstone Church in San Antonio. His letter warmed my heart.

I wanted to take the time today to write you to say that the Body of Christ has not forgotten you and that you are loved. I can't begin to imagine what you must think or feel locked behind the walls, but know of a certainty you are our brother who is going through a Lion's Den experience and God Almighty will bring you out. . . . Jim, be assured you are in our thoughts and prayers and beyond this vale of tears the sun will shine again. You will smile and laugh again, and all will be well.

One letter was both encouraging and amusing. It came from Melvin M. Belli Sr., the old famous lawyer who was the first attorney who offered to represent me in the dark days of March 1987. I could almost hear Melvin's gravelly voice as I read his encouraging letter. The blustery lawyer had once referred to me as the "best damn Christian I know."

Another surprising letter came from Sonny Singer. More than forty years earlier he and I had been best buddies in Muskegon, Michigan, when we were between the ages of seven and twelve. Sonny was Jewish and knew of my deep love and concern for the nation of Israel, and although he and I were of different religious persuasions, his letter reverberated with tremendous faith. I was surprised that he expressed such confidence in my early release from prison in light of my long sentence. Sonny wrote:

> Jim, before you know it, you'll be out of prison, but the waiting must drive you crazy. Keep busy, write a new book. . . . Keep active and the time will fly. When you are out again, we'll walk the beach together under the sun and moon. We'll talk and laugh like old times.

The Christmas card I received from my eighty-four-year-old dad nearly ripped my heart out. Of all the people who suffered because of my mistakes at PTL, nobody hurt more deeply than my dad. He cried for me almost every day and often told me: "I wish I could take your place, son." Daddy wrote in his Christmas card to me:

> We know that your Christmas will not be like so many Christmases in days gone by, but God will be with you there. We are sure God will vindicate you soon. The jury is out now about the civil suit that some of the Lifetime Partners are supposed to have instigated. The best thing about this is that you are not guilty.
>   I am feeling much better. Mother is okay, considering her age and all.
>
> We love you much!
Mother and Daddy
> P.S. Greet the inmates with a Merry Christmas for us.

One of the cards that touched me most deeply during the holidays was from a woman I had never met. She wrote:

> In June of 1978 we went to PTL. My husband was not a believer and drank very much. But after watching you on TV he said we could go, although he did not believe. When we arrived at PTL, he was convinced the ministry was of the Lord. When we got back home, he chose to support your ministry financially. He told his friends, "I gave to the drinking places in this town for ten years and all I got was nothing. But these people are helping to change lives from a way that has no end but hell." He felt so strongly about your ministry, because you were real. I praise God for seeing a man coming home drunk change into a man in

church with our two girls, praising God. My husband went to be with the Lord in 1981, but I want you to know, I am to this day so grateful for what your ministry did for our family.

That dear woman's card was one of the best Christmas presents I could have gotten that year.

Because I was receiving so much Christmas mail I wanted to send out some sort of Christmas greeting to the many people who had written to me. An inmate, who was a friend of mine, sketched a charcoal line drawing of me holding baby James during Tammy Sue's last visit. He was a true artist and the drawing came out beautifully. I wrote a free-verse poem, describing my prison experiences to date. I sent the sketch and poem home and Tammy Faye and her staff reproduced the drawing on the front of a card with my poem inside, and they sent it out as a Christmas card from me. I had asked Tammy Faye to put my name on the computerized mailing list to receive one of the cards, since I had not seen the finished product. Just before Christmas, the card arrived at the prison. When the guard checking the mail saw a card *from* Jim Bakker *to* Jim Bakker, red flags popped up in his mind. *Something must be wrong here*, he must have thought. *Nobody sends cards to himself. This must be some sort of con.* He turned the card over to the lieutenant's office. The prison official called me in to interrogate me concerning this strange phenomenon.

I tried to explain to the official that Sam Houston, the unit manager of Building Two, had suggested the idea of having my wife send out the card from Florida, since I had so much mail to answer. I explained that the card had been part of a computerized mailing, and my name and address were on the list, so I automatically received a card.

The officer stared back at me as though I were speaking a foreign language. He simply could not comprehend this. "No, there must be more to it," he insisted.

I tried to think of another way of explaining it to the man. "Have you ever seen an address machine? That is what this is." I pointed to my address on the envelope. "The machine printed a card from me to me. That's all there is to it."

The officer refused to believe me and demanded that I appear before the prison council. I was called in to give an account before the prison counselors, case managers, and other prison bigwigs.

I began to explain to this group in rudimentary terms how I received the card. This group of individuals worked every day with computers and other modern mailing equipment, and I had no sooner begun my defense than the entire roomful of people burst out laughing. When they realized the foolishness of the charges, they dropped them.

I had told Tammy Faye that I preferred that she not come for Christmas that year. Of course I wanted to see my family, and Tammy had been trying to find inexpensive airline tickets for her and the children, but the best she had been able to do was $515 each. I hated to see her spend that sort of money, plus several hundred dollars more for a hotel bill, when they did not have much money in the first place. Besides, I remembered how painful it had been for all of us last Christmas when my family had visited, and I did not want to put them through that again. I told Tammy, "The only gift I can give you this year is for you not to have to spend Christmas in prison again." I insisted that my family members not come, even though my heart was aching to see them. They reluctantly agreed to spend Christmas in Florida.

Since my family would not be coming for Christmas, Tom Brandon and I volunteered to serve at the Christmas dinner sponsored by the prison Jaycees for the inmates and their family members on Christmas Day. There was some question as to whether the prison officials would allow me to be involved in the Christmas dinner. After all, more members of the public might see me, and the prison brass was adamant about me maintaining a low profile. I signed the volunteer list anyhow.

On Christmas Day, all the members of the Jaycees who had volunteered to serve Christmas dinner were paged over the intercom: "Report to the chow hall." I walked over to the chow-hall door, lined up with the other volunteers, and waited to be allowed in to begin working. When the guard opened the door to let in the volunteers, he checked each man off his list as we passed by. Tom and I reported and swept right by him. Surprisingly, the guard did not say a word to me. Somehow my name had made it onto the list of approved workers. We later discovered that the list of volunteers working at the Christmas dinner had not been reviewed by anyone in an upper-level position but had in fact been approved by an inmate working in one of the offices!

Once inside the chow hall, the volunteers separated into groups. Tom and our friend Richard were busboys. Others were to pass out the Christmas presents that the Jaycees were allowed to distribute to the children of the inmates. The job they gave me? Maitre d'. At least that's what Tom called me.

My responsibility was to greet and help each family as they came through the serving line. This was probably the last job the prison officials

269

would have wanted for me, since it meant that every single person coming in to eat that day would see Jim Bakker. "I can see the headlines now," Tom said with a laugh, as he went by carrying a stack of dirty dishes on a tray. "Jim Bakker—The Official Host of Prison Christmas Dinner!" All the guys helping on the serving line broke up in laughter. I was having a ball, smiling at everyone coming in the chow hall, wishing them a Merry Christmas, pointing them in the direction of their utensils and food, and helping the elderly ladies with their food trays.

Late in the afternoon, the prison warden, other top officials, and Dr. Westrick came into the chow hall. When they saw me serving as host, their mouths dropped wide open, but nobody said a word. I greeted them as I had all the others, with a hearty welcome and a Merry Christmas. Dr. Westrick, in her usual charming manner, immediately began moving among the tables, greeting the inmates and family members of inmates and the Jaycees volunteers. The warden looked as though he wanted to say something to me, but decided against it. Perhaps the Christmas card incident was still fresh in his mind, and he did not want to say anything unkind. It was too late anyhow. I had already greeted almost everyone who had come through the doors that day.

I spent most of the remainder of Christmas Day in my bunk. Working with the Jaycees and serving the Christmas dinner to the inmates and their families had kept me too busy all day to become depressed over the fact that my own family was all the way across the nation. Then, as I lay in the dark, I missed my family terribly, and I could not prevent myself from sinking into despair.

Earlier in the week, Tom and I had attended a special presentation by a singing group that had come to spread a little Christmas cheer inside the prison walls. The group did okay until near the end when they sang, "I'll Be Home for Christmas." I nearly lost it, as did many other inmates who were in attendance.

Christmas was now over, the new year was about to begin, and I was a year older. I was studying the words of Jesus and asking the Lord to answer many of the tough questions with which I had always grappled but had never taken the time to truly seek answers for. Now I had the time. Of course, one of the questions that still occupied my thoughts frequently was, "How long, oh Lord? How long will I have to stay in prison?"

With my appeal now in the hands of the judges, Tammy Faye was hoping and praying for a speedy release. I was not quite so optimistic. One of us was about to be proved right.

27

Back in the Pits

JANUARY 1991 WAS THE BEGINNING OF ONE OF MY WORST downhill slides into one of the worst periods of depression I had known since coming to prison. Although I had encouraged my family to stay away at Christmas, I missed them horribly. Despite being surrounded by hundreds of fellow prisoners, I felt alone and abandoned. It was not my family's fault that I spent Christmas, New Year's Eve, and my birthday alone. Yet it was the first Christmas of my life that I had not celebrated with my family. It was the first time I had not been with my family on my birthday. My emotions took a nosedive.

Adding to my depression was the news from Charleston, South Carolina, that I had lost another legal battle. In 1987 the people who took over PTL and put it into bankruptcy hired a lawyer to instigate a multimillion-dollar class-action lawsuit against me, PTL builder Roe Messner, David Taggart, one of my top assistants at PTL, and our accounting firms of Laventhol & Howath and Deloitte, Haskins, & Sells. The suit alleged a conspiracy between PTL's builders, banks, accountants, and of course, me, to launder money and use it for our personal gain. It was a lawsuit seeking more than $575 million in damages. Even if the case would have had legitimate merit—which I felt it did not—I had no money anyway.

Most of the Lifetime Partners who expressed their sentiments to me wanted nothing to do with the lawsuit. They knew I had not defrauded them of anything, that their "Lifetime" gifts were just that—a gift or a donation to the PTL ministry. Many of the Partners were convinced that if I had been allowed to return to Heritage USA, they would have received everything they anticipated at PTL and much more. Hundreds of Partners wrote to U.S. District Judge James McMillan on my behalf. Many stated that they wanted their names to be withdrawn from the suit, because the suit did not represent their feelings toward PTL or toward me. As a PTL Lifetime Partner, if a person did not specifically write and ask to be removed from the civil litigation, he or she was automatically included.

Originally, those bringing the suit had hoped to win a large sum of money from our accounting firms or possibly from Roe Messner. When it became obvious that there was no misconduct on the part of our accountants or builders, one part after another of the case was dropped off the suit. In the end, the only defendant left was me. After more than three years of legal wrangling, the civil case against me was resolved. A panel of judges decided that I was innocent of criminal charges, but the judges found me guilty of civil charges of defrauding my Partners of $135 million. In other words, if I had any money, people would have been standing in line for it. At the front of the line, of course, would have been the lawyers who "won" the case.

In prison, I was almost oblivious to what was going on in the world outside the razor-wire fences. My struggle was trying to stay alive and dredge up enough will simply to get out of bed each morning and face another day. I could do nothing about the case, and I was trying my best just to keep my head above water emotionally. When I heard the news of the judges' decision, however, I was devastated. I hurt not so much for myself—I was already in prison with little chance of getting out—but I was concerned for the Lifetime Partners, who were now embroiled in a battle not of their own making. My dream of Heritage USA as a unique base for worldwide evangelism and a beautiful place where Christians could fellowship had truly turned into a nightmare.

I had lost another battle. Beyond that, I wondered if the decision of the civil judges could adversely affect the decision of the appeals judges. I could not help but think that it would.

About this same time, I received another defeat, though it was on a much smaller scale. Because of budgetary restraints, the prison officials refused Tom's and my request for new films and other materials to help enhance the smoking cessation course. It seemed that some of the prison officials were intent upon inhibiting the very program that Dr. Westrick had asked us to develop. It didn't make any sense. Already, our class had been moved to a poor, noisy location, in which it was hard to maintain the men's attention. The juices that leading health experts felt were an important physiological help to the guys as they were trying to stop smoking had been refused.

Tom Brandon was irate. "If our class helped prevent one inmate from getting cancer, it could literally save the Bureau of Prisons hundreds of thousands of dollars in long-term medical costs. But they are squawking about paying a few bucks for juice."

Furthermore, when Tom and I had been reassigned to cleaning toilets as well as being allowed to work as teachers, Sam Houston had informed me that I had not been receiving "good time" for the months of work I had already spent preparing for and teaching the class. Nor would Tom and I be paid our eleven cents per hour for our efforts. I didn't mind being deprived of the money—it takes a lot of hours to earn enough money to buy commissary items at that rate—but losing my "good time" really bothered me. Under the law, I was allowed to receive up to ten days per month—good time—for doing exemplary work and being a model prisoner. An inmate's good time could be deducted off his sentence. Good time is a prison's way of offering inmates an incentive to behave, especially for prisoners with long sentences such as mine. Of course, an inmate was not always "awarded" all his good time every month, but every day was worth working toward. Now I learned I had worked from April to December and would receive not a single day's reduction of my sentence for the effort. It was discouraging.

My awful feelings of homesickness for my family, the disappointments concerning the smoking cessation course, and of course the blow delivered by the civil case verdict and its possible effect on my appeal multiplied the effects of my depression. I did not want to do anything. I did not want to eat, drink, shave, or bathe. I began to allow myself to become more and more disheveled and unkempt, making little to no effort to clean up. I began to grow a beard, not because I thought it would enhance my appearance, but because I no longer cared about my appearance. Always known as a fastidious dresser—even in prison I wore sharply pressed clothes, with crisp creases in my shirts and pants—my clothes now went unpressed and often unwashed. With my hair uncombed, my body unwashed, and stubble covering my face, I looked like a homeless person. Friends and foes alike who were accustomed to seeing me on the set of *PTL* well dressed with every hair in place would have had difficulty recognizing me.

Despite the news that doctors from Mayo Clinic wanted to come and sit in on our course in January, I told Tom I could not possibly teach a class in January. I was in the pits myself.

When Paul Olson, my friend for over thirty years, visited me on February 1, 1991, he noticed immediately that my demeanor had changed for the worse. Five years later, Paul revealed to me what he had written in his journal that day:

> To my surprise, Jim was wearing a full beard. It's mostly gray and makes him look much older. Nearly a year and a half in prison has put not a few wrinkles in Jim Bakker's face. He looks so weary. It was his eyes that caught my attention. They were filled with sadness. As he walked through the door, my spirit sank. It was the lowest I have ever seen Jim Bakker.

"What are you doing here, Paul?" I asked as I embraced him in the visitation room. I was upset with him. I had not wanted any visitors and had even canceled several scheduled visits that some other friends had planned to make. We sat down at one of the tables and began to talk.

"Are you still teaching your antismoking class, Jim?" Paul asked.

"I'm supposed to start a new class next week," I responded, "but I think I'm going to give it up."

Surprise registered on Paul's face. My friend knew how much that class meant to me and what a sense of satisfaction it gave me.

In my depressed state, I continued to ramble on to Paul about how the prison officials had informed us that the prison was establishing a new policy limiting the amount of normal street clothes an inmate could keep in his cell.

"It's silly. It could possibly cost the prison thousands of dollars to box up and mail all those items back to the inmates' families. Inmates have so little. An inmate losing a favorite shirt or pair of pants here on the inside would be equal to a person losing a house or a car on the outside. It's all the prisoner has he can call his own."

Paul listened compassionately as I told him that I was also going to drop out of my activities and clubs that, despite my personal doldrums, had helped to keep my mind off my troubles.

"Why, Jim? I don't understand."

"I've just given up, Paul," I answered, fighting back the tears. "I still believe in God, but I have lost all hope of getting out of here soon. It seemed to me like my lawyers botched my appeal so miserably. . . . I don't know what the decision of the judges will be, but I have resigned myself to the fact that I will be in prison for at least ten years. That would be the earliest I would be eligible for parole with a forty-five-year sentence. Frankly, I don't even have much hope that I will get out in ten years. The system does not readily parole high-profile prisoners.

"Tammy Faye gets down, but she always manages to get back up again. During the trial, Tammy cheered me up by saying that God would not let me go to prison. Then she said that God would bring me out soon. I just can't get up anymore, Paul. I can't take the emotional roller coaster. Bit by bit, the prison system has chipped away at me until I have no hope left."

My friend would not allow me to concede defeat. "You can't give up, Jim, no matter what," he told me. "I am going to pray hard for you. God will do something, you'll see."

Paul Olson was not the only person who expected something unusual to happen regarding my case. Tammy Faye wrote effusively throughout the months of January and early February, encouraging me that God was about to do something. Because I missed her so terribly, her letters—many of them written on lovely, feminine stationery—were bittersweet. For example, in January, she wrote: "I am just sitting here missing you. I wish you were here! I would give anything in the world if you could just walk in the door. But I know that one day soon that is going to happen. I could not live if I didn't believe that!"

In another letter, Tammy wrote: "I miss you so badly that sometimes I don't think that I can stand it another day. But I believe that this is about to come to an end. I expect *victory*! And I live in that expectancy! Every day! I am always saying and thinking, 'Next week Jim will be back home!' And I believe that."

In letter after letter, Tammy encouraged me, "Don't give up! We're on the brink of a miracle." In one of her letters, she told me that our friend, singer and songwriter Mike Adkins, had stopped by to visit briefly. "Mike feels that God is going to get you out of there soon and that He is going to use you greater than ever before," she wrote.

Mike also said that when he was praying for us, God showed him a fishing line that was so tangled that there was no way to untangle it. He said that God came down and cut the fishing line and all the tangled mess floated away on the water. I really believe that is what God is going to do. We need to quit trying to untangle the mess, cut the line, and keep fishing with new line.

275

I also got a letter and a tape from Pat Boone. He said that he and Shirley still love us, that they pray for us every day, and that God is going to work it all out for us.

About that same time, I too received an uplifting letter from Pat Boone. Echoing the sentiments he had expressed to Tammy, Pat wrote:

Shirley and I have been your friends for years, and continue to be. As I hope you know, we defended you and Tammy everywhere, not faults or mistakes, but your hearts and accomplishments and desires to serve the Lord, which you did so admirably in so many ways. I just want you to know that Shirley and I still love you, are still your friends and brother and sister, and will always stand ready to help in any way we can. I'm sending you a song I wrote and produced, "The Fallen Giant." Whenever I have sung it, and I have on a number of Christian television programs, I've always mentioned you by name and urge people to pray for you, and to stand by a wounded and fallen brother. Our hearts hurt especially for Tammy and the family, but no less for you. And we are confident that the Lord will not only see you through all this, but is still working everything together for our good, because we do love Him and are called according to His purpose!

In His love and ours,
Pat

Surprisingly, at a time when I was at a low point in my prison experience, having lost all hope of ever getting out soon, I received one letter after another exhorting me to keep trusting God and to keep believing that He would bring me out of prison much earlier than I anticipated. For instance, Dr. Basil Jackson wrote:

We continue to pray hard about your appeal and just wonder what the Lord has in store. But my faith has never wavered in this regard. I feel that God has a special function for you and a special ministry for you in the years ahead and that you will not be spending the rest of your life in prison in Rochester.

C. M. Ward wrote once again at the beginning of 1991. His encouraging letter was a beam of light. C. M. wrote:

You are never far from our conversation and we value you as a friend and a talented minister. I'm sure, should Jesus tarry, and spare you, we will see you brought out into a prominent place of God's destiny and to a testimony for the nation. My faith toward this is stronger every day.

Many of the letters I received in January and early February of 1991 referred to the Christmas card I had sent out, bearing the picture of baby James and me on the front cover and the poem describing prison on the inside. Many of the responses were similar to one I received from gospel music pioneer Eva Mae LeFevre. In her seventies now, Eva Mae wrote:

I got many Christmas cards in 1990 but the one that touched me most was yours. I can't believe everything that has happened in the last three years where you and Tammy are concerned, but I . . . know thousands just like me are sending up prayers twenty-four hours a day. I am 73 years old but I pray that God will let me live to see the day that you are a free man again. Since there is nothing impossible with God, it could happen in 1991.

Owen Carr came to visit me in late January and was surprised by my disheveled appearance and especially my beard. During his visit, I confessed to Owen that I felt like a piece of dirt. When Owen returned to his home in Tulsa, he wrote back to me:

In the eyes of some, you may be "nothing" as you stated. However, that is not true in the eyes of the Lord. Worth is determined by cost. Think of the price God paid for your redemption, and you will have an idea of your worth. . . . I can see you now, as you used to wave good-bye to the audience at PTL, and with your infectious smile, exclaim, "God loves you! We love you! You're going to make it!" We continue to pray concerning the appeal. God is able. Jim, you are greatly loved, deeply appreciated, and prayed for often. They may rob you of your liberty, but they can never rob you of your victory.

As always, Owen's words were a tremendous encouragement to me, and his rich spiritual insights were extremely helpful. Nevertheless, I could not overcome the desire to simply give up and die. In a letter I received from Tammy Faye near the end of January, she included a list on which members of our congregation in Florida routinely wrote down their prayer requests, asking for the other members of the church to pray for them. On the last Sunday morning of January, there among all the other requests on the list, in his own handwriting, was the name "Jay Bakker." Beside his name in the prayer request column, Jamie had printed only two words: *My Dad.*

When I saw the unadorned prayer request of my boy, I burst into tears. No wonder I was a basket case when Paul Olson showed up on the first of February.

Looking back, I can see where God always had something to keep me going when all hope was seemingly gone. This time was no different. Once again, undetected by me, the Lord used ordinary circumstances to literally pull me out of my bunk and back into the mainstream of life in prison.

I had maintained my association with the Growth Awareness Development Association, the predominantly black group desegregated only by Lyndon LaRouche and me. I have always had a great affinity toward the black community, and for some reason, I have always been accepted among most black people. As far back as the mid- to late 1960s, when I was working at the Christian Broadcasting Network in Portsmouth, Virginia, and doing *The Jim and Tammy Show*—our daily children's program, and *The 700 Club*, I had begun to invite members of the black church community to appear on our programs. At that time most churches were black or white; few congregations were integrated. But Tammy and I wanted to minister to the whole community, not simply the white segment of the Tidewater, Virginia, area. To our surprise, however, we experienced great difficulty in getting black children to come on our show. Finally, I contacted the pastor of one of the black churches and said, "Pastor, we can't get black children to come on our show, and we want them. Can you explain this to me?"

The pastor answered straightforwardly, "We have been told in so many ways for so long that we are not wanted by the white community, not even by the white churches, that we will not attempt to push our way in."

"But you are wanted on our program. Won't you please come?" After about a year of calling and scheduling black churches to come and bring their children to our show, black children finally began coming. At times as many as 50 percent of the children on our program were black. Our efforts had paid off.

While at CBN, I invited Doris Akers, who had written the classic song "Sweet, Sweet Spirit," to come and lead a racially mixed choir on our live television show. We never knew who was going to show up for the rehearsals in those days, but amazingly, every night that Doris was there, we had an even 50 percent mix of black and white singers. The same mix held true the nights the choir sang on *The 700 Club*. Everyone involved felt that God was giving us an obvious lesson in race relations. Some of the best long-term benefits of the choir were the new friendships formed between white and black people, who had previously been unaccustomed to speaking to each other, let alone working together for the glory of God.

We did something similar later at PTL. We even rented an auditorium in downtown Charlotte and did an exciting live recording of Doris's mixed choir.

At Heritage USA, the black community was especially welcome, and they knew that, and they came. Over the years, I had numerous black guests on my programs. Pearl Bailey, E. V. Hill, Mahalia Jackson, Mr. T, Kim Fields, Della Reese, Willa Dorsey, Rosey Grier, my beloved board member Dr. Evelyn Carter Spencer, Meadowlark Lemon, "Mother" Smith, Carlton Pearson, Clifton Davis, Marla Gibbs, Lillie Knauls, and many, many others graced our set. Tammy and I especially loved black gospel music. Some of our outstanding musical guests included the great Shirley Caesar, Andrae Crouch, Candi Staton, Jessie Dixon, and the legendary black songwriter Thomas A. Dorsey, who wrote "Precious Lord Take My Hand" and "There Will Be Peace in the Valley." I was also honored to have working with me black artists and ministers such as Derek Floyd, BeBe and CeCe Winans, Brenda Davis, Bob Bailey, Howard McCrary, Reverend Russell and Sandy Hosey, Pastor Hank and Emily Walker, and the host of the African *PTL* program, Benson Idahosa.

Race was never an impediment to my friendships. I had grown up in a racially mixed neighborhood in Michigan where blacks and whites mixed freely. Moreover, I always felt that if there was any place where people should be color blind, it was in the Church.

In 1990, Bruce Solomonson, another Caucasian, had joined GADA. Bruce is the son-in-law of former Vice President Hubert Humphrey, and like his father-in-law, Bruce was a concerned social activist. Tammy Faye and I had gotten to know Bruce and his wife in the visiting room. A quiet, mild-mannered couple, they nonetheless had a passion for people who were hurting, especially those to whom an injustice had been done. Their social conscience had been pricked even more deeply by Bruce's prison experience. Bruce's wife was particularly incensed at the way her husband was being treated, since Bruce was a heart patient in dire need of a transplant.

Bruce had been responsible for working with GADA's sponsor to invite outside guest speakers to the annual Black History Banquet and other events in 1990. He had been instrumental in getting Allan Page and Tom Timpton, two outstanding black communicators, for GADA programs in the prison the year before. The following year, because the guys had selected me as chairman of the religious activities committee, the responsibility to help secure an inspirational speaker for the Black History Banquet was passed on to me. I had a hard act to follow, since Bruce's choices had been so phenomenal. Because the stated goals of GADA were to improve the educational backgrounds of its members and to provide constructive leadership programs that would help the inmates return to their home communities as assets rather than liabilities, I naturally hoped to bring in a speaker who would bring both a practical and a spiritual dimension in his message.

One of the first names to come to mind was Dr. James E. ("Johnny") Johnson, the first black man ever to serve as the assistant secretary of the U.S. Navy. A former marine with a dynamic personality, a contagious smile, a quick wit, and a keen intelligence, Johnny Johnson is a man who immediately inspires confidence. I had known Johnny for many years. He had once been a member of my board of directors in the early days at PTL, and I knew he was a dedicated Christian. I also knew he was fiercely loyal to his country and his ideals and hopes for his fellow blacks. In Johnny's stellar career, he had achieved over a hundred "firsts" for the black race. For instance, Johnny was the first black to become a commissioned warrant officer in the United States Marine Corps. He was also the first black to run for the U.S. Senate from California. He was the first black to be elected vice president of the Boy Scouts of America, and the list goes on and on.

In the latter part of 1990, when Johnny had agreed to come to the prison to speak at the GADA banquet, I was elated. To have a speaker of Johnny's caliber would be a treat indeed. Since I was the chairman of the committee that had been instrumental in helping our sponsor contact Johnny, I had been asked to introduce Johnny before he spoke. At the time, I had agreed, as long as it was okay with our sponsor. But by early 1991, as I was wallowing in my own personal doldrums, I would not even have attended the GADA banquet, much less introduced the speaker, had it not been for my friend Johnny Johnson coming to speak. Once again, God was not going to allow me to waste away in my bunk. He used my friendship with Johnny and my prior commitment to force me back onto my feet.

On February 8, 1991, the evening of the GADA banquet, I shaved off my beard, showered, and put on fresh, clean, sharply pressed clothes for the first time in weeks. Anyone who had not seen me in recent weeks would have been unaware of the deep depression into which I had dropped. The banquet was scheduled to begin at 5:15 P.M., so after the 4:00 P.M. count had cleared, I walked across the compound from Building Two to the chapel. The program was to be held in the large multipurpose room in the chapel basement, so I went early to help set up the room and to wait for my friend to arrive.

Johnny's plane was late that evening, so by the time he got to the chapel basement, the inmates and prison officials attending the banquet were already seated at their tables. As the person who was to introduce Johnny, I was seated at the table across from the guest of honor's table. When Johnny came in, he was seated at the head table, right next to the warden. Johnny nodded discreetly to me and flashed his trademark smile as he sat down.

When it came time for Johnny to speak, I got up and walked directly past the warden and up to the platform. The warden looked shocked to see me going to the podium, especially in light of the prison's efforts to maintain my low-profile status. I was not deliberately trying to violate the prison's wishes; I was merely fulfilling my obligation as chairman of the religious activities committee.

I was nervous as I stood behind the podium in front of the large room filled with people. I had spoken in front of our smoking cessation class, which was frightening enough, but this was a much larger group of people. I had not spoken before such a sizable group in several years. As I began introducing my friend Dr. Johnny Johnson, I relaxed a bit and started listing some of his many accomplishments. Soon, I was sharing stories and telling the banquet guests interesting tidbits about Johnny. The inmates were fascinated, but the longer my introduction went on, the more agitated the warden and prison officials looked. The warden's facial expression said plainly, "How did Bakker get up on that platform?" Although I was not reprimanded or punished in any way at the time, I would not always be so lucky.

Finally, I finished my introduction, much to the relief of the prison brass, and Dr. Johnson bounded up the stairs to the podium. He made some kind remarks about me and then launched into his talk. In a matter of moments, the inmates were on the edge of their seats as he chronicled his rise from a poor, black family to the top of the military ladder. Throughout his speech, he interspersed stories of humor and pathos that reached right inside the inmates' hearts.

Johnny told us about the death of his twenty-three-year-old son, Ken, who had died in the operating room during a relatively routine procedure in which the doctors failed to notice that oxygen was not getting to the young man's brain. Johnny's son had a cardiac arrest on the operating table. He remained alive, through the use of artificial life-support systems, for nearly two more weeks. As Ken's heartbeat slowed to an agonizing halt, Johnny leaned over his boy and whispered, "I'll meet you in heaven . . . I promise."

Johnny told us, "If you keep God ahead of all things, you will succeed." His idea of success related to one of his son's favorite sayings: "It isn't important what you do for yourself, because that will die with you. But what you do for others will live on afterward." When Johnny Johnson finished his speech, the inmates gave him a rousing round of applause. More than that, I knew that we had heard a message from God. I decided that I could not allow myself to hide in my bunk. If I had to live in prison every day for the rest of my life, I was going to make those days count.

CHAPTER

28

Good News

I WAS BUSY TEACHING THE SMOKING CESSATION COURSE ON the morning of February 12, 1991, when I heard a commotion at the door. Tom Brandon opened the door and walked into the room a few steps. "I'm sorry to interrupt you, Jim, but would you please come out in the hall for a minute?"

I stared at Tom. He had never before interrupted one of my sessions. "Excuse me, please," I said to the class, as I followed Tom out of the room.

Out in the hall, I saw my friends Rod Netherton and Tony, the president of the Jaycees. They were grinning as wide as their mouths would allow.

"All right, you guys," I said. "What's going on here?"

Rod suddenly blurted, "Your appeal has been granted!"

"What do you mean?" I stammered. "Come on, you guys. Don't joke with me. That's not funny." I looked at Tom Brandon, my cellmate, and the one guy of the three whom I could count on to tell me the truth. Tom was smiling and nodding his head. "It's true!" he said, echoed by Tony and Rod.

I started to cry right there in the hallway. I was shaking and said aloud, "Oh, God! Can it be true?"

"It's true! It's true!" my friends assured me. The guys did not know any of the details, but someone had seen the news on television. I wanted to call Tammy Faye immediately, but somehow I managed to contain my excitement enough to go back into the classroom to complete my session. My spirits were buoyed by the news, but it was almost too good to be true. I did not want to allow my hopes to rise too high only to have them dashed again.

Back in Florida, Tammy Faye was doing the housework when the telephone rang. She picked up the receiver and heard Tammy Sue's voice on the other end of the line, sobbing into the phone, "Mama, Mama! Have you heard the news about Daddy?"

"What is it?" Tammy Faye screamed into the phone.

"Mama, they have dropped Daddy's forty-five-year sentence! I just heard it on the news!"

Tammy Faye dropped the telephone and raced to the television to turn on the news. Sure enough, the reporters were still talking about the fact that my sentence had been overturned by the appeals court. Tammy Faye and Tammy Sue, both weeping, began praising God for His goodness to us. Then, as the full impact of the news set in on Tammy Faye, she realized that she had to get to Jamie at school before the media did. She said a hasty good-bye to Susie and quickly called the school and asked the school officials to get Jamie out of class to come to the phone for a very important call.

When Jamie came on the line, with little warning, Tammy Faye said, "Jamie, they have dropped the forty-five-year sentence against Daddy!"

Our fifteen-year-old son suddenly began to cry. "Are you sure, Mom? Are you sure? Oh, Jesus! Oh, Jesus! Thank You, Jesus!" he cried out. Then suddenly the phone went dead.

A few minutes later, Tammy Faye's phone rang. It was Jamie. "Mom, I'm sorry I hung up on you," he said. "I was hyperventilating! I had to calm down so I could breathe. Now, Mom, please tell me about it again . . . *real slow*." Tammy reassured Jamie that the news was true, and that the reporters were saying it was possible that I might be freed immediately on bond while I awaited a new resentencing hearing. To my family members, the news meant one thing: I was coming home soon!

About the time Jamie hung up the telephone, I was on the phone from prison to Tammy Faye. "Tam! What is happening?"

Tammy told me what little information she had been able to gather from the television news reports. Suddenly, a call came over the prison loudspeaker system: "Inmate Bakker, report to the warden's office." I quickly said good-bye to Tammy and walked as fast as my legs would carry me toward the administrative offices.

I was called into the assistant warden's office, where I was officially informed that my appeal had been decided by the three-judge panel of the Fourth U.S. Circuit Court of Appeals in Richmond, Virginia. In a businesslike fashion, the assistant warden explained to me the good and bad news of what had happened. The good news was that the federal appeals court had thrown out my forty-five-year sentence. At that moment, I no longer had a prison sentence. The bad news was that the same court had upheld my original conviction on all twenty-four counts of wire fraud, mail fraud, and conspiracy charges for which I was imprisoned. I was to be returned to Charlotte, North Carolina, within the near future to be resentenced by a different federal judge. The best news that the assistant warden told me was that since I had been allowed to be home on bail during the time between the original verdicts and the original sentencing, I would probably be allowed to return home on bail while I awaited my resentencing as well.

In the meantime, he told me, I needed to be ready to move out on a moment's notice. If a court order came through granting my release on bond, I would have to be released within a twenty-four-hour period or placed in solitary confinement for my own protection until I was able to make arrangements to get home. Even now, since technically I had no more sentence, the assistant warden asked me whether I wanted to waive solitary confinement and remain in the general prison population while we waited for the decision on my bond. I certainly did not want to spend the next few days in the hole, so I readily signed a waiver stating that I had chosen to remain in the general population until further word was received regarding my case.

I walked out of the assistant warden's office not knowing whether to laugh or cry. Realistically, I had given up all hope that I would actually win my appeal and that the verdicts would be overturned. Attorney Allan Dershowitz had been quite blunt in informing me that the other attorneys involved in my appeal had botched their efforts. In fact, as I was later to learn, my team of attorneys had lost my appeal on every point except one: that Judge Robert Potter had improperly allowed his own religious prejudices to influence him in sentencing me. Specifically, the appeals court declared inappropriate Judge Potter's statement spoken during the sentencing, "Those of us who do have a religion are ridiculed as being saps from [by] money-grubbing preachers or priests." In rendering the opinion reached by Judges J. Dickson Phillips Jr., John D. Butzner Jr., and himself, Judge J. Harvie Wilkinson III wrote:

285

As the community's spokesperson, a judge can lecture a defendant as a lesson to that defendant and as a deterrent to others. If that were all that occurred here, the court would have been properly exercising its discretion, and we would be loathe to disturb what surely is an integral part of the sentencing process. Sentencing discretion, however, must be exercised within the boundaries of due process. . . . In this case, the trial judge exceeded those boundaries. Courts have held that sentences imposed on the basis of impermissible considerations, such as a defendant's race or national origin, violate due process. . . . While these cases focused on a defendant's characteristics, we believe that similar principles apply when a judge impermissibly takes his own religious characteristics into account in sentencing.

Our Constitution, of course, does not require a person to surrender his or her religious beliefs upon the assumption of judicial office. Courts, however, cannot sanction sentencing procedures that create the perception of the bench as a pulpit from which judges announce their personal sense of religiosity and simultaneously punish defendants for offending it. Whether or not the trial judge has a religion is irrelevant for purposes of sentencing. Regrettably, we are left with the apprehension that the imposition of a lengthy prison term here may have reflected the fact that the court's own sense of religious propriety had somehow been betrayed. In this way, we believe that the trial court abused its discretion in sentencing Bakker. Consequently, the sentence is vacated and the case is remanded for resentencing. This resentencing will be carried out by a different district judge to ensure that the ends of due process are achieved.[1]

An hour later, after I returned from the assistant warden's office, I called Tammy Faye again. This time I could barely contain my excitement. "Tam, it's true! I'm going to be resentenced. They just told me that I could be released from this prison on bail at any time. I am going to go start getting my things together!"

Tammy screamed with joy through her tears.

We had no sooner hung up when one of my lawyers called Tammy to confirm the news. He told Tammy that a hearing would be held soon concerning the bond issue, but he saw no reason why the judge would deny bond and not allow me to be released until my resentencing. One of our good friends told Tammy Faye that he would gladly post the bond money, and my family began getting ready for me to come home.

Although my family, my friends, and I considered the vacating of my original sentence to be a victory, the resentencing itself held no guarantees that I would receive a lighter sentence. The same prosecutors who argued the original case were bent on asking the new judge for the identical sentence—forty-five years. Since they had won their case and the convictions had withstood the appeal, they must have felt confident that they could persuade the new judge that I deserved the same sentence. The new judge would have great latitude in handing down a new sentence. He could uphold Judge Potter's sentence, and nothing would change. On the other hand, he could reduce the sentence to "time served," and I would walk out of prison a free man. Or, he could cut the original sentence in half or thirds. We really had no idea how the judge would rule.

Nevertheless, my family and I were more excited about the possibilities of my release than ever before. Tammy Faye prepared a press release for the media in which she said, "My family and I are very grateful to the appeal court judges for their decision to drop the forty-five-year sentence given to my husband by Judge Potter. So far, that is all we know, as we have not yet talked to Alan Dershowitz, our lawyer. I just talked to my husband. Everyone is excited for him. I believe that before this is all over, my husband will be totally exonerated."

In Cambridge, Massachusetts, Alan Dershowitz was equally ebullient, commenting to the media, "Tammy says this is a great victory for Christians. I told her it was a Jew that did it, so let's call it a great victory for religious freedom in America. She agreed."[2]

Other attorneys who had worked on my case were openly optimistic, including George Davis, my octogenarian trial lawyer. With his usual "I told you so" aplomb, George told reporters, "I said from the day the sentence was given, that that sentence was an outrageous abuse of process by the judge. I'm surprised that the conviction wasn't reversed. I would think that commonsense justice would require that he should never have been incarcerated during this appeal."[3]

The response of our friends was immediate. Calvin Bacon, our former pastor in Charlotte, was in Florida with his wife at the time the announcement hit the news. The Bacons stopped by to rejoice with Tammy Faye. Well-wishers and interview hounds jammed our office telephone lines in Orlando. Television shows and tabloid magazines called incessantly, hoping for any shred of information.

In prison, cards and letters poured in during the days following the announcement that I was to be resentenced. One of the first, of course, came from Owen Carr.

Hallelujah! We saw it first on our local ABC station. Then we saw it
on the evening news with Peter Jennings. We have just now
watched Tammy and your attorney on *Good Morning America.* When
our local ABC station showed it, they talked about James Bakker,
and showed a picture of James Baker, Secretary of State. I couldn't
help but laugh.

Another early letter came from Pastor Hugh Morgan of Tarkenton
Memorial Pentecostal Holiness Church in Athens, Georgia. Although I
had never met Pastor Morgan, he had written to me faithfully during my
first sixteen months of prison. Pastor Morgan wrote: "I heard the good
word on television, radio, and read about the appeals court overruling your
unfair sentence. We, at Tarkenton Memorial, are praying for God to give
you a merciful judge who will set you free."

The following day I received another letter from the same pastor. As
always, he included words of encouragement and spiritual insight: "I trust
that you will be released from prison very soon as you wait to be resentenced. My prayer is that you will find favor. Remember Proverbs 21:1,
'The king's [judge or judges] heart is in the hand of the LORD, as the rivers
of water: he turneth it whithersoever he will' [KJV]."

My dear friend, and one of my favorite singers, James Blackwood and
his wife, Mim, wrote as soon as they heard the news that I was to be resentenced: "Well, praise God . . . part of what we have been praying for has
happened! Now we are praying for your release on bail and your complete
release." Still singing in his mid-seventies, James went on to fill me in
about his most recent concerts.

Another pastor whom I had never met, yet who wrote to me regularly while in prison, was Steven Todd of the Vineyard Christian Fellowship
in Colorado Springs. "I rejoiced when I read about a possible resentencing
trial for you. I have always believed that the outrageous sentence would be
overturned, and at the least, modified significantly."

Others spoke out publicly to the press. Ben Kinchlow, cohost of *The
700 Club,* called the judges' decision an answer to prayer. "I am delighted,"
he said. "I hope this is the end of it."[4]

Evangelist Bob Gass reflected, "Clearly the judge was trying to sentence him for the sins of all the media preachers. But Jim Bakker has
served enough time."[5]

Again, the "hurry up and wait" syndrome set in and was perhaps the
most difficult part of the resentencing process. On Valentine's Day, 1991,

two days after it was announced that my sentence had been thrown out, the job of resentencing me was assigned to U.S. District Judge Graham Mullen in Charlotte. The previous day, Harold Bender, one of my original lawyers on the case, filed a motion with the court asking that I be released on bail until the resentencing hearing could take place. There was no guarantee that the judge would accept Harold's motion. A hearing would have to be held to determine whether I could be permitted to return home until my resentencing hearing.

The bond hearing took place in Charlotte, before Judge Graham Mullen, at 1:30 P.M. on March 1, 1991. Although I was not allowed to attend, Tammy Faye and my sister Donna drove from Orlando to attend the proceedings. The judge's decision whether to allow my release on bail hinged on two main points: Was I a danger to the community, and was I a flight risk?

The prosecutors contended that I was a risk to the community because if I were let out on bail, I would begin soliciting money or Tammy Faye would do so in my name. Judge Mullen rejected this argument as unpersuasive. Next, the judge dealt with the matter of whether there was a risk I might try to escape the country or otherwise try to escape. The burden of proof was on my lawyers to show that I was not a flight risk. To that end, they called as witnesses Tammy Sue; Eddie Knox, my former attorney and the former mayor of Charlotte; Reverend Douglas Pyle, a pastor at New Covenant Church in Orlando; and the psychologist with whom I was counseling in prison, Dr. Daniel Foster.

All of the witnesses spoke confidently that they did not believe I would try to escape before my resentencing hearing. Dr. Foster, who had flown in from Rochester just for this purpose, spoke eloquently on my behalf, providing his opinion from a psychological perspective that I was not a flight risk.

When the witnesses had all been heard and cross-examined by the prosecutors, Judge Mullen dismissed the courtroom until he made his decision. On March 6, 1991, the day before Tammy Faye's birthday, Judge Mullen rendered his decision:

> While Dr. Foster no doubt is sincere, and even on sound professional grounds, in giving his opinion that the defendant is not a flight risk, this still falls short of meeting the defendant's heavy burden. The speculative nature of any psychological evaluation, combined with Mr. Bakker's previously demonstrated susceptibility to aberrant behavior in stressful situations, prevents this court from concluding that the

defendant is clearly and convincingly not a flight risk on the basis of the evidence presented.

Accordingly, the defendant's motion for release pending resentencing is Denied.[6]

Denied! Tammy Faye was stunned. She had totally expected me to be released on bond. After all, I had been released on bond between October 6, 1989, when I had been found guilty and October 24, 1989, when I had been sentenced originally. And I had already spent over a year in prison and had been what some call "a model inmate" with no negative marks against my record.

Tammy Faye burst into tears. Denied! I would remain in prison. I would not be sleeping in the same bed as my wife. I would not be able to hug my children every day. I would not be allowed to see my grandsons, one of whom I had yet to see. No amount of bond money would get me out of prison.

A brief trip to the assistant warden's office was how I found out that I would not be going home anytime soon. For some reason, I accepted the news in stride. The prison axiom, "You ain't got nothin' comin'," had been drilled into my head by my fellow inmates. More and more I was beginning to understand it and accept it as a philosophy of life inside prison. Consequently, I was not surprised that the bond hearing had turned out negatively, nor was I devastated. I went back to my cell and unpacked my belongings.

I went to the phone and dialed the operator to place my collect call to Tammy Faye. As soon as the operator put us through, Tammy asked, "Jim, are you okay?"

"I'm fine, Tam. I'm just numb."

For the next few minutes we tried to encourage each other. Our best attempts seemed futile, and before long, we hung up.

Just before we said good-bye, Tammy said, "I just don't know how many more shocks we are going to be able to stand."

Not many, as I was soon to find out.

CHAPTER

29

Burnout

ON APRIL 4, 1991, TAMMY FAYE AND SHIRLEY FULBRIGHT boarded a plane from Orlando to Wichita, where Tammy was to do her first-ever ticketed gospel music concert. The concert was scheduled to be held at the Crest Theatre and was sponsored by Wichita promoter Christopher Love, a former professional wrestler. Chris met the women at the airport and transported them to the Terradyne Hotel and Country Club, owned by my good friend Roe Messner.

Wichita was Roe's hometown, and he was excited and happy that Tammy had chosen to sing there. Knowing that Tammy was unfamiliar with the many details involved in ticketed concert promotions, I had talked with Roe a few days before and had encouraged him to watch out for Tammy and to take care of her.

Roe and his wife, Ruth Ann, visited with Tammy Faye and Shirley at the hotel on the evening of April 4. Ruth Ann especially went out of her way to welcome Tammy Faye to Wichita.

The following night, nearly six hundred people almost filled the theater to hear Tammy Faye sing and speak. When the local media showed up to interview Tammy Faye prior to the concert, Roe sprang into action in his role of "road manager" and protector of Tammy Faye. A dispute broke out between Roe, members of the press, and Christopher Love, the concert promoter, who had assured the press they could cover the concert. Roe insisted that members of the media be cleared from the building before Tammy Faye would perform. Finally, the matter was resolved and the press was cleared, except for Channel 10, the local ABC affiliate in Wichita.

The show went on, and from all reports, Tammy did a fine job. All reports, that is, except those fed to ABC. Late that night, I called Tammy at the hotel and she gave me a glowing report about the concert. The following day, however, I was listening to an ABC station on my radio when I heard a report about Tammy Faye's concert. The report panned Tammy Faye and claimed that the concert had "bombed." When I heard the negative review, I wondered, *What is going on here? Why am I getting two different stories?*

In Wichita, the Messners treated Tammy Faye like a queen. Ruth Ann hosted a lovely luncheon for Tammy with many of the leading women of the city. Then a number of the women piled into a large black limousine Ruth Ann had arranged, and the limo whisked Tammy Faye, Ruth Ann, and the women off for a shopping spree. All in all, Roe and Ruth Ann Messner went to great lengths to provide Tammy with one of the nicest weekends she had known in a long time.

At first I was glad I had asked Roe to look out for Tammy. A few days later, when Tammy sent me some of the photographs taken that weekend, I wasn't so sure. One photo bothered me particularly. It was a photo of Tammy and Roe, with Roe's arm around Tammy's waist, pulling her snugly toward him. I winced when I saw the picture, but I quickly put jealous thoughts aside. Tammy was my wife of thirty years . . . and Roe was my best friend.

One of the reasons I was able to not dwell on negative thoughts about my wife and best friend was because I had been immersing myself in the words of Jesus. For many hours every day, I pondered the true message of the Gospel accounts and what it really meant to see everything and everyone as Jesus did. I was also receiving a tremendous amount of spiritual insight from another book sent to me by Sue Williams in New York: *Spiritual Burnout* by Malcolm Smith.

As I read Malcolm's book, it was as though he had a computer printout of my innermost thoughts, describing what had happened to me during my last years at Heritage USA. In those days, often at the end of a day's activities—preparing for and doing our daily television program, attempting to raise almost $3.5 million a week to keep everything going, overseeing our many building projects, and planning for new ones—I would be totally exhausted. I was not exaggerating when I told friends that by the end of the day, I had to literally tell my feet to lift up and take another step.

I worked feverishly and constantly; I could do nothing less, because in my heart and mind, I felt I was doing it all for God.

Malcolm Smith placed a mirror in front of my face when he said: "The man or woman who does not reach for the top will never suffer from burnout; it is a condition found only among those who want the best."[1]

That was me! In my high school annual, I listed my future goal as "To do the best at everything I do." And I tried to. Malcolm Smith's book, however, helped me realize that although it was not wrong to want to do my best, I had allowed a warped concept of God to color my efforts. I had developed an obsession with trying to do the best for God. I was striving to do great things for God in an attempt to earn His favor. I never truly grasped the meaning of God's grace, which would have helped me understand that I already *had* God's favor; nothing I could possibly build or do for God would ever earn His favor because He had already bestowed it on me as an undeserved gift.

As I devoured Malcolm's words, one truth after another leaped off the pages. I did not always like what I was beginning to realize. One of Malcolm's statements struck me right between the eyes: "The spiritually exhausted person needs more than the singing of a few inspirational worship songs—they will only momentarily make him feel good. He needs a completely new perspective on the way he thinks about life. When that happens, the inspiration will last a lifetime."[2]

Yes! I began to detect a pattern in what God was showing me through my prison experience and my newfound understanding of the words of Jesus. God was performing major surgery on my heart. He was giving me an entirely new perspective on how He wanted me to live.

Malcolm's words smacked with a truth for me:

It's hard to believe God loves us when His people reject us. . . . Although some of God's misguided children have thrown you out as a useless reed and written you off as a burned out, embarrassing flax, God hasn't. He says, "Now you are ready to let Christ be your life."[3]

Ready? I was more than ready! I could hardly wait to see what God was going to show me next. It was this:

Are you wounded and lonely, ridden with true guilt? With everything people are saying about you, it may be difficult to believe, but your first step is to realize that you are loved. You need to understand that you have failed but, having done so, you need to know God says that He accepts you.[4]

Oh, how I needed that message! Yet Malcolm was not espousing a message of "easy believism" or as Dietrich Bonhoeffer referred to it, "cheap grace." Oh, no. Smith's message drove home my responsibility to repent.

> Before the grace of God can take our mistakes and turn them into strengths, there must be a response to Him. That response is repentance and faith.[5]

I racked my brain and examined my heart. In truth, I *had* repented. Again and again I had poured out my heart to God, repenting of my sins and seeking His forgiveness.

I asked God to reveal any areas in which I still needed to repent, but step-by-step I found that repentance was not the paramount issue on God's agenda for me. He was speaking to my heart about issues that went even beyond repentance. Malcolm Smith's words helped focus the issues for me:

> We think that we would be healed if we could see God judging all the people who have disappointed us or, at least, making them come and tell us how wrong they were! . . . We come to God and demand a formula, a series of steps we can tell others we followed to get out of the pit of spiritual exhaustion. God frustrates us, He doesn't give us a formula. . . . He gives us Himself![6]

God had been showing me in many ways that the primary reason He had allowed me to be imprisoned was not to punish me, nor was it so I could minister to other prisoners; I was in prison so I could get to know Him. Some people might find it ironic that a preacher who had spoken to millions of people about how to find God needed to be sent to prison to renew a relationship with Him himself. But I am convinced there was no other way God could have gotten my attention. God wanted me to quit worshiping bricks and mortar, programs and talents, and get back to worshiping Him.

I discovered that I could go no farther until I confronted the matter of forgiving the people toward whom I harbored bitterness and resentment over the events that had landed me in prison. Again, Malcolm Smith clarified the issue:

> A major step for returning to spiritual vigor and strength is to forgive all who have been part of the hurts of life. Forgive those who have failed you, who were not there when you needed them the most. Forgive the gossips who carried the news of your exhaustion and problems to every believer in the vicinity. Forgive those leaders and elders who have hurt you with their words and actions. And forgive those who you thought were spiritual giants, but were found to have feet of clay and a set of weaknesses just like everyone else.[7]

Ouch! Malcolm, couldn't you mince at least a few words? Apparently not, because the author went on hitting me right between the eyes. "We become the slave of the person we hate. . . . Unforgiveness hurts the unforgiver more than the unforgiven!"[8]

It didn't take a theologian to interpret what God was saying to me.

I began to see several glaring areas in which I had been wrong in the past. For one, I had been so busy building Heritage USA—ostensibly for God—that I had lost my intimate relationship with Him.

A second area that came into focus was my relationship with my children, especially my relationship with Jamie Charles. Someone had sent a picture to me of four-year-old Jamie in Hawaii, sitting on the stage with several PTL band members, playing his little ukulele. As I put the picture up on the wall of my prison cell, I asked myself, *Where was I?*

Someone else sent me a picture that tore my heart apart. The picture showed me at one of the many building sites on which construction was being done at PTL. I was wearing blue jeans, cowboy boots, and a construction worker's hard hat, which was my customary dress following most of our *PTL* programs. After I had ministered to the audience for about half an hour after the program, I would hastily change clothes and head for the construction sites to oversee our building projects, often simply grabbing an apple for lunch.

In the picture, I was standing at one of the sites with a bodyguard at my side, and in the background, looking on from a distance was my little boy, Jamie. When I saw the photograph, I literally wept in my cell. I could not believe that I was so intent on building Heritage USA that I had missed my little boy growing up. I thought, *He was so cute! Why didn't I spend more time with him?*

Certainly, I had tried to be a good father to my son. Like any good dad,

I had taken him places, done fun things with him, and tried to create special memories together with him. Yet somehow I had become so obsessed with "the work of God" and "saving the world" that I was oblivious to the painful, longing look in my little boy's eyes. The look that said, "I need my dad."

Instead of Dad, Jamie's constant companion was a PTL bodyguard. During the 1980s we had received several death threats, reported to us by our chief of security, Don Hardister. Although no attempts were successfully carried out against our family, an insane man once came to Heritage claiming that God told him he was supposed to rape and kill Tammy Sue. The man was apprehended and sent back to the asylum. We also received numerous bomb threats. Merited or not, we lived with a constant awareness of danger. Consequently, our children had bodyguards who hovered near them most of the day. While growing up, Jamie's closest friends were his adult bodyguards, Tommy Stamps, Don Hardister, and Carlos Fisher.

The bodyguards drove Jamie from place to place. They played with him while I was busy erecting another building. They picked him up after school. In contrast, I hardly remembered Jamie Charles's childhood. He had just been born when we had started PTL in an old furniture store in Charlotte. Then we moved to a twenty-five-acre site we called Heritage Village, and our ministry began to take off, multiplying exponentially. Analysts from IBM Corporation estimated that we grew 7,000 percent over the next year and a half. We could barely keep up—things were happening so quickly. Before long, we were building Heritage USA and sending gospel programming to fifty-two nations. In the midst of the swirl of spiritual activity, I lost touch with my family, and especially with Jamie. I was not there when he needed me.

Like many other ministers, I had made a tragic mistake: I had confused the *work* of God for God Himself.

I was wrong.

God's work is a poor substitute for God Himself. I am now convinced that God must come first in our lives, then our family, and *then* the work that we are doing for God. If we allow the order to get out of whack, we run the risk of losing our most important relationships in life. And if our family crumbles while we are out trying to serve God, we have missed our primary ministry. Yet that is exactly what I allowed to happen. Not intentionally. It happened so subtly, imperceptibly, while I was busy doing what I thought was important work for God.

My self-imposed responsibilities at Heritage USA were massive. I was the president of The Inspirational Television Network, seen on two hundred television stations and on over eight thousand cable systems. The television production center and the twenty-four-hour-a-day programming on our satellite system all came under my oversight. Of course, I served as executive producer and host of our daily flagship programs, variously named *The PTL Club*, *The Jim and Tammy Show*, and simply, *Jim Bakker*, seen live in all fifty states and in many foreign countries.

I was also the senior pastor of Heritage Village Church and Missionary Fellowship, with a congregation of several thousand people attending services each week. I preached at most of the Sunday morning services, unless I was out of town. As pastor, I was responsible for a staff of twenty-five assistant pastors, an active Sunday school program, and the usual fare of church ministry programs for all ages as well as special ministry needs, including weddings, funerals, baptisms, and communion services. We were not simply a television program. We were a bona fide church.

Although at one point I had nearly three thousand employees—including many dedicated, hardworking supervisors—plus thousands of volunteers who helped make Heritage USA function smoothly, sooner or later, the ultimate responsibility fell to me. Besides the television and church, I also had spiritual oversight of all the other ministries at Heritage USA, including: New Vine Fellowship, a ministry to help alcoholics and drug addicts get free of their addictions and stay free; Heritage School of Evangelism, where we trained college-age young people in the techniques and methods of evangelism; Heritage Academy, a kindergarten through grade twelve Christian school; Heritage Day Care; The Heritage Preservation Society (formed to help preserve our religious heritage, such as the childhood home of Billy Graham, which was moved from Charlotte and restored at Heritage USA, with the help of Dr. Graham's brother, Melvin); Fort Hope, a center where street people and former prisoners could find help, a home, job training, and spiritual development; Heritage House, a home for pregnant women; Tender Loving Care Adoption Agency, to help place babies in Christian homes; People That Love Centers, over nine hundred centers nationwide that provided free food and clothing and helped with job placement; Prison Ministry, placing Christian literature and Bibles in prisons; *Together* magazine, our full-color monthly magazine; Kevin's House, a home for disabled children; and The Upper Room Prayer Center, a replica of the Upper Room in which Jesus and His disciples ate the Last Supper before His crucifixion. The Upper Room was staffed twenty-four hours a day with pastors and a worldwide phone center for those seeking spiritual counseling and prayer.

In addition to these responsibilities, I was president of Heritage USA, the world's largest Christian retreat center. At the height of our efforts, our dedicated staff provided eighty-six religious services each week. According to PTL security figures, more than six million visitors came through the gates at Heritage USA in 1986, the last full year I served as president. We had seven restaurants, three swimming pools, three trains, 3,336 lodging rooms and campsites built or being developed, Mainstreet USA shops and religious bookstore, a dinner theater where inspirational musicals and plays were performed with full orchestra, Heritage Island, a huge, $13 million, state-of-the-art water park staffed by seventy lifeguards per shift, the Heritage Passion Play, a dramatic presentation of the life of Christ in a multimillion-dollar outdoor amphitheater, and much more. We also had time-share lodgings and a retirement village, which included single-family homes, high-rise condominiums, apartments, and duplexes, in various stages of construction.

Oh, yes, we also had a hotel. At the time of my resignation the five-hundred-room Heritage Grand was completed and the five-hundred-room Heritage Grand Towers was under construction and would have been completed within a few months. Besides all that, I was our chief fund-raiser, responsible to raise the money to keep it all going, which, in 1986, was almost $170 million.

It was little wonder that I burned out. Although my intentions were good, I was obsessed with building what some might call a modern-day Tower of Babel. I had allowed my attention to become centered on the packaging rather than on the Gift.

Now, as I sat in my prison cell, staring at the pictures of my boy who had gotten lost in all the buildings, I would have traded my entire life's work for just one full day that my boy and I could spend together, doing whatever Jamie wanted to do. How I wished I could make up for lost time with him. But those opportunities were gone. My little boy was now a young man . . . and I had plenty of time to regret that I had missed so many special moments in his life. I prayed that somehow, some way, I would have another chance to be a real father to my son. Although I could not have imagined it then, that time was soon to come.

"Big Doc"

IN THE EARLY PART OF 1991, I LEARNED THAT DR. TOM Brandon would soon be leaving Rochester prison. I was happy that Tom was getting out of prison, but I was sad to know that my best buddy was leaving. We knew that our February smoking cessation class would probably be our last. Despite the fact that Tom and I had been teaching the class for almost a year, every new guard that came into our unit gave us flak about why we were not cleaning toilets every day. Usually, when we mentioned Dr. Westrick to the inquisitors, they backed off and allowed us to continue our studies and preparation.

On one occasion, as Tom and I were walking down the hall with our arms loaded with books, handouts, and other materials used for our class, a young guard approached us about only cleaning toilets on weekends. The guard persisted in questioning how Tom and I were allowed to spend our time studying instead of cleaning. He seemed intent upon getting us back to cleaning bathrooms full-time again.

Finally, Tom pulled his glasses down on his nose—he looked like Jerry Lewis in the 1960s movie *The Nutty Professor*—and peered at the guard's name tag. "What is your name, sir?" he asked and then read the guard's name aloud in a professorial tone of voice. "I will have Dr. Westrick call you and tell you what Jim and I do under her supervision."

When the guard heard Dr. Westrick's name, he started backing up, holding his hand over his name tag. "You don't know me!" he said. "We didn't have this conversation! Just forget it. I don't care what you do, but do not have Dr. Westrick call me!"

Tom and I never learned why the guard had such fear of our "guardian angel," but we were glad the guard stopped giving us trouble.

Although Tom lost his license to practice medicine when he was incarcerated, he never ceased to care for people. One day, Tom was in the chow hall when he saw an inmate stretched out on the floor. Tom recognized the man immediately as a fellow from Building One who had attempted suicide by putting a .357 Magnum in his mouth and pulling the trigger after he was caught trying to rob a bank. His suicide attempt failed, but he did succeed in blinding himself and blowing away a large portion of his palate. As a consequence of his injuries, the man had difficulty in swallowing hard foods. He actually was supposed to eat a special diet, but for some reason, that day he had tried to eat a cheeseburger and it had gotten stuck in his throat. As Tom approached the scene, besides choking to death, the man was beginning to have a cardiac arrest.

Several prison officials were desperately attempting to apply the Heimlich maneuver, but it was not working. Tom knew what he had to do. He was going to have to apply mouth-to-mouth resuscitation. He had only one question: *Does the man have AIDS?* As Tom jumped into the center of the chaos, the victim's body was already turning an ashen gray. The doctor in Tom took over, and as he wiped the vomit from the man's mouth and covered it with his own, he thought, *If I get AIDS, I get AIDS, but I have to try to save this man's life.* After several minutes of Tom's blowing air into the man, the choking man began breathing on his own again. The prison officials quickly transferred the man to the hospital and his life was spared. Tom sighed with relief when he later learned that the man did not have AIDS.

Since November, when Sam Houston had informed Tom and me that we would have to clean toilets on the weekends if we wanted to continue teaching our smoking cessation class during the week, we had spent every weekend, every holiday cleaning the rest rooms. Our lives revolved around shining porcelain bowls, mopping tile floors, and scouring shower stalls with our long-handled brushes.

Each day, the guards inspected our work, and regular monthly inspections were done as well. As an incentive to keep our living quarters clean, the inmate unit section with the cleanest facilities was permitted to line up first in the chow line, which amounted to about fifteen minutes earlier than the others. As such, it was a big deal that Tom and I kept the bathrooms as clean as possible.

That job was made much more difficult on weekends because the inmates were in the unit. When we were doing the same job during the week, most of the men were out of the building at their respective jobs. On the weekends, however, many of the guys were "home." After trying several times to do my work on the weekend only to have other inmates tramp over the still-wet floors and flush the commodes that I was disinfecting, I inadvertently discovered a way to keep the other inmates out of the bathrooms until I had time to complete my cleaning.

One of the inmates tramped across my wet, freshly cleaned floor and was about to use one of the commodes in which I had just placed a dose of A-500 chemical cleaning agent. I usually allowed the disinfectant to sit in the toilet bowl for ten to fifteen minutes, causing the water to turn bright yellow. When one of the guys came in and used the commode before I was done, I'd start the process over. This time, however, when the man saw the bright yellow water in the commode, he pointed and asked, "What's that?"

"Oh, that's the stuff the prison gives me to kill all the bacteria in our bathrooms," I said, adding nonchalantly, "including the AIDS virus."

When the man heard me say AIDS, he backed up immediately, throwing his hands up in front of his body as if to defend himself as he quickly retraced his steps to the door.

"AIDS virus! You go right ahead, Bakker. Don't let me bother you. I'll be back when you're done."

From that day on, anytime I wanted to keep the men from using the bathroom in which I was working, I would tell them I was disinfecting for viruses, including the AIDS virus. Inevitably, they would suddenly find the energy to make the short walk to the next bathroom down the corridor.

In addition to my other studies, I had been working through the temperaments course provided by Drs. Richard and Phyllis Arno of the National Christian Counselors Association (NCCA). Because I had been an ordained minister and had been counseling people for years, the NCCA gave me credit for my work in the field. So by completing this course of study, I would also have a professional counselor's license and the ability to administer and help interpret a wide variety of tests used in formal counseling situations. Part of my training required that I test and counsel a number of people, with the help of my instructors.

Tom Brandon volunteered to be one of my first guinea pigs. Shortly before Tom left F.M.C. Rochester, I administered a Temperament Analysis Profile to him. If completed honestly the short test is designed to reveal a

301

person's true nature. It is an easy, enjoyable test to take, but it is remarkably accurate in revealing the relationship between what a person expresses toward the world around him or her and what the person really wants deep inside.

Ordinarily, the results of a person's test were to be discussed over as much as a six-month counseling period, dealing with a limited amount of material in a series of one-hour sessions. But since Tom was a "captive audience," and we knew that he was going to be transferred soon, he and I went over Tom's entire test in one night.

Tom sat on his bunk in our cell and I sat on his desk chair, facing him, as I began to describe some of the characteristics about Tom revealed by the test. I had been counseling regularly with Dr. Foster, so I knew the routine well.

"It says here that you are an extreme introvert, a compulsive loner," I told Tom, "that you are a very private person, a homebody, someone who would rather stay home than go out and socialize."

"Well, I could have told you that." Tom laughed as he brushed off the comment. I could tell, though, that the description had hit home and that he was thinking about it seriously. "What else does it say?"

"Well, it says that you are very task oriented. That you relate well to tasks and systems, but you have little understanding of people."

"Hey, what can I tell you? That's why I became a doctor!" Tom laughed again.

"The report says that you are unwilling to allow anyone to control you. That you have low self-esteem, and that it is almost impossible to make you feel loved and accepted. It says here that you are an extremely lonely person." I stopped and looked up at Tom. He wasn't laughing now. We talked briefly about some of the areas the test revealed before I went on.

"Apparently, in an effort to lessen your loneliness, you are prone to undertake sexual sins. But the sexual relationships don't mean much to you." I knew this to be true about Tom. He had admitted to me that he had slept with over one thousand women over the course of his lifetime. He was not simply looking for love in all the wrong places, he was not looking for love at all. To him it was just sex, nothing more. He was not seeking affection. As his test results revealed, to him, physical touch had to lead to sex or else it was a waste of time. He didn't care about the women with whom he slept and he didn't want them to care about him. "The report says that your deep relationships are few and far between." Again the piece of paper was right on target. I could not recall Tom having a visitor, and he rarely got personal letters. Most of his mail was magazines and medical journals.

"The report also says that you have a strong tendency to use alcohol and drugs to lessen the pain of living your everyday life." It was true. Tom had been an alcoholic. Part of the reason he was in prison related to his drinking problem. He slumped down on his bunk and stretched out, facing the ceiling. I was beginning to feel like a psychiatrist.

In one area after another, the test results seared into Tom's inner person. He was disturbed by the inside look at himself. He had never allowed anyone to know the things about himself that I was now reading off the test report.

We talked well into the night about the various characteristics about Tom reflected on the test, as well as the recommendations made by the National Christian Counselors Association concerning how Tom could use the information about himself. To Tom, the test was life-changing. For the first time in his life, he began to understand some of his predispositions toward certain types of behavior, and that although his temperament was "set in stone," he could take positive steps to avoid the circumstances that had gotten him in trouble in the past. It was as though he saw the real Tom for the first time.

As part of the course requirements for my license, I tested numerous other inmates as well. Many of them were excited about it; they genuinely wanted to know about themselves and what made them tick. More than one man said, "This test must be right on. My wife has been telling me things like that for years!"

When I gave the test to my friend Rod Netherton, he became so fascinated with the self-discovery process that he wrote to the NCCA and paid to take the entire counseling course! He eventually became a licensed counselor while still in prison.

A few days before Tom was transferred to a state prison, I wrote out a "prescription" for him from "Dr. Bakker." Since Tom was a medical doctor, I knew he would appreciate my effort to give him a "Prescription for Life." I included instructions for Tom to get married and maintain a monogamous relationship with only one woman; I encouraged him to attend regular Alcoholics Anonymous meetings; I cautioned him against ever taking another drink, because it would likely throw him right back into the destructive patterns of his past; I also instructed Tom that he was to read his Bible regularly and to find a good Bible-believing church he could attend, and to take care to maintain and develop his faith in Jesus Christ.

When Tom read the prescription, he smiled and nodded his head. I sensed that Tom truly appreciated that my concern for him stretched beyond the prison fence.

It was tough to say good-bye to Tom. He had been my cellmate, my coteacher, and my best friend in the Rochester prison. I was going to miss him badly. Toward the end of April we got word that Tom was going on the "Merry-go-round," one of the last trips an inmate takes around the prison compound, securing release signatures from each department head, including the inmate's unit manager, the chaplain, the inmate's day guard, as well as somebody from the recreation department. It was sort of a last check to make sure that the inmate did not have any work or forms to be completed before release, and a last good-bye to everyone too. It usually took an inmate all day to work his way around the "Merry-go-round."

On the Friday night before Tom left, we decided to have a going away party for him. Around 7:00 P.M., at a time when most of the prison officials except the guards were usually gone for the evening, we assembled in the "Quiet Room," a twelve-by-twenty-foot room where the inmates played cards or went to read and study. The guys went all out and got our usual assortment of food including prison pizza and mop pails filled with ice and cans of soda pop. At least twenty-five guys showed up and were standing around talking, eating, and laughing when suddenly the door opened and in walked Sam Houston, the unit manager.

Instantly, silence enveloped the room. It was not against the rules to assemble in one place, but it was against the rules to eat in the card room. We had been caught.

Sam Houston instantly recognized what was going on. Had he wanted to be nasty, he could have had each of us thrown into the "hole" for being at the party. Instead, he walked slowly around the silent room and greeted each man by name, pausing an extra few moments to chat with Tom, the guest of honor. When he got back to the door, he addressed the room full of inmates.

"Carry on, gentlemen," he said with a hint of a smile. He turned around and walked out the door.

For a moment nobody said a word. One of the guys broke the silence by saying, "He's not such a bad guy after all." At that everyone cracked up and Tom's going-away party continued.

I have never liked good-byes. To this day, I am not good at them. Nevertheless, my friend Tony and I walked Tom over to the building through which all prisoners enter and leave the Federal Medical Center at

Rochester. There he would go through the final strip search and change of clothes before exiting the prison and boarding the bus to "someplace else."

Just before we got to the R & D area, Tony and I stopped and embraced Tom. Men in prison do not usually touch, but when a fellow inmate is leaving, it is considered acceptable to give him a brief hug or a slap on the back. We said our good-byes. We did not prolong them.

Tom waved good-bye one more time and then stepped inside the door to R & D. I have never seen him since. Nor have I been allowed to talk with him because of parole regulations that prohibit fellow inmates from contacting each other for an extended period of time after they are released. The last I heard, Tom was back on the outside, going to AA meetings, rebuilding his life and his medical practice, and married. He has been actively involved in helping other alcoholics beat their addictions. I may never see him again, this side of heaven, but I will always be grateful to "Big Doc."

31

Partners for Life

A FEW WEEKS BEFORE TOM BRANDON WAS TRANSFERRED from F.M.C. Rochester, I had my progress review at the prison. Once again I was called before the review team, which included numerous prison officials, my counselors, and Sam Houston. Although everyone in the room knew that I was to be resentenced, it was obvious that I was still going to be calling Building Two my home for a while. My resentencing hearing had been delayed until May 31, 1991, over a month away.

The review team considered every aspect of my prison experience, including my work habits, mental and physical health, my volunteer activities, and my overall attitude. They reported that by my working "in toilets," and with other funds taken from my commissary account, I had been able to pay $1,050 toward the five-hundred-thousand-dollar fine imposed on me by Judge Potter when he had sentenced me in October 1989. The review also noted that my release date was October 15, 2034, but my projected release date was Tuesday, December 15, 2015. This included the thirteen days of "good time" I had earned. No matter how I looked at it, my report said that I was going to be in prison a very long time.

Despite the report, I was relatively upbeat. My request to be released on bail until the resentencing had been denied, but I still held on to hope that my resentencing might result in a reduction of the amount of time I would have to stay in prison. Tammy Faye had convinced Alan Dershowitz to stay on the case to handle my resentencing hearing even though Alan had readily admitted that he was an appellate lawyer and resentencing was not his area of expertise. Nevertheless, knowing that Alan was on the case gave me some hope.

More importantly, though, I had been immersing myself in the words of Jesus more and more. In addition to the Bible, I was also studying several books that I felt had been providentially sent to me.

I had read Malcolm Smith's book, *Spiritual Burnout*, over and over to the point that I could quote many passages of it almost verbatim. Another book, sent to me by the same woman in New York who had sent Malcolm's book, was also having a profound impact on me. *God Meant It for Good*, by R. T. Kendall, minister of Westminster Chapel in London, is a study in the life of Joseph. Although I didn't know it at the time, the book was destined to become a "manual" for me during the remainder of my prison years.

When Pastor Phil Shaw came to visit me in April, he noticed the change in my attitude and demeanor immediately. Phil later called Tammy Faye's office and talked to Shirley Fulbright. He told her that for the first time since he had known me, he saw hope in my eyes and in my spirit. He said the change was phenomenal and he attributed much of it to the book I was reading. Phil was right.

One day one of the inmates brought me a newspaper article that someone had sent him from the March 9, 1991, edition of the *Chicago Tribune*. The headline read: "PTL Materials Used as Textbook." The article described a college course at the College of Charleston, taught by Associate Professor Gary Tidwell, a former attorney with the U.S. Securities and Exchange Commission Division of Enforcement. The course studied the business practices at PTL, and on at least one occasion, students had even taken a field trip to visit Heritage USA after I had gone to prison. According to the article, students taking the course ostensibly were to "find and analyze 'red flags' in their PTL materials that are inconsistent with ethical business practices and that signal trouble ahead."[1]

Ordinarily I ignored most newspaper and magazine articles about me that crossed my path in prison. But for some reason, my interest was piqued. Perhaps because I was interested to see just how someone could develop an entire college course out of our business practices at Heritage USA, I read the article.

It laid out in bite-size, simple terms why I had been put in prison. As strange as it might seem, I had been asking myself and a few of my fellow inmates for just such an answer for nearly a year and a half.

"Why am I in prison?" I would ask my friends.

Usually they would laugh and make some sort of wisecrack.

"No, really," I said. "What crime did I commit? I want to hear your answer."

"Well, you know," my friends would say, "you . . . er, ah . . . well, you know, you stole all that money."

"What money? How much?" I asked.

"You know!" They insisted. "That $190 million you bilked those people out of. . . ."

"No, I do not know," I replied.

"Yeah, right," some of the guys would answer. One fellow said, "I'll bet you have that $190 million stashed away in a Swiss bank account."

Another fellow even wanted me to help set him up in business when he got out of prison, with the money I had supposedly stolen.

But those closest to me said, "What do you mean, you didn't steal all the money, Jim? Where did it go? If you didn't steal the money, what are you doing in here?"

When I read the *Tribune* article, for the first time since before my trial in 1989, I began to understand why, from the government's perspective, I was in prison. The article said it succinctly: "Overselling the hotel space and reneging on the lodging promises was at the core of Bakker's convictions in both a criminal fraud trial and a civil class action trial."[2]

For some reason, despite the five-week trial in 1989, I had never fully realized this before. Now, there it was right in front of me, in black and white: I was in prison for overbooking our lodging space at Heritage USA. Syndicated columnist and radio commentator Paul Harvey had first raised his eyebrows at this possibility in his article that ran in the Sunday papers less than two weeks prior to my sentencing. Harvey asked: "Are we really going to send Jimmy to prison for 120 years for overbooking his resort when hotel managers almost every day promise more rooms than they can provide? Airlines also almost every day overbook flights. Let's keep this in perspective."[3]

As I read the article about Professor Tidwell's course, I was appalled at the errors it included or implied. I pointed out several of the errors to one of my friends, and he encouraged me to write to the professor to help provide him with firsthand factual information for his course.

So on April 14, 1991, in my cell, late at night, I began drafting a letter to Professor Tidwell. I first asked the professor to identify what I did wrong. "What is my crime?" I asked him. "The article says I was tried, convicted, and sentenced for swindling my supporters. How much did I steal?

(Give facts, dates, and amounts)" I then wrote about points of the article that weren't true.

Tidwell's students were apparently shown videotaped highlights of past *PTL* programming.

> The students hone in on those parts where Bakker gets down to business—such as segments where he announces a 25,000-person-limit on "lifetime partnerships" for the 500-room Grand Hotel; and later, a 30,000-limit on the 500-room tower addition. Both of those partnership plans guaranteed three nights free lodging every year for life.
>
> Despite those promised limits, court documents revealed that more than 68,000 partnerships were sold for the Grand Hotel. Another 63,000 were sold for the hotel's tower addition, which was never built as PTL went bankrupt.[4]

It was the last line of that statement that really got to me—reporting that the hotel's tower was never built, and implying that I had bankrupted PTL. The twenty-one-story Heritage Grand Tower *had* been built while I was still at PTL. The Tower was only about two to three months from opening when news of my sexual immorality with Jessica Hahn and subsequent resignation as president of PTL hit the press. The rooms in the Tower had already been carpeted through the tenth floor and had been wallpapered through the thirteenth floor. Most of the custom-designed furniture for the rooms had already been manufactured and was in local warehouses. Many of the hotel's accoutrements had already been purchased and were on site, ready to be installed as soon as the interior work was done on the Tower. Ironically, Professor Tidwell's own students would have had to have seen the Tower during their "field trip" to Heritage USA. To say that it had never been built was simply not true. I sent Professor Tidwell a photograph of the Tower as proof.

To his credit, at least Professor Tidwell encouraged his students to go tour Heritage USA for themselves. That was more than the jurors had been allowed when my original case had been tried.

What also bothered me was the implication in the article that I had taken PTL into bankruptcy. I wrote to Professor Tidwell, "PTL was not bankrupt when I left. Our debt-to-asset ratio was one-to-six on book value with no consideration for the appreciated value of the property." My estimation of the actual value of Heritage USA and The Inspirational Television Network was closer to $500 million, when the ministry and the eight thousand cable affiliates were fully functioning. When we purchased the property, we paid $1,200 to $1,500 per acre. By 1987 when I resigned, the least expensive land contiguous to the four square miles of Heritage USA was selling for $45,000 an acre.

I asked Professor Tidwell to supply the date that I put PTL into bankruptcy, which I knew, of course, was impossible for him to do. PTL had not filed for bankruptcy under my watch. It was several months into Jerry Falwell's leadership of PTL that the ministry was plunged into bankruptcy. Frankly, I would never have taken PTL into bankruptcy; I would have died before I put PTL into bankruptcy. More importantly, there was no need to be concerned about bankruptcy. In 1986, we had experienced one of our greatest years since beginning the ministry. Literally millions of people had visited Heritage USA that year, and although we had the financial pressures that any rapidly burgeoning company might have, we were having a banner year financially. We took in nearly $170 million in 1986. A large amount of money came in through our Lifetime Partnership programs. These were undesignated funds, money that was available to be used throughout the ministry, as it was needed. Although it seemed in my twenty-five years of pioneering Christian television, we were always playing financial catch-up, 1986 was by far the best year in our history and our fixed assets had a book value of over $140 million.

Professor Tidwell made much of:

A 1985 memo from Peter Bailey, chief financial officer for PTL, stating that while the ministry was generating a whopping $700,000 a week, its bills amounted to $1.2 million a week. The difference was made up by drawing from the "lifetime partners" accounts that were supposed to pay for building hotel rooms.[5]

Again, this reported another common misconception of PTL. Professor Tidwell's course looked for unethical business practices at PTL. Why then, I asked the professor,

. . . was I tried on memos, and not on audited financial statements? The Audited Financial Statement for fiscal year 1985 (May 1984 to May 1985), shows that the Ministry's income was $120 million for that year. . . . The 1985 fiscal year figures show average weekly income was approximately $2.4 million. That was twice the needed $1.2 million stated in the memo.

At PTL, we hired some of the best accounting firms in the U.S. We paid hundreds of thousands of dollars for their expertise. I personally instructed our accounting firms to make sure we were doing things exactly right. If there was a question of whether we were liable for a particular tax or not, or whether a certain item was a legitimate business expense or not, I encouraged our accounting firms to be stricter with us than necessary. I always told representatives of our "Big Eight" accounting firms, "I want our financial operations to be squeaky clean."

Concerning the government assertion that we had oversold lodging space at Heritage USA, and that I had willingly conspired with Reverend Richard Dortch to defraud the Lifetime Partners, I wrote to Professor Tidwell:

> When I gave the 25,000 Lifetime-Partner number for the five hundred-room Grand Hotel, it was true. We then added more lodging and camping facilities to the Lifetime Partner program. The growth and development of the Lifetime Membership program was shown and explained on our television program almost daily. The tapes will prove this.
>
> Here is a question of ethics I would like to ask you and your class. If Mr. Hilton said in 1982, "I am going to build a five-hundred-room hotel on this site; that is all the rooms there will be!" In 1984, business was so great he expanded the hotel. Should he go to prison for lying even though, in 1982, he firmly believed what he said was true?

It was well after midnight when I closed my letter to Professor Tidwell by saying,

> I take full responsibility for what happened to PTL and for my moral failure. I made many mistakes, but I did not conspire to defraud anyone and I am not guilty of any of the government charges. If I had read all the newspapers, and watched all the TV shows, or even looked on at my trial without knowing the other side of the story, I would have come to the same conclusion you have.

I signed my name to the letter, turned out the light, and crawled beneath the cover on my bunk. I didn't know if sending this information to a college professor whom I had never met would be of any value or not. When I awakened the next morning, I sent the letter. I also called Tammy Faye and had her send Professor Tidwell further information about PTL.

311

A few weeks later, I received a kind, cordial letter, dated April 29, 1991, from Professor Tidwell. He thanked me for my letter and my concern that his students be taught the truth and that his research be accurate. The professor assured me that he would incorporate the information I had given him into his lectures and the required reading material for his students. Whether or not he did, I never knew. I later learned, however, that in 1993 Professor Tidwell published a book, *Anatomy of a Fraud: Inside the Finances of the PTL Ministries*, in which the erroneous information about which I had challenged him was presented as fact.

Regardless of what Professor Tidwell did with the information I supplied to him, my correspondence with him sparked a fire within me. I began to realize that much of the information I was giving Professor Tidwell had never been heard in a court of law. For a variety of reasons, none of which made sense to me, my original lawyers did little to contest the prosecutors' case against me. My lawyers spent most of their time trying to discredit the government witnesses and may have even succeeded had I not demanded that my lawyers "not hurt anybody."

Following their lead, my appeal lawyers, except for Alan Dershowitz, had simply tried to poke holes in the government's case against me. They did not base their arguments on information such as I gave to Professor Tidwell. Consequently, I had lost again. Now, it was too late to do anything about my appeal. The only recourse I had was to appeal to the Supreme Court, which was unlikely to hear the case. I had neither the money nor the will to pursue the appeal any farther.

I did, however, think that the information I had given to Professor Tidwell might be of value to Alan Dershowitz as he prepared for my resentencing hearing, now scheduled for the end of May. Over the next few weeks, I fired off several letters to Alan, bringing up points I thought might be helpful, information that I should have emphasized two years earlier.

First and foremost, I told him, I never "sold" Lifetime Partnerships at PTL. The fraud charges brought against me by the government and propagated by the press implied that I had been selling "time-shares." In my letter to Alan Dershowitz I quoted from several of our television program transcripts in which, from the early days of the Lifetime Partnership program, I emphatically told our viewers that Lifetime Partnerships were not time-shares.

February 20, 1984: This is not in any way a time-share, so there are no fees. We don't guarantee anyone a particular room.

February 28, 1984: There are no fees, no maintenance fees, no yearly fees—it is not time-share. You are saying, "Jim and Tammy, we want to be a part of your ministry.

September 17, 1984: It is not time-share.

September 25, 1984: This is not time-share. You don't have a guaranteed time of the year. You come when you can book it in, and you have no fees to pay; there are no maintenance costs for you at all. . . This is a Christian ministry, we are a church, this is a religious organization, and we are here in fellowship together and that is what this is all about.

Similar statements could have been found hundreds of times on the voluminous videotapes of our programs housed in the PTL videotape library. As normal practice, we filed a videotape and a written chronicle for every program we produced. Unfortunately, none of these tapes or program logs, except those selected by the prosecution, were used in my trial. My lawyers did not access the PTL master-tape library at Heritage USA. They used only footage provided by the government in the "discovery room," a large suite of offices across from the courthouse, housing the portion of PTL financial records and videotapes that had been selected by the prosecutors for possible inclusion as evidence in the trial.

Another key point was that the monies sent in to PTL by the Lifetime Partners were not what the Internal Revenue Service calls "designated funds." The IRS is extremely stringent that money given to a nonprofit organization to be used for a specific, designated project must be used for that project, and that purpose alone. At PTL, we were careful to make sure that any money given to build a designated project was always used for building and operating that project. For example, if someone sent in fifty dollars to be used in our missions program in Africa, that money was used for missions in Africa. We did not put that money toward buying a television camera to be used in South Carolina. Had we done so, that would have been an improper use of designated funds.

On the other hand, money that was given to PTL, or any nonprofit organization in the U.S., that was not specifically designated to be used in a particular manner could be used as needed anywhere in the organization. The money received from the Lifetime Partnership fell into this category. Most of our building projects at PTL were not self-funded by designated monies, but rather were paid for out of the general fund.

As I explained to Alan Dershowitz in my letters, our brochures about

313

the Lifetime Partnerships always included a statement such as: "This gift is for the worldwide ministry of PTL." Every receipt that we sent back to donors made it clear that their gifts were to be used wherever they were needed in the ministry. Over and over again, in our magazines, newsletters, and updates, we emphasized that when people gave to PTL, they were giving to the variety of ministries at Heritage USA.

On our live program aired February 22, 1984, I stated, "When you give this thousand-dollar gift . . . you are not just receiving a Lifetime Membership of four days and three nights at the Heritage Grand, [You are] helping us to build a conference center and a preaching center and a school and all the things that are going on here, reaching out in the prisons, reaching out with the People That Love Center, and the People That Love Home."

A few days later on February 28, 1984, I reiterated the message: "When you give, I want you to say to God, 'I am bringing my gifts to You. I am giving this thousand dollars in the name of Jesus. I am giving this Lifetime Membership because I want to go to all the world and preach the gospel to every creature. I want to be a part of the worldwide ministry of prayer. . . . I want to be a part of Your ministry of love that is reaching out to this generation, all of this scope of ministry, of the entire worldwide scope of PTL.' You are saying, 'I want to be a part of it and I want to sow a thousand-dollar seed.'" Clearly, from the inception of the Lifetime Partnership program, it was stated that the money given by the Partners was to be used for the overall ministry, not simply to build hotels and the other lodging places at Heritage USA.

Another area I clarified for Alan Dershowitz was the accusation that Tammy Faye and I had stolen $3.7 million from the ministry over a period of five years.

We never denied receiving this amount of money in salary, bonuses, and benefits over the five years. All of our financial remuneration, however, was voted on by the PTL Board of Directors and was duly noted in the board minutes. In most cases, I left the room while discussions of Tammy's or my financial picture were being held by our board. Had our board said, "Sorry, Jim, we just can't afford to pay you a penny this year," I would have worked at PTL for no salary at all. I never once got out of bed and thought, *I can't wait to get to work today! Am I ever going to make a haul!* Quite the contrary, I felt I was building something great for God and His people. I often suggested to the board that I did not need a pay raise. But board members always said, "You are worth it, Jim. Many sports stars, secular television personalities, and entertainers make much more than that!"

Whether that was true or not is debatable, but I know I worked very hard to build and maintain the ministry of PTL. If from no other standpoint than that of a fund-raiser, the board justified my income. During 1986, for example, I helped raise almost $170 million for the ministry. Had we hired a professional fund-raising organization to do the same and paid the normal going rate of 10 percent for such services, PTL would have paid $17 million in fees during one year alone. Of course, my responsibilities extended far beyond fund-raising, to the general oversight of the entire ministry, not to mention a daily television program that could be seen all over the U.S. and in various foreign countries.

Please understand: I do not want to justify the past. I am merely trying to share my mind-set at the time concerning what was happening. If I had it to do over again, I would not have allowed myself to receive the salary I did. It was a terrible mistake in judgment.

I know some will find this hard to believe, but I would have paid the board of directors for the privilege of being a part of the ministry at PTL.

For a three-year period, during which time the government would claim we were receiving exorbitant salaries, Tammy Faye and I donated almost 100 percent of the royalties earned from our many books, records, and tapes. Peter Bailey, PTL's vice president of finance, testified in court depositions given under oath that the estimated amount of our royalties during this time was $8 million. Richard Dortch attested to the same. They also confirmed under oath that these royalties went right into the PTL ministry, not Tammy's and my personal pockets. Beyond that, an album of Christian music, recorded by our daughter Tammy Sue, brought in another $1.6 million to the ministry in 1986. Tammy Sue was not on the PTL payroll and did receive $50,000 in royalties from that recording.

Legally, nothing required us to donate our royalties to PTL, but Tammy Faye and I felt that since our materials were publicized primarily on our television programs, it was only fair that the money should go to the ministry. I have had numerous advisers tell me since then that we would have been better off to have taken our royalties, as is normal practice, and taken less salary from the ministry. Apparently so.

While the prosecution painted me as a conniving, thieving charlatan, never letting up on the fact that Tammy and I received over $3.7 million in five years, Peter Bailey's and Richard Dortch's testimonies concerning the estimated income to the ministry from our books, tapes, and records were never used in my trial.

The prosecutor peppered members of PTL's Board of Directors on the witness stand with questions such as, "If you had known that PTL was bankrupt, would you have voted Jim and Tammy Bakker bonuses and raises?" Each board member answered emphatically, "No." Of course they would not have. But as I mentioned previously, PTL was not bankrupt at the time the remunerations were voted upon.

Similarly, the prosecutor asked each member of the board, "Did you vote for a $500,000 bonus for Jim Bakker?" One by one, the board members answered, "No." The implication was that I had stolen the $500,000. In fact, at the November 1986 meeting, the board *had* voted for various elements of a financial package that when added together totaled $500,000. Each part of the package had been voted on separately and had been recorded in the official minutes. The board had not, however, voted for a bonus in the same amount. The prosecutors omitted this detail, making it look as though I had stolen the money. My attorneys did not contest the point, despite the fact that I called it to their attention.

Nor did they ever call as a witness Shirley Fulbright, our executive assistant and the recording secretary of the PTL Board of Directors, who kept meticulous records of all PTL board meetings and other PTL activities. To this day, I wonder why neither side called Shirley as a witness. Shirley could easily have explained not only the bonuses and salaries, but she was also aware of all major decisions at PTL while the ministry was under my direction.

I was hoping that Alan Dershowitz could somehow use all this information in his preparation for my resentencing hearing. I also stressed to Alan what I considered to be one of the most important points in my case, in light of the insight I had received as a result of the Tidwell article—namely that we were building more than enough space at PTL to handle all of the Lifetime Partnerships.

The Lifetime Partnership program began in 1984, when we constructed the Heritage Grand Hotel. At that time, we decided to offer to anyone who donated one thousand dollars to the ministry four days and three nights of free lodging at the Grand every year as long as the donor or his or her spouse lived. The offer expired at the death of the donor. The Lifetime Partnerships were not transferable. Nor were they stock options in the hotel. They were simply a "gift" we offered to those who donated one thousand dollars to the ministry at that time.

When we first developed the idea, we felt that we would be wise to let the hotel pay for itself by allotting 50 percent of the five hundred rooms to paying guests and the other 50 percent would be available to the Lifetime Partners free on a first-come, first-served basis. We established the number of 25,000 Lifetime Partners as a feasible number needed to raise the money to build the hotel, while the income from the rooms reserved for regular paying guests would pay for the hotel's operating costs once it was constructed.

The ministry owned the entire hotel, and the 50 percent was a figure we imposed upon ourselves. When we initiated the plan, we were not legally required to set aside 50 percent of the rooms for paying guests and 50 percent for Lifetime Partners. We could just as easily have terminated our management contract and committed the entire hotel for use exclusively by the Partners.

We expected a good response to the offer of Lifetime Partnerships, but we were overwhelmed. We quickly realized that our initial numbers were too small. The hotel was large all right, but even more people wanted partnerships than we had anticipated. The Grand Hotel was such a massive undertaking that it was hard to conceive that we would ever need more rooms in the near future. But as early as September of 1984, we had already exceeded our expectations. We recognized that we would have to change our Partnership program.

The first step we took was to include in the Partnership program the already built ninety-six-room Heritage Inn and add a bonus night for Lifetime Partners who chose to use that lovely facility. The twenty-one rooms located in the Lakeside Log Lodges were added to the Partnership program. We also added the 396 campsites located in the beautiful Fort Heritage Campgrounds. Lifetime Partners by the thousands chose to use their membership for ten nights, filling the campground with travel trailers, motor homes, and tents. To many of the avid campers, the extra seven free days at Heritage USA were a delightful bonus.

We immediately began designing and building other facilities, and all the while, the partners who had donated one thousand dollars to the original program were free to enjoy the benefits of it. Eventually the number of Lifetime Partners topped 150,000. Thousands of Lifetime Partners visited Heritage USA and stayed in the Heritage Grand Hotel four days and three nights each year free of charge. Others stayed in the Heritage Inn and Lodges for four days and four nights, while others enjoyed our campground for ten nights. Many of the Lifetime Partners were among our most generous contributors when offerings were received for various ministries at Heritage USA. In short, the Lifetime Partners believed in what we were doing, and they put their money where their hearts were.

So many reservations were coming in, we added scores of operators to our phone system. As the various lodging places were built at Heritage USA, the Lifetime Partners were informed of the changes and how they could use their free days of lodging in the new facilities. On our daily television program, by newsletter, and our monthly magazine, we constantly talked about our new building programs and how the Partners could adjust their visiting plans accordingly. In addition to the Grand Hotel, the ninety-six-room Heritage Inn, the twenty-one rooms in the Lakeside Lodges, the Fort Heritage Campground with 396 campsites, and 350 Wilderness Camping sites, we began building five hundred more family units in Bunkhouses, air-conditioned minisuite units that could sleep six people in a rustic decor at Farmland USA. Thirty-two rooms in two Bunkhouses were already completed by the end of 1986. And we were still building! As already mentioned, the Heritage Grand Tower was near completion and would add another five hundred rooms when construction was finished.

I want to make something clear: Our building program was interrupted in progress. While I was at PTL we never stopped building. We did not say, "Sorry, folks; that's all the space we're going to have." We were building as fast as our contractors could put up buildings. Three months before my unplanned departure, we had broken ground for The Crystal Palace, a new thirty-thousand-seat conference center, and the Grand Mansions, small hotels done in the same architectural style as the Grand Hotel. Eventually, I had hoped to develop a Crystal Palace Hotel as well. We had blueprints done and land cleared for at least seven other projects. Had I been allowed to continue, within two years I had planned for Heritage USA to have a minimum of 3,336 rooms and camping sites available to our Lifetime Partners. If these lodging facilities were used as we originally formulated—50 percent for paying guests and 50 percent for free use by the Lifetime Partners—we would have easily provided free lodging for 211,062 Lifetime Partners per year! One hundred percent of the campsites were available to the Lifetime Partners year-round. At 100 percent usage, our already built and planned lodging facilities could serve 356,147 Lifetime Partners each year.

Granted, it was difficult for partners to reserve space at busy times of the year, such as the Fourth of July or during the Christmas season when Heritage USA was transformed into "Christmas City," with 125 million lights, complete with pageants and special programs. The partners understood that, for the most part. Some protested, but of course anyone in the travel industry is well aware of this kind of seasonal problem.

The Lifetime Partners knew that everyone could not possibly book into the hotel or other accommodations on the same day. Most of the partners were willing to choose alternative dates. Some were not. Any partners who were disgruntled because they could not get space in our lodging facilities when they wanted, or were dissatisfied for any reason at all, were allowed to get a full refund of their donation. I personally had this policy put in effect, and it was implemented and overseen by Vice President of Hotel Operations, Charlotte Whiting. Were we happy to have partners request refunds? Certainly not. But while I was at Heritage USA, when refunds were requested, to the best of my knowledge, they were always given. Not only did we refund a Lifetime Partner's money if it was requested, we refunded *anybody's* donation if it was asked to be returned for any reason, as long as we had a record of the original contribution. Some of my top managers were not happy with this policy, and after my departure the policy was rescinded.

I can recall incidents in which we refunded money to someone who had given money over a period of time and he contacted us and said that he needed the money back because he was going to have an operation. We sent the money back. Others said they had lost their jobs and could use the money back. We sent it back. In at least one case, we sent money back to a grandchild of a PTL donor after the grandparent had died! The grandchild notified us that he wanted the money back, so we returned it.

To the best of my ability I had tried never to intentionally hurt anyone. If there was one group of people whom I would not want to hurt, it was the PTL Lifetime Partners. Sadly, I know I did hurt them by my moral failure and other unwise decisions and actions. I deeply apologize and ask their forgiveness. These were the people who believed in the dream I showed them. Many of them had such tremendous confidence in me and in what God was doing at Heritage USA that they were willing to contribute their money whether they ever got any free days of lodging or not. One partner and his wife had ninety Lifetime Partnerships! They are still some of my dearest friends to this day.

I would never have defrauded anyone intentionally, and I especially would have done everything in my power to avoid hurting the wonderful, godly group of people known as the PTL Lifetime Partners. In fact, for the first few years of my prison sentence, I awakened every day with one primary passion—to somehow restore the PTL Partners. When close friends would ask me in prison what they could pray for me about, I always answered, "Please pray that I can one day restore the PTL Partners." To me, the Lifetime Partners were just that—it was not simply a catchy phrase I used. I was committed to those people *for life!*

In prison, I was nearly as obsessed with finding a way to provide the Lifetime Partners all the benefits they deserved as I had been in building Heritage USA for them in the first place. I was willing to do anything to see them given their rightful place.

I had no idea how high a price I would ultimately pay in my efforts to see that obsession come to pass.

32

French Lick

ONE OF THE MOST DESTRUCTIVE THINGS THAT WAS DONE BY the new regime after my resignation as president of PTL was choosing not to honor the Lifetime Partnerships. Over the years I had served at PTL, our mailing list had included more than a million people. Within this vast number, we had a core group of donors numbering nearly 600,000 people. Not all of these were regular contributors, but about 200,000 people sent donations of some amount each month. Nearly 160,000 of these people were Lifetime Partners. These were the people who made Heritage USA work. Most of these people were also the monthly financial mainstay of the ministry, and they gave their prayers and spiritual support as well, making PTL what it was.

I knew that when the Lifetime Partnerships were canceled, it was the death knell of the ministry. Had the leadership at that time not disenfranchised the Lifetime Partners but allowed them to continue coming to Heritage USA, I have no doubt those good people would have continued to support the ministry, whether Tammy Faye and I were there or not. In fact, literally tens of millions of dollars were raised for the ministry over the spring and summer of 1987, between the announcement of my resignation and the decision to take the ministry into bankruptcy. Who can forget the picture of Jerry Falwell going down the Heritage USA water slide dressed in a full suit? Ostensibly the money raised—and the reason for Falwell's slide—was to be used to complete the five-hundred-room

Heritage Grand Towers and to pay PTL's bills, including money owed to contractor Roe Messner. The Tower's rooms were never completed and Roe Messner later told me that he never received a dime of that money.

Originally, the entire concept of Heritage USA was based on the idea of the old-time campground, where families used to go for rest and spiritual refreshment. I wanted a place where people could come for help, healing, and encouragement and enjoyment—basically a modern-day equivalent of the old camp meeting only with comfortable facilities rather than the dark, dank cabins and dormitories so many of us grew up with at church camps. The partnership programs were simply a way to help pay for the facilities and to help accommodate the people when they came.

As a boy, I had worked side by side with the men, women, and children of our church family as we built our new sanctuary in Muskegon. I remember learning how to lay tile flooring in our church. I recalled hearing how my forefathers had built their first church, Creston Street Gospel Tabernacle. In the church minutes from back in the Depression era, the church secretary, my dear Aunt Maude, had written concerning the congregation, "They had a mind to work."

In my heart and mind, I believed that Christian people could do just about anything if they could work together. To me, what we were doing at PTL was like an old-fashioned barn raising, in which the people could be a part of the building process and share the benefits of it. Of course, our "barn" was a bit bigger than that which many people were accustomed to seeing built by Christian ministries at that time.

On our PTL television programs, I likened the Lifetime Partnership program to the time-honored custom of "buying a pew" in the local church. Church members contributed the money to pay for the seat, and in some cases, even had their names engraved on a small brass plate on the edge of the pew, but that did not mean the seat belonged only to them. They used the seating, but the pew belonged to the church. If a family moved to another location, they did not take their pew with them; it stayed in the church, to be used by others. If the original donors died or decided that for whatever reason they did not wish to attend that church any longer, their pew was not returned to them at their departure. Similarly, the PTL Lifetime Partners understood that the lodging space they had contributed toward building there was to be used by them and others.

During the months following my departure from PTL, tens of thousands of partners wrote letters of support and encouragement to me in care of PTL. Unfortunately, I never received those letters and I would not have known that they existed had it not been for the loyalty of former PTL "readers." This was a staff of nearly fifty secretaries whose main job was to read the mammoth mounds of mail that arrived at Heritage USA daily. We had developed a rather elaborate system of reading the letters and passing them on up the line to various ministry or administrative personnel who would respond to each letter as needed. We had an entire staff of people whose ministry was to counsel people seeking spiritual help by mail. Every letter that came to PTL was read and passed along to the appropriate person. No letters were ever simply scoured for money and then discarded.

After I resigned, it was announced on the *PTL* television programs—which were still on the air—that all mail sent to the ministry for members of my family or me would be forwarded to us. It was not. No letters sent to PTL in 1987 ever reached Tammy or me at our home in California. Instead, they were burned, buried, or otherwise discarded.

When our family returned to Tega Cay briefly in 1987, several friends who were still at Heritage USA brought stacks of Tammy Faye's records and my sermon tapes to the house and told us that there were literally truckloads of our mail and ministry materials being buried out by the original water tower at Heritage USA. Some of my most trusted maintenance men told me personally that they had been instructed to bury huge bags containing mail that was addressed to Tammy Faye and me. The same men told me that they were no longer allowed to go near the landfill where large volumes of mail and other materials were being burned under the watch of Pinkerton security guards. One of my most trusted employees had been ordered to burn the materials buried at the water tower, but he informed the new officials that vital communication lines ran underground through that area. The officials told him simply to bury the materials instead. I was deeply grieved to hear all of this.

Living in California, watching events unfold at PTL on the television and reading about them in the newspapers, I felt I had to do something to help restore the Partners. I was contacted by a man who owned hundreds of acres of beautiful property in the Palm Desert area of California. This man offered to help me build a "Heritage USA West." Another man proposed a means of financing the new "Heritage USA West" by offering stock options on the public market. I even went so far as to meet with the city leaders to discuss the plans. Heritage USA builder Roe Messner drew up the site plans and rough sketches and was ready to go to work on the new project at a moment's notice.

Previously, I had been approached by one of the top hotel brokers and owners in the country. He had once served as the chief executive officer of one of the leading luxury hotel chains in the world. A limousine pulled up to our house one day, and the chauffeur got out and handed a letter over the wall to one of our security guards. In the letter, the man said he was Jewish but he had watched our television programs regularly. He asked for an appointment and we met for dinner in one of the nicest hotels in the Palm Springs desert area. He offered to turn over to me the $100 million-plus property with no money down. The eventual price tag, however, was enormous. Beyond that, the hotel was located in one of the posh desert communities, and I did not think the residents of the area would appreciate my efforts to turn their leading luxury hotel into a Christian retreat center. Furthermore, the hotel owned one of the finest tennis stadiums anywhere in the world. When I saw the facility, I had begun dreaming of having evangelistic crusades and gospel concerts there. But the community codes restricted the use of the stadium to major tennis championships once a year. In light of my recent public troubles at PTL, I was in no mood for a fight with powerful people who governed the area. Looking back, I think I had been so bludgeoned by my fellow ministers that I had lost my confidence. A few months prior to this, I would have taken on any project of any size. But now, fear had taken over, and my old feelings of insecurity and inferiority came storming back.

Or maybe it was God who kept me from going any farther until He had completed the renovation work in my own life.

After several months, I moved our family back to the Charlotte area. Granted, I missed PTL and wanted to return to the ministry that I had poured so much of my life into building. Furthermore, by that time, I had come to a full realization of the duplicity of many of the key players in my demise as president of PTL and recognized that I had been deceived. Nevertheless, I can honestly say that my primary hope for possible return to Heritage USA was to somehow restore to the Lifetime Partners that which I felt they deserved.

From July through September of 1988, I thought that I might be able to purchase Heritage USA. I had been working diligently trying to arrange financing with a group who purportedly represented a consortium of Greek shipping magnates. My offer to purchase PTL had no sooner been made public when I discovered that the money brokers with whom I had been dealing were a front for a colossal scam. They wanted me to pay them up-front money as "earnest" money and "transferring fees" to secure the rest of the needed funds from overseas banks. It was one of the oldest scams in the book, and in my desire to get back PTL, I almost fell for it.

Despite my disappointment, I refused to give up. Next came my efforts to go back to PTL through Sam Johnson, my former employee who now headed the ministry of Heritage USA. This avenue required a green light from the official channels of the Assemblies of God denomination. Those efforts also ended in failure. After that, for a while, it looked as though "Red" Benton, one of the early trustees of PTL after it was placed into bankruptcy, might allow me to lease the facilities. Tammy Faye and I, along with some of our friends, set about a calling and letter-writing campaign in hopes of securing enough pledges of financial support to convince the bankruptcy officials of our viability. We had actually raised enough pledges when the offer was withdrawn by Mr. Benton.

Tammy Faye, Jamie Charles, and I moved to Florida in 1988, and although I had given up hope of getting Heritage USA back, I never gave up hope of finding some way to restore the Lifetime Partners. I looked at several properties in Florida that friends had said might hold some potential for a new Partner Center. One such piece of property was at Rainbow Springs, once a beautiful tourist attraction before the new highways had passed it by. We also looked at another old, rather run-down hotel on Ormand Beach. Nothing seemed quite suitable.

Even in prison, I never lost sight of the dream to restore the Partners. I pored over every newspaper or magazine that carried advertisements of large, resort-type properties. An inmate named Bill had run a company that had purchased old hotel properties and turned them into retirement facilities prior to his incarceration. Each month, Bill received several hotel magazines and other publications and he allowed me to read them. I looked at Bill's hotel magazines the way some of the guys studied their hunting, fishing, or race-car magazines. I'd get excited every time I saw another property for sale that sounded as though it might be a suitable place for the PTL Partners.

I read of one hotel south of Miami that had been beautifully restored, but then had gone bankrupt. I told Tammy Faye about it, and she sent out feelers to check out the facility, but we never seriously considered it. We were still hoping and praying to find something similar to Heritage USA, no small order. Then one day during the early part of the summer of 1991, I was sitting outside in the prison compound, when Bill excitedly approached me waving a full-color brochure. "You are going to be very interested in this!" he said with a broad smile.

The brochure described French Lick Springs, a resort in southern Indiana that was to be auctioned at 1:00 P.M. on August 1, 1991. As I thumbed through the twelve-page brochure, my heart began beating faster. The place was incredible! A huge, stately 485-room historic hotel—about the same size as the five-hundred-room Heritage Grand Hotel—

324

was situated on 434 acres of land. An adjoining piece of property was also for sale, making the property only slightly smaller than Heritage USA. French Lick Springs boasted seven restaurants, sixty thousand square feet of convention space, a complete spa and health club, a bowling alley, eight indoor and outdoor tennis courts, an indoor swimming pool with a retractable dome, a ranch and stables housing thirty-two horses, with over thirty miles of riding trails, two eighteen-hole golf courses, one of which had been designed by Donald Ross, one of golf's premier course designers, and had hosted both the men's and women's PGA Championships.

Besides that, French Lick had its own old-fashioned steam locomotive that was owned and operated by the Indiana Railway Museum. The trains had always been popular at Heritage USA and were one of my favorite features of our complex. At French Lick, the locomotive pulled authentic passenger cars on a ride of almost two hours through twenty miles of the Hoosier National Forest, through breathtaking limestone rock cuts, and the 2,200-foot Burton Tunnel, one of the longest railroad tunnels in the state. Uniformed crew members helped transport passengers back in time as they enjoyed the scenic train trip. All that, and I did not have to build a thing! It was already there.

In the 1920s and '30s the resort had reached its peak popularity when the mineral waters and casino of French Lick Springs had attracted a continuous bevy of America's rich and famous. Franklin D. Roosevelt had announced his candidacy for the presidency in the hotel's convention center in 1931. Gangster Al Capone gambled at the casino; actress Lana Turner, actor John Barrymore, composer Irving Berlin, the Vanderbilts, and President Harry Truman had all graced the guest lists at French Lick.

By 1991, however, the world had passed by French Lick Springs. People were not beating a path to southern Indiana to spend their vacation dollars. Instead, the once elegant resort center had experienced a steady decline, despite a $3 million renovation effort. Hotel insiders guessed that the property, estimated at more than $65 million, might sell for as little as $1 to $2 million.

For me, sitting in prison, with barely enough money to pay for a plane ticket for my wife and children to visit, the price tag on French Lick might just as easily have been $100 million. I had no money. But I had a great dream. I called Tammy and told her about French Lick. Then I called my friend, Roe Messner.

Tammy Faye, Jamie, my sister Donna, and Roe Messner visited me in prison during the latter part of June, shortly after I had received the information about French Lick Springs. Pastor Phil Shaw and his wife, Faith, accompanied them. My excitement and enthusiasm about the resort were contagious. Soon we were all sitting in the prison visiting room, making plans about what we could do with the tremendous French Lick property.

"The auction is coming up in August," I said to Roe and Tammy. "Why don't you two and Jamie plan to take a trip to French Lick sometime in July to check out the property? Roe, you know what sort of structure we need. Tammy, see if you think the Partners would enjoy the facilities."

Tammy's eyes lit up as I spoke. "Jamie doesn't really need to go," she said.

That was all Jamie needed to hear. "Dad, I don't really want to go," Jamie complained. "Can't I stay here with Pastor Shaw and his family?"

"Oh, I think you need to go with Mom and Roe," I replied. "Besides, it would be good to know what you think the resort will need to meet the needs of the partners' children."

"But I'd rather stay right here and spend the time with my friends," Jamie continued. Tammy Faye had told me that Jamie had been carrying on a long-distance romance with a young lady from Minnesota, so I was not surprised that he wanted to stay.

"Oh, you can come if you want or stay if you want," Tammy Faye spoke past me to Jamie.

"Good, I'll stay here," Jamie responded.

"I really think it would be a good idea for you to go along," I said to Jamie as I shifted uneasily in my seat.

"No, no. Jamie can stay here. Roe and I will go check out the resort and report back," Tammy Faye said breezily.

I caught Phil Shaw's eye ever so briefly. The gentle, even-tempered pastor did not say a word, but I could tell he disapproved of the arrangements. I tried once more to dissuade Tammy Faye from going alone with my best friend to French Lick Springs. I did not want to sound as though I didn't trust her, or Roe for that matter, yet at the same time, since she and I were such frequent fodder for tabloid rumor mills anyhow, it seemed extremely foolish to fuel the fire by having Tammy Faye and Roe seen together at French Lick.

Tammy Faye seemed to have read my mind. "Don't worry, honey," she said with a wave of her hand and a laugh. "We'll be discreet. I'll wear a disguise of some kind." We all broke up laughing at the thought of Tammy in a disguise.

On July 7, 1991, Tammy Faye and Roe Messner checked into separate rooms at French Lick Springs. It was the first of many trips during which

I later discovered they were booked in hotels in separate rooms. It was only a matter of time before the sparks began to fly.

As expected, Roe reported back to me that the French Lick Springs complex was a tremendous value. It needed $10 to $15 million in refurbishing, but the structure was sound, and the layout was gorgeous. We began to make plans. Throughout the summer of 1991, I studied every detail of French Lick Springs's layout. Although I had never been there, I felt as though if I walked onto the property, I could almost give a guided tour of the complex. It was good therapy for me to focus on something besides prison and my resentencing. Of course, the upcoming resentencing, which had been postponed again, held out the hope of a possible lighter sentence and an earlier release date.

Roe found some investors in Canada who were willing to underwrite the purchase of French Lick Springs. Our plan was to purchase the property and have Tammy Faye do a television program from French Lick. We planned to restore the Lifetime Partners and allow them to use the free days of lodging they had been deprived of at Heritage USA. With the prospect of a new sentence, it was not totally unrealistic to dream about the day I would get out of prison and go back on television with Tammy Faye.

We bandied about dozens of possible names for the new center and finally settled on "Heritage Springs International." I began making notes to call many of our friends and staff members who had helped us at Heritage USA, including Joyce and John Westheim. I had known Joyce since my teenage years. She had actually encouraged me to attend North Central Bible College. Joyce had a beautiful singing voice. Her husband John was a professional food-service manager. I hoped to invite Joyce and John to join us at French Lick Springs, Joyce to sing and John to handle our food services. I also made a note to contact Charlotte Whiting, my former vice president of hotel management at Heritage USA, to help with the redecorating of the rooms and the selection of the furniture and pictures in the hotel. In addition, I planned to contact ministers such as Bob Gass and Mike Murdock, and seek a year's commitment from them to help get the ministry started. As we had done at Heritage USA, I wanted to have seminars and workshops featuring special Bible teachers, prayer meetings, and gospel music programs every day.

In prison, my fellow inmate and former hotel expert, Bill, and I began making lists of activities, management plans, marketing plans, and flowcharts of our new organizational structure. To us, it was as though we were playing Monopoly. We were like little kids building sand castles on the beach, dreaming our best-case scenarios, hoping all the while that

Tammy Faye and Roe might be able to pull off the real thing. Roe Messner and I designed plans for a new television studio to be constructed in the facilities of the hotel. I even dreamed up press announcements for Tammy to use at the appropriate time after the purchase was concluded. Beyond that, Tammy and I began working on a letter we planned to send to our Partners immediately after the deal was closed. Heritage Springs International was about to happen. My dream that the Lifetime Partners would be restored was about to come true!

On August 1, 1991, Roe Messner attended the auction at French Lick Springs. He carried with him the $250,000 cashier's check required of all serious registered bidders. Unfortunately, the bids soon topped what Roe's Canadian backers had authorized him to spend, and Roe had to drop out of the auction. French Lick Springs was sold to Luther James, a Louisville, Kentucky, businessman, for $2.6 million.

Undaunted, Roe and Tammy arranged to meet with the Canadian financial backers at French Lick Springs. Roe had already met with the new owner of French Lick Springs and had convinced him to sell the complex, offering him a profit of $1 million. The new owner countered with a request for $1.5 million in profit, not a bad deal, considering the ink had barely dried on his check to purchase the property! When the Canadians toured the resort and saw the potential, they readily agreed to the purchase. All that was left was for the details to be worked out. While Tammy and Roe surged ahead with plans to put Tammy back on television from French Lick Springs, I had to focus my attention on the upcoming resentencing hearing, now scheduled for August 23, 1991.

CHAPTER

33

Hope for Freedom

THROUGHOUT THE SUMMER OF 1991, I LEARNED MUCH concerning French Lick Springs, but I spent most of my free time continuing my in-depth study of the words of Jesus. The more I studied the words of Jesus, the more convinced I became that much of what is being presented in many contemporary religious circles is not consistent with the actual message of Jesus Christ. Worse yet, as I read, dissected, and wrote down the recorded words of Christ, the study was raising serious questions in my own mind concerning many of the things I had believed and taught while at PTL.

For instance, I had taught for years that Christianity was not a religion of "do's" and "don'ts." But when I began to closely examine the recorded words of Christ, I soon learned that much of what Jesus expected of me fell into the category of "Do this" or "Don't do that." Jesus was not encouraging legalism; He was simply instructing me how to live.

I concluded that about 75 percent of Jesus' statements were positive commands—He said, "Love God and one another"—and 25 percent were warnings against sin and negative conduct or attitudes—"Don't fear or worry." I discovered at least three hundred specific instructions in the words of Jesus, reduced them to an easily remembered rule, and wrote them out as a sort of guidebook for life. When taken at their face value, the words of Jesus explain clearly what a Christian is to do and not to do.

One of the most important principles I learned as I studied the words of Jesus was something I had read hundreds of times throughout my lifetime, yet had somehow never allowed to permeate my understanding. After Jesus had been fasting in the wilderness for forty days, Satan tempted Jesus to turn a stone into bread to satisfy His hunger. Jesus resisted the temptation and rebuked the devil by quoting an Old Testament passage, Deuteronomy 8:3, saying, "It is written, 'Man shall not live by bread alone, but by every word that proceeds from the mouth of God'" (Matt. 4:4). I had read this passage, quoted it, and preached on it at PTL, but there in prison, suddenly for the first time, the word *every* practically leaped off the page toward me.

For years, I had taught that we are not to live for food or any other sort of physical gratification, but we are to guide our lives by the Word of God. I was prone to speaking about *a* word of God or *the* Word of God, but amazingly I had missed the point of Jesus' statement. He was not saying that we are to live by one biblical principle; nor was He implying that it was okay to pick out our favorite verses from the Bible and make those our guiding lights. I began to realize that I had fallen into the trap of taking a verse here and a verse there and making the Bible say what I wanted, rather than what God wants.

Jesus was saying that we are to live by *every* word of God; we are to take the Scriptures as a whole rather than building our theologies on a particular verse or phrase that suits our needs at the moment. To accurately understand the Bible, we must study the moral principles established in the Old Testament as well as the New Testament. Certainly, as Christians we no longer live according to the letter of the Old Testament laws. We no longer sacrifice animals to come into God's presence, because Jesus became the ultimate sacrifice; He fulfilled the Old Testament laws and prophecies. Because of Jesus, we have the New Testament, the new covenant, which supersedes the old, but that does not mean we are to ignore the Old Testament.

On the other hand, I began to realize that since Jesus' life fulfilled the Old Testament, it was only possible to truly understand the Old Testament through the life of Christ. Where I found an Old Testament principle, I compared it to the words of Jesus. As it lined up with the life of Christ, I accepted it as a rule for my life. If something seemed not to coincide with Jesus, I studied further. Inevitably, when I took the time to search the Scriptures, I discovered that God's Word was consistent with itself from Genesis to Revelation.

This way of approaching the Scripture, looking at everything through the life and words of Jesus—as obvious as it may seem—completely revolutionized my understanding of the Bible. It also established a firm foundation upon which I could begin to build a new life.

My study of the words of Jesus challenged many of my ideas about theology, but Christ's words also gave me tremendous faith at a time when I sorely needed it. As my resentencing date grew nearer, I was concerned, but thanks to the encouragement I was receiving from the Bible, I prepared to go to Charlotte with a quiet confidence that God was in control of my life no matter what the judge decided about my sentence. Of course, I hoped for a sentence reduction or possibly even to be sentenced to "time served" and to walk out of that courtroom hand in hand with my family. On the other hand, I was also aware that the prosecutors had not changed their attitude toward me one bit and would be pressing the judge to sentence me to a time equal to that which Judge Potter had meted out. Regardless, I was determined not to worry, but to trust God.

On August 19, 1991, I packed all my belongings into a large, military-type duffel bag and took it to be inventoried by a prison officer. I would leave F.M.C. Rochester the way I came in, with only the clothes on my back. The only additional items I was allowed to carry with me were my legal papers regarding my court case. The good news was that at least I would be allowed to wear street clothes during the trip rather than a prison jumpsuit. The bad news was I would have to wear those same clothes throughout my transfers. Everything else must stay—my Bible and other books, my hat, my radio, even my toothbrush had to stay behind when I went to Charlotte. Since there was a good possibility that I would not be returning to Rochester, all my personal belongings were to be stored while I was "out on writ," out on order of the court, until it was determined where I would be going next.

Most of my fellow inmates did not expect to ever see me again in prison. Consequently, the day before I left for my resentencing, a number of guys asked me if they could have a picture taken with me. I readily agreed, and we went over to the recreation building where the inmates turned in their tickets purchased at the commissary to the Jaycee member who was taking the pictures in front of the mural in the hall. Word had already gotten around that I was leaving and probably would not be back, so when other inmates saw me posing for pictures with their buddies, they too wanted a picture with me. Before the day was over, I posed for around 125 photographs with individual inmates.

I left Rochester the morning of Wednesday, August 21, wearing my favorite blue-and-white-striped shirt, black slacks, and my leather boots, traveling by means of a small, private prison jet along with several other inmates and federal marshals. We flew from Minnesota to North Carolina, stopping once or twice for inmates to be removed from the jet, before finally arriving in Charlotte, where I was taken immediately to Mecklenburg County Jail. The guys at Rochester had warned me about county jails. "County jails are the worst places in the entire prison system," they told me. "The cells are small, the food is so bad you don't want to eat it, there is very little room to exercise or even to walk around, and they are usually filthy."

I took one look at my "home away from home," and I thought, *The guys back in Rochester didn't lie to me!* The cell was stark and small, obviously not meant for long-term occupancy. Two bunks hung off the wall, with the headboard almost touching the sliding door made of steel bars.

Almost everything about the county jail that night seemed to have a dirty feel to it. Even the bright orange jumpsuit I was given to wear seemed soiled. The blanket on the hard pillowless bunk smelled as though someone who had not washed in a long time had been sleeping on it before it had been issued to me. Despite the dank aroma all around me, I barely noticed the conditions of the jail. I was too busy, writing furiously everything I thought my attorney Alan Dershowitz should tell the judge the next day. I needn't have bothered. Alan had his own plan in mind.

Harold Bender, my other lawyer, stopped by to see me shortly after my arrival at the county jail. It was obvious that Harold knew his way around the place. Harold and I spoke briefly about what to expect in the resentencing hearing. Before leaving, he handed me a twenty-dollar bill to use to purchase snacks from the jail's small commissary shack.

I jumped back as though Harold had handed me a live rattlesnake. "I can't take that!" I cried. "They'll put me in the hole!" All legal commerce at Rochester took place by using our commissary cards. We were allowed to have a limited amount of change for use in the prison vending machines, but I had not touched paper money in several years.

Harold laughed aloud. "It's okay," he said. "You're allowed to have some money in a county jail."

"Are you sure?" I asked.

"I'm sure," Harold replied as he walked toward the door. "I'll see you in the morning. And be sure to shave."

Later that evening, Tammy Sue visited me in the county jail. She was not permitted to bring baby James or Jonathan Douglas, my new grandchild. During Tammy Sue's visit, we talked through a glass window. We could not touch. I had not seen her in a long time, and despite the circumstances, I was still glad to see her face and hear her voice.

Earlier that day, Tammy Faye had landed in Charlotte and was accompanied by Roe Messner, the man who had become my best friend over the past few years. When Tammy arrived at the Adams Mark Hotel, she was met by numerous PTL Partners who called out, "You can make it, Tammy! Don't give up." For reasons unknown to me, the county jail officials refused Tammy's request to visit with me that evening before the resentencing. She dropped off the clothing I was to wear in court the following day and returned to her hotel.

On Thursday, August 22, I was awakened by a guard around 5:00 A.M. He handed me a small toiletry kit and instructed me to get cleaned up and ready to go to court. He opened the cell door and pointed to a shower stall across from my cell. I thanked him and headed toward the shower.

I opened the toiletry kit and looked inside. A stomach-wrenching feeling swept over me. There in the toiletry kit was a bar of soap imprinted with the logo of the Heritage Grand Hotel. Once again the awful irony of my circumstances smacked me right in the face. Here I was only a few miles from the beautiful hotel and conference center, the construction of which I had personally overseen, but now I was climbing into a scuzzy shower stall in open view of other prisoners.

I was taken to a R & D area where I was allowed to shave and was given my street clothes. I was told to get dressed and was then taken down a long, tunnel-like hallway to another room where I was told to wait for a marshal to come to get me. There, I was placed in a tiny white holding cell with a high ceiling. I sat on the edge of the bench like slab and stared at the wall in front of me. The walls were covered with foul graffiti and names of prisoners who had once occupied these quarters. Dried semen spotted the walls and the floor areas, where men had masturbated while waiting to be transferred to the courthouse. I was almost afraid to sit down for fear I might catch a disease. I glanced toward the top of the cell, where high on the wall, someone had gone to great effort to write in large letters: "It's a sad, sad, world." *Yes, it truly is*, I thought.

I remained in that room until about 9:00 A.M. when the marshals finally came for me. I was cuffed, shackled, and transported in a prison van to the same federal courthouse in which I had been tried, convicted, and sentenced nearly two years previously. We drove down to the back loading dock, the same loading dock from which I had tried to wave good-bye following my sentencing by Judge Potter. As the marshals helped me from the van, I fought back fearful thoughts of what had happened on these grounds two years earlier, and tried to concentrate on the hope that perhaps this judge would view my case differently. I had heard that Judge Graham Mullen, the man who would preside over my hearing and make the decision regarding my sentence, was a strict judge but a fair one.

Once inside the courthouse, I was taken to another small holding cell, where I was given the suit of clothes Tammy Faye had brought from Florida for me. Tammy had chosen a sharp-looking, dark blue, pinstriped, double-breasted suit for me to wear during the resentencing trial. I felt the fine fabric between my fingers and rubbed it against my palms. I had not worn such a suit in nearly two years. I quickly changed into the outfit and was ready when the marshal called for me.

I heard the small courtroom erupt in a commotion when I walked in the side door escorted by the marshal. As I walked across the room, the first sight to catch my attention was Tammy Faye sitting next to my best friend, Roe Messner. Both Tammy and Roe were nattily dressed, but Tammy Faye looked incredible! She wore a chic, tailored, close-fitting black dress with large white polka dots. A matching black-and-white leather bag was at her side. White, half-moon-shaped earrings decked her ears, while several gold bracelets and a watch, which I had given to her as a Christmas present years before, graced her left wrist. On her right wrist were several white plastic bangles. She had gold rings on almost every finger. What I noticed most, however, was her hair and makeup. Gone were the simple, close-cropped curls and the massive amounts of mascara she had worn around me. Instead, her auburn-colored hair was long, big, and poofed. (I later found out that it was a wig.) Her makeup was much more subdued, and natural looking. Tammy Faye looked svelte, tanned, and healthy. In many ways, she looked like the girl I had married thirty years earlier. I had to tear my eyes from her as the marshal took me to my seat between my lawyers at the defense table, but not before I saw Roe slip his arm around Tammy Faye to comfort her.

Tammy Faye whispered from behind me, "Honey, I love you. You can make it!"

The courtroom had a surreal familiarity to it, almost as if I were reliving scenes from two years previously. It did not take long for the prosecutors to begin their relentless hammering away at my credibility once again. They presented the same videotape collage they had used during my trial. The tape was edited in an attempt to show that I had willfully deceived the Lifetime Partners by overextending the program beyond what the lodging facilities at Heritage USA could accommodate. They did not show a single instance of the literally hundreds of times I told our viewing audience that the Partnership program had expanded and that we were building more beautiful lodging facilities that would accommodate every one of our Lifetime Partners within a short period of time.

Hoping to get me off with time served, as a sort of unofficial plea bargain Alan Dershowitz suggested to Judge Mullen that he might release me and impose upon me a wide variety of probation restrictions, including a ban on me being on television for any length of time, and a total barring of my involvement in any fund-raising activities. Dershowitz told the judge he would guarantee I would never again engage in the mixing of religion and money. Alan convincingly challenged the prosecutors' contention that I had defrauded people of $158 million, pointing out as the first government-appointed trustee had done two years earlier, that most of that money was right there invested in Heritage USA, just as it was supposed to be. The Harvard law professor made a strong case that the amount of the supposed fraud was "wildly inflated."

Judge Mullen ignored Alan's suggested bans and chose not to place any such restriction on me. By the end of the day, I felt as though my life had been dragged through a washing-machine wringer once again. But in some ways, the worst was yet to come.

When Judge Mullen dismissed court for the day, the marshals quickly swooped onto the courtroom floor and surrounded the defense table, ready to escort me back to Mecklenburg County Jail. Before they could usher me out, I leaned over the railing and kissed my daughter, Tammy Sue. Then I kissed my mother, whom I had not seen in nearly two years. Finally, I kissed Tammy Faye, and by that time, the marshals were at my side, insisting that I go with them.

We returned to Mecklenburg County Jail just as we had come, first stopping long enough for me to change out of my suit into my street clothes, then back to the holding area where I changed out of my street clothes back into the same soiled orange jumpsuit I had worn the day before. I was placed back in the same filthy cell where I had spent the night.

Later that afternoon, when a guard offered the inmates a mop and scrub bucket to clean our cells, I put my Rochester cleaning expertise to good use. I not only mopped my own cell, I cleaned the common areas of the entire cell block. As usual, some of the guys did not understand. "Bakker, what are you doing?" they chided. "Quit working so hard for the guards."

"Hey, we're staying here, not the guards. I'm not working for them; I'm working for us," I answered.

335

That night after supper, Tammy Faye and Roe Messner came to visit me. The officials at Mecklenburg County Jail were kind enough to allow us to use a vacant office for the visit rather than the jail's visiting room. The office was drab but private. A desk sat to one side of the room and several metal, institutional-looking chairs were arranged in front of it. A guard sat off to one side of the room, mercifully trying to be as inconspicuous as possible. Tammy Faye and Roe sat together on two of the chairs facing me.

The picture of my wife and best friend sitting together, with Tammy Faye making no effort to move closer to me after having been away from me for two years, impacted me powerfully. I had detected a cooling in our relationship in recent months, most notably during our daily telephone conversations. Where Tammy Faye had once talked freely for hours, now she was always in a hurry to get going. She had to go somewhere or do something, or someone was coming to the house. I knew she was busy. I never faulted her for having to break off our phone conversations to attend to one of the many details of her life. I recognized that I was in prison with nothing but time on my hands, but she was still on the outside trying to function as normally as possible. Before long, however, her indifference on the phone increased to the point where I could no longer fool myself into believing that she was simply overly busy. I'd seen these signs before.

Nevertheless, I was not prepared for Tammy Faye's blatant shifting of allegiance the night before my resentencing. As I looked at her and Roe, I could not deny the truth any longer.

My wife and my best friend were a couple.

I could see it in their eyes, the way they looked at each other. I could hear it in their voices, the way they talked to each other. They shared a camaraderie that is born only out of a close relationship. As I looked at the handsomely dressed man and woman sitting across from me, it was as though some unfamiliar *couple* had come to visit—Tammy with her crisp, stylish new look and Roe with every hair in place and his dapper clothes sharply pressed. I became increasingly aware of my own disheveled hair and the stinking, soiled jumpsuit in which I had cleaned the floors only a few hours earlier. We talked about the hearing, but I really did not hear what the couple was saying. We talked about French Lick Springs, but I could not get my mind off the *couple*. Fortunately, they did not stay long. I'm not sure how much more I could have taken. I never mentioned a word to either one of them concerning their relationship. I did not confront them in any way. We all went through the motions as though everything were simply normal. Tammy Faye and I kissed in a perfunctory manner, totally devoid of passion on her part. Roe stood nearby, looking on.

And then she was gone.

My wife walked out of the room with my best friend, and the guard walked me back to my cell in silence. It was almost as though he was embarrassed for me.

The small courtroom in the federal courthouse was packed with spectators, mostly members of the media, when the marshals escorted me in, wearing the same clothing I had worn the day before. I had already been awake for hours, as we had gone through the identical routine in transferring me from the jail to the courthouse in downtown Charlotte. Prison procedures allow little room for variation.

Once again the prosecution attempted to shred my character in their closing arguments, encouraging the judge to reinstate the original forty-five-year sentence. To counter, Harold Bender pointed out that I had been a model prisoner since my incarceration, citing my work with the prison Jaycees and the various other groups of which I was a part. In what I'm sure was meant to be a positive image, Harold went on to tell the judge that I had also served on the prison's United Way fund-raising committee.

Totally ignoring Alan Dershowitz's plan to play down my fund-raising expertise, Harold rambled on in what I could only assume was meant to be a comment upon my exemplary community service in prison. "They raised, among the inmates, several thousand dollars," Harold told Judge Mullen. "It was *the* most successful United Way campaign they've ever had."

Thanks, Harold.

I glanced over at Alan Dershowitz while Harold was extolling my fund-raising capabilities. Alan's face looked as though he might explode at any moment. Had we not been dealing with my life, it might even have been funny.

At 10:22 A.M. Judge Mullen said, "Mr. Bakker, it is now your right to address the court on your own behalf. Do you have any remarks you wish to make on your own behalf, sir?"

Judge Mullen's politeness caught me off guard. I was not accustomed to being addressed as "Mr. Bakker" these days, let alone as "sir." I answered, "Yes, sir."

"All right, sir, you may," Judge Mullen replied.

I rose to my feet and began to speak. "Your Honor," I began, "I am deeply and seriously remorseful for my moral failure and for the hurt that I have caused so many people. I have failed so many people who trusted in me—my own church congregation, this community, my Partners, the church world as a whole, and myself and my God, and my dear family that I love so very, very much."

As I was talking I recalled the message I had seen in the holding cell in Mecklenburg Jail, so I told the judge about it. "I looked up on the wall, and there was some writing and it said, 'This is a sad world.' And prison is a sad world. It's the land of the living dead for many. It's not just the strip searches and that kind of thing, it's the separation from your family, from your loved ones.

"I have a wife of thirty years who has stood with me through thick and thin, through an affair—a fifteen-minute affair that happened almost a decade ago—but she has stood with me and forgiven me, and I love her. We built Heritage USA together, even after our marriage had broken up and was put back together. I know even the bad times become good times as you look back in history, because you've stood together.

"I have a fifteen-year-old son who was ten years old when this happened. He's taller than I, and he needs a father. I need to be with my son. This will be [my] third Christmas in prison away from [my] family.

"I have a daughter and her husband here in this room. My daughter is the apple of my eye. She gave my wife and [me] two beautiful—" my voice cracked at the thought of Tammy Sue's children, and I had to pause before continuing. "She and her husband gave us two beautiful grandbabies, Jonathan and James. Jonathan is eleven months old. I have never seen him. I have never held him.

"I got to see my mother in the courtroom yesterday for the first time in two years. She just turned eighty-five. My dad will be eighty-five next month. I have failed my family, and I have asked their forgiveness."

Judge Mullen listened attentively to every word I spoke and his respect seemed to carry over to the spectators. I continued. I wanted to let the judge know that I never intended to hurt anyone or renege on any of the promises I made to my partners or to anyone else.

"Even though I planned to be honorable in all of my commitments, as leader of my church and family, I choose to accept full responsibility for the actions that I am now being sentenced for. I do not blame anyone else nor minimize my responsibility as the pastor and president of Heritage Church and Missionary Fellowship. . . .

"There's not been a day gone by that I have not grieved for the Partners and the Lifetime members who lost Heritage. Heritage USA did not belong to me; it belonged to the people who supported it. . . .

"I have asked God, and I don't have the answers, but I wish to God and pray to God that somehow they could be restored and I would do anything to do that and see that happen. . . .

"I have [said it] in the past, and I would say it again in front of this witness and this courtroom and Your Honor, I ask all that I have hurt to please forgive me. I have begged God for heavenly forgiveness, and I beg this court for human mercy. Thank you, Your Honor." I sat down. I had spoken for approximately five minutes. It would have taken hours to tell the judge everything I was feeling inside, but I did not want to prolong the judge's decision. I felt that I had said enough.

Both the prosecution and the defense were allowed closing statements. In his final effort to influence Judge Mullen, Harold Bender suggested to the judge—as he had done to Judge Potter two years earlier—that he might consider "punishing" me by making me go back to Heritage USA at a minimum salary and "make good on my promises" and "make restitution." Harold latched on to a descriptive phrase used by the prosecutors and admitted that this idea might be akin to a "fox in the henhouse" approach, but it might work. Even reporters were scratching their heads at Harold's meandering logic.

Finally it was time for Judge Mullen's decision. "I am impressed with the fact that Mr. Bakker has made a remarkable adjustment to confinement," Judge Mullen began. "I could resentence Mr. Bakker under the new guidelines, but I choose not to do so." He then went on to explain the way he had divided the counts against me. At last he came to the sentence itself—five years, five years, five years, and three years. Judge Mullen had reduced my sentence to a total of eighteen years. As part of my original sentence, Judge Potter had fined me $500,000 in addition to the forty-five years in prison. In the new sentence, Judge Mullen decided not to fine me at all.

The judge dismissed the court and it was done. *Eighteen years.* I was not going home. In fact, I would not be going home for a long, long time. I was going back to prison. I would be seventy years of age by the time my sentence was completed. The marshals were coming again.

I turned quickly to Tammy Sue, who was seated just behind me on the other side of the railing. I kissed her and said, "I love you, baby." I reached for Tammy Faye. I hugged her and kissed her good-bye.

I turned to my soon to be eighty-five-year-old father and said, "Tell Mother I love her."

A marshal's voice boomed across the courtroom, "Let's clear the courtroom. It's over."

Tammy Faye slumped to her seat, sobbing and clutching a package of tissues. Roe quickly joined her and put his arms around her, comforting her.

The exit routine seemed all too familiar. Change your suit. Put on your street clothes. Handcuffs. Shackles around the legs. All right, let's go. Out the back door. Down the loading dock steps. Duck your head. Get into the car. You're on your way back to prison.

Meanwhile, Tammy Faye was standing in front of the courthouse speaking to members of the media. "I'm understandably very sad today," she said. "I was hoping Jim would be able to come home sooner." She thanked the PTL Partners for their support, about fifty of whom were standing nearby wearing yellow ribbons. She concluded her remarks in chipper tones by reciting the "Serenity Prayer," which she had learned at the Betty Ford Center.

I sat dumbfounded in the back of the marshal's car as they whisked me back to the airport. The prison plane was waiting for me. Television crews followed my every move. I tenuously made my way up the steps to the small jet's doorway and ducked inside. Several other men were already seated in the jet. I shuffled to the first empty seat, sat down, and stared out the window. I talked only when absolutely necessary. I'm not sure that I flinched a muscle during the entire trip back to Minnesota. It was a strange, sinking feeling as I reentered the gates of F.M.C. Rochester. Although I had been afraid to expect any positive results from my resentencing hearing, I guess deep down I had indeed entertained hope that I might walk out of that courthouse in Charlotte a free man. Now, as I was being processed through R & D, strip-searched again, and sent back to Building Two, my "home" for the past two years, the disappointment over my eighteen-year sentence hit me full force. Walking back into prison caused my stomach to churn. I hated imprisonment, yet at the same time, my reentry to prison was far less traumatic than my original introduction to the federal prison system.

Once I had cleared R & D, I was free to walk back across the compound toward Building Two. It was still light enough that many of the inmates were outside. A number of the guys came up to me and congratulated me.

"For what?" I asked.

"For your victory," someone replied. They had seen the reports on the news concerning my sentence reduction. I soon realized that they considered a reduction from forty-five to eighteen years a major victory. They thought I had won.

I didn't feel like much of a winner. But I was about to discover that I was more of a winner than I had ever dreamed. It all began as I encountered the life of another imprisoned dreamer. . . .

CHAPTER

34

God Meant It for Good

BACK INSIDE THE GATES OF ROCHESTER FEDERAL MEDICAL
Center, I was more convinced than ever that I would not be released from
prison until God wanted me out, until I had learned whatever it was God
wanted me to learn through this experience. I was certain that my incarceration had much more to do with God's plan than Judge Mullen's opinion that I should remain in prison for eighteen years.

Upon my return, I learned that my former cell was now occupied by
two new men. As I walked toward Building Two to be reassigned to another cell, my friend Rod Netherton met me. "Jim, welcome back. We all
thought you were out of here, but as soon as we heard the news about your
resentencing, I went right to work. Guess what! I put in a request to have
you move in with me, and Sam Houston approved it."

"You what?"

Rod was one of my best friends. I enjoyed his energy and enthusiasm
and I liked hanging around with him, but he was one of the last guys in
prison that I would have chosen as a cellmate. Our personalities were so
opposite. Rod was a world-champion sky diver, a drug smuggler who had
made his living parachuting out of airplanes. He was daring enough to land
planes in the middle of a South American jungle to pick up his next cache
of drugs. He was an outgoing, self-assured, confrontational sort of guy—
he had loved arguing with Lyndon LaRouche just for kicks.

Rod was also by his very nature a controlling, persuasive type of person.

He convinced the prison authorities to allow him to teach a skydiving class in prison on the theory that most of what a person needs to learn about parachuting must be learned on the ground, rather than in the air. Rod always said, "You better know what you are doing before you get up in an airplane and plan to jump out!" I even took Rod's course, which he conducted with all the skills of a drill sergeant.

When I went "out on writ" to my resentencing, I was told that my cell would be held for me. It wasn't. Consequently, upon my return I accepted Rod's offer and moved into his two-man cell.

I appreciated Rod looking out for me; had he not requested that I room with him when I returned from Charlotte, most likely I would have been placed in another four-man cell since no other two-man cells were open at the time.

More importantly, within a matter of months I would learn that my rooming with Rod was no accident.

Back in the routine of prison, I once again plunged into activities to deaden my disappointment in my new sentence. I started working out at the weight room every day with Rod and enrolled in a college-credit computer course and a sociology course. I had never had the opportunity to complete my college education, and these classes fascinated and challenged me. I also began reading the latest book Sue Williams sent me, *God Meant It for Good,* by Dr. R. T. Kendall, a minister of London's famous Westminster Chapel. It was like a wake-up call from God. Along with the Bible, this book, which drew lessons from the life of the biblical character Joseph, who was sold into slavery by his brothers and later rose to power in Egypt, became my handbook while in prison.

God instructed me about many areas of my life through this book, especially three key areas I had struggled with for years: self-pity and my desire to be vindicated, God's timing, and total forgiveness.

Both my worst critics and my strongest supporters have chided me concerning my propensity toward self-pity. Even Tammy Faye regarded my self-pity as one of my worst traits. Often when the press were beating me up, to escape the pressure I simply curled up and went to sleep. When problems arose at PTL with one of our building projects or one of our programs, rather than lashing out I withdrew into myself, becoming less and less accessible to others. To Tammy, this was a sign of weakness. Tammy handled her problems by letting the whole world know about them. If anyone was unsure of her mood, she gladly clarified it. If Tammy was hurting, she went shopping, to see a movie, or out to eat at one of her favorite restaurants. Her motto was, "When the going gets tough, the tough go shopping."

Early on in my prison experience, self-pity frequently got the best of me. For example, one day during the first few weeks I was at Rochester, I was called to the warden's office. When I arrived, the warden had someone in his office, so I stood in the reception area while I waited. Pictures of the warden and all the assistant wardens covered the walls of the reception area, so to pass the time I began studying the faces of the various prison personnel so I might be able to recognize them when I saw them.

Out of one of the offices walked a tall man, a prison official of some sort, I was sure. He took one look at me and bellowed, "Bakker! What are you doing here?"

"I was called by the warden," I replied tentatively.

"Well, you can't stand here!" he said, referring to the small carpeted section of the reception area. "Go down the hall and wait," he ordered, pointing out the tile-blocked hall area about twenty feet away.

"Yes, sir," I answered. As I hurriedly exited the reception area and headed down the hall, I felt like a little schoolboy being told to go stand in the corner.

Waiting in the stark prison administration building hallway, it suddenly struck me that just a few years before I had been comfortable standing with presidents in the White House. Tammy Faye and I had been guests of both President Carter and President Reagan. I had met privately with Vice President Bush. Now, my mind drifted back to late 1979 when I had been invited aboard *Air Force One*. I had been sitting in one of the powder-blue chairs near the doorway of a sitting room aboard the aircraft, along with Johnny and June Carter Cash and other celebrity guests. When President Carter entered the compartment, I was the first person he saw. As he paused to greet me, he said softly, "Jim, I want you to come to my private suite in a few minutes." I nodded as the president moved around the small room shaking hands with each visitor. He completed the circle and came back to me. "Please come with me now."

I followed the president of the United States back to his private suite on *Air Force One*. When President Carter and I were alone in his quarters, we sat down to talk. It was obvious that he was under horrendous stress. The date was October 31, 1980; it was right before the presidential election, and American citizens were still being held hostage in Iran. After a while, President Carter asked me to pray for him. I was glad to oblige.

I reached over to him and laid my hands on the president while I prayed for him, as is the custom in the denomination in which I was raised. I prayed that God would grant him wisdom to deal with his responsibilities and that God's will would be done in his life. President Carter thanked me sincerely.

In later years, I would meet with President Reagan in the White House and at his California home. I had been to breakfast with the president in the White House. Tammy Faye and I had been allowed to roam the White House freely, without a security guard, a rarity in White House protocol.

Now, however, it suddenly hit me that I was no longer good enough to stand on the cheap, all-weather carpet in the warden's reception area. I felt thoroughly degraded and self-pity poured over me like a flood.

As I studied the life of Joseph in Dr. Kendall's book, however, I began to see the folly of self-pity and recognize it for the first time in my life for what it really is—a sin. Dr. Kendall pulled no punches: "It never does any good when we blame another person; we only condemn ourselves." "The person filled with self-pity is looking forward only to saying, 'I told you so.'" "Self-pity wants sympathy." "We become absorbed with ourselves and our own feelings. We don't realize we are hurting people." "When a person is filled with self-pity, he is making no real progress." Kendall concluded, "I can safely say there is nothing at all good about self-pity."[1]

Kendall's book showed me that I mustn't allow myself to slip into the quagmire of self-pity.

His words seared into my soul:

> Are you suffering right now because somebody has said something about you that is not very nice? Has somebody done something to you that is not very kind? Do you yearn for the moment of vengeance, for the moment when everybody will see the truth? Of course you do. But if you can't keep quiet about it, and you begin instead to act as a busybody, trying to protect yourself and your self-esteem, God will back off from the whole situation. He will let you handle it, and you will lose the war. The wisest thing one can ever do when mistreated is to be quiet about it.[2]

In prison, I had to come to grips with the fact that I might never truly be vindicated of the charges made against me, but it no longer mattered. I knew the truth and those involved knew the truth, and more importantly, God knows the truth. If He chose to clear my name, I would be delighted for the cause of Christ and for my children and their posterity. If not, I could live with that, but I must not allow myself to slip back into the pit of self-pity.

A second area in which Kendall's book spoke to me was regarding

God's timing. The Bible is clear that God has a perfect time for everything. Like most people, however, I wanted God to move *now*. Moreover, I had expected God to do something long before this point. Frankly, I had believed that God was going to do something supernatural, or at least highly unusual, to keep me from going to prison in the first place. When He did not, I was shocked and eventually shattered by what I considered to be God's abandonment of me. Again and again, I cried with the psalmist, "How long wilt thou forget me, O LORD? for ever?" (Ps. 13:1 KJV). *How long must this go on?* I wondered. *Is this really Your plan for my life, God?*

Through Kendall's book, however, I realized afresh that God had not abandoned me. He was preparing me, molding me, shaping me into the man He wanted me to be. In His time, the rest of the story *would* unfold.

Kendall listed five ways we can know when God's time for us has come. "First, we know that God's time has arrived when we have come utterly to the end of our own strength. . . . This is something that comes hard to us. We don't like to think that we are utterly helpless."[3] It is human nature to want to manipulate people and events to our advantage.

Looking back, I realized that I had done something similar by subtly believing that Alan Dershowitz and Judge Mullen might be my ticket out of prison. I had spent relatively little time in preparation for my resentencing because I had committed it entirely to God, but there was still a temptation to think that if Alan and I could convince the judge of my innocence, I might be able to walk out of that courthouse a free man. When Judge Mullen resentenced me to eighteen years in prison, I was reminded again that I was utterly powerless to orchestrate my release by mere human intelligence, persuasiveness, or personality. Like Joseph, God's time had not yet come for me.

Second, "God's time has come when he does a work utterly outside ourselves." Kendall explained:

When has God's time come? When all human resources fail. When has God's time come? When the wisdom of men comes to nothing. When has God's time come? When something appears for which there is no natural explanation. . . . God delights to show the world that for which there is no known explanation. . . . As long as there is a natural or traditional explanation to something, men may well debate it. But when all explanations fail, God's time has come.[4]

345

A third indication that God's time is at hand "is when God works successfully at the precise point we have failed."[5]

Another sign that God is working in your situation is "when someone pleads your case (and knows all the facts) without your opening your mouth."[6]

Fifth, we know that God is working things out for us "when God reaches us where we are without any effort on our part."[7]

As I read Dr. Kendall's words, it was almost as if I was having a conversation with the author. "Are you in the equivalent of a dungeon at this moment?" Kendall asked.

"Yes!" I wrote in the margin of the book.

"Are you afraid that God does not see you?"

"Yes! That is my greatest fear."

Kendall's words were reassuring. "He does see you and he's come right now. All is in God's timing."[8]

Kendall's emphasis upon God's timing was a liberating concept, especially as I remained incarcerated. I realized that my circumstances were not obscured from God's vision. He knew exactly what I was going through. I slowly but surely began to believe that He could use even this experience for good.

The third major area in which Dr. Kendall's book helped me was the matter of forgiveness. I had been actively trying to forgive everyone involved with the demise of PTL since the very public, scandalous days of March 1987. Furthermore, as I had been studying the words of Jesus, I could not ignore the imperative message of forgiveness. Jesus emphatically stated, "For if you forgive men their trespasses, your heavenly Father will also forgive you. But if you do not forgive men their trespasses, neither will your Father forgive your trespasses" (Matt. 6:14-15).

Malcolm Smith had reminded me in his book, *Spiritual Burnout*, that a major step toward returning to spiritual health and well-being was to forgive all who had been a part of the hurt I had experienced. Now, Dr. Kendall's book took me farther into the matter of forgiveness by helping me realize I must not only forgive those who had hurt me, but I must pray for them and want the best for them as well.

Dr. Kendall proposed five principles of total forgiveness: First, total forgiveness is demonstrated when we do not want anybody else to be hurt because of what was done to us. Once again, Dr. Kendall's incisive words sliced into my heart. "It is the unforgiving spirit that wants to let the world know our own hurt. Love hides a multitude of sins. It is hate that wants to let the cat out of the bag. Hate wants everybody to know we have been hurt: 'Here's what so and so did to me.'"[9]

Kendall continued, "Second, total forgiveness wants to make a person feel completely at ease."[10]

Third: "Total forgiveness will not even allow the person to feel bad or angry with himself. . . . When we really forgive another person, we want them to feel good."[11]

Fourth: "Make it easy for that person to forgive himself; we do it in such a way that it is obvious we really do forgive."[12] "Finally," says Dr. Kendall, "total forgiveness is demonstrated when we keep someone's sin hidden from the person who means the most to him."[13]

Kendall's pen continued to hit the bull's-eye of my heart:

> If you are a Christian, there will come a day—it may be soon—when the unexpected, the unthinkable happens to you. Your immediate question will be "God, why did you let this happen?" The temptation will be to let yourself be filled with bitterness, hatred, and desire for revenge. . . .The brothers of Joseph acknowledged what they did. Sometimes, however, we are called upon to forgive people who refuse to acknowledge that they have even done anything wrong. And there are those who don't think they have done anything wrong. But you have to forgive them, too—they are the hardest people to forgive. . . . It is one thing to say, "I have forgiven him for what he did"—we can say it and think we mean it—but it is another thing to truly and totally forgive.[14]

Kendall's words resonated in my heart as I read them, but that did not make it any easier to forgive everyone involved with my imprisonment. I knew I had to forgive the prosecutors in my trial. I felt I must forgive several of my own lawyers for their bungling of my case; and I had to forgive the judge for giving me a sentence of forty-five years. Beyond that, I had to forgive the people who did not come to my aid—individuals who could have actually stopped the madness but chose not to do so—as well as church leaders and friends who I felt had abandoned me. I also had to forgive my church denomination, for defrocking me when I needed the church more than ever.

In addition to forgiveness, Jesus also said, "Love your enemies, bless those who curse you, do good to those who hate you, and pray for those who spitefully use you and persecute you" (Matt. 5:44). Not only did I have to forgive those people who had taken advantage of my sin, failures, and mistakes to orchestrate my downfall, I had to start praying for them!

I had a long list of people I began to pray for by name almost every day. When my cellmates were gone, I sat at my desk or on my bunk and prayed aloud for individuals, both friends and foes. In addition, I prayed every day that God would prolong the lives of my mother and father until I could get out of prison. I also prayed daily for my wife and children, that God would take care of them.

From my study of the words of Jesus and the reinforcement I received from reading Dr. Kendall's book and others, I knew that I had to pray for all the major players in the fall of PTL including Jessica Hahn, Jerry Falwell, Norman Roy Grutman, Jerry Nims, Reverend Dortch, Jimmy Swaggart, John Ankerberg, and many others. At first, I had awful difficulty praying that God would bless some of these individuals, but I tried my best not to judge their motives, and I simply prayed for them.

I quickly found that this sort of prayer was impossible to fake. Perhaps it may have been possible to make a pretense of these prayers had I not been in prison, but in the isolation of my cell, where nobody could hear me, and nobody was paying any attention to me, the prayer either came from my heart or not at all. I confess, there were days when praying for my long list was too laborious for me. On other days, I simply hurried through my list of names, just to get it done. Some days, I merely read the list of names aloud to God, because that was the best prayer I could muster.

Some inmates whom I let in on the secret that I was praying for the people who had hurt me, tried to dissuade me from my practice. So too did many of the people who wrote to me, people to whom I had written letters encouraging them to forgive all those involved in my nightmare. Some people got angry at me and asked, "How can you forgive those people? I'm not going to forgive them! I will never forgive Jerry Falwell. I will never forgive Jimmy Swaggart."

I wrote back, "But we must forgive. We do not have any other options. If you or I harbor unforgiveness toward any of those individuals involved in the downfall of PTL, Christ will not forgive us." I became deeply concerned that the worst fallout from the events surrounding the explosion of PTL might be unforgiveness on the part of many believers.

I felt compelled to communicate my forgiveness to all the key players in the demise of PTL, whether they accepted it or not. Over a period of months, I wrote, telephoned, or talked face-to-face with many of them. I received several letters asking me for forgiveness and apologizing for actions and statements that were made against me. Those were pleasant surprises.

Besides my own spiritual health, I recognized that I had to lead the way in forgiveness for my family. I did that by encouraging them to forgive the people who hurt them, including me. Looking back, I can now see that had I allowed bitterness and resentment to fester, I could have destroyed my own family.

During this time, I discovered something else: As I was forgiving those who in some way had been a part of my downfall, I had to confront my own culpability. For instance, as I prayed to forgive Jessica Hahn, I also began to realize that regardless of Jessica Hahn's attitude, I was responsible for my own actions. I cannot blame her or anyone else for my sin.

Similarly, as I expressed my forgiveness of Jerry Falwell and his questionable motives in taking over PTL, God reminded me that I can complain that I was hoodwinked until the day I die, but I cannot ignore the truth that *I allowed it to happen.* That was my responsibility, and I had to pray, "Dear God, please forgive me for disobeying You."

When our hearts and minds are clouded by unforgiveness, our perception of the truth is blurred and distorted. All we can see is the other person's fault. But when we forgive, it moves the dark cloud away, and we can see more clearly our own responsibility. We can then admit, "It wasn't all that other person's fault; I had a part in this too." Yes, I had to forgive those who hurt me, but I also had to accept my responsibility as well and acknowledge that my sin opened the door to the entire debacle.

It is not arrogant to forgive other people; we must forgive. God has commanded us to forgive those who have hurt us. It is only as we are willing to forgive that we begin to realize that even though other people may have meant their actions and words for evil, God turns them into something He can use for good.

At the close of his book, Dr. Kendall listed four proofs to know for sure that we have forgiven those who have hurt us. "The first is that you don't want the other person to be afraid."[15] I want all those men and women who spoke and acted so bitterly against me to know that I harbor no resentment toward them. They have nothing to fear from me. I am not out to get even. If Christ can forgive me, after all the pain and hurt my actions have caused Him, I can forgive anyone.

According to Kendall, "The second way of knowing that you have really forgiven someone is that you refuse to take advantage of any superior position you might be in."[16] Joseph could have caused his brothers to cower in fear of him for the remainder of their lives, but he chose not to do so. Instead, when Joseph's brothers acknowledged their sin, Joseph replied, "You meant evil against me; but God meant it for good, in order to bring it about as it is this day, to save many people alive" (Gen. 50:20).

Dr. Kendall points out:

To be able to say "God meant it for good" is an attitude. It is an attitude we must feel toward those who will not admit they intended to harm us. After all, what does it matter whether or not they admit it? We ought to be able to see the hidden hand of God in anything. Why should it matter whether they come clean? It doesn't matter. If you see the hidden hand of God, that matters. When you know that all things work together for good, that God has your life in his hands, and that whatever affects you affects him, you are beginning to get free. . . . It doesn't matter, then, whether anybody admits to what they have done. In a way, it is better if they don't. For that gives you a greater test, a greater victory. Because what you want to see is that God is in it for good. The Christian is a person who has the opportunity to show that he sees God's hidden purpose in evil.[17]

I am convinced that God did not send me to prison to punish me for my sins, even though I deserved it. God put me in prison so I could study His Word, get to know Him, and learn the meaning of forgiveness. Had I been seeking God daily, studying the Bible, and living by its principles all along as we built PTL and Heritage USA, I have no doubt that I would never have gone to prison. I would have seen the error of my ways reflected in God's Word, and I would have taken the appropriate corrective measures. But because I had allowed my relationship with God to grow cold and had ignored His Word, God put me in a position in which I had only two choices—either get right with God, or die.

"The third proof that you really have forgiven another person," says Dr. Kendall, "is that you bind up the wound so completely that you show that all that happened really was *meant* to be."[18] Joseph told his brothers, in essence, "This was meant to be." And he meant it. I feel the same way about what I have experienced.

The final proof that you have really forgiven the other person is that you keep on forgiving them. . . . You know you really have forgiven and that it is not just a burst of emotional feeling because you keep on doing it. Total forgiveness holds two months later. Six months later. Two years later. Forever.[19]

That is the way God forgives us, that is the way He expects us to forgive each other, and that is the way I decided to forgive.

I wish I could say this was an easy process, but it was not. I found that I had to relearn the lessons on a frequent basis. While I knew that forgiveness was a matter of my will and required a choice, I also discovered that forgiveness was an ongoing process. I honestly forgave everyone involved with my ouster from PTL and I held no grudges. Yet from time to time, when an inmate brought another erroneous article to me or another attempt was made to vilify me in court, I found that I had to express my forgiveness again and again. Even in the writing of this book and reliving so many experiences I had tried to forget, once again, I have had to work through forgiving certain individuals.

I have anguished over the dilemma of how I could tell this story without violating the principles of forgiveness that have set me free, and without hurting anyone or dragging everyone back through events and circumstances that many besides myself have hoped to forget. Yet because so many of the events within these pages were played out before the public, I feel strongly that I have a responsibility to lead in publicly extending forgiveness and encouraging others to do the same. I believe asking for forgiveness and extending forgiveness are going to be integral parts of my life for as long as I live.

Through my study of forgiveness, God impressed upon me that I was not going to get out of prison until I had forgiven—from my heart, not simply in my mind—every last person who had said or done anything against me. Nevertheless, as the Minnesota summer turned colder, and the autumn chill began to set in, I would never have dreamed that two of the main objects of my forgiveness for the rest of my days would be my best friend and my wife.

35

Tammy Faye

AS SOON AS WORD OF JUDGE MULLEN'S DECISION TO REDUCE my sentence from forty-five years to eighteen years hit the media, reactions came fast and furiously. Some people thought the judge was too lenient with me; many thought the new sentence was still much too stiff. Letters soon poured in to Tammy Faye in Florida and to me in prison. One letter that particularly piqued my interest was dated August 27, 1991, and was written on Liberty University stationery. It was from Mark DeMoss, the young public-relations director and administrative assistant to Jerry Falwell who had witnessed firsthand the events surrounding my pseudoresignation from PTL in March 1987 through Jerry Falwell's departure from PTL on October 8, 1987. Mark's letter was brief and to the point:

> As you may know, Dr. Falwell has publicly said many times that your
> 45-year sentence was outrageous, unreasonable, and unfair. When Judge
> Mullen reduced the sentence last week to 18 years, we issued a news
> release stating that the sentence was still excessive and that Dr. Falwell
> would have supported your release. Yesterday, he referred briefly to
> your situation on *The Old Time Gospel Hour*.

I have mixed emotions about this letter. Another letter, also dated August 27, 1991, came from Owen Carr and was specifically addressed to Tammy Faye. Owen expressed his love to Tammy on behalf of his wife,

Priscilla, and himself. He tried to console Tammy Faye concerning my resentencing: "Of course, eighteen years isn't as bad as forty-five, but it is still outrageous. There is no possible way to align this with 'justice.' Or to align it with what others are given who have committed crimes much worse than that with which they have charged Jim."

Owen went on to encourage Tammy Faye: "We are back to basics: trusting Jesus! We can't explain. We can't understand. We can't rationalize. Nothing seems to fit together. So we place our hand in His, and walk with Him through the long, dark valley, over very rough roads. And we *trust* Him."

Suddenly, Owen Carr's letter took on a different tone, still one of loving concern, but also expressing his pastoral caution:

> Tammy, I feel impressed to warn you again, as I did early in this nightmarish experience. You have already been separated from Jim for a long time. And now, the prospects are that you will be away from him for an even longer time. There is bound to be a loneliness. You can't afford that. No one else can really take Jim's place—either in your home or in your heart. How you must long for his companionship. Just to be with him. Just to talk with him—when no one is watching or listening. Just to be held by him and to hold him.
>
> Be very careful, Tammy. The devil will take advantage of this, and someone else may offer to provide "special attention." Even some preacher, who feels sorry for you, and wanting to empathize with you, may lead you into Satan's trap. Be very careful. Be alert. Be on guard. The Bible tells us, "We are not to be ignorant of his devices."

Unfortunately, even as Owen Carr was writing his words of admonition to Tammy Faye, she was already back at French Lick Springs . . . with Roe Messner. She and Roe were meeting with the Canadian financial backers who were putting up the money to purchase the resort from the man who had bought it at the auction. The Canadian backers also offered to put up $500,000 to get Tammy Faye back on television. On August 28, Roe wrote to me in prison concerning his plan to get Tammy Faye on TV before Christmas.

> It was good to see you in Charlotte. I was very disappointed in the new sentence. . . . We continue to pray every day that the Lord will give you the strength to carry on. Keep a positive attitude and don't let bitterness

set in. I realize this is easy for me to say and probably hard for you to do. We have to believe that God is still in control.

. . . Who do you think we should hire or consult with to get the TV set up? Please give me any input you have on operating the hotel. I don't think I will have any trouble operating the hotel and overseeing the TV operation. . . . Tammy seems to be holding up pretty good. Do you have any suggestions on working with her?

Your friend,
Roe

A week or so later, I received another letter from Roe, informing me of further details that were being negotiated toward the purchase of the property. The close of his letter was interesting. Roe wrote, "How are you doing, now that you are faced with such a long sentence? How are you spending your days? Is there anything you want me to do for you?" As he had begun doing more frequently in recent days, Roe signed his letter, "Your friend," and included a Scripture reference below his name. As much as the circumstances said otherwise, I could not bring myself to believe that my best friend was trying to steal my wife away from me.

In October, Tammy Faye traveled to Nashville to record another album of Christian music. The recording included such songs as "It's Mercy Time," "I'm Looking for the Samaritan Man," and "You've Not Heard the Last Word from God." The album was produced by Rick Goodman, son of our good friends and renowned gospel singers Howard and Vestal Goodman. In a letter shortly after Tammy's visit to Nashville, Vestal Goodman wrote to me exclaiming how pretty Tammy Faye looked during the trip. Vestal said she encouraged Tammy to "always look pretty, stay sweet, and hold steady for Jim."

No doubt, Tammy did look especially pretty that week, but it wasn't for me. Roe Messner had checked into the hotel where she was staying.

About that same time we received word that one of Jamie's best prison-visiting-room friends had died. His name was John and he was a giant of a man who weighed nearly 450 pounds. John owned a music store and had been a promoter of rock concerts. He frequently visited an inmate at Rochester F.M.C. and before long, he and Jamie struck up a friendship. John sent Jamie about one thousand dollars' worth of compact discs recorded by some of Jamie's favorite music artists. John often called to talk with Jamie at home or insisted that Jamie call him collect whenever he just needed to talk to another older male.

The last time Jamie talked to John was the day of my resentencing.

John had called Jamie at home to help him through the disappointment of finding out that I was not coming home but was on my way back to Rochester. Less than two months later, John was found dead in his own home. He had been shot four times in the chest.

John's death shook Jamie dramatically. It was the first time anyone that close to him had died, let alone been murdered. When I talked to Jamie by phone, I tried to console and encourage him. He seemed especially anxious to come visit me at Thanksgiving.

Back in Rochester, I was struggling through another bout with despair myself. During one stretch of down days, a prison guard paged me and instructed me to report to the visiting room. I was fighting a battle just to keep my head above water emotionally, and I did not want to spend several hours talking to anyone. I had specifically requested that nobody be permitted to visit me.

I had just finished cleaning bathrooms and I was still dressed in my work clothes. I reeked of cleaning solutions, my hair was unkempt, and I had not bothered to shave in several days. Reluctantly, I peeled off my work clothes and hurriedly replaced them with the khaki clothes required to be worn in the visiting area. I did not take time to wash before changing clothes.

Irritated and looking like I'd just crawled from under a rock, I made my way across the prison compound and into the visiting area. "I am Inmate Bakker, 07407-058," I said as I checked in with the visiting room guard. The guard grunted his acknowledgment of me.

My eyes quickly scanned the visiting room to see who had the gall to intrude upon my self-imposed, depression-laden ban on visitors. Coming toward me was the apple of my eye, my daughter Tammy Sue . . . and she was holding in her arms a beautiful little baby boy—my grandson Jonathan Douglas, whom I had never before seen! Behind Tammy Sue and Jonathan were her husband Doug and baby James, who was now all of two and a half years old. My feet barely touched the floor as I flew to them as fast as I could move without running. I was never so happy to see my daughter in all my life!

Tammy Sue's and Doug's limited income had prevented them from making the trip to Minnesota for more than a year. It had been through the generous gift of our friends Faye and Ray LaForce that they could afford to make this trip.

For four glorious days, I was able to spend time with Tammy Sue, Doug, and my grandchildren. It was exhilarating to get to know little Jonathan; each day I cradled him gently in my arms until he fell asleep. Then James and I played together like we were old friends, which in a way we were. Although I had been in prison since the time of James's infancy, Tammy Sue had placed my picture on their refrigerator. Every day of my imprisonment, Tammy Sue pointed out my picture to baby James and said, "This is your grandpa, Paw-Paw Jim." By the time James finally "met" me, he was already well acquainted with me, thanks to a mother who loved her child and her dad enough to build a bridge between us.

James and I played with the old blocks stained by the thousands of little hands and teeth that had played with them and chewed on them in the visiting room. With them we built houses, boats, and anything else James's or my imagination could conceive and our blocks could accommodate. When he tired of the blocks, I read stories to him from the well-worn children's books available in the visiting room.

Each day, our little family group ate sandwiches purchased from the visiting-room vending machines as we talked and talked. James, of course, had questions about everything. He was amazed at the massive prison complex, even though he could actually see very little of it. He realized that the prison was much bigger than his home. One day upon his arrival at the prison, James looked up and exclaimed to Tammy Sue, "Paw-Paw Jim has a *big* house!"

Later when Tammy Sue related to me what James had said, I replied, "No, Paw-Paw Jim is *in* the big house!" We all laughed heartily. It felt good to laugh, although that was one of the few times I could recall ever laughing about being in prison. Only baby James could have brought me out of depression to laughter.

All too soon our four-day visit came to a close. Tammy Sue and her family returned to South Carolina. It would be nearly nine months before I saw my grandchildren again.

Near the end of October, Tammy Faye ministered in Louisiana at Metropolitan Christian Centre pastored by our friend Marvin Gorman. She spoke and sang for the church's women's group, headed up by Mary Helen Bryant, one of New Orleans's top interior designers. Tammy Faye also performed in Reverend Gorman's televised Sunday morning service, and again in the evening service. Reverend Gorman was so pleased he invited Tammy Faye to return to his church for a special Mother's Day service in May. Marvin wrote me a glowing letter, praising Tammy Faye and expressing appreciation for her ministry.

For her part, Tammy Faye was not quite so enthusiastic. In her letter describing the services to me, Tammy wrote:

Reverend Gorman's church went really well. But I thought it would
leave me more satisfied than it did. I thought I would love the evangelistic field again . . . and I don't! I could never live that life again! I
know that television is where I am supposed to be, and I guess I will
never be happy in ministry again until I am back in my place, doing the
thing I best know how to do. If that does not work, then I feel that I
want to leave the ministry forever. There are other ways to serve the
Lord.

The tone of Tammy's letter stunned me, but it did not surprise me. I
could tell that she was changing. Nevertheless, I could not help wondering, *Is this the same woman who started out with me thirty years ago, traveling to
our first meetings on a Greyhound bus we caught at the local bus station?* Later, as
we became better known, we bought a Holiday Rambler travel trailer in
which we lived as we moved from place to place conducting church revival
meetings. In those days, Tammy Faye had a consuming passion for lost
souls and for God. She sang from the depths of her heart, "I'd rather have
Jesus than anything," and I knew she sincerely meant it. Now, Tammy was
saying that she could never live an evangelistic lifestyle again.

Another bittersweet legal decision was rendered on November 4,
1991, by Judge William Thurmond Bishop, a U.S. bankruptcy judge in
Columbia, South Carolina. Jerry Falwell had placed PTL into bankruptcy
proceedings on June 12, 1987. At that time, the court appointed a trustee
to oversee the property and all activities regarding PTL. On June 30, 1988,
while I was still trying to find a way to buy or lease back Heritage USA, a
small group of Lifetime Partners, represented by three private individuals,
filed a suit before the Court against PTL's trustee, Mr. M.C. "Red"
Benton. In their suit, the Lifetime Partners claimed that the PTL Lifetime
Partners should receive priority in the disbursement of PTL's assets
because they had paid a deposit of money and had not received the benefits they had expected. On October 25, 1988, the court made a decision
allowing this small group of Partners to represent *all* Lifetime Partners,
even though many Lifetime Partners showed little interest in the case.

After nearly three years of legal wranglings, Judge Bishop finally rendered his decision:

It was not contemplated that Lifetime Partners would be entitled to a specific hotel room, condominium, or unit on the premises [of Heritage

357

USA] nor, more importantly, were Lifetime Partners promised availability of rooms or any other benefits for the use of their partnership. . . .

Payments made by Lifetime Partners were not, in any sense of the word, deposits. The word deposit does not appear in any of the promotional literature attached as exhibits to either the Plaintiffs' or the Defendant's pleadings. Moreover, no trust relationship is alleged to have been created with respect to the Lifetime Partners' monies, nor have the Plaintiffs alleged that the Lifetime Partners' payments were, or should have been, segregated by the Debtor. In essence, the rights and responsibilities of individual Lifetime Partners and the Debtor were both fully operative and were being delivered and provided prior to the filing of the bankruptcy petition. . . . Further, the undisputed testimony of Plaintiff class representative . . . demonstrates that the Lifetime Partnership benefits were, in fact, delivered and provided before the commencement of the case.[1]

What all that meant was that in the court's decision against the PTL Lifetime Partners who had filed the suit, it had admitted that the PTL Lifetime Partners were in fact receiving all that they had been promised while I was president of PTL. The judge acknowledged the difficulties that Partners sometimes had in booking lodging space at Heritage USA during our peak seasons but did not consider that as a breach of our promises. Furthermore, he plainly acknowledged that the money donated by the Lifetime Partners was not meant to be "segregated" and used for construction purposes only.

The good news was that Judge Thurmond Bishop was saying that two of the basic premises on which I had been tried—that I had defrauded the Lifetime Partners by purposely overbooking our lodging space at Heritage USA, and using the money donated for projects other than construction— were false. The bad news was that I was still in prison serving eighteen years. Although Judge Bishop's decision had not been rendered for the purpose of exonerating me and had absolutely no legal impact on me, it was at least a sort of moral victory. Finally, somebody in the legal system had said in essence, "Bakker did not defraud the PTL Lifetime Partners. That which had been promised to them was being delivered."

A few days after Judge Bishop's decision, on November 10, Reverend Richard Dortch was released from a halfway house in Florida, where he had been since June. He had served sixteen months at a minimum security prison at the Eglin Air Force Base federal prison after he made a deal with prosecutors to testify against me. The week before Thanksgiving, the

North Carolina District Council of the Assemblies of God, headed by superintendent Charles Cookman—one of my former board members—voted unanimously to return Reverend Dortch's ministerial credentials. The denomination's national board approved the action as well. In commenting to the press, Superintendent Cookman stated, "I am convinced that Richard Dortch never, in his wildest imagination, thought that he would ever defraud anybody of anything."[2]

Although I was glad for Reverend Dortch, his release was yet another reminder that I was still looking at eighteen long years in prison. I had lost any hope of an early release and had resigned myself to my state. Nevertheless, when Tammy Faye, Jamie, and Donna arrived on November 22 for our Thanksgiving visit, I tried my best to put on a positive face, in spite of the fact that Roe Messner had accompanied my family to Minnesota.

Over the summer and fall of 1991, I had begun to suspect that something was going on between Tammy and Roe, but I refused to believe it. I could not help noticing, however, how abrupt Tammy Faye's and my telephone conversations had become. Where we had once spent hours talking by phone, now she was always in a hurry to end our conversations. "I have to hurry, honey," she would tell me. "The girls from the ministry are coming to go out to lunch with me, and I have to get ready. I love you, bye!" Her excuses became more and more strained as the months wore on.

I called less frequently during the fall of 1991. When I did telephone, our conversations were full of mundane matters. "How are the kids? How are you feeling? Are you making it okay financially? How is the church doing?" We expressed few of our true emotions at that time.

Regardless, I was delighted to see Tammy Faye at Thanksgiving. I had not been in the same room with her since the resentencing at Charlotte in August. Just to see her smiling face brightened my spirits. Tammy Faye was so perpetually perky.

We had our usual vending-machine Thanksgiving dinner and tried to pretend everything was normal. Nevertheless, I could tell that something was wrong during our visits. For one thing, Tammy Faye seemed to have difficulty looking me in the eyes. As we sat at our low table in the visiting room, she appeared nervous. We had been married for over thirty years, so even in the awkward environment of the prison visiting area, it was impossible not to notice the difference in our relationship. To anyone unfamiliar with us, it might have been hard to know that we were even married.

Tammy Faye, Jamie, and Donna visited each day from November 22 through December 2. Roe left over Thanksgiving and returned the following week. I assumed that he had gone home to spend the holiday with his wife.

After a few days of visiting, I could tell Tammy Faye was bored. She talked more to the wives of the inmates sitting near us in the visiting room. When she and I talked, she talked more about her excitement at going back on television at French Lick Springs than anything else. I knew the inactivity of our visits was tough for her; she was used to going, going, going all the time. No doubt it would have been difficult for her to stay in one place for five or six hours each day under any circumstances, much less the growing coolness between us. On several days, I encouraged Tammy to leave the visiting room a bit early. She was reluctant to go, but I could tell that it was useless for her to stay.

On the last day of Tammy Faye's visit, I was determined to reach out to my wife any way I could. We were still husband and wife, she was the mother of my children, and I still loved her immeasurably. I did not want to lose her, especially after all we had come through together. I was not about to allow thirty years of marriage to simply slip away without a fight.

I could hardly stand it as I waited to hear my name called: "Inmate Bakker, you have a visit." I had taken extra care the night before to make sure my prison khakis were crisply pressed. I wanted to look my best for Tammy Faye. I hurried through the prison routine for entering the visiting room. When I completed my check-in procedures, I looked for Tammy Faye's beaming face.

Today, however, her face looked less than radiant. The extra thick makeup she had applied could not conceal her somber look and her smile seemed forced. She seemed so emotionally detached; it was as if a mannequin of her body sat there. Her lips merely grazed mine as we hugged and kissed. I tried to hold her close to me for an extra moment or two as we had done on previous visits, but I could feel Tammy pulling away. "Jim Bakker, behave yourself. Do you want to get into trouble and be sent to the hole?" she scolded with a fake laugh. She whirled away from me, pulled out a chair, and sat down . . . on the opposite side of the table from me. Almost immediately she began telling me about all the things she needed to get done as soon as she got back to Florida.

By the end of the day, my heart was pounding. I could hardly tear my eyes away from Tammy Faye for more than a moment, almost as if I was afraid that if I glanced in another direction, she would disappear. Deep feelings of love and desire for her overwhelmed me.

Toward the time when we knew we would soon hear the guard's voice calling "Wrap it up," Tammy Faye and I walked back to the rear visiting room, to the window near the vending-machine area. Normally at this time of day, the vending area was the closest thing we could find to some semblance of privacy, as most of the inmates and visitors congregated in the main room before the end of visitation time. With nobody around us, Tammy Faye and I stood in front of a soda pop machine, both of us facing the window as we had done on other occasions just to sense a moment of intimacy. It had been more than two years since I had slept with Tammy in our own bed, and every fiber of my being was straining to touch her and to be touched by her.

I knew I was taking a chance—the prison strictly prohibited expressions of affection except upon greeting and saying good-bye. But to me, it was worth the risk. I pressed my body against Tammy Faye's, placed my hands as inconspicuously as possible on her waist, and gently pulled her toward me. For a long delicious moment I basked in her warmth, as I allowed the heat of my body to intermingle with hers. She smelled so good. I wanted to kiss her and sweep her up in my arms and carry her away to some private place where we could be one once again. My body responded to her softness. I was lost in the moment. . . .

Suddenly, Tammy Faye whirled around, took a step backward, straightened her dress, and said icily, "Don't start something you can't finish."

I stood there aghast. I was so stunned I could not even respond to her. I could not believe we had come to this. I mumbled something about it must be time to go, and we went back to where Jamie and Donna were waiting for Tammy Faye. We all said hasty good-byes, Donna's and Jamie's eyes filled with tears. Tammy's eyes were dry.

My head and heart were still reeling as I watched them go out the door. That was the last time I ever touched Tammy Faye Bakker.

36

Billy Graham

I HAD ALREADY TOLD MY FAMILY MEMBERS THAT I THOUGHT it would be a better Christmas for all of us if they celebrated at home again this year, so as the holiday approached, I had no sense of anticipation whatsoever. In fact, I was dreading another Christmas in prison. In the past, I had always enjoyed showering my family members with special Christmas gifts. I had looked forward to one day being able to do the same for my grandchildren. Now, however, I had no way to give my children and grandchildren anything but pottery I had made in the prison crafts room.

I tried to console myself with the knowledge that Christmas was a time at which we celebrate Jesus' birth, but frankly, I wanted to forget all about Christmas in 1991. This was to be my third Christmas in prison, and I had now been incarcerated long enough to truly understand the hatred with which most inmates regarded the holidays. An unspoken pall permeated the entire prison compound. It was as though everybody knew something awful was approaching yet nobody wanted to admit it.

Tammy Faye's Thanksgiving visit had left me discouraged and depressed as it was. On top of that, shortly before Christmas, I started coming down with the flu. The Minnesota winters chilled me to the bone, and to make matters worse, for some reason, the heat in my end of Building Two was not functioning correctly. At night, the cold ceramic-covered brick walls in our cells felt like the inside of a refrigerator. To keep warm, I put on both of my jogging suits and piled on as many extra covers as Rod Netherton and I had been able to borrow. I still froze. Often in the middle of the night while I was sleeping, my hand fell up against the wall and remained in that position. In the morning, I could hardly move my fingers. I had developed arthritis in my hands, and the cold caused my knuckles to become stiff. The pain was almost unbearable when I banged my knuckles against the faucets as I cleaned the bathroom sinks.

One cold morning, a week or so before Christmas, I finished cleaning the hallway and bathrooms on my floor and returned to my cell. Still in my work clothes I climbed onto my bunk and pulled a blanket that was folded at the foot of my bed over the top of me, trying to get warm. We were not allowed to sleep under the regular covers during the day, no matter how cold it was. Our beds must remain made at all times during the day in case of surprise inspections. The thin cotton blanket did little to warm me. My nose was running, my head was pounding, my body ached; all the symptoms of the flu were catching up with me. I felt miserable. I had just shut my eyes, hoping to get a few minutes of relief, when I heard a guard's voice echoing in the hall over the prison paging system, "Inmate Bakker! Report to two-one guard station."

"Oh, no," I moaned as I rolled off my bunk. *What now?*

I half-walked, half-staggered down the hall to the guard station. There I saw a familiar-looking box sitting on the desk. It was a box containing an artificial Christmas tree and the same sort of scrawny Christmas tree ornaments I had used to decorate the Christmas tree the year before . . . and the year before that.

"Bakker, take these ornaments and go put up the Christmas tree and decorate it. There's an electrical outlet across the hall from the Coke machines," the guard said. "Make it look good, ya hear?"

The look on my face must have given me away.

The guard softened his tone a bit and said, "Well, make it look as good as you can."

I carried the box back up the hallway toward the spot where the Christmas tree was placed each year. It was like the rerun of a bad movie. *The third year in a row*, I thought. *Is this just a coincidence or is it some kind of cruel trick that the guards are making me decorate the tree again?*

I did my best to make the sparse tree appear festive. As hard as I tried, however, I could not shake the thoughts of the Christmas decorations at Heritage USA in past years. Now, here I was again, decorating a tree that nobody wanted to see—not even me.

The prison officials were not oblivious to the antipathy with which most inmates regarded Christmas. Consequently, the prison offered numerous activities to help prisoners make it through the holiday season. The prison sponsored special holiday sports contests and games, and for those who wished to participate, special chapel services and visits from outside choir groups were permitted.

One night my friend Tony asked me to go with him to hear a singing group comprised of senior citizens; the group was known as "Young at Heart." I reluctantly agreed. Sure enough, like most choral groups who performed at the prison during the Christmas season, the senior citizens had in their repertoire the classic, "I'll Be Home for Christmas," which they sang with deep emotion. As the dear golden-agers sang their hearts out for the guys, they little realized that they were tearing the hearts out of the inmates. Many inmates in attendance simply couldn't take it and they got up and walked out of the concert.

The singers meant well, so I stayed and sang "Jingle Bells" with them and "Silent Night." Afterward, light snacks were served and I got to greet many of the singers. I appreciated them taking the time to come to the prison, but I wished that the singers could have avoided such a troubling song.

On Christmas Eve, I walked over to the chapel to see if perhaps another shipment of the cards provided by the Hallmark company had arrived. None had, but while I was there the chaplain spotted me. In over two years, I had not violated the prison officials' mandate that I refrain from being involved in any position of spiritual leadership. The only time I attended chapel functions had been when special guest speakers or singers came to the prison.

So I was shocked when the chaplain approached me and asked me if I would be willing to read the Christmas story from the Bible during the ecumenical Christmas Eve service to be held that night. I agreed to do it.

The Christmas Eve service was a beautiful candlelight ceremony. We sang several familiar Christmas songs, and then it was time for me to read the Christmas story. I stood to my feet and walked slowly to the front of the chapel and stepped behind the pulpit. As I looked out into the faces of the group of men gathered in the chapel that night, my mind flashed back to a picture of me standing in front of the large congregation at Heritage Village Church so many times before. Now, however, as I stood in front of this relatively small group, I was shaking in my shoes. This was the first formal chapel activity in which I had taken a participatory role since entering prison in 1989.

I had studied and marked the passage to be read. I slowly pronounced every word. I sincerely wondered if my brain had been damaged through my trial, sentencing, and imprisonment, because I had no confidence in my ability to speak in front of a group of people. *How did I ever appear on television in front of millions of people?* I wondered.

Christmas Day was relatively uneventful. I tried to eat the traditional Christmas dinner, but I didn't have much of an appetite. The flu was definitely catching up with me now, so I was glad for a day off work, just to rest. I stayed in bed most of the day, getting up only for the prison's mandatory 4:00 P.M. count and to call my family. I talked briefly with each of my family members, Mother, Dad, Jamie, Tammy Sue, Doug, the grandchildren, and Tammy Faye. Tammy Faye acted as though her rebuff of my affection only a few weeks before had never happened. She told me that basically it had been a good Christmas. I was glad I had encouraged the family to stay at home this year.

On January 2, 1992, I "celebrated" my fifty-second birthday. I spent the day in self-imposed exile, talking to as few people as possible. Tammy Faye spent the day in Des Moines, Iowa, having her teeth worked on by Dr. Jim Boltz, a friend of ours who had done much of our dental work over the years. I later learned that Roe Messner accompanied her for her dental trip.

By early January, I finally succumbed to the flu. Besides the physical misery, a deep sadness plagued my heart and mind. Nevertheless, I got up each morning and went to work, but as soon as I finished cleaning the bathrooms and halls, I returned to my cell, closed the door and crawled back onto my bunk, still wearing my work clothes.

On the day I had the worst fever, I lay in my bunk, trying to "sweat it out." Suddenly, my cell door opened and a guard appeared in the doorway. "Bakker, come with me," he commanded.

I groaned and rolled out of bed. I had not showered or shaved yet that day. I knew I looked awful, but I was too sick to care. I did not even bother to comb my hair; I simply ran my fingers though the increasingly thin strands and left it at that. I started to put on my good tennis shoes and stopped short. I had no idea why the guard wanted me. *Maybe he wants me to clean up a mess somewhere or help push the trash carts over to the dumpster,* I thought. *No use ruining my good shoes for that.* I had two pairs of tennis shoes in prison, one pair I wore while I cleaned the rest rooms, and the other I wore to exercise, walk the track, or during after-work hours. The old tennis shoes I wore mopping and cleaning rest rooms were tattered, torn, and filthy. I decided to put them on.

I reported to the guard, wearing my work clothes and work shoes. He looked at me strangely, but he didn't say much. He simply told me to sit down and wait.

Although I had been in prison for more than two years, fear of the unknown still caused me to be extremely nervous. *Have I done something wrong?* I wondered. *Did I miss something when I did my cleaning chores today?* I retraced my steps and activities over the past few days, carefully examining my words and deeds.

After about fifteen more minutes, another guard came over to me. "Get your coat," he said. I walked back to my cell, retrieved my heavy, green, army overcoat with its bright orange lining, and returned to the guard station.

"Let's go," the guard said. We walked out of Building Two into the bitterly cold air, toward the front of the prison compound. It eventually became clear that we were going to the warden's office.

The guard and I entered the building. I noticed a number of people buzzing around a doorway, some familiar faces, others who were not. *Something is up*, I thought.

A high-level prison official approached me and whispered, "Somebody is here to see you, Bakker. Do you want to see him?"

"See who?" I asked, honestly surprised. I was expecting no visitors. *Why would they be making such a fuss over somebody coming to see me? And why are we in the administration building, rather than in the visiting room?*

"Hasn't anyone told you who it is?" the official asked.

"No, sir," I responded.

"Why, Billy Graham is here to see you!" the prison official gushed.

"Billy Graham?" I repeated. "He's here? To see me?" I looked down at my shoes. The gaping holes in them stared back at me.

"Well, you do want to see him, don't you?" the official asked.

For a fraction of a second, I almost said no out of sheer embarrassment. The last time I had seen Billy Graham face-to-face had been when he had appeared on *PTL* along with George Beverly Shea and Cliff Barrows. Billy's opening line to Tammy Faye and me that day had been, "You feel just like family, you have been in our home so much." On that day, I had been dressed in one of my best suits of clothes, with every hair in place. Now, I was in rumpled, prison work khakis, totally disheveled. How could I allow the great Dr. Billy Graham to see me like this?

But then I thought, *Billy Graham has come here . . . to this place . . . to see me.* There was no way I was going to refuse his visit.

"Yes, I would like to see him," I replied. I took off my old green overcoat and tried to straighten my hair. It was no use. I took a breath and walked into the warden's conference room where the prison officials had indicated that Dr. Graham was waiting along with Dr. Westrick and other prison officials.

As I walked through the door, Billy Graham turned toward me and opened his arms wide. Immediately, I felt his total acceptance and love. I wanted to run into his arms like a little boy would run into his daddy's arms. As I looked at him, the tall, distinguished gentleman looked back at me with absolute compassion. I had not seen such compassionate eyes in a long time.

We stepped toward each other and embraced. "Hello, Jim," he said in his rich Carolina accent. "How are you?"

"Hello, Dr. Graham. I'm sorry you have to see me like this." Billy Graham simply waved my apology away.

We sat down beside each other at the conference table and began to talk. The room was still swirling with people, but I felt as though Dr. Graham and I were in our own separate world. We talked quietly but freely. He told me that he was glad to be able to see me. "I wanted to come sooner," he said almost apologetically.

His wife, Ruth, was in Mayo Clinic for some tests, which is why they were in Minnesota in the first place. He told me Ruth was especially insistent that he come to visit me. "She sends her greetings and her love," said Dr. Graham.

Billy Graham asked about my family and about my life in prison. He seemed genuinely concerned, so I shared with him some of the good points and the bad.

He then told me about his most recent overseas crusade and how God had done such great things there. He was clearly pleased that so many people had accepted Christ. He noted that satellite television had extended the crusade coverage to the four corners of the world.

I told him about Dr. Ruth Westrick, whom I could see out of the corner of my eye. "This woman is the Mother Teresa of the prison system," I told Dr. Graham. I told him of Dr. Westrick's compassion and loyalty to the inmates, and about the dignity she had given me. I got the feeling I was not telling Billy anything he did not already know.

Before he left, Billy Graham offered to pray with me, and as he began, the activity in the room instantly ceased. Time seemed suspended during Dr. Graham's visit, so I have no idea how long he stayed. Probably not long, but I will never forget that the man who had just been voted one of the most influential men in the world and who has ministered to millions of people took time out of his busy schedule to come minister to one prisoner. Amid my depression, flu, filth, and hopelessness, Billy Graham had come. I felt as though Jesus Himself had come to visit me.

I said good-bye to Dr. Graham, and we hugged each other one more time. The prison officials stood by, looking on. I put on my green army coat and headed for the door. Dr. Graham waved good-bye from across the room. "Ruth and I will be praying for you, Jim," he said.

I made my way out of the room and back across the prison yard to my unit. As I walked down the hall toward my cell, still trying to grasp all that had just happened, I noticed the pay phone was not in use. *I have to tell Tammy*, I thought. I grabbed the receiver and dialed our phone number, collect, of course. When Tammy Faye came on the line, my first words to her were, "Tam, guess who came to see me today?"

CHAPTER

37

Dad, Mom Is Leaving You!

THE IMAGE OF BILLY GRAHAM STANDING IN ROCHESTER prison with his arms outstretched to me and his eyes filled with compassion will be forever etched upon my heart. Although I did not know it just then, his visit was providentially timed. God must have known that I was going to need an extra boost in my spirit to make it through the next difficult days.

As excited as I was about Billy Graham's visit, the next news I received was even better. Jamie had turned sixteen years of age on December 18, and he wanted to come to the prison to see me! Jamie had visited me several times previously, but always with Tammy Faye, Donna, or Tammy Sue, never by himself. As much as I tried to spend time with him when he came, he felt that he had to compete with our family's women for my attention. Now that he was sixteen, however, prison rules allowed him to visit me alone, without being accompanied by Tammy Faye or another adult.

I could hardly wait to see my boy.

The first thing I noticed when I saw Jamie was that my *boy* was now a man. Almost overnight, it seemed, he had grown up. In many ways, Jamie was much more worldly wise at sixteen years of age than I was at fifty-two.

The collapse of PTL after the public exposure of my moral failure had wreaked havoc in thousands of people's lives. Godly, dedicated men and women who had moved to Heritage USA to be a part of the ministry were suddenly jobless and spiritually disillusioned. It wasn't just Jim and Tammy whose lives and homes were hurled into disarray. Hundreds of lives were directly and devastatingly affected on a daily basis because PTL had been destroyed. But of all the thousands of horror stories that came out of the fall of PTL, I believe nobody suffered more than my own son, Jamie Charles.

Jamie had just turned eleven when the PTL scandals hit the news. Granted, his life at Heritage USA had been anything but normal—how many eleven-year-olds have their own bodyguards? Nevertheless, Jamie had grown up in a comfortable home with the love and nurture of caring Christians all around him. Even when Tammy Faye and I had been preoccupied, Jamie still had Tammy's parents and mine living at Heritage, schoolmates and teachers from Heritage Academy, and hundreds of PTL staff members who loved him and doted over him constantly.

Suddenly, after March 1987, Jamie had nobody. Tammy Faye and I were consumed with trying to keep our lives together, Tammy Sue had run off and gotten married, and most of Jamie's closest friends, including his bodyguard buddies, were back at Heritage and had been encouraged to have no further contact with him.

Our family moved to Florida just as Jamie moved into his teenage years. Besides struggling with all the notoriously cruel things pubescent teens say to each other, Jamie also had to deal with the barrage of legitimate press reports and tabloid scandal sheets shredding what little respectability our family had left. At a time when most teenage boys crave acceptance at almost any cost, Jamie was treated like a leper. It should not have surprised us that Jamie then gravitated toward some wilder kids. After I went to prison, Jamie defended my virtue before his friends. Once, a large student sitting in the back of the classroom accused me of having homosexual relationships in prison. Jamie went ballistic. He leaped to his feet and began picking up the desks between him and the boy in the back of the room. One by one, Jamie heaved the desks out of his way. When he reached the boy, Jamie shoved him up against the classroom window. Jamie later confessed that he had intended to punch the boy literally through the window and out of the classroom, but just as he reared back to swing, his teacher stopped him. Later Jamie chased the boy all the way to the school bus, fighting his way through several of the kid's larger friends and screaming, "I'll kill you!"

By the time Jamie was fourteen, he was already smoking cigarettes and drinking beer with his friends. At fifteen years of age, he was smoking marijuana and had experimented several times with LSD. During the summer of 1990, I could tell that something was wrong with Jamie when he came to the prison to see me. His face was drawn and gaunt, and his eyes had a hollow look. He later confessed to me that he and some friends had been drinking and using LSD at the Kahler Hotel all week long while he had been in town along with Tammy Faye to visit me. The boys partied well into the night. The next morning, Jamie was an emotional basket case when he came to see me. He burst into tears at odd moments and seemed to be disturbed and disoriented much of the time. When Jamie went back to the vending machines in the visiting room, I told Tammy Faye that I feared Jamie was on some sort of drugs. I would have been horrified had I really known what my son was doing.

About that same time, seeking love and affection, Jamie became sexually active. By the summer of 1991, at the age of fifteen, he was deeply embroiled in a bona fide love affair with a young woman named Suzanne, a first-year college student. Before long, his world revolved around Suzanne. She was his first true love. He was so head over heels in love that he hardly paid any attention to what was developing between Tammy Faye and Roe.

Jamie's first clue that something wasn't quite right came one night when he and Suzanne were at our home in Florida. Tammy Faye had been gone for several hours and had come home late. She rang the doorbell to get into the house. Jamie answered the door. "Mom! What's wrong?" he asked her.

"Well, um, I locked my keys in the car at the grocery store, where I had gone to walk around for a while. . . ."

The grocery store was only a few blocks down the street from our home. Jamie was suspicious but didn't say anything at the time.

Another night toward the end of 1991, Jamie and Suzanne were eating dinner at our home when Tammy Faye came home upset. She told Jamie and Suzanne, "An article is coming out in one of the rag mags that says Roe and I are having an affair. I just want you to know that it's not true. It's just a bunch of garbage."

Jamie made light of Tammy's comment. "Man, those people will write anything, won't they?"

Early in January 1992, Jamie and Suzanne broke up, by mutual consent. They had been together almost constantly for more than a year. Jamie later confided to me that breaking up with Suzanne was one of the most devastating moments in his young life. Tammy Faye was absorbed in running the church in Florida, while trying to get everything together at French Lick Springs to purchase the resort and go back on television.

371

Meanwhile, I was languishing in prison. Without Suzanne, Jamie's emotional props were knocked out from beneath him. She had been his friend, confidante, and security. His relationship with Suzanne had also provided Jamie an escape from the pain of his father being in prison and his mother coming down on him for drinking on the weekends. Now, Suzanne was gone, and Jamie plunged into a deep depression.

He repeatedly told Tammy Faye, "I have to talk to Dad. I need my dad! I want to go see Dad."

"All right," Tammy Faye said. "Roe says he will be glad to fly up there with you so you can go see your dad."

"Great, let's make the reservations," Jamie answered.

On Friday, January 17, Jamie and Roe flew to Rochester. They arrived in Minnesota after prison visiting hours so they were not able to see me that day, but I knew Jamie would be at the prison first thing the next morning.

Early Saturday morning, Roe and Jamie left the Kahler Hotel for F.M.C. Rochester. As they started to get into the car, Roe stopped, handed the keys to Jamie, and said, "You drive, Jamie."

"Me?" Jamie replied. "I don't drive yet, Roe. I don't even have a license."

"That's okay," Roe answered. "Go ahead. I'll teach you."

It was a cold, winter, Minnesota morning and the ground was covered with snow and ice.

"I'm afraid I might mess up the car if I drive," Jamie said.

"Oh, you'll do fine," Roe replied.

Jamie had never driven a car before, but fortunately, he negotiated the icy roads safely and arrived at the prison without incident.

Roe left Jamie at the prison entrance and drove off. Jamie was on his own for the first time as he went through the visitor's entry process. As soon as I saw Jamie, I recognized that he was deeply discouraged and depressed. It wasn't long before he began to bare his soul concerning his breakup with Suzanne. Jamie told me how lonely he felt without her, and for the first time, I could honestly empathize with my son. As I looked at him, I couldn't get over how much he resembled me when I had been his age.

"Jamie, when I was in high school, I was always a loner," I told him. "I was active in school programs, but deep inside, I was lonely."

"Really, Dad? You felt that way?"

I went on to tell Jamie how much I now missed Tammy Faye, and how lonely I was for her. Jamie looked back at me with an understanding that far surpassed his years.

The longer we talked, the more open we both became with each other. He spoke straightforwardly of his involvement with drugs, alcohol, and sex. I told him candidly and in detail of the events leading up to my tryst with Jessica Hahn. I tried to explain to him again how I had lost PTL. We talked for hour after hour; we laughed a lot, we cried a bit, and for the first time in his sixteen years, Jamie and I spent one entire day alone together. The irony was not lost upon me that it took me going to prison before I could spend the day with my son, giving him my undivided attention.

No subject was off-limits that day. Whatever Jamie wanted to talk about was fine with me. We talked at length about his relationship with Suzanne and about his other friends. We talked about Jamie growing up to be a man, as well as the experiences he had already known as a child. I told him that I was concerned about how thin he looked. Jamie countered by telling me how he always felt self-conscious about being pudgy as a little boy. We both laughed as Jamie recalled how as a child he used to wander the grounds of Heritage USA and well-meaning people would feed him anything he wanted, ice cream, candy, soda pop, whatever.

"You know it's true, Dad," he said laughing, "You're the one who hung the sign around my neck that said, 'Please don't feed me!'"

"I never did such a thing!" I poked Jamie as we both laughed.

Throughout the day, I did my best to listen to Jamie more than I advised him. I was careful not to condemn him about anything but attempted to remain open and accepting of even those things about which I disagreed with Jamie. It was the father-son talk we should have had five or six years previously.

Toward the end of the day, Jamie and I were laughing about something when suddenly, he said, "Hey, Dad! What do you think about that rag-mag article that is supposed to be coming out, saying that Mom and Roe are having an affair? Isn't that crazy?" Instantly my mood turned somber. I bowed my head momentarily and then looked up at Jamie, and said, "What do you think?"

Jamie stopped in the middle of a laugh and sat up straight in his chair.

"What do you mean, Dad? You don't think it's true, do you?" Jamie asked.

I looked down at the table for a moment. Finally, I said quietly, "Jamie, I think it is true. I think your mother is . . . I think your mother is seeing Roe."

Jamie was horrified. "No, Dad; it's not true. Mom would tell me.

She's always been honest with me. You know how much Mom hates lying."

"Jamie, Jamie, Jamie . . ." I said.

"Dad, it's not true. Mom would not lie to me. Dad, I swear, it is *not* true!"

Jamie was so adamant that Tammy Faye and Roe were not seeing each other, it was almost reassuring to me. Perhaps they were not, in fact, having an affair. After all, I wasn't really sure.

Jamie and I let the subject drop and moved on to talk about other things. By the time Jamie was ready to leave, both of our spirits had risen once again.

"I'll be back tomorrow, Dad," Jamie said.

"Great!" I answered. "What time do you think you'll be coming?" I asked.

"I'll be here first thing in the morning, as soon as they open the doors!" Jamie answered.

"Don't you want to sleep in a little bit?" Like most teenagers, Jamie loved to sleep late when he could.

"Oh, no, Dad. I want to spend as much time as I can with you."

"Okay. I'll be waiting. I'm not going anywhere." Jamie and I both grinned.

Just before Jamie left the visiting room, he turned to me and said something I will never forget.

"Dad, this has been the best day of my life. All my life I have wanted to have you all to myself for a whole day."

I nodded my head and hugged my son. No words were possible. No words were necessary.

Jamie went through the prison exit procedures all by himself, and then waited outside for Roe to pick him up. Once again, Roe insisted Jamie drive the car, so Jamie got in and pointed the vehicle in the direction of the hotel.

Jamie had made arrangements to eat dinner with some of his friends who lived nearby in Rochester, but when Jamie and Roe returned to the Kahler, Jamie received news that one of the friends had to work late, so their plans were postponed until later in the evening. Jamie was hungry since he had not eaten an actual meal all day long, so he said, "Roe, do you want to grab a bite to eat downstairs in the hotel restaurant?"

"Sure."

As Jamie and Roe were eating dinner, they talked about me. Jamie's mind was in turmoil. Finally, Jamie looked across the table and said, "You know what's crazy? My dad said today that he thinks that my mom might be leaving him. . . ."

Roe swallowed his food and gulped hard. "Well, Jamie, I'm afraid to say that it is true."

Jamie later said he felt at that moment as though someone had just shot him with a shotgun at close range and splattered him against the back of the chair. He and Roe had been seated in the nonsmoking section of the restaurant, but immediately, Jamie reached into his pocket, pulled out a cigarette, lit it, took a deep drag, and blew the smoke in Roe's direction.

"Really?" Jamie said nervously. "And Dad thinks it might be because of you."

"Well, Jamie, there is some truth to that. If, ah . . . well, er, if your mother, ah . . . if your mother leaves your father, um, I have . . . I have some interest in her."

"Some interest?"

"Why, yes, Jamie. I would like to ask your mother to marry me."

Jaime took another deep puff on the cigarette, looked squarely in Roe Messner's eyes, and asked point-blank, "Are you sleeping with my mother?"

Roe stammered, "Um, er . . . ah, of course not, Jamie. But I would want to marry your mother. . . . "

Jamie slammed his fist down on the table and jumped to his feet. Instinctively, Roe flinched backwards. Jamie stormed out of the restaurant.

That night, Jamie did not sleep. He paced back and forth in his hotel room, smoking one cigarette after another. "I've got to tell Dad," he kept saying over and over to himself. "I've got to tell Dad . . . but how? How does a son tell his dad that his wife is leaving him to marry his best friend?"

The next morning, true to his word, Jamie was one of the first visitors into the prison. He had driven to the prison with Roe in silence.

I entered the visiting room in an almost exuberant mood, expecting to pick up with my son where we had left off yesterday. But from the moment I saw Jamie in the prison visiting area that day, I could tell something was wrong. His face had a sallow appearance, his eyes had dark shadows under them, and he looked as though he had been crying. I checked in with the guard, gave him my commissary card, and quickly went to where Jamie was sitting. He saw me approaching and stood to meet me. He did not smile. Jamie hugged me and held on to me tightly, as though he was afraid to let go of me.

"Hi, Dad," he said softly.

"Jamie, what's wrong?" I asked. He had been so up when he left the prison less than eighteen hours earlier. Jamie sat down in a heap and slumped down even farther in the chair. I noticed the tears beginning to form in his eyes.

"Dad, promise me that you'll never leave me. . . ."

"Leave you? Jamie, of course I'll never leave you. What are you talking about?"

Jamie was adamant. "Dad! Just promise that you will never leave me!"

"What on earth is wrong?" I asked.

Jamie looked up with a pained look in his eyes and leaned forward in the chair. "Dad! Mom's leaving you!"

My entire body went numb. My greatest fear had come to realization. My wife of nearly thirty-one years was leaving me.

Jamie started to sob. Other visitors stared at us. We didn't care.

For the longest time—I have no idea how long—both Jamie and I sat, grieving, yet speaking not a word to each other.

Finally, I asked, "How do you know?"

Slowly, Jamie poured out the story of his conversation with Roe the night before. He told me that Roe denied he and Tammy Faye were having an affair but admitted that she was planning to leave me and that Roe was waiting with open arms. He was planning to leave his wife, Ruth Ann, and their four children, and marry Tammy Faye.

Neither Jamie Charles nor I spoke much the remainder of the day. We spent over six hours, the entire visiting period, bonded together in our mutual distress. Occasionally, we moved from our table to the vending-machine area, but still we remained quiet.

What a contrast to yesterday when Jamie and I had talked nonstop for six hours, ending with Jamie exclaiming, "Dad, this has been the best day of my life!"

How could we go from the best day in my sixteen-year-old son's life to the worst day in his life—and in mine—all within twenty-four hours?

My heart and mind refused to accept the truth. *My wife of thirty-one years, my best friend, the mother of my children cannot be leaving!*

"Visiting hours are over," the guard called. "Wrap it up!"

My handsome son—now a young man in more ways than I had ever hoped he would be at sixteen years of age—hugged me tightly. With tears in his eyes, he said, "Good-bye, Dad. I'll be back soon."

"Good-bye, son." I started to say, "Take care of your mother," as I had done on so many occasions before, but the words would not come. "Stay close to Jesus," I said instead. The words sounded hollow as Jamie nodded his head and turned away toward the door.

I was unable to cry. My emotions were numb. I walked slowly to the strip-search area and mechanically pulled off my khakis. The guard went through the normal routine. Eventually, I put on my clothes and moved in the direction of my building. As I walked across the compound, I felt no emotion at all.

Later, as the full realization wrapped its clammy fingers around my heart, I wrote in my journal:

> I only live because I do not die . . . My God, my God, have mercy on me! My heart cannot stand the pain.
>
> A projector keeps running movies on my imagination's screen— moving pictures of my wife making passionate love with her new lover . . . in our bed . . . laughing, having fun. The projector will not shut off. It runs when I lay down on my bed; if I get up to go to the bathroom, the film is still running.

Prison makes few allowances for heartrending experiences. Consequently, I had to go on with the normal routine of prison life. One night, while standing and looking in the commissary window, waiting for my order, I left and hurried back to my cell. I felt as though I was about to explode with grief.

I put on my robe, grabbed my bag of toiletries, and made my way down the hall to the shower room. The small cubicle was the only private area open to me in the entire prison at that hour. I stepped inside the shower stall and pulled the curtain. The moment I closed the curtain and turned on the water, I began weeping uncontrollably. I cried so hard I thought I was going to vomit. I could not stop.

My wife of more than thirty years was leaving me.

I wept . . . and wept . . . and wept. . . .

377

CHAPTER

38

War of Words

"MAYBE YOU SHOULD PUT ON A SEAT BELT" JAMIE SAID TO Roe as they drove toward the Minneapolis airport. Once again, Roe had encouraged Jamie to drive the car from the prison after his visit with me. With one hand on the steering wheel and the other holding a cigarette, Jamie looked over at Roe, took a long drag from the umpteenth cigarette he had smoked that day, and blew the smoke in Roe's direction.

"Oh, that's all right, son. I don't need to wear a seat belt," Roe replied.

Jamie's eyes burned into Roe as he said firmly, "Don't ever call me 'son.'"

Jamie later confided to me that the thought kept going through his mind that all he had to do was to crash Roe's side of the car into a wall and he could take care of Roe once and for all. Jamie had never hurt anyone in his life, but at that point he was barely in control of his emotions, much less his actions.

When Jamie and Roe finally arrived at the airline ticket counter, Roe upgraded their tickets to first class. Jamie felt that by doing so, it was as if Roe was saying, "See, you flew out here in coach, but you're going back with me first class." Before boarding their flight back to Florida, Roe and Jamie stopped at a fast-food restaurant in the airport. While Jamie was eating, Roe made an issue of pointing out his good qualities to my son.

"You know, Jamie, I have never taken a drink in my life. I've never had a taste for alcohol or cigarettes."

"Uh-huh, cool," Jamie replied.

"I always played sports and tried to take good care of my body. . . . "

Jamie picked up on Roe's comparisons immediately. He thought, *My dad never played sports, and neither have I . . . and I smoke . . . and I have tasted alcohol. . . . I am nothing like you, Roe, and you are nothing like me. And you are nothing like my dad!*

Jamie then boarded a jet and flew across the country, seated next to the man with whom he was now convinced his mom was having an affair. To say their conversation was stilted would be an understatement. Eventually Roe ceased trying to make small talk and Jamie retreated into the solitude of a headset.

When the plane landed in Orlando, Tammy Faye and Shirley Fulbright met Jamie and Roe at the airport. Jamie had thought that he and Tammy Faye would be going home in one car, and Shirley would be dropping off Roe at a hotel somewhere else. Much to his chagrin, all four of them piled into the same car. "Well, hi! How was your flight?" Tammy gushed.

"Fine," Jamie replied.

"Are you doing okay?" she asked him.

"No," Jamie again replied angrily.

"Are you upset?"

"Yes!"

Jamie simply could not believe that Roe was returning to our home with them. It so angered him, Jamie went into his bedroom, quickly tossed his clothes into a suitcase, and moved out of our home and in with one of his buddies.

On the way out the door, Jamie turned to Tammy Faye and said, "I'm leaving. I'm going to live with one of my friends. I'm mad at you and don't want to talk to you right now. I can't believe you lied to me. I can't believe you did this to Dad. He's sitting there in prison, and you've done this to him. You make me sick!"

Tammy Faye tried to defend her actions by saying, "Well, Jamie, there are a lot of things that you don't understand. . . ." Jamie cut her off mid-sentence and walked out of our family home.

Back in prison, my life plunged into a deep, dark abyss. I flipped back and forth between stomach wrenching anger and overwhelming love for Tammy Faye.

On January 21, Tammy Faye mailed an urgent letter to me. No doubt she was alarmed over Jamie's visit and that her involvement with Roe had been exposed. She wrote:

379

Dear Jim,

Please call me. We need to talk! I am so sorry for what happened when Jamie was there with you. Jim, I wouldn't hurt you for anything in the world. I am not planning on rushing into anything! I am so confused, and hurting so bad, and so mixed up about life. Please don't shut me out! I feel so far away from you, and sometimes feel as if I hardly know you anymore, and it is sure hard to "feel married" when you have been apart for such a long time. I am so lonesome.

I hate prison so bad, and lawyers, and courts. I get really sick to my tummy when I have to be involved with any of it anymore.

Please try not to worry. I am not going to do anything fast or fool-ish. I just need some time to sort out life. I have to rethink so many things, the ministry, Christians, TV, I just don't know what to do in life anymore. I want to get out of the ministry so bad, yet what can Tammy Bakker do except what she knows? Who would hire me? I keep trying to have faith, yet I pray and there is no answer. . . . I don't want to travel and do meetings; I am called to TV and that mountain will not move in my direction one bit. I blame you and yet I don't blame you. I am so confused, I just sometimes want out of everything. Even life! I know that you feel that way, too. So please, Jim, give me time. Please pray for me. I won't do anything fast.

Love, Your wife,

Tam

As I read Tammy Faye's letter, I was amazed at how easily I began to feel sorry for her—and she was the one who was walking away from our marriage. Her letter made me feel as though it was my fault that she had fallen in love with Roe Messner.

When I called Tammy Faye a few days after Jamie left Minnesota, I did not have to broach the subject or confront her in any way. Though at first, she tried to deny that anything was going on between her and Roe, grad-ually she realized that I knew much more than she had thought. She never came out and said, "Yes, I'm having an affair with your best friend," but she did confirm the fact that she was leaving me. She said she just couldn't take any more. When I hung up the phone, I knew that our marriage was indeed over.

I talked very little to my friends. I took part in few things in the prison that were not absolutely mandatory. What little food I consumed, I made from ingredients I purchased at the commissary. I ate in my cell; I did not want to go into the chow hall with the other inmates and try to put on a happy face. As the days wore on I ate less and less. I just wanted to be left alone to mourn. I did my work as necessary, went to my college classes, and talked to Dr. Foster. Then I would return to my cell and curl up on my bunk.

I began pouring my feelings into letters. I fired off a letter to Tammy Faye, beginning what would become like a series of missiles sent screaming back and forth between Minnesota and Florida. I readily admit I tried every technique at my faculties—I resorted to my old friends of self-pity, guilt, manipulation, and others—in my attempts to bring Tammy back to me. I tried pouring out my love to her. I tried explaining psychological principles and temperament needs I had learned about in my studies with the National Association of Christian Counselors. I tried preaching at her, reminding her of scriptural principles that I knew she understood as well if not better than I did. I reminded her of ministry opportunities and responsibilities, sometimes telling her what a great job she had done, hoping to evoke a desire within her to do even more, and sometimes subtly hinting that if she chose to continue her course of actions, she could not continue in the ministry. When all else failed, I reminded Tammy Faye of our two wonderful children and the impact her actions might have on them.

In one of my first letters I wrote:

The last days have been filled with the deepest pain I have ever experienced. I want to scream out from the depths of my soul a primal sound that I cannot express with words.

After the massive betrayal by those I loved and trusted at PTL, and the media hate . . . and then being thrown into prison to die a little each day, I thought there could be no more pain inflicted on me. I was wrong. . . .

Please do not come to see me. I cannot stand the hurt of hearing you say again, "Jim, I don't love you any more." Those words at Waikiki are burnt in my brain cells. I live with the knowledge, as you said to the group in Palmdale, "I never loved Jim." [Tammy had confessed this to the Palmdale team of counselors when she and I had sought help after our marital stress in 1980.]

I would fight for you, but I know you don't love me and perhaps, as you said, you never did. You have tried to get free of me for a long time.

381

I cannot look into those blue eyes I fell in love with so hard thirty-some years ago and see only cold pity coming back. I cannot take any more pain.

I don't want you and Roe to try to explain how, "We didn't plan for this to happen; we just fell in love." I knew for a long time you did not love me when you pulled back from my kisses and would refuse even to touch my hand or leg. There is no human touch in this prison, and I was dying for your touch, but you were touching someone else.

Almost every time I called, you were busy going out to eat or going shopping. Even though for many months, I knew you were meeting Roe around the country, I kept hoping it was not true. It just could not happen with the man I trusted most, my last, best friend. It is like the last act of a bad movie. I understand your loneliness and pain, and I can't really blame you, but I am so sorry for all the people who believed in us and defended us. My heart also aches for our children, but they are strong, and with God's help, they will make it. Please, for their sake, let's be kind and not feed the hate through a messy divorce.

I still love you and always will! From the day I first met you, I have been in love with you only. I know I have failed you and made many mistakes. I have been a fool and a simpleton.

My dream was your nightmare.

Sleep does not come to me much in these last few days. Visions of you and Roe making love I will admit have made me jealous and lust-ful. My thoughts return to the night I first made love to you in our lit-tle third-floor walk-up apartment. I have relived all the good and the bad times, especially all the hours we spent together. The birth of Tammy Sue and how happy we were, and how I wanted to have a boy and how I could not be there for his birth. What a fool I was.

As I was looking at the cards I had picked out for Valentine's Day for you, I realized that this would be the first Valentine's Day I will not give you a card in thirty-two years. Remember our first Valentine's Day, I sent you a heart candy box and roses to your room? Do you remem-ber the white poodle with the purple bow? I'm rambling on like a senti-mental slob.

As you can tell, I still love you, and when they put me to rest, only then will they be able to say, like the George Jones song, "He stopped loving her today."

But I have to face reality. (1) You are in love with someone else. (2) You are not in love with me, and perhaps never have been. (3) You are unhappy. (4) You don't want to do the work we felt called to do anymore.

(5) You have someone to support you and take care of you. (6) You have tried to leave me for many years. (7) I am in prison.

The list could go on, but I will close. As much as I love you, I won't try to convince you to stay with me. I know it is too late for that anyway. Be happy; stay as close to the children as possible. Don't give up on God.

Jim

My next letter, after finding out that Tammy Faye was leaving me, was to my "best friend," Roe Messner.

Roe,

Tammy Faye is the love of my life. She is the only one I have been in love with for thirty-two years. She was my best friend and lover, and, of course, the mother of my children.

You were the one last friend I thought I could trust—with my life, and my wife—a man of real integrity.

I can almost hear you saying, "But Jim, we did not plan for this to happen."

Roe, we are not sixteen anymore. We know when to back away from the fire. Tammy has a great need for love and affection, and during this time of separation was very vulnerable to anyone who would take advantage of her loneliness and pain. I'm sorry she has to bear the added pain of the media saying she is an evil woman stealing another woman's husband, while her own husband is in prison.

If you were going to betray me and my trust, why did you have to flaunt it from coast to coast, even in front of my children. . . . I knew it was going on for a long time, but I just didn't want to believe it of you. It just could not be.

I know the excuses. I've heard them all before:

"It's all your fault, Jim. You didn't pay enough attention to her."
"She was going to leave you, anyhow."
"She did not love you."
"My wife didn't love me and I was so lonely."

As I told Tam, it's like the ending of a bad movie for me. My wife of thirty-two years rides off into the sunset with my best friend. What a conclusion to six years of hell! . . .

Several days later, I wrote Roe again. Roe never answered my letters.

383

A few days later, I received a letter from Tammy Faye in response to my letter to her, a letter I told her might well be my last that I would ever write to her. Tammy's mood sounded somewhat conciliatory if not downright apologetic. At 3:14 A.M., she wrote:

> I have cried my false eyelashes off and my tummy hurts so bad my whole body feels sick. I have read and reread your letter—the last one you say you will ever write me.
>
> Sissy and Doug and the kids and I spent the day today at Disney World. All we did all day was reminisce. I could almost feel you there with us, and wished with all my heart you could have been there with us.

As I read Tammy's comments, I realized afresh how differently she and I faced pressure points in our lives these days. When something bad happened to me, I would retreat to a bed or couch, curl up, and either try to figure a way out of the mess or anesthetize myself with sleep. When something awful happened to Tammy Faye—such as her husband finding out that she was leaving him—she went to Disney World! Even at Disney World, however, Tammy Faye could not escape the obvious:

> Jim, every time I look at a music box I think of you. Every time I see a giraffe, every time I go to a theme park, I always think of your building Heritage USA. Every time I look into the eyes of our kids and grandkids, I see you mostly, and a tiny bit of me. Jim, everything in life reminds me of you and me together. Jim, I would not hurt you for anything in the world. Please believe that! My heart has ached for you until I think it finally just broke! I could not live in hurt anymore. My stomach was sick all the time, I always had a lump in my throat, tears stayed on the surface of my eyes constantly. I lived and relived that horrible day they took you away over and over and over. I think there is only so much pain a human mind can take and then something happens.
>
> I feel as if my whole existence was torn away from me—everything familiar; everything comfortable; everything warm; my home—I loved Tega Cay; my job—I loved our work; my security—you, whom I loved. I was left by myself in a strange town, a strange house, left to raise a teenage boy, support us both, plus Sissy and the children, try to keep a ministry together that I was not called to—I am not a pastor! I have never been so lonely in my whole life, have never felt so raw and so scared, and so absolutely friendless.

I entered a terrifying world of lawyers, courts, judges, trials, juries, handcuffs, news media, prison, debts—a horrible world of betrayed friendships, betrayal by Christian leaders, watching the singers I trained for TV now doing their own TV shows on Christian television, while I sit at home and cry and hope like some pitiful little kid that someone will help me to get back on the air.

I understood what Tammy Faye was saying, but somehow she conveniently seemed to forget that my sending her to French Lick Springs with Roe in the first place was to explore the possibility of purchasing the property and getting her back on television. Even as she wrote to me, she and Roe were still committed to going ahead with the original plan to get Tammy Faye back on the air. Her letter continued:

Jim, I'm so tired of feeling lonely, pitiful, so full of hurt and near hate at what has happened to you and me. I find myself screaming, "If only Jim wouldn't have given PTL away! If only! If only he would have listened to my begging him, 'Please, Jim! Don't give up your place on the Board of Directors.'"

I'm afraid that if you and I stay together, I will only make you miserable. I would resent all the hard work of building everything back up again. And I don't think my health would even take trying to make it to the top again. My blood pressure is so high. My heart is doing strange things. My whole left side goes totally numb. My nerves are so bad, Jim! My body just sort of takes over and there is nothing I can do to control it. I must find some peace—somewhere! I am so disappointed in Christians—and yes, even in God. I really love God and always will, but. . . .

I feel I just need to get out of the ministry for everyone's sake! I need to get away from the public eye! But that is my problem.

Jim, don't ever put yourself down! You are a great man! You are handsome, talented, kind, and so good! You're really too good. Your heart wants to "save the world," wants to make everything wonderful for everyone—and that is just how it should be. But that is you, Jim. It is too heavy a burden for my heart and health to carry anymore. You are going to make it—again. I know you are. You might not if you have to carry me and all my hurts and disappointments. Please try to understand what is going on inside of me. Jamie and I are going to California for counseling. I pray that it will help me.

I, too, hate to let down all of our faithful partners. I feel I have disappointed and let down the whole world. I am so sorry, so very sorry.

Love,

Tam "Still your wife"

P.S. I wanted to touch you in prison, but you told me it wasn't allowed. And it's awfully hard to kiss too long with 100 people watching you. Now I've got to try to stop crying and try to go to sleep.

Tammy Faye had once again succeeded in making me hurt for her. I wrote back to her:

Dear Tam,

Today I had to let you go. I know I must not write you anymore. If the pain and grief that I have been living with does not stop, my health will not hold up much longer.

Today I took all the pictures of you down off the corkboard in my prison cell. So many of the pictures were of you and the children and you and the grandbabies. It is hard to tuck those pictures in a shoe box and say a final good-bye. I've loved you so desperately for three decades and I can't just cut off my love.

I'm so hurt that you could throw me away with such an ease and cold heart. You talk about your pain and hurt and how you want to be happy. How I worked to make you happy! I felt we had something that no other couple had going for them, a special bond. Most all wives of inmates leave their husbands if they are in prison for two years or more, but I thought we would beat the odds. Jim and Tammy were going to make it; they are not average America. We are children of the most high God.

Tonight was my final exam for my computer course. It was so hard to concentrate on the test. I fought off thoughts of you and Roe making love. Later I tried to watch a movie on TV, but every girl in the movie made me think of you, so I came back to my cell to write to you. We used to lay in bed and talk for hours. There is no one in the world I want to talk to, but you—is that not a kick? So I have these little talks with you on paper.

How does love turn to hate? I'm told my great love for you will go away. Some even say I will be happier than ever with a new life. God is the only one who can take my love for you from my heart.

Our lawyer, Jim Toms, said you and Roe talk every day by phone and spend much time in conversation. I'm so jealous how he has taken my place in every way. Oh, how I needed someone to talk to and love me. How I longed for your touch, your voice, your encouraging words, just to hear you say, "I love you." I feel like a chain saw has cut us apart. Jim and Tammy were one flesh. Now you and Roe are one flesh—how that hurts me! I'm going to try to sleep in my narrow bunk and fight off visions of you and Roe making love in our king-size bed. What hell is wrought in our minds.

Good night, my love,
Jim

Thinking that perhaps I had shut the door too soon on Tammy's and my relationship, a few days later I wrote to her again:

Dear Tam,
The last letter I wrote you was going to be my final correspondence with you, but I feel I owe you, after thirty-two years, an explanation why I'm giving you a divorce. I realize that I have been obsessed with you all these years, to the point I know now that I smothered you. My love for you is so great that I didn't think I could live without you. You excited me and challenged me. Even your outrageous traits made life exciting. I worshipped you and wanted to please you, sometimes putting you before God in my life.

As I said before, I have been in love with you and you only since the day I met you. I tried to give you lots of love and all the good things of life, giving you what you wanted, or at least, needed the most.

Since Jamie told me you were leaving me, my life has been hell. I have eaten and slept very little. I hate myself that I have such a hard time giving you up. I do get the picture, but my heart won't stop loving you—there's that stubbornness in me that you hate so much.

I don't want your pity or platitudes. Even though I deeply want you to love me, I'm not trying to win you back. I did that before. I have faced the fact you just don't love me. My mistakes and sin lost our life's work and material possessions. I have not been the spiritual covering for you that I should have been and I left you open to Satan's attacks. I am so sorry I was not the spiritual leader in our home. There is not much left of me and believe me, you made the right decision. I don't like Jim Bakker, either.

I can hear you say, "There he goes, feeling sorry for himself," and you're right! I had it all and lost it. No longer can I live in the pain I brought on myself, perhaps freeing you will help ease my hell. I see

387

how you were like a little bird I tried to keep and protect, but the little bird wanted to fly and be free.

You are free. You can check with our lawyer, Jim Toms, on signing the final divorce papers.

I want you to be happy and pray that you and Roe will find the happiness you have been seeking for so long. Roe was one of the best friends I ever had and I am sure he will be a good husband. Perhaps God will give us both a new start in life. I'm not sure anymore what His will is for me—perhaps nothing, but whatever, I'm willing to abide by His will.

On February 16, Tammy responded to my letters. She began by admitting that she had led a comfortable life:

I have started so many letters to you and they are all wrong. I wish that we were somewhere we could just talk this thing out. Letters leave so many unanswered questions.

First of all, you have given me *everything* a woman could ever want. Fine homes, fine cars, beautiful jewelry, more clothes than most women will have in a lifetime; I have traveled to lots of wonderful places, eaten at the best restaurants. I have had maids, beautiful offices; I have had fame and fortune, plus a very powerful man to love me. Two wonderful children—I have had it all! God and you have certainly been good to this gal from International Falls, MN. The oldest of eight kids, outdoor bathroom and all—sounds like a Cinderella story, doesn't it? And perhaps it was.

Her letter then quickly changed in tone:

You have once again succeeded in making me feel like an ungrateful wretch! No, a sinful, ungrateful wretch! I feel like I don't deserve to even live. I am letting Jim Bakker (who is in prison for something he didn't even do) down; I am letting down two kids; I am letting down our partners (who have been so faithful to us); I am letting down God who has taken such good care of me since you have been gone. I feel lower than low! I would commit suicide but that "just ain't my style!" I'm too chicken to do that. . . .

Jim, I am not ungrateful to you or to God. In fact, I really do feel as if I have lived a "fairy tale life." I love God more than anything in this world, and am so grateful to Him for all He has done for me. But somewhere, something went wrong. I cannot even tell you what it is or was. I know you are going to say that the only time things went wrong for me was when I sinned by getting too close to other men. But *why* did I feel I needed that closeness? You were always there for me. I don't know! I wish I did. My heart hurts until I can hardly breathe. I feel so ungrateful, so unworthy. But that still doesn't stop the awful hurt inside of me. I don't have any tears left to cry. I feel numb.

I don't want to hurt anybody, especially you and God. But something has been missing for years that even prayer won't fill. Believe me, I have prayed and cried out to God until I had no strength left.

The thought of going back into our whirlwind life sends me into a "panic attack." It really does, Jim. Trying to start all over again in TV, going from church to church preaching to a lot of Christians that were so cruel to us, raising money just to hear people condemn us for the car we drive, the house we live in, or the clothes we wear. You know that I have *never* enjoyed sitting in church; I have never been able to even bear the thought of being a pastor's wife. I'm tired, Jim. I need a rest from it all. My mind hurts. . . .

I need to listen to someone else preach for a while in a church where I can just be me. I desperately need friends that don't need anything from me. I feel like a balloon ready to explode!

Then Tammy Faye launched into a part of her letter that was most devastating to me. She compared Roe Messner and me:

About Roe—No, he isn't the "knight in shining armor" that you talk about. He is a very simple man. In many ways, he is a lot like you. He is kind, gentle, and even giving. You are all those things. He is tall and lanky and casual, where you are short, well-built, and very elegant. You are both very hard-working men.

Roe is grass roots—baseball, football, golf. You are not really grass roots—you are artistic, creative, a genius. Roe is very even—you are very moody. Roe golfs out his problems; you sleep out your problems. Neither is wrong. Roe and you are almost in the same condition financially since he has had to file bankruptcy. He is no longer a wealthy man.

"Then, why, Tam?" you ask.

I don't know, Jim.

Except when I think of Roe, I think of peace. When I think of you, I think "high energy, big, no stopping."

Roe is not better—just different.

It's a different time of life for me, Jim. I have changed so much. I think I have reverted back to "that little girl from International Falls" again. That little girl just doesn't fit into the mold you want to make anymore. Maybe she never did. . . .

Tammy then picked up on a statement I had made in a previous letter, which she interpreted as me encouraging her to go ahead with a hasty divorce. Actually, I had hoped to shock her into reality. Unfortunately, my attempt backfired:

You are urging me to go ahead with the divorce. You put it, "Quit cutting me up a little piece at a time. Get it over with."

Jim, I will do that for you if that is what you really want. I don't mean to drag it out. I don't want to hurt you any more than you are already hurting. I would never do that! I was going to wait till the end of the year, and leave the ministry and move to California. But I will file right away if you want me to. I will not remarry right away. I want some time. Roe also realizes the importance of taking time. I want to wait at least a year. . . .

Your letters have helped me a lot, Jim. You make a great teacher, and, needless to say, you're still quite a preacher! Please know that *I have counted the cost*. I will probably be "the world's most hated woman"! But they make fun of me as it is, so it could not get too much worse. They have called me everything they can call me—and that was before I was guilty of anything.

You will always have a very special place in my heart, Jim. I have not forgotten the good times; I have wonderful memories. Everything I look at, you gave to me. I remember the time and place.

And I cry!

Love,
Tam

About that same time, Tammy Faye sent me a copy of a letter she planned to send to our friends and the partners who had supported us in our ministry in Florida, informing them of her plans. I could only imagine the impact it would have upon our faithful friends as they read Tammy's words:

I am experiencing many emotions as I write to you today. Great sadness . . . fear of your rejection . . . and relief that I am able to be totally honest with you. It is a letter that I have needed to write for a long time. I do not expect your understanding, but please try not to react cruelly. Cruelty cannot help anyone nor can it change any situation.

Jim and I are getting a divorce. I can almost hear you gasping . . . saying, "It's not possible! How could they get a divorce with Jim in prison? How is this going to affect the Christian world?"

First of all, I am not being forced to write this letter. *I have chosen to do so!* I feel that, for too long, you have had to get your information from TV and newspaper articles that contained just bits of the truth . . . the rest of the story just figments of someone's overactive imagination. . . .

Jim and I were married very young. I was eighteen and he was twenty-one. Our marriage started out as everyone else's . . . full of excitement and dreams for the future. God had placed a calling on our lives and we were determined to win the world for Jesus!

But somewhere along the way, we got our priorities mixed up. God's order for things is God first, husband or wife second, children third, then comes ministry or whatever job you do. Over the years, God was always first in our lives, but somehow ministry became second, our partners and Heritage USA third, and our family followed.

For years, I have been pretending that everything is all right . . . when in fact I hurt all the time. I cannot pretend anymore. Pretending becomes too hard on the physical body. I have been suffering with high blood pressure, anemia, asthma, hyperventilation—all the doctors tell me—related to stress and severe nervous strain.

Jim and I have had marriage counseling many times. We even separated at one time in an attempt to work things out between us. We have never kept our marriage problems secret from you. As you know, the marriage workshops at PTL were started as a result of our own hurts. I have spent the last few weeks once again in Christian counseling and through that counseling have made this decision.

I still love the Lord with all my heart. *Nothing will ever change that!* God's calling is still a fire that burns within me. Nothing can change that.

Jim and I will always remain friends. We are still in constant communication. We both remain open to God, and to whatever His will is for our lives. I have decided to complete the divorce proceedings before he gets out of prison. I feel that having been apart for over two years anyway, the hurt will be less this way. Neither one of us can take much more hurt.

391

I want to say thank you from the bottom of my heart for the love you have shown to me these last two years. You have helped me build a beautiful ministry. Tammy Sue, our daughter, will be taking my place at New Covenant Church.

Please pray for our dedicated staff as they make this difficult transition, and please continue to support Tammy Sue as she endeavors to keep the ministry alive until Jim gets home from prison. More than anything else in the world, I desire to have a strong foundation for Jim to build on when he gets home.

All I have ever wanted to be is a Mom and someday a Grandma . . . I am now both. My dreams have been fulfilled. I am Tammy Sue's and Jamie's Mom, and James' and Jonathan's Grandma. God has been so good.

When I read Tammy Faye's last letter to me and her letter to our partners, I was decimated, yet I continued to try to win her heart. This time I tried a different tact:

After reading your last letter and your letter to the partners, I realize that you know what you are doing and that you know right from wrong. I think, as you said in your letter, that I thought of you as that little girl from International Falls who I needed to protect and save from her own decisions, when in fact, you are a grown fifty-year-old woman who is capable of making her own decisions and living with the consequences. . . .

You said in your letter: "That little girl just doesn't fit into the mold you want to make anymore." Tam, no one has ever been able to fit you into any mold. I did not try to fit you into my mold. You were called of God the same way I was called. I always let you do your own thing. When I met you . . . you said everyone was always trying to change you. You wrote a book, *I Gotta Be Me*. If you are ever going to be happy, you must get to know the real Tammy Faye and deal with her. You have an inborn need to control others, and according to your temperament chart, you are unwilling to allow anyone to control you. Tam, if you would stop to study your own temperament needs, you could really be in control of your life, with God's help.

Just as you said, one of my traits is moodiness. My temperament analysis says that my mood swings respond to the environment in which I am living. Now that I know this is an inborn trait, I know I must fight moodiness. Also, I mask anger as hurt feelings so to deal with hurt feelings, I must recognize my hurt is really anger and deal with it constructively, which I am doing now at the gym and by writing to you. . . .

You keep talking about how no one cares for you and how mean the press and everyone is to you, that you get no respect. Tam, you are very wrong. You have probably reached the highest level of respect and love you have ever had from the public. I'm sending you an article using you as an example of a woman who "stood by her man." Of late, you have been portrayed as a beautiful woman, with a soft, classy look, and very loving. Whoever is telling you otherwise—even if it is you—is wrong.

By now you probably have signed the divorce papers. It looks like it will be final about on our anniversary. It might be good if they could make it April 1, then we would have only one sad day to remember.

You said, "Maybe you never did fit my mold," and maybe you were never called of God but followed my calling. Maybe I am your April fool after all. Forgive me for saying that, but it's how angry I feel when you talk like marrying me was the great tragedy of your life. I don't take rejection very well, you know! We had a very full and exciting life.

I felt that I was beginning to get in touch with many areas of my life just about the time Tammy Faye decided to leave. I knew that if we could just weather this storm, I would be a much better husband, a much better man, a much better person. I hinted at that to Tammy in my letter:

I am still wearing my wedding ring. It will be hard to take it off. But I have been doing better each week, and I'm much stronger than I have ever been. Dr. Foster said there was a part of me that did not grow up because of something that happened to me as a child. He told me today that he is impressed with the progress I have made. I have dealt with every part of my life. . . .

I will try not to preach to you anymore. As you said in your letter, "Please know that I have counted the cost." If you truly have, then I can do no more. You are paying a great price which may include your eternal soul. I hope you have not let your compulsive inborn temperament traits and needs and feelings lead you from the will of God. Our feelings are so destructive. I love you and want God's perfect will for you.

Love,
Jim

Tammy's next letter was paradoxically upbeat, despite the doom and despair of its contents. She began:

Hello Mr. B,
And how are you doing today? I always try to picture your life there and what you are doing. I know that it is so hard to get up every day and face it. I'm at home and at times can hardly face another day. But at least I can go to a shopping center, and get my mind off things by walking, and getting away from people. . . .

About what I am planning to do. I am not going to rush into anything, Jim. I would like to give myself a year if you don't insist on "pushing me." What is another year in light of what we have already been through? It looks like things are going to be fine here at the ministry, in spite of the "rag" magazines. I have received some of the nicest letters I have ever received. I want to keep the ministry strong for you so you will have a solid foundation to rebuild on . . . so far, nothing has changed with the ministry.

Hang in there, Jim. Remember, "It's not over till it's over."

When I read Tammy's letter in its entirety, I was livid. I could not believe that she wanted to continue on in the ministry, while her loyalties were so divided. On February 17, the day my friend *Charisma* columnist Jamie Buckingham died, with my emotions raw, I sat down and wrote Tammy a searing letter:

Dear Tammy Faye,
Your letter has put me in a state of shock. I can't comprehend what you want!

You told me and the children you were in love and planned to marry. You told me on the phone you and Roe were going to live in Dallas. You were angry when I stopped the divorce [by refusing to sign the divorce papers] and said that you would have to be the one to file. You said you hated the church and were not called to pastor and be a pastor's wife and preach the Gospel and would not help me rebuild a TV ministry.

Now, you want to keep the church for a year. It looks like you want to make this delay so Roe Messner can hold his business together and get his divorce and then you can divorce me and walk away from the ministry and let it crumble.

Tam, you keep playing me for a fool. You have trampled on my deep love for you. While in prison, I longed to talk to you on the telephone,

my arms ached to hold you. Out of thousands I received, the only letter
I looked for was the pink envelope from you. The saddest day of my
life was Valentine's Day when, for the first time in thirty-two years, I
didn't receive a Valentine from you. I am sure you and Roe exchanged
loving Valentines.

For the last year, I needed your love and support and you were in
the arms of Roe Messner. Now you want to keep up a front with me
until Roe is ready to receive you and has his ducks in a row. You make
me feel like a piece of dung. You have been more of a wife to Roe
Messner than to me. I can't understand why he will not support you.
You have been paying for his travel and hotel rooms and rental cars. If
you were my lover and I was a free man, I would take care of you like a
queen. . . .

I was shocked to find how you and Roe were together almost
everywhere you traveled for the last nine months and even spending
many days together in our own home. You and he flew to California for
the Women's meeting November 11 to 16. I am sure you enjoyed visiting San Francisco while you were there. Even when you cut your
record, you had adjoining rooms in Tennessee. Of course, I know you
were together on trips to French Lick.

My sarcasm began to get the better of me as I slammed my pen onto
the paper, writing:

Then the wonderful fun-filled acts in Las Vegas. Then, we don't want
to forget the romantic and happy days at the Kahler Hotel in Rochester
while you and your lover were visiting Prisoner 07407-058. And, of
course, there was Thanksgiving at the Kahler. We must not forget the
trip to Charlotte while the lovebirds went to see "poor Jim" at the
county jail, dressed in his orange Pierre Cardin prison jumpsuit, and
then back to French Lick for some more fun. Then the one that hurt
the most was my birthday celebration you and Roe had in Des Moines
at the Marriott, with lots of room service.

Once I got all that venom out of my system, I went back to the issue
of Tammy staying on as a minister at the church in Florida:

Tam, you said I am "pushing you." . . . You tell me you want out of our
marriage and the church, and I give you what you ask for and then you
say I am pushing you!

Tam, you have not said, "Jim, forgive me," or "I am sorry"; only, "Just let me stay on at the church." You act like you don't care about me or my feelings. There is not a man on earth who would put up with his wife and former best friend living like they are married while he looks on. *You have misjudged my undying love for you as weakness!* It is time for you to do what you plan to do and not play me for the fool anymore.

I have lived through the deepest hell that any human being could go through for the last four weeks. Coming to prison or losing Heritage USA was nothing compared to giving you up. I feel as though I have lived through our divorce already. Do you know what it is like to be in prison and find out your wife has been making love to your best friend for almost a year and to hear you say, "I want a divorce." I will not go through this hell! It is worse than death. Tammy, someday you may hit bottom and find out what it is like to break the bonding of thirty-two years.

How can you live with Roe in adultery and pastor the church, making believe you love me to the partners and to the public? Tam, you have some decisions to make. You can't have it both ways. Just remember, because you feel the anointing of God when you sing or preach does not mean that God has stamped His approval on what you are doing. God says His callings are not without repentance. That means, once He gives the gift, He does not take it back. Think of the preachers we have known that have preached the Gospel under the anointing of the Holy Spirit and lived an ungodly life. "Not every one that saith unto me, Lord, Lord, shall enter into the kingdom of heaven; but he that doeth the will of my Father which is in heaven."

I tried to appeal to Tammy Faye's deep-seated, sincere love for the Lord. Besides, I wanted to emphasize to Tammy Faye that her relationship to God did not depend on me, but on her own obedience to the Lord. I told her:

You are deciding if you are willing to pay the price to serve God or not. You can leave Jim Bakker and go to heaven, if you live a godly life. But if you can rationalize that what you and Roe are doing is not sin, you are in a fearful state. My sin or Roe's wife's sin does not justify more sin and what you and Roe are doing. You have the biggest decision of your life to make and I or no one else can make it for you. Tammy Faye, are you going to serve God or the devil?

We are one heartbeat from God, as Jamie Buckingham's death today so dramatically demonstrated. You ran the race for fifty years. Are you going to turn your back now?

Tam, for God's sake, read the Word and pray. You need to be where the Word is taught and be around godly people. I am afraid you are out from under God's covering. Sin opens the door for Satan to have a heyday. You also stepped out from beneath my covering as your husband. I have been fasting and praying for the last several days that God would not let you make an eternal mistake and go to hell.

If you know without a shadow of a doubt you have made up your mind to marry Roe and you know that is what you want and it is God's perfect will for you, then call Jim Toms and sign the divorce papers today. Don't play with my love by saying, "It's not over till it's over" if you know full well you and Roe plan to be married. Love in a marriage is commitment. You can't be committed to two men. If you are committed and pledged to Roe, then be honest with me and sign the divorce papers today and walk away. If you want to give up Roe and stay with me, then get on an airplane and come and see me and tell me so. But, after that, I will not put up with one phone call or meeting between you and Roe.

You said you received some of the nicest letters. Tam, I am receiving the same kind of letters. Almost everyone is saying how much Tammy Faye loves me and how wonderful she is to have stood by her man. I think if only they knew every time I read them it is like a knife going through me. Jim and Tammy are no more. My heart is broken. I always felt as long as we had each other, we had a foundation to make it. Oh, how I loved you.

Tam, all your life you said people were trying to change you and to tell you what to do. Tammy, you rejected those who loved you and wanted the best for you because you have an inborn temperament that you must be in control at all times. It is not a fault, but a fact. Now, you have complete control of your life. I pray someday you will realize serving God is surrender, and love and marriage is a commitment, not good feelings.

I love you and forgive you and have committed you to God.

It is your decision.

Thinking that perhaps I had been too hard on Tammy Faye in my previous letter, the following week, I sent Tammy another letter, outlining what I felt were the only acceptable conditions for her to stay associated with the ministry in Florida. I began once again by reminding her of her own temperament:

> Your temperament chart warns the counselor: "You must not try to control her, tell her what to do or interfere with her independence. She will be angry and become cruel if you try to control her and will take on any behavior to maintain control."
>
> Tam, there is no way in the natural you can bow to the leadership of anyone else including God, without God's help and your own strong will to let go of your controlling mechanisms.

Thinking that I had established the fact that I had no intentions of trying to control Tammy Faye in any way, I dared to suggest a course of action to her—a course which I now realize was unrealistically dogmatic, and yes . . . an attempt to get Tammy Faye to do what I felt was right.

> Actually, I am asking you to consider two alternatives: One is to help meet my needs, and the other to do what you will and simply walk away.
>
> If you want to stay, I need:
>
> You to seek God and read your Bible every day, at least a chapter each day, reading through the entire New Testament.
>
> For you not to call or receive calls from Roe Messner or see him or any other lovers . . . no contact.
>
> For you and me to talk every day or night on the telephone.
>
> For you to get good regular Christian counseling, at least two times per week.
>
> For you to let me help you understand yourself and your temperament traits.
>
> For you to write me every day.
>
> For you to come to see me often.
>
> For you to be faithful to the church and the partnership and spend regular time working at the office.
>
> For you to be faithful to me as long as we are married.
>
> You to face the fact your inborn personality traits make you demand to be in control and that you will ask God to help you turn control to Him. (Actually, you are not in control. Your temperament is controlling you to do the opposite of what anyone tells you to do, making you in reality not to be in control.)

I want you to work on your anger and temper, which you use to control people, and ask God to help you surrender your will to Him.

For you to love and demonstrate love to our children and grand-children and spend much time with them.

For you to sign the divorce papers. I will not sign them if you live up to this agreement.

Or, you can walk now.

Tam, I love you dearly, but this roller coaster you are on and putting everyone around you on must come to a stop. As I said before, your conflict is because you are trying to live two lives and it just will not work. Even the law allows for only one husband at a time. Your life and future is in your own hands. If you will endeavor to find out what makes you tick, you will become at peace with yourself, and you will understand and be able to deal with your feelings with God's help. Then, you will like and forgive yourself.

When will you stop running? Before you crash, I hope.

I love you,
Jim

After this letter, all I can say is that it was probably a good thing I was already in prison for my own protection—not from hardened criminals, but from Tammy Faye. Since she was too far away to wring my neck, she wrote a scathing response. The prison guards probably had to handle the letter with asbestos gloves!

Tammy Faye came out swinging: "There are two words that came to my mind when I read your last letter. They were: 'Pompous Ass!' Excuse the language, but I remember you calling other men that many times at PTL."

Tammy was correct; I had referred to several of the huffing, puffing, strutting preachers who "graced" PTL's sets as pompous asses. I had actually adopted the phrase from my good friend and mentor, C. M. Ward, who could inflect his voice in such a way when he said it that everyone in the audience understood C. M.'s disdain for the proud-as-peacock type of preacher.

Tammy quickly got more specific in her letter:

You tell me to quit putting the people around me through so much. You forget the horrible emotional roller coaster they put me on for months when they all were fighting and hating each other so bad that I was going to close down the ministry. I nearly lost my mind, if you

399

remember. So please don't tell me I must make a decision "for their sake."

You tell me it's time for me to "meet your needs." How easily you forget the last two years of hell you have put me through. Telling you every day, "You can make it," "Don't give up," "Trust in God," "The people love you." Sometimes I have nearly lost my mind trying to keep you from losing yours. I have followed you around this country from prison to prison; I have faced TV cameras and news media in your defense; I have faced ridicule and hate and embarrassment defending what you did or did not do at PTL. I have had to do it alone! I have had to stand by and watch as the whole country has made fun of *me* because of *you!* I not only have had to hold you up but your children and the partners! I have raised thousands of dollars to pay lawyers, have held *your* ministry together so you would have something to come back to. I have cried until I had no more tears to cry. And you did not hear me complain or have a temper tantrum over any of it! I have tried to live trusting the Lord, and believing in you. I don't think that there is another woman on the face of this earth that could have gone through what I have gone through and still be sane! So don't give me all this "bull" about "meeting your needs"! That is the ultimate put-down! When is someone going to care about *my* needs? You sure haven't.

So let's cut all the psychological crap and get down to where the rubber meets the road.

Don't tell me about "controlling mechanisms"! You have used controlling mechanisms on me for years. But instead of temper—which is at least an honest emotion—you have used "Oh, poor me, feel sorry for me" control. "Nobody loves me. Nobody appreciates me." These are controlling mechanisms in my way of thinking. Even Sister Fern Olson picked up on that years ago. She told you that you have a way of "making people feel sorry for you so that they wanted to help you." She said for you never to take advantage of that.

And who are you to tell *me* to read the Bible every day and pray? There were months while you were in prison that I bet you never once opened the Bible or said a word of prayer. Besides, you cannot *demand* that anyone read the Bible and pray, Jim. That is too personal of a thing. That is between God and me, not you, me, and God.

You said that I had to "write you every day." "Talk on the phone to you every day." What in the world do you think I have been doing for the last two years? I have been paying $800 a month phone bills for some reason. So don't give me that crap!

I will *not* go to Christian counseling twice a week! I have been through more than any Christian counselor that I know. I could counsel *them!* I will not waste the money on it. Besides, you didn't like or agree with the advice the last Christian counselor in California gave me. You said that what she said did not agree with the Word. And that she was wrong! That little visit cost me $1,400 for her and $2,000 in airline tickets!

You said that I had to "come to see you often." I have come as often as I could possibly afford. I spend at least $2,000 a trip. Where do you think that comes from, Jim? Do you think money grows on the palm trees here in Florida? Plus, you want me to pay to send Tammy Sue and Doug and the kids, and your sister, which I have done time and time again. I think I have done pretty good. Give me some *credit*!

You asked me to be faithful to the church and partnership. Why in the world do you think that our church is full, and our partners are still writing and supporting *you?* Because I have been unfaithful to them?

There are two things I can do in your ten commandment list. I can stop seeing Roe, and I can sign the divorce papers.

I would have thought you would be happy for me to wait six months if indeed you care about me as much as you say you do. I will keep the church together and write the monthly letters, and take care of Jamie and his household. I will talk with you on the phone and I will write to you, but *not* every day on either account. I will visit you as often as the money allows.

You cannot ask more of me than that. You have absolutely no right to!

If you should share this letter with your counselor, please also share the one with him that I speak about today—your ten commandment letter.

I am not promising *anything* in our personal relationship. We need to just take one day at a time and see what happens. If you are not happy with things, then *you* can sign the divorce papers.

Tam

As I read and reread Tammy Faye's response to my last two letters—especially my "ten commandment letter," as she referred to it, I realized what a difficult position in which I had placed her. There was no way she was going to agree to all of my demands, and I probably knew that when I wrote the letter. I was trying to get her to react to me . . . and she did. I knew that for all intents and purposes I had already lost her, but I was acting out of desperation, with much the same attitude as I had when I had tried to make Tammy Faye jealous by having sex with Jessica Hahn. I had been wrong then, and I was wrong again now.

Within days after Tammy had mailed her rebuke to me, I received a beautiful greeting card from her, apologizing for her last letter. She even joked about our age. The reality was, however, that I owed her an apology for being so arrogant.

Tammy's mention of our age reminded me that her birthday, March 7, was approaching. I decided to send her one last birthday card. In it I wrote:

One last Happy Birthday—I hope the card does not offend you.

As I read Richard Dortch's book, I realized that even he had not caught the vision of what I was building. I had a dream in my head and I saw Heritage USA complete and beautiful. While I was building on this dream, all he saw, and now I realize, all you and others saw, was a driven man building something that looked helter-skelter. I understand your feelings of not wanting to go through that again. Neither do I. I had wild faith that Heritage USA was of God and He would bring me through.

Science says that many people cannot see pictures in their minds like others can, so don't feel badly that you could not see my dream. I look at a blueprint and see a completed building; you see lines on a paper.

I was a driven man with a dream and a burden to raise the money to build it. I want to apologize for the hurt and pain I caused you by my intensity and immaturity. With God's help, I don't think I will ever build a major project again. I have come to believe God's will is not to build His kingdom on earth, but in heaven. He does not want us to worship buildings or fall in love with places or things. He wants us to fall in love with Him.

The French Lick project helped put you and Roe together and when it fell apart I realized it was not of God. My dream was that Roe and I would rebuild or restore Heritage together, but of course, Roe and I can never work together again. God has closed the door and I believe He is telling me I will not be doing much building. God has restored my first love of soul-winning and I have fallen in love with Jesus and I feel His presence, like we used to. I may do something with the vast information I have learned from my temperament studies; it can help so many people get control of and understand their inborn temperament needs. Every young couple should be tested before they get married to see what their inborn needs are and if they are going to be compatible after the honeymoon.

I'm sure you will be leaving for California any day now. So if this is the last correspondence I have with you, please forgive me for all the hurts. I loved you and wanted to make you happy. I will always remember our life together.

Still friends I hope,

Jim

Finally, I had come to grips with Tammy's feelings toward Heritage USA and my obsession to build it. More importantly, I had resigned myself to the fact that Tammy Faye was leaving me. Nevertheless, that did not make the finality of the divorce any easier to take when it came the following week.

39

The Dreaded Day

FRIDAY, THE THIRTEENTH OF MARCH, 1992, DAWNED A COLD, crisp Minnesota morning. It was a normal day in prison, and I arose as usual to clean the toilets and hallways. Everything was the same, yet in a way, I knew that from this day forward, everything would be different. I was unusually hyper, aware that a drama was being played out in a Florida courthouse that morning that would change my life as much or more than anything I had experienced in the past five years. Tammy Faye had decided to proceed with our divorce.

A few days previously, I had been paged to report to the unit manager's office in Building Two. Sam Houston, who had been in charge of my building when I had first arrived at Rochester, had been transferred to an addiction unit on the other end of the first floor. A new unit manager, Doug Brendle, was now in charge, a man whom I did not know well, and who did not seem too interested in getting to know me. Mr. Brendle was an unbending, military-style manager, who believed in going by the book 100 percent of the time. He often authorized guards to conduct surprise "shakedowns" of our cells, searching for contraband items such as extra blankets, extra clothes, or too many books. Brendle's name did not connote a picture of compassion in the minds of most of the inmates.

Earlier that week, I had received a phone call from Tammy's and my lawyer, Jim Toms, informing me that the preliminary divorce papers would be arriving at the prison and that I would have to sign them.

Nevertheless, when the call came to report to Mr. Brendle's office, it felt as though clammy, cold hands began to wrap around my heart.

I walked into the unit manager's office and waited to be told what to do next. A prison staff member was already there, ready to notarize the papers.

"Sit down, Bakker," Brendle commanded, as he began spreading some papers in front of me. Technically, the papers were an "acceptance of service" stating the terms of the divorce. I took time to read the divorce papers before signing. In essence, the papers confirmed that I was not contesting the divorce. Nor were there any property considerations involved. I had already agreed to give Tammy Faye any of our belongings—what was left of them—that she wanted. Anything that she did not want was to be placed into storage. Tammy Faye was to receive legal custody of our sixteen-year-old son, Jamie Charles. The most devastating part of dealing with the divorce document was seeing the bold, flowing signature of Tammy Faye Bakker on the paper. I could no longer live in denial. Tammy Faye, my wife since April 1, 1961, had signed the papers, declaring the dissolution of our marriage.

The entire process was so cold, stark, and clinical. How could it be that with a few strokes of a pen, a vibrant relationship would come to an end? I knew that the marriage was basically over long before this point, but there was still something horribly *final* about seeing the papers in front of me. I had hoped that at some point—at any point—Tammy Faye would have backed off from the divorce. She hadn't. It was over.

I signed my name. The deed was done.

Jim and Tammy—a single entity for nearly a third of a century—were no longer related. A relationship that I had shared for over thirty-one years was severed in a moment.

No doubt the officers in the unit manager's office had witnessed such proceedings many times previously, but today they seemed unusually aware of my grief. I later learned that for several days before and after this day, the guards and prison officials were watching me more closely than usual out of concern that I might attempt to commit suicide.

As the clerk notarized the papers and gathered them together to be sent back to Jim Toms, Brendle sat back in his chair.

"I know a little bit about what you're feeling, Bakker," he said more kindly than usual. "I went through a heartrending divorce myself."

I never established the same sort of relationship with Doug Brendle that I had with Sam Houston, but I will always appreciate the man's willingness to be vulnerable at a moment when I needed him to.

On Friday the thirteenth, Tammy Faye and Shirley Fulbright left Orlando about 4:30 A.M. to make the four-hour drive to Tallahassee. There they met Jim Toms at the office of B. K. Roberts, a former judge and a highly respected lawyer who was a friend of ours, and who had agreed to be Tammy Faye's counsel in the divorce proceedings. I had already signed papers giving Jim Toms authority to represent me. After meeting briefly with Roberts, the group traveled to the Tallahassee courthouse where Hal S. McClamma, a judge who was a friend of B. K. Roberts, perfunctorily went through the divorce papers. Shirley, our longtime friend and cowork-er who had been living with Tammy Faye at the time, was the corroborat-ing witness who had to testify that the basis of the divorce was because of irreconcilable differences. The judge asked Shirley, "In your opinion, is this marriage irretrievably broken?"

Shirley answered affirmatively. Judge McClamma then signed the dis-solution papers and ordered the proceedings to be filed the same day. Ordinarily, before a divorce became final, a waiting period of several weeks was required under Florida law on the chance that the couple seeking divorce might change their minds and be reconciled. To avoid any unnec-essary publicity, however, the waiting period was waived in our case. By midday on March 13, 1992, Tammy Faye and I were legally divorced. After nearly thirty-one years of marriage, the final dissolution of our union had taken less than twenty minutes.

After the judge had signed the papers and the matter was officially closed, he told the group that he had visited Heritage USA and that he was an admirer of both Tammy and me. He indicated his appreciation for our "tremendous achievements."

Following the judge's decision, Tammy Faye, Shirley, and Jim went out to lunch with Justice Roberts at The Governor's Club. Throughout the morning, Tammy Faye had been extremely serious and quiet. At lunch, however, Tammy Faye was more animated. She expressed her pleasure that the proceedings had gone so smoothly and quickly. Tammy Faye conclud-ed that because she had received a peaceful arrangement, it was an indica-tion of God's favor. In reality, it was Judge Roberts's longtime friendships in Tallahassee that had expedited matters.

Shortly after lunch on Friday, Jim Toms telephoned the warden's office at Rochester prison. He spoke with the warden's assistant and asked him to take the word to me that the dissolution of Tammy Faye's and my marriage was final. At the same time, Toms cautioned the prison official concerning the strong likelihood of my being bombarded with interview requests. He needn't have worried. As I had done before, I did not grant a single interview.

Earlier that morning I had gone to my regularly scheduled counseling session with Dr. Daniel Foster. I had developed a deep trust in Dr. Foster since coming to Rochester, and had become accustomed to divulging the darkest secrets of my life to him, including some things I had never before confided to another human being. I had chosen to trust Dr. Foster with my honest feelings and Tammy Faye's letters since the discovery of her relationship with Roe Messner. During our session on that Friday morning, as he had been doing since learning that Tammy Faye was planning on leaving me, Dr. Foster once again gave me "permission to grieve."

"There is an appropriate and necessary amount of grieving that must be done for every loss, Jim," Dr. Foster told me. "You have suffered a major loss and you must now grieve the loss of your wife. It is almost like experiencing a death in the family."

"No, Dr. Foster," I said. "Divorce is worse than death."

"I understand," he replied, "but you must allow yourself to grieve. Don't fight against it. If you do not avoid the grieving process, it can be speeded up considerably. On the other hand, by not grieving, it can lead to a low-grade depression that can last for many years."

"But Dr. Foster, I think I can handle it. Tammy Faye and I have been dealing with our problems for the past ten or fifteen years, so this has been a long time in coming."

"Jim, I give you permission to grieve," Dr. Foster reiterated quietly and calmly. "You cannot short-circuit the grieving process. The more deeply you grieve now, the sooner you will recover. No significant healing can take place as long as you refuse to ignore reality. Tammy Faye is gone. You are divorced. That relationship is dead."

"Then what should I do?"

"Be kind to yourself," Dr. Foster answered. "Avoid a heavy schedule of activities for a while. Do your work; take part in your classes; enjoy your hobbies, but don't overload yourself right now. Take one step at a time.

"Let me encourage you to explore the full implications of your loss, even though it might mean the intensifying of your depression for a while. That's okay. It will facilitate the grieving process. The more effectively you experience the low times, the quicker you'll get better. Trying to fight off the depression or trying to avoid it or minimize the pain will only serve to prolong it. Let's keep talking about the pain. We won't try to run away from it. Nor will we move through it too quickly. These are important days for you, and I will walk alongside you each step of the way.

407

"Face the reality of your loss, Jim. Tammy Faye is gone," Dr. Foster said again. "Let her go. If you insist on living in denial, you will only prolong your depression. It is wishful thinking to try to restore your relationship with her, or to avoid your grieving any longer."

"But Dr. Foster. . . ."

"Grieve, Jim," Dr. Foster said compassionately but firmly. "It is all right for you to cry. In fact, it is very important when men or women experience significant loss that they have a good cry. I understand the danger of being vulnerable to predators in prison, but you must cry. I give you permission to cry."

I had been taught all my life not to cry. Now, here was Dr. Foster, a strong, tough, articulate man among men telling me that it was okay to cry. He told me the more effectively I expressed my grief, the quicker I would recover.

Dr. Foster's tone softened even further. "God has provided you with the resources you will need to heal emotionally, but you must do your part too. Grieve, Jim. Grieve."

Five days after our divorce, Roe Messner filed to divorce Ruth Ann, his wife of thirty-six years.

Almost immediately the word of Tammy's and my divorce hit the airwaves. All afternoon friends dropped by my cell to console me and offer their condolences. Many of the inmates had suffered through a divorce themselves since coming to prison. Statistics suggest that there is an over 80-percent possibility that a couple will divorce if the husband goes to prison for two years or more. My friends knew what I was feeling.

One of my friends was a large, gray-haired Italian man named Dominic, who lived in the cell across the hall from Rod Netherton and me. Dominic was a kind, grandfatherly sort of man in his late sixties or early seventies. The constant twinkle in his eyes and quick smile caused most inmates to wonder about the rampant prison rumors that Dominic had at one time been a prominent member of the Mafia.

As soon as news of my divorce circulated inside our cell block, Dominic came across the hall to cheer me up. Several other guys were already there. Dominic voiced the sentiments of many of the inmates as he tried to comfort me with his worldly wisdom, "You should be really happy, Jim. You're a free man now. When you walk out of this place, you'll be free as a bird!"

"Yeah, just think of all the women who will be chasing after you once you get out of here!" one of the guys exclaimed. "Think of all the women you can date," another agreed. "You're free, man!"

I didn't want to be free. I hadn't dated anyone in over thirty years and the thought was far from my mind. The only woman I wanted would soon be on her way to California to start a new life with my former best friend. I appreciated my friends' efforts to lift my spirits, but I was inconsolable. I was glad when they all left and I could be alone with my thoughts again.

That night, however, one of the fellows who worked in the prison bakery baked a cake and brought it to my cell.

"It's your divorce cake," he told me. "It's sort of a tradition around here that when anyone gets divorced, we have a cake." Before I knew it, my cell was crowded with guys, laughing, joking, and relating their own awful divorce stories. It was a strange but wonderful camaraderie, and I was grateful for a bunch of guys who cared enough to share my pain.

Despite the encouragement of my friends and the emotional fatigue I was feeling from the stress of the day, I slept very little that night. I was up at the crack of dawn on Saturday morning. In the flurry of activity and the nightmare of Tammy's and my divorce, I had almost forgotten that a good friend of mine was coming to speak for a special Saturday morning event at the prison chapel. On January 9, Pastor Phil Shaw received a letter from Dave Roever confirming that he would be able to come to F.M.C. Rochester on Saturday morning, March 14, 1992. Looking back on it now, I can see that Dave's visit was providentially planned.

It was a bitterly cold morning as I made my way across the prison compound to the basement meeting room of the chapel. My heart was broken, my spirit was crushed. Given a choice I would have spent the entire day on my bunk in my cell. The only reason I was going out one day after Tammy's and my divorce was because Dave Roever was an old friend who had appeared on *PTL* programs many times. Dave was a Vietnam veteran who had had half his face blown off by a grenade in Nam and had spoken at Rochester before. As he stood in our prison chapel that morning, Dave's face was still a mass of scars, but for the first time since I had known him, I didn't really notice his disfigurement. All I saw was love in the eyes of my precious friend. Dave and I threw our arms around each other and hugged—not exactly a familiar sight in prison—and the moment he saw me, Dave began to cry. Few sights in life are more heartrending than Dave Roever crying. I struggled to hold back my own tears as Dave and I embraced. Almost immediately my friend began ministering to me, encouraging me, and comforting me. I knew I had to excuse myself before

I lost my composure. I told Dave that I would be right back, and I hurried into the rest room to hide my eyes from the sight of my fellow inmates.

When I returned, the program was about to begin. Dave's message that morning was about scars. "Many of us are more scarred on the inside than on the outside," Dave said.

Dave went on to relate how people who stood by his bed after his tragedy would say things such as, "I know how you feel." Yet they had never had their face half ripped away by a grenade or their body burnt beyond recognition by a fireball. It is only the person who has experienced the scars who can truly say, "I know how you feel," and mean it.

Dave's message spoke to me. It had been eight weeks since I had first learned that Tammy Faye was leaving me. I had counseled other men that divorce was sometimes more painful than death; now I was experiencing the truth of my own words. Never again would anyone be able to say to me, "You don't know how I feel." I now had the inner scars to prove that I understood their hurt.

As Dave continued to pour out his heart, I noticed some words written on a chalkboard behind his head. Even as Dave was speaking, the words on the chalkboard seemed to shout at me, "Life is 10 percent what happens to you and 90 percent how you react to what happens to you!" As I listened to Dave Roever recount his story, I was watching and listening to the living embodiment of those words.

For the next few days following Dave's visit, I continued to ponder the message of the words on the chalkboard. I determined in my heart and mind that the message was true, but experientially I was still trapped in a cavern of grief. Everywhere I went I saw things that reminded me of Tammy Faye and our life together. One night I forced myself to go to the chow hall for dinner, one of the few times I had done so since learning the truth about Tammy Faye and Roe. The meal that night was turkey. Instantly, my mind went back to the way Tammy Faye and I always had prepared our Thanksgiving turkey together. We cooked that turkey all night long at a low temperature and by morning the pleasing aroma of turkey dinner wafted throughout the house. Prison turkey neither tasted or smelled anything like the wonderful meals my family and I had shared, but the sight of the turkey caused the memories to roll over me like waves in the ocean, and before I knew it tears welled in my eyes again. I left the chow hall in a hurry without eating much of anything.

Another night I went to the prison commissary, where I ordered some items with which I could make a meal in my cell. As I picked up my groceries, my eyes focused on a bag of corn chips near the top of the bag.

Again my mind went instantly to Tammy Faye as I recalled her eating and laughing in one of her favorite Mexican restaurants. Although Dr. Foster had encouraged me to let go of Tammy Faye, I kept seeing her everywhere. As I did, I slid further and further into a pit of utter despair.

I didn't want to do anything. I didn't want to get out of bed. If I did muster the energy to get up, I didn't want to leave my cell. I didn't care to eat, but Dominic, my Italian friend from across the hall, brought food for me that he had made in the hall microwave.

"Jim, you must eat," he would say in his grandfatherly way, as he slipped some of his special spaghetti or other pasta in front of my face.

At the close of the day, I tried to write in my journal. The words came slowly:

Today the pain of loneliness began to descend upon me like a dense fog as denial turned into a sad reality. My heart is breaking; it aches like an unbearable weight is crushing my chest. I can feel my heart—it is as if a meat hook has been plunged into it. Each day it feels like more weight is being added to that hook. The feelings of total rejection are taking over. My teenage bride, the love of my life, has just walked away. Each day brings new feelings—feelings of love, hate, anger swing like a pendulum in a grandfather's clock from day to day, digging the hole of depression deeper and deeper.

Another night I wrote:

Today memories of thirty-one years will not stop coming—our wedding, our first apartment, ministering together in churches, on television, putting our house together, having and raising our babies, all the years of making love—the good and the bad times blend together in my brain. It was our time, our history, and it was like our marriage was being ripped apart by a chain saw.

Of all the marvelous miracles I now see that God performed for me while I was in prison, the temporary transformation of my cellmate Rod Netherton remains the most amazing to me to this day. Rod was a fascinating fellow, a persuasive motivator, and a good man. He could also be horrendously stubborn and demanding.

Even before I found out about Tammy Faye and Roe, to pass the time in prison, I had begun working out, exercising regularly and lifting weights in the recreation building. Rod was a fitness fanatic, so before long, he and

I were working out together. Rod was a taskmaster when it came to lifting weights. He would not simply spot for me, guarding against a sudden lapse of strength, but he would drill me as I went through my regimen. "Watch me!" he shouted as I lifted weights. "Keep your eyes on me. Stop daydreaming! Don't look to the left or to the right," he ordered. "Keep focused on what we're doing! Your muscles will grow faster when you concentrate and use your brain."

During my first year at Rochester, Rod had grown as a Christian. When I took the course from the National Christian Counselors Association, Rod became so fascinated, he paid to take the course too. He became a licensed counselor while in prison. Although Rod's heart had been changed, his basic temperament remained the same. He was still a choleric, controlling type of person.

When I first learned about Tammy Faye leaving me, I lapsed into depression, but my condition did not take God by surprise. Months before it all happened, He had already prepared someone to counsel me and minister to me—my cellmate Rod Netherton.

Night after night, for a period of sixty days, Rod Netherton sat on a chair at the foot of my bed and counseled with me and ministered to me. Amazingly, throughout that entire period of time, Rod was a changed personality. My normally confrontational cellmate was transformed into a gentle, compassionate counselor. Beyond that, he espoused wisdom far beyond his years or learning. It was as though the Holy Spirit was speaking directly through the man. I had never before heard such wisdom coming from a man, nor have I since. It was so out of character for him, I could hardly believe my ears. But I was hurting so badly, I savored every syllable that came out of Rod's mouth. At the close of each session, Rod prayed with me and for me. It was as though God knew that I needed intensive care on a daily basis, so He had prepared my cellmate in advance to be the vessel through which He could minister to me.

Perhaps the most fascinating part of this experience came at the end of the sixty-day period. Abruptly, without any warning, Rod changed back into his normal, inborn temperament, and he never again exhibited the same kindness, gentleness, or compassion toward me for as long as we lived together in prison.

40

Pulling Out of Depression

I DID NOT SUDDENLY STOP GRIEVING OVER TAMMY FAYE after the divorce. Nor did God miraculously and instantaneously remove my pain and despair at losing the person I loved more than life itself. In many ways, I am not "over" the divorce to this day. I grieve a little more each time I think of Tammy Faye, see her picture, or hear some news about her.

Yet life goes on . . . even in prison.

Looking back, I can now see how God used numerous people, events, and circumstances to help me through those difficult days. Rod Netherton and Dr. Foster were invaluable in their willingness to talk with me. Dr. Westrick, too, called me to her office shortly after hearing about the divorce and welcomed me to come to her office any time I simply needed to talk. Sam Houston also went out of his way to encourage me after he learned of Tammy's and my divorce. Although technically I was no longer under his charge, he called me into his first-floor office at the end of the wing and echoed Dr. Westrick's words, "If you ever need someone to talk to, please stop in any time."

No doubt some of the prison officials were concerned for my mental health and stability after the divorce. I had, after all, lost my ministry, my life's work, my home, almost all of my material possessions including my life's savings and retirement accounts, my reputation, and most of all, I had lost my freedom. Now, added to that, I had lost my wife. No wonder the counselors were concerned that I might try to put an end to it all.

Yet God kept giving me a reason to take one more step. At the darkest moments, He always provided a ray of light.

Prior to the divorce I had been taking a Bible course offered by North Central Bible College's Correspondence Institute. The course was on the book of Acts. I took my first test on March 7, Tammy Faye's birthday. Despite the fact that my mind was distracted by the knowledge that Tammy was filing for divorce, I scored 99 percent, answering seventy-four of seventy-five questions correctly.

Tammy Faye and I continued to communicate by mail even after the divorce. Although I was trying to let go of her, my heart would not allow me to do so. On April 1, our anniversary, I wrote:

> Your letter arrived today on our thirty-first wedding anniversary. It was a very sad day for me. I wanted to talk to you and tell you how much I still love you. The pain had eased up, but today it came back with full force.
>
> Don't get me wrong. I fully know you made the decision to divorce me to marry Roe Messner and I can't change those facts, but my love does not just switch off because you chose to leave me. . . . One of the hardest things for me to accept is that you are no longer related to me. The children will always be, but the one I had those children with and chose to be my wife is not a part of me anymore.
>
> Tam, stay close to Jesus and stand on His Word and you will be okay. I ask Him every day to take care of you. Don't worry about me; God has a perfect plan, and I trust Him.
>
> Love,
> Jim

In the midst of my doldrums, I received a surprise letter from Richard Dortch, my former top aide at PTL who had been released from prison in November of 1991. Reverend Dortch had gone to prison for the same charges that had been pressed against me: mail fraud, wire fraud, and conspiracy to commit fraud. Dortch, however, had made a plea bargain with the prosecution and in return for pleading guilty and testifying against me, was sentenced to eight years in prison, of which he served less than two at a minimum security facility. I, on the other hand, had pleaded not guilty and was originally sentenced to forty-five years in prison. I had not heard from Reverend Dortch since 1987, so I was quite interested in what he had to say:

Just a few hours ago was the first opportunity I have had to write to you. Thank the Lord it is over, so I will be writing to you. Obviously, so much has happened in the four years-plus since we last visited. I want to tell you quickly that you are in our prayers daily. You are in our thoughts so often. Mildred and I know where your heart and intents are. Our respect for you as a brother in Christ [is] unchanged. Both of us have been so pulled from every direction that we will need time to work through our differences and resolve our conflicts. That will come in due season. . . .

As I read Reverend Dortch's letter, I could not help wondering what "differences" and "conflicts" he meant. While I had served at Heritage USA, I had never known of any differences or conflicts that needed to be resolved between us. It was not until the subterfuge that went on at PTL in March and April 1987 and the events that followed that Richard Dortch and I took separate paths. His letter continued:

I remember you telling me on one occasion that people forget what they read, get it mixed up, and things lose their punch after time. We have seen that demonstrated in the past few weeks. People are already asking, "Richard, what is it you did?"

I'm sure you have heard that I have written a book. It came out last week. I am sure many will give you their opinion of it, but please wait until you have read it *all* yourself. I know you will not agree with some things, but the book is about what I believe to be the truth. What I have written about you is not written to offend, but to give my honest view of what I have been through. . . .

I'll be in touch,

Your friend and brother,
Richard

True to his word, Richard Dortch was in touch soon; I received a request from him to visit me in prison. On March 20, my longtime friend Paul Olson deliberately broke my visitation ban and simply showed up in the visiting room. I was still hurting deeply from the finalization of the divorce the week before, so Paul sat with me for a while, commiserated with me, and prayed with me. By most indications, it had been a nondescript visit, but had not Paul been bold enough to break through my wall of silence, I may not have accepted the request for Richard Dortch to visit or anyone else. I had gone from Jamie's visit in January to Paul's visit in

415

March without allowing a visitor to see me. A week after Paul visited, my cousin George Bakker came to see me. With George's visit, I was over the hump and lifted the ban on people visiting me. As such, I was willing to see Richard Dortch if the prison system would allow it. Much to my surprise they did allow the visit.

Actually, I looked forward to seeing Reverend Dortch —I had several important questions I wanted to ask him personally and privately— although I recognized that our meeting might be a bit awkward. When I walked into the visiting room, the first thing I noticed about Reverend Dortch was how much he had aged in the few years since I had last seen him—but then, so had I. Prison will do that to a person. Reverend Dortch, however, had been sick while in prison, and he now looked gaunt, tired, and worn.

We embraced each other and sat down at one of the low tables to talk. Phil Shaw, who had helped facilitate Reverend Dortch's visit, stayed nearby as I had requested. Reverend Dortch and I talked freely about the one thing we had in common lately—prison life. We compared stories of prison food, clothing, and prison terms that neither of us had ever heard before being thrust into the prison culture. We laughed a bit, which eased the tension.

We talked about Tammy Faye, and Reverend Dortch told me that he had met with her in an attempt to talk her out of the divorce. She had treated him with respect, but she remained determined to proceed with the divorce.

We also talked about our last years at PTL. We both agreed that we had made a mistake in trying to beat *The Charlotte Observer* at its own game. Reverend Dortch smiled when I reminded him that someone had warned us, "Never get in a battle with someone who buys ink by the barrel." Rather than trying to defend and justify ourselves to the press, we should have answered their questions as simply and as forthrightly as possible and kept our focus on the work that God had given us to do.

We talked about Jerry Falwell's role in the demise of PTL, and the duplicity of the man who supposedly came in to help us. Reverend Dortch knew full well now that he had been deceived by the men from Lynchburg. I admitted to Reverend Dortch that Jerry Falwell would have had no inroad if the Hahn incident had not occurred.

As the conversation went on, I decided to go ahead and confront Reverend Dortch as to why he pleaded guilty to crimes we did not commit. He told me that he had not testified against me, but that he answered the prosecutors' questions as honestly as he could. He said that he never confessed to any crime, although he did confess to offering Lifetime Partnerships on our PTL television programs and by mail. Since he had done so with me, the charge of conspiracy was included, as well. Reverend Dortch insisted that he did not consider any of these things to be a crime. I listened thoughtfully as Reverend Dortch explained his position to me. I understood that he had decided to plead guilty for expediency's sake, because his lawyers had advised him that his case would probably go better for him if he did so.

I looked Reverend Dortch right in the eye and asked him whether he thought that I had conspired with him to commit any crime. Reverend Dortch did not flinch. He answered, "Absolutely not."

To make sure I understood him correctly, I made the statement personal. "I did not commit a crime, nor did I conspire with you to commit a crime."

Reverend Dortch agreed wholeheartedly.

The visit was bittersweet. I was glad to hear that Reverend Dortch had not believed that he or I was guilty of the government charges. Yet, like the conclusions of the bankruptcy judge in November 1991, it did nothing to ease the pain of being in prison. If anything, it served only to increase it.

Reverend Dortch's visit also reminded me of how much I missed the people who had been a part of our programs at PTL. Maybe that's why I was especially delighted to learn that three special friends were coming to visit me on April 27, from three separate parts of the country. Jerry Barnard, a pastor from California, Mike Murdock, a singer-songwriter-evangelist from Texas, and James Blackwood, the outstanding tenor for the world-famous Blackwood Brothers Quartet from Memphis, were all coming to F.M.C. Rochester on the same day. All three of the men had appeared on *PTL* programs numerous times. None of the three men knew that the others were coming.

Phil Shaw accompanied the men to the visiting room. It was still chilly in Minnesota but the sun was shining and it was a beautiful spring day, so we decided to take our plastic chairs outside to the "visiting yard." The visiting yard was actually a bleak cement area just off the main visitation building; it was about the size of a small backyard, surrounded by a narrow strip of grass upon which inmates and their visitors were not permitted to sit. The outside visiting area was usually heavily populated by smokers since smoking was not permitted inside the visitation building.

On this day, however, only a few visitors and inmates were outside. The five of us huddled in the sunshine to keep warm. We talked and laughed and reminisced about better days we had known at PTL. Suddenly

417

I had an idea. *All three of my visitors today are outstanding singers. Wouldn't it be tremendous if these guys could sing a song?* Ordinarily, the prison officials frowned upon anything that hinted at what they considered excessive noise, but since we were outside, and because there were only a few people in the visiting yard, I could not resist asking these great singers to sing me a song. It had been *so* long since I had heard a gospel song, it was worth going to the hole for, if necessary.

"Would you guys sing something?" I asked. "You'd have to sing quietly, because we are not allowed to disturb anyone else, but I would love to hear a song or two."

The men all nodded in understanding. "What do you want to hear?" Jerry asked.

I smiled at Jerry. He was known throughout the world for his rendition of the song "It's Real." I asked him to sing that song.

Outside, sitting in the prison visiting yard, Jerry began singing as softly as he could, "It's real! It's real! I know it's real!" His voice began to get louder as he sang the chorus again. My heart welled with joy. I didn't care how many guards heard the singing. It was worth it!

Next, James Blackwood began singing the old hymn "The Eastern Gate." James's rich tenor voice pierced the cool April air like a supersonic jet racing through the sky. James tried his best, but he just does not know how to sing softly. As the legendary tenor got wound up on the chorus, singing, "I'll meet you in the morning, just inside the eastern gate," I thought that at any minute we might all be transported to heaven.

Then Mike Murdock softly began to sing a song he had written and Tammy Faye had recorded back in the mid-1980s, "You Can Make It." There they were again—those familiar words that kept coming back to me throughout my prison experience. Mike sang a verse and chorus of the song. Then, as if on a divine cue, he began singing another song that he had written and that Tammy had recorded. The song was "God Is Not Through Blessing You." As Mike sang, the lyrics sounded as though he was describing my life:

> A man lost every dime to his name,
> His best friends even said he was through.
> But God said, "Job, your best days are just ahead,
> 'Cause I'm not through blessing you."
>
> God's not through blessing you,
> God's not through blessing you.

Never give up; what He said He will do;
God's not through blessing you.

Have you ever prayed for something, day after day,
And nothing happened?
Have you ever asked God for a miracle
  and it seemed the answer would never come?
That very moment, that very second,
  you might feel like letting go, quitting,
You may not realize it, friend,
  but you might just be a moment from your miracle.
Don't quit, don't let go,
'Cause God's not through blessing you.

Mike went back to the chorus, only this time as he sang, he substituted the words:

God's not through *using* you,
God's not through *using* you.
Never give up;
What He said He will do;
God's not through *using* you.[1]

The faces of all five of us—grown men—glistened with tears. I had felt for so long that God had abandoned me. Then slowly but surely as I studied the Scriptures I began to sense His hand was still upon my life. The words of men who had so boldly and absolutely proclaimed that I was through, that I would never preach again, that the "Bakker ministry is done," still rankled in my mind. Now, it was as though God had sent a special trio of singers to remind me that He had not given up on me.

As I listened to these three men singing, for the first time since coming to prison, I missed being on television. One of my great joys during my twenty-five years on television had been to present to the world talented singers and gifted speakers. Now, as the beautiful voices transformed the prison visiting yard into an outdoor amphitheater, it seemed so unfair for me to be having this heartwarming, inspirational "concert" in private and not to be sharing it with the world. I actually felt guilty having these great singers all to myself. I made a mental note that when singers and speakers wanted to come to visit me, I was going to try my best to encourage them to minister to the entire prison population as well.

To me, it was a turning point. From that day forward, I began to pull out of my spiritual tailspin.

It was a clear sign to me that I was making progress when one night after chow time I turned to my tough, athletic cellmate, and asked, "Rod, would you teach me how to catch a ball?"

Much to my surprise and relief, Rod did not laugh. He merely looked back at me and waited for me to explain.

"My father was always too busy to teach me how to play ball," I told him. "He worked two jobs and he didn't have much time or energy left for playing ball. I don't think his dad had time to play ball with him either. I always wanted to learn, but I was too afraid to risk it. Even at family reunions when I was a child, there was always a softball game, but I avoided it because I was embarrassed. I didn't know how to throw or catch a ball."

"You never played ball as a kid?" Rod asked in disbelief.

"No, I was always too afraid."

"Okay, come on," Rod replied. "It's getting dark out, so we won't have much time tonight, but let's get started."

We went over to the outdoor recreation area and checked out a softball and two mitts.

"First, you need to know a few things," Rod began explaining in his usual instructor's manner. "The key to catching a ball is that you must keep your eye on the ball. Got that?" Rod moved the ball around in a circle in front of my face. "Keep your eye on the ball," Rod repeated. "Don't watch my body; don't watch my eyes because I will fool you; just keep your eye on the ball."

Rod went on to explain the rudiments of how to use a baseball glove. I wasn't even sure which hand to put it on! "Since you throw right-handed, you need a mitt on your left hand to catch the ball," Rod went on as though he were teaching a six-year-old. "Keep your fingers loose and flexible so you can squeeze the mitt closed when you feel the ball land in it." Just as he had done when Rod was teaching how to skydive, he went through the entire mental process of catching and throwing a ball before he ever allowed me to touch the softball.

"Okay, let's go."

We went to a less populated area of the recreation field. It was a huge step for me to be seen trying to catch a ball. I certainly didn't want to be mocked and made fun of by any inmates, but I was willing to risk not being able to catch the ball and making a fool of myself. It didn't matter to me anymore—and it felt great to be free.

Rod began by tossing the ball to me from only a few feet away. At first, I had difficulty coordinating my glove and hand movements, but after a bit more instruction from Rod, I began to get the hang of it.

Inch by inch, Rod began to move back farther and farther.

"No, no!" I called. "Don't go back any further." I was afraid if Rod went back too far, I would not be able to catch the ball. Rod, however, kept moving back, throwing the ball harder . . . and I caught every one! At fifty-two years of age, in prison, I learned how to play catch for the very first time.

Next Rod taught me how to throw the ball overhand so it could fly a long distance. "You throw like a girl," Rod told me.

I was humiliated by Rod's comment, but I did not know any other way to throw. I received the rebuke from him without becoming offended, because I knew he was trying to help me. He taught me how to stand, how to move forward when I threw the ball, bringing the ball straight down over my shoulder to get the maximum thrust on the ball.

A few of the guys who were standing by watching began to chortle. "Ha! He really does throw like a girl, doesn't he?"

Rod immediately realized his mistake and fell back into a fatherly instructor's mode. "Don't pay any attention to those guys," Rod told me. "Keep your eyes on the ball."

He began throwing the ball high in the air—I was scared stiff that it was going to come down and smack me right in the face—but I caught it. Again and again we threw the ball back and forth. I could do it!

Rod and I played catch until the sun disappeared. My hand turned red from the ball smacking into the glove, but I didn't care. I was playing ball. Finally, the guard called out that it was time to get back inside before dark. We checked our gloves and ball back in with the rec. guard and returned to our cell.

I was euphoric as I sat inside my cell. All my life I had thought that I couldn't play ball. All my life I was afraid to risk playing. Now to find out for the first time that I could do it—and that I was actually pretty good at it, because I had good hand-eye coordination—it was overwhelming.

I thought, *I could have been doing this all my life!*

That night I couldn't sleep. Not from the excitement, but from the pain! Every muscle in my body ached. Muscles I didn't even know I had, screamed almost aloud, "You overdid it!" But I didn't care. I felt as though

I had been released from my own personal prison. I could throw and catch a ball.

For the next several weeks, Rod and I played catch almost every evening after chow time. Eventually he taught me how to swing a bat and the basic rules of baseball. I enjoyed the game, although I didn't feel confident enough yet to enter into the prison ball games, especially when teams from the outside came to play some of our prison teams. I enjoyed going to the games and watching, sitting on the sidelines, dreaming of the day that I might be good enough to play on such a team.

CHAPTER

41

The Hole

BACK IN LATE FEBRUARY 1992, I RECEIVED A MOST INTERESTING request in the mail. The students of Harmony School in Bloomington, Indiana, invited me to write an introductory article for their annual yearbook. The Harmony School Yearbook is a high school annual unlike any I had ever seen. The yearbook is different from most others in that it follows a selected theme and each of the school's 140 or so students is given his or her own page to contribute an insight or comment. Many of the students include their baby photos as well as current pictures and answer such questions as "What is your favorite smell?" and "How many years do you think you will live?" *Yearbook* is an inadequate word to describe what the staff of students puts together each year in their off-the-wall yet wonderfully creative publication.

As a special addition to the yearbook, the editorial staff solicits commentary, photos, and articles contributed by a wide variety of famous (or infamous) people. The 1991 yearbook included articles or signed photos from Richard Nixon, children's television personality Mr. Rogers, Orville Redenbacher, Tommy Smothers, and Federico Fellini. In more recent years, the yearbook has included material from Woody Allen, John Travolta, Timothy Leary, Bill and Hillary Clinton, Al Gore, Clarence Thomas, Leonard Nimoy, Penn & Teller, Dr. Joyce Brothers, Jack Kevorkian, the Dalai Lama, Mickey Spillane, Allen Ginsberg, Mikhail Gorbachev, General Colin Powell, Jonathan Winters, Vanna White, James

Earl Jones, Jerry Seinfeld, Tonya Harding, and a "special blessing" from Pope John Paul II.

With a lineup such as that, how could I refuse?

The theme of the 1992 yearbook was "Why We Left Omaha," an off-beat approach to something each writer had left behind, a place, a career, a state of mind. As I read the request several weeks after my divorce, I thought, *Yes, I know something about leaving things behind. I left an entire life behind when I entered that courthouse in Charlotte in October 1989*. I assumed the students had probably invited me to write an article for their yearbook as a novelty, or perhaps because my name had become so familiar through the media. But in a way, I was honored that they had thought of me at all. My sense of self-esteem had been so shattered that anyone at all who would be interested in reading something I had written—even a bunch of kids from an alternative school in Indiana—buoyed my spirits.

I wrote an article entitled "What I Left Behind" for the 1992 edition of the Harmony School Yearbook. It read:

> When you go to prison, you leave everything behind except your memories. I lost my life's work, my home and car, my life savings and retirement fund, almost everything. Those things are not really important, but since coming to prison, I have lost my wife of thirty-one years, the most important person in my life.
>
> I miss my family most of all, my sixteen-year-old son Jamie Charles, my twenty-two-year-old daughter Tammy Sue, her husband, Doug, my two wonderful grandsons James and Jonathan, and my ex-wife, Tammy Faye.
>
> My daughter and her family spent my last night of freedom with me. I had a great time playing with my namesake, grandson James. As I went from prison to prison, the only thing I was able to keep was a picture of baby James. My faith in God and that little face kept me alive those first frightening months. It was a happy day when he ran into my arms in the visiting room of the prison on his first visit.
>
> Let me close with this true story. An elderly lady, who just lost her husband, was looking over her beautiful chinaware that she had never used, and she was weeping. "I was saving my good china for special company and now I realize my husband was the best company I ever had."
>
> The moral of my little time with you is, "Don't fall in love with things; love each other, and use your good china before it is too late."

424

The yearbook staff printed my article just as I wrote it, messy handwriting, misspelled words, and all. Harmony School has continued every year since to extend an invitation for me to impart my "words of wisdom" and I have been glad to comply.

Another much-needed boost to my self-esteem came as a result of my cousin George Bakker's visit with me in prison. George and I grew up together in Muskegon, Michigan. We played together as boys, attended the same church, and shared most of our childhood experiences. At the time George came to visit me in prison, I had not seen him for several years. During his visit, we enjoyed reminiscing about old times and talking about old friends. As we talked, George remembered that he had recently received a letter from my old girlfriend, Sally Brown. Actually, Sally had written a letter to me, but not knowing how to contact me through the prison system, she had sent the letter to George.

Sally Brown was my high school sweetheart. She was a talented singer and gifted actress. We performed in several school plays together and walked home from school together almost every day. We genuinely cared for each other. We had even considered marriage until I felt called to enter the ministry and decided to attend Bible school at North Central Bible College in Minneapolis. At that point, Sally and I went our separate ways, but we parted as friends. She eventually married and divorced a few years before I went to prison. I had not seen her in over thirty years and had corresponded with her only once during that time.

When George forwarded Sally's letter to me, I was excited to receive it. I wrote Sally back and we began to correspond throughout the summer of 1992. She sent me a photograph of her and her children, and I was not surprised to see that Sally was just as beautiful as she had been thirty years previously. She and her daughter could have passed for sisters.

Our letters were strictly platonic. Much of Sally's writing revolved around her telling me about the new man in her life, whom she planned to marry, and eventually did. She described her career as a college professor and her work for AIDS research. She was most excited about the new line of dolls she was creating. In return, I wrote to her of prison life and many of the day-to-day events I was experiencing. Neither of us had any illusions about rekindling the long-extinguished fire of our teenage romance. Yet I must admit that in a wonderful way, corresponding with Sally filled a major void in my life left by the departure of Tammy Faye. Until the time shortly before our divorce, I had written or called Tammy Faye almost every day. I even wrote to her after the divorce, but it was not the same. As the weeks turned into months following our divorce, I wrote to her less and less.

Writing to Sally and receiving letters from this good-looking, articulate and upbeat woman provided not only an outlet for emotional expression, but a boost to my severely damaged ego as well. I stopped writing to her after she got married because I did not want to create a problem between Sally and her new husband or to give the wrong impression concerning our correspondence. I did miss her letters, though.

I kept busy during the summer months, often working out with Rod at the "iron pile," the stack of dead weights outside near the recreation field. With Rod's help and the coaching of a bunch of other guys, I was getting myself into better physical shape than I had ever been in my life. Besides lifting weights, I walked several miles most days, going around and around the track that surrounded the soccer field. Physically, my strength and stamina were returning; spiritually, I was studying the Scriptures sometimes for as many as sixteen hours a day. Emotionally, I was beginning to accept the truth that Tammy Faye was gone.

In addition to my other activities, once each week, members of the local Toastmasters group in the Rochester area held a class in the prison for those who wished to learn how to speak better in public. Although I had spoken to millions of people on television, I was still nervous about standing in front of a group of people to talk. Especially since coming to prison, I had lost my confidence as a communicator. My brain seemed so damaged from my experience over the past several years, I sometimes had difficulty even putting a sentence together.

I quickly learned that I had much to gain by attending the weekly Toastmasters meetings. The organization was comprised of a wonderfully supportive, caring group of men and women who volunteered their time to come into the prison to work with the inmates. Most of the Toastmasters from the outside were gregarious, intelligent individuals, some of whom actually made their livings as professional speakers. Each week they taught the inmates principles of how to select a topic, write a good speech, and deliver it most effectively. We had numerous paper handouts in the class, often exchanging agendas, "table talks," speech topics, critiques, and notes with the other members of the group. A prison guard stood nearby, watching and listening to everything that was said and done.

Well, almost everything.

One evening, several months after my divorce had been finalized, I attended the Toastmasters meeting as usual. We were especially active in passing papers around our group that night, so nobody thought much about it when an attractive woman who helped regularly with the class passed me a piece of paper on which she had written a critique. I started to read it but then stopped short when I realized that the woman wasn't critiquing my speech topic; she was writing a personal note to me! I hurriedly folded the piece of paper and stashed it in my pocket. I smiled at the woman and she smiled broadly back at me. I quickly turned my attention to the person who was presenting a talk and tried to avoid prolonged eye contact with the woman for the remainder of the class.

Later that night, after I had returned to my cell, I took out the woman's note, unfolded it, and read it by the light of my small bed light. It was a good thing the room was dark other than my reading light because I'm sure I must have blushed as I read the complimentary note.

A few days later, the woman sent me a greeting card in the mail, again effusively complimenting everything from my appearance to my intelligence to my speaking ability. I purchased a nice card at the Vietnam Veterans' card sale and sent it to her, thanking her for her kind words and letting her know how much they meant to me. I truly did appreciate her compliments. I had not heard such glowing sentiments directed toward me in a long, long time, and I lapped up her words like a thirsty man in the desert.

The next week I received another letter in the mail, this time including a photograph of my new friend. I naively pinned the woman's picture onto my corkboard in my cell, placing the woman's picture in clear sight with my family photos and spiritual reminders.

Having the woman's photo on my corkboard was not in itself a breach of prison rules. Guys had all sorts of photos plastered on boards. But having a picture of a prison volunteer worker was considered inappropriate, although I didn't know that at the time. It wasn't long before somebody saw the picture on my board and turned me in for breaking the rules. I never learned who snitched on me.

Within days after I had put the woman's picture on my corkboard, a high-ranking female guard stopped me in the hallway one Friday afternoon.

"Hold it, Bakker," she commanded. "Do you have a picture of a woman in your wallet?"

Wallet? What wallet? I wondered. *Inmates aren't allowed to have wallets.* Surely the officer knew that.

"No, I don't have a picture in my wallet. I don't even have a wallet," I replied to the officer.

"What about on your wall?" she asked. "Do you have any pictures on your corkboard?"

"Well, sure," I answered.

"I want to see them right now," the officer said.

"Sure, okay," I replied, confused but unconcerned. I knew I had no contraband items on my corkboard, so I wasn't worried as we walked down the hall toward my cell.

The female officer walked into my cell, over to my corkboard, and without asking about any of the other individuals in photos on my corkboard, the officer pointed to my Toastmasters friend and asked, "Who is that?"

I knew immediately that I had been set up by a snitch.

"That is Denise Jones," I replied.

"Is she a family member?"

"No, she is no relation at all. She is a volunteer at the Toastmasters meetings."

"Well, you are not allowed to have that picture. Take it off the board and give it to me."

"Not allowed to have that?"

The female officer wasn't entertaining any questions. "Come with me, Bakker. You're going to the hole," she said matter-of-factly. She had already turned and started to walk out of the cell. "Leave your things here. You won't be needing them," she nodded at my clothes in my locker.

The hole? Not the hole!

I had been in prison since October 1989 and had meticulously avoided doing anything that might get me thrown into solitary confinement. Memories of the hole at Butner Federal Prison still haunted my mind. The last place on earth I wanted to go was to the hole. Stories I had heard other inmates tell about the hole in Rochester were rather benign, nothing like what I had experienced at Butner, but the hole was nonetheless the most feared and hated punishment inside the prison system. It was the prison within the prison. Making matters worse, the hole was located in a section of the building directly behind Rod's and my cell, separated by only a narrow strip of grass and the solitary confinement cages used for exercise by those inmates in the hole. Inmates often came into our cell to yell out our window across the chasm to their friends who were serving time in the hole. I had heard firsthand of the loneliness, monotony, and the sheer maddening impact of the hole.

428

And now I was going there.

The female guard escorted me back down the hall in the direction of the entrance to the hole. As we passed other inmates, I whispered to anyone I knew even vaguely, "Get Dr. Foster. I'm going to the hole! Please, get hold of Dr. Foster." What upset me the most about going to the hole—besides the awful feeling of being incarcerated in solitary confinement—was the fact that my children were coming to visit the following day. I had come to grips with Tammy Faye's departure and had accepted the fact that we were now divorced. I certainly wasn't over her, but I had at least turned the corner and pulled out of my deep depression. I had been feeling good; I had been exercising outdoors regularly so my body was toned, tanned, and fit. My clothes were all sharply cleaned and pressed. My shoes were shined. My mental attitude was better than at any time since being incarcerated. I had gotten all A's in my college courses. I was ready to have the most positive prison visit possible. I had really been looking forward to having a wonderful time with my children.

Now, I was going to the hole.

The female guard escorted me as far as the entrance to the hole, where another guard opened the door and I stepped inside a "security chamber." The heavy door closed and locked behind me, with the same awful sucking sound as all the prison cells at Rochester. Once I was inside the security lock, the guard inside the cell block on the other side of the chamber unlocked the next door and I stepped into the cell block known as "the hole." The guard slammed the door shut behind me, locking it instantly.

As soon as I stepped inside the cell block, the guard put me through a strip search and took away my clothes. He issued me a rumpled jumpsuit and pointed me toward a solitary confinement cell on the left side of a row of solitary cells. The guard unlocked the cell, and I walked inside. The door slammed shut behind me, seeming to pull all the air out of the room at the same time.

I looked around the stark cell. Our regular cells were small and sparse, but this cell was ridiculously stark. The only furniture in the cell was a slab-type cot, and a commode and sink along the wall. The cell reminded me of a tomb. In the back of the room was a window out of which I could see my regular cell in the wing across the way.

I walked over to the cement slab cot, sat down, stared toward the tiny window in the cell door, and waited . . . and waited. I knew that nobody got out of the hole quickly, not without going through a trial-type hearing before the unit manager and other prison officials. That usually took time. Meanwhile, there was nothing to do but wait. Eventually, I tired of staring at the window in the cell door, hoping to see a friendly face. I rolled over onto the thin mattress covering the slab and tried to sleep.

I had been in the hole for two or three hours and had already begun to feel the walls closing in on me when suddenly I saw a guard's face in the window of my cell door. The guard opened the door and said coldly, "Okay, Bakker. Let's go."

Somehow, someone had gotten a message to Dr. Foster, late Friday afternoon. It was a miracle of almost biblical proportions that he was able to investigate the reason for my punishment and have it overruled on Friday afternoon, right before many of the senior prison officials went home for the weekend.

Bless you, Dr. Foster! I thought as the guard expedited my release and sent me back into the general prison population. Or perhaps it was Dr. Westrick or some other unseen benefactor, but I was sure glad to be out of there. The guard on duty on my floor gave me a large, army-green duffel bag that contained my belongings, all of which had been thoroughly searched while I was in the hole. I walked back to my regular cell and began to put my things back in their usual locations. All of my pictures had to be remounted on my cork bulletin board as well. One picture was conspicuously absent from my photo montage. Nonetheless, my prison cell never looked so good.

It was chow time, so even though I wasn't really hungry, I wanted to find my friends and let them know that I had been released. When some of the guys who had been in prison for a long period of time saw me walk into the chow hall, they could hardly believe their eyes.

"Nobody gets out of the hole that fast!" they said with genuine astonishment.

Tammy Sue and Jamie arrived the following day. Our visit truly was one of the best we had in Rochester. Perhaps I especially appreciated the visit because I was so grateful to be out of the hole and back in the familiar confines of my cell. Had I known what horror was coming, however, I might have opted for the safety and security of solitary confinement.

42

My Worst Nightmare

I HAVE ALWAYS ENJOYED EXERCISE, BUT PRIOR TO GOING to prison I had never been comfortable with working out in public gymnasiums or exercise rooms. Part of my reluctance went back to my childhood days, when I had a secret desire to be a gymnast. Yet I never dared step onto the gym floor to try. My gym teachers often made fun of me as a young boy because I did not run and jump as well as the other boys. My first day in gym class, my teacher gave me a failing grade for poor posture. I hadn't even done anything yet, and the man had flunked me already!

In prison, most inmates know that if they do not make a conscious effort to exercise, they will soon become lethargic and overweight. An inactive lifestyle will quickly take a toll on a person's body in any environment, but especially in prison, where inmates have nothing to look forward to but the passing of time.

Beyond the physical benefits of exercise, there was a sort of unwritten respect for the inmates who took good care of their bodies and exuded a tough, macho image. In that area, my cellmate Rod was concerned for my well-being. He said, "Jim, you walk like a girl. You walk like a victim. You have to walk tough in prison, or somebody is going to try to take advantage of you."

I knew Rod was right. In prison, because I was so nervous and uptight, I walked fast, keeping my eyes down, no matter where I was going. I have always walked with a short step, sort of like a bandy rooster, so I have always walked quickly. I'd never had a macho image. When I used to see videotapes of myself walking across a television stage, I always thought that I walked sort of funny compared to other people, and it always bothered me. As a teenager, one of the bullies in our school teased me that I walked like a "fairy."

Apparently, my walk was one of the first things people noticed about me in prison. Dr. Foster later admitted his concern upon my arrival because I looked vulnerable when I walked. Added to my overall timid demeanor, Dr. Foster feared I would be a sitting duck for predators in prison if I did not adapt quickly and present a tougher look. Most of my friends in prison realized the same thing, so before long, some of my black buddies tried to teach me how to walk with "soul." "You gotta get loose, Jim," they'd tell me.

In an effort to help me defend myself if necessary, Rod taught me some rudiments of boxing. He also taught me some basic techniques of street fighting, how to use my fingers to poke an aggressor in the eyes, and how to leverage my weight to turn my body into a battering ram if I were attacked.

Rod helped design a regimen for me, using free weights at the indoor workout room. On nice days we exercised outdoors at the iron pile. Rod also developed a vigorous regimen of exercises for toning my body on the days I was not working out with free weights. Rod took on my exercise program as though he were preparing one of his skydiving students for an important jump. Olympic athletes and movie stars never had a better, more committed personal trainer than I had in Rod.

One afternoon I finished my cleaning work early, so I obtained permission from the guard to go out to the iron pile to work out. Most of the other guys were at work so except for men moving from one place to another on the compound and on the track, I was relatively alone at the pile. I went about my usual weightlifting routine, quickly becoming immersed in my regimen. Rod's reminders that I must focus on my exercises if I hoped to gain maximum benefit from them reverberated through my mind.

I was sitting down, doing arm curls on the "preacher's bench," a small metal structure with a slanted, padded top similar to a kneeling bench. Although I was always on alert in prison, constantly aware of my surroundings, I was concentrating so intensely on my weight lifting I barely noticed when a new inmate sat down on another workout bench a few feet away from me. When I did finally look in his direction, I saw that the

The main sanctuary of Heritage Village Church and the location for nightly camp meetings. Also located in this complex of buildings were seminar and Sunday School rooms, a nursery, day-care, and a K-12 school. This building was nicknamed the "Big Barn Auditorium."

My associate pastor, Richard Dortch, joins me in serving Holy Communion to our congregation.

(following page) The beautiful, state-of-the-art 1,500 seat television studio where Tammy and I originated our daily programs. Often, over 2,000 people packed this studio while several thousand more watched on closed-circuit, big-screen TV in the Big Barn Auditorium.

On July 4, 1982, we dedicated to God what I consider the nerve center and very heartbeat of our ministry, the Upper Room. Modeled after the historic Upper Room in Jerusalem, this prayer center never closed. Pastors and phone counselors were stationed there 24 hours a day.

Prayer and communion service being held in the Upper Room.

Camp meetings, gospel "sings" and teaching seminars were held 365 days a year at Heritage USA. Eighty-six religious services were conducted each week.

The family center served as a hub for Heritage USA youth activities: basketball, roller skating, pizza parlor, and worship, music, and teaching activities.

One of the greatest passion plays in America was presented in the beautiful outdoor setting of the Jerusalem amphitheater.

Live music and singing were performed daily on Main Street Heritage USA and in the fellowship lobby. During the summer months, musical presentations were performed throughout the park, including the lakeside amphitheater.

In July of 1984, we opened the beautiful Heritage House for expectant mothers who chose birth rather than abortion. A 24-hour hotline for women in critical pregnancy situations and the Tender Loving Care Adoption Agency were also formed around the same time.

Our ministry developed a nationwide network of nearly 1,000 People That Love Centers to help feed, clothe, and provide furniture, counseling, and employment assistance to people in their time of need. This outreach touched nearly 10 million people a year.

The childhood home of Dr. Billy Graham was slated for destruction to make way for a building complex. PTL friends and partners moved the house piece by piece to Heritage USA and furnished it in the same style of the period as when Billy Graham was a boy. One of our goals at Heritage USA was to preserve our spiritual heritage for future generations.

Kevin's House, built to accommodate severely disabled children in a homelike setting.

On January 2, 1987, in one of my last official duties at Heritage USA, I broke ground for our new church and conference center which, when completed, would have seated 30,000 people.

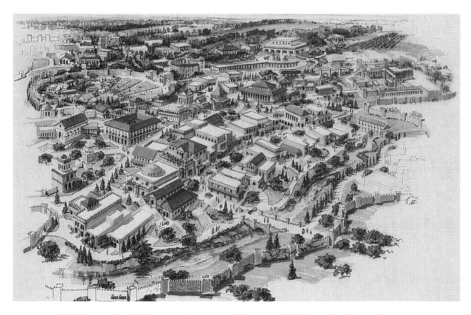

Old Jerusalem Village was just one of the new facilities already on the drawing board for a future lodging and ministry center at Heritage USA.

One of the happiest days of my life, shortly before I entered prison, was when Tammy Sue presented me with my first grandchild and namesake, Baby James.

I debated long and hard before including this picture in my book. This is one of the lowest moments of my life—a time during my trial when I suffered a nervous breakdown and was put into what I call an "insane asylum" inside the prison at Butner, NC.

This picture is the only possession I was able to somehow take with me into almost every prison to which I was assigned. There were times when simply looking at this picture of my grandbaby gave me the will to hold on just a little longer.

My last night of freedom for almost 5 years. This picture was taken the night before Judge Potter sentenced me to 45 years in prison. I took care of Baby James throughout the night, giving him bottles. It was a joy to be with him.

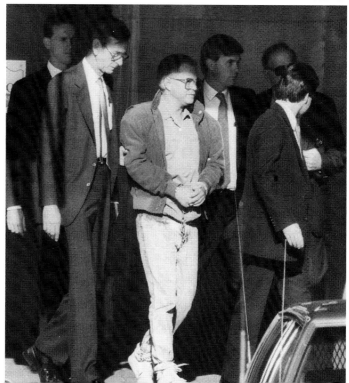

Being led in chains from the courthouse to begin my 45-year sentence.

The first Christmas we "celebrated" in prison. This picture was taken on Christmas Eve of 1989. Pictured with Tammy and me are my sister Donna, Tammy Sue's husband Doug, Tammy Sue, Baby James, and my son Jamie Charles.

April 1, 1990: Our first wedding anniversary in prison.

Two of my best friends in the world, Rev. Phil Shaw and Rev. Paul Olson, who visited me in prison every chance they got.

My parents holding the vase that I had poured and painted for them while in prison.

Jamie Charles had just turned 16, and was able to visit me by himself for the first time. As he started to leave, he declared, "Dad, this has been the best day of my life." This picture was taken that day.

A scene from prison that I had scribbled down on a piece of paper.

It was always a happy day when Baby James came to see me in prison. One day, as he walked in with his mother, he exclaimed, "Paw Paw Jim has a big house!"

What a thrill it was after two years to finally see my parents again.

(far right) In the deepest days of despair and despondency, even shaving became a difficult task.

While I was in prison it seemed as if my son grew up overnight. One day when he walked in, it felt as if I was looking at myself 30 years before. Pictured here, I am preaching during my Bible College days, and Jamie Charles is standing on the platform of our church in Orlando.

What a wonderful day when James Blackwood came to the Jesup prison and brought his quartet to perform a gospel concert on the prison's loading dock. The prison guard even allowed me to visit with them on their bus, though he had to accompany me.

Franklin Graham not only visited me in prison, but he ministered in our chapel programs, bringing with him Dennis and Danny Agajanian.

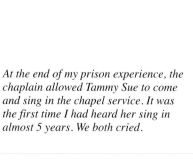

At the end of my prison experience, the chaplain allowed Tammy Sue to come and sing in the chapel service. It was the first time I had heard her sing in almost 5 years. We both cried.

One of my favorite gospel singers and old friend, Candi Staton Sussewell, came to the Jesup prison and ministered in concert to an enthusiastic and receptive house.

Professor Jim Albert from Drake University rallied to my cause and provided valuable legal insight and encouragement.

Inmate and former Pastor Larry Wright became my best friend in the Jesup prison. He was like a pastor to the entire compound, conducting a Bible study each morning at 5:30, evening Bible studies and church on Sunday night.

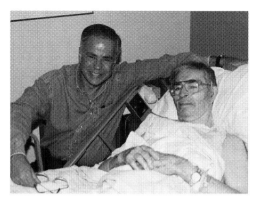

On my brief furlough from prison. I visited my father in the hospital after he fell and broke his hip.

Jamie Charles and I visited with Uncle Henry and Aunt Susan while on a 48-hour furlough to visit my ailing father. Years before Uncle Henry had vowed to keep his Christmas tree up until I was released from prison.

On the way back to the Jesup prison from my furlough, Jamie and I stopped at the spot where our home in Tega Cay had burned to the ground. We shared a sad moment as he brushed the sand from what was once the floor of our garage. There, etched in the concrete, was a message Tammy Faye had written almost a decade and a half before. It read, "Tammy loves Jim. Eating fish tonight."

This is the painting I did in my cell the night that our Tega Cay house burned to the ground.

The living room of our Tega Cay home, where we raised our children. I watched from a prison television as this home burned to the ground.

Another of life's happiest moments was photographed here. This shot was taken just moments after my release from prison. Jamie Charles likes to call this photo "the flight to freedom."

Being fingerprinted as I was admitted into the halfway house at the Salvation Army in Asheville, NC.

This was a welcome sight as my family greeted me just hours after my release from prison.

Welcome Home
Dad
We Love You!!!
July 1, 1994

A happy reunion in the North Carolina mountains with my parents, my sister Donna and my brother Norman. My nearly 90-year-old parents and I rejoiced that God had answered our prayers that they would live to see me walk out of prison.

Most of this book was written in a small rented farmhouse, surrounded by the beautiful mountains of North Carolina. The farmhouse was a place of solitude and refuge for me as I continued to seek the will of God for this next chapter of my life. This picture was taken in my barn.

Accompanying Aunt Susan to the memorial service for her husband and my friend, Uncle Henry. This was my first sermon following my release from prison.

man's stern, cold-as-steel, blue eyes were fixed on me, not a good situation in prison.

I quickly took stock of him. I did not recognize the man, so he must have been recently transferred to Rochester F.M.C. He was a husky man of muscular build, in his midtwenties I guessed, and I recognized that despite my intense physical regimen, I was no match for this fellow. I continued doing my arm curls as he continued to stare at me unflinchingly, even now that I had taken notice of him. I became acutely apprehensive. I had no idea whether this man was angry with me for some unknown reason—perhaps he felt that I had stolen money from someone close to him, as so many of the press reports had stated concerning me. I did not know whether he was going to curse me, punch me out, or try to kill me. I continued doing my curls, keeping him constantly in my peripheral vision . . . and he continued to stare.

Suddenly, without a word of introduction, the stranger blurted loudly, "Why does God hate me?"

His words caught me off guard. I looked up at the man and realized that the same eyes that had been so cold only moments before were now two of the saddest eyes I had ever seen.

"God doesn't hate you," I replied. "God loves you."

The man introduced himself as Craig and we struck up a conversation. I listened as he told me how his wife had moved in with another man and he no longer knew where she and his four-year-old daughter were living. He felt totally abandoned by his family, friends, and even by God. He could only conclude that God hated him, that God was somehow or other trying to get even with him.

As we talked, I explained to him that God was not trying to get even with him for doing wrong things. God had already gotten even for our sins by sacrificing His own Son, Jesus, on the cross. The Bible clearly says, "He has not dealt with us according to our sins, Nor punished us according to our iniquities. For as the heavens are high above the earth, So great is His mercy toward those who fear Him; As far as the east is from the west, So far has He removed our transgressions from us" (Ps. 103:10-12). Then I told him about some Scripture passages that had helped me deal with my own sense of being abandoned in prison. I quoted Hebrews 12:6, "For whom the Lord loveth he chasteneth [punishes], and scourgeth every son whom he receiveth" (KJV).

I then surprised Craig by asking, "Are you a bastard?"

"No, I'm not a bastard," Craig retorted.

I really shocked Craig when I continued by quoting verse eight of the same chapter: "But if ye be without chastisement, whereof all are partakers, then are ye bastards, and not sons." I explained to Craig that God might be trying to get his attention by allowing him to come to prison, and that whomever God loves, He disciplines, not to hurt us, but to help us. Ironically, the same words I was telling Craig, I needed to be reminded of again and again myself.

In fact, I was beginning to wonder if some of my former "feel good" messages that I had preached, teaching that Christians could have a pain-free, problem-free life if we only believed, might be wrong. Had I been encouraging Christians to give birth to spiritual "bastards" rather than legitimate children of God? The Bible clearly teaches that it is the trial of our faith that God uses to refine us and to bring us forth as "pure gold," yet I had been encouraging a theology that avoided any trials. I went so far as to refuse to have guests on our *PTL* television programs whose problems did not have a happy ending. Our programming took on a "Pollyanna" tone, leaving people with the unrealistic impression that Christians did not have to struggle, or at least they lived "happily ever after" if they did encounter troubles.

In prison, however, I was coming to grips with the fact that everyone is battling with something in their lives. I was reminded again and again of a T. H. Thompson quote that I had read in Tim Hansel's book, "Be kind. Remember that everyone you meet is fighting a hard battle." I was being hit in the face with the fact that much of what I had been teaching at PTL had given the impression that unless Christians were extremely successful, they were living a second-class spiritual life. It crushed me as I realized that like Craig, millions of people might be feeling that God does not love them because they have not been able to attain a happy-go-lucky, pain-free existence. The words I was sharing with Craig had been forged in my own experience as I slowly but surely came to understand that God did not hate me just because I was going through tough times.

Craig admitted that he had been heading in the wrong direction in his life. He had been in business and had lost a large sum of money; he had gotten in debt and could not pay his bills. Needing money desperately, he had robbed a bank and gotten caught. Nevertheless, it was difficult at first for Craig to accept the fact that being sent to prison was actually an expression of God's love toward him.

Over the next few weeks, my new friend frequently worked out with me or played catch with me when Rod wasn't available. Craig and I also walked the track together, and he poured his heart out to me as we walked. He listened intently as I told him how God had been helping me and would help him too. With heavy conviction, I shared with him one of the verses that had been so meaningful to me in my life, "That the trial of your faith, being much more precious than of gold that perisheth, though it be tried with fire, might be found unto praise and honor and glory at the appearing of Jesus Christ" (1 Peter 1:7 KJV). I told Craig the Old Testament story of Joseph that had meant so much to me, and I reminded Craig that it was hard for Joseph when he was in prison to think he was in God's will or that God was working in his life. "But God had a plan for Joseph," I explained to Craig, "and it was a plan for good, not evil. When you turn your life over to Christ and trust Him, you can be assured that what God has said in Romans 8:28 is true, that all things work together for good to those who love Him and are called according to His purposes." I suggested to Craig that even prison had to work out for his good someday, somehow.

We also talked about the fact that the only way our pain of rejection and loneliness would go away was for us to embrace it. We agreed that if we tried to run from the pain, it would seek us out and destroy us. I told Craig, "I believe our pain will turn to peace if we stop running." Craig nodded in understanding.

I continued, "I think this is what God meant when He said we would be more than conquerors when we face our fears, our depression, self-pity, and our loneliness. We don't have to overcome them, but we move into a state of peace we have never had before."

Craig was listening intently, so I went even further, "When we face our sins and deal with them, confessing them to God and perhaps to a faithful counselor or friend, they no longer have control over us. We more than conquer, we overcome and attain peace."

"That's what I want," Craig replied sincerely.

Craig began reading *The Living Bible*, a modern paraphrase of the Scripture; he started praying and seeking God's help and direction. In the weeks and months that followed, I saw a new peace and faith coming into his life.

Eventually Craig's wife wrote to him saying that she had broken up with her lover, and she wanted to know if it would be okay for her and their daughter to visit him. Craig was ecstatic. When Craig's wife and daughter came to see him in prison, I "happened" to be in the visiting room that day. Craig's darling little girl would not let go of her daddy. It was a sight I will never forget! At that moment, Craig had no doubt that God really loved him.

Chris was another inmate I became friends with at the iron pile. I was working out one day when a strong, athletic looking young man asked me to be his workout partner. After a few weeks of exercising together, I found out that Chris was actually a former national championship bodybuilder.

What I did not know at the time was that my new friend was also a snitch. While in prison, Chris had learned he had cancer caused by the steroids he had used in his bodybuilding career. He had been given an extremely long prison sentence for his large-scale drug dealing, and in an attempt to get his sentence reduced, Chris had agreed to return to his home area to testify against the drug dealers he had once bossed. When a photograph of Chris and an article about him hit the newspapers, it also hit the prison. Photocopies of the picture and article describing my friend's actions mysteriously started showing up on bulletin boards all around the prison compound. The word was out on Chris. His former friends wanted him dead.

One day as I walked across the compound with Anton, another one of my workout buddies, a big, strong, strapping man, Anton spoke quietly and seriously. "Do you know who that guy you're working out with is?"

"Yeah, I sure do. He's a championship bodybuilder," I answered.

"Well, stay away from him," Anton warned. "Don't hang around with him. He's a snitch and he's coming down."

"What? Why? Chris is my friend. What do you mean, 'he's coming down'?"

"He's coming *down*, Jim," Anton repeated angrily. "Stay away from him! If you're near him when he comes down you're gonna come down too. Do you understand?" I felt that Anton was just blowing smoke, but he sure was angry.

I had no special place in my heart for snitches. Nevertheless, Chris was my friend. I felt that I should not abandon him; I had to keep working out with him.

I tried to explain my position to Anton. "You see, Anton, I am a Christian. I have to do what I think Jesus would do. And He would be a friend to everyone. I gave my word to Chris. I said I would be his friend, just as much as I'm your friend."

Anton trounced away in a huff. For several months, he refused to speak to me, even though he saw me regularly in the halls and in the exercise areas.

Providentially, just as the word got out that Chris was coming down, he was called out again "on writ" to testify. He succeeded in having his sentence reduced because of his testimony. The government succeeded in trapping a few more drug dealers, and I succeeded in maintaining my integrity.

I believed that God had protected me in the situation with Chris. But my confidence was about to be severely tested.

As I mentioned previously, the positive aspect about being assigned to cleaning toilets in prison was that I was often able to complete my work early in the day and then, before the other inmates returned to their cells, have the time left to study the Bible or write. With most of the men out on work duties, the relatively quiet afternoons were extremely conducive to concentrated study and writing. Often I became so absorbed in what I was doing, I was oblivious to the normal prison sights and sounds around me.

On one such afternoon, when my cellmate Rod was out of the building, as were most of the other inmates, I was busy studying and writing letters in my cell when suddenly I glanced up, and to my horror, I saw a huge man standing right next to me.

Already shocked that someone had been able to enter my "space" without me hearing the door, I was terrified when I saw that the man had unzipped his fly and was exposing himself. "You want this, don't you," he growled, leering at me.

I was terrified, but I sat stoically, not making a move. I knew the only way I could possibly rebuff him was to be equally gruff.

"No!" I growled back, doing my best to sound surly and authoritative. "Get out of here before I call the guards!"

I turned back toward my work and kept my eyes straight ahead toward my desk. I dared not move. The man could easily have killed me; he could have snapped my neck in a moment. But God gave me courage and an unusual power to my words.

The man taunted me again, "You know you want this."

Then as quickly and as quietly as he had entered the room, he whirled around and left, pulling up his zipper as he went.

I sat there quaking in the chair. I had heard horror stories of attacks in prison, and for the first few months at Rochester, I avoided prolonged eye contact with other inmates unless absolutely necessary. I did not know whom I could trust, if anybody. Books and movies give the impression that everyone in prison is either a predator or a victim. In truth, some inmates do engage in homosexual contacts, especially those who have been incarcerated without conjugal visits for a long period of time. After being in prison for more than two and a half years, however, I had not had any incidents in which another inmate had tried to attack me. Aside from a death threat by an insane inmate in Building One, and a few threatening comments by another inmate, I had not experienced any real trouble from anybody. Consequently, I was beginning to let down my guard slightly, to be more at ease in the prison environment, if that is possible.

Then out of the silence came a huge man with evil intentions.

A few days later, once again during the midafternoon when Rod was out of the room, I was lying atop my bunk sleeping. I had been out walking the track after work and had come in to take a nap before all the other inmates returned from their work duties. I was wearing a T-shirt and a pair of tennis shorts. With my back to the door and my face to the wall, I had just fallen into a comfortable sleep when I was abruptly awakened by hands groping inside the backside of my shorts. The man was back!

As he rammed his fingers toward my rectum, I twirled on the bed, pulling my body away from him, screaming at the top of my lungs, "Get out of here! Get out! I'm going to call the officers."

The giant man glared at me but backed off when I screamed. Like a dangerous wounded bear, he hunkered toward the door, glowering at me one more time before leaving.

I fell back on my bunk and stared at the bunk above me. Undoubtedly, had I not responded so vociferously, the person who had sent me the letter early in my prison experience expressing the hope that I would be raped by the biggest black man in prison would have gotten his wish. I knew I had to do something about this situation, but what?

Toward the end of my next session with Dr. Foster, I tentatively brought up the subject of the recent assault. Dr. Foster maintained his usual cool, professional demeanor, but I could tell he was agitated by the news. He asked me if I knew the name of the man and I told him that I did not. I wasn't lying. I had a general idea where the man lived, but I didn't know him.

"Jim, the prison system has rules that say you cannot perpetrate a crime on another inmate and remain in that same prison. If you will tell me his name, I will see what I can do to have the man transferred for your safety."

Again I told Dr. Foster that I didn't know the name of the perpetrator. He then asked me to describe the man in detail and provide as much information about him as possible, but I refused. I didn't want to become known as a prison snitch. I knew how other inmates regarded snitches— on the same level as child molesters—and in most prisons snitches didn't last too long.

I knew I could not be a snitch and tell Dr. Foster anything about the man who had accosted me. I was afraid of the predator, but I was more afraid of the consequences of snitching.

What I did not know at the time was that Dr. Foster was understating his concern. Dr. Foster had been around the prison system long enough to know the true dangers. He had seen inmates who had been literally decapitated . . . usually for one of three reasons: harassment, unpaid gambling debts, or sexual rejection.

Dr. Foster recognized the seriousness of the offense committed by the man who had violated me. Although he didn't tell me at the time to avoid frightening me any further, many years later, Dr. Foster explained to me why he had been so concerned. First, the man had entered my cell, my *space*, uninvited. That was a prison taboo. The man knew that stepping into my cell while I was sleeping and not waking me up immediately was a serious infraction of the unwritten inmates' code. Second, he had put his hands on me in an intimate way. Contrary to popular movie grist, most inmates do not touch in prison. Dr. Foster emphasized that fear of being labeled a homosexual is so high that rather than run the risk, most inmates do not touch at all unless they are actually intimate with each other. Bad enough that the man had made an overt homosexual pass at me, but the fact that I had rejected him would most likely cause him to kill me to prevent news of my rebuff from circulating in the prison and "ruining his reputation." Third, the man was black and I was white. Although the prison officials attempt to maintain good racial relations, it is an incontrovertible truth that racial tension exists in most prisons, just as it does in much of society. Many ethnic groups in prison form gangs. I don't know if my attacker was a gang member. But if he was and word got out that I had stood up to him, Dr. Foster knew that it was not unlikely that I could meet some tragic "accident."

Although I appreciated Dr. Foster's concerns, I knew that if I snitched on my attacker, he would probably be shipped to a tougher prison. But I would not be forgotten by his fellow gang members. Even though Rochester was considered a relatively safe prison, sooner or later—perhaps while I was being transferred from one prison to another—my attacker's gang members would catch up with me.

Consequently, as Dr. Foster continued to press me for the name or description of the man who had crossed the line, I just as adamantly refused to snitch. It was one of the moments in my life where I felt I had to grow up and be a man, to do what I felt was right, regardless of the consequences to me.

In the meantime, the man stalked me any time he saw me, hovering nearby when I was working out at the iron pile or walking across the compound. He never said a word, but he was always there, lurking in a place

439

where he was certain that I saw him, just glaring at me, taunting me by his perpetual presence. It was as though he were saying, "You're mine, Bakker, anytime I want you."

One day, a friend and I were working out at the iron pile and, as usual, my attacker soon showed up. He made no effort to lift weights or do any exercises; he simply stood off to the side and stared at me. Seeing him hovering, as if waiting for the best opportunity to strike at me, had a different effect on me that day. Ordinarily, I was frightened when I saw the man stalking me, but for some reason, on this day I became extremely angry instead. So incensed was I that this man could dominate my life to such an extent, I exploded with anger.

I had not told anyone except Rod and Dr. Foster about the attacker, but I was so enraged at the moment, I broke my self-imposed code of silence and blurted out, "He won't leave me alone!" My friend knew immediately what I meant and guessed what was going on; I didn't have to tell him the details. He waved his hand as if shooing away a mosquito and picked up a heavy free weight. "No problem, Jim," my friend said as he lifted the weight high above his head. "I'll get rid of him for you."

I nearly dropped the dumbbell I was holding. "No! No way! Don't you ever do anything like that. Don't! God will take care of me."

My buddy, a bear of a man himself, laughed aloud as he dropped the weight to the ground. "Okay, okay. Take it easy," he said with another laugh. "I was just trying to help."

Later when I was alone in my cell, I committed the matter of my safety to God. I knew I was no match for the attacker if he really came after me. There was little I could do to defend myself and no place in prison to hide. If he wanted me, sooner or later, I'd be dead meat. On the other hand, I knew that God could protect me if He chose to do so. Or if He chose not to spare my life, I knew I was ready to walk into heaven.

Dr. Foster had a great faith in God's ability to protect me from harm, too. Nonetheless, his knowledge of prison far surpassed my own. He had stood over too many dead bodies in prison to believe that my attacker would soon forget about me and merely move on to a more willing subject.

Dr. Foster finally realized that I was not going to back down and tell. "If you are not going to let me help you," he sighed, "at least do something to protect yourself."

"Like what?" I asked.

"Take the lock off your locker at night—or any time you are in your cell alone—and put it inside a heavy sock. Keep it with you under your pillow as you sleep or somewhere you can reach it immediately in an emergency. If the predator attempts to attack you again, use the lock and sock and whale the tar out of him. Hold the top of your sock closed tightly, and bash him with the other end. Hard. Don't worry, you probably won't kill him, but you might be able to frighten him away."

I was shocked that Dr. Foster, a man pledged to helping inmates make peace with themselves and others, was actually suggesting that I beat another man with a combination lock. Only then did I begin to realize the seriousness of my situation. Yet I couldn't bring myself to take the precaution Dr. Foster suggested. As I had done previously in my life, I felt that if God could not or would not take care of me, then either I wasn't worth taking care of, or He had a different plan in mind. I slept soundly each night and left the combination lock on the locker.

My prayer life improved dramatically, however.

Amazingly, within three weeks, the man who had accosted me was transferred to another prison. As far as I know, Dr. Foster had nothing to do with the man's transfer. To this day, I have never revealed to any inmates the name of the man who had attacked me and I never will. I believe, however, that God knew his name and decided that he needed a new address.

I confess, I was tremendously relieved when I heard the man had been shipped to another location. Not that I didn't believe God could have taken care of me had the man remained in Rochester. But I felt like a person who lives through a violent hurricane. Certainly, God could take care of me if the circumstances reoccur, but for the time being, I was content to count my blessings.

On the other hand, the attack in prison served to focus my attention on an issue that I had never been willing to deal with. This was, after all, not the first time I had been violated by a person of the same sex.

441

43

My Darkest Secret

DR. DANIEL FOSTER WAS ALMOST AS RELIEVED AS I WAS THAT the man who had attacked me had been transferred. In my next counseling session with the psychologist, we talked at length concerning my feelings about the situation. I told Dr. Foster that I now had a more vivid understanding of rape. Fear, anger, intimidation, a sense of being violated by another person, I experienced all of that.

That sense of being violated was something that Dr. Foster and I had already been discussing for more than a year. As our sessions continued week after week, I gradually came to feel that I could trust him with some of my innermost secrets and fears that stemmed back to my preteen years. Dr. Foster had informed me of the wide spectrum of human sexuality issues with which he had dealt in clinical situations. Although Dr. Foster would never have said it directly, I got the impression that Dr. Foster had seen and heard it all, and nothing I ever told him was going to shock him or cause him to think less of me.

I wanted to tell Dr. Foster my darkest secret, but each time I came close to opening up about it, I backed away. Dr. Foster didn't push me any further or faster than I was ready to go, and he respectfully backed off once he sensed that I wasn't ready to continue. We skirted the issue for some time. After each session, I returned to my cell, wishing that I had had the courage to be totally open with him. During our next session, I once again wrestled with whether or not I should trust this man with my ghost from the past.

Finally, one cold morning, as I sat huddled in my big, heavy overcoat in the large easy chair in Dr. Foster's office, I decided I would open up to him. He listened patiently. The story was not easy to tell.

With several weeks remaining during her pregnancy, my mother was trying to turn a heavy mattress by herself. The strain caused her to go into labor and I was born prematurely. I was an extremely tiny baby, so small that my mom and dad had to leave me at the hospital when Mom was discharged. I was placed in an incubator. While I was in the incubator, the heel of my right foot was severely burnt on a heating element, permanently scarring my heel and prolonging my hospital stay. Even after the doctor allowed me to come home, I was small enough to fit into a shoe box. Mom and Dad considered me so fragile that they didn't allow my brothers and sister to even breathe on me as I lay in the bassinet. A gauze material perpetually covered the bassinet during the first months of my life.

Consequently, during my first crucial hours, weeks, and months as a baby, I never experienced the sensation of my family members' touch. My family was not overly expressive of affection anyhow, and I was deprived of what little touch and affection my parents and siblings were accustomed to giving.

As I grew older, my stern, Dutch family members were comfortable with hello and good-bye hugs, but little more expressions of affection than that. Years later, I sometimes joked with my siblings that I was not sure how Mom and Dad ever spent enough time in close proximity to achieve our conception. Our parents were kind, loving, and committed to the family, but affection was not one of their stronger points. Consequently, during my preteen years, although I didn't know it, I was starved for physical touch and attention.

One Sunday night after church, when I was around eleven years of age, I was standing on the front porch of our church, along with a number of other children and adults who had congregated outside after the service to talk. Russell White (not his real name), a young man in our congregation in his late twenties or early thirties, approached me and cheerfully asked, "Hey, Jim, how would you like to go with me over to the drive-in for a hamburger? I'm kind of hungry, aren't you?"

Of course I was hungry, but I was even more awed that this adult would want me, an eleven-year-old boy, to accompany him to the drive-in burger shop. I had heard people say—when they thought they were out of my earshot—that I was very mature for my age and that I had grown up quickly over the past year. I would never have guessed, however, that an adult man would invite me to go someplace with him. My dad was a hard worker who worked his entire adult life at Seal Power Company as a tool and die maker. In addition he was always working one or more part-time jobs selling everything from lightning rods to storm windows to baby cribs in his efforts to support our family; he rarely had the time or energy to take us kids out for hamburgers or anything else.

"Sure, you bet!" I said. "But I better ask my mother and father if it's okay first. I'll be right back." I darted through the crowd into the church and located my parents. I asked permission to go with the family friend. They knew Russell because he and his family were longtime attendees of our church and he was a friend of my brother and sister, so Mother and Dad readily consented. In a flash I was back at Russell's side, and we were walking toward his car.

I felt so big sitting in the front seat of Russell's car, like I was one of the "big guys." I sat up as straight as possible so I could wave good-bye to my friends as Russell and I pulled out of the church parking lot.

Russell took me to the drive-in restaurant, bought me whatever I wanted to eat, and gave me his undivided attention. I felt wonderfully special.

It was almost 10:00 P.M. by the time we finished eating. Russell revved the engine of his car and pulled out onto the highway. I thought it slightly strange that he did not turn the vehicle in the direction of my house. After all, it was getting late, and I had school the next morning. *Maybe Russell has to stop for gas or something*, I thought. But I could see the gas gauge, and it was on full.

Within minutes, Russell had driven the car to the edge of town and was still going.

"Where are we going, Russell?" I asked.

"Oh, I just thought you might like to take a little ride," he answered pleasantly. As soon as the car cleared the city limits, Russell suddenly reached across the seat and placed his hand on my leg. Even through the heavy material of my new Levi's, Russell's hand seemed to sear into my skin.

"I hear you are a big man," said Russell as he slid his hand up my thigh. He smiled at me in the darkness.

I was apprehensive about what was happening, so I didn't answer Russell, but I was extremely aware of where his hand was resting.

As an eleven-year-old boy, I had no prior sexual contact. I hadn't kissed a girl yet at my young age. Like most preadolescent boys, I was, however, becoming increasingly self-conscious about my rapidly maturing body.

Not long before this time, my mother had given me a little booklet designed for Christian boys to inform them about sex. I had no other knowledge about sexual matters; our family did not discuss sex. From reading the book, however, I learned that babies somehow came from sperm.

Once as a pubescent child, I had touched my genitals to the point that a small amount of semen was emitted from my penis. I was horrified! I thought that I had done something really bad. I wanted to put the semen back in me, I was so afraid! That was the extent of my sexual information and my sexual experience before going to the drive-in with Russell.

Russell drove the car onto a deserted dirt road. Other than the beam from the car's headlights, no other lights could be seen anywhere. I was scared, but Russell was so friendly and kind, he allayed my concerns about his probing fingers. When Russell pulled off the road, turned off the car's ignition, and unzipped my jeans, I was alarmed. But as Russell kept talking to me about how great I was, I felt almost proud that Russell would give me so much attention. I thought, *So this is what having a buddy is all about! This must be what the big guys do.*

Russell continued to reassure me that what he was doing was okay. Maybe he could tell that I was nervous, so he kept telling me that everything was fine, that "this was nice." Carefully but deliberately, he reached inside my underwear and put his hand on me. I was frightened at first, but Russell was not being mean to me, so I assumed that what he was doing was okay.

(Parents, please never assume that your children know what is right or wrong when it comes to "good touches and bad touches"—especially if you do not talk to them honestly and frankly about the subject of sex.)

Russell then unzipped his pants and instructed me to do to him what he was doing to me.

"No!" I said, "I'm too scared. It's dirty."

"Oh, don't be afraid. It's okay, I'm clean. I just took a bath," Russell said kindly. He never raised his voice to me or was mean to me in any way. He simply told me how special I was. Many people assume that child molesters beat their victims into submitting to their desires. I am convinced the exact opposite is true in most cases. The molester gives the child the love, attention, self-esteem, or kindness that the child may not be getting from his or her family or friends. That's what Russell did to me.

He did not force me to do anything, but he kept pressuring me gently

445

until I did everything he wanted me to do. When it was over, he drove me home and dropped me off. I went inside the house and went to bed. I did not talk to anyone about what had happened to me. I had no desire to tell anyone, nor would I have known how to explain what had happened to me. Instead, I kept the secret hidden deep within me.

Over the next few years, Russell was a frequent figure in my life. Often he took me out after church, ostensibly for a hamburger, but usually for much more. Sometimes he took me to isolated construction sites; at other times we simply stopped along the road somewhere. Occasionally, my parents naively permitted me to mow the lawn at Russell's house. Russell took advantage of those opportunities. He took me up to his bedroom and molested me. He did not have to purchase my cooperation with candy or gifts, as many child molesters do. I allowed Russell to do whatever he wanted to do to me and I tried to comply with his requests because he lavished attention and caring touches upon me. I realized from the first that something was wrong, but my deep need for attention was being met. I felt ashamed, but who could I talk to about such a thing?

Soon I became interested in girls and enjoyed an extremely active dating life throughout junior high and high school. I saw Russell less and less, and eventually he faded from the scene, but for nearly forty years, I would live in fear that what he had done to me would one day be discovered.

I wanted to have sex with some of the girls I dated in high school, but in the 1950s, most girls did not have sex before marriage, and most boys respected the young woman's wishes. Certainly some teenagers were having premarital sex in the fifties, but it was not a socially accepted practice, and unmarried mothers were frowned upon. Furthermore, as I came into a genuine relationship with Jesus Christ during my late high school years, I learned that God intended marriage to be a sacred covenant relationship between a husband and a wife. According to the Bible, all sex outside of marriage is sin.

Knowing the truth from God's Word did not keep me from being tempted sexually. I experienced all the usual sexual temptations that teenagers encountered and more. I spent many evenings parking down at the lake necking and "petting" with my dates. Inevitably, if I dated the same young woman for any length of time, the relationship took on sexual overtones. Nevertheless, because the message of the Bible was beginning to take hold in my heart, I knew there were lines I could not cross. For the most part, I was able to restrain expressions of sexual intimacy until Tammy Faye and I married and established a loving, vibrant sexual relationship.

For years I thought that what had happened between Russell and me had been my fault, that somehow I had brought it on myself, that I had encouraged his attentions. I wondered, *Did I invite Russell's actions? Could I have avoided them?* After all, Russell hadn't physically forced himself upon me. He hadn't held a gun to my head or threatened me with bodily harm if I didn't do things with him sexually. As a child, I had willingly consented to his attention, so perhaps there was a part of me that was not heterosexual, but homosexual. In my worst moments, when I experienced rejection or severe criticism of almost any kind, the ghosts swarmed through my thoughts.

Those ghosts were never very far from the television studio sets upon which I had spent most of my career. Especially frightening were the worries that someday, someone was going to stand up in one of our PTL audiences, and announce, "I know something about you, Jim Bakker."

At times I wondered if maybe someday God Himself would require me to stand up and reveal what had happened to me as a child to our studio audience and to the world. Stranger things had happened on our sets as we tried to spontaneously and immediately obey the Holy Spirit's directions.

Worse yet, what if I shared with the world what had happened to me as a child and nobody believed me? In the 1970s and '80s our society rarely discussed child abuse in public. Child molestation and its long-term effects have only recently become topics of a plethora of magazine articles and titillating talk shows. When Heritage USA was booming and our PTL programs were garnering their best Arbitron ratings, I felt that to reveal my secret past to our audience would be the kiss of death. So I held the secret inside, telling no one.

I certainly couldn't reveal the details of my past to the church at large, or to other pastors, or to my denominational leaders. At that point in our Christian history, the impression was given—and had to be perpetuated at all costs—that things such as child molestation did not happen in "nice" Christian families and churches. It was easier for the church to pretend these things didn't happen than to open up and deal honestly with the broken lives that still carried the unspeakable pain.

Consequently, for over forty years, I lived with the fear of exposure. I never told a soul about what had happened to me as a child and how it had impacted my sexual identity. I had hinted at the subject with Vi Azvedo, head of our pastoral counseling ministry at PTL, but could never bring myself to discuss such a sensitive subject with her. Vi was a good friend and a counselor, but she was also part of my staff.

I didn't even tell Tammy Faye. I was afraid she might reject me if she ever

447

found out about the molestation. Looking back, I now think she could have handled it. At the time, however, I dared not risk her rejection, so I lived every day in fear that somehow, some way, some day, she would find out.

Perhaps it took going to prison and losing everything I had ever held dear for me to finally muster the courage to tell someone about my past. Dr. Foster was the first person to whom I chose to reveal my true self.

Dr. Foster exhibited no signs of surprise at my intimate revelations. Quite the contrary. Because of his dealings with cases of molestation, he had suspected that something such as what I told him had been a part of my past. He said that incidents of child molestation were much more common than most people think and that I was not some sort of freak for having experienced it. He did, however, tell me that because of the molestation, it was likely that a part of me had never truly grown up emotionally. Part of my emotional growth was stalled back in the 1950s as a little eleven-year-old boy.

As Dr. Foster and I began to deal with what had happened to me, one of the first things he did was to help me understand that I had not brought the attentions and perverted actions of Russell upon myself. I had not gone after Russell in any way, trying to seduce him. He pursued me.

All my life I had thought that the molestation had been my fault. But Russell was an adult; I was a boy. I had not been sexually active; Russell was the first sexual encounter in my lifetime, and unfortunately, the relationship scarred me for life.

Throughout the years of 1991 and 1992, Dr. Foster and I walked together through almost every aspect of my life. One day after we had been working through many of the effects my childhood experiences had had upon my adult life, I could no longer avoid the one question that had haunted me throughout my life. I looked Dr. Foster straight in the eyes and asked, "Am I gay?"

Dr. Foster did not blink. "No, Jim. You are not a homosexual."

I sat back in my chair, relieved at last to hear someone whom I trusted, a professional in his field, tell me that my fears were unfounded. Dr. Foster confirmed to me that I am heterosexual, an avid heterosexual. He jokingly said, "No man can love women as much as you do and be a homosexual. It is obvious you're not gay."

Dr. Foster pointed out that I was the perfect victim for a child molester. I was compliant, responsive to the requests and demands of adults, shy, not too likely to talk, especially reluctant to talk in a group setting, and yet I had good social skills. I could keep up appearances; I could maintain a public persona even when I was falling apart internally.

Dr. Foster and I discussed how my situation was tragically replicated in the lives of many pastors and missionaries, who know how to present a persona that is perfectly appropriate for the public, but they try to maintain that same persona in private and it is impossible to do so. When they need to be pouring their hearts out to God, to their marriage partners, or to their closest associates, they are unable to do so because they are afraid of exposure. It is not until they crash and burn that people find out that there was something wrong all along.

Dr. Foster noted that some of the most hurting people he has had to deal with over the years in his profession have been pastors and pastors' wives. Just because they can speak well, wear nice clothes, and present a positive image in public doesn't mean they have it all together in their private lives. Part of the reason is that when they realize they have a problem, there is no one they feel they can turn to, nobody with whom they can share their innermost thoughts and fears. In the past, career-wise, it has not been safe or expedient for ministers or their family members to seek help for personal problems. By sharing my experience, I hope that aspect of the ministry will change for some people.

In time, Dr. Foster and I went on to discuss how my sexual identity had been confused by my childhood experiences. Dr. Foster told me that I was not alone, that sadly millions of men secretly worry that they might be gay or have homosexual tendencies because of something that happened as a child or as a teenager. In some cases, men may seek to compensate for and overcome this fear by being excessively rough, tough, and macho. Dr. Foster and I also discussed my fear of exposure at PTL and throughout my life. I admitted to him that, perhaps because of my simple upbringing, or possibly because of my experience with Russell, I had always felt like something of an impostor. I feared that someday I would be exposed, because like many successful men, I had a fear that I really wasn't good enough to be where I was, especially at the top of the Christian world. Something inside of me kept saying, "You know you really don't belong here. You aren't good enough to be here."

About this time I came across another helpful book, *Emotional Freedom*, by Dr. Mario E. Rivera. In his book, Dr. Rivera suggested that one of the best ways to diffuse our fear of being discovered for who we really are is to

Accept God's unconditional love for you. The basis of fear is the belief that you are not acceptable. As long as you determine that you are not loved, you will have fear. But if you accept God's unconditional love for you, your fear and your pride will vanish. This is clearly seen in 1 John 4:18: "There is no fear in love; but perfect love casteth out fear. . . ."[1]

I determined in prison that I was going to start believing what I had always preached, that "God loves you, He really does." I had to admit to and take responsibility for my moral failures, which I have done. I had to forgive Russell for his actions and I had to forgive myself for mine. I realized that my healing would be moment by moment, event by event. I can say with confidence that I am not now, nor have I ever been a homosexual. But don't expect to hear me lashing out at gay men and women. I never railed at homosexual men and lesbian women in my past ministry, and I am certainly not going to start doing so now. I understand some of the hurt and pain they are going through. I don't have all the answers, but I know some of the questions. I want always to express Christ's love and compassion.

If Christians are truly going to live up to our name, we must ask, "What would Jesus do?" What would Jesus do with a girl who finds herself today with an unwanted pregnancy, the man obsessed with alcohol, and the drug dealer or user, the homosexual or lesbian, the prisoner, the poor and the homeless? I believe if Jesus were physically walking our streets today, you would find Him with His arms around the people at the abortion clinic, in the gay bar, and in the AIDS ward, in the prisons, and sitting on the curb with the homeless and the drug addicts. If we stopped playing our religious games long enough, we might hear Him saying, "Come unto me, all ye that labour and are heavy laden, and I will give you rest. Take my yoke upon you, and learn of me; for I am meek and lowly in heart: and ye shall find rest unto your souls. For my yoke is easy, and my burden is light" (Matt. 11:28-30 KJV).

As for me, I am free. I no longer have to fear exposure. I no longer have to placate people, especially unscrupulous people, for fear that they might snoop around in my past and discover some deep, dark secret.

I knew that I was well on my way to facing reality when I was able to sit down in the prison visiting room with Tammy Sue and Jamie Charles and tell them the entire story of being molested as a child. They accepted it much better than I expected.

God was truly changing me. But the next change surprised even me.

44

What Went Wrong at PTL?

HAVING FINALLY RESOLVED SOME OF THE ISSUES THAT HAD dogged me all of my life, I should not have been surprised when God began to really bear down on me in prison. God continued to take away the last vestiges of my pride. I had nothing left to cling to other than God Himself—which was exactly what He wanted.

As difficult as it was, I realized that I had to let go of Tammy Faye as well. I still loved her and would have taken her back in a moment, but I had to face the fact that she had decided to go a different direction in her life. She was no longer my wife and, from all indications, would most likely soon be the wife of someone else. It hurt me to do so, but finally, many weeks after the divorce, I took off my wedding ring and mailed it to my son, Jamie Charles. I knew Jamie was having a difficult time accepting all that had happened, so I wanted him to know that I felt as he did. I wrote to him:

> The pain of losing your mother and the grief I bear will not go away. I still love her very much. When I married her, it was for life, "till death do us part." It is hard to accept that we are no longer married, but I must face reality.
>
> Today I took off my wedding ring, and I want you to have it. Jamie Charles, I love you more than I have words to tell you. I want the best for you. Please always put God first in your life. Remember, God looks

at the big picture; we only see a little part. Keep your hope in God and your eyes on heaven.

Stay close to Sissy. She really loves you; take care of each other. I love you and am proud of you!

Love,
Dad

After Tammy Faye moved to California following our divorce, Jamie moved from Orlando to St. Petersburg. The move was difficult for Jamie; he had to leave what little security in life he had, but with Tammy Faye gone, our church doors closed, and my daughter moving her ministry offices to Largo, there was little reason for Jamie to stay in Orlando.

Our friends Bob and Molly D'Andrea gave Jamie an apartment in which to live, right next door to their home. Bob was the president of the Christian Television Network, based in Largo, Florida. Ironically, it was a telethon at Bob's flagship station, WCLF Channel 22, that took me to Clearwater in 1980, where I met Jessica Hahn. If anyone in Christian television had a right to be angry with me and unforgiving, it was Bob D'Andrea.

Instead, Bob gave my boy a home while I was in prison. Not only did he give Jamie a place to live, he also gave Jamie a job.

I received a letter from gospel singer Nancy Harmon in which she wrote: I just returned from Tampa. I got the shock of my life at Channel 22. Who was behind one of those cameras but Jamie Charles Bakker! He looks great! "What a joy: What the devil meant for destruction, God has made good!"

Nancy went on to encourage me: "God loves you! And He remembers all your hurts and fears! But He also remembers all the good you have done! It's not over yet!"

I appreciated Bob D'Andrea taking care of my son when I was unable to do so, and I appreciated Nancy's letter of encouragement. About the same time, I received a letter from Pat and Shirley Boone:

You'd be surprised how often Shirley and I think about you, and how many times we pray for the Lord to comfort and strengthen you, as you continue to go through this incredible ordeal. I hope that you've taken great solace from the story of Joseph, who "did time" almost entirely because he had tried to serve God. I'm convinced, as so many of us are, that what you have been going through is principally because you have been an outspoken leader and done great exploits in the Kingdom, and the enemy of our souls has done his best to negate the great good you've done — though we know he is defeated, and God will more than make it up to you.

Pat, too, expressed hope for my future:

I hope your days are being spent profitably, and I am quite sure the Lord is ministering to you, assuring you of His love, and also preparing you for more good to come. We'll look forward to the first opportunity we have to hug your neck, when the Lord makes that possible. Just know you continue to be loved and respected by those who've seen the real Jim Bakker.

Your brother,
Pat

Not everyone who wrote to me during this period shared the Boones' gracious sentiments. Some people were still extremely angry at me for allowing PTL to be devastated by scandal and for the repercussions that flowed out of Heritage USA in ever-widening circles. One such person was Margaret Anderson Mauzy. Margaret and I had been classmates at Muskegon Senior High School in 1959. Her father, Ken Anderson, was a pioneer in Christian films, founding first Gospel Films and then Ken Anderson Films in Winona Lake, Indiana. Margaret's initial letter to me expressed what many people may have felt but were unwilling to say:

I've wanted to write to you for a long time, but it's probably a good thing I didn't. You've come to mind often, and I've committed you to prayer each time. But to be honest, for the longest time I really struggled dealing with the damage created by your situation at PTL. You'll never know, Jim, how Satan has used you to hurt the church. [Financial] giving to Christian organizations has been affected unilaterally, but the skepticism I've found toward Christianity by so many of my nonChristian friends cuts deeply.

When people find out I went to school with you, the first thing they are anxious to ask is almost always the same: "What was he like?"

I have to tell them that I didn't know you well, but from what I remember, you seemed like a really nice guy. They are always skeptical about that. People just can't seem to accept that you took money, "In God's Name," often from people who didn't have much, and took so much for yourself. I guess I have the same problem. We've known Billy

Graham for years. I admire him so much. Although he lives comfortably, he lives within his means. He has a reasonable salary, and he took the proceeds from his books. How I wish you had done the same thing.

I tell people that I'm sure you started your ministry with all the right intentions. Most people don't understand the pressure of fundraising, and how when an organization mushrooms as yours did, it becomes a burden just to keep it going. I'm sure it was easy to feel the end justifies the means.

My parents could be wealthy today themselves, were it not for the way they have shared any profit they ever made with the Lord. God has used them in a mighty way, and blessed them with seven children who love the Lord with all their hearts. Same with spouses. And all their grandchildren, all 13 of them, have made a profession of faith.

I hope you don't look at the secular world as the reason you are in prison, but really come to grips with the fact that God never asked for anything in His name to be grandiose . . . at least not in the material sense. PTL got to where it spent more energy raising money than it did saving souls. I don't find anywhere in the Bible where we are to come before God's people pleading for money all the time. And yet, toward the end of your time at PTL, and on all the televangelists' shows currently on TV, that seems to be the primary reason they are on the air.

But you are paying for your mistakes. Too harshly, in my humble opinion. I don't think the justice system has been impartial in the way they have handled your sentencing. I'm glad to see that your time has been reduced. But in comparison to other crimes of equal severity, I feel your sentence was unfair.

So I'll continue to pray for you, Jim, to remember you as that kid I knew walking the halls of Muskegon Senior High. Thank goodness all our sins are forgiven at the Cross. I'm sure it is very difficult and depressing in prison, but it's my understanding that although times are tough for you, you are clinging to your faith in Jesus Christ. My prayer will be that you will remain strong. That you will continue to grow in Christ. That you will be able to help others who are hurting. And, when you leave prison, you will be in a position to really make a difference in people's lives. Not to start another PTL as it was known. The guy who runs it now goes around pleading and begging just as before. But that you will know God's true will for your life, and in a simple, quiet way, go about the business of living for the Lord.

Keep your head up, Jim. God isn't finished with you yet.

Margaret then went on to describe her work with an organization known as InterComm, which her family founded to take gospel audiovisual materials overseas. She asked me to consider praying for their work. She then closed her letter by saying:

> Hope I didn't offend you in any way. I just wanted you to know that someone from your past, who was not involved in any way with PTL, still remembers you in Christ's love and prayer.
>
> Your friend,
Margaret Anderson Mauzy

When I first received Margaret's letter, I was deeply hurt. I had received other critical letters since coming to prison, but this was from one of my high school classmates. More important than that, I had always highly respected Margaret's father as an innovator in communicating the gospel message. I had even appeared in one of his films when I was a teenager. For Margaret to be so upset was deeply disconcerting to me.

I had already apologized to the Christian community as best I could; I didn't know what else I should do. I continued to grieve deeply over the negative fallout my sin caused to the entire Body of Christ. No amount of apologizing could ever make up for the worldwide denigration of the role of evangelists and television ministries that resulted from my moral failure. Most important of all, I had besmirched the name of the Lord Jesus Christ, my blessed Savior and the lover of my soul. What could I possibly do to ever make up for that?

At times, I honestly felt that the only thing that would have satisfied some people that justice had been done would have been for me to die a horrible death or to commit suicide. I quickly recognized, however, that such thoughts did not come from God, but from the evil one, whose goal was to destroy not just my ministry but my soul. Furthermore, I had to grapple with the truth that as far-reaching as my sin was, nothing that I could do would ever erase the effects of sin. Only the blood of Jesus could do that. For me to think that there was anything I could do other than to humbly apologize to those whom I had hurt, would be the height of arrogance and an insult to what Jesus did on the cross when His blood paid for all our sins, even the far-reaching ones.

For these reasons, I knew I could not change Margaret's mind or her heart, yet I felt compelled to answer her letter. I wrote:

Dear Margaret,

Thank you so much for your thoughtful letter. It was with mixed emotions that I read it. I was happy to hear from someone I went to school with and whose father I have admired throughout my entire life. I even had a small part in a 1950s gospel film called *Teenage Rock*. On one hand, I am keenly aware of the hurt I have caused the Body of Christ and I am deeply sorry and have asked God's forgiveness and that of the church world. I hope you will find it in your heart to forgive me.

You brought up things in your letter that hurt because they are not true. It is hard sometimes to sit in prison year after year and not try to vindicate yourself. But God's Word says, "Dearly beloved, avenge not yourselves, but rather give place unto wrath: for it is written, Vengeance is mine; I will repay, saith the Lord" (Rom. 12:19 KJV). About 90 percent of what the press has written [about PTL and me] is not true, or was a great distortion of the truth.

You said, "Billy Graham has a reasonable salary, and he took the proceeds from his books."

Tammy and I gave nearly 100 percent of our proceeds from royalties to the ministry from our books, records, and tapes. We personally gave over $8 million in royalties to PTL over our last three years there.

I then went on to explain to Margaret the many ministries in which PTL was involved.

I am not trying to justify myself to you, but I wanted to share a side of the story not told and that no one seems to want to hear. I take full responsibility for my moral failure and the fall of PTL, but I did not commit the crimes I have been accused of and am in prison for. Contrary to popular belief, I am not a rich man. All the money I have in the world is in my commissary account here in prison. I have no home, or car, or retirement. My sixteen-year-old son is living in an apartment loaned to him by friends. My daughter has been living below poverty level since I have been in prison. I am not asking for your pity—I actually believe self-pity is a sin. My heart is right with God and I feel that I must believe the Word of God and accept the fact that all that has happened will somehow work together for good.

Please forgive me for talking about the past. God has taught me so much as I have studied His Word. I do not want to go back to things the way they were. We are facing the last days and a time when only those who are sold out totally to God will be able to stand for Jesus

Christ. . . . Since I got your letter, I have prayed for you and your
father, Ken Anderson Films, and InterComm. May God bless you and
supply your needs as you reach out to a world without Christ.

I had Tammy Sue send Margaret some of the letters I had sent to the
people who had written to me in prison, one of the letters I sent to Alan
Dershowitz explaining some of the details of my trial, and some other
materials about PTL.

Two weeks later, I received another letter from Margaret. In her letter,
she acknowledged that her first letter reflected her own heart that was
hurt, and that of so many Christian ministries that had been hurt because
of what I had done, and that she had vented her hurt and pain on me.
Margaret wrote:

> I apologize for the self-serving nature of my first letter. While it might
> have made me feel better, as a Christian, I should have been more sen-
> sitive to how it would make you feel, since the circumstances that have
> put you in prison are in the past, and I have no control over them. You
> are correct when you say it is God's right to judge, but I'm sure you
> understand the human element we all face when we are made aware of
> difficult circumstances such as your involvement at PTL. Thank good-
> ness God is so forgiving, as I require His forgiveness on a daily basis.
>
> So, of course I forgive you, and appreciate the forgiving nature of
> your letter to me. . . . Reading from the depths of your heart, I believe
> God is preparing you so when you are released, you will have a new
> ministry for which you will be especially prepared. And upon your
> release, you will have a certainty of how God wants you to use your tal-
> ents for Him.

From that day on, Margaret Anderson Mauzy and I became good
friends. We corresponded regularly while I was in prison, and she and her
family prayed for my family members, as I prayed for hers. Her letters
teemed with encouragement and hope for a strong future ministry for me.
Margaret also wrote kind letters to my children and even secured a copy of
the movie *Teenage Rock* for them from her dad's film archives. My kids got
a huge charge out of seeing their father at age sixteen in the movie.

Among the surprise letters I received during this time was one that
came from Thomas E. Trask, then general treasurer of the Assemblies of
God and the heir apparent to the top spot. His letter took me by surprise,
not because he was not kind and godly, but because much had been made

457

of the fact that I had been defrocked by the Assemblies after the scandal had broken in 1987. Moreover, when I had attempted to be reconciled to the denomination in 1988, I found the doors closed. Now it seemed the doors were opening just a crack. Reverend Trask told me that he had been preaching in Arkansas that week, and the special music for the services was provided by Bob and Jeanne Johnson, former singers at PTL. Reverend Trask wrote:

> When they introduced me, I made comment of their ministry and the good days of PTL. After the service, when we had time to fellowship, Bob said, "Brother Trask, I was happy to hear you refer to the good days at PTL." And they were just that, Jim, good days. In fact, you can't travel across America and in our churches without finding people who were ministered to or helped in some way by PTL.

Many of my friends who wrote to me during this time expressed the belief that God had something more for me. My friends had much more faith in that regard than I had. C. M. Ward, for example, wrote to me, "It won't be long until you are circulating again. We know in our hearts that things are going to look up for you. Keep the faith!"

One letter particularly touched my heart. It came from Dr. Evelyn Spencer, one of our former PTL Board Members, a vibrant black woman whom we affectionately referred to as "Rev. Ev." The name stuck, and before long, Dr. Spencer took to calling herself Rev. Ev.

The interesting thing about Dr. Spencer's letter was that she started out by asking me about myself, how I was doing, how I was feeling, and then filling me in on some current events in her life. Suddenly, however, Rev. Ev stopped writing a personal letter and began writing prophetically, as though she were expressing God's heart and His thoughts were flowing through her pen.

> Be encouraged my son. All is well though outward circumstances may not appear to be. I know your heart. Fault-finding is not my forte. I am in the blessing business. I and only I can make the crooked road straight. I bring mountains down and valleys up and give you a plain path. I have a definite purpose and plan for you, and it shall come to pass. This is not the end. Hold on to Me as you have never held before. Give up everything but never give up on Me, the Lord your God.
>
> Some things must be removed, not for punishment, nor for vindication, but for the best to be manifested. Know this, the latter glory

shall be greater than the former. Your foundation is sure. The buildings were built with untempered mortar. But now, you shall rise as the phoenix from the ashes. Your life is not over. Your work has just begun. It is the end of an era and a new beginning. Little did you know when your compassion—which was really Mine—for your fellow hurting clergy with no pensions, no homes, no one to reach out and touch them in the midst of their hurt, only those turning their backs, caused you to reach and make provisions. Little did you know that you would be a first-hand partaker. But realize this, My son. All great work for Me is done first in the individual soul of the worker.

Hold fast to your crown. Let no one take it from you. Maintain your own heart pure in the midst of adverse circumstances. You must not expect to live in a world where all is harmony. You must not expect to live where others are in unbroken accord with you.

You can't put things right. That is My job to do. I am Wisdom. Only My wisdom can rightly decide anything, settle any problem. So rely on the Lord your God. *All* is *well*.

It is against the tide you must direct your efforts. Your effort, My blessing, work hand in hand. Be encouraged, get up, and get in the flow, listen for My voice.

Know you are loved and cared for. The end is in sight. An opening to new vistas.

Rev. Ev made no comments on this portion of her letter; she simply closed her letter and let me grapple with the application of the message.

What am I to make of these things? I wondered. If I truly was in prison to get to know God better, what was it that He wanted me to learn? Through my counseling with Dr. Foster, I was learning how to forgive myself for my past failures. I was also doing a fairly good job of forgiving those people who had hurt me. At times, though, I still had difficulty reconciling my circumstances and how I came to be in prison with God's plan for my life.

Beyond that, although I was thrilled to have finally faced reality about who I was as a person, and as a Christian, I often wondered if I had any future. Was I washed up? Was I out of the ministry for good? Had I sinned so badly that God had replaced me, never to use my life for His glory again? I was not concerned about ever having a megaministry again. I no longer desired to be the head of anything, but as a Christian, grateful for what Jesus had done for me and the forgiveness that God had given to me, I wanted to give my life back to Him in some sort of service. I knew that God could use me somehow inside prison, and I was honored and satisfied with that.

Sometimes I felt that if I ever got out of prison alive, I should just go find a cabin in the woods and live as a hermit, not trying to be involved in any sort of ministry. Nevertheless, I still wondered at times if there was some larger purpose for all of this. Was there something else God wanted to do in my life?

Questions still plagued my mind: "God, what are You doing to me? What do You want from me? Lord, so many people have been saying so many conflicting things—what is the truth? What is Your Word on these things? Were those preachers correct back in 1987, when they said that I was through, that I would never preach again? Their words echoed in my mind, "The Bakkers' ministry here is over."

I had been studying the words of Jesus, so not surprisingly, as I sought the answer from God concerning the questions that rankled in my heart and mind, He directed me to the words of Jesus, specifically, Matthew 7:15.

As my eyes settled on the verse, I began to shudder. For a moment, I thought that perhaps I was trying to do what I had done so many times at PTL, focusing on a particular Scripture that said what I wanted to find. I searched my heart and asked God once again to show me in His Word where I could find the answers. Again and again, I felt God leading me back to Matthew 7:15. The verse read, "Beware of false prophets, who come to you in sheep's clothing."

What was this? *False prophets*? I had always assumed that false prophets would come blatantly preaching antichristian messages, the Beast-of-Revelation type of messages, and we Christians would recognize them, stand up, and shout, "Aha! That is a false prophet!" Here, however, God was showing me that the false prophets were more likely to appear innocuously, that they would look and sound like sheep in the Father's fold, but actually they are ravaging wolves. *The Living Bible* says these false teachers, these wolves, "will tear you apart" (7:15).

As I read on, I was even more stunned. These were some of the most radical words I had ever read, and this passage of Scripture literally changed my life!

The Scripture said, "You will know them by their fruits" (Matt. 7:16). For most of my Christian life I had evaluated other believers and especially myself according to our *works*. It suddenly hit me that God was not all that impressed with our works; He wants to see spiritual fruit in our lives. I began to understand that spiritual fruit did not merely mean bringing in a harvest of converts to Christianity, as important as evangelism is to God. The Lord was showing me that He was more concerned with the charac-

460

ter of our lives rather than what we could do for Him. I remembered the Scripture, "But the fruit of the Spirit is love, joy, peace, longsuffering, kindness, goodness, faithfulness, gentleness, self-control. Against such there is no law" (Gal. 5:22).

As I looked at my own life as well as the lives of the people involved in toppling me from the presidency of PTL, I asked, "Where is the spiritual fruit?" God was showing me that I should not try to evaluate anyone on the basis of their actions, words, works, or abilities, but only by their spiritual fruit.

How can you tell whether a man or woman is a real Christian, a person who is in love with and living for Jesus? Ask yourself, "Does that person have love? Joy? Peace? Is he or she patient? Gentle?" The Bible says we will know them by their fruits, not by their talents. We don't have to judge them; we will automatically *know* them by their fruit.

One of the worst mistakes I made during my tenure at PTL was that I became enamored by men and women who had talent, gifts, and abilities. I stood in awe of great preachers, teachers, singers, and musicians, often knowing that some of them were not living according to the standards of the Bible . . . but they had such talents!

I was aware that sometimes at PTL we had people on our programs or on our staff who were living with willful sin in their lives. I knew it, and I winked at it because of their spiritual gifts. I knew what they were doing, and I allowed individuals to sin flagrantly and repeatedly, without calling them on it.

Perhaps I was reluctant to confront someone else about his or her misconduct for fear that someone might point a finger at my own sin. Regardless of the reason, I was wrong; I was the leader, the spiritual head of the ministry, and I should not have tolerated known, willful misconduct simply because of a person's ability to sing, preach, or perform miracles in Jesus' name. Admittedly, at times, I tried to give individuals the benefit of the doubt. At other times, a member of my staff or I confronted certain individuals about their conduct, and in an effort to restore them, we forgave them, counseled them, and kept them on our payroll. Unfortunately, that was not always possible with some people. In later years, some of my most virulent attackers were individuals whom we finally had to let go because of repeated, flagrant infractions of not simply the standards of our work environment, but the principles of God's Word.

On the other hand, I tended to overlook some of the things I saw and heard backstage at PTL before and after programs because the person involved was so talented. One of the things I did not fully understand was that it is possible to preach about God, play an instrument or sing for God, and even perform miracles in His name, yet be totally out of step with Him in our personal lives. The reason this can happen is twofold: First God's gifts and callings are irrevocable (Rom. 11:29 NIV). God does not take back His gifts, even when we use them unwisely or for our own glory rather than His. What evil and damage can be done by a man or woman who has a gift of God but whose heart is far from Him. Second, God honors His own Word and the faith of His people. That is why it is possible for people to be converted, filled with the Holy Spirit, blessed, healed, and all sorts of other things, even while the minister or musician who is bringing the message is an utter reprobate.

As I continued studying Matthew 7, however, my eyes began to open. Jesus repeated the concept of recognizing true men and women of God by their fruits, and then He drove home the message even more emphatically. Jesus said,

> Not everyone who says to Me, "Lord, Lord," shall enter the kingdom of heaven, but he who does the will of My Father in heaven. Many will say to Me in that day, "Lord, Lord, have we not prophesied in Your name, cast out demons in Your name, and done many wonders in Your name?" And then I will declare to them, "I never knew you; depart from Me, you who practice lawlessness!" (vv. 21-23)

I thought, *That doesn't make sense. How could Jesus not know them? The Bible says He knows when a sparrow falls to a ground, and how many hairs are on our heads. If somebody was casting out devils in Jesus' name, surely He would know him, wouldn't He? How could Jesus not know someone who was a prophet? Or someone who was performing great miracles in His name?*

I was puzzled. Certainly I had read this passage before, but I had always applied it to people who did not really regard the Bible as authoritative. As I read the passage carefully, however, and studied the words in the original Greek language, I noticed that the people to whom Jesus was referring had legitimate gifts. They really did prophesy, not only speaking forth the truth of God's Word, but declaring predictive prophecies as well. They actually did cast out demons; they did perform mighty miracles. They did "many wonders," all in the name of Jesus (v. 22). I looked up that phrase in the Greek and I discovered that the root word for the phrase was *dunamis*, which in various forms can mean, "power, powerful, able, capable, miraculous, abundance, a worker of miracles, strong, or mighty." It is the root from which we get our words *dynamic* and *dynamite*.

As I reread the passage with that understanding, I realized that Jesus was describing people who would say to Him, "Jesus, we did powerful things in Your name. We had dynamite choirs. I was a dynamic preacher. We built wonderful buildings in Your name. We did wonderful works, all in Your name."

Yet Jesus said that He did not know them!

The point was not lost on me that we had done all those things at PTL. We had dynamic singers and musicians. We hosted some of the greatest preachers in the world. And yes, we built a great television network and a fabulous Christian retreat center. Beyond that, we had some miracle workers at PTL who astounded me with their supernatural gifts. The horrifying thought struck me, *Could it be possible that after all we had done at PTL, that our buildings, programs, and talented ministers were not really what God wanted from us?*

I had to find out. What did Jesus mean, He did not *know* those gifted people who had done such great exploits in His name? Once again, I went back to the original language of the New Testament and began looking up the various words for *know* that are used. What I discovered nearly scared me to death!

In Matthew 7:23, the word translated as "know" comes from the Greek word *ginosko*. It is the same word that is used in Luke 1:34, when Mary was first informed by the angel that she was to conceive and give birth to a child. Mary innocently replied, "How shall this be, seeing I know not a man?" (KJV). Mary was saying, "I have never been intimate with a man. I have never known a man in the most intimate way a woman and a man can know each other."

I found that in other places in the New Testament, a different word is used for *know*. For instance, on the night before Jesus was crucified, Peter, one of His inner circle of friends, denied three times that he knew Jesus. Peter's most vehement denial can be found in Matthew 26:74: "Then began he to curse and to swear, saying, 'I do not know the Man!' Immediately a rooster crowed."

The word for *know* used here, I discovered, was *eido*, meaning "to perceive with the physical sight." It is a completely different word than the one Mary used to describe an intimate relationship . . . and the word Jesus used to describe the lack of such an intimate relationship between Himself and the miracle workers in Matthew 7:22-23.

Jesus was saying, "Yes, these people did wonderful works in my name, but I never knew them. I never had an intimate relationship with them; they never had an intimate relationship with Me!"

463

I thought about myself during my years at PTL. I had gotten so busy trying to do something great for God and for His people, I totally missed the point. Although I talked a great deal about Jesus—and in my heart I truly loved Him—I allowed myself to be drawn away from my first love. Instead of fostering an intimate relationship with Him, I loved the spectacular, the supernatural, the signs and wonders.

For instance, when I heard a great song on one of our programs, I was prone to think, *My! What an anointing of God!* Now, I realize that sometimes it was God's anointing, but oftentimes it was not. I loved music, and still do; music can be a tremendous tool to help us praise and worship God. Music itself, however, is a neutral element. Some people can go to a Broadway show or a rock concert and be moved equally as much as I was at PTL by a great performance.

Similarly, I thought that because a man or woman had a spiritual gift, he or she must be close to Jesus. At PTL, we sometimes went bonkers over the ministries of individuals who I knew were not in a right relationship with God. With some I wondered if they had an intimate relationship with Jesus. With others I wondered if they had any relationship with Jesus at all! But because they had a healing ministry, or a gift of discerning spirits, or were gifted in "a word of knowledge," which was often expressed by an ability to look into people's lives and accurately describe certain circumstances, I thought that these ministers must be of God. Now I am not so sure about some; others I am positive were not.

Because I was so enamored with talented people and laid such emphasis upon the ability to perform, I now realize that I was setting people up, preconditioning them to accept an Antichrist who will be able to perform great miracles. But the power source for those miracles will not be God. Jesus said that in the last days, "For false christs and false prophets will rise and . . . deceive, if possible, even the elect" (Mark 13:22). The apostle John warned, "For they are spirits of demons, performing signs" (Rev. 16:14).

Jesus became upset with people who were always looking for another sign, another miracle to prove who He was. Jesus said, "Unless you people see signs and wonders, you will by no means believe" (John 4:48). He wants us to believe in Him for Himself, not simply for the miraculous, wonderful things He can do.

At PTL, I was always looking for a new spiritual sensation, a new truth, a new revelation, preaching a gospel "of stuff," when all the time, I was missing one of the most basic truths of all: Jesus wants us to have an intimate relationship with Him.

Not that we did not emphasize Jesus at PTL. We did! And millions of lives were impacted as a result. That's the good news.

The bad news is that because we were trying to do so much in our own energy the attention often got sidetracked from Jesus and placed on men and women and their human achievements. Back in the early days of Heritage USA, for example, when we were trying to complete The Barn, we ran out of money. That in itself was nothing new; we were always running out of money at PTL because we were always starting some new project or ministry. This time, however, the financial crisis severely threatened the viability of our entire ministry. Construction stopped cold for nearly a year. With the wind whipping through the unfinished structure, The Barn stood as a monument of defeat.

When we finally were able to complete the facility, thanks to the sacrificial financial giving of the PTL viewing audience and the dedicated people working with me, we wanted to mark the event by having a parade, a time of celebration and thanksgiving unto God. Complete with people singing praises to God and waving palm branches, we marched from the entrance of Heritage USA all the way to The Barn, which was at the back of the property. We promised God that we would hold this parade each year to remind us of the great miracle He did in rescuing Heritage USA. Each year, the parade got a little bigger and more grandiose. After a few attempts at having the celebration at various times of the year, we eventually declared July Fourth as the official "birthday" of Heritage USA and turned the parade into a colossal birthday party.

What started out as a simple celebration honoring Jesus soon degenerated into a parade of floats, with Christian celebrities and preachers riding in convertibles. The renowned concert pianist Dino Kartsonakis was perched upon a float shaped like a grand piano while riding down the street. Tammy Faye and I rode on a float waving to a crowd of onlookers as we basked in their love and adulation. Our final parade was the most elaborate of all, an "Electric Light Parade," with all the floats lit up with thousands of lights powered by portable generators. The Electric Light Parade opened the 1986 edition of Christmas City, so we had "Uncle Henry" and "Aunt Susan" Harrison dressed up as Santa and Mrs. Claus and riding a sleigh pulled by reindeer on a float. The celebration went on all day, culminating in an extravagant fireworks display over the waters of Lake Heritage at night.

What happened?

As with so many things done under my leadership at PTL, we started out with the best of intentions and somehow got sidetracked onto a path

465

of pride, arrogance, and indulgence. We got trapped in the subtle snare that says, "big is better." If a little celebration was a blessing, just think how pleasing it would be to God to have a *huge* party. That was wrong, and I was wrong for allowing it to happen.

Another area where I went wrong at PTL was the balance between faith and works, and my understanding of what sort of "works" were truly pleasing to God.

Throughout my ministry, I thought that hard work was of God, and that I was proving my faith by my hard work. At PTL, I believed that by constructing large buildings, a great television network, and other marvelous, big programs and far-reaching ministries, I was showing my faith through my works.

I became obsessed with building Heritage USA. What had begun as a vision to build a modern, comfortable retreat center became an ever-increasing monster, something like the old science-fiction movie *The Blob*. As the Blob overwhelmed and sucked up people and resources, it kept growing larger and larger, demanding more and more people to maintain its energy supplies, feeding on the very people it needed to survive. All the while, I sincerely believed I was working for God.

During my first few years in prison, I wrestled with the question, *What went wrong at PTL?* I understood that my sin had opened the door to attack, but I could not comprehend why God did not merely remove me and allow the ministry to carry on unabated. So many good things were happening at Heritage USA, so many lives were being positively changed, why did it have to come to an end?

I knew God had given me the vision to build a Christian retreat center, a place where people could gather to rest, relax, vacation, and be refreshed physically and spiritually. I grew up in an era when multitudes of people gathered at great camp meetings to fellowship together, and most of all, to hear the gospel proclaimed. Many of today's Christian grandmothers and grandfathers can trace their initial experiences with God back to the brush arbors and rugged campgrounds that still exist in America.

During my boyhood in Michigan, I often attended a camp in which the services were held in an old, wooden tabernacle with a sawdust floor. The lodging facilities were little more than rustic, stuffy cabins with lumpy, stained mattresses. Indoor plumbing or bathroom fixtures were rare at most of the camps I attended as a youth. For recreation, we played in the large, vacant field when it was not being used as a parking lot, or we went swimming in the chilly waters of the lake or the muddy waters of the old swimming holes. Neither option was too inviting. Even as a child, I began to dream of a place where God's people could gather in beautiful, pleasant surroundings with modern facilities.

Attendance at camp meetings began to dwindle during my lifetime. I believed at least part of the decline could be attributed to the facilities, not the message being preached there. I recognized that the drab, outmoded campgrounds I had attended as a child would no longer appeal to a generation accustomed to vacationing at clean hotels and theme parks and other recreational centers, a generation to whom "roughing it" meant the hotel had only an outdoor pool. Consequently, I felt that God birthed within me a vision to build what I called a twenty-first-century, total-living community modeled on the old-time camp meetings, but where the entire family could come and enjoy both a beautiful park and plentiful opportunities for spiritual growth. Since I considered it an expression of my faith, I worked year after year with all my heart and energy to build the vision.

I designed the buildings and worked with the architects and contractors; I walked the land and laid out the roads, parks, sidewalks, water towers and water lines, underground electrical lines, fiber-optic phone lines, and other community facilities. I oversaw every aspect of the building of the four-square-mile Christian retreat center.

Tammy Faye and I personally picked out many of the furnishings for the Partner Center, which included the Heritage Grand Hotel. We attended auctions, estate sales, and flea markets, searching for just the right "period" pieces for the shops and stores at Heritage USA. I personally selected much of the wallpaper, furniture, drapes, pictures for the walls, lighting fixtures, and hardware for most of the lodging facilities at Heritage USA. It was a mammoth undertaking that required every ounce of energy I had and ten times more.

In addition to overseeing the construction of Heritage USA, I also had the primary responsibility to raise the funds to pay for it. Most of what we built prior to my departure in 1987 was built debt-free, paid for by the contributions of the *PTL* viewing audience.

I was consumed with building Heritage USA. When evangelist James Robison preached a week of "camp meeting" services—ours were now held in the air-conditioned and carpeted Barn auditorium—he confronted me about my "mistress."

"Jim, you are committing fornication with brick and mortar," he told me.

Although I responded politely to James's face, I resented his remark. I was working night and day just to keep everything at Heritage USA afloat.

467

I thought angrily, *Who is he to come here and tell me something such as that?* Others who tried to warn me to slow down or to take stock of what I was doing received little appreciation from me.

The day before our highly touted, $13-million water park was to open, we discovered a problem that caused the wave pool to tug the sand from the beach area back into the pool. The sand had to go. The contractors told me that they could move in heavy equipment to move the sand, but doing so would most likely crush some of the concrete pool edges, thus delaying our announced and heavily publicized grand opening the following day. I decided to dig the sand out by hand.

Some staff members and PTL Partners volunteered to help, so I dispatched several of them to go find shovels with which to work. Knowing that every minute counted, I refused to wait until the shovels arrived. I began digging out the sand with my bare hands. Was I obsessed?

When the workers returned with shovels, we shoveled by hand literally tons of dirt, cleaning out the pool and removing the sand from the area. We worked long into the night, but we did it. The pool was ready to open the following day. At the opening ceremonies, I could hardly walk, I was so sore from shoveling sand the previous night.

Besides being obsessed with building Heritage USA, I was also fanatical in my efforts to maintain it and keep everything running smoothly. I constantly trouble searched, at first writing reminders to myself about things that needed attention as I spotted them. Later, I carried a micro-cassette tape recorder with me most everywhere I went, so when I spotted things that needed attention—light bulbs that were burned out, trash that needed picked up, a pot hole in the road, or a problem in one of the many shops at Heritage USA—I recorded the reminder and had my executive secretary transcribe my comments and notify the appropriate departments. When I went on trial in 1989, some of the transcripts of my taped comments were used to show what an "overbearing dictator" I was in managing PTL. The truth is, I wanted every detail to be right; I wanted our physical property to be clean, wholesome, and beautiful. I wanted our partners, many of whom planned all year long for the time when they could come to Heritage USA, to receive the best attention and service we could possibly provide.

Oftentimes I was so busy building Heritage USA, I ignored or purposely attempted to avoid the very people for whom Heritage USA existed. "Oh, Jim, can I talk to you?" someone would call out as I hurried from one project to another. "Can I get a picture taken with you?" someone else requested. I was glad to meet and talk with the many visitors who came to

PTL every year, but at times when I was stressed and stretched to the limits, I became easily irritated by the interruptions. On several occasions, I resorted to wearing a disguise simply so I could move around the grounds with a minimum of delays. Inevitably people recognized me and wanted to talk. I tried always to be kind, but no doubt there were times when I was curt with some people. Often exasperated at my inability to get everything done that I had hoped, I sometimes complained to friends, staff members, or to myself, "Don't these people realize that I am building this place for *them?*"

Perhaps one of the worst mistakes I made at PTL was to ignore the spiritual health and nourishment of the people around me—my coworkers, our staff, and employees. When we first started at PTL, we had prayer every day and staff meetings every week. Eventually we backed off to meeting once a month or so. I asked everyone to attend, if possible, for a time of Bible study, prayer, praise, and worship. We literally pulled as many of our people as possible off the grounds for an afternoon time together in which we could focus on the Lord. The meetings were designed to last an hour or an hour and a half, but sometimes, when the Holy Spirit moved mightily in our midst, the meetings extended twice that time and longer. We didn't care. God was there, and His presence in the place was the most important part of what we all did.

Our staff members were paid during the time they attended the meetings. As our payroll reached a peak of nearly $30 million and three thousand employees, my financial advisors repeatedly reminded me that it was costing us between $250,000 and $300,000 in wages and salaries while our people were listening to a sermon or praising the Lord at the staff meeting. I foolishly agreed to limit the number and frequency of our staff meetings, and as PTL grew, the meetings became fewer and further apart. Granted, with a twenty-four-hour-a-day, seven-day-a-week operation, it was becoming increasingly difficult to pull all our people together at one time anyhow. We did encourage our department heads to open each day with prayer. Nevertheless, by eliminating the spiritual focus, we were making a subtle statement that money was more important than ministry. Slowly but surely that attitude began to pervade much of the leadership of PTL during the mid 1980s. I should not have let that happen.

One night in prison, I had a dream in which I saw many of our PTL Partners at a huge, sumptuous banquet back at Heritage USA. Large tables were overflowing with all sorts of food, some of the best food in the world. The people were feasting and having a tremendous time, and a seemingly endless supply of food was always available for them. One of my staff members approached me at the banquet and begged, "Jim, we're hungry too."

In my dream, I reached into my back pocket, took out my wallet, and I placed it between two pieces of bread. I handed the "sandwich" to the staff member and said, "Here, let them eat this."

When I awakened from the dream, I felt that God was rebuking me for not providing spiritual nourishment for our staff. Looking back, it was easy to rationalize that we had eighty-six services a week at PTL, and almost any time of the day or night, a spiritual smorgasbord was available if our employees wanted to avail themselves of it. In truth, however, so many of our employees worked so hard trying to meet the many needs of our ministry, they had little time or energy left for attending services. Some staff members were so burned out from the constant drain of ministering to others, like me, they were becoming dangerously dry in their own spiritual lives.

One of the questions asked me again and again in prison (and frequently asked to this day) was, "If you had it to do over again, what would you do differently at PTL?"

The most important change I would make is this: I would not emphasize the physical structure, but I would encourage people to fall in love with Jesus. I always felt that Heritage USA was merely the box in which we packaged the gospel, a big box, a beautiful box, but just a box, nonetheless. Unfortunately, the box began to get more attention than the gift inside. Eventually, we spent so much time, energy, and money trying to build a bigger, better box, we neglected the priceless gift of Jesus Christ. If I could somehow be transported back in time to PTL in the 1980s, I would keep my attention off the physical, material plant, the place known as Heritage USA, and keep my eyes on Jesus.

My vision was not eternal. It was simply a group of buildings. What made Heritage USA so special were the people, the people who loved Jesus and each other. God can still use Heritage USA, just as He can use a cathedral, a stadium, or a cowshed. I've come to realize that the works that please God most have little to do with buildings. The church is not the building; the building is simply the box. The real Church is the Body, the true believers of Jesus Christ.

About the same time that I was coming to grips with the message of the Scriptures and how far away from it I had been at PTL, my pen pal Jim Dickinson from St. Paul, Minnesota, who wrote to me almost every week and often sent me challenging books at Rochester F.M.C., sent me *Life*

Together by Dietrich Bonhoeffer. The book was old, yellowed, and slightly tattered, but the message was intact. Dietrich Bonhoeffer was a pastor in Germany during the time Adolph Hitler and the Third Reich were coming to power. Because Bonhoeffer dared to buck Hitler's system, the theologian was thrown into a Nazi concentration camp, where he died.

God had been showing me that one of my most tragic mistakes in life was in allowing my vision of Heritage USA to become the focal point of PTL rather than keeping the gospel of Jesus Christ as our top priority. When I read Bonhoeffer's words, they seemed to leap off the pages at me. Written in 1938, two years before I was born, Bonhoeffer wrote:

> Innumerable times a whole Christian community has broken down because it has sprung from a wish dream. The serious Christian, set down for the first time in a Christian community, is likely to bring with him a very definite idea of what Christian life together should be and to try to realize it. But God's grace speedily shatters such dreams. . . . God will not permit us to live even for a brief period in a dream world. He does not abandon us to those rapturous experiences and lofty moods that come over us like a dream. God is not a God of the emotions but the God of truth. . . . A community which cannot bear and cannot survive such a crisis, which insists upon keeping its illusion when it should be shattered, permanently loses in that moment the promise of Christian community. Sooner or later it will collapse. . . . He who loves his dream of a community more than the Christian community itself becomes a destroyer of the latter, even though his personal intention may be ever so honest and earnest and sacrificial.[1]

Ouch! Bonhoeffer's words hit me right between the eyes. I did not like to see myself reflected on the pages, especially to think of myself as the destroyer of the very community I had hoped to build because of my love for my dream. But the message got worse before it got better: "God hates visionary dreaming; it makes the dreamer proud and pretentious."[2]

What? Surely, Mr. Bonhoeffer, you must be joking! After all, my friends and admirers had been telling me for years that I was a visionary, a dreamer of great dreams. I saw myself that way and considered my visionary dreaming to be one of my better qualities. Surely there must be some mistake. . . . There was, and I had made it.

As Bonhoeffer's words sank into my heart, mind, and spirit, I was suddenly more deeply grieved than ever before that Heritage USA, my dream, had been the cause of so much infighting, hurt, and shame in the Body of

Christ. I never intended it to be so, but as Bonhoeffer said, that is irrelevant. My dream turned into a nightmare. The world watched as Christian leaders fought over who would get "the box." Fellow believers betrayed one another in their efforts at gamesmanship. Money and buildings were more important than obedience to God's Word and reaching the souls of men and women with the gospel. When the world looked and saw PTL, they saw Christians, a relatively small number of Christians to be sure, at their worst . . . and that included me.

We had so much going for us. People were meeting Jesus at Heritage USA. Lives were truly changed. Marriages were restored and healed. Unborn babies were saved, and unmarried mothers were supported as they began a new quality of life. The gospel was broadcasted daily around the world. Witnesses to the transforming power of Jesus Christ were trained to reach the world with the gospel. We had so great an opportunity . . . and we lost it, because we got our eyes on the box rather than keeping our attention on Jesus.

My dream was that Heritage USA might be a modern-day City of Refuge, a place where hurting people could find the help and healing they needed, a place of refreshment and encouragement. My ideas concerning a Christian community were flawed, but I was soon to learn the awesomeness of what a true Christian community was all about.

CHAPTER

45

Rule 35

THE PHRASE "TIME FLIES" IS SELDOM HEARD IN PRISON. NOR did I ever hear an inmate nonchalantly say something such as, "It seems like it was just yesterday that I came to this place!" On the contrary, time in prison seems to stand still, life becomes drudgery; it is interminable, and it is intended to be so. Nevertheless, although I cannot say that the time passed quickly, at least for me, the summer of 1992 was filled with activity.

When I wasn't working, I was busy studying the Bible, especially digesting the words of Jesus. I was also nearly done with a college correspondence course on the book of Acts. I had already completed two computer courses and a sociology course taught by local college professors in the prison. Overall, although I was doing time, I did not feel that I was wasting it. Besides exercising my brain, I was also exercising my body regularly, walking the track and doing extensive weight lifting in the gymnasium and at the outdoor iron pile. I was in the best physical condition of my life.

Jamie, Tammy Sue, Doug, and the grandchildren came to visit me on the Fourth of July, just in time for the annual Inmates' Families Picnic. I was so excited to see them! Unfortunately, the Minnesota summer suddenly turned cold and the temperature plummeted to near freezing. The prison officials rolled out huge laundry carts filled with coats and allowed inmates' family members to borrow the old, green army coats to help stay warm during the gathering in the prison yard. My family members and I felt a strange but wonderful sense of comradeship as we huddled together, all of us dressed in our prison-issued jackets.

As we packed back into the visiting room, the guard called out, "Visiting time is over!" He ordered the visitors to go to one side of the room, near the outside door, and all the inmates to go to the other side of the room, near the door that leads back into the heart of the prison. As I was standing with a group of prisoners, waiting to go into the processing room to be strip searched, I looked down, and there was little three-year-old James, making his way through a crowd of inmates, with his hands outstretched to me. He was too young to know that he was violating the prison rules. I picked him up, and he said, "Paw Paw Jim, I lovvvvvvve youuuuuuuu!" He gave me a big kiss.

I said, "James, I love you too!" I put him down and James left the forbidden zone and ran back to his mom.

I was encouraged by my family's visit because for the first time, it felt as though they were finally able to get on with their lives. Tammy Sue was singing in churches and was excited about the possibility of cutting a new album. Jamie was working part-time at the television station and was taking a course to help him get caught up on his education. He had missed so much schooling over the past two troubled years of his life, and I was proud of him that he was willing to start again. As I had told him so often, everyone makes mistakes and falls down once in a while, but it is the person with courage who gets back up.

After Tammy Sue's family and Jamie left, I felt that I needed to do something, anything to try to reenter my boy's world, to let him know I was interested in some of the things in which he was interested. I could have picked any number of things. Instead, I decided to surprise him by learning to play the drums. The prison had some instruments in the recreation building, and some practice rooms, so I ordered a five-dollar set of drumsticks through the commissary and started taking lessons from one of the inmates. I never became a great drummer, but I gained a great appreciation for the manual dexterity of those who are expert drummers.

I practiced my drum lessons by beating on magazines on my desk while trying to play along with the rhythms of songs I heard on my portable radio headset. Apparently I was really getting into it too, because I hardly heard when the inmates in the cell next door began doing some drumming of their own . . . on the wall! "Bakker, you better tone it down," one of my friends advised, "or the next thing you know, they're going to be drumming on you."

I practiced on the drums in the recreation building as often as possible. One of the guards saw and heard me there so often, he joked, "When you get out of here, Bakker, you are probably going to be playing with Guns and Roses." I laughed along with the guard, even though I didn't know at the time that Guns and Roses was a hard rock band.

Although I loved playing the drums, I had always wanted to learn how to play guitar as well. Jamie Charles too had a great love for the guitar. By early August, I had saved enough money in my commissary account to order a Martin dreadnought acoustic guitar. The Martin guitar company allowed prisoners to buy their slightly imperfect guitars at half price. To me the flaws were imperceptible; I never discovered the reason why it was not considered first-rate. To me, it was wonderful. When it arrived, I was the talk of the wing. Guys from cells up and down my floor came to my cell to play my guitar. I let so many inmates borrow the Martin, especially Christian guys who wanted to use the guitar in small worship groups and for their personal practice, I never really got around to learning to play it. But that guitar brought a bit of happiness to our prison world, so to me, it was worth every penny.

One of the best and worst days of the summer was August 10, the day my mother and father first visited me in the Minnesota prison. Along with my sister, Donna, Mother and Dad had made the long, arduous trip from Fort Mill, North Carolina, to Rochester by automobile.

Mother and Daddy still lived at Heritage USA in the house Tammy Faye and I had purchased for them. Living there among so many memories was a bittersweet experience for them. Nobody grieved any more deeply at my ouster from PTL than my parents, especially my dad. He often said, "I just can't stand it. I wish I could take your place in prison, Jim. I would do it." Long after Tammy Faye and I were gone, every direction my mother and father looked, they saw something that reminded them of what once was. I can't even imagine the pain they endured as PTL went through its traumatic changes. On the other hand, because my parents had remained living at Heritage USA, they had a group of godly friends and neighbors around them, people like Joyce LaBaron, who stopped in every day and cooked, cleaned, and cared for my mother and father.

When I heard that my parents wanted to visit me in prison, I was thrilled and worried at the same time. At eighty-six years of age, my mother was especially feeble; she could no longer stand up straight when she walked and had a great deal of difficulty performing even menial chores around the house. I wasn't sure she could handle a cross-country trip by car. Daddy, though much more spry than Mother, was also only a month away from being eighty-six years old, and was beginning to show it.

Overshadowing their visit was the awareness that this could well be the last major trip my mother would ever take, and most likely the last time I would ever see my parents this side of heaven. At present, I was serving an eighteen-year sentence. Even if I was able to get paroled after twelve years, my parents would be close to one hundred years of age before I could get back to see them at home.

When I walked into the visiting room, Mother and Father were sitting at one of the low tables waiting for me. I signed in and quickly went to them. Mother tried to rise to greet me, but I knew how much effort that would be so I leaned down and hugged her in her seat. "Oh, Mother, please don't try to get up. I am so glad to see you. Stay right there in your chair."

My mother was desperately trying to hold back her tears. Mom was embarrassed because of her tears. "I promised myself that I wasn't going to do that," she said.

I turned to embrace my dear dad, who was now standing to greet me. I know it must have been extremely hard for him to see me in prison, but he handled it well.

After the initial shock subsided, Mother, Daddy, Donna, and I sat down at the table and began to talk. They brought me news of what was happening among the members of our extended family, and I explained to them many basics of prison life. Mostly, though, I was excited to tell them about the new discoveries I was making in my study of the Bible. Mother and Daddy always had loved to hear me preach, so they were delighted to listen patiently while I explained the truths I was learning from my study of the words of Jesus.

We talked about Grandma Bakker coming to America from the "old country." We talked about Donna's and my childhood, growing up in Muskegon. Donna joked, "Jim, you were so quiet, always playing by yourself, we hardly knew you were there. I can hardly even remember your childhood!"

I didn't want to tell my family members that I remembered the awful hurt of my childhood only too well. To this day, I have never discussed with them my being molested as a child. We were having a marvelous time reminiscing about the "good old days"; there was no reason to bring up the painful part of my childhood experiences.

Later that day, my family and I ate the usual visiting-room dinner, procured from the vending machines in the back of the room. Mother and Dad didn't seem to mind. We were together; that's all that mattered to

476

them. We had our pictures taken by the Jaycees cameraman, then went back to our table to talk some more. I didn't want the day to end. I hated to see my mother and father leave, driving all the way back to Charlotte. In a few days, they would celebrate their sixty-sixth wedding anniversary, and of course, I would not be there with them.

Before my mother and father ever reached their home, I received bad news. Kevin Whittum, the adopted son of my cousins, David and Ione Whittum, had died. Kevin was twenty-three years old when he died; he weighed about forty pounds and was only thirty-four inches tall, victim of a lifelong brittle-bone disease, that prevented him from walking and stunted his growth. He had to be carried, moved on a gurney or in a wheelchair everywhere he went.

I met with Kevin in the summer of 1986 when, at seventeen, he appeared along with his parents on one of our television programs at PTL. Kevin had already lived sixteen years longer than the doctors ever expected. At the time, he and his family lived in Michigan. Kevin and I talked about Kevin's dream, to help provide housing for other handicapped children like himself.

Kevin's faith in God and his upbeat, positive attitude despite his severe handicap so inspired all of us at PTL that we caught his vision. Before long, we were making plans to build a facility to house special children, severely handicapped children that most adoptive parents would not want or for one reason or another were ill-equipped to handle. I went on the air and presented the plan to our *PTL* viewers. Kevin's parents agreed to move to Heritage USA and run the home. David and Ione had been in pastoral ministry with the Assemblies of God, and they obviously had a heart for this type of ministry. They had adopted another child, Carolyn, a beautiful girl who had no legs. The Whittum home was always filled with children. Over the years, they had taken in, cared for, and helped raise more than twenty-five foster children.

I explained to the *PTL* viewers as tactfully as possible that Kevin was already living on borrowed time. "There is a sense of urgency in building this because of Kevin's health," I said on the air. We dubbed the project "Kevin's House," though, of course, the group children's residence was intended to house many more children than him alone. The viewers responded by pouring in enough money to build, furnish, and operate a 13,000-square-foot, thirty-six-room Victorian home in which Kevin and the disabled children could live. Roe Messner and his construction crews outdid themselves, working with a sense of mission and passion, night and day. While the cameras watched twenty-four hours a day, they finished the house from start to finish in only thirty-two days!

When Kevin, Carolyn, and their family moved in, the home was fully functional for handicapped and disabled children. We had installed all the necessary handicapped-equipped bathrooms, ramps, and railings. The home was a lovely haven for crippled children. In the fall and winter of 1986, after the home was occupied, a dispute arose about the building codes. We already had secured licenses for the residence to operate as a group home, so I was surprised when the problem occurred. Regardless, had I been given enough time, I would have rectified anything necessary to comply with the local codes. Unfortunately, I was not able to help resolve the problem as I was in California with Tammy Faye while she worked to get free of her drug addiction. By the time I got back to PTL, Jerry Falwell and his new leadership board were in charge of Kevin's House. They decided to close it.

Throughout the tumultuous days of March 1987, Kevin and his extended family lived at Kevin's House, under the loving care of David and Ione Whittum. In late 1987, after the Falwell regime had departed the scene, a judge ordered Kevin and his family to be evicted. The Whittums were reluctant to leave the house that was built and named for Kevin, and fortunately nobody forced them to go. They stayed until 1989 before returning to Michigan, when Heritage USA for all intents and purposes shut down until the Malaysian businessmen reopened it June 27, 1992, two weeks before Kevin's death. The new owners turned the home built for disabled kids into a bed-and-breakfast.

When I learned of Kevin's death, I was deeply moved. He had been such a courageous little guy who loved God and loved other hurting people, especially hurting children. The world had lost a true hero. Although I refused to be interviewed about Kevin's death, I did write out a statement to be distributed to the press.

I was equally shaken and totally surprised when Kevin's mom, Ione, died within three months of Kevin's death. She had poured out her life for her son and others like him. She was sixty-one years of age at her death.

Death seemed intent upon knocking on my family's door during 1992. That same year, Tammy Faye's mom, Mrs. Rachel Glover, was found dead in her home at Heritage USA. At seventy-three years of age, she was still a vibrant woman right up to the day she died. She had been sitting in her chair, waiting to be picked up to go to church. She was believed to have died from a heart attack or a stroke. Tammy Faye was shocked at her mom's death. I wrote her a letter, conveying my sincere sorrow. She wrote back kindly and gratefully.

About that same time, another special person in my life passed away. Annie Regina was the first person to be housed in the efficiency apartments for senior citizens and others that we built at PTL. Annie was a fixture around PTL. When the ministry went under in the late 1980s, Annie moved to a nursing home in Florida, where she died.

Perhaps Annie's death hit me even harder since I had just been reminiscing with two special friends who came to visit me in prison. Mary Davidson and her sister Francis Waite lived together and cared for their aged mother, who was bedridden and in a coma. Francis was mentally handicapped and childlike, a dear human being, but not really much help in caring for their mother. Mary didn't mind. She had enough love for both of them. Francis could not speak, but she attended every Sunday service and all the broadcasts of my programs at PTL, always sitting right down front, smiling and laughing. I loved Mary and Francis dearly and was always glad to see them, but never more than when I saw them sitting in the prison visiting room. I simply could not believe that these two women, both senior citizens, had made the long trek to Minnesota to see me.

About that same time, I received a letter from Charlie Crowley, a middle-aged man who had a muscular disease that had caused him to be confined to an electric cart in order to get around Heritage USA. But get around he did! He was everywhere, and everyone at PTL knew him, loved him, and watched out for him. His life, which he had once thought to be over, had been filled with meaning at Heritage USA. He lived at the apartment complex at PTL. He said in his letter that he had received a notice of eviction. I was deeply grieved, but there was little I could do for him from prison.

I had hoped that Heritage USA would be a place where people such as Annie, Francis, and Charlie could live out their days in a loving environment, surrounded and cared for by God's people. Now, as I received Charlie's letter telling me of his eviction notice, I realized again that not only had my dreams and those of my family been dashed, but the hopes and dreams of so many others had been destroyed at PTL as well.

I had numerous other visitors throughout the summer of 1992. One strong, spunky woman who came to visit during that time was Irene Lindquist, whose late husband had founded North Central Bible College and pastored one of the premier churches in Minnesota. As pioneers in my former denomination, Frank and Irene were dear friends of Fern and Russell Olson, so Irene and I spent the afternoon reminiscing about my younger days at the college and then in the ministry with Fern and Russell. Irene had lots of great stories about her own experiences with God. She was a tremendous encouragement to me and helped balance the barrage of negative news I was receiving that summer with her positive spirit.

I was amazed and humbled that people came from all across the country, taking time out of their schedules that summer to visit me and encourage me. My cousin Beverly Halgren came from Michigan; my cousin Marge Klages and her daughter Karen came all the way from California. Gerald Derstine came from his Christian Retreat Center in Bradenton, Florida. Sandra Simms, the woman who produced my television programs at PTL, and Herman and Sharon Bailey came from WCLF in Clearwater, as did Bob D'Andrea, who brought along my son Jamie. PTL Partner Karl Garmager came from Michigan to see me; Partners Helen Reeves and Barb Jukich traveled by car all the way from Charleston, South Carolina, to visit with me. Vern and Mary McLellan traveled from Charlotte to visit me. Vern had headed up the worldwide missions program at PTL. Words cannot express the debt of gratitude I owe to the many people who came to visit, at their own expense, simply to encourage me. More than I had ever known before, I realized in prison that the Body of Christ, true believers from all walks of life, across the denominational spectrum, had not abandoned me. They were there for me when I needed them.

Throughout the summer and into the first days of fall, one of the things weighing heavily on my mind was my upcoming "Rule 35" sentence-reduction hearing before U.S. District Judge Graham Mullen in Charlotte. The hearing had been postponed several times, creating even more interest in the case and stress for me. Everyone seemed to have an opinion. Even Billy Graham weighed in when questioned about my eighteen-year sentence in an interview with *The Charlotte Observer*. Dr. Graham said, "I thought that was an awfully heavy sentence for that when you see people like [Michael] Milken and [Ivan] Boesky and people in that area getting lighter sentences".[1]

One man who had a strong opinion about my case was a man I had never met before. James A. Albert was a professor of law at Drake University in Des Moines, Iowa, a graduate of Notre Dame Law School, and an Episcopalian. Professor Albert was never a "Jim Bakker fan," nor did he share my religious beliefs.

James Albert was a legal educator who had served on Drake's faculty for twelve years, teaching broadcast law. He had been voted Professor of the Year three times at Drake and had been selected as the outstanding law professor in the nation by the Delta Theta Phi International Law

Fraternity. He was also an outstanding, active lawyer, specializing in cases dealing with administrative law and broadcast law. In the previous sixteen years before meeting me, he had read and briefed every wire fraud case that had been decided.

In August 1991, as my lawyers were preparing for the initial resentencing hearing before Judge Mullen, after Judge Potter's sentence had been thrown out, Jim Albert wrote me a letter. In his letter, he explained that he had read a twenty-five-page article in the April 23, 1990, edition of *The New Yorker*, which had extensively analyzed my trial and conviction on federal fraud and conspiracy charges. The article piqued Professor Albert's interest. He was convinced that from all that he had read, I had not received a fair trial. Wire-fraud cases and broadcast law, he said, are a bit more complicated than most normal trial lawyers assume; most lawyers who may be excellent at forging a solid defense in other criminal or civil cases have little experience with the voluminous intricacies of broadcast law. Professor Albert did not criticize the lawyers who had handled my initial defense, but he strongly hinted that they may have been working in an area outside their expertise. Perhaps, he offered, he could be of help—free of charge—to my legal team as they prepared for my resentencing hearing. Professor Albert told me right up front that his motive for offering was twofold: one, that he felt an injustice had been done in that I had been tried more on my religious beliefs than on facts; and two, he hoped to one day write a magazine article on what he found as he explored the case.

I was excited by Jim Albert's credentials and his awareness of my case. I wrote back to him and told him I would welcome any help he could give us.

Jim Albert traveled to Minnesota at his own expense to talk with me about my case; he was not paid a dime to do so. We talked at length and I answered all of his questions concerning the original trial as best as I could recall. Some parts of the trial seemed as though they had taken place light-years ago and others were indelibly lodged in the frontal lobe of my brain. I couldn't believe it! For the first time, I felt that somebody was asking all the right questions. Besides his own exhaustive research into my case, Professor Albert incorporated the help of volunteers from his classes to search out information and comparisons of other cases similar to mine. After Professor Albert had met and talked with me, he asked his classes, "How many of you would be interested in volunteering to help do the research on Jim Bakker's case?" To Professor Albert's surprise, the number of volunteers totaled almost 100 percent of his students. For more than a year, my case became their pet research project.

Professor Albert read all eleven volumes of the court transcripts of my original trial. Each volume had over five hundred pages of material, but eventually, Jim Albert read every line of testimony in the entire trial, making notes as he read. In the process, he became convinced that I had been wrongfully convicted, and he felt strongly that he could prove it.

As I thought of Jim Albert's unsolicited interest in my case and his commitment to seeing the truth revealed, I could not help but be reminded of R. T. Kendall's poignant words about how we will know when God's time for working in our lives has come: "When someone pleads your case (and knows all the facts) without your opening your mouth."[2] I marveled at God's providing me just such a man in Professor James A. Albert.

On October 1, 1992, I notified Harold Bender that I had officially asked Jim Albert to be an uncompensated member of our legal team as they prepared for the Rule 35 hearing. I wanted Jim's expertise in broadcast law and his knowledge of my case to be presented at the hearing. For the next six weeks, Professor Albert worked closely with my lawyers, Harold Bender and Jim Toms. He and his students represented a wealth of research into not only my case, but every other wire-fraud case in American history. They made their conclusions readily available to Harold. When the Rule 35 hearing came, we would be prepared.

In the meantime, my family sent out a letter to our friends, asking them to write to the judge and appeal for mercy. Hundreds of letters poured in to Judge Mullen's office, begging him to be compassionate and merciful to me as he made his decision regarding a possible sentence reduction. I was able to see copies of many of the wonderful letters, but I'm sure I will never know all who extended a hand of compassion toward me during this time.

The list of everyday folks as well as Christian leaders who were concerned enough to write to Judge Mullen read like an edition of *Who's Who*— Chuck Colson, president of Prison Fellowship; gospel singer James Blackwood; psychiatrist Dr. Basil Jackson; Jim Henry, pastor of First Baptist Church in Orlando; John Hagee, pastor of Cornerstone Church in San Antonio; Bishop Alfred A. Owens Jr.; Gregory C. Tibbetts, family law attorney; Carlton R. Reichert, attorney-at-law; author and speaker Judson Cornwall; James Brumbaugh, mayor of Astatula, Florida; Jimmy Dolan, pastor of Argo Presbyterian Church in Springville, Alabama; Charles Roundtree, principal of Palnez Academy in Plant City, Florida; evangelists Charles and Frances Hunter; Pastor Tommy Reid of Orchard Park, New York; Bishop Earl Paulk of Decatur, Georgia; Oral and Richard Roberts; Billy James Hargis, author and evangelist; Sid Kleiner, southeast coordinator of B'nai

B'rith Jewish Prisoner Services; Don Argue, president of the National Association of Evangelicals; famed lawyer Melvin Belli; Dan Betzer, *Revivaltime* radio speaker; actor Pat Boone; author Harold Bredesen; evangelist Philip Cameron; Glen Cole, executive presbyter, southwest region of the Assemblies of God; author and minister Kenneth Copeland; Karl Strader, pastor of Carpenter's Home Church in Lakeland, Florida; evangelist James Robison; Clarence St. John, district superintendent of the Minnesota District Council of the Assemblies of God; Bill Swad, Chevrolet auto dealer; Cecil Todd of Revival Fires Ministries; David Mainse, host of *100 Huntley Street* television program; George Otis, president of High Adventure Broadcasting; Dr. James McKeever, noted Bible teacher; Dr. John Osteen, pastor of Lakewood Church in Houston; Charles Morgan, attorney-at-law and husband of noted author Marabel Morgan; Gerald Derstine of Christian Retreat Center; Jamie Buckingham, editor in chief of *Ministries*; Bob D'Andrea, president of the Christian Television Network; Loren Cunningham, president of Youth With a Mission. Almost all of my friends who visited me in prison wrote to Judge Mullen, including my daughter, Tammy Sue. I myself wrote, outlining my activities in prison and my family needs and pleading with Judge Mullen to be merciful in his decision. I reiterated to the judge that "I made many mistakes, but I never conspired or intended to defraud anyone. I take full responsibility for all my actions and for all that has transpired under my leadership of (Heritage USA)." I could do nothing else but wait. The rest was up to God.

In late September, I was working out with weights one day, doing leg presses, the type of exercises in which I had to lie on my back and push a heavy weight up and down a slide. A friend asked me a question about a point in the Bible that he was contesting, and for a fraction of a second, I violated one of Rod's cardinal workout rules: I stopped focusing on what I was doing. The heavy weight came crashing down, pushing my legs and hips almost back up to my chin. I had been trying to keep up with the young guys in my workouts, but I suddenly felt my age.

The next morning, I could hardly get out of bed, the ache and pain in my hip was so severe. I forced myself to get up and ready by 7:30 A.M., and although it was difficult to stand upright and walk, I went to work cleaning the bathrooms, as usual. When I got done, I went back to bed. That was my routine for the next few weeks, with the added exception of going to physical therapy at the prison hospital where they tried to stretch me back into shape. The physical pain and the seemingly endless postponements of my Rule 35 hearing sent me spiraling into an emotional slump.

The Lord was gracious, though, sending several dear friends to visit me during my recuperation time, which helped to lift my spirits. Don Argue was such a friend. Don had been the president of North Central Bible College and had recently been elected as president of the National Association of Evangelicals. He was so busy, yet he took time to visit me. He seemed in no hurry during his visit, as though I were the most important person in the world at that time. I felt such love, concern, and compassion from Don, and he truly blessed me with his words of encouragement and his prayer.

Reverend Herman Rohde, a state executive with the Assemblies of God and a pastor of a large church in Minnesota, also visited around that time, as did Gordon Weekly. Gordon had been a prominent pastor in the Charlotte area when I founded PTL there. He had fallen into sin and become an alcoholic who made his home in the cemetery next to the church. He subsequently got back on track with God, got his life back together, and opened a ministry known as Rebound Christian Rehabilitation Center, a place where Charlotte's street people, homeless, alcoholics, and other down-and-outers could find help. I asked Gordon to tell his testimony on one of our early programs, and as Gordon says, "scattered across the airwaves the story of his fall and subsequent restoration." Gordon's story was eventually written in the June 1992 edition of *Reader's Digest*. Gordon never forgot our kindness to him at PTL, and I appreciated his visit with me in prison. He well understood how I felt, having lost everything but finding a new, deeper relationship with Christ as a result.

Old friends Ray LaForce, Dr. and Mrs. Basil Jackson, Ken Gaub, Owen Carr, Bob Gass, Shirley Balmer, Rhoda Lee, Mike Murdock, and my most frequent visitors, Phil Shaw and Paul Olson, also came to see me. Reverend Dortch and his wife, Mildred, visited also, as did Stephen Winzenburg, chairman of the communications department at Grand View College in Des Moines, Iowa. Alan Langstaff, host of the Australian *PTL* visited in the fall, as did Charles Capps, noted author and speaker.

Richard Wurmbrand, another man who could identify with my prison experience, visited in November. We felt an instant bond of Christian love and understanding between us. Richard had been tortured in Communist prison camps because of his faith in Christ. As part of the Communists' torture, they had severely beaten Richard's feet. He could not stand for long without great pain. Consequently, Richard was the only person who ever visited me in prison whom the guards allowed to put his feet up on the small table as he talked with me. Richard Wurmbrand really ministered to me. To have a man who had suffered so much for Jesus' sake visit me was like having a visit from the apostle Paul.

I also received an assortment of encouraging letters about this time. Interestingly, many of the letters came from former PTL staff members. Several members of the orchestra wrote glowing letters, including trombonist Jim Winters, who now lived in Maine, and former trumpet player Karl Seivers, who was now an assistant professor of music at Wright State University in Dayton, Ohio. Sonny Burnette wrote, as well. Sonny had played saxophone in our *PTL* band from 1979 to 1988, staying on until the end. Sonny was now teaching music theory at Georgetown College in Kentucky.

Roger Breland, founder and musical director of the musical group Truth, who often performed on *PTL*, wrote a warm note of encouragement, as did Steve Wike, publisher of the *National and International Religion Report*. Robert and Joleen Vander Maten, former *PTL* singers, also wrote and requested permission to visit. One of the most touching letters I received from former employees came from former *PTL* singer, Brenda Davis. Brenda became a cohost of the flagship television program after Jerry Falwell's people departed and left Sam Johnson in charge of PTL. Tenderhearted Brenda, whose only desire was to serve the Lord, lived through the PTL changes and emerged disillusioned, but wiser, more committed, and closer to Jesus. Her letter, addressed to both Tammy Faye and me, was a breath of fresh air.

Several people wrote to me during this time telling me how PTL had helped launch their ministries. Jeff Park had headed up our prison ministries at PTL and now served as executive director of COPE, Coalition of Prison Evangelists, working with more than 360 prison ministries around the nation and in foreign countries. Gene Bailey had been a student in our college in 1978. Now, he and many of his friends from PTL were in key television ministry spots all over the world. Mark Muirhead had been our youth minister at PTL. He wrote to tell me that he was now serving with Speed the Light, a national missions outreach of the youth ministry of the Assemblies. Through these letters, God was showing me that although I had allowed Heritage USA to become an Ishmael—a child born and manipulated by my own presumption—to me, He had done much good there in the lives of many people. What I had done in the flesh was gone, but the eternal work that God did by His Spirit was being perpetuated and expanded all around the world, even while I was in prison.

On November 16, U.S. District Judge Graham Mullen and the lawyers arguing my Rule 35 case finally convened in Charlotte. Judge Mullen was the same judge who had reduced my original sentence from forty-five years to eighteen years. That was both good news and bad news when it came time for a Rule 35 plea for mercy. For the judge to lower the sentence further might be interpreted by some as the judge saying, "I made a mistake when I first decided this case." That, or if he reduced the sentence without the inclusion of new evidence, such an action might be interpreted as being "soft on crime," and no judge in the mid1990s wanted to have that reputation.

On the positive side, Judge Mullen had been compassionate enough to reduce the sentence once; he might be willing to reduce it further. I certainly hoped so. Beyond that, the decision to grant a sentence-reduction hearing was at the judge's discretion. He was not required to hear the case. Relatively few cases ever get heard, and fewer yet yield positive results for the person asking for mercy. The simple fact that Judge Mullen had agreed to hear my case was cause for hope. My hope was tempered, however, by the prison adage "You ain't got nothin' comin'," combined with my own realization that I was not going to get out of prison one day before God so directed. Consequently, although I was excited that the decision was going to be made, my expectations were not running wild.

As with my initial appeal, I did not attend the hearing. I remained imprisoned at Rochester while the lawyers duked it out in Charlotte. The testimony opened with my lawyers calling to the witness stand Dr. Daniel Foster. Like Professor James A. Albert, Dr. Foster had read the transcripts of my trial and knew the details better than I. Again, I was reminded of R. T. Kendall's claim that you will know God's time has come when somebody else pleads your cause, somebody who knows all the facts.

When asked to describe my conduct since being incarcerated, Dr. Foster replied,

> Mr. Bakker, because of his notoriety and because of the heavy, heavy media attention, it was determined by our warden at the time that he arrived that I would be personally involved with him. . . . Upon arrival, he was, as are many of our men when they come to us, pretty broken just by life's circumstance, the whole issue—a lot of grieving, a lot of loss: nearly everything that he held important.
>
> In the course of the three years that I've known Mr. Bakker, I've seen him make substantive progress just in terms of coming to terms with his loss, but also coming to terms with bigger life issues. I've seen a quiet and

substantive maturation process. . . . His work reports have been good to outstanding on a consistent basis, and he's received extra-good bonus pay for his work as an orderly, also with the smoking-cessation program. Since his assignment at F.M.C. Rochester, Mr. Bakker has been primarily cleaning the bathrooms in the work cadre. . . . He's taken the task seriously in the sense of he receives outstanding work reports with a lot of humility. He's been patient, hasn't complained or asked for a job change. Typically, we don't keep people in that particular position for more than three to four months. For whatever reason, Mr. Bakker has been sustained in it now for three years.[3]

The lawyers then asked Dr. Foster to describe how I had grown as a person since being in prison. He replied,

When Mr. Bakker came to us, he was quite naive as to prison culture and the street culture broadly. He had not lived among people of whom a portion were primarily predatory and very physical in earthy ways. He wasn't accustomed to the kind of language that many Americans speak in a normal course of their day . . . and the various cultural and ethnic styles that are represented within a prison in the white, black, the Hispanic, the American Indian community. I think he was a bit shell-shocked upon arrival. . . . It was a pretty tough and lonely road for him.

He's matured a lot in those ways in terms of not just sophistication, but in terms of his own emotional stability and his own confidence in living in an environment that for many Americans would be very, very difficult . . . and he's done well. He's been able to resolve the various conflicts and challenges thrown at him.[4]

Dr. Foster went on to list the various activities in which I had busied myself in prison and emphasized that I had not requested or expected any special treatment. He then answered several questions relating to my feelings following Tammy Faye's and my divorce and my concern for the effects upon Jamie.

The prosecuting attorneys made much of the fact that I was not the only inmate to suffer a divorce while in prison, that in truth, most prisoners get divorced if they are incarcerated for any length of time. The implication was, "Who does Bakker think he is to ask for mercy on the basis that his family is falling apart? Everyone who goes to prison should expect his or her family to dissolve."

Next the prosecutors pressed Dr. Foster to tell them whether I had ever admitted that I had knowingly defrauded the PTL Lifetime Partners. Although I had explained to Dr. Foster that I had not defrauded anyone, he wisely deferred to the judge for a decision about the confidentiality of our conversations.

The judge decided that Dr. Foster did not have to discuss privileged information between a doctor and his patient. At that, the prosecutors were no longer interested in hearing from Dr. Foster.

The next witness was Jamie, the only family member to testify at the hearing. Tammy Sue and my parents were in the courtroom, but the lawyers did not invite them to testify.

Both Tammy Sue and Jamie were scheduled to testify, but Harold Bender had not wanted my children to take the stand in my defense. I'm not sure why. Only after the insistence of Jim Albert, our expert consultant, and a last-minute phone call from me the morning of the hearing did Harold relent and allow Jamie to testify. He never called Tammy Sue to the stand.

Even the prosecutors admitted that Jamie's testimony was heartrending. Jamie confessed that he was lonely and angry. "I have never hurt so bad before," he said. Jamie told the court that he talked to me by phone each day, and that I wrote to him nearly every day. Because of his dyslexia, Jamie admitted that he was embarrassed to write to me.

"Do you need your father?" Harold Bender asked.

"More than anything I've ever needed in my whole, entire life."

"Do you love your father?"

"More than anybody in the whole, wide world. He's my best friend," Jamie replied.

The prosecutors had no questions for Jamie.

As the final witness, my lawyers called Benjamin J. Malcolm, an expert on the U.S. Parole Commission. Ben had been appointed to the commission in 1977 by President Carter and had served for seven years. He was the commissioner of corrections for New York City before that and had also taught at John Jay College. Since 1984, Ben had operated a private consulting agency to attorneys and inmates concerning parole issues.

Ben Malcolm gave a strong testimony that said in essence, based upon his knowledge of how the federal parole commission works and information he had garnered from hundreds of cases, that if the judge did not reduce my sentence, it was doubtful that the commission would grant parole. Under my present eighteen-year sentence, I would not even be eligible for parole until I had served six years, which even with the time off for good behavior, the "good time" I had earned, would not be before

August 30, 1995. In Ben's expert opinion, because of the large amount of money in my case, he felt parole would be refused no matter what. Basically, Ben Malcolm was saying that if the judge wouldn't let me out of prison earlier, I would be there for the full extent of my sentence, which, considering time reduced for good behavior, would still be at least twelve years.

Ben compared my case to that of Ivan Boesky and Michael Milken, both of whom were convicted of white-collar crime and received much shorter sentences than mine. The prosecution countered that the reason the two men whose crimes involved far more money received sentences that were much lighter than mine was because they "cooperated" and pled guilty to their crimes. I had pled not guilty, and had never admitted to committing a crime. Attorney Deborah Smith complained that my "lack of cooperation" cost the government a sixteen-month investigation that could have been completed in one month. The prosecution also cautioned the judge to keep in mind that Jamie Charles's testimony was an attempt to play upon the sympathy of the court.

In his closing arguments, Harold Bender suggested to the judge that he put me on probation for five years and order me to serve no fewer than one thousand hours of community service. Doing that large amount of community service, Harold said, would

> Show to the world that he has been punished and that he will continue to be punished, and if he doesn't walk the straight and narrow, he's going to have to go back to prison for a term of thirteen years. . . . We're asking you . . . show some compassion and mercy on Jim Bakker and his family and allow him to see the light at the end of the tunnel and get out of prison and go about doing good, because he's capable of doing good and he will do good. Thank you.[5]

With that, Harold rested our case.

In his closing arguments, attorney Jerry Miller contended that the PTL Lifetime Partners were victims who would never get a penny of their money back. Mr. Miller conveniently failed to mention that in bankruptcy court on November 4, 1991—over a year earlier—Judge Thurmond Bishop had ruled that the Lifetime Partnerships "were being delivered and provided," that the money given to PTL by the Lifetime Partners was considered a gift, and that the partners were not eligible to be reimbursed. Nor did he mention that most of the Partners had given their contributions to further the Lord's work and did not ask for or expect their gifts to be returned.

In her closing words, Attorney Smith lamented that if Judge Mullen reduced my sentence further it would be sending a wrong message and would create "a tremendous problem for law enforcement" because I was asking for the same sort of leniency granted to Boesky and Milken, who had admitted their guilt, yet I had the audacity to walk out of the courtroom and announce that I was innocent. Attorney Smith also presented a thinly veiled accusation of insincerity on my part when I said that I accepted full responsibility for my moral failure and the wrong priorities at PTL. Attorney Smith continued:

> Mr. Bakker has been very successful so far in walking this very thin line, trying to convince the Court he's accepted responsibility so that he gets the benefit from playing on this Court's sympathy and mercy while at the same time turning to all of his friends in the industry of televangelism and all his followers and saying, "I was merely naive; I won't let it happen again. I accept responsibility for what I did," but it is always in the vein of, "I'm the captain of the ship. I accept responsibility for what happened on my watch, but personally I'm blameless because I didn't intend to defraud anyone." His campaign has been remarkably successful. . . . We think before any reduction of sentence is provided, Your Honor, it's really vital that Mr. Bakker admit that he knowingly lied to people to get them to send him money. That's one very large difference between he and Mr. Milken that I think is almost insurmountable in this case.[6]

At the conclusion of the proceedings, the judge gave the lawyers on both sides permission to submit twenty-five pages of written material within two weeks. He promised to then render his decision expeditiously.

I woke up every day for the next month wondering if it might be the day I would hear the news of Judge Mullen's decision. I went to bed each night disappointed that it had not yet come. I knew better than to hope for much; after all, Judge Mullen had already reduced my original sentence by more than half.

To keep myself from dwelling on the Rule 35 decision, I threw myself into getting ready for the holidays. Since this was to be my family's first holiday season since Tammy Faye's and my divorce, I knew it was not going to be easy. Nevertheless, I committed myself to making this year's celebration as special as possible.

As had happened in past years about this time, the bitterly cold

Minnesota weather caught up with me, and once again I came down with a bad case of the flu the first week in December. I was miserable. The flu dragged on day after day; the week before Christmas I still had it and instead of getting better, I felt as though I was close to lapsing into pneumonia. I was weak, tired, and cold most of the time, especially at night. Even after I had been able to borrow several blankets, accumulating five blankets on my bunk, I was still shivering all night long. During the days, I did my work and then returned to my cell; I piled on the blankets and tried to keep warm and rest.

On Tuesday, December 22, I wanted to send out some more Christmas cards, but I was too sick to even stand up. I curled up in my bunk and fell into a fitful sleep. Suddenly, through my grogginess, I heard a guard calling my name at the door of my cell, "Bakker, you're wanted in the Warden's office."

Oh, no. What now? I wondered. I had barely been out of my bunk for several weeks so I knew I hadn't done anything to get in trouble. I figured I had received the usual pre-Christmas batch of interview requests, and I had to go refuse them again. I looked at my watch as I rolled off my bunk and began folding up the extra blankets. It was 2:00 P.M.

Because of the flu, I simply had not been able to get warm, so I was wearing three sweatshirts and two pairs of sweatpants. I had not shaved for days. I didn't care what I looked like just then. I only wanted to go do whatever it was I had to do, and then get back to bed as soon as possible. I threw on my old army-green parka and a pair of tennis shoes and headed in the direction of the warden's office in the administration building.

As I made my way across the compound, it suddenly occurred to me that this might not be another interview refusal; this might be the day for which I had been waiting for so long, the day when I learned the results of my Rule 35 hearing! My stomach—already soured from the flu—began to churn, as I thought, *Could this be the day? Has the answer to my Rule 35 come down from the judge?*

By the time I stepped into the reception area of the Warden's office, my stomach was turning flip-flops. "Have you heard?" the Warden's secretary asked, shifting papers in her hands as she walked across the room from her desk toward me.

"Heard what?" I asked tentatively.

"The judge has reduced your sentence," the secretary told me.

A dozen questions popped into my mind instantly, but none came out of my mouth because the secretary was speaking again.

"We don't know what it all means yet. . . . " Her words trailed off.

I desperately tried to read the papers she was holding in her hands. I couldn't see much of what was written on the top sheet, but the words I saw were enough for me: "Indeed on further reflection, the sentence seems unduly harsh . . . and grants the defendant's motion."

Just then the assistant to the warden called me into his office. He told me that members of the press had been calling, saying that my sentence had been reduced. The courthouse in Charlotte would be faxing the paperwork any time now, as soon as all the figures were fed into the computer and the calculations were made concerning my new sentence and release date, whatever it was, and the actual dates I would be eligible for parole.

I sat there dumbfounded. Release date? Parole? Those were welcome but foreign concepts. My heart was pounding with excitement, my palms were sweating as I waited to hear the news. Could it really be happening? Could freedom be near?

At exactly 3:22:47 P.M., on December 22, 1992, the prison computer determined that, "James O. Bakker, 07407-058, was eligible for parole as of April 29, 1992.

April 29? That was eight months ago!

Judge Graham Mullen had cut my sentence from eighteen years to eight years, saying that he felt that the eighteen-year sentence was "unduly harsh." The judge's decision made me eligible for parole immediately!

Parole! I might be going home! I might be getting out of prison! My lawyer estimated that the parole commission would not hear my case for three more months, but three months seemed as though they were a moment compared to forty-five years or even eighteen years.

My mind was a blur. Jamie had just turned seventeen a few days earlier, on December 18, so I blurted to Robert McFadden, the warden's assistant, "This is the greatest Christmas present, aside from the birth of my son, that I have ever had!"

Being eligible for parole did not automatically guarantee that the parole board would grant it. But surely the parole board would concur with the wisdom of the appeals judges who had thrown out my original sentence; surely they would accept the decision of Judge Mullen who had reduced the sentence twice. Surely, they would allow me out of prison on parole!

Or would they?

CHAPTER

46

A Taste of Freedom

WHAT A CHRISTMAS THIS WAS GOING TO BE! EVEN THOUGH I was physically suffering from the flu, my attitude was soaring. For the first time in three years, I felt a glimmer of hope that I would not be spending the remainder of my most productive years in prison.

I applied for parole as soon as I could after hearing the news of Judge Mullen's decision. I knew parole was not going to be an overnight process. The parole board that would decide my case came to the prison quarterly and usually spent about three days there, reviewing potential parole cases. After interviewing the inmates under consideration for parole, the board then made a decision whether to recommend parole to the regional board, which had the authority to release an inmate. I had no idea how long everything was going to take, but I recognized that I had to keep busy because I would still be living in prison for a while. I was about to find out how long "a while" could be!

Even before Judge Mullen's decision, I had been keeping busy getting ready for my fourth Christmas in prison. I wanted to make this a special Christmas for my family, especially since it would be the first Christmas following Tammy Faye's and my divorce. I had saved a little money in my commissary account and planned to purchase a few small Christmas presents for my family members. It would be the first time I could actually buy them Christmas presents since 1988.

Pastor Phil Shaw helped me select my Christmas gifts by collecting all sorts of mail-order catalogs and sending them to me in prison. I scoured the Christmas catalogs, searching for items I thought each member of my family might enjoy. When I settled on the items from the catalogs, I withdrew the money from my commissary and sent it to Jamie so he could pay for them and arrange to have the gifts sent to Tammy Sue's home. It was such fun to be able to feel like a real person again at Christmastime. It felt especially good to be able to give again. Contrary to popular belief, I have always enjoyed giving more than getting.

Phil also helped me in putting together a special "prison Christmas card" that I could send out to all the many people who had written to me in prison and those who had been corresponding with Tammy Sue. It was a major project! I wanted to make up our own card with a picture of Canadian geese on the front. Those geese had special meaning to me.

Shortly after arriving at F.M.C. Rochester in 1989, one day I had been walking across the prison compound from one building to another, when suddenly I heard a loud honking sound in the air. I looked up and to my surprise, I saw thousands of geese—thousands of large, lively, loudly honking Canadian geese. Each one looked as though it might weigh as much as twenty pounds, with wingspans of four to six feet. I could not believe my eyes. Still in a bit of a stupor upon my arrival at Rochester, the first time I saw this amazing flock, I rubbed my eyes to make sure I wasn't dreaming or hallucinating. Sure enough, the birds were real.

As the geese drew closer to passing over the prison compound, the noise of their honking grew louder. Finally, when the entire flock could be seen, it was almost as though someone had thrown a huge canopy over the prison, sort of like a domed stadium made of goose feathers. When I worked up enough courage to ask someone about the geese, they told me that the birds fly over the prison almost every single day. The prison, I was told, was in a direct line between the field where the geese fed and the warm waters of Silver Lake, which, because of a power plant located there, doesn't freeze even in the coldest of winters. I was intrigued.

A few weeks later, in the midst of a blizzard, I was once again making my way across the compound through the snow. I closed my heavy, winter parka tightly and pulled its hood over my face, leaving only a small slit for my eyes to be exposed to the elements. Suddenly, I heard the now-familiar sounds of the geese honking high in the sky above me as they traveled their daily route over the prison compound. It was snowing and the wind was blowing so hard that I couldn't understand how the birds could stay aflight in such awful weather.

I looked up, peeking through my parka's opening, as I clutched the hood around my face. The sight was so awesome, I let go of my parka and let the hood fly off my head, as I peered through the snowflakes. Gracefully swooping over the prison compound were my new "friends," thousands of them, honking to each other as if they were on a Christmas outing, having the time of their lives. The sight of the birds against the gray sky dashed with a driving white snow nearly took my breath away. What particularly interested me was that most of the birds in the front could not be seen by the geese in the back because of the bad weather, but they all kept honking encouragement to their leader as if to say, "We're still here!" Many months later, I would read Tim Hansel's book, *Through the Wilderness of Loneliness*, in which he says, "It's the geese in the back who honk, letting the leader know that they're following and all is well. I am sure, too, that if people thought we would be constantly honking encouragement to them, our churches would be standing room only."[1]

For some reason, at that moment, standing in the middle of a prison compound, completely surrounded by razor-wire fence, I felt incredibly free.

Over the next several years, I studied and learned much about my fine, feathered friends. Pastor Shaw sent local information booklets about the geese of Silver Lake and other materials from his personal collection. I was able to find further information about the birds in the prison library. What I discovered fascinated me.

For instance, I discovered the reason why geese fly in a V formation. By flying together in a V they lift up each other by creating an upward air current through the movement of their wings, each bird getting 71 percent greater flying range than if it flew on its own. The flock actually flies in the shape of one great bird.

I thought instantly of the people in the Church: The comparisons were striking. How much more we could accomplish if we mobilized and helped each other, instead of going off in our own directions as individual "Lone Rangers," or worse yet, flying in the face of the entire group in our efforts to draw attention to ourselves.

Other things fascinated me about the geese as well. I learned that they migrate together, they feed together all summer, and fly south together in the winter. The reason the geese stopped at Rochester was because of the warm lake. The male mates with the same female for life, and the gander shows great interest in the young while they're being hatched and raised. The family group of geese stays together during migration.

When the warm weather finally came to Minnesota, I noticed three geese had landed in our compound near the dining hall. The inmates instantly adopted them. Each day, some of the inmates saved scraps of food from their own meals and smuggled it out to feed the geese. Soon we realized that the reason the trio had left the flock for the "security" of the prison compound was that the mother goose had laid eggs in a nest next to the chow hall door. I wondered though, *Why three geese? Why not just the expecting goose and the nervous daddy gandy?* At first I thought that the female goose had two husbands. Then I read that if one goose is hurt or wounded, two geese fall out of formation and follow the hurting goose to the ground, to help and protect the injured goose. The two geese stay with their fellow goose until he or she can fly again. Tim Hansel commented, "If people knew we would stand by them like that in the church, they would push down the walls to get in."[2]

Every day, eight hundred prisoners lined up for "mainline" and watched over this new life experience being played out before their eyes. When the goslings were born, with their soft, downy coverings, they were the pride of the prison. Almost everyone felt a sense of ownership of the goslings, as an attitude of parental protectiveness filled the compound concerning the geese. On some days, the inmates brought out enough food for the new family to feed a whole flock. One inmate built a tiny pond with a piece of plastic next to the nest so the baby geese could swim. The concern and compassion the "hardened criminals" showed to those creatures was amazing and is incompatible with the image most people have of inmates.

The new family of geese might have become permanent pets at the prison, but eventually the order was given to the guards to shoo the baby geese out of the prison yard, where they were snatched up and eaten by the huge hawks that constantly hovered near the prison. The following day, the three adult geese came back to what they had obviously believed to be a safe place. The geese were wrong. Their babies were gone, victims of a prison system that seemed intent on sucking out all vestiges of life, rather than revitalizing what life is there.

Throughout my stay at F.M.C. Rochester, I continued to study and learn from the geese. Often, spiritual principles came alive to me as I watched the way God had built in protective tendencies in the geese. For instance, the geese circle a long time before landing, trying to detect a fault or irregularity in a situation that might spell danger. After the geese land, a few members of the flock, the sentries, stand guard. They keep a constant vigil while the remainder of the flock feeds. If a sentry spots any sign of danger, he will sound a warning, bringing the entire flock to immediate attention. As I read the information about the geese, I thought, *What a beautiful picture of what the family of God should be like! We should be helping each other, watching out for one another, rather than seeking an opportunity to better ourselves at someone else's expense.*

The worst danger to the flock is deception, being fooled by a decoy or something that makes an imitation goose call. The skillful hunter uses a goose call to mimic the "All is well" honk of the geese. The hunter must know the "language" of the particular geese he is trying to deceive if he hopes to trick them. If the hunter can deceive and entice the flock into believing that the false geese or decoys are peacefully feeding in an area, the hunter can attract other birds to land. It is deadly for the goose, however, if he is deceived by the decoy, or the imitation goose sounds. If the goose is that gullible, he will quickly fall prey to the hunter's gun.

Again, I saw a spiritual similarity: It is equally as deadly for a Christian to be deceived by people who look and sound as though they are members of God's flock but who in reality are deceivers and decoys. Jesus called them wolves in sheep's clothing, "ravening wolves" (Matt. 7:15 KJV). He said,

Take heed that no man deceive you. . . . Many shall come. . . . False prophets shall rise, and shall deceive many. . . . There shall arise false Christs, and false prophets . . . signs and wonders . . . if it were possible, they shall deceive the very elect. (Matt. 24:4, 5, 11, 24 KJV)

All of my life I had heard the expression, "If it looks like a duck and sounds like a duck, then it is probably a duck." Those prison geese taught me not to be so naive.

For my 1992 Christmas card, Phil Shaw secured the services of a photographer who captured the geese on film while they basked in the warm waters of Silver Lake on a cold but sunny day. The ground and trees were all decked in ice and snow against a deep blue sky background. It was perfect. Phil sent me a copy of the photo, and I laid out the artwork in prison, picking out the type from a card I had found at the prison chapel. I sent it back to Phil and he arranged the printing, addressing, and mailing of the cards with Tammy Sue and Shirley Fulbright. The amount of coordination and work it took to get out a simple card was astounding. But it was worth it. Numerous people over the years have commented to me how deeply meaningful that 1992 Christmas card was to them. You can imagine how much it meant to me.

As Christmas grew closer, I talked by telephone with Tammy Sue almost every day, helping her plan the party for Jamie's seventeenth birthday on

December 18 and discussing the many details concerning her planned visit to Rochester for Christmas. I was really excited to see Tammy Sue and her family.

Mrs. Winger, a faithful friend who had baked many delicious cakes for my family over the years at PTL, created one of her wonderful specialties for Jamie's birthday party. Tammy Sue and her mother-in-law worked for days getting ready for the party on a limited budget. It was always astounding to me how creative Tammy Sue was; she could make a dollar stretch further than any woman I had ever known.

Tammy Faye flew in from California for Jamie's party; she spent four days with the children and got to enjoy a bit of the fun and chaos of an early Christmas celebration with two-year-old Jonathan and three-year-old James. I had purchased small Christmas presents for everyone else in the family, so it only made sense to me that I should purchase a present for Tammy Faye too. For Christmas 1992, I had ordered her a leopard-patterned, lightweight jacket. It had that "Tammy Faye" look, but it was a far cry from some of the more luxurious coats I had bought her in the past.

That same week, as I was struggling to overcome the flu, a nasty cold spell locked onto the Minnesota weather map. One day, shortly before Christmas week, the windchill factor reached thirty-six degrees below zero. I hated to think of the children standing outside in such cold weather, waiting in the visitors' lines to get in to see me, so I reluctantly called Tammy Sue and told her that I thought it might be best if they stayed home for Christmas. I tried to mask my disappointment as best I could, but Tammy Sue understood. Since she and the family were planning on coming to Rochester for Christmas, she had allowed the boys to open some of their Christmas presents early with their "Mama Faye," as the children refer to Tammy Faye. Tammy Sue told me over the phone about their excitement, and in my mind, I tried to picture what it must have been like to watch as the children and grandchildren opened their presents.

Tammy Sue described to me how her boys opened the presents I had purchased for them through the catalogs. I had given them some wooden building blocks, similar to the kind we had in the prison visitation room— only without the dirt and the teeth marks. Tammy Sue told me in detail about what the boys were building with the blocks and how they loved to stack them up and knock them over, just as James and I had done in prison. They also loved the wooden train I had given them. I was thrilled. I called every chance I got, trying to celebrate Christmas vicariously.

I telephoned Tammy Sue and Jamie on Christmas Day to express my love and to wish them the best Christmas ever. When Tammy Sue answered the phone, immediately I could tell by her voice that something was wrong. "Grandpa Bakker has been in a wreck and he is in serious condition," my daughter told me.

Instantly, my first response was, *Oh, God! Please don't let Dad die! Not yet. Not now!* The one thing that my mother and father had prayed every day for the past three years was that they would live to see me free from prison. *Please God! Don't let him die now.*

"What?" I cried into the phone. "Is he okay? What happened? Where is Grandmother? Is she okay?" I was firing questions at Tammy Sue off the top of my head as the bad news settled in on me.

Tammy Sue was tearful but she remained calm as she told me, "His pelvic bone is broken and he is bleeding internally. He's been transferred from one hospital to another one that has a trauma center that could better care for him. His car was broadsided on his side, and the car was totaled. Grandmother is okay."

My mother and father were en route to have dinner with members of the family and to open presents, a Bakker family tradition on Christmas Eve. Apparently, my eighty-six-year-old dad had been making a left turn at about 6:40 P.M. He did not see any traffic coming so he pulled into the intersection where he was hit by another auto going around thirty-five miles an hour. The car slammed into the driver's side door. My mother was with him and was shaken up quite a bit but not seriously injured. Dad, however, because of the internal bleeding, was in bad shape.

I asked Tammy Sue and Jamie to go to the hospital immediately to be with Grandpa and Grandma Bakker. Tammy Sue agreed and said that my brother, Norman, was already there as well. As soon as I hung up the phone, I tried calling the hospital where my dad had been taken, but the hospital would not accept my collect call, and inmates are not able to call direct. I called my attorney Jim Toms in Hendersonville, North Carolina, and asked if he could find out any details about my dad's condition. Jim promised that he would get back to me as soon as he knew anything for certain.

I tried to find Doug Brendle, our unit manager, to let him know that I was waiting to hear from the hospital or from my lawyer about my father's condition. The guard on duty said that the unit manager was unavailable, that he was in the prison compound somewhere, but his whereabouts were unknown. The guard suggested that perhaps Brendle was in the chow hall or the visiting area, helping to escort prisoners' families in and out of the prison for the Christmas dinner. In my concern over Dad, I had almost forgotten that it was Christmas Day, the most hectic day of the year in prison. Besides that, since many inmates want to make Christmas calls, inmates must line up to use the pay phones and must limit their calls to fifteen minutes in length. I rotated in the phone lines, calling family and friends, trying to find out about my father's condition.

Finally Brendle came down the hall. He came right to me and said, "I heard your father has been in an accident."

"Yes, sir. That's correct." I filled in the details for him as best as I could with what I knew of the situation back home.

"Come up to my office." He nodded toward the stairway. "You can call the hospital from there."

I thanked him and gladly gave up my place in the phone line to the next man. I followed Brendle upstairs to his office and called the hospital direct.

When I finally got the doctor on the phone, he explained to me that my dad's blood count was dropping and that they would do another test at 6:00 P.M. If the count continued to drop, they would give him blood and perhaps operate. The doctor then talked to Brendle and recommended that I come home immediately, if possible. I later learned that the doctor's own father had died recently from a similar set of medical circumstances.

After talking with the doctor, Doug Brendle placed an urgent call to the warden. They talked for a few minutes, while I waited, wondering, *What is going on?*

When Brendle turned his attention back to me, he spoke matter-of-factly but compassionately. "We are going to try to get you home to see your dad. The warden is working on clearance from Washington, D.C., right now. We can't promise anything, but we will try."

I was flabbergasted. *Home! To see my dad! And my mother! Home!* I tried to temper my emotions. I had been in prison long enough now to know better than to ever get my hopes up.

Besides, it's Christmas, I thought. *No one will be available in Washington to even consider giving me clearance.* Brendle instructed me to return to my cell and said he would contact me as soon as he heard anything, one way or the other. I appreciated his concern. Such promptness is not usually extended to prisoners.

About midnight on Christmas night, Brendle gave me the news. "Your trip is approved," he said. "You'll be going home in the next two days to see your father. That's as soon as we can get you there." He explained how it was possible for me to get out on leave. "Because of your sentence reduction this past week, the warden is giving you a new inmate classification. You will be able to travel, without handcuffs and legcuffs."

At that point, I wasn't too concerned how I was going to travel—I was going home to see my dad! It was to be a one-day-only trip, to see my dad in the hospital, then straight back to prison in the same day. The cost of the trip for both Mr. Brendle and me would come out of my commissary account.

I was dressed in street clothes as Brendle and I met to begin our trip by car from the prison to the Minneapolis airport. We were to travel by commercial airline to Charlotte rather than "Con Air," the prison transportation system. Just walking out the front gate of the prison without wearing handcuffs was a thrill. Once in the car, I was fascinated to see the scenery of the countryside surrounding the city of Rochester. I had arrived at Rochester in the middle of a snowstorm in a daze, so I had never really seen much of the local terrain. As I looked around now, the frozen, snow-covered Minnesota rolling hills and lakes looked wonderfully refreshing. Cold, perhaps, but free!

Walking through the airport without restraint was my next tiny taste of freedom. Did it ever feel great! *Freedom*, I thought, as we passed the bustling passengers, *should never be taken for granted*. I was slightly scared that people would recognize me and wonder how I had escaped from prison, and maybe even curse me or attack me. At times in prison, I felt as though the whole world hated me, so I wasn't sure what to expect on the outside.

On the plane, I was nearly overwhelmed by a simple question from a flight attendant. "What would you like to drink?" she asked pleasantly.

I could hardly make up my mind. There were so many selections, so many choices. For three years in prison, I had been told what to do, when and where to do it, and for how long. Now as the friendly flight attendant waited patiently for my reply, I was having trouble making a selection. Finally, I ordered apple juice. Later, when the flight attendant brought breakfast, I ate every bite. Airline food was delicious compared to prison food.

A police car was waiting on the tarmac when we landed. We exited the plane quickly and hustled into the back seat of the waiting car. I had so many mixed emotions about Charlotte. I had spent some of the best years of my life there, and some of the worst. The officer driving the car from the airport to the hospital was friendly and talkative, which helped take my mind off the past. He told me that crime in Charlotte had shot up significantly since I had been gone. I wasn't quite sure if he was joking or being serious.

When we arrived at the hospital, we were ushered upstairs by a security guard, and I was allowed to go into the intensive care unit to see my father. Even with all the tubes in him and monitors attached to his body, my father was a sight for sore eyes! My mother was sitting by his bedside as I entered the room. Dad tried to lean up in bed when he saw me, so I went to him quickly. I embraced my dad first and then turned to hug my mother. Dad was in good spirits, despite his banged-up body. He told me about the accident; he said he never saw the other car coming. I was just glad he was alive!

A few minutes later, Tammy Sue and Jamie arrived. My brother, Norman, came in shortly thereafter. What a family reunion we had at my father's bedside! Tammy Sue told me that the grandbabies were in the waiting room. I couldn't wait to hug those precious little boys. It was a special moment when I got to see my grandbabies, in the hospital or not. What fun we had. I read them a story from their new sound-effects storybook they had received for Christmas.

The head nurse arrived bearing good news. The internal bleeding had stopped and my father was to be transferred to another room in the trauma ward, a room in which the whole family could be together, even the children. My dad's condition seemed to improve just from seeing everyone around him.

Tammy Sue's husband, Doug, and Jamie went out and bought food for everyone—Kentucky Fried Chicken and Pizza Hut pizza. When they brought it into the room, it looked like a king's banquet to me. Real food. It's one of the things prisoners dream about. Tammy Sue later said that I looked like a starving man! I was holding a piece of chicken in one hand and a piece of pizza in the other.

For six wonderful, fantastic hours we were a family once again, even though one of us was injured. Actually, we were a family, plus one. Doug Brendle sat outside the hospital-room door the entire time. He tried to remain inconspicuous, that is, until someone suggested that we take some family photographs of the occasion. "No pictures!" Brendle ordered. He offered no explanation of his ban on photos, but I assumed he was worried about publicity.

It was heartwrenching to say good-bye. No doubt it would have been difficult under any circumstances, but to leave while my dad was still hospitalized made it even tougher. On the other hand, my family was extremely appreciative of Mr. Brendle and the prison system for making it possible for me to come home at all. We all hugged good-bye, and the family members prayed for me to be released on parole so we could be back together again soon.

Jamie Charles did not want to let go of me when it came time to leave.

He sobbed as if his heart was breaking. "Dad, I need you," he said again and again. Tears streamed down Tammy Sue's face as well. All the good-byes in prison were tough, but this one was the worst. Maybe it was because I had actually been back home rather than the family coming to see me in prison. Perhaps we felt as though this was a teaser, a tantalizing taste of what *could be* if I did not have to go back to prison. Then too, the circumstances that brought us together made it more difficult to leave. Whatever the reason, as I walked out of the hospital into the chilly Charlotte night, I felt as though it had all been a dream—a good dream, to be sure, in many ways, but nonetheless a dream.

Prison was my reality . . . and it was to there I was returning.

After rushing me away from my dad to get to the airport on time, by the time Mr. Brendle and I arrived at our gate, a terrible ice storm was turning Charlotte's roads into a giant skating rink. We were told that our plane had not yet even left Washington, D.C., and would be more than an hour behind schedule. The airline allowed us to wait in a pilots' lounge to avoid a potential scene in public. We waited . . . and waited . . . and waited. After about three hours, Brendle decided he was going to rent a vehi-cle and drive me to the nearest federal prison, where I would spend the night. I didn't understand his logic. We could just as easily have stayed in a hotel. Later on, I was told that with my new inmate classification, we could have stayed in a hotel without getting Brendle in trouble. For that matter, we could have stayed right there in the pilots' lounge if necessary. Other people seemed resigned to staying put at the airport . . . but not us.

A stickler for prison rules and routines, Brendle was committed to making sure I slept that night in a federal prison—any federal prison at this point. It had been a long day for him. No doubt he just wanted to sleep someplace where he didn't have to worry about watching over me. A fed-eral prison was a logical choice. Unfortunately, the closest federal facility was three hours away . . . in Butner, North Carolina!

When Mr. Brendle told me he was taking me to Butner, the very place I had experienced the worst of prison's indignities during my midtrial psy-chological examination, my heart jumped into my throat. I had not felt such abject terror in several years. Just the thought of going back to that hellhole sent shivers up my spine.

Getting to Butner was no easy chore, either. Brendle rented a jeep-type vehicle hoping to get better traction on the icy roads, but when the weath-er turns nasty in the South, traction is irrelevant, especially in an ice storm. Most southern states are ill-equipped to deal with an arctic blast such as we were having that night. It was the type of night when most people didn't even want to let the dog out, let alone drive three hours. But Brendle was not most people. We headed toward Butner, inching along at times over the treacherous roads.

When at last we pulled into the prison at Butner, I had to force myself to get out of the vehicle. The cold wind coupled with my fear chilled me to the bone. Brendle handcuffed me and walked me toward the front door—the same door, I presume, that I had entered slightly more than three years earlier. I walked in the door and down the corridor. Oddly, I had no recollection of the place. My mind had been in such a fog the last time I was at Butner, I now felt as though I was entering a different prison.

Even at that late hour, coming into the prison with a unit manager from another major federal facility, I was strip searched. Once again, while standing naked in front of strangers, every crevice and orifice of my body was checked. I was processed quickly and led to a cell—but not just any cell. I was put in a solitary-confinement cell—the hole, the same sort of cell as that in which I had been incarcerated during my first experience at Butner. I shouldn't have been surprised. If they had put me in solitary as an unconvicted, free citizen, why should I have expected any better treatment coming back to the place as a federal prisoner? Fortunately, I was not put among the insane inmates again. Other than that, the cells were the same—ten by twelve, with the only "furniture" being a steel sink and toilet. I nearly gagged as I recalled the filth and bile that had backed up into my commode the last time I was here.

The "bed" was a metal, shelflike structure covered by a three-inch pad. The door was solid steel with the awful horizontal slots through which food was handed in and inmates were cuffed before being brought out. A guard gave me a blanket and a sheet. I tried to sleep, but my body started to shiver. I was still getting over the flu. In the flurry of activities and the adrenaline rush of going home, I had not paid much attention to my physical condition. I was chilled to the point of shaking; I was so cold I couldn't get warm. I slept little that night, or what was left of it.

The following morning, Brendle and I boarded a flight—also to be paid for from my commissary account—from Raleigh-Durham Airport to Charlotte, where we connected to a nonstop flight back to Minneapolis. By 5:00 P.M. that afternoon, I was back in prison at F.M.C. Rochester. The inmates there welcomed me back as though I had been on vacation. Several of my friends said that they had seen me on television newscasts. Most of my buddies were more interested in hearing how my dad was doing than anything else. They seemed genuinely concerned.

This was the second time that I had been outside of prison for a few days, the first time to go to my resentencing trial, and now to visit my dad at the hospital. Reentering the Rochester prison this time, however, I had less a feeling that I was coming "home." On the contrary, I had a sick feeling, an awful, imposing awareness that I was locked up again. I had tasted a sliver of freedom, and I longed for the day that I would walk out the front gates at F.M.C. Rochester and never have to come back.

With my sentence being reduced, and having already applied for parole, it was a real possibility that I had spent my last Christmas in prison. Maybe by Easter I would be home with my family . . . maybe. . . .

505

47

The Last Appeal

AFTER MY SENTENCE REDUCTION TO EIGHT YEARS WAS made public, I received a deluge of congratulations letters, including notes from Melvin Belli, Marvin Gorman, Franklin Graham, Howard and Vestal Goodman, and of course, a glowing letter from C. M. Ward. One of the most enigmatic letters of congratulations I received came from Rich Oppel, editor of *The Charlotte Observer*, the newspaper that had run more than nine hundred articles on PTL and me in 1987. Most of those articles had a decidedly negative tone. Oppel and his paper won a Pulitzer Prize in 1988 for their coverage of the PTL scandal. That same year, Oppel was honored as Editor of the Year by the National Press Foundation for his coverage of PTL. Since my imprisonment, the newspaper had been much kinder toward me in its coverage of my experiences.

On January 2, 1993, Phil Shaw helped me celebrate my fifty-third birthday in the visitor's area in prison. We bought a cupcake out of a vending machine, tore out a make-believe candle from a piece of paper, and stuck the fake candle in the middle of the cupcake. It wasn't a fancy birthday party, but I greatly appreciated Phil being there with me on that day. We talked at length about some of the things that were going on in our country at the time. Some friends had given me subscriptions to *The New York Times, The Wall Street Journal,* and several major news magazines, so I kept fairly well abreast of current events. The big news in January of 1993 was the upcoming inauguration of Bill Clinton as president of the United

States. Phil Shaw and I discussed the reaction of many Christians who had been surprised and sorely disappointed by the election results. Many of the letters I had been receiving questioned God's sovereignty in the election process.

I understood their dismay. Having once been enamored with the power of Washington, D.C., myself, I understood how easy it was to wrap Christian imagery around a political candidate and think that the answer to all our problems rested in simply electing "our kind of politicians" to office. I also recognized that as a highly visible television minister, I had a measure of influence that I needed to guard carefully. Merely by being seen with certain political figures I was tacitly endorsing them, so I always sought to be fair in my support of both major party candidates.

Since being in prison, however, and studying the life of Christ, I had come to realize afresh that Jesus had no political agenda. He did not call for the toppling of the Roman emperor in order to touch people's lives with love, to reach out in compassion to the hurting and the poor and to bring the kingdom of God to earth. Jesus was neither Democrat nor Republican nor Independent—and shock of shocks to some people, He wasn't even an American! Jesus was God.

To allay the concerns of my friends who were fretting whether the world would survive the 1992 U.S. elections, I wrote a long letter outlining my perspective on Christians and politics. *The Charlotte Observer* got hold of a copy and printed an edited version. Although the paper downplayed the biblical quotes, the editors captured the essence of my message:

> Over the last few weeks since the election, many dear friends have written to me in different stages or states of depression, despair, defeat and devastation. They have a defeatist attitude that doomsday is here. They are so far down, dejected and despondent, I'm sure they don't want to get up in the morning. They sound like God has decamped or disappointed them somehow when their candidate lost the election.
>
> One of the greatest tragedies that has brought about catastrophic consequences is the church's involvement in the political system. Before I go on, let me make something very clear: I believe godly people should vote, run for political offices and, as Jesus taught, be the salt of the earth. But when churches and church leaders started endorsing candidates and political parties, it has brought about division and the greatest polarization and—I know some will scoff at this thought—unless stopped, could lead to violent conflict and even civil war within our nation.

507

If I could say one thing to our church leaders today, I would plead with them to stay out of politics and get back to preaching Jesus Christ and His Good News. We make a great mistake by judging a man by his political beliefs.

What would Jesus do?

Do we love a hurting world, or do we just join in political action to control those we disagree with? Even the disciples, when they were with Jesus the last time just before He ascended into heaven, wanted to know if, at this time, He would restore the kingdom to Israel. They wanted an earthly kingdom and an earthly throne. The disciples wanted to change political systems and Jesus wanted to change them and change the world with His Holy Spirit.

I would beg our church people to not be a part of this campaign by the so-called "religious right," but to do as God's Word instructs us to do and to pray for all those in authority. It's time to pray for our country and to lift up Jesus and His love from our pulpits and turn from messages of hate and fear. "For God has not given us the spirit of fear, but of power and of love and of a sound mind."

I want to make it very clear, I love and respect those who choose to affect the political process. But I feel for those who fill the sacred desk that there is a higher calling, which is to proclaim the Gospel of Jesus Christ in the power of His resurrection. Our dear brother in Christ, Billy Graham, has stood beside presidents of both parties on Inauguration Day and prayed for them and our country without being a part of the political process. Critics have petitioned Billy Graham to withdraw from appearing publicly with our new president.

How sad for Christians to have a "fort" mentality when Christ said we are to be the salt of the earth. The Rev. Graham is a preacher of righteousness to this generation. He has not shirked back from preaching in Russia, where he was accused of giving aid and comfort to communism. When asked if he felt he was being used, "Of course," he said, "but I'm using them too, to get out the Gospel." For those who believe in the power of the Gospel, let's put down our carnal weapons and pick up the Word of God, which is sharper than any two-edged sword.

Interestingly, after the "Letter from a Rochester Prison" ran in *The Charlotte Observer*, the paper received letters to the editor suggesting that I be set free from prison.

Although my new sentence made me eligible for parole, there was no guarantee I would get out of prison before serving every day of my sentence.

That decision was up to the parole board and I was scheduled to meet with two parole-commission examiners on Maundy Thursday, April 8, 1993, at 8:00 A.M. Dressed in my best prison khakis and accompanied by my lawyers, Jim Toms and Harold Bender, and parole expert Ben Malcolm, I walked across the compound to a room in the chapel building to meet with the examiners. I knew that if I wanted out of prison early, this was the first group of people I would have to convince that I was worthy to be set free. I was confident, upbeat, and hopeful, but extremely nervous.

I walked in and met the examiners, two large men, one black and one white, both dressed in business suits. They greeted us cordially and instructed us to sit down. My lawyers and I sat on one side of a conference table and the two men sat on the other. Stacks of inmates' files sat on the conference table in a heap. As part of the parole board, these commission examiners went from prison to prison, listening to story after story, every inmate trying to win his freedom.

I was no exception. I would be given about half an hour, my case manager had told me in advance, to make my case. The examiners would then decide whether it was worth recommending me for parole or not. If they responded positively, the case would be referred to the regional office where the decision to grant parole or not would be made. If they reacted negatively, I would have to reapply.

The examiners wasted no time in questioning me. I answered their questions and had the opportunity to present any statements or new evidence in my case that might help them in their decision. I presented the actual lodging records of the Heritage Grand Hotel, documents that showed that the Grand Hotel had space available to accommodate Lifetime Partners during most of the year except during our peak occupancy periods such as the Fourth of July and Christmas. These documents had not been presented in my original trial or in any of my resentencing hearings.

Thomas Sima, a student at University of North Carolina at Chapel Hill, was working as a law clerk for my lawyer, Jim Toms. Jim regarded Thomas as one of the brightest young clerks he had ever employed. As part of his job, Thomas Sima searched the PTL class-action suit files of Leventhol & Horwath, PTL's former accounting firm. Looking for anything that might be of help to me there in the files, Thomas discovered the hotel lodging records for the entire Heritage USA complex, including the much-disputed Heritage Grand Hotel. Thanks to Thomas, for the first time in my case, I was able to present clear, easily understandable, verifiable information.

My lawyer Jim Toms made a few brief statements on my behalf, followed by Ben Malcolm's presentation regarding the options the parole board might have in my case.

The examiners didn't rush us. They didn't limit our presentations or cut anybody off from making a statement. After about fifty minutes, the examiners asked my representatives and me to leave the room while they deliberated. In a few minutes, they called me back and said, "We are going to recommend that you be released this December, which is the maximum sentence under the federal guidelines for your case."

I wanted to stand up and shout "Hallelujah!" or something! Instead I held my emotions in check and smiled. "Thank you very much," I said softly but emphatically.

The black examiner looked me right in the eyes and said to me, "I believe you're innocent."

I thanked him. I was so excited. I might be getting out of prison soon!

Later, when I was alone with my representatives, Ben Malcolm told me, "Jim, in all my years in dealing with parole boards, I have never heard an examiner tell an inmate that he thought he was innocent."

The examiners sent their recommendation to the U.S. parole commission in Kansas City, the regional commission that had jurisdiction over my case. In most cases, an inmate who was recommended for parole was notified of the Regional Commission's decision within twenty-one days.

Real hope that I might be getting out of prison never was any higher than the days following the hearing with the parole examiners. I felt confident too because Ben Malcolm had prepared a masterful summary of my case for the regional commissioner, prior to the hearing. Using the government's own printed material on my case, Ben addressed the major allegations against me:

From 1984 to 1987, Bakker and other officials solicited lifetime partners to fund the construction of facilities at "Heritage USA." In return for their gift, partners were promised lodging based on the availability of space.

The Preliminary Sentencing Information (PSI) indicates that PTL received a total of $172 million as a result of the sale of 152,903 fully paid lodging partnerships. The PSI also states that $64.9 million was spent on construction at Heritage. The remainder of the funds went to cover operating expenses at PTL. The record also states that more than $4 million was paid in bonuses to Bakker and Codefendant Richard Dortch. Of this amount, Bakker received $2,780,000 spread over a four-year period.

His wife Tammy received $685,000 and Codefendant Dortch $550,000. In addition, Codefendant Dortch paid $275,000 into a trust fund to be paid to Jessica Hahn to prevent her from publicly accusing Bakker of sexual misconduct. Of this amount, she (Hahn) received only $20,000.

To clarify Jim Bakker's total remuneration from 1984 to 1987, inclusive, the PSI lists a total on his tax returns for $4,321,496. These were joint returns for Bakker and his wife and include salary and bonuses for both of them. Therefore the total, spread over a four-year period, averages out to $1,080,374 for both Bakker and his wife. It should be noted that approximately 60 percent of their taxable income was paid to the government as income taxes. It should be further noted that Bakker was not a greedy person who tried to steal from PTL; instead, he and his wife made large contributions to PTL. Codefendant and Chief Elder Richard Dortch testified that Jim Bakker and his wife assigned their royalties for tapes, books, LP's, etc. to PTL.

According to the record (PSI), it appears that the salary and bonuses paid to Bakker since 1984 were not fraudulently received. Salaries and bonuses were approved by the Board of Directors. What the record does not allow for is a retroactive compensation for all the very lean years from 1974 to 1984 when he received no bonuses and a very small salary.

One of the major allegations against Heritage USA and Bakker was that they oversold, that there were no vacancies and that this constituted a fraud. At the outset, the plan in the Grand Hotel was to set aside 50 percent of the rooms to Lifetime Partners and 50 percent to the general public. Lifetime Partners would make a donation of $1,000 in return for an annual stay of 4 days and 3 nights for the rest of their natural lives. Documentation clearly shows that there was always space at the Grand Hotel and the Heritage Inn, with the exception of July and August, 1985. There were a total of 125,191 vacancies during the years of 1985, '86, and '87.

Finally, it has been alleged that the Lifetime Partners *purchased* for $1,000 four days and three nights for the rest of their lives. Nothing could be further from the truth. For the sake of argument, a well-to-do parishioner or church member could contribute $1,000 a month or more. Does the parishioner purchase part of the establishment? Absolutely not! This is a gift, no different from the gift of the Lifetime Partners. The average age of the Lifetime Partners was approximately 50 years. Given a conservative life span of 20 years, a Partner would be entitled to a total of 80 days and sixty nights lodging at Heritage USA. This averages out to approximately $16 per night. Where in America can you get that kind of bargain?

511

Even so, during the trial held in the Federal Court of the Western District of North Carolina, numerous Lifetime Partners testified that they considered the $1,000 paid as a gift to the ministry and nothing else.

Unlike most frauds in which the defendants designed a scheme to solicit large sums of money and intended to defraud the public, Bakker did not intend to defraud the Lifetime Partners. It appears that his intentions were good, as stated by the Probation Officer on page 13 of the PSI. Therefore it is my opinion that the offense behavior is a Category Five because the fraud is more than $200,000 and the appropriate guidelines (before granting parole) should be 24 to 36 months (in prison). . . . By the time Bakker has his hearing in April 1993, he will have been incarcerated approximately 43 months. It is recommended that he be paroled after service of 45 months, on June 10, 1993.[1]

Most of my friends in prison believed as Ben Malcolm that I would be released before the summer of 1993. Everybody thought I was "going out," that I would soon be freed to at least a halfway house or possibly home. Even the warden seemed to think that I would soon be gone. "Hi, short-timer," he quipped, when he passed me on the compound using a term that implied I would not be at F.M.C. Rochester much longer.

My case manager at Rochester too told me that because of my clean prison record, she thought I might be released to a halfway house for six months, which was still considered prison time, but was far less restrictive than being incarcerated in a medium-security facility such as F.M.C. Rochester. That was good news indeed.

Jim Toms cautioned me about getting overanxious. Because mine was a high-profile case, it would probably be sent on to Washington D.C., for a ruling by the full U.S. parole commission. Most likely that would take a minimum of sixty days for the commission to make a decision.

Jim was right. On May 3, I was called to the warden's office. I should have known that the news was bad, because everyone who talked with me around the office was somber. Robert McFadden, executive assistant to the warden, broke the bad news to me that the regional office of the U.S. parole commission had disagreed with the decision of the parole board and had sent the case on to Washington, where it would be decided. I wasn't surprised, but the news was disappointing.

In 1993, the United States parole commission consisted of five members, two of whom were appointed by President George Bush and three who had been appointed under Ronald Reagan. On May 11, they handed down their decision concerning my case:

Parole Denied.

The national commission determined that I must serve every day of my sentence until it expired. The commission denied parole on the basis that the amount of money involved in the case was in excess of $1 million, which made it a Category Six offense. They rejected Ben Malcolm's suggestion that my case was a Category Five offense because it involved less than $1 million. Instead, they accepted as fact the figure of at least $130 million in fraud and therefore said that my case was more than one hundred times the cutoff amount which would have made the offensive behavior a Category Five offense. Parole guidelines suggested an offender serve between forty and fifty-two months for a Category Six offense. I had already been in prison for more than forty-three months. The parole commission wanted me to serve all fifty-two months before they would consider letting me out on parole.

Beyond that, the board wrote in their explanation of why they had turned down my request for parole: "You abused the trust implied by your chosen profession and the fact that you were a highly respected public figure."

Friends and family members who had anticipated my impendent release were floored by the news. My dear friend and former cohost, Henry Harrison, summed up the sentiments of hundreds of people who sent cards and letters to me within days of the news. Henry wrote, "How I wish there were some way I could ease your disappointment at this time!"

"Completely shocked and devastated at the news I heard today," wrote Helen and Jim Reeves.

Vestal Goodman also wrote to express her confidence that God was at work in my situation, and He would not fail to meet my needs.

One letter that particularly ministered to me came from Dr. R. T. Kendall, minister at Westminster Chapel, in London, England and author of the book that had so profoundly touched my life in prison, *God Meant It for Good.* I had written to Dr. Kendall, thanking him for his book and the deep meaning it had helped me find in my prison experience. When Dr. Kendall heard that my parole had been denied, he wrote to encourage me:

> It is my own view that when Joseph was not allowed to be released
> from prison . . . it was then he really began to get to know God in an
> intimate manner. I predict you are going to find this to be true. I
> believe that the best is ahead for you at the spiritual level. God wants to

513

know you at a level of intimacy that you have never before experienced
and that is what is in store for you next.

I thanked God for wonderful words from good friends, but still the
shock of being turned down by the U.S. parole commission sent me reeling. Jim Toms and Ben Malcolm, however, were not going to allow me to
stay down for the count.

I was permitted to appeal the U.S. parole commission's decision, but
time was of the essence. The appeal must be filed within thirty days. To
make the case for the appeal, I had to present the facts as best I could and
answer the same questions the examiners had asked me, only with the dis-
advantage of not being able to appear in person.

Phil Shaw and Jamie, who had come to visit me and was staying with
Phil's family, flew into action. Together with Shirley Fulbright in Florida
and Jim Toms in North Carolina, we began to gather materials to present
to the commission. We included pictures of Heritage USA to prove that
we had, in fact, built the lodging facilities we had announced. I even had a
friend take pictures of the almost-completed twenty-one-story Grand
Tower and the two completed bunkhouses to prove they existed. We found
brochures and newsletters describing the Lifetime Partnerships, all clearly
stating that the donations were intended for use by all the ministries and
operations of Heritage USA, not simply for construction costs.

We also showed examples of the various changes in the Lifetime
Partner program. We included a chart to show that if we chose to use 100
percent of our facilities, once constructed, we would soon have room for
356,147 Lifetime Partners. At the time of my resignation, we had only
152,903 Lifetime Partnerships. In other words, had we been able to finish
the projects that were under construction or in blueprint stages at the
beginning of 1987, we would have had more than twice as much space as
needed to accommodate all the Lifetime Partners on any given day. Using
the information procured by Thomas Sima, Jim Toms's law clerk, we provided charts showing that we had 125,091 vacancies at the Heritage Grand
Hotel and Heritage Inn during the years 1985 through 1987.

I attempted to explain to the parole commission in simple terms how
our original Lifetime Partnership program expanded with the full knowledge of those people involved. I told them we began in January 1984 to
build a Partner lodging center at Heritage USA, our church-sponsored
retreat center. This new project became the Heritage Grand Hotel. To help
defray construction costs, we offered a "Lifetime Partnership" to anyone
who donated $1,000 to the ministry of PTL. As a way of saying thank you

for their gift, the Lifetime Partners received four days and three nights free lodging at the Hotel every year for life. I had said on television and in mailings sent out to our mailing list that only twenty-five thousand of these Partnerships were available. Once they were gone, we would close the offer.

We didn't. We kept on receiving more Lifetime Partners and simply changed our original lodging offer by adding to the program other already built properties such as the ninety-six-room Heritage Inn and the massive Fort Heritage camping facilities to accommodate them. This brought the Partner total to 69,142. All the while, we were dramatically expanding every facet of Heritage USA and the ministries that flowed out of there. The crowds kept coming, both in person and by means of television, and soon I announced the second expansion of the Lifetime Partnership program. We began building the twenty-one-story, five hundred-room Heritage Grand Towers, which was nearing completion at the time I foolishly resigned from PTL in March 1987 on the advice of Jerry Falwell, Richard Dortch, and others.

The reason I was accused of fraud, I explained to the parole commission, was because by 1987, we had more than 150,000 Lifetime Partners. The government's case against us said that there was no way we could accommodate all those people and that we did not intend to do so, but were merely pocketing the money for ourselves. It was like being stopped in the middle of building a house and being told, "You never really planned to build it, anyhow!" Regardless, we were not prepared for the landslide of response we received from people who wanted to become Lifetime Partners and the thousands more who were coming to Heritage USA every week to enjoy the eighty-six religious services and Christian fellowship.

In putting together my appeal to the parole commission I also tried to answer some of the most pervasive questions, such as: "Who gave the money to PTL and where did it all go?"

Contrary to the impression given by the prosecutors in my trial and subsequently trumpeted without substantiation in the media, PTL did not receive a major portion of our donations from poorly educated, little old ladies. According to Dr. Patricia Kyle of FacFind, Inc., a marketing research company PTL hired to tell us about the demographics of our support base, the most frequent contributors to PTL were between the ages of twenty-six and thirty-five. The *least* frequent contributors were senior citizens over sixty-five years of age. The majority who donated and became Lifetime Partners were of above-average incomes. Overall, visitors to Heritage USA had higher income levels than the national averages. An overwhelming majority of PTL contributors also contributed to at least one other television ministry; most supported two television ministries on a regular basis. Forty-one percent of the contributors to PTL had at least two years of college education.

Where did the money go?

One man who knew exactly where the money had gone was William Robinson. Mr. Robinson was the first government-appointed trustee of Heritage USA after Jerry Falwell took it into bankruptcy. It was William Robinson's responsibility to inventory everything at Heritage. Later, he stated on television "that the numbers show us that the money that came in basically is here at Heritage or has been used to support the projects that are here at Heritage over the past five or six years."[2]

I now felt that I had taken too large a salary during my final years at PTL and had allowed some of the top people on our staff, such as Reverend Dortch and others, to receive salaries that were unwise for a ministry to pay. Because of the rocket-like speed of our growth, we made many mistakes. We sometimes spent money unwisely. Nevertheless, apart from the money spent on payroll, TV airtime, and missions, the bulk of the money contributed to PTL was right there on the property.

The financial figures I included in this section of my appeal all came from certified audits done by the highly respected "Big Eight" auditing firms who handled PTL's accounting for the years 1984 through 1986. Unfortunately, the figures provided by the auditors were never introduced in my original trial. Neither the prosecution nor my own lawyers paid much attention to the figures from the companies who knew the most about PTL's finances, the accounting firms. The prosecutors had been content to mainly introduce memos from our financial officer to paint a picture of what was happening at PTL on a daily basis. The figures in the memos did not match those in the certified audits.

It is easily understandable why the prosecutors did not focus on the audits as evidence. What puzzled me, both then and now, is why my own lawyers didn't present the audited figures to counteract the implied accusations of mismanagement of funds. When I asked my lawyers that question, they replied that we did not have enough money for outside research work to be done on my case. The lawyers used the same excuse when I asked them to subpoena videotapes of the television programs I had done while at PTL. The tapes, which are still in existence today, would have established my case because I specifically and emphatically stated two things: One, I repeatedly announced when the Lifetime Partnership programs were changing, so nobody could say we were trying to deceive them, and two, I repeatedly reminded the viewers that even though they were able to stay at Heritage USA in return for their financial gift, they were not purchasing time-shares by becoming Lifetime Partners. Rooms were on an "as available" basis. The Lifetime Partners had no guarantee of a certain room or date to visit, nor could they sell or will their memberships. They were donating the money to the ministry to be used wherever it was needed.

Shirley Fulbright and Jim Toms sent some books and brochures from which I cut pictures with my prison-purchased, blunt-edged, mustache scissors and pasted them onto separate pages, laying the spread out in such a way to tell the story so even a child could see the many projects and buildings on which the money was spent. Again and again, I pasted in the question: "Where did the money go?" and then tried to show a photo of some aspect of Heritage USA, with the amount it cost to build and maintain it. For instance, using the auditors' figures only from the years 1984 to 1987, the years during which we had implemented the Lifetime Partnership programs, I listed and illustrated with photos:

$171 million to build and equip Heritage USA between 1984 and 1987 (many structural parts of Heritage USA had already been built before that time period).

$35 million for general operating expenses.

$13 million to build Heritage Island (the famous water slide and giant swimming area).

$22 million for food, retail shops, and lodging costs besides the Grand Hotel and the Grand Towers. This included food and housing for the many guests on our programs, as well as the cost of the food available throughout the grounds.

$1 million for the Passion Play presented in the amphitheater nightly during the summer months.

$17 million to pay interest on loans, accounting fees, and legal fees.

$91 million to pay for television time to stations that aired our program and broadcasting on our own satellite broadcasting system.

$101 million for wages and salaries. In 1987, we employed approximately 2,400 people and had a $25-million payroll.

$17 million for Bibles and books.

$15 million for printing and postage.

$21 million for real estate development. This was the area in which we were building houses and condominiums for the people who wanted to live at Heritage USA all year long.

$1 million per year to put on our annual Christmas City display.

$15 million for maintenance and utilities. This included water towers, wells, sewage treatment plants, phone systems, electric power, roads, landscaping, maintenance, and warehousing. These things are often taken for granted by the average visitor to a public place, but the costs are gigantic.

We also included in the appeal copies of the court record showing the shocking disparity between what the government said I had built at PTL and the projects for which I had actually overseen the construction. The government had contended, "Bakker used relatively few of the funds solicited from the partners to construct promised facilities. In fact, of the proposed Heritage Village facilities, only the Grand Hotel and one bunkhouse were actually completed."[3]

Few of the funds! Only two buildings! Anyone who had ever come within camera range of Heritage USA could have disproved that statement. Yet it went uncontested in my trial and my appeal. In truth, during the time I was president of PTL, we built over one hundred buildings! Granted, many of them were not lodging facilities, but the impression given by the prosecutors was that I had somehow used millions of dollars on my own lavish lifestyle while the people who donated money to PTL were being ripped off because we did not build what we said we were going to construct.

All the while, we were in the process of building everything we said we were going to build. Even while Tammy Faye and I were in California attending the Betty Ford program, construction continued at Heritage USA. Had I not resigned in March 1987, we would have continued to build according to our master plan that I had shared with the community leaders of Fort Mill in January of that year. I believed in a God who could do anything. God had always helped me through the most desperate financial situations in the past, so I had no reason to doubt that, with His help, we would make it even then. The Bible says, "Now faith is the substance of things hoped for, the evidence of things not seen" (Heb. 11:1 KJV). The government and the media dealt in hard facts and figures, however, and they were convinced that PTL had been tottering on the precipice, ready for a great financial fall, even before my resignation. To those of us who had worked in Christian ministry, it was just normal, everyday life.

All of this information and much more we put into the 144-page appeal to the parole commission. Phil Shaw then had the pages copied and bound together in plastic binders. Jamie Charles and a group of volunteers put together fifty color copies and hundreds of black and white copies of the appeal and sent them to significant pastors and Christian leaders who might be willing to write to the parole commission on my behalf or recommend that others do so. We also prepared five sets of the material for the national commissioners.

At the same time Phil, Shirley, and I were working on the written appeal, Jamie was on the telephone trying to drum up support from Christian leaders. He spent hours every day calling Christian leaders all across the country—at Phil Shaw's expense—asking high-profile Christians to send a letter to the commissioner and to encourage those within their sphere of influence to do the same. The responses were mixed, but many pastors and leaders readily agreed to write and to help any way they could. Ironically, the calls that yielded the least fruit were to people whom I had greatly helped when I was in a leadership position. I was shocked and Jamie was disappointed at how many of them refused his calls.

The call that most surprised Jamie was to Jimmy Swaggart. Jimmy and I had never been close friends before the disclosure of his or my moral failures, nor were we close friends afterwards. We had corresponded twice by mail, however, in 1992. Jimmy's letters were encouraging, yet noncommittal. Jimmy continued to deny that he had had anything to do with my demise at PTL. To me, it didn't matter anymore, but to Jamie, it was a major issue. Jamie always had a love and respect for Jimmy Swaggart as a man of God. Much of that had been eroded by the events of the past few years, but Jamie decided to call Swaggart anyhow and ask him to help get me out of prison.

Jamie dialed the number, reached a secretary, and after he had identified himself as "Jay" Bakker and had given the purpose for his call, Jimmy Swaggart came on the line.

"Well, hello, Jay," Jimmy's big voice boomed into the phone. "What can I do for you?"

Jamie explained that he was calling pastors, television preachers, and other Christian leaders in an attempt to generate support for me at my upcoming parole hearing.

"How can I help?" Jimmy asked without Jamie having to ask.

Not expecting Jimmy Swaggart to be so cooperative, Jamie stumbled around for a moment before suggesting, "Well, you could put the address of the parole commission on the screen during your TV program and encourage people to write on Dad's behalf."

"All right, I'll do it," Jimmy answered.

"You'll do it?" Jamie asked.

"Yes, son, I will. I've always felt that your dad's sentence was grossly unfair." Jimmy and Jamie talked for a while longer and Jamie asked Jimmy Swaggart to forgive him for the hard feelings he had held toward the man since 1987. It was the beginning of changes in my son's heart.

Another of Jamie's life-changing phone calls was to Mark DeMoss, Jerry Falwell's young associate. Since I had first met Mark at the Maxim's Hotel in March 1987, several major changes had taken place in his life. Mark had married and now had three children of his own. He had continued to work with Jerry Falwell, serving as his administrative assistant and director of public relations until August 1991, when he moved to Atlanta and established his own public relations firm.

Mark had lost his fifty-three-year-old father, the famous philanthropist Arthur DeMoss, when Mark was Jamie's age. Seven years later, Mark's twenty-two-year-old brother was killed in an auto accident. Perhaps these losses and the fact that he had now become a father himself had given Mark a better understanding of the impact the awful experiences we shared had made upon my children, especially Jamie. Mark had been in contact with Jim Toms and had written to me in December 1992 expressing his sincere concern for Jamie Charles.

In May, Mark had mentioned to Jim Toms that he would be willing to contact some nationally known Christian leaders, requesting a letter of support to be sent to the parole commission in my support. Jim had encouraged the idea but in attending to all the other details of my case, had not pursued Mark's suggestion.

In mid-June Mark DeMoss traveled to Des Moines, Iowa, to meet with Jamie, Phil Shaw, and Jim Albert, the law professor from Drake University. They spent five hours together, and Jamie tore into Mark, telling him in no uncertain terms how he felt about the coup that Mark had been a part of that eventually led to my imprisonment. Mark listened patiently and graciously to Jamie's tirade. He did not attempt to dispute Jamie's accusations or defend his former boss's actions or motives for involving himself in PTL. Mark merely listened and let Jamie know that he wanted to be his friend.

During the meeting and again afterward, Mark mentioned that he would be glad to encourage some high-profile national Christian leaders to write to the parole commission on my behalf. I had not asked Mark to do any such thing, nor was I aware that he was doing it until after he had already sent out a letter. On his own accord, Mark stuck his neck out for me.

Thanks to the efforts of Jamie, Phil Shaw, Tammy Sue, and Jim Toms, more than three thousand letters poured into the parole commission in Washington. Meanwhile, Mark DeMoss collected letters from numerous well-known Christians. Some of the people who wrote on my behalf had done so before. Pat Boone wrote another kind letter, as did Charles Colson. Both of these extremely busy men had written to Judge Mullen during my resentencing and Rule 35 proceedings.

Other letters came from several unexpected sources. Art Linkletter, for example, wrote a kind letter on my behalf. A pioneer in television, Art had appeared on our program crusading against drug use after his own daughter died a drug-related death. Bill Bright, president of Campus Crusade for Christ, also wrote at Mark DeMoss's request, as did Beverly LaHaye, president of Concerned Women of America, and Robert P. Dugan Jr., public affairs director of the National Association of Evangelicals.

Mark also elicited a few surprise letters—surprising to me, at least. One kind letter came from Dr. David Clark, chairman of the board for the National Religious Broadcasters. More intriguing, David was a former employee at the Christian Broadcasting Network and had served as a federal bankruptcy trustee of PTL for seven months in 1987 and 1988.

Another rather unexpected letter came from Focus on the Family President James Dobson. Dr. Dobson's compassion was not unexpected, but I also knew of his reluctance to become involved in anything that might hurt the image of Focus on the Family. It was risky for him to take up my cause and I sincerely appreciated him putting his name on the line for me. Others who wrote on my behalf included former PTL board member, A.T. Lawing; renowned Christian psychologist, Dr. Richard Dobbins; former president of the National Religious Broadcasters, Ben Armstrong; and well-known Christian ministers Kenneth Copeland, Oral Roberts, Rex Humbard, C. S. Lovett, George Otis, and Don George.

Perhaps the letter that surprised me the most came from none other than Reverend Jerry Falwell. Jerry had expressed on several occasions that he had felt my forty-five-year sentence and the reduced sentences of eighteen years to eight years were unduly excessive and unreasonable. He had spoken in such terms from his pulpit in Lynchburg, Virginia. Jerry passed on those sentiments to the parole commission.

Similar concerns were addressed by members of the legal community. David A. Funk, professor of law at Indiana University School of Law, wrote to the U.S. parole commission, "In my view, for what it is worth, the conviction and imprisonment of this man truly does constitute the greatest American miscarriage of justice of the twentieth century."

Of all the letters written to the parole commission, nobody understood the case better than Professor Jim Albert of Drake University Law School. He had studied my case for more than a year, had read every page of the transcripts of my trial, and had made notes throughout that raised points he felt should have been addressed or could have caused a mistrial. Most gratifying to me, Jim Albert was convinced beyond a doubt of my innocence, not on the basis of my personality, spirituality, or past positions, but on the sole basis of the evidence and the facts. Although he had not been a supporter of PTL or Jim Bakker, he became convinced that the case was not only an insult to me but to people of faith in general and especially to all branches of Christianity.

Jim began his letter by relating some of his formidable credentials, which formed the foundation of his opinion. He explained how he came to be involved in my case:

As a broadcast law scholar and student of fraud litigation, I was intrigued by an article I read in the April 23, 1990 New Yorker, which extensively analyzed in twenty-five detailed pages Jim Bakker's trial and conviction on federal fraud and conspiracy charges. At that point, I began researching the trial for myself and read every single page of the voluminous trial transcript, interviewed several witnesses who testified and corresponded with and visited Mr. Bakker in the federal correctional facility in Rochester, MN. From this exhaustive research, I have nearly completed a lengthy in-depth magazine article about the trial. A modified version will be offered to law journals.

What I have learned about that trial prompts several questions about its conduct. The transcript is clear that the trial judge allowed the prosecution to belittle some of Mr. Bakker's key witnesses, including Arnold Santjer, whose evangelical religious beliefs were mocked and ridiculed by the prosecutors in the presence of the jury. It appears that in that way the focus of the trial was wrongly shifted from the question of fraud to the reasonableness and acceptability of Mr. Bakker's religious beliefs. The government's major emphasis on Bakker's lifestyle, with testimony the first day ranging from jewelry purchases and cars to Jessica Hahn, belies the prosecutors' often stated explanation that this was a garden variety fraud case. I don't think it was tried as one—they kept beating the jury over the head with testimony and evidence of the elegance of Bakker's lifestyle. The strategy was obviously effective, but I think they got an inordinate number of bumps and plenty of free mileage toward the fraud counts with that kind of red meat for the jury. It surely doesn't read like a fraud case.

I have interviewed Mr. Santjer at length and was staggered by what he told me. Not only did the jury laugh and giggle when the prosecutor belittled his statement that God had made it possible for him to earn the money that he did in his life (he was asked whether God had signed his paychecks, if that was indeed the case and the prosecutor smirked and the jury erupted in laughter), but I have now talked to two people who were in that courtroom during Mr. Santjer's testimony who have told me that while Mr. Santjer was testifying Judge Potter sat shaking his head with his fingers in his ears. One focus of my article is the signals that the Judge was sending to the jury and the permissiveness of the Judge allowing the prosecutors to humiliate Mr. Bakker's witnesses and belittle their religious beliefs. It could credibly be argued that, as a result, Mr. Bakker was denied a fair trial. I have researched the narrow question of prosecutorial misconduct which takes that exact form, *vis* belittling the religious beliefs of witnesses and found rock solid authority for the proposition that such conduct violates the constitutional fair trial right of an accused. *United States v. Ballard*, 322 U.S. 78 (1944); *Munn v. Algee*, 924 F.2d 568 (5th Cir. 1991).

I wish that these points had been raised on appeal, but they were not. Based on the case law that I have cited, I think they would have been most relevant on the appeal of the case and would have justified the Fourth Circuit overturning the conviction. I present these facts to you, then, as new information which in your discretion may warrant a parole at this time.

Jim Bakker was probably careless and inattentive to matters financial, relying on others, but I haven't seen any persuasive evidence of intent. He was a man of the cloth, one whose whole life was his religion. He preached an optimistic, miracle-filled and abundant evangelism that admittedly inspired millions of people. I think that a person like that operates on a completely different plane than most of us in the sense that he believed in miracles and in the Holy Spirit moving him to raise money and to build a Christian retreat and vacation center at Heritage USA. His broadcasts were always spontaneous and, in a sense, stream of consciousness outpourings by he and his wife as they were moved on the air to talk optimistically about all that they were doing and planning to do. I have read the transcripts and, for the life of me, I can't see the intent to defraud in them. I have also seen the fund-raising brochures and the solicitations mailed to the PTL contributors and each of those solicitations contains a very plain legend that the monies received would be used for any of the ministry's purposes. And, I have read the November 6, 1991 decision of United States Bankruptcy Judge William Thurmond Bishop which concluded that the premise upon which the government convicted Jim Bakker in that courtroom in Charlotte was simply invalid. As you know, Judge Bishop found that "[i]t was not contemplated that Lifetime Partners would be entitled to a specific hotel room, condominium, or unit on the premises nor more importantly, were Lifetime Partners promised availability of rooms or any other benefits for the use of their partnership." He also found that "the benefits of the Lifetime Partner memberships were being delivered and provided" by Mr. Bakker.

I would submit that the analysis of these same facts provided by Judge Bishop also constitutes the kind of new information which would justify a parole. The consideration given by Judge Bishop certainly stands in sharp contrast to the hostility which Judge Potter openly displayed toward Mr. Bakker, his witnesses and their religious beliefs in the presence of the jury in the fraud trial and in sharp contrast to the atmosphere that prevailed in that courtroom when jurors were laughing out loud at the sincere and honest answers concerning the religious beliefs of Mr. Bakker's witnesses.

I also strongly disagree with the position taken and representations made by the prosecutors in their May 3, 1991 sentencing memorandum and the affidavit of John Brugger which is attached to it to the effect that the unbelievable forty-five year sentence imposed was appropriate for the crime for which Jim Bakker was convicted. Mr. Brugger makes reference to the sentence imposed on Michael Milken as an example of the strict punishment justified in these cases. Of course, Milken is now free and I've got a file two inches thick of wire fraud and securities fraud opinions where the fraud perpetrated was far more serious than that proved in Jim Bakker's case and the sentences imposed significantly less severe. Particularly, people in these cases are simply not incarcerated for eighteen or forty-five years. That is even more true given the lack of intent to defraud on Mr. Bakker's part and the purposes for which he was raising that money. It was certainly not to defraud those contributors. If he had intended to do that, he would not have built a five star hotel and furnished each room as elegantly as he did. Each room was fancier than the nicest hotel I've ever stayed in. I've seen the pictures. They were poshly appointed. Bakker chose the furnishings himself. If he really was raising this money to defraud his contributors and "rip them off," it seems to me he would have built a less elegant hotel and decorated it more cheaply given the premise that he knew he was overselling and the contributors wouldn't ever see or use those rooms.

I honestly believe that Mr. Bakker's trial was tainted in the ways I've suggested. The *New Yorker* concluded that, as well, Mr. Bakker was not provided a vigorous defense. Jurors that magazines interviewed were quoted as saying that they were waiting to hear Jim Bakker's side of it and his defense to the charges but that it never came. That is a provocative aspect of this, too and one that I find coalesced with Mr. Bakker's own lack of any appreciation of his true legal exposure in the case. Whether it was a fair fight or whether an attorney more experienced in defending public figures charged with crimes could have successfully defended him is something that haunts me.

Please allow me to share some of my impressions of Mr. Bakker as they relate to the fairness in allowing him to be released from prison now. He has obviously been pulling himself up by his bootstraps from that sinkhole that was the national humiliation of being convicted and shackled and ridiculed on television sets in tens of millions of homes. He is taking college courses in prison through a community college there in Rochester and a Bible College in the Twin Cities. He is becoming computer literate. His correspondence to me has been intelligent, positive and insightful. He has really pulled his life together and I think stands as a model prisoner.

I have spent several days over the past twelve months with Mr. Bakker in Rochester. I have been struck by his repentance, his introspection and his forgiving and nonmalicious outlook on life. He has certainly been broken. Everything he owned has been taken away. His wife has left him. And he is attempting to raise, as a single parent, his son who has remained in Florida and who is very close to his dad. His son happens to be dyslexic, as is my own son and I know something about how important it is on a day-to-day basis for a child with a learning disability to have the nurturing and support that only a parent can provide. And Mr. Bakker is doing it from prison, but that child is having trouble getting through high school and is now in a computer therapy program. I would simply urge that some compassion be shown for that child which would allow him to be reunited with his father and permit him to receive the daily parenting that is necessary for someone like him with a mental disability to cope in this world. These dyslexic kids are great and they are sharp and often so sensitive, but they have trouble on a day-to-day basis that others don't and they just can't make it alone.

I honestly believe that to release him would not only recognize all that he has done to deserve it, but would provide you an opportunity of historic dimension to reflect the compassion and forgiveness which [have] always defined this country.

Even more importantly, I believe a wrong has been done here and that it should be righted. The trial was turned into a referendum on whether that jury thought the religious beliefs of Mr. Bakker and his followers were acceptable. To have voted to acquit after the focus of that trial was thus shifted would have required a juror to embrace those evangelical beliefs. And that is why I am so troubled by that trial. If the framers intended nothing else by the First Amendment, it was to prohibit that type of inquiry in a court of law in this country. Jim Bakker's religious beliefs were put on trial.

I could see other benefits to society in releasing Mr. Bakker. The new Jim Bakker, down but now rehabilitated, preaching a message of forgiveness and compassion himself, could be a boost to this country. Frankly, in the context of all the gloom and doom I see on television today, the euphoria and optimism of Jim Bakker's programs would be refreshing again. I would think that he could be a powerful role model with a message of hope and belief in God even when a person is at the very bottom in their life.

He is not vindictive in any way, shape or form and I am sure would not use his freedom to seek vengeance from those who toppled him. He would not be looking back, he would be looking forward. He is not a hateful man. There does not appear to be a mean streak in him and I certainly can't see him abusing his freedom by attacking his accusers or the system that I think failed.

I am a believer in the system. If I were not, I couldn't send hundreds of law students each year into it. And I believe that, at some point, justice will be done in Jim Bakker's case. I hope that you are the ones to do it and I thank you for considering these comments.

Sincerely,
James A. Albert
Professor of Law
Drake University Law School
Michael G. Galligan Law Firm, P.C.

Professor Albert sent me a copy of his letter to the parole commission and I included it in my appeal. If they had not read it previously, they had another opportunity to do so as they considered my case. As I read and reread Jim Albert's insightful and moving letter, I could not help remembering R. T. Kendall's words once again, "This is another sign that God's time has come: when someone pleads your case (and knows all the facts) without your opening your mouth."[4]

Thank you, Professor Albert.

Thank you, R. T. Kendall.

Thank You, God!

I knew the U.S. parole commission could totally disregard Professor Albert's opinion and that of all the others who had written on my behalf. Certainly I wanted to be set free. More than ever, though, I felt that my case was completely in the hands of God. He had raised up Professor Albert to plead my case; if God wanted me to be free now, the commission could not prevent it. On the other hand, if God had more for me to learn in prison, the best-argued case to the parole commission would not win my freedom. As Chuck Colson had advised me during his visit with me in prison, I had fought my case, but I had to let go of it. This was the last round; I had no further recourse after this appeal. It was now in God's hands.

On Tuesday, July 27, 1993, *Los Angeles Times Syndicate* writer Cal Thomas made my parole the topic of his column. Cal had been a close associate of Jerry Falwell and the Moral Majority during my tenure at PTL. He and I had never met; we were in the same kingdom but at different poles. That's why I was surprised when Thomas wrote:

> While Bakker was one of a number of TV evangelists who had succumbed to the temptations of several deadly sins, he was the only one convicted of a crime and sent to prison. One of the reasons given by those who favored a prison term for a first offense was that an example had to be set. Presumably, other clergy who used television to proclaim their messages would be so petrified over the treatment given to Bakker that they would try honesty as a new tactic. . . . But perhaps Bakker should never have been sentenced to prison. He was a nonviolent, nondangerous offender and there are already too many of them being warehoused expensively in federal and state institutions. They take up space that could be used for those who are serious threats to the public. In fact, because of overcrowding, the truly dangerous get out early, often serving just a fraction of their sentences. Restitution and community service for

Jim Bakker and for many white-collar criminals would be far preferable to several years in prison. . . . The public interest is not served by continuing Jim Bakker's incarceration. He has been punished enough. He has cleaned toilets in prison, his wife divorced him, and he is a broken man. It would be cruel and unusual punishment to attempt to extract additional pounds of flesh from a man who has no more to give.

Jim Bakker could have a greater influence outside than inside prison. Perhaps he could visit some of his former friends who remain on television and "evangelize" them to be honest and to preach the truth, instead of taking advantage of simple people who mistake snake oil for the Word of God.

The parole commission should let Jim Bakker go and the occasion should be used to begin an examination of the entire federal prison system, preferably before the "tough on crime" demagoguery of the next election cycle begins.

It's long past time to renovate the way we handle nonviolent, nondangerous offenders. If Jim Bakker is a catalyst in that, we will all have something for which to "Praise the Lord."[5]

The same day Cal's article first appeared on newsstands across the country, the U.S. parole commission was meeting in Washington and deciding my case. They must not have deliberated long,; the response came almost immediately.

Knowing that my freedom from incarceration had already been decided by a higher court did not lessen the blow when it came.

Parole denied.

Denied? How can this be? All those letters? Jim Albert's pleading my case? The fact that I have already served three and a half years. . . .

Denied. On July 27, 1993, the national commissioners rejected my appeal and affirmed their previous decision in its entirety. I was to stay in prison the maximum length of time the law allowed for my sentence and for an inmate with my exemplary record in prison. It was as if all of our massive efforts had not even made a dent in the parole commission's opinion. In explaining their decision, the commission stated,

You argue that whenever you solicited donations for various hotel and lodging projects at Heritage USA, you invariably informed potential donors that (a) the promised lodgings would be only "as available" and (b) the money would be spent not just on hotel construction, but on general operating expenses of your "whole ministry." You also point out that donors who have received "life time memberships" which purported to give them annual free lodging at Heritage USA, did not acquire legal ownership or contract rights that made the donors priority creditors in bankruptcy. You are correct in that contention.

Nonetheless, you were convicted of 24 counts of mail and wire fraud, conspiracy and aiding and abetting the same. Even though the people who gave donations in response to solicitations by you were not purchasing any secured ownership rights, they were induced to part with their money on false premises, i.e., promises by you of lifetime "partnerships" that you ultimately knew you could not fulfill.[6]

Basically, the parole commission was saying, "We believe that you never intended to build enough lodging space for all the Lifetime Partners." The Commission's report continued:

You claim that no promise was ever made that the entire donations solicited would be used other than for your ministry. This is correct. You conclude that the donors were therefore not victims of any fraudulent misrepresentation. The Commission disagrees. The fraudulent misrepresentation was that (a) the hotel and other forms of lodging would actually be constructed in the near future and (b) there would be free lodging for each "partnership" on a reasonably available basis. Therefore, you were not free to abandon your hotel construction projects while continuing to solicit (and to receive) money on the strength of the promised "partnerships." Over $100 million was solicited for construction projects such as $74 million for the Towers Hotel which were never completed. Your scheme was criminally fraudulent because you kept soliciting money with promises of free lodging long after you knew that your operating costs made construction of those lodgings impossible.[7]

I began to wonder if the commission even read my appeal. In full-color photographs, I had pointed out to the commission that not only were we going to construct the Tower, we had done so! The twenty-one story building was there! As long as I was president of PTL, construction was continuing on not only the Tower, but numerous other projects as well. The Tower was only weeks away from being completed and stands at Heritage USA to this day.

The commission's report went on:

529

Moreover, in the case of the completed Grand Hotel project, you failed to limit the membership to 25,000 as promised, but exchanged 66,683 "partnerships" for donations. Thus, you deliberately "oversold" partnerships and made it impossible for your donors, as a group, to receive the promised free lodging on a reasonably available basis.

The fact that you used the available funds primarily to pay for the many operating expenses of the PTL Corporation does not affect the fraudulent nature of how you acquired those funds. Further, what you spent on your lavish lifestyle seems to contradict your argument that you meant well but were just overwhelmed by circumstances. Therefore, it is fair for the Commission to conclude that your fraud offense consisted of having solicited and received over $100 million on false pretenses, from donors who never received the benefit you promised.[8]

I could not believe my eyes! All of our charts, explanations, and pictures were for naught. These people wanted me to stay in prison . . . apparently God did too.

48

I Was Wrong

DURING MY TIME AT F.M.C. ROCHESTER, I OBSERVED something that it seemed to me had gotten nearly every inmate into trouble. It was something insidious, pervasive, something that I too had tried to cover and push aside in my own life—the love of money. The underlying reason why some of the bankers, Wall Street businessmen, doctors, and others are in prison is because of something they did to get more money. I realized that of the 60 percent of inmates who are in prison because of drug-related crimes, most are not there because of an addiction to drugs; they are there because of an addiction to the drug of money. It was their insatiable desire for more money that led them to selling drugs in the first place, not a desire to ruin someone else's life by getting him or her hooked. Unimpeded, that lust for money carries the potential to destroy both the buyer and the seller.

About the time of my parole hearing, I completed my study of all the words of Jesus in the New Testament. To my surprise, after months of studying Jesus, I concluded that He did not have one good thing to say about money. Most of Jesus' statements about riches, wealth, and material gain were in a negative context.

Even "The Prodigal Son," one of my favorite stories told by Jesus, took on new meaning as I read it for the first time with an overview of Scripture in mind. I quickly noticed that the story began with the younger brother saying to the father, "Give me! Give me my part of the inheritance" (Luke

15:12). He didn't even say, "Please give me." He simply demanded. Before long that young man landed in the pigpen. I began to see that the fastest route to the pigpen begins with "Give me" . . . and the fastest route to the "big pen," the federal penitentiary, often begins with the same phrase, "Give me!"

I was amazed at this "new" revelation, but beyond that, I was deeply concerned. As the true impact of Jesus' words regarding money impacted my heart and mind, I became physically nauseated. I was wrong. I was wrong! Wrong in my lifestyle, certainly, but even more fundamentally, wrong in my understanding of the Bible's true message. Not only was I wrong, but I was teaching the opposite of what Jesus had said. That is what broke my heart; when I came to the awareness that I had actually been contradicting Christ, I was horrified.

For years I had embraced and espoused a gospel that some skeptics had branded as a "prosperity gospel." I didn't mind the label; on the contrary, I was proud of it. "You're absolutely right!" I'd say to critics and friends alike. "I preach it and live it! I believe in a God who wants to bless His people. Look at all the rich saints in the Old Testament. And the New Testament clearly says that above all, God wants us to prosper even as our souls prosper. If your soul is prospering, you should be prospering materially as well!"

I even got to the point where I was teaching people at PTL, "Don't pray, 'God, Your will be done,' when you're praying for health or wealth. You already know it is God's will for you to have those things! To ask God to confirm His will when He has already told you what His will is in a matter is an insult to God. It is as though you don't really trust Him or believe that He is as good as His Word. Instead of praying 'Thy will be done' when you want a new car, just claim it. Pray specifically and tell God what kind you want. Be sure to specify what options and what color you want too."

Such arrogance! Such foolishness! Such sin! The Bible says we are not to presume upon God, but we should say, "If the Lord wills, we shall live and do this or that" (James 4:15).

I may not always have been so blatant about it, but I often preached a prosperity message at Heritage USA and on our *PTL* television programs. But when I began to study the Scriptures in depth while in prison, something I am embarrassed and ashamed to admit that I rarely took time to do during the hectic years of constant building and ministering at PTL, I was very distressed at what I discovered.

I realized that for years I helped propagate an impostor, not a true gospel, but another gospel—a gospel that stated "God wants you to be rich!" Christians should have the best because we are children of God, "King's kids," as I often put it. And shouldn't the King's kids have the best this world had to offer?

The more I studied the Bible, however, I had to admit that the prosperity message did not line up with the tenor of Scripture. My heart was crushed to think that I led so many people astray. I was appalled that I could have been so wrong, and I was deeply grateful that God had not struck me dead as a false prophet!

How could I have taught and even written books on the subject of "how to get rich" when Jesus spoke so clearly about the dangers of earthly riches? One of the statements of Jesus that kept echoing in my head and heart was in the parable of the sower, where Jesus said that "the cares of this world, the deceitfulness of riches, and the desires for other things entering in choke the word, and it becomes unfruitful" (Mark 4:19). *The deceitfulness of riches.* The more I thought about it, the more I had to admit that I had fallen into that snare. I had allowed the quest for material possessions and the deceitfulness of riches and the lusts for other things to choke the Word of God in my own life and in the lives of my family members and coworkers. As PTL grew larger and our ministry more widespread, I had a financial tiger by the tail, and just coming up with enough money to meet the daily budgets dominated my thoughts and my time.

In prison, I decided to dig into the Scriptures further to see what else Jesus had to say about money. I noticed that He said,

> Do not store up for yourself treasures on earth, where moth and rust destroy, and where thieves break in and steal. But store up for yourselves treasures in heaven, where moth and rust do not destroy, and where thieves do not break in and steal. For where your treasure is, there your heart will be also. (Matt. 6:19-21 NIV)

Another Scripture that seared into my heart was Matthew 6:24, "No one can serve two masters. Either he will hate the one and love the other, or he will be devoted to the one and despise the other. You cannot serve both God and Money" (NIV). In that same passage, I discovered that God's priorities were much different from what mine had been.

Jesus said,

> Therefore I tell you, do not worry about your life, what you will eat or drink; or about your body, what you will wear. Is not life more important than food, and the body more important than clothes? . . .

So do not worry, saying, "What shall we eat?" or "What shall we drink?" or "What shall we wear?" For the pagans run after all these things and your heavenly Father knows that you need them. But seek first his kingdom and his righteousness, and all these things will be given to you as well. (Matt. 6:25, 31-33 NIV)

Other teachings of Jesus scored direct hits upon my heart, as well:

"But woe to you who are rich, / for you have already received your comfort" (Luke 6:24 NIV).

"Then Jesus said to his disciples, 'If anyone would come after me, he must deny himself and take up his cross and follow me'" (Matt. 16:24 NIV). This verse dramatically illustrated the stark contrast between what Jesus taught and what I had been teaching. I had taught that Christians could have the best of both worlds, the best that this world had to offer and heaven too. Jesus said, "Deny yourself."

Jesus taught, "How hard it is for the rich to enter the kingdom of God! Indeed, it is easier for a camel to go through the eye of a needle than for a rich man to enter the kingdom of God" (Luke 18:24 NIV). Unwittingly, I had tried to explain this verse away with the help of modern scholarship. I had taught people that the "eye of the needle" of which Jesus spoke was a low arch in the Holy Land. Supposedly, a camel carrying a heavy load had to get down on its knees to slip through the "eye of the needle." This was the explanation that I had heard from other prosperity teachers whom I admired and respected, so I simply passed on their explanation as fact without really examining the verse carefully, especially in the original Greek. Nor had I consulted any Bible dictionaries or encyclopedias. If I had done so, I might have found that not a shred of reputable archeological or historical evidence supports the camel-through-the-arch theory.

In prison, however, when I took time to study the meaning of Jesus' words in the original Greek language, I discovered that Jesus was not talking about camels walking on their knees at all. The word He used was one commonly used to describe a *sewing needle*, not an archway. In other words, the verse meant exactly what it said: It may not be impossible for a rich man to enter heaven, but apart from a miracle of God, he doesn't stand a chance!

In my cell, I studied the Bible long hours into the night. Often as the sun rose in the eastern sky, I was still poring over the Scriptures. The more I studied, the more I had to face the awful truth: I had been preaching false doctrine for years and hadn't even known it!

Tragically, too late, I recognized that at PTL I had been doing just the opposite of Jesus' words by teaching people to fall in love with money. Jesus never equated His blessings with material things, but I had done just that. I had laid so much emphasis upon material things, I was subtly encouraging people to put their hearts into things, rather than into Jesus.

Was Heritage USA of God? I believe it was; I believe the original concept was His and that He planted it in my heart. But as I said before, Heritage USA—with all its facilities and buildings—was the box, the package. The box was meant to enhance people's appreciation of the true gift, Jesus Christ, but before long, many people began to worship the box . . . and I allowed them to do so; no, I encouraged them to do so by what I was teaching and by the manner in which I was living. I lived the prosperity message I was preaching. I should have taught people to fall in love with Jesus rather than the trappings.

Sadly, long after I left Heritage USA, some people still wanted to worship the box. Others compromised their values trying to be the boss of the box, and still others nearly sold their souls in attempt to get . . . what? The box? So many people tried to save the box, saying they wanted to save the ministry, but I have never heard a building preach a sermon or a box reach out and help a hurting person. How sad. The box is empty without Jesus.

I began to share some of the things I was learning with several of the Christian inmates with whom I often discussed the Bible. I was stunned by their responses. Rather than being excited that I had finally come to a knowledge of the truth, they were aghast that I was denying what they considered to be sound spiritual principles taught by sincere men and women of God.

"I was sincere about what I taught too," I told them, "but I was sincerely wrong. Just because somebody repeats something often or loudly does not make it true. The big question is: 'What does the Word of God say?'"

To their credit, the guys replied, "Well, what *does* the Word say?" In response, we looked up verse after verse as I pointed out to them what Jesus had to say about money. The guys accepted Jesus' words as authoritative, but then they developed a bad case of the "Yes, buts."

"Yes, but doesn't Jesus also say that He came that we might have an abundant life?" asked David, an inmate whose background was steeped in the prosperity message. We turned to John 10:10 and read, "I am come that they might have life and that they might have it more abundantly" (KJV). It was a wonderful statement by Jesus Himself, so I could easily see how David had related it to material prosperity. As we looked up the words in a Greek-English dictionary, however, we found that the Greek word for "life" used in this verse was *zoe*, a word indicating "life in the spirit and soul" rather than the word *bios*, which is used to refer to physical, material life. Of the two words, *zoe* is usually considered the more noble, higher word. Basically, Jesus was saying, "I want you to have an abundant life in the spirit, which is My highest and best for you."

"Hey, that verse doesn't have anything to do with material prosperity," David said, as the light turned on in his heart and mind. "If abundant life meant having houses, cars, riches, parties, and entertainment, then I guess the world is experiencing abundant life. Yet we have more hatred, disease, and pain than ever."

"Not only that," piped up Jorge, a Spanish guy with a big smile who had walked into my cell and was leaning up against the bunks as he watched David and me searching through the Bible reference books, "but if you're figurin' how much God loves you by how much money you have or what kind of car you drive, or how big a house you live in, what happens when all that stuff is gone?" Jorge had hit the nail right on the head.

The next night after work, David and Jorge were back. David had talked to his Christian girlfriend on the telephone that afternoon and she had told him, "Of course God wants us to prosper, David. You know the Bible even says so in 3 John, verse two."

I knew the verse well. It had been my favorite "prosperity verse" for years; it was the premier New Testament verse upon which I had built my prosperity message and lifestyle. The verse reads: "Beloved, I wish above all things that thou mayest prosper and be in health, even as thy soul prospereth" (KJV).

I had preached on this verse for most of my ministry. It said exactly what I believed—that God wanted His people to prosper, and by that, I interpreted it to mean prosper financially and materially, in other words, to get rich. Again, I never really examined the true meaning of the text, nor did I ever seriously consider why this verse, on the surface anyhow, seemed to contradict so much of what the New Testament said in other places. I simply pulled this verse out of context and took it to the bank—literally!

"First of all, let's look at this verse, David," I said. "We have to take the whole counsel of God's Word, just like Jesus says in Matthew 4:4, 'Man shall not live by bread alone, but by *every* word that proceedeth out of the mouth of God.'" We began going through the verse, word by word, deciphering the meaning from the Greek with the help of a few Bible reference books someone had sent me. I didn't tell David that I had been tearing this verse apart for nearly two years and trying to find where it fit with the message of Jesus.

It did not fit. No matter how hard I tried to make my former interpretation of 3 John 2 consistent with the words of Jesus, the verse as I had understood it simply did not make sense. How could John be saying, "above all things, I want you to prosper"? First, David and I looked up the meaning of the word *prosper* in a dictionary. The various forms of the word all had one common meaning: "to increase in wealth."

"David, tell me something," I said pausing and pointing to the Bible. "Jesus said that our number one concern was to love God supremely; after that we are to love our neighbors as ourselves. Why, then, would John say that 'above all' I should have wealth?"

"I don't know, Jim," David replied. "What do you think?"

I ignored David's question and asked him another. "Do you think God wants you to have money above your soul's salvation?"

"No. Of course not!"

"Well, then let's find out what these words mean," I suggested. I suddenly remembered one of my Bible professors warning me never to look up biblical words in an English dictionary, because the words might have a completely different meaning than in the original biblical languages. I pulled a Bible dictionary and Greek lexicon off the shelf.

We looked up the meaning of the word *prosper*. We found the word translated "prosper" in the King James Version of the Bible came from a Greek word, *euodoo*, which is made up of two Greek root words, *eu*, which means "good," and *hodos*, which means "road, or route, a progress, or journey." We did not find a single reference in the Greek to money, riches, or material gain from the word translated *prosper* in the King James Version.

The apostle John, the writer, was saying simply, "I wish you a good, safe and healthy journey throughout your life, even as your soul has a good and safe journey to heaven."

John was not saying "Above everything else, I want you to get rich. Above everything, you should prosper and make money." That is not even implied in the true meaning of the verse. Yet I had based much of my philosophy at PTL and even before that on this one verse that I had totally misunderstood!

Just to make certain that we were not unfairly placing too much emphasis upon the words in this passage, I began looking up other places where the same words were found in the Bible. I found *euodoo* again, for example, in Romans 1:10. The apostle Paul wrote, "Making request, if by any means now at length I might have a prosperous journey by the will of

God to come unto you" (KJV). Paul often took special care to make sure that his motivation could not be misconstrued or maligned because of money. It would be unthinkable for the apostle to say, "Please pray for me that somehow or other I might obtain wealth by coming to preach to you," or "Please pray that I will make a lot of money on this trip." Yet that is how Romans 1:10 would have to be interpreted if we took the King James Version's translation of *euodoo* to mean wealth or material gain. Clearly, that was not the intent of the apostle Paul. He was saying simply, "I sure hope God grants me an opportunity to visit you soon. Please pray that I will have a good journey on the road as I travel to see you."

The apostle John was saying something very similar when he said, "Beloved, I wish above all things that thou mayest prosper and be in health, even as thy soul prospereth." It was a greeting, a prayerful desire of the apostle's, not a principle suggesting that Christians should be wealthy.

David reluctantly agreed that to base a prosperity doctrine on this verse would be shaky indeed, but he was not yet ready to abandon his belief in the prosperity message with which he had been indoctrinated. He took some of the notes from our study sessions and wrote to several leading "prosperity preachers," some of whom were close friends of mine. Day after day, David was back, armed with more books sent to him by prosperity teachers.

"Jim, look at this!" David said as he pointed to a passage in the Old Testament. "Look here. It says right here that God has given us the power to get wealth. Now, why would God give us that power, if He didn't expect us to use it?"

I looked at the passage to which David was pointing. I wasn't surprised to see that he had been referred by some of my friends to Deuteronomy 8:18. I had used the verse myself in countless messages and appeals for money. The verse reads, "But thou shalt remember the LORD thy God: for it is he that giveth thee power to get wealth, that he may establish his covenant which he sware unto thy fathers, as it is this day" (KJV).

At first glance, the verse did seem to support the idea that God is the one who gives us the power to get rich. When David and I read the verse in context with the entire passage of Deuteronomy 8:1-18, however, it took on a different meaning. We realized that what God is actually saying to His people in this passage is, "When I bring you out of Egypt into the Promised Land and you are enjoying the blessings I have given to you, don't think that you have been successful in your own strength. Don't say that it is your own power, that you did all this yourself." The Lord then warns His people to remember that He is the one who deserves the glory.

All God was saying was, "When you get into the Promised Land, don't forget who brought you there and gave to you everything that you have."

David and I dug into the words in the passage, looking especially at the word translated *wealth*. By looking up *wealth* in a Hebrew lexicon, we discovered that it comes from the Hebrew word, *chayil*, which is used 232 times in the Old Testament. In almost every case, the word is meant to imply "might, strength, power, ability, virtue, valor," and, oh, yes: "wealth." It is used most often to describe valiant men and women and armies.

As David and I read the passage with new understanding, we concluded that God was not saying, "I am the one who gives you riches." What He was really saying was: "Remember, it is God who has given you the power to receive everything you have. He is the one who has given you strength. He is the one who has given you a house, land, or other possessions."

I admit, in the past I had used this verse to make it sound as though it was God's will to make everyone wealthy and if any of His people were poor, it was probably due to lack of faith or not applying the biblical "formulas" correctly. That was an improper interpretation of the passage. Yes, it is God who gives us the power to receive all that we have, but to assume that He wants all His people to be wealthy based on this Scripture is an illegitimate extension of that truth.

As David and I studied the Scriptures concerning material wealth, he became convinced that the Bible does not teach that God wants us to be rich in material possessions. "But Jim, doesn't God want to bless His people?" David asked.

"Of course He does," I replied, "but we don't have to twist the Scriptures into saying something they don't mean. There are plenty of passages in the Bible that tell us that God will provide for us, and as we honor Him by using the resources that He gives us for His glory, He will continue to pour out even greater blessings upon us." We turned in the Bible and read,

> Bring ye all the tithes into the storehouse, that there may be meat in mine house, and prove me now herewith, saith the LORD of hosts, if I will not open you the windows of heaven, and pour you out a blessing, that there shall not be room enough to receive it. And I will rebuke the devourer for your sakes, and he shall not destroy the fruits of your ground; neither shall your vine cast her fruit before the time in the field, saith the LORD of hosts." (Mal. 3:10-11 KJV).

God also gives us the principle of sowing and reaping, what we sow we are going to reap. "He which soweth sparingly shall reap also sparingly; and he which soweth bountifully shall reap also bountifully" (2 Cor. 9:6 KJV). But God does not intend for this principle to foster lust for money and things or to support attitudes of greed, both of which are totally contrary to the teachings of Christ. This principle does not give people a license to love money under the guise of sowing seed, reaping a huge personal harvest and assuming that their gain is a sign of godliness.

God has promised to bless those people who put Him first in their lives. That principle has never changed. I still believe that God blesses His people and will meet their needs. The sin is falling in love with and seeking after money and material things. He doesn't want us to equate mere money with godliness. In fact, the apostle Paul said that "If any man teach otherwise, and consent not to wholesome words, even the words of our Lord Jesus Christ, and to the doctrine which is according to godliness . . . supposing that gain is godliness: from such withdraw thyself. But godliness with contentment is great gain" (1 Tim. 6:3, 5-6 KJV).

For the first time, I began to really understand what Paul meant when he wrote,

> But they that will be rich [which I discovered meant: "they that want to be rich"] fall into temptation and a snare, and into many foolish and hurtful lusts, which drown men in destruction and perdition. For the love of money is the root of all evil: which while some coveted after, they have erred from the faith, and pierced themselves through with many sorrows. But thou, O man of God, flee these things; and follow after righteousness, godliness, faith, love, patience, meekness. (1 Tim. 6:9-11 KJV)

For years I had glossed over that passage of Scripture. I ignored it, made excuses for it, or tried to explain it away. I refused to accept the obvious interpretation. I now see that the message was right there all the time, so plain that even a child could see it and understand it. I was wrong.

I knew I could not keep this newfound information a secret. I had influenced so many people to accept a "prosperity message," I now felt that I had a responsibility to tell my friends what I had been learning from my studies of the Bible. I wrote a simple, straightforward letter and sent it to some of the people who had written to me in prison. In the letter, I told of the verses I had used improperly and what I had discovered by studying the true meaning of those verses. I apologized for preaching a gospel that emphasized earthly prosperity rather than spiritual riches. I wrote, "I

540

ask all who have sat under my ministry to forgive me for preaching a gospel emphasizing earthly prosperity. Jesus said, 'Do not lay up for yourselves treasures on earth.' He wants us to be in love with only Him." I went on,

> Many today believe that the evidence of God's blessing on them is a new car, a house, a good job, etc. But that is far from the truth of God's Word. If that be the case, then gambling casino owners, drug kingpins and movie stars are blessed of God. Jesus did not teach riches were a sign of God's blessings. In fact, Jesus said, "It is hard for a rich man to enter the Kingdom of Heaven." And He talked about the "deceitfulness of riches. . . ." There is no way, if you take the whole counsel of God's Word, that you can equate riches or material things as a sign of God's blessing.
>
> If we equate earthly possessions and earthly relationships with God's favor, what are we to tell the billions of those living in poverty, or what do you do if depression hits, or what do you say to those who lose a loved one? Many "in name only" Christians would curse God if they lost all of their material possessions.
>
> Jesus said, "Narrow is the way that leads to life and few there be that find it." It's time the call from the pulpit be changed from "Who wants the life of pleasure and good things, new homes, cars, material possessions, etc?" to "Who will come forward to accept Jesus Christ and the fellowship of His suffering?" Jesus calls us to come and die, die to ourselves and to the world, so He might give us true life.

The letter was not meant to be published to the world. I didn't know how *The Charlotte Observer* got a copy of my letter, but the paper ran portions of it on the front page under the headline: "Ministry of Prosperity Was Mistake, Bakker Tells Friends." Other publications picked up on the story, and ran excerpts of the letter as well.

Soon I began receiving mail from all over the country concerning the letter. Some people were appalled that I—a person they considered as a primary propagator of the prosperity message in the twentieth century— had disavowed my former teaching. Others who wrote to me were delighted that I had "finally seen the light."

Franklin Graham wrote:

> I saw the article in *The Charlotte Observer* today with excerpts from a letter you wrote to some of your friends. The article, I think, should

encourage you. . . . The statements you made, Jim, were excellent and productive. . . . Be of courage and good cheer. I think of you often. God bless.

Your friend,
Franklin Graham

One letter especially took me by surprise. It was from Mark DeMoss, Jerry Falwell's young assistant who had helped convince Richard Dortch of Jerry's good intentions in helping me stave off a "hostile takeover" of PTL. Mark wrote:

It has been 5 1/2 years since we met under rather unusual and difficult circumstances at Maxim's Hotel in Palm Springs, CA. I cannot count the times I have thought about and prayed for you and your family during those years. Several things have prompted me to write you at this time.

First, I have followed you and your legal case as closely as I can and have been impressed by everything I have seen and heard. . . . I have spoken with several people who have visited you in prison, including Richard Dortch, Chuck Colson and Franklin Graham. . . . Next, I was moved by your letter to friends and by your heart and spirit which was obviously behind those words. I took the liberty of sharing that letter with a number of pastor friends and evangelical leaders. . . .

Next, I have been burdened for your family and particularly for Tammy Sue and Jamie Charles. . . .

As you may know, Jerry [Falwell] was publicly very critical of your original prison sentence as well as the reduced sentence of 18 years. He addressed it on *The Old Time Gospel Hour* from his pulpit as well as at various news conferences and media interviews. . . . Jerry and I would also be interested in visiting you. . . . In the meantime, I will pray for God's presence and guidance to be perfectly clear to you at all times. I look forward to hearing from you and I trust you will feel the freedom to let us know if there is something we can do to help you.

Sincerely,
Mark DeMoss

Some people saw the reversal of my position on prosperity theology as self-serving, as an attempt to curry favor with the judicial system. Others were concerned that my years in prison had skewered my perspective on the Christian life in a different way, that just as I had gone overboard on the prosperity message previously, I was now going overboard on a message of austerity and self-sacrifice as a result of my prison experience. Some said, "It's understandable that prison has had that sort of influence on Jim. He has nothing, therefore it's easy for him to believe that Christians should have nothing. We'll see how he feels about things once he gets out."

Frankly, I was not greatly concerned with what the critics or the skeptics had to say about my speaking out against the prosperity message. I knew what God had clearly shown me from His Word. I had studied every word of Jesus over a period of two years, and I was convinced that the prosperity message was at best an aberration and at worst "another gospel" contrary to the gospel of Jesus Christ. Although I still believed that God blesses His people, the prosperity message I had preached for many years was wrong.

In retrospect, one of the main reasons I slipped into believing and preaching a distorted doctrine was because of my lack of understanding of what it really means to allow Jesus to be Lord of my life.

In prison, I began a fascinating study of the titles ascribed to Jesus in the New Testament. I discovered that the term used to describe Jesus more than any other is *Lord*. The word in the Greek is *Kurios*, which means, "might, power, master, owner, and possessor." As such, we do not simply accept Jesus Christ as our Savior; we must allow Him to be our Lord, our Master, Owner, Possessor, and our Mighty and All-Powerful God. Jesus is called "Lord" 618 times in the New Testament.

I had accepted Jesus as my Savior and with my lips I had called Him "Lord," but in my heart and lifestyle, I now realized that He was not the Lord of my life; I was. As I came to grips with Jesus' words in Matthew 7:21, however, I was shattered. Jesus said, "Not every one that saith unto me, Lord, Lord, shall enter into the kingdom of heaven; but he that doeth the will of my Father which is in heaven" (KJV). Jesus was saying, "You can sound religious; you can do great works in My name; you can even preach the gospel, cast out devils, and do wonderful things—ostensibly for God—and still miss heaven."

Although I was committed to following Jesus, I wanted to do it my way rather than His; I had given my life to Him, but I was still in control of it. As a result, although I knew and used the correct words and terminology, Jesus was not in fact Lord of my total life. Unwittingly, I had attempted to compartmentalize my relationship with Him, giving Him control of certain parts of me, yet not surrendering to His absolute Lordship. To put it another way, I wanted Jesus to be in my life, to be the engine, the power in my life, to be the motivator and the enabler who supplied the resources to do great things for God on earth and eventually take me to heaven, but I wanted to keep my hand on the controls.

In prison, I came to the end of Jim Bakker. God was teaching me that I must "die" daily and that the process would continue for the remainder of my life. The more I studied the Word of God, the more I realized that I have so much further to go . . . but I have made a start.

I truly believe that one of the reasons God allowed me to go to prison was to learn this principle. It was only then that I was ready to leave F.M.C. Rochester.

49

Diesel Therapy

THE LAST YEAR THAT I WAS IN F.M.C. ROCHESTER, WINTER lasted nine months, it seemed. It was so cold. And dark. It seemed as though the sun rarely came out all winter long. Those Minnesota winters had become so depressing to me, locked inside prison walls. Throughout my prison sentence, I had resigned myself to going wherever I was ordered to go, and I did so without appealing to any prison officials and only occasionally appealing to God to transfer me to another environment. During the cold winter of 1993, however, I began praying, "Oh, God, please let me go someplace where the sun is shining and it's warm."

At my next meeting before the prison review committee, I requested to be transferred to a prison camp in a warmer location and, more importantly, a location closer to my children and my aging parents. It was normal procedure and within my rights to request such a transfer now that my sentence had been cut to eight years. I had heard that the minimum-security prison camp at Eglin Air Force Base in Florida was as good as the prison system gets. Also Reverend Dortch, when he had visited me in Rochester, had told me of his experiences there and I felt as though I knew a bit about the place. The prison review team promised to process my request but made no promises concerning if or when it would be approved. Most requests took several months to arrange. Until then, I simply bundled up and tried to keep warm through the bitterly cold winter.

Even if my hands and feet were chilled, my heart was warmed by a letter I received from a group of ministers known as "Shepherds of Charlotte." The group was comprised of pastors from various denominations who met together with the purpose of praying for each other, encouraging one another, and working together to spread the gospel in Charlotte. It was before this group of pastors and church workers that I had first taken public responsibility for my sin and the hurt my actions had inflicted on the Body of Christ. The meeting took place in 1988 and few members of the press decided it merited reporting.

The Shepherds of Charlotte appreciated my actions then, just as I appreciated theirs now. Their letter resonated with love and compassion. The group expressed their joy that my sentence had been reduced and assured me that I would be accepted and welcomed by them if or when I returned to the Charlotte area.

The letter was signed by seventeen pastors who were members of the Shepherds of Charlotte. I was sincerely moved that my brothers in ministry would welcome me so openly.

Another person who was already thinking about my release was Franklin Graham. Franklin had been keeping up on my condition in prison and had written me several times. He was also well aware of and in fact inspired Mark DeMoss's efforts to encourage Christian leaders to write to the parole commission to encourage them to allow me to be released on parole. Franklin had offered to help in any way he could. Three weeks before the Commission rejected my appeal, Franklin wrote:

> Jim, let me just say that one of these days you will be released. I don't know what the terms will be, but I would like to invite you to join me on an overseas trip to see what God is doing through Samaritan's Purse. I would love to take you to Kenya to see Tenwek Hospital, a work that you have had a vital role in. I think it would bless your heart and give you great encouragement. Please be thinking about this.
>
> I have just returned from Tokyo, where I preached a series of rallies in advance of my father's crusade there this coming January. I leave next week for Croatia and Bosnia.
>
> Please stay in touch. God bless you.
>
> Your friend,
Franklin Graham

Once again, Franklin had amazed me with his kindness toward me and his acceptance of me.

Jamie Charles visited me on Father's Day. We hoped that it might be my last Father's Day in prison. Jamie had been staying with Phil Shaw's family while we all worked on my appeal to the parole board. He had come for the weekend and was still there six weeks later!

Around that same time, I received some wonderful news from another inmate. He told me that I was leaving! He had been working in one of the administrative offices and he had seen my transfer approval papers on a desk. He had read them upside down, but he was certain he had seen the name Jesup, Georgia. It would be another three weeks before the prison officials would inform me of my transfer.

I was elated to learn that I would be leaving Rochester. Although I had made many friends there, including Dr. Westrick and Dr. Foster, I welcomed a change.

The good news was I was being transferred to a minimum-security facility work camp in Jesup, a small town about sixty-five miles southwest of Savannah and about three hundred miles from Heritage USA where my parents still lived.

The bad news was that I was being transferred to Jesup by way of El Reno, the most feared facility in the entire prison system. That meant I was going to have "diesel therapy."

"Diesel therapy" was the name the inmates used to describe the prison system's method of transferring prisoners from one location to another when there was no hurry involved in moving them, or, as the inmates assumed, when the prison officials wanted to get even with an inmate. Rather than sending the inmate on a direct flight to the location to which he was to be transferred, as had been done to me when I was returned to Charlotte for my resentencing, the inmates believed that the prison officials purposely routed the inmate the long way to his destination, with layovers at various federal prisons or county jails along the way. On such trips the inmate may start out traveling by plane but usually ended up traveling by bus. Thus the name: diesel therapy.

Diesel therapy usually took a dramatic toll on the inmates. I had personally known and seen inmates who had been called to testify in court (or "go out on writ") and had been given diesel therapy as they traveled to and from their destinations. Oftentimes a strong and robust, emotionally stable inmate returned as an emaciated basket case. One of the worst parts about diesel therapy is that the inmates are not told where they are going, how long they will be there, or when they will return. It's almost impossible for family members to keep track of their loved one who is on diesel therapy. I wondered if at times it was not difficult for the prison system

547

itself to keep track of its travelers on diesel therapy. Inmates only half-joked that some of their friends are still out there . . . somewhere . . . lost in the system. Several inmates told me they knew of prisoners whose testimonies were potentially damaging to politicians, so the inmates were kept on diesel therapy until the crucial days of the election campaign were over.

The most frightening parts of diesel therapy are the stopovers—often at one of America's large, maximum-security prisons. In these facilities, besides being a newcomer in unfamiliar surroundings, the inmate on diesel therapy is often thrown in with hard-core prisoners from throughout the prison system who are in transit, as well as the local prison population. Just the names of certain prisons around the country sent shivers through the average inmate, prisons such as Terre Haute, Lewisburg, Atlanta penitentiary, and worst of all—El Reno.

I had heard many hellish accounts of what inmates had encountered at El Reno. Several guys told me how they had to sleep side by side with hundreds of men on cots in a large common room that looked like an old train station. Many of the windows were broken out, so the birds would fly freely inside the building and hover overhead, defecating on the inmates below day and night. Other inmates told me that the prison was always jammed with prisoners in transit and there was never enough bathroom space.

Cockroaches at El Reno were notorious. One inmate told me that the prison dispenses a lot of Kool Aid-type drinks, made in large plastic containers, with spouts in the side. He recalled that when the spout was turned off, it sometimes dripped several drops of Kool Aid onto the floor. Immediately, hundreds of cockroaches raced to the spot.

Another inmate who had been there told me that he slept with cotton in his ears and his mouth covered, because the roaches would crawl in a guy's ears or in his mouth while he was sleeping. El Reno was one of the most dreaded stopovers in the prison system.

And the inmate who had read my transfer papers said he thought sure I was going to Jesup by way of El Reno.

Even though a prison official assured me that I would not be put in with murderers or violent criminals, for the next several weeks, fear and uncertainty mounted in my heart with every passing day. I was delighted to be going somewhere, anywhere. But the thought of diesel therapy terrified me.

It may not have been necessary for me to have gone on diesel therapy. Because of my reduced sentence, I had a new prisoner status known as "out-custody," which allowed me to travel by conventional means, by myself or in the company of a federal officer. It was possible to have a federal marshal accompany me and fly directly to the major airport nearest the facility to which I was being transferred. Such special transfers were permitted, but the expenses for both the inmate and the marshal had to be paid by the prisoner. I didn't have much money left in my commissary account, but when I learned that the alternative travel plan might take me through El Reno, I figured a direct flight was worth the price, no matter what the cost.

Beyond that, brutal memories of being transported from Charlotte to Butner in chains, like a wild animal and being paraded in front of the world's press corps still haunted me. I would have done almost anything to have avoided the humiliation of being dragged in front of the media again.

Consequently, when I found out that my transfer had been granted and that I was probably heading to Jesup, I mentioned my concerns to Jim Toms. Jim immediately contacted the prison in Rochester to see if we could arrange for a marshal-accompanied transfer.

Jim ran into a stone wall with the official who was in charge of my travel arrangements. When Jim suggested that he was concerned for my safety as a high-profile prisoner, the official retorted, "I've transferred thousands of inmates. I know how to transfer people. I have never lost an inmate yet!" As my lawyer persisted in trying to arrange for a direct transfer, the prison official became irate. His position solidified further with every call from my lawyer. No doubt part of his consternation resulted from the fact that my lawyer was already trying to arrange transfer details and the official had not yet even informed me that I was in fact being transferred!

When the official confronted me about it and confirmed my fears, he angrily answered, "Well, if you're afraid to be transferred through the normal prison procedures, you're not ready to go to a camp yet! Don't worry. You won't be in with any violent criminals such as murderers or rapists. The prison system keeps the various types of inmates separated."

I knew then, I was definitely going on diesel therapy.

A few days before I left Minnesota, evangelist James Robison visited me in Rochester on June 28 along with my friend Phil Shaw. I had not seen James since our meeting with Sam Johnson in 1988 back at Heritage USA when we had discussed the possibilities of my return to the ministry there. I was glad to see James again. We laughed heartily when James told me the story of how on the way from the airport to the prison, he had asked Phil Shaw for a breath mint. As Phil drove along, he reached into his pocket and pulled out a package of white tablets and handed them to James. James popped one in his mouth and chomped down hard. Suddenly James started spitting up all over his coat sleeve. He quickly leaned over and tried to spit the candy out the window, but he had not lowered the window far enough and he ended up drooling down the glass.

"What are you doing to me, man?" James bellowed, half-laughing, half-crying.

Phil took his eyes off the road long enough to look at the packaging on his container of breath mints. In dark green letters, the print said "Excedrin."

That's what I liked about James Robison, though. He was the kind of guy who would expectorate first and roll the window down later. Despite my concerns about diesel therapy, we had a good time visiting together. I reminded James that he had warned me years before that my love affair with bricks and mortar was going to get me in trouble.

"You were right, James. I was wrong."

We had a wonderful visit sharing the truths that God had been teaching both of us.

Just before the Fourth of July weekend, I got the official word—I was moving out. We had always celebrated the Fourth in a big way back at Heritage USA. This year, my celebration of freedom would have a slightly different twist.

"Pack up your things," the guard told me. I packed everything I owned—my Bible, my books, my toiletries, my toothbrush, my clothes, my pictures on my bulletin board—I packed everything into a large green duffel bag and took it to the mail room to be inventoried and shipped to my destination. I kept only the clothes on my back—my prison khakis, my glasses, and my inventory sheet, a single sheet of paper listing all my items that were being shipped in the duffel bag. Then I returned to my cell to wait. Since it was the weekend, I assumed that I might not actually leave Rochester until Tuesday, since the federal holiday fell on Monday. True to form, I went the entire extended weekend with no personal belongings except my allotment of prison clothes and my glasses.

I made my rounds, saying good-bye on Sunday. I had already bid farewell to Dr. Westrick and Dr. Foster. I then went person to person to my friends. It was a strange feeling; in some ways, I hated to part with these people who, for the most part, had been so good and kind to me, and on the other hand, I couldn't wait for a change of scenery. Somebody suggested taking a few pictures and I readily agreed. We went over to the recreation building and had the Jaycees photographer snap some shots in front of the usual wall mural.

That Sunday night, I posed for literally dozens of pictures with the guys, because we all knew that I would be leaving at any time. I then gathered as many of my friends as I could for a group picture. In a few minutes, I rounded up more than fifty guys for one last group picture, sort of the "Class of '93." When I got back to my cell, guys were still dropping by to say good-bye. Several men were laughing and talking in my cell and outside the door when Dominic, my Italian friend from across the hall, came in to say good-bye. Dominic had brought me food he had made throughout my stay and especially during the time of my deep depression when Tammy Faye left me. He may have been a tough man at one time— I never asked about his past—but the grandfatherly man I knew who lived across the hall was a deeply caring human being. Dominic told me, "Jim, you've served your time with more dignity than any man I have ever seen." Dominic hugged me good-bye and then, right there in front of the other inmates, tears began to form in the eyes of this tough man. He tried to brush the tears away, but they kept coming, so he turned away and quickly left my cell.

I didn't sleep much the night before I was to leave F.M.C. Rochester. I would not have had much of a chance to sleep, anyhow. A guard came to my cell in the middle of the night—actually in the wee hours of Tuesday morning—and ordered me to get dressed. I started to put my prison khakis over my underwear and I had to laugh. The undershorts I was wearing were the exact same shorts I had been wearing the day the marshals brought me in to the prison. They were the same shorts I had worn the day of my sentencing, when they had first whisked me off to Talladega prison. That one pair of underwear was the one item of clothing that somehow had made it with me throughout my prison journey so far. I smiled to myself as the guard waited for me to get dressed, and I wondered if I could possibly make it all the way home with these well-traveled underwear.

When I got to R & D on my way out of F.M.C. Rochester, I was strip searched one last time. The guard made me take off my underwear and toss them into a bin. It was the end of the line for those shorts. After I was searched, the guard handed me a pair of mint-green jockey shorts. Most of the prison-issued shorts were dark army-green or white, but I had never seen any articles of prison-issued inmate clothing that were mint green.

The only mint-green clothes I had seen in prison were associated with the hospital units. I could only assume that the mint-green shorts had gone to the laundry with the doctors' and hospital workers' garb. At that hour in the morning, however, I didn't much care what color the underwear were; I just wanted to put some clothes on and get out of there. The color of those underwear, however, would soon take on extreme significance to me.

I was only one of a group of men who were being transferred that day. We were given the usual prison travel clothes, the navy blue, slip-on canvas shoes and the lightweight brown khaki pullover shirt and elastic-waisted pants. The guards put the usual handcuffs, leg irons, and chains on us. A few of the nicer guards said good-bye. Most said nothing at all. The guard who put my leg irons on did not fasten them real tightly around my ankles. At first I thought that was a blessing, but I soon discovered it was the opposite. Every time I took a step, the irons rubbed up and down my leg, flipping back down onto my ankle bones. By the time I got to Georgia, my ankles and feet were bruised from the irons.

Once our handcuffs were fastened to the chains around our waists, the other transferees and I were marched out to the compound and ordered to stand in a straight line. There, bound in shackles, I got my last look at F.M.C. Rochester. I almost did not mind being chained this time. I had seen so many other guys chained and lined up, ready to go out the gate. Now, at last, it was my turn.

Along with the other inmates, I marched several hundred feet in my shackles to the front gatehouse of the prison. The large gate opened and we were herded into a chamber that reminded me of a studio sound lock, with a locked door ahead of us and the closing door behind us. Inside the lock, along the left side was a man behind what looked like a ticket window.

"Inmate Bakker, sir," I said. "07407-058." The guard glanced at me, wrote something on his clipboard, and nodded toward the gate. The front door opened into a large prison lobby area.

Outside in the parking lot, I could see the prison bus waiting. This vehicle was nothing more than a cell on wheels. At the top of the steps was another heavy steel door. All the bus windows were lined with heavy steel mesh. I slowly walked down the aisle and sat down in the first empty seat.

I stared into the morning darkness with mixed emotions. I was exhilarated that I was finally going somewhere, I knew not where. As I sat waiting for the other inmates to board, I thought back to the many times when my friends and I watched as airplanes flew over the prison yard. We'd look up and almost every guy would say something such as, "I don't care where that plane's going, I wish I was on it!"

Almost every prison I have ever seen is built near the train tracks, perhaps to facilitate prisoner transfers in days gone by. F.M.C. Rochester was no exception. Every time I heard that mournful train whistle blow, I'd think, *I wish I was a hobo, stowing away in a boxcar on that train.* Now, sitting in a bus to nowhere, at least part of my wish was coming true.

Finally, the bus pulled out just as the morning sun rose in the sky, exposing the surrounding area to my sight. I had seen the countryside around Rochester only twice before, once when I arrived in the snow and again when I went home to see my dad in December. This was the first time I was able to see the green grass of the Minnesota rolling hills, the many lakes and the rows of "built-to-take-it" homes we passed in the bus. I gawked out the window. I had been here for nearly four years yet I had little concept of what the area surrounding the prison looked like. I wanted to see it at least once before I left.

Before long, the bus rumbled to a stop at the Rochester airport. A large plane was waiting for us on the tarmac. I hadn't traveled aboard this sort of prison plane. The planes I had traveled on since being incarcerated had all been small, executive-type jets. The plane on the tarmac looked similar to a large, commercial airliner. The bus driver pulled the vehicle as close to the plane as possible. The jet was surrounded by officers with shotguns in their hands.

After another wait, we were instructed to line up again on the tarmac. Once more we had to give our names and numbers to the marshals. With our chains clanging, the other prisoners and I were then led up a steep set of steps at the back, in the tail of the aircraft. With each step, the leg irons ground against my ankles. Once inside, I realized that the plane was already loaded with prisoners from other places, so I shuffled up the aisle and sat down in the seat the marshal directed me to, about midway in the plane on the left-hand side. The inside of the plane looked similar to any other commercial jet airliner, except that all the passengers were dressed alike, we were all chained, and there were no flight attendants. In their places were government marshals, stationed throughout the plane. I looked around, hoping to see a familiar face, but of the approximately 130 other inmates on board, I found nobody that I recognized. My buddies were all gone. I was on my own.

The aircraft began to taxi toward the runway. Looking around at the chained passengers, it suddenly hit me, *If this plane crashes, we don't stand a chance. There would be no survivors, only a mangled mess of charred, chained corpses.*

553

As the large plane lumbered down the runway, I prayed that God would keep the old bucket of bolts in the air. I tried to keep from thinking about the stories I had heard about how poorly these prison planes were maintained. One inmate whose friend worked on prison aircraft said that most of them have oil leaking out of the hydraulics. I didn't know what that meant, but it improved my prayer life.

Once airborne, the marshals gave us a bag lunch with a bottle of water. I knew that the inmates always prepared the food, but I had no idea where this food had come from, so I didn't eat it. I didn't have much of an appetite anyhow. Nor did I drink my water. It was not bottled spring water. I had visions of some disgruntled inmate filling the bottles and spitting in each one, or worse! From my travels overseas, I had learned never to drink the water if you were not sure it was safe. I gave my food and water to a big man sitting across the aisle. He was really thirsty and he was glad to have the extra water. When a marshal saw that the man had two bottles, he blew his stack at the man and wanted to know where he had gotten it. I thought, *Oh, no. I'm in trouble now*. Apparently, the guard thought the big man had forced me to give him my water. I explained and everything calmed down.

The big bird's landing gears pulled up and the pilot banked the plane hard to the west, pointing it toward the Dakotas. *That's an odd way to go to Georgia*, I thought.

Throughout the day, the plane made several stops at other prison towns, dropping off inmates and picking up others. I didn't move out of my seat, not even to go to the bathroom. Late that afternoon, the plane landed in some flatlands and the marshal called my name to get off.

"Where are we?" I asked the man next to me.

The man looked at me as if I had just stabbed him with a knife. He answered in an anguished tone, "El Reno."

Actually, although no official said for sure, we thought we had landed in Oklahoma City. We did the bus routine in reverse, this time as the shotgun-wielding marshals loaded us onto another drab looking prison bus. After what seemed like a forty- to sixty-minute ride, the bus pulled up in front of a huge, old looking building.

El Reno Penitentiary.

My worst fears were realized as I stared out the wire-mesh bus windows at what looked to be a dilapidated Dracula's Castle. True to what I had heard about the place, I noticed that numerous windows were broken out of the higher sections of the building, and sure enough, I saw birds going in and out of the windows. I remembered the stories my friends had told me about trying to sleep in that room with the bird droppings falling on them and the roaches crawling over their faces.

I thought, *Oh, God, I'm really here.*

Outside in the parking area, prison buses were lined up in front of the bus on which I was sitting. I couldn't tell how many buses were ahead of ours, but there were enough to make the lot look like a bus stop at a busy tourist attraction from hell. We sat chained in the bus for more than two hours, waiting for our turn to unload at the processing area.

When it was finally our turn to unload, we were marched to a concrete pad alongside the barbed razor wire and made to stand, still chained, facing Dracula's Castle. The guards made us stand there for a while in a single file, just staring at the place. I thought, *Are they trying to impress upon us the horror of this place?* It was as though they wanted to psych us out. Whatever the reason, I was beginning to realize that I was going to get the full "diesel" treatment.

After another count, we were herded inside to a narrow bull pen holding cell with backless benches along the sides. Inmates from many prisons around the country were jammed together in that room; another bull pen crammed with hot, sweaty inmates was next to the one in which I was placed. Perhaps as many as two hundred men were confined in those cramped bull pens. The crowded, rank room evoked images of cattle waiting to be slaughtered. The noise was intense. Everyone was talking at the same time, and it seemed to me, they were all talking about me!

I sat down on one of the benches and instantly men were pressed against me on every side, shoulder to shoulder. The man sitting next to me began to talk wildly. First of all, he told me that he was Martin Luther. Then he told me that he was Joan of Arc. Suddenly, with a dark, dead, glassy look in his eyes, he leaped to his feet and, still chained, jumped up onto the bench. He kept jumping up and down right next to me, yelling at me, telling me that he was Satan. He was either pitifully insane, demon possessed, or both. I thought sure that at any moment he was going to pull his chains over my head and choke me to death.

This is where I will die, I thought seriously. I thought for sure that I would be raped, beaten, and killed before this night was over. Thankfully, some of the other inmates got the deranged man to calm down. One inmate then told me that "Satan" had tried to kill a large number of people by locking up a skating rink with the people inside, then setting it on fire. Encouraged by the demented man's outbursts, some of the inmates from the Terre Haute prison began telling "war stories" about some of their experiences in that facility. The more I listened to their garish tales, the more convinced I became that it would be only the goodness of God if I were still alive in the morning.

The middle door clanged open and the guard ordered us to file out to have our chains removed. The inmates lined up and the guards spread out through the ranks removing the chains and cuffs. The guards then ordered us to take off all our clothes and toss them in the big barrels and bins, all except our undershorts.

I suddenly became extremely aware of the mint green undershorts I was wearing. *Nothing like being conspicuous*, I thought. We were then herded into another long, narrow bull pen, with a toilet and sink at the far end. Backless benches lined the sides of the pen as well as the middle. Another identical bull pen was alongside ours, separated by a heavy steel mesh.

"Hey, Bakker," I heard a rough voice call my name from behind me. I turned around to see a man holding out his inventory sheet and the small pencil used for filling out medical records and other forms in the bull pen. "How about an autograph?" he asked.

I gladly signed the man's paper. As soon as I signed one inventory sheet, another was thrust in front of me. "Yeah, me too. Will you sign one for me?" I signed the paper.

In a matter of minutes, I was signing autographs like a home run slugger at a ballpark. Guys in the bull pen next to ours began rolling their inventory sheets up into tight, pencil-thin tubes and passing them through the wire mesh so I could sign them. A large group of inmates gathered around me and began asking questions while I signed the autographs. They wanted to know all about Tammy Faye and the many things they had read in the newspapers and rag magazines. Some of the guys even wanted to know where they could get Bibles and other Christian books.

All of a sudden, the picture of me sitting in my underwear signing autographs hit me and I started laughing out loud. There I was, scared to death, thinking this might be my last night on earth in this cramped dungeon with a couple hundred guys, sitting there in my mint-green underwear, talking and signing autographs! *What a picture this would make*, I thought. *If only my friends and family members could see me now!*

More hours went by and brown-bag lunches, comprised of an apple and prison "mystery meat" sandwiches, were passed out to all the inmates. I ate my apple, but I thought of a better use for my sandwich. I decided to trade it for "protection."

Another man sat down next to me after "Satan" had been subdued and moved to the bench across from me. The man who now sat next to me was a big, friendly black man from Terre Haute. He and I had struck

556

up a conversation, and he had been telling me awful stories about some of the things he had seen in prison. He told me about a young man who had been raped by twenty-two guys and left to die during a movie in the recreation room. He told me about the guys who had rats for pets. And he told me about the way men were stabbed on the way to chow by somebody slamming a "shiv," a makeshift knife, into the inmate's back as he was pressed against the other inmates trying to enter the chow hall. His horror stories weren't exactly calming my nerves.

My mind thought back to the prison official in Rochester who had promised, "Oh, don't worry, Jim. You won't be in with any hardened criminals. The prison system keeps various types of inmates separated. You won't be in with any violent prisoners, such as murderers or rapists."

I knew some inmates loved notoriety so much that they would do almost anything to get their names in the paper. Because I was considered a "high-profile" prisoner, it was not out of the question that somebody might be tempted to attack me just for the publicity that would surely follow. I was getting along rather well with the big guy from Terre Haute, so I decided to take a chance. I asked him straight out, "Would you sort of watch out for me tonight? I'll give you my lunch if you'll be my bodyguard tonight. If we get placed in that big room with the birds and the roaches and all the cots side by side, will you see to it that nobody rapes or kills me?"

Looking back, I can hardly believe I did that, but at the time and under the circumstances, it made perfectly logical sense.

My big friend acted as though I had appointed him as a Secret Service agent to the president. He threw back his shoulders and replied, "I sure will!" He pointed to some of his friends from Terre Haute and said, "And they'll watch out for you too. Nothin' is gonna happen to you tonight."

I knew the guy could be a con and that he might be lying to me through his teeth, but for some reason, I believed him and trusted him.

It was getting late in the evening, as we sat with our clothes off in those bull pens hour after hour, waiting to be processed. I was the only man in the crowded room who was wearing mint-green underwear. Guys from various prisons had different colors of underwear; some had army green, some had light brown, but only one man had mint-green underwear—Jim Bakker.

After several hours, we were told to line up and march to an inspection area, a section about one-fourth the length of a football field, built for the processing of inmates. Huge racks of bundled prison clothing, all separated by size, lined the back wall. A row of guards separated the inmates from the clothing. We were ordered to strip naked and the guards began strip searching entire lines of inmates at one time. The naked men stood little more than an arm's length away from each other, in front of the guards.

When it was my turn, as I started to take off my underwear, the guard who was inspecting me said in an extremely sarcastic tone of voice, "Where did you get those green panties?"

I had been up most of the night before and it had already been a long day. I was tired and in no mood to play along with his silly head games. In the roughest, gruffest voice I could muster, I answered, "They issued them to me at Rochester."

The guard shrugged and began examining me.

"Hold your hands up," he ordered.

I mechanically obeyed. I knew this routine only too well by now.

The guard inspected each part of my body and was satisfied that I didn't have drugs, weapons, or other contraband. He turned to the clothing racks and grabbed a bundle of clothes and tossed it to me. I opened the bundle and started putting on my new clothes, which were nearly twice my size. I continued putting them on, knowing it would have been useless to complain. At that time, I was wearing pants with a twenty-eight-inch waist, a small. The clothes the guard had given me were extra-large. I had to hold my pants up with my hand as I walked into another room where I deposited my medical paper. Next stop was a window where a man asked me, "Do you have any cause to fear for your life?"

What sort of question is that? In this place, I have a feeling that everyone fears for his life!

"Have you testified against anybody?" the man was asking.

"No, I haven't," I replied.

"Do you want to go into isolation?" he asked matter-of-factly.

"That's up to you," I answered.

The man looked at me a moment. "I think we better put you in solitary," he said.

Considering the rooming possibilities in that place, I was delighted to have a private room for the night—a cell with no birds overhead—even if it was in solitary confinement, the hole. I was taken to another waiting area and finally, a full eight hours after I had arrived at El Reno, I was taken to a cell. It was well past midnight when I was finally alone. I was dead tired.

I had not been in my cell much more than an hour, lying on the bunk, still wide awake, when a guard came to the door and commanded, "Get dressed. You're leaving." He gave me a brown paper bag. In it was what he described as breakfast, a hard-boiled egg and some bread. I tried to eat it, but I had no appetite. The food was unappetizing and I was nervous.

I couldn't believe it, but it was true. It was about 2:00 A.M. Along with two bull pens full of inmates, I was brought out of my cell and we reversed the procedure we had just gone through coming into the prison.

Back through the lines we went. We gave them our prison clothes back. Another strip search. The guards gave us new traveling clothes, back to the bull pens, another long wait, and from there, the guards prodded our only half-conscious bodies back toward another prison bus.

By 7:00 A.M., we were back in the buses, ready to head toward the airport. The bus radio, tuned to a local rock 'n' roll morning show, was blaring. As we were sitting there, waiting to depart for the airport, the raucous disk jockey announced, "Guess whose birthday it is today? Why, it's Jessica Hahn's birthday!"

There I was, cuffed and chained, along with a busload of inmates, and the morning guys on the radio were going through an entire Jessica Hahn and Jim Bakker routine.

I wanted to crawl under a bus seat and hide. Fortunately, most everybody was too tired to make jokes or harass me, but I couldn't help thinking, *How much more?*

At last the bus pulled out, drowning out the sound of the morning show. We traveled all the way back to the airport, at least a forty-minute ride. When we arrived at the "Con Air" prison plane, however, we were not permitted to board. We sat in the buses on the tarmac for a long time. I could tell something was wrong. I had been around enough planes in my lifetime that just by watching the flurry of activity on the ground around the plane, it was obvious that there was some sort of mechanical problem. The plane was not ready to fly. Con Air had broken down. I watched as a tow unit pulled the big bird back into the hanger. After sitting there for what seemed like hours, the decision was made. The buses turned around and headed back over the same roads we had just traveled. We were going *back* to El Reno!

We went through the entire laborious process once again, doing the exact routine we had done the day before.

This time, I received clothes that fit. Nevertheless, it was nearly noon before I was finally assigned to a cell. I had not slept for two full days. Nor had I gone to the bathroom that entire time.

The guards decided to put me into a cell block with other prisoners in transit, so I was taken to a blood-red, basement cell. Even the bars were red. In the cell block were some tough looking guys and others who looked more like businessmen than hardened criminals. I was assigned a top bunk in the first cell in the unit.

For the next several days, the red cell block was my home. One night, an older man was put into our unit. I didn't recognize him, but by the way the other inmates deferred to him it was obvious that he was fairly famous and a man to be held in high regard. Men gathered around him outside my cell, asking him questions, much as they had surrounded me when I first arrived. Soon the man was telling his story.

Apparently, he had been involved in a well-known standoff between government law officers and some sort of dissident group. As he related the story to the inmates, it was so fascinating, I slipped down from my bunk and joined the circle of guys standing around him, listening in rapt attention. He told how the agents had shot his wife and how he had run to his pickup truck, dove inside, reached down, pulled a gun, and shot and killed a government agent. I didn't know anything about his story, but the other men seemed very familiar with it, asking him more details about what they had read concerning him in the newspapers.

All I could think of while he was telling the tale were the words of the prison official back in Rochester, "Oh, Jim, don't worry. You won't be in with any violent criminals such as murderers or rapists."

Right in the middle of the man's story, he suddenly stopped cold. He stared at me for a moment then burst out, "Why, you're Jim Bakker! How are you?" The killer thrust his hand in my direction to shake hands. He got so excited, he forgot to tell the rest of his story. He said he was over-whelmed at meeting me, "Why, my mother watched your TV show. She just loves you!" he gushed the classic line I had heard so many times in prison.

I had now been housed in the end cell of that cell block for several days. During that time I rarely went outside or to the chow hall. I simply did not want to go across the compound and take the risk. Some of the guys brought back items of fruit or bread for me, and that was the only food I ate at El Reno. I could feel myself getting weaker and weaker.

A few days later, while I was still in the basement cell, a doctor came to examine me. Jim Toms had contacted the prison and asked the officials to check on me to see if I was okay, because nobody was hearing from me. "That's not like Jim; he must be sick or something," he told the officials. While the doctor examined me, he asked me some personal questions about my physical and mental well-being.

"Come to think of it, I haven't gone to the bathroom in days, since I left Minnesota," I told him. I had not eaten much and I had drunk only a little in several days. My stomach and nervous system must have been a mess.

"You what?" the doctor exclaimed. He looked me over again and said, "You're dehydrating. You need to get some food and water into you right away."

I told him that I didn't want to go to the chow hall and I was not able to drink the water, but he was adamant. Reluctantly, I went to the chow hall and ate a meal.

Whether it was a coincidence or the doctor recommended that I move to a different environment, I never discovered. The next day, however, an officer came to my basement cell and said, "Get your stuff together, Bakker. You're going next door."

"Next door?"

"That's right, next door. There's a prison camp right across the way. Because you're a minimum-out status, you can be over there." My minimum-out status meant I could be outside the walls of prison without chains on. The officer led me out of El Reno penitentiary, past the maze of walls and barbed razor wire.

When we stepped out into the sunshine, I hesitated. I noticed the guards in the gun towers brandishing their weapons. I suddenly realized that I was outside the prison and I didn't have any chains on me, and I was terrified. I expected to be gunned down at any second.

"Come on," the guard ordered me firmly but kindly.

"Are you sure?" I asked tentatively.

The guard was on his radiophone talking with somebody. "I'm sure," he replied with a slight smile. "But the minute you get over there, change your clothes. If they see you out here without me calling them," he nodded toward the gun towers, "you're gonna be shot. The clothes you're wearing mean you're supposed to be inside the walls of the main prison."

The guard ushered two other men and me past Dracula's Castle, past the broken windows, the horrible, ugly walls and across a driveway. I couldn't believe it. I thought, *Any minute now, several guards are going to come and tackle me*, as I had seen them do to erring inmates at Rochester. Worse yet, I might be gunned down.

Nothing happened. We walked over to a fairly new-looking prison camp with modern buildings, well-manicured grass, and basketball courts . . . all with no walls or electrified fences. The camp looked almost like a college campus.

Once we made it to the camp, the guards inside took me to a laundry room and got me some clothes, a dark-blue shirt and pants. They took me to a cell, which was a four-man, open-door, cubelike room. Three guys were already in the cell and they welcomed me like a long-lost brother—which in a way I was, because all three men in that cell were Christians. One fellow had worked at the Assemblies of God headquarters at one time in his life. I never ceased to be amazed at whom I met in prison . . . some of the nicest people!

"What am I supposed to do here?" I asked the guys.

"You can do whatever you want," one man replied, with a slight laugh.

"But there are no fences, no walls. Where can I go?"

"Well, that road over there is Old Route 66. You can't go over there," the man said with a twinkle in his eye. The other men in the cell laughed out loud. "And don't cross that road down the opposite direction. Other than that, you can go pretty much where you please. I wouldn't go back over to the big house, though, if I were you." Everyone laughed again.

I was shocked. I could not get over the fact that yesterday I was in the closest thing to hell I had ever seen and now, here I was, looking out over the flat, wide open expanses of Oklahoma terrain. More than that, to think that somebody actually trusted me to walk around outside with no razor wire to define my parameters. It was overwhelming. Before I stepped out into the yard, I once again asked an inmate, "Are you sure it's okay for me to walk out there?" I realized that I had become thoroughly "prisonized," conditioned to living in confinement.

"I remember that feeling," one of the inmates said with a laugh. He then patiently reviewed with me the legal limits within which I could walk.

It was still daylight, so I went outside and just walked around. I noticed that it was almost hot, but I didn't mind. I thought back to the many times when I had felt so cold and so cooped up in Minnesota and I had prayed, "Oh, God, please let me go someplace warm. Let me go where I can see some land, some fields and trees. Let me go someplace where I can see forever."

Now as I looked out across the Oklahoma plains, I realized that God had answered my prayer. I continued walking and looking and the plains kept spreading out further in front of me. It seemed as though they had no ending. I will never forget that sudden appreciation of freedom that I experienced there. To look out over those flatlands with no fences and to feel unfettered left me dizzy, almost euphoric, with a sense of liberty. I knew I could never take freedom for granted again. I felt the tears begin to trickle down my face, and I prayed, "Oh, thank You, God, for bringing me to a place where I can see forever."

That evening I went to chow with my new Christian buddies. There I got a real surprise. The inmates were allowed to eat with silverware—real metal flatware, not the plastic stuff. At first, I couldn't bring myself to touch it, especially the knives. When I tried to touch them, my hand jerked away as if I had touched a hot stove. "It's okay Jim, it's okay," my cellmates would tell me. "You're allowed to use the silverware here. It's not like where you were before. This is a prison camp." Finally I picked up the knife and fork. Like a little child, I clanged them together to see if they were real. The guys roared with laughter, but they all understood. Touching the silverware was a tiny step back toward becoming a human being again. Beyond that, it was a statement, subtle to be sure, but real: "You have some worth. You're not an animal; you can eat with silverware."

On Sunday morning, I did something that I had not felt free to do when I was first incarcerated in Rochester—I went to chapel. It was a wonderful service and such a great time of Christian fellowship. For a few moments, I almost forgot I was in prison. I realized that God was at work, even in the federal prison system.

Later that night, however, I received a graphic reminder that this was not utopia. A female officer called me into her office and informed me bluntly that there had been a threat on my life.

"Do you want to go back to the penitentiary to spend the night?" she asked. "We can put you in solitary confinement and you'll be much safer there, much more protected."

"No, thank you," I answered. "If I can, I'd rather stay right here." I was like a caged animal that had been set free in the open. I did not want to give up my newfound sense of freedom.

"Okay, fine," she replied. "But if you get any notes on your bed, or a threat of any kind, let us know immediately." She dismissed me and I went back to my cell. I told my cellmates and they all promised to keep an eye out for any signs of trouble. My awesome sense of joy at being free overrode any fear of being killed. After two or three days of relishing this tantalizing taste of freedom and the encouragement of a strong Christian group of guys, I received word that it was time to move on. I had more diesel therapy awaiting.

I had to go back through the processing systems at the "big house" at El Reno. Once again, it was an all-night ordeal, just getting ready to go. Strip searches, clothes changes, chains, the long bus trip back to the airport and finally boarding the plane to the next stop in the twilight zone. When Con Air landed this time, I was in Atlanta.

The Atlanta Federal Penitentiary was an old, huge, complex. Our prison bus pulled up and we unloaded at the front door. Shackled once again, we were led up a long set of stairs, into one of the most feared prison facilities in America. For most of the day after processing, I was by myself in a large holding cell. Oddly, I was in a place where female prisoners passed by. When they recognized me, some of the women were very friendly. Some were lewd. I was glad when a guard finally came and moved me into a cell block.

An inmate told me that the cell block in which I was being housed had once been occupied by Al Capone. My cell was a very old, six-man cell, with high ceilings in which the pipes were exposed and looked as though they were ready to fall right out of the ceiling. The whole place looked dingy.

In my cell block, I met a man who had once been a banker in Charlotte, an officer in one of the smaller banks in town. He recognized me and we struck up a conversation. He told me there was another former Charlotte resident in our cell block—the very man who had been outside the courthouse during my trial, making fun of me. The man had written and recorded a song about Jim and Tammy and PTL and had been hawking it on the lawn of the courthouse.

When the songwriter saw me in Atlanta Penitentiary, he came right up to me. We had never officially been introduced during the trial days, and now he was shocked to actually meet me in prison. He apologized to me for what he had done and he asked me to forgive him.

I told him, "Of course I forgive you. I don't have any animosity toward you whatsoever." I then went on to explain to him some of the things God had shown me during my time in prison, especially that I had to forgive everyone involved in those hurtful last days of PTL, and that included the street vendors outside my trial.

Later, I heard that the man felt that God had purposely allowed our paths to cross in prison so he could make amends. The man went on to become a Bible study leader in prison.

The Atlanta Penitentiary was equally as fearful as El Reno, especially because of the thousands of inmates congregated there from prisons all across the country. I was kept there for several days before it was moving time again.

The final session of diesel therapy was from Atlanta to Jesup, Georgia, my new home away from home. Once more, the other inmates who were being transported and I were awakened in what seemed to be the middle of the night to process out of the penitentiary. When we finally boarded the bus on Wednesday, July 14, I again had no idea where we might be going. I didn't know if we were flying or driving.

We ended up driving all the way to Jesup, a distance of about two hundred forty miles in one of the bumpy prison buses. At one point, we were bouncing along a road when the bus passed a church. As I looked through the mesh-covered windows of the bus, I saw the name of the church and had an instant panic attack. The church was of the same denomination as the man who more than any other, in my mind, had been responsible for orchestrating the fall of PTL and my eventual imprisonment. My adrenalin shot up as the bus churned past the church. Never before in my life had I looked at a church with fear in my heart.

As I slowly regained my composure, I began to think about what had just happened. *How horrible*, I thought, *that the sanctuary to which people should be able to freely turn for safety and comfort could be a trigger for fear, condemnation, and hurt.* I have a feeling that I am not the only person who had ever felt that way about the church.

It was a long drive to Jesup and the usual long processing ordeal when we arrived. Like El Reno, Jesup has both a large major penitentiary and a prison camp on the premises. After several hours in the big house, a group of inmates and I were led to another bus for the short ride to the prison camp. The only reason we rode the bus across the compound to the camp was that it was pouring rain.

I boarded the rickety old bus and took a seat and looked idly toward the driver as we began to pull out. To my amazement, the driver was an inmate. And there were no guards on this bus. And no fences around the prison camp. What kind of place was this Camp Jesup? After a two-week journey on Diesel Therapy to get there, I was about to find out.

50

"Camp Jesus"

IT WAS OBVIOUS THAT JESUP WAS A DIFFERENT SORT OF camp; the usual contingency of guards waiting to strip search us was absent. Instead, we were met by a congenial officer with a deep Southern accent. He told us where to go to get our issuance of new clothing, the dark-blue outfits like the sort I had worn in the El Reno camp.

I stumbled down the sidewalk, physically and emotionally exhausted. All I wanted to do was get to a bunk and fall asleep. My bones ached, my eyes drooped, and it felt as though strands of my hair were falling out.

Just then I was met by a group of inmates standing in front of me. Everyone was welcoming me with outstretched hands. "Hi," said a small wiry guy. "I'm Chuck." "Welcome, Jim! My name is Jimmy," a large black man with a huge smile greeted me. "Hello, I'm Rick. Glad you made it okay." I started shaking hands with one man after another. "Hi, I'm Blair." Paul, David, Petie, George, David, Ronnie, and Sam were there, all talking excitedly at one time, volunteering to help me get my clothes, pointing out the laundry room, and being extremely helpful. I wasn't used to this sort of reception in prison. I was overwhelmed by their friendliness and appreciated it immensely, but I was exhausted and just wanted to sleep. Nevertheless, I tried my best to be friendly in return.

"Hi, Jim! I'm Larry Wright," said a big, friendly looking fellow as he stuck out his hand. Larry had sandy hair, just beginning to gray; he wore eyeglasses and a contagious smile. "We've brought you a few things that you might need until your own items arrive," he said as he handed me a bag of toiletries, shower shoes, stamps, and a small New Testament. "We're part of the Christian brothers here at Jesup," Larry nodded toward the other guys who were also smiling and nodding, most of whom I had already met and shaken hands with, "and we're available to help you any way we can. Is there anything you need right now?" Larry asked.

"No, no. I'm fine," I replied.

"What you probably need most right now is some sleep," Larry offered knowingly. "Why don't you get some rest? We'll check on you later to make sure you are okay."

"Thank you," I answered. *How could there be so many Christians in one prison?* I wondered. We had a good group of Christian men in Rochester, and the Christian guys in El Reno were a strong group too, but I had never before seen a Christian welcoming committee in prison! I later found out that they were not doing anything for me that they were not doing for almost every new inmate at Jesup. The Christians there were putting their faith and words into a tangible meeting of needs.

Soon I was on my way to a cell block, which at Jesup was not really comprised of cells at all, but cubicles enclosed by painted cement-block walls about half the distance between the floor and ceiling, about the height of the partitions in a business office. The room housing about sixty men was open above the cubicles. No doors or bars slammed shut in the Jesup cell block, because there were none.

I stopped in the bathroom before I went on to my bunk. When I caught a glimpse of my reflection in the mirror, I was shocked. I hardly recognized myself! I looked like I had aged twenty years in a few weeks' time.

I went to bed and slept for nearly three days, getting up only for orientation information and count. I had not yet been assigned a work duty, so it was easy for me to lay on my bunk and sleep. Truthfully I just wanted to lie in my bunk and sleep the days away.

But the body of believers at Jesup was not about to let that happen. True to Larry's word, he and the other Christian men kept a close watch on me. After they allowed me to rest for a while, they began to tug and pull me out of my bed.

Chuck kept nagging and cajoling me like a small bull dog, trying to get me out of bed and back into the land of the living. "Go away, Chuck. I'm tired. I just want to sleep," I told him over and over.

"You've slept enough. It's time to get up and on with your life. Come on, there's a service over in the chapel. We can go together."

"Oh, Chuck, I don't want to go to chapel. I just want to stay here and sleep. You go ahead and you can tell me about it later."

Chuck was not to be deterred. After I had spent the majority of several days in bed and had not attended any of the various Bible study or chapel programs, Chuck was exasperated. "Are you backslidden?" Chuck asked me bluntly. "Don't you ever go to chapel? How are you supposed to be spiritually encouraged if you neglect the fellowship of believers? Why don't you go to chapel?"

"Okay, Chuck, okay. I'll go."

Smiling broadly, Chuck extended a hand to help pull me from my bunk. "Good, it's about time."

And it was time, time for me to begin functioning as a human being again, time for spiritual nourishment and healing to take place in my life, and also time to get back to work. One of the female officials had given me a work assignment—picking up the cigarette butts in the yard, out in front of the main part of the prison.

When I first was called to see the attractive, young black woman who was designated as my "counselor," I was not prepared for her behavior. Almost immediately, she started yelling at me. I later learned that she yelled at everybody, but she caught me off guard when one of the first things she said to me was, "Bakker, don't ask for a furlough, 'cause you're not gettin' one."

A furlough? I didn't know it was possible to earn a short furlough from prison camp. I was accustomed to a medium-security prison, from which furloughs could only be granted for unusual circumstances, such as in the case of my father's accident. What the woman was basically saying to me was, "Don't ask for any special treatment around here, because you are not going to get any!"

Camp Jesup itself was relatively new. It was well kept, clean, and had beautiful landscaping, including South Georgia palm trees, lots of flowers and green grass. The complex was located in a swampy area, and since there were no fences around the minimum security camp, the guards incorporated the natural elements as part of our orientation. "Don't go across that field, because the swamp over there is filled with poisonous snakes and alligators," they warned. "Even the grass beyond the field might be dangerous because of the brown recluse spiders. If you get bitten by one of them, get help fast. Otherwise, your flesh will rot right to the bone." I didn't know whether they were exaggerating or not, but I had no intention of finding out.

The best part of Jesup's location was that it was much closer to my parents and family. Again, to me, it was part of God's provision. Camp Jesup was halfway between Tammy Sue's home and where Jamie was now living. Had I been placed in the camp at Eglin, Florida, it would have been much farther away from the ones I loved.

Of course, I wanted to be out of prison completely. I had hoped to be out on parole, at least. Looking back, however, I now believe God knew that I was not yet ready to go back out into the world. I needed a sort of decompression time. I needed to be emotionally healed and spiritually strengthened before I could ever be of help to anyone else. God was not going to allow me to live in burnout as I had done at PTL for the last years of my ministry there. He was not going to allow me to stand up in front of a group of people and do a spiritual routine, as I had sometimes done at PTL. For that I was wrong. I beg the forgiveness of anyone who may have been hurt by that.

In Jesup prison, God began to show me what true ministry is all about—people caring for one another, teaching the Word, devouring the Bible. As a result, every week, more men—some of them so-called hardened criminals—came to trust Jesus Christ as their Savior and Lord. Evangelism was the natural outgrowth of the functioning Body of believers and I needed to learn more of how the true Body of Christ is meant to function. So God sent me to Camp Jesus, er, Camp Jesup.

We had a wonderful group of Christians at PTL—men, women, and children who had dedicated their lives to Christ and telling the world about Him. But the body of Christian believers at Jesup prison was the strongest example of the functioning Body of Christ I have ever seen anywhere. The Christian men in that prison held Bible studies, prayer meetings, or other services almost every night after work. I soon started getting up at 5:00 A.M. so I could get to the morning time of prayer and Bible study at 5:30. Some of the guys were getting up at 3:00 A.M. to pray for the 5:30 Bible study group! Our morning study on the life of David was one of the most practical, productive, and inspiring Bible studies I had ever attended.

Larry Wright, I quickly discovered, was one of the Christian leaders in prison. He was also one of the godliest guys I had ever met. A former Wesleyan pastor, Larry's ministry on the "outside" fell apart when his wife left him. Not only did he lose his wife, he lost his church and his ordination as a pastor because of his marriage failure.

"My spiritual brothers and sisters didn't want to have anything to do with me anymore," Larry told me. "They wouldn't even talk to me."

I understood well. When I went through my lowest valleys, much of what we refer to as the "organized church" was not there for me. But the

569

Body of Christ, that group of people who believe and trust in Jesus and are committed to obeying His Word regardless of their denominational tags, *they* were there for me. And, of course, Jesus never forsook me, even in my darkest moments.

Since Larry Wright felt cast off by his church, he put his formidable gifts of teaching, preaching, and the power of persuasion to work making money. He found that he was good at it. Very good, indeed. So good that he built a multimillion dollar corporation. He got in some sort of business trouble and was sentenced to prison. There in prison, Larry Wright found that he did not have to be in a beautiful church building to be a minister of Christ's love and compassion. He began reaching out to inmates with the love of the Lord, teaching them the Bible and pointing them to Jesus Christ.

By the time I met Larry at Jesup, he had become one of the finest Bible teachers I had ever heard. An inmate is not going to put up with fluff or motivational, get-rich teaching or tricky formulas passed off as Bible truths. He wants to know, "Does this stuff work in the prison in which I'm living? Does God really care about me, when everything about this system seems designed to reduce me to a worthless, barely human number? Can that Jesus you talk about so much really do anything in my life?"

You don't want to preach in prison if you don't have any answers. Larry Wright had answers—a whole book full of them, the Bible, and he was able to help guys find not only answers, but The Answer.

One of the main characteristics of the Christians at Jesup was that the guys cared for each other in godly, practical ways. For instance, when one of the men received a "Dear John" letter from his wife or girlfriend and wanted to curl up on his bunk and die, the brothers at Jesup would not allow him to do it. They pulled him out of his bunk and said, "Come on, we're going out to walk the track," or, "We're going to Bible study and you're coming too. We're not going to let you roll up in your self-pity and die. We are your brothers and we are going to take care of you, even when you don't care enough to take care of yourself."

The gift bag that the Christians passed out to all new inmates at Jesup was a tangible expression of the care of the brotherhood. Since inmates were not allowed to collect money in our Sunday evening chapel service, we brought toiletry items, shower shoes, and other items purchased at the commissary. We collected them in what we called "The Chest of Joash," alluding to the Old Testament Hebrews who collected items for charitable use. The large chest was kept in the chaplain's office and the brothers could draw items out of it to help meet the needs of others.

I strongly disliked picking up cigarette butts as my work duty. It wasn't the work I minded—that part was easy. It was the location. Because of my notoriety, I felt extremely uncomfortable working out in front of the prison complex where everyone could see me. When an opening among the orderlies occurred, I volunteered to switch jobs. Guess what my new job was?

Back in the toilets again.

Each morning after Bible study, I walked the track, listening to my little transistor radio as I walked. Usually I listened to radio preacher Reverend David Jeremiah as I walked. When the program was over, I knew I had just enough time to clean my room and get to work.

As the bathroom orderly, I scrubbed the showers, sinks, commodes and laundry room every morning. Throughout the day it was the orderly's job to make sure the bathrooms were kept clean. About sixty men lived in my wing at Jesup. If you think your bathroom is a mess sometimes, imagine what one looks like that has been used by sixty guys each morning! Is it any wonder that I now refer to myself as a "porcelain expert"?

As I got to know Larry Wright better, he and I began to meet each day around lunchtime. We made our own meals of rice and . . . something. Usually the something was canned chicken, tuna, or chili beans, but we tried lots of experimental recipes, using whatever food was available from the commissary. As we ate lunch, we studied the Bible. We went from Genesis to Revelation. We were like two little kids who had just discovered candy. "Oh, look at that!" one of us would say as we found a new insight from the Bible. It was wonderful to rediscover that "Look what I found!" attitude about the Bible.

Larry and I also shared our deepest questions, pains, and joys. It was great to have a friend I felt I could trust.

In the afternoons, I worked out with weights regularly, much as I had at Rochester. I had committed myself to a completely low-fat diet after seeing all the grease and fat in the food in prison, so with the combination of diet and exercise, I was more physically fit than ever, though some of my friends on the outside worried that I was getting too thin.

Many evenings at 6:30 P.M., I went to some sort of church service. After being discouraged from attending the chapel programs during my early years at Rochester, I felt like I was feasting at a spiritual smorgasbord now that I was at Jesup. We had a vibrant Prison Fellowship group, the organization founded by Charles Colson. We also had a regular Bible study in

571

addition to the basic Bible doctrine class Larry taught using the *Christian Life Study Bible* as his source. We had Sunday school, taught by seventy-two-year-old Dr. John Boatwright, a black inmate who had been a pastor on the outside. There were Sunday morning worship services conducted by the chaplains; Christian video nights, featuring Christian movies, music, and preaching videos; and Christian support-group meetings. On Saturday mornings, we had "Marriage Builders," a class for guys who were married or hoping to be married, and on Saturday night, Larry Wright taught a "Servants" class, a class for spiritual leaders, using author Larry Crabb's material, *Encouragement: Key to Caring*. At one point, we were averaging twenty Christian services a week!

I had many memorable visitors at Camp Jesup. One of the most unusual and most loyal visitors was a dog named "Einstein." I first saw Einstein while I was walking the track at the back of the prison compound. His shivering, emaciated form cowered at the edge of the swampland that surrounded the prison.

Many of the inmates offered him food, but, at first, Einstein refused their kindness and ran off into the swamp. I figured he must have been cruelly treated, to not trust those who were offering him food when he looked so hungry. He looked as though he hadn't eaten a square meal in weeks. The outline of his ribs showed through his belly. His hair was dirty and matted. He was truly a pitiful sight.

Each day, the inmates left some food out by the track for Einstein. When he thought nobody was looking, Einstein crept along the track, picked up the food, and then bolted back into the brush. Slowly but surely, Einstein began to rebuild his trust in human beings. Eventually, he became the best pet a prisoner could have.

The inmates called him Einstein because they claimed he was the smartest dog in the world. Einstein was especially brilliant at eluding the guards . . . now that I think of it, that may have been one of the things the inmates most appreciated about the dog. Dogs, after all, are not permitted in prison. Those few dogs that happened to make their way onto the Jesup camp complex were usually rounded up and sent to the dog pound. Not so with Einstein. He had an uncanny ability to differentiate between the guards and the inmates. He took off before a guard came anywhere near, but he walked the track with the inmates as comfortably as old friends walking in the park. He was smart enough to never set one paw onto the main part of the prison compound. One of Einstein's favorite tricks—and another validation of his name—was to walk in front of an inmate who was trying to exercise by walking the track. Einstein would suddenly stop, causing the person exercising to have to stop and go around the dog or fall right over him. Einstein continued his interruptions until some inmates would simply pick up the big mutt and carry him as they walked the track. Einstein got a free ride along with the attention and human affection he craved.

Einstein greeted me nearly every morning at 7:00 and walked a few laps with me. It was as though he knew my schedule. He rarely missed a day. It was so wonderful to pet a dog after so many years. I wanted to have my picture taken with Einstein, but I did not want to betray my buddy. I knew all pictures were reviewed by prison officials and if they saw Einstein, he would be gone. Einstein remained my special friend until the day I left Jesup.

Another visitor who came to see me made a much sadder impression. The man was a world-class speaker, one of the best camp-meeting speakers in the world, a great organizer and a very successful pastor. When he walked in the visiting area, he emanated a sense of class and sophistication. He was dressed in a top-name designer suit. A silk handkerchief was in his breast pocket, perfectly highlighting the colors in his silk necktie. He was wearing alligator shoes and a gold wristwatch. He had all the trappings I once equated with success.

For the first part of our visit, he attempted to maintain an image he apparently thought that I expected. When I began to explain to him some of the things God had been doing in my life by bringing me to the point of brokenness, the man's veneer cracked and then crumbled. He burst into tears right there in the visiting area and said, "Everyone has deserted me. . . . I'm all alone." He then told me his all-too-familiar story.

A few weeks before his visit with me, my friend was the pastor of one of the fastest growing churches in his denomination. Speakers and musicians regularly beat a path to his door because they wanted to be associated with him and in doing so, be given the opportunity to perform at his church. In his obsessive quest for success, however, his marriage fell apart and his wife left. Within twenty-four hours, for all intents and purposes, he went from the top of the ladder to the bottom. He lost his pulpit, his church, his ministry, his reason for existence.

I hurt with that man. I knew the inner turmoil through which he was going. We talked for several hours that afternoon, and I tried to help him understand that God loved *him*, not just the things he was doing ostensibly in God's name. I felt free enough at Jesup to pray for the man right there in the visiting room.

Much of the spiritual openness at Jesup had to be attributed to the

573

leadership of the chaplains. Chaplains David Morton and David Grooters were two of the best chaplains I encountered in the prison system. Overworked and stretched to the max, they were nonetheless enthusiastic about inviting all sorts of special speakers and musicians to Jesup. We were blessed to have Bob and Jeanne Johnson do a concert for us. Bob and Jeanne had been part of my music team at *PTL* and it was great to see them again. Mylon LeFevre also came for a meeting, and the former rock musician with a famous musical family background related well to the inmates. Many prisoners decided to follow Jesus after Mylon's performance.

Deanie King, former Miss Arizona, came to our chapel, which was really the prison library, and sang to us. One of my favorite singers and longtime friend, Candi Staton, came and did an entire concert of gospel music. Candi did a tremendous job, and again, a number of inmates committed their lives to Christ.

Roger Breland brought his entire musical troupe, Truth, and gave a magnificent performance. James Blackwood brought his quartet to Jesup. Attendance at the concert was not mandatory—inmates were never required to attend any spiritual programs—but it seemed that nearly the entire camp population gathered on the prison loading dock to hear the renowned singers. The inmates loved the Blackwoods and especially the antics of bass singer Ken Turner; they were on their feet nearly every song. The inmates appreciated some of the old songs for which James was famous, such as "The Eastern Gate" and "I'll Meet You in the Morning." Tears streamed down many faces as the music evoked good memories from the past.

The prison authorities were extremely kind to James and his group. They allowed the quartet to give pictures to the inmates, which the inmates promptly asked them to sign. The group spent an hour autographing the pictures and inmates' Bibles. The guards even allowed me to go on the Blackwoods' tour bus, which was backed up to the loading dock where the singing took place. I was allowed to spend a few minutes in conversation and prayer with my friends as the guard looked on, apparently enjoying my visit with these musical legends as much as I was.

Franklin Graham came to Jesup, and, as he had done when he had visited me in Rochester, he brought music artists Dennis and Danny Agajanian with him. The inmates went wild over the Agajanians and were impressed that Franklin Graham, son of the world's most famous evangelist, would take the time to come and minister to them. I felt the same way.

Franklin's mother, Ruth Graham, was also active in our prison ministry, although few people knew it at the time. We had a constant need for Bibles because we were giving so many away to the new inmates as they arrived. When Mrs. Graham learned of the need, she went around her house and packed up as many of her family's old Bibles as she could find, including many of Dr. Graham's personal Bibles. She sent them to us to be given away without fanfare to the new inmates. Later, Mrs. Graham used some of her considerable charm and influence to convince a Bible publisher to supply us with the Bibles we needed for the inmates.

Dr. David Lewis came and presented a fascinating two-day seminar on the subject of biblical prophecy as it related to current and future world events. My dear Jewish friend Dr. Sid Roth and his coworkers came and spoke at our Prison Fellowship group and later began a regular weekly Bible study in the prison camp. Sid had appeared on *PTL* numerous times and I was always fascinated to hear him expound the Old Testament Scriptures from a Jewish perspective. My good friend Owen Carr, who had written me so often and with such encouragement, also came to Jesup and conducted a three-day revival series!

John Brevere, author of *Victory in the Wilderness*, a book that meant a great deal to me in prison, came to visit and to preach in chapel. I had never before met John, but his book spoke to me in such a profound way, I wrote to him and asked him to come visit me at Jesup. That was the only time I had ever written to a stranger with such a request. I just couldn't believe that someone who had never gone through a prison experience was teaching such meaningful truths. I wanted to see if he was for real. He was. John not only came to visit me, he came back to preach in the chapel and did a masterful job.

The Jesup chapel services were so popular, we had more inmates wanting to attend chapel than the library could handle. Since the room couldn't accommodate much more than one hundred people, guys had to alternate going to chapel. Interest in the things of the Lord was so high among the inmates that instead of referring to our camp as Camp Jesup, we soon began using the term Camp *Jesus*.

In addition to the many services and Bible studies conducted at the camp, Larry Wright and I did a great deal of biblically based counseling. The inmates had so many questions and were so in need of direction, Larry and I could have spent twenty-four hours a day counseling if we would not have had other responsibilities at the prison camp. To expand his counseling abilities, Larry took the same course as the one I had taken from the National Christian Counseling Association. Consequently, we always had a backlog of men waiting to be tested and advised concerning their temperaments and spiritual opportunities. Tammy Sue's ministry paid for all the testing and sent in hundreds of Bibles and encouraging Christian books to the Jesup prison. The inmates latched onto the literature within minutes of its arrival. No matter how many Bibles and books we received, we always needed more because new inmates were arriving constantly and many were becoming new Christians.

Not everything about Camp Jesup seemed like an old-time camp meeting. Besides the big house looming across the road in the background, there were still plenty of other reminders that this was prison, not a spiritual party. One night I will never forget was the night the federal authorities raided their own prisons and rounded up the Cuban inmates.

In the middle of the night, suddenly the doors of Camp Jesup burst open and in swarmed an army of prison guards. They went to every cell where prisoners of Cuban descent were sleeping, woke them up, chained them, and moved them out toward the road where a line of prison buses was waiting. Men screamed out, "I didn't do anything. Where are you taking me? Please! Why are you taking me? Where am I going? I didn't do anything!"

My heart ached for them. It was like a bad dream. For me it was reminiscent of when the federal marshals had seized me in the middle of my trial. Worse still, it was something one could imagine happening in a Russian gulag, but not in a "civilized" prison camp in America. Rumor had it that on the same night, Cuban prisoners all over the country were being singled out and transferred to someplace in Louisiana to await deportation. Some of the men who were rounded up at Jesup were members of our Christian fellowship. Many of them we never heard from again.

On another occasion, I woke up between 4:00 and 5:00 A.M. and got out of bed to go to the bathroom. As I walked up the corridor toward the bathroom, I noticed several guards in the bathroom doorway. That struck me as unusual, especially since the guards didn't use the same bathrooms as the inmates. Then I saw the blood.

A pool of blood stretched at least five feet across the bathroom floor. It looked as though someone had thrown a bucket full of blood onto the floor and then let it spread. The blood must have been there for some time. While some parts of it were still red, much of it looked as though it had already begun coagulating into a brackish, blue-black color, with what looked like grotesque blue berries jutting up here and there throughout the pool of blood.

The guards were talking quietly about the scene when I suddenly realized that it was going to be my responsibility to clean up this mess! Sure enough, one of the guards nodded to me and said, "Better go get your cleaning materials."

I went back to my cell and put on some clothes, then went to the mop closet and gathered my bucket, cleaning agents, and a new pair of rubber gloves. I had to use a hose to get all the blood off the floor, the black and blue chunks turning bright red as the water splashed on them. I hosed the blood down the drain, scrubbed the floor, and disinfected everything in the bathroom. It took me until 6:30 A.M. just to get the place cleaned up. The entire time I was working, I thought, *Somebody must be dying. A person can't lose that much blood and survive without medical attention.*

As soon as I was done, I went to one of the officers and said, "Somebody's dying in here."

"Yeah, I know. We're all dyin' a little bit more every day in here," he answered sarcastically.

I went to one of the women who worked in the counselor's office and told her the story. She seemed concerned, but she didn't do anything.

I went to two other guards and said, "An inmate is dying in this prison, somewhere." I told them about the blood and said, "You can't lose that much blood and not be dying. Somebody in here is bleeding to death."

"Oh, don't worry about it," one of the guards responded carelessly. "If he doesn't stand up for count, we'll know he's dead." Count was still six hours away!

The insensitivity of the guards and my sense of utter helplessness to do anything to assist a fellow human being nearly drove me crazy. Sure enough, at the midday count, in a cubicle not far from my own, a young man did not stand up for the count. He remained in bed as the guards called his name. When the guards pulled the covers off him, they discovered that he was covered with blood. The wall next to his bunk was spattered with blood. They stood him to his feet and his blood-soaked clothing clung to his body.

"Get him into the shower and get him dressed," a guard commanded.

I couldn't believe that they were going to try to clean him up before dealing with the situation. Eventually, the boy was taken to the hospital. We were told that the young man was going to be okay, but the prison rumor mill reported his death. Regardless, he never returned to Jesup.

Most of the guards at Jesup were kind, compassionate human beings. Others were sometimes less than that.

Because there were only two chaplains at Jesup and they had so many inmates with which to deal, they often allowed Larry Wright to do the preaching on Sunday nights. Larry's prison record was impeccable and he was known, even to the guards, as a man of integrity. During one evening chapel service, when Larry Wright was the speaker, he asked me to pray. I gladly consented. Just before I prayed, however, I read a small portion of Scripture to help focus our prayers on God rather than on our needs. I made a few comments and began to pray fervently.

When a guard who had been walking by saw me behind the podium, he immediately went to the guard station and began calling out over the P.A. system, "Recall! Recall! Recall!" In other words, he was ordering everyone in the entire prison back to his cell for an immediate recount. Later, some of the more amiable guards informed me that the unhappy fellow who ordered the recall had thought that I was preaching—which in his mind I should not be doing—which, in truth, I had not been doing. It was a commonly accepted rule that inmates were not permitted to practice their professions in prison, unless an inmate possessed a skill needed by the prison, such as plumbing or carpentry. Apparently, that guard preferred to shut down the whole prison rather than let me preach!

For their sixty-seventh wedding anniversary, my mom and dad made the three-hundred-mile trip from Heritage USA to Jesup. They were both eighty-seven years of age at the time and my fears at Rochester, that they would never be able to take another trip together and that I might never see them again, proved unfounded. My brother, Norman, and sister, Donna, joined my folks and me for an anniversary celebration in the prison visiting room.

My children and grandchildren visited me often at Jesup. We spent hours just talking about the past, but even more time talking about the future, things we hoped to do once I was released from prison. As we had done at Rochester, we purchased our lunches from the visiting-room vending machines. The grandboys didn't mind a bit. They'd eat their junk food and romp and play in the visiting yard. I loved every minute I could spend with them and was reminded of the Scripture, "An old man's grandchildren are his crowning glory" (Prov. 17:6 TLB).

One day I was going through my normal routine when over the prison paging system I heard, "Attention on the compound and in the housing units: Jim Bakker, report to the administration building." Instantly, I began to review my recent activities. When my name was called in prison, I never knew whether I was being summoned to answer interview requests, take a random urine test for drug usage, or perhaps an officer had decided that I had too many books or pairs of underwear. Sometimes the pages brought good news, but often the news was negative.

The week before, I had been paged to the office and told my daughter, Tammy Sue, was in the hospital and sick with pneumonia in both lungs. But there was nothing I could do for her. That same week, Jamie came down with the flu. Again, there was nothing I could do to help. The normal bumps and bruises of life become exacerbated in prison, especially when they involve your children. Any parent who has ever had kids suffer some sort of sickness or calamity where you could not be there for them understands that awful feeling of helplessness.

I learned in prison that I could not always be there for my children when they needed me. I could not always bandage every bruise. I discovered, however, that I could always depend on our heavenly Father to take care of them, even when I could not. The verse "Thou art the helper of the fatherless" (Ps. 10:14 KJV) became much more than a verse to be read casually. It became a promise of God upon which I depended. I realized afresh that the same God who was with me in prison could take care of my family members. And God was always faithful to bring them through even the toughest of times.

That morning, as I made my way across the compound to the administration building, I didn't know what to expect. Once inside, I learned that it had been the senior chaplain, David Morton who had paged me. The chaplain dropped a bombshell on me that day. "The Reverend Jerry Falwell has requested permission to visit you," he told me.

Falwell! Visit me? What does he want with me? All sorts of thoughts raced through my mind.

I had prayed much about Jerry Falwell long before this day. Similarly, I had put the past behind me and had asked God's forgiveness for my mistakes and sins and I had received His forgiveness. I did not want to open any old wounds. I had extended forgiveness to Jerry Falwell in my heart and had even written him a letter telling him so and asking for his forgiveness. Wasn't that enough?

I asked the chaplain for some time to think and pray about Reverend Falwell's request. I went back to the cell block and found Larry Wright. I explained the situation to Larry, and we prayed for quite a while. When we were done, there was no question about what I should do. Larry and I both felt that the only right and biblical alternative I had was to meet with Reverend Falwell. I told the chaplain that I agreed to the visit. For me to be convinced I should meet face-to-face with Jerry Falwell was one thing; for my kids to be convinced of the same was something else. I wasn't sure how they would respond to the idea. After all, in their minds, Jerry Falwell had not only stolen our ministry but had thrown them out of their home, me into prison, and them into impossible circumstances.

579

When I broached the subject by telephone to Tammy Sue, I was surprised when she was elated. She thought that meeting my former accuser face-to-face would be a positive step in my own healing.

"I think it's the right thing to do, Dad," she told me.

Telling Jamie Charles would not be so easy. Of all my family members, Jamie Charles seemed to be carrying the deepest scars from the wounds inflicted by the take-over of PTL in 1987. Jamie was only eleven years old when the world as he knew it came to an end. Suddenly, his friends were no longer allowed to play with him; his house and his room were no longer his; he no longer attended the same school or church; he was uprooted from every bit of security he had known. Not to mention the pain, embarrassment, and teasing he endured when I went to prison. In his young mind, nearly all the major hurts he had experienced in his life were directly or indirectly attributable to one man—Jerry Falwell. It is impossible to overstate the bitterness and resentment Jamie felt toward the man who had requested to visit me.

I knew Jamie could better handle the news of the planned visit if I were able to tell him face-to-face rather than over the telephone. Jamie was scheduled to visit me the Friday before Falwell's visit, so I decided to wait until then to break the news to him. Unfortunately, it didn't work out that way.

Since late May 1993, when Jamie moved in with Phil Shaw and his family in Rochester for six weeks, Jamie had been obsessed with contacting everyone he could who might be able to help me get out of prison. He had worked feverishly with Phil to help put the copies of my appeal into the hands of influential people across the country. He even contacted the White House in his efforts to see me freed. Even the rejection of my appeal by the U.S. Parole Commission did not deter Jamie's efforts.

After I was transferred to Jesup, Jamie moved in with Bishop Earl Paulk's brother's family in Atlanta so he could be close to me. The Paulks had offered to educate Jamie and give him a home while I was in prison. Don and Clariece Paulk became like a mother and father to Jamie; their son, Donnie Earl, who was about Jamie's age, became like a brother to him. The two young men struck up a fast friendship. Besides giving my son a home and driving Jamie to Jesup to see me week after week, the Paulk family had a profound influence on Jamie's spiritual life as well. He grew deeper in the things of God and began taking an active part in the youth ministry in the church. All the while, Jamie continued to work, trying to find someone who could help in some way to get me out of prison.

Just before his scheduled visit to me, Jamie contacted my lawyer's office to see if there were any new developments he could tell me about. When my lawyer mentioned the Falwell meeting, it was like hitting Jamie with a speeding train. He felt betrayed and angry that such a meeting could be arranged without his knowledge. More than that, he was afraid for me. Jamie felt sure that Jerry Falwell was going to try to hurt me in some way. He begged me not to go through with the planned confrontation. "When you come to see me on Friday, we'll talk about it," I promised.

Jamie arrived early on Friday morning, as always, hoping to be the first in the visitors' line at the prison. When I walked into the visitors' area, I could tell Jamie was distraught. He was visibly shaken. We spent the day together and we talked a great deal about the planned Falwell meeting. "Dad, please! Don't do it!" Jamie begged. "The man has heard that you're close to getting out of prison. Don't trust him. He will destroy you." Nothing I said could calm Jamie's fears.

The next morning, Jamie was back at 8:30. He had not changed his mind overnight. That day I was able to bring my Bible into the visiting area and Jamie and I went through the Bible, talking about forgiveness. When we came to Matthew 6:15, "If you do not forgive men their trespasses, neither will your Father forgive your trespasses," I knew we had found a key. I had always taught my children to forgive those people who said or did things that hurt them, but this hurt went much deeper than anything I could imagine in Jamie's life. I realized that God wanted Jamie to be involved in the healing process that was going on between Jerry Falwell and me.

Jamie, however, remained adamant. "Dad, you are not going to meet with him!" He simply would not hear of me meeting with Falwell. It was not a forgiveness issue with him; it was fear that Falwell was going to harm me.

Finally, I hit upon an idea. I said, "Jamie, would you like to meet with Jerry Falwell before I do and see how you feel about our meeting together?"

Without a moment of hesitation, Jamie said, "Yes, I would."

I told him, "I'll make a deal with you. If you go meet with Falwell and you don't feel that I should meet with him, then I won't do it. But if after meeting with Reverend Falwell, you feel that it is right, then you come with him and bring him back here to meet with me." Jamie agreed to my proposal.

Jerry Falwell was in Jacksonville, Florida, that night, preaching at a large Baptist church. He was planning to come see me the next day at the conclusion of the series of services there. I contacted Jim Toms and asked him to arrange a meeting between Jamie and Jerry for the following evening after the service. Jim took it from there.

The next day, Mr. Toms picked up Jamie and the two of them left for

Jacksonville. As he departed, I prayed, "God, if You want this meeting to take place, then You're going to have to work in that boy's heart and in the heart of Jerry Falwell."

What happened next surprised even me!

51

Reunion

EVEN THOUGH WE HAVE FORGIVEN A PERSON IN OUR HEART, sometimes it helps to put a face with the person we forgive. That is what I needed to do with Jerry Falwell. Although I had forgiven him time and again in my heart for what I considered to be his deceit in getting me to resign and turn PTL over to him, I still needed to express it to him in person. It's one thing to forgive a person you see only from a distance; it's quite another thing to look that person in the eyes and say, "I forgive you." Tougher still to say is, "I was wrong to hold onto the bitterness and resentment I have felt against you. Would you please forgive me?" Yet I knew something like that had to take place between Jerry and me, not only for our sakes, but for the sakes of our families, and for the sake of the Body of Christ at large.

Our family advocate, Jim Toms, and Jamie traveled together to Jacksonville and arrived in time for the evening service at the church where Jerry Falwell had been speaking. Another man was preaching that night, so when Jerry entered the room accompanied by Mark DeMoss, he walked to a reserved seat on the front row of the church . . . right in front of Jamie. Before being seated, Jerry looked at Jamie as though he recognized him, but he didn't acknowledge my son in any way. Jamie later admitted that his anger toward Jerry Falwell surged to the surface and was almost uncontrollable. There was Falwell sitting within inches, and with his back to Jamie! For a moment, Jamie thought, *If I were that kind of guy, I could reach my hands around his neck and strangle him!* Jamie blinked hard and tried to drive the nasty thoughts out of his mind.

When Jerry Falwell was introduced from the podium that night, many people in the audience jumped to their feet, giving him a standing ovation. Jamie remained seated.

Ironically, the speaker of the evening touched upon prisons and prison sentences in his message that night. As Jamie recalls it, the speaker said something such as, "These kids who are committing crimes should spend more time in prison!" Jamie nearly got up and left the service.

Jamie was ready to meet with Jerry Falwell, but the preacher was busy with well-wishers. Jamie went back to his hotel room and waited for a call from Mark DeMoss, indicating it was time to meet with Jerry. Jamie and Jim Toms waited for several hours in their hotel room and Jerry Falwell never showed up.

Around midnight, the telephone rang. It was Mark DeMoss, and he wanted to speak with Jamie. Mark informed Jamie that Jerry Falwell was tired and would meet with Jamie the following morning. Jamie was livid. He felt sure that Falwell was trying to play a game with him. Mark DeMoss assured him that was not the case, but that Jerry had been preaching all weekend and was simply tired. He invited Jamie to his room so the two young men could talk. Jamie accepted the invitation and went to Mark's room, where he poured out his heart to Mark.

Jamie said to Mark, "I can't stand what Jerry Falwell did to my dad."

Mark was understandably defensive "Well, Jamie, a lot of strange things happened back then."

Mark would neither confirm nor deny Jamie's accusations against Jerry Falwell, but he listened as Jamie emphasized that Jerry Falwell had acquired the leadership of PTL through less-than-honorable means and that he knew the details of what had happened in the fall of PTL. He told Mark, "I feel that Jerry Falwell's influence is a major part of why my dad is in prison right now."

Mark contested a few details, but he didn't attempt to change Jamie's mind about anything that had happened in the demise of PTL. He and Jamie talked for quite a while and parted amicably.

About 8:30 A.M. the following day, Mark called Jamie and said that Jerry was ready to meet. Jim and Jamie had just ordered breakfast, so Mark told them to bring it along. With his breakfast in hand and Jim Toms at his side, Jamie marched into Jerry Falwell's hotel suite. Jerry Falwell immediately rose to greet them.

"Well, hello, Jamie. I'm glad to meet you," Reverend Falwell said, extending his hand.

Jamie shook Jerry's hand, but he did not reciprocate niceties.

They opened the meeting with prayer. Afterward the group sat down at a table in the suite and Jim Toms initiated the discussion, saying, "We wanted to meet today because Jamie has some concerns and wanted to check things out before Reverend Falwell sees his father."

Mark DeMoss responded, looking at Jamie, "Yes, this is why we want to see your dad. . . . "

Meanwhile Jerry Falwell and my son sat across the table from each other, not saying a word.

Finally, Jamie blurted, "Just why do you want to see my dad?"

"Well, Jamie, I just want to visit him to see how he is doing."

"Okay. Well, Jerry, I just want to let you know that you are a life-changer. You changed my life. And I want to let you know how you did it."

Jamie proceeded to tell Jerry Falwell how he had cried when our family was kicked out of the Tega Cay house where he had spent most of his life. Jamie told him how it hurt to hear Jerry Falwell call his father a homosexual on national television. Jamie was extremely blunt. He challenged Reverend Falwell saying, "You can't deny it. I saw and heard you do it. I have it on video. If you'd like to see it, I'll send you a copy."

Jerry Falwell remained quiet and simply let Jamie erupt. Jamie went on to remind Reverend Falwell of what he already knew. "My parents are divorced, my dad's in prison, all sorts of bad things have happened. . . . " Jamie told Falwell about his own bouts with drinking and drugs.

After Jamie's verbal outpouring he shifted gears in his inimitable, rapid-fire way. "I want you to know that I forgive you for what you have done to my family. And I want you to forgive me for hating you for so long."

Jerry Falwell chose his words carefully. "Well, Jamie. I thank you for forgiving me. Forgive me for anything I might have done, or you think I might have done. There are some things that you don't understand."

Jamie took a deep breath and let it out slowly. Those were not the words he had come to hear. Yet he suddenly realized that as much as he would like to have heard Jerry Falwell admit his manipulation of the events of 1987 that eventually culminated in me going to prison in 1989, Jamie suddenly felt liberated in his own soul having extended forgiveness to Falwell and asking for Jerry's forgiveness.

Jamie responded, "Well, like I said, you are a life-changer. You have changed my life again. Now I can go on being a free man, because I don't hate you anymore."

Jamie and Jerry Falwell talked for nearly an hour and a half. At the close of their session, Jamie and Jim Toms asked to be excused and went into the interior room of the suite to discuss what should happen next.

"What do you think?" Jim asked Jamie. "How do you feel about it? Do you think your dad should meet with him?"

Jamie responded, "Yes, I think they should meet." Jamie later said that his sole reason was the sense of peace he had experienced in his own heart after talking with Reverend Falwell and extending forgiveness personally. "I just can't deny my dad that feeling of incredible peace. Dad must experience what I have experienced."

Once the decision was made, Mark DeMoss and Jim Toms immediately went to work implementing the plan. Jerry Falwell had a speaking engagement that night not far from Jesup. It was decided that Jamie and Jim would accompany the Falwell group aboard Jerry's private plane and fly into the airport adjoining the prison at Jesup. Jim Toms alerted the chaplain at the prison and as soon as the group checked out of the hotel they were on their way to Jesup.

Meanwhile, I had been anxiously waiting to hear from someone whether the visit was on or off. I fully intended to abide by my promise to Jamie, that if he did not feel right about Reverend Falwell and me meeting in person, I would forgo the visit. As I did my usual work that morning, I kept waiting to hear a call to the administration building. When it didn't come, I began to wonder whether the visit would actually take place.

At last, around noon, I heard my name over the prison P.A. system, calling me to the administration building. I was still uncertain as to the status of the proposed Falwell visit.

When I walked into the building, I saw Jerry Falwell, a man whom I had not seen in person in more than seven years, standing next to my son. Jamie looked as though a heavy weight had been removed from his shoulders. I hugged my son, and then Jerry Falwell and I embraced. I had been a bit nervous about seeing him. After all, this man had impacted my life more than any other human being outside of my own family members. At one time, I felt Jerry Falwell was the most evil man I had ever met. All that, however, was in the past. Now, I was not fearful or hateful; I had already dealt with that when I had studied *God Meant It for Good*. I was tense due to the circumstances, but as I embraced Jerry Falwell, I felt no animosity or resentment. At that moment, I knew that God had done His work in my life.

The prison chaplain took Jerry Falwell and me back to his office. Jamie stayed at the front entrance while Jerry and I talked. Once in the room and out of earshot from the others, both Jerry and I seemed to sense the awkwardness. The last time we had sat in a room together, we had discussed his helping the leadership of PTL for a period of thirty to ninety days, after which I would return to my previous position. That was nearly seven years ago, and Jerry had since repeatedly and publicly disavowed those details of our conversation.

Now, as we sat together in a room again, it would have been easy to dredge up all the sordid mess from the past. I was not even tempted to do so, and apparently, Jerry had no desire to relive the past either. Instead, I asked Jerry Falwell to forgive me for the hateful statements I had made about him. Jerry asked me to forgive him as well though he was not specific. We talked briefly about my activities in prison and some of the things I had learned. He stayed for about twenty minutes to half an hour and then said that he must be on his way to his speaking engagement. We prayed together, said our good-byes, embraced again, and he was gone.

I had so many feelings, so many emotions pulsating through my heart as Jerry and I sat together. I felt awkward being with Jerry, yet in that moment, I knew that I had forgiven him. I was free of bitterness. It felt great!

Nevertheless, I couldn't help wondering why Jerry Falwell had really come to see me. Was Jerry more concerned about the future than he was over the past? Was this the last act in a play that began in Palm Springs in March 1987? Our conversation was relatively low-key, mundane, and uneventful, but perhaps more was going on than either Jerry or I was aware.

I will never know for sure why Jerry Falwell got involved in my life. God knows, and He will judge all of our words and deeds. But I have settled the matter in my heart, that regardless of Jerry's motives or anyone else's involvement, God used the circumstances of losing PTL to bring me to a place of genuine brokenness, repentance, and surrender for the first time in a long, long time. It hurt. And the losses my family and I have endured have been many and irreplaceable, but in the light of eternity, it will be worth it. Jamie was allowed to see me for a few minutes while the Falwell group said their good-byes to the prison personnel. Jamie was euphoric about the way things had turned out. He quickly briefed me on his meeting with Jerry Falwell and told me that he and Jim Toms would be flying to the place where Jerry was speaking that night, and from there he and Jim would catch another flight back to Jacksonville where their car was waiting.

As I watched my son walk away that afternoon, I felt at that moment, my "little boy" was more of a man than I had ever been. He had confronted his worst fears and had turned what he had perceived to be a grizzly bear into a human teddy bear. This visit had not been for me only, but for my son. God had done a miracle that day, but it was not in bringing Jerry Falwell and Jim Bakker together; it was the healing of Jamie's heart.

Perhaps it was a little easier for me to deal with forgiveness issues concerning Jerry Falwell, because a few weeks earlier, I had been grappling with even more difficult issues of forgiveness. My former wife, Tammy Faye, and my former best friend, Roe Messner, were married.

Tammy Faye had written a letter to Tammy Sue and Jamie informing our children that she was planning to marry Roe on October 3, 1993. Of course, she didn't discuss her marriage plans with me. I had heard several rumors indicating that marriage was in the offing for her, but it was still a shock when someone came into my cell at Jesup and showed me a copy of *People* magazine with Tammy Faye on the arm of Roe. She was wearing a gorgeous white wedding dress, and she and Roe were smiling contentedly at one another.

About fifty people attended the Sunday evening wedding held at a country club near Tammy's home in Rancho Mirage, California. Tammy Faye sang "Jesus Loves Me" during the ceremony. After the wedding, Tammy Faye and Roe went off to Hawaii on a honeymoon. It hurt deeply for me to read or hear about Tammy and Roe's marriage. It pierced my heart every time I saw a picture of my wife of more than thirty years kissing another man. Had it not been for the encouragement and healing help I received from the Christian men at Jesup, I might have crashed emotionally, as I had done when I first learned she was leaving me. Thanks to Larry Wright and many other inmates who had been through the stomachwrenching pain of divorce, I was able to maintain my balance. They understood what I was going through, and they refused to let me go through it alone. As a true Body of Christ, they were there for me in my time of need. They cared for me all through the aftermath of my former wife's marriage to Roe Messner. They prayed with me and for me. And they encouraged me to forgive her.

Forgiveness is rarely a one-time deal, especially for something like divorce. I soon discovered that I had to deal with the issue of forgiving Tammy and Roe every time it came up and every time I saw another photograph of the two of them. Yet God had seared into my heart and mind the Scripture, "And when you stand praying, if you hold anything against anyone, forgive him, so that your Father in heaven may forgive you your sins" (Mark 11:25-26 NIV).

It was easier for me to forgive Tammy Faye than Roe. I was still in love with Tammy Faye, as much as I knew our marriage vows had been severed. Roe was a different matter. He was the man who had betrayed my trust and stolen my wife. I had regarded Roe Messner as a modern-day John Wayne, a paragon of virtue, a man of impeccable business ethics, and a man I could and did trust with that which was most precious to me: the care of my wife. When Roe betrayed that trust, regardless of the reasons, it was as though he had taken a large knife, stabbed me in the back, and continued to twist and turn it until I dropped.

Nevertheless, I knew that I couldn't avoid forgiving Roe. Even if I could somehow circumvent the many Scriptures on forgiveness—which I did not attempt to do—I couldn't get away from Jesus' command to "Love your enemies, bless those who curse you, do good to those who hate you, and pray for those who spitefully use you and persecute you" (Matt. 5:44). Whether I regarded Roe as a friend or an enemy, I was locked into forgiving him and praying for him.

At one time, Roe and I shared dreams of building the greatest Christian center the world had ever seen. When I learned that he and Tammy were seeing each other while I was in prison, I wrote to him and told him that he and I would never lay another brick in another building together. Amazingly, though, during those difficult days at Jesup and afterward, I forgave Roe so completely that if in the future God instructed us to build something else together, I could do it. I don't plan on building anything else with Roe, but I am free enough to do it.

Looking back, I can now see I should never have placed him in the position of trying to care for Tammy Faye while I was in prison. Yes, they must take responsibility for their own actions, and they must give an account before God, but I should have trusted God more and a man less when it came to taking care of my wife. I thought friendship superseded wisdom and common sense, and I was wrong.

Of course, I had to forgive Tammy Faye as well. I do not want to give the impression that forgiveness came easily. It did not, but it did come. At this writing, Tammy Faye and I have no contact except through our children, but I harbor no resentment or animosity toward her. At times, my heart grieves for her. I understand the pain and loneliness she suffered during those early prison years better than I once did, and I hurt for her.

Almost every week, I receive mail from well-meaning people who are praying that Tammy Faye and I will someday be remarried. I appreciate their kind and loving words, but I am also a realist. I recognize that just as when we break an egg and scramble the parts, it is difficult to undo the results and put everything back together again. I know God often does what mere humans regard as impossible, but I also know that both Tammy Faye and I must move on with our lives. We are both so different now. At times, I have seen Tammy in print or on television, and I have wondered, *Were we really married for more than three decades?* Yet she remains the mother of my children, and that is reason alone to always love and honor her. I truly want God's best for Tammy Faye and Roe. I pray that God's will may be done in all our lives.

Back at Jesup, having worked through forgiveness and receiving the inner healing so necessary in my own life, it looked as though I might be ready to get out of jail!

52

Return to Heritage

AS MUCH AS I WOULD HAVE BEEN DELIGHTED TO HAVE A furlough, which was standard procedure for inmates at prison camps who have complied with the rules, I really did not anticipate having one granted. My counselor had repeatedly emphasized that because I was a high-profile case, my chances of receiving a furlough were nil.

The first week in April 1994, my eighty-eight-year-old father fell down while he was working in his garage. He was in severe pain, but he hobbled back into the house and sat down in his favorite recliner. He sat there all night, barely moving a muscle. By morning, my father's pain was so intense, he and my mother had no choice but to call an ambulance to take him to the hospital. After a quick X ray, the doctors gave Dad the bad news—he had broken his hip. And to think he had sat up all night on it!

Because of my parents' advanced ages, the prison officials kindly allowed me a thirty-hour furlough to go see my dad in Charlotte. Jim Toms made the arrangements, and he and Jamie came to meet me at Jesup shortly after 1:00 P.M. on Saturday, April 10, 1994. Before I left the compound, my counselor warned me that I must be back by 8:00 P.M. Sunday night, or I would be considered an escapee, and could possibly be returned to the big house. I assured the counselor that I understood and would be back on time.

Although I was concerned for my father's well-being, it was an exciting moment when I walked out of that prison, without a guard walking next to me, and without shackles and handcuffs and chains. I felt like a real human being.

I met Jamie Charles and Jim Toms out front, and together we piled in an old, dilapidated car, borrowed from the manager of the local airstrip, for the short trip from the prison to the tiny airport. Jamie had just gotten his driver's license a few days earlier, so Jim let him drive the car. The old former police vehicle had more power than the car Jamie had learned how to drive, and when Jamie tramped down on the gas, we took off like a jet! I thought, *Oh, no. Only two minutes out of prison and we're already breaking the speed limit.* Jamie quickly got the car under control and smiled at me. He was so proud to be driving his dad away from prison. I was proud of him too, and thrilled to be free, riding in what Jim Toms called our "getaway car."

We boarded the small plane for our trip to the Carolinas, and as we lifted off the runway, I looked down at my prison home below. From this vantage point, it looked like a well-kept college campus. I breathed a sigh of relief. It felt so good to be flying away from incarceration—even if for a few hours. I still had on my prison blues, which Jamie insisted that I remove immediately.

Jamie had brought along one of his blue denim shirts and a pair of pants he borrowed from a friend. I changed out of my prison blues and put on the borrowed street clothes in the back seat of the airplane. The fit wasn't the greatest, but after wearing prison jumpsuits, khakis, and blues, anything seemed stylish to me.

The airplane, piloted by one of Jim Toms's friends, landed at its home airport near Greenville, South Carolina, where Jim had left his car. We were anxious to get to the hospital, but Jim Toms insisted that everyone would feel better if we stopped to get something to eat. We pulled into a lovely Italian restaurant, where Jim and his wife, Susan, had eaten many times. I was somewhat apprehensive; it had been nearly five years since I had last eaten in a restaurant. Beyond that, I wasn't sure how I might be accepted back in public society.

When we walked in, the hostess said they were no longer serving lunch, and the restaurant would not be open for dinner until after 5:00 P.M. Since Mr. Toms had eaten at this restaurant many times and he knew both the owner and the chef, Jim asked if he could speak with one or both of them. Jim talked briefly with the restaurant owner, who then came out and ushered us to a beautiful table in the center of his charming dining room. Since his regular serving hours were over, we had the restaurant to ourselves.

As I looked around the dining room, I was struck by the sheer beauty of it. The elegant table was set with real china, placed perfectly upon a clean, starched, white linen tablecloth and decked out with Williamsburg-blue linen napkins.

A strange fear suddenly came over me. I worried that I might not be able to remember proper etiquette and table manners since in prison I had grown accustomed to merely eating to survive, rather than as a social custom. Often in the Jesup Prison chow hall, our food would be simply heaped onto our trays, especially on days when bowls were in short supply.

As we sat down to order, I was in culture shock. Instead of an inmate yelling for me to hurry up and finish my food so he could clean up and get out of there, a fresh-faced waitress dressed in a crisp, clean uniform stood waiting to take my order. I almost lost my composure when she asked me kindly, "What would you like?" In prison it was usually, "Take this and like it." I could feel the tears welling up in my eyes. I felt like a foreigner in my own country. I was out of my element, and try as I might, I could not remember the simplest of social graces that had once been such a natural part of my everyday existence. I sat frozen, not wanting to reveal my learned prison behavior by devouring my food "inmate style."

The congenial restaurant owner, a tough, former football coach, sat next to me and realized I was having difficulty readjusting to life outside of prison. He quickly said, "Let's pray." He reached out his hands and we formed a prayer circle around the table as he called on God to be with us in a special way.

The kind restaurateur quickly came to my rescue as I hopelessly looked over the mouthwatering selections on the menu. He said, "I'll have the chef prepare a little of everything for you." The chef made each of us an Italian platter, with veal, chicken, spaghetti, and even the owner's special homemade Italian sausage. Each of the delectable dishes was doused in rich Italian tomato sauce, another specialty of the house, and some of the best I have ever tasted.

"I could get used to this," I quipped to the group around the table. I had no illusions about delicious, home-cooked meals in my near future. I was due back in prison in less than thirty hours.

After the meal, we loaded back into the car and Jamie drove the remainder of the way to the hospital in Charlotte. When we arrived at the hospital, we found my mother sitting at my father's bedside. My dad was still groggy from some pain medicine, but he was thrilled to see us. He was in a great deal of pain, as the doctors had just operated and placed a pin in his broken hip. The prognosis looked good. If we could keep him from working in his garage, he would most likely be fine in a few months.

After we had visited for a while, I could tell both my mother and father were getting tired, so we decided to go home.

My mother and father still lived in their home at Heritage USA. Jamie and I were to spend the night at my mother's place while Jim Toms was going to check in at the Heritage Grand Hotel. As we drove onto the grounds of Heritage USA, I had a queasy feeling in my stomach. I had not been back at Heritage since 1988. It still looked the same, yet it seemed a lifetime ago that I had been here. A young man with a familiar face was at the gatehouse to greet us. His mom and dad, Buddy and Marty Sheppard, had helped develop and operate our first farm at Heritage USA. The last time I had seen him, he had been a little boy running around the old farm at Heritage USA. Now he was a security officer, making sure that no intruders came onto the grounds at night.

The first residents to greet us were Uncle Henry and Aunt Susan Harrison. Henry had been my cohost on our television programs for many years, but now he was unable to walk and had to get around on a motorized cart. He and Aunt Susie had church in their home on the hillside location that I had personally selected for them a number of years ago.

Uncle Henry and Aunt Susan insisted that we come in and see their Christmas tree.

Christmas tree? What are they doing with a Christmas tree in their house during the second week of April? I wondered.

Sure enough, inside their home was a fully decorated Christmas tree. Uncle Henry explained to me that he had made a commitment that he was not going to take down the Christmas tree until I was released from prison. It had been up for several years now, and it still looked stunning. Henry turned on the tree lights and ran them through their beautiful displays of flashing colors and patterns. He was proud of his beautiful tree, and it was quite a contrast to the prison trees I had decorated the past five Christmases.

Sensing my emotional exhaustion, Aunt Susan suggested that I lay down on Uncle Henry's big recliner bed. We talked and laughed, and I rubbed the tummy of their dog, "Mushy Love," who had jumped up beside me and rolled over. It was like old times except we were all much older, sadder, and hopefully wiser. Aunt Susan woke Grandma Ruthie, a sweet, old woman who had volunteered her services at PTL for years, and who now lived with Uncle Henry and Aunt Susan. Grandma Ruthie had written to me faithfully while I was in prison.

"Look who's here!" Aunt Susie said as she gently nudged Grandma Ruthie awake. "Somebody has come to see you," she said in her singsong voice.

When Grandma Ruthie opened her eyes and saw me, she looked as though she had seen a ghost! When she finally realized it was me, she relaxed and said, "I can die now. You're home."

"Oh, no, Grandma Ruthie," I told her, as I leaned over and kissed her. "We need you around here a lot longer."

I was glad to have been able to spend a few minutes with these dear folks. As difficult as the past years had been on them, I was grateful that God had blessed them with a good life and many friends who still lived at Heritage USA.

As we drove down the gently winding road that led to the Heritage Grand Hotel, where Jim Toms was going to spend the night, it was like traveling back in a time machine for me. As difficult as it may be for some people to believe, at times in prison I actually wondered if Heritage USA was all a dream. But as we crossed the railroad tracks, which I had driven over so many thousands of times before, and I caught my first glimpse of the Heritage Grand, I realized that it was no mirage after all. It had been six years since I had seen the Grand, but now the memories of it all, from blueprint stage to seeing every brick put in place, to the madcap dash to open it on time, and the many celebrations we held there, all came flooding back to me.

Jamie drove right up to the front of the hotel, under the canopy. No doubt, had I been driving or giving directions, I would have chosen a side entrance. Not Jamie. It was right up front or nothing. Jim Toms went inside to check into the hotel, and Jamie and I remained in the car. As we sat silently for a few moments, my mind replayed scenes in which thousands of people had gone through those front doors to one of the many functions we had held inside the hotel or in the Grand Ballroom. I thought back to the grand opening. It had been a high moment in my life. Who would have guessed that this hotel, so beautiful, so majestic, would be the crux of the court case that would send me to prison? The pathos of it all swept over me as we sat in front of the hotel.

"Come on, Dad," Jamie was saying. "Let's go inside."

"Oh, no, Jamie. We can't do that."

"Why not? Come on! It's past midnight and there aren't many people around. Besides, I've really wanted to see it for so long. Come on, Dad. It will be fun."

Fun?

Finally I consented and Jamie and I stepped inside the hotel. Only a few people were milling around, and nobody seemed to pay much attention to us as we walked past the front desk, around the corner, and down the hall toward the shopping area known as "Main Street," an indoor street lined with Victorian shops, all decorated in a turn-of-the-century motif. Main Street was nearly deserted at that hour, but its soft blue ceiling created a beautiful sense of warmth and serenity even now.

My mind raced back to Tammy Faye's and my twenty-fifth anniversary, as our family walked together down that cobblestone street, the band playing, the old-fashioned street lights lit, the twinkle lights sparkling in the trees, confetti flying, and people shouting words of love and encouragement. Now, on this night, Jamie and I walked down the deserted streets alone, the sound of our shoes echoing through the long corridor. One lone family sat at a table next to the Trolley Car, a refreshment stand that sold hot dogs and other short-order food items.

Because it was so late, all the stores in Main Street were closed, but Jamie insisted that we walk the length of the street and on around to the Grand Ballroom, the spacious hall where so many great Christian artists and speakers had once graced the stage.

"Jamie, let's go home." It had been a long, emotion-packed day already. I was tired, and the memories were too vivid; they were tearing into my defenseless heart. I felt that at any moment I was going to explode from trying to hold in my emotions at the memories of what once had been. Jamie, however, was still energized by it all. We got in the car and circled past the famous water park, the log chalets, and Heritage Inn. We drove by the tennis courts, Olympic-sized pool, and the recreation complex. Past hundreds of campsites, then down to The Barn auditorium and television studios. We drove near the Upper Room, the twenty-four-hour-a-day center for prayer and counseling that I had initiated after driving the streets of Charlotte looking for an open church in which to pray one night in the midst of Tammy Faye's and my problems. As Jamie and I passed by, I wondered if there were any ministers available at this hour in the Upper Room. We came upon the great amphitheater looming like a large abandoned castle in the darkness. At one time, thousands of people praised God in the amphitheater as their hearts were warmed by the Passion Play, depicting the life, death, and resurrection of Christ. Now, the amphitheater cast an eerie shadow across the grassy knoll.

Out past the Youth Center we drove; Jamie wanted to see it all. Even in the dark, I knew every bend in the road, and each turn brought back wonderful yet heartrending memories.

After what must have been an hour or more, Jamie and I made our way back to the residential area of Heritage USA to my mother and father's home. That night, I slept in my dad's bed, the first real bed I had slept on in a long time. It felt so soft, so comfortable, I felt as though I was sinking a foot deep into the mattress. I slept like a baby.

The next morning, I had my first bath in almost five years. Prisons have shower stalls only, so baths were a "luxury" I sorely missed. Oh, to be able to simply lie back and relax in a hot tub of soapy water! I now had a new appreciation for even the simplest of life's pleasures.

As I was shaving with my dad's razor that morning, I heard a knock on the bathroom door. I opened it and there was Jamie, standing, smiling at me. "Dad, that was the best night of sleep I have had in several years, just knowing that you were in the house with me."

"Thank you, son," I replied. Jamie stood in the doorway and watched me shave, as he had done so many times as a little boy. Over the past two years especially, Jamie had often told me that he lived for the day I got out of prison and he and I could be together. "It's neat to see you shave again, Dad." Jamie said.

My mother seemed more like her usual spry self that morning. She seemed physically revived by the fact that we were home with her. She wanted us to eat breakfast at her home, but I had promised Tammy Sue's family that we would have breakfast with them, even though she was still in Russia on a missions trip. I was sorry to have missed my daughter, but I was not going to miss a chance to see my grandbabies, James and Jonathan.

The time went so quickly; the clock simply refused to slow down. I knew that we had to hurry. I dared not be late. Hopefully I would have other opportunities to visit with my family in the near future, but if I returned to Jesup after 8:00 P.M., it might be many years before I saw them again.

"Hurry, Jamie," I said. "We have to get going."

When we arrived at the hospital on Sunday, Dad was feeling much better. He was still groggy, but the pain had subsided a bit. His room was filled with dear friends from our former church congregation at Heritage. While we chatted, a nurse brought Dad a tray of food for his lunch, which I fed to him like a little child, just as my dad had done for me as a little boy. Now it was my turn.

Just before Jim Toms, Jamie, and I left the hospital to begin our trip back to Jesup, we joined hands with everyone in the hospital room and prayed. We said heartfelt but hasty good-byes and thanked the hospital staff for their kindness and care toward my dad. We had to hurry. Time was running out. And there was still one important stop I wanted to make before leaving.

We drove out to Tega Cay, the sight of our former home that had burned to the ground while I was in prison. I had seen the inferno on the news in the prison, but nothing could have prepared me for the shock of seeing the charred remains of what had once been our home. Very little was left, only a cement slab on the hillside overlooking the lake and the beautiful, old-fashioned lampposts that had once lined the driveway in front of our home. The glass in the lamps nearest the front of the house was partially melted in a grotesque pattern.

Jamie and I roamed around to what had once been the back of the house. As I gazed numbly at the patio where I had cooked so many hamburgers for our family, friends, and half the neighborhood, my thoughts drifted back to so many good times at that house. Sunday afternoons were always special times for us. After I had preached at the morning worship service at The Barn, I came home and started cooking up the burgers.

We never knew how many people we would be having for lunch on Sundays. It was always open house at the Bakkers' after church, as our family members and friends congregated on the patio next to the swimming pool. Our neighbors Howard and Vestal Goodman and their family were regulars around our grill, as were the legendary gospel singer Doug Oldham and his dear wife, Laura Lee, and their children. Dale Hill, the director of our television programs, routinely showed up with his wife, Brenda, and son, Steven, as did our neighbors, Vi and Eddie Azvedo, and Dr. Blair Bycura and his wife, Judy, and their children, Darrin and Ryan. Everyone was always welcome at our home for Sunday afternoon burgers. And were they ever good! I always made the burgers extra big and thick. Tammy's specialty was her brown-sugar baked beans. We called them "Tammy Beans."

When we had more time and weren't quite as rushed to get food on the table as we were after church, I loved to fry up a huge batch of seafood for the family and friends who dropped by—shrimp, scallops, flounder, oysters, and my famous homemade battered onion rings. For a moment, I was back there. I could smell the fish frying. I could hear the laughter of family and friends gathered around the table. Each batch of fish I delivered to the table disappeared as fast as I could fry it. . . .

Jamie's voice jolted me out of my daydream. "Dad! Dad, come here, quick! Look what I found!" I looked over to where Jamie was standing on the concrete slab where our garage had once stood. The garage was one of the first parts of that creaky, leaky house that we renovated. Shortly after we bought the place, the garage began threatening to fall down. When we rebuilt it, we put in a concrete floor and eventually tiled it over so the kids could also use the garage as a playroom when the cars were not inside. The blaze that had burnt up the house also destroyed the garage, including the tile that had once covered the cement. Now that the asphalt tile had been burnt off, Jamie had discovered some scrawlings in the still-intact concrete. I brushed the dirt off the writing, revealing Tammy Sue's childlike signature and that of the Bycura children. Jamie brushed away more debris and discovered his name written in the concrete as well. I could see some more writing, just beneath some sand, and as I pushed the sand off the concrete, I read the words, "Tammy loves Jim. We're eating fish tonight." The date of June 19, 1981, was scratched above a heart with an arrow through it.

Both Jamie and I stood there speechless. Time had been frozen in that concrete, a happy time that seemed so long ago. The memories of what once was enveloped us. It was almost as if we were looking at Tammy Faye's handwritten epitaph on a tombstone, only in this case, the tombstone marked the passing of the Bakker family as it once was.

Jamie and I reluctantly pulled ourselves away from the remnants of our former home and climbed the hill to where Jim Toms was waiting in the car. We jumped into the vehicle and Jim drove as fast as we dared all the way back to Jesup, Georgia. We arrived with just twenty minutes to spare. As I was hurrying into the prison to report, my dear friend Dave Roever was walking out. It seemed so strange to be able to stop and hug him outside the visiting room. In the whirlwind of events surrounding my father's fall, it had slipped my mind that this was the weekend of Dave's visit. I was sorry I missed Dave's message, but I knew I would be hearing all about it from Larry Wright and the other guys upon whom Dave's impact would be profound.

We said hasty good-byes and I hurried in so the guards could check me in on time. Almost before I knew it, I was back in prison, but not for long.

53

Released!

THE ANCIENT PROVERB SAYS, "A FRIEND LOVES AT ALL TIMES, / and a brother is born for adversity" (Prov. 17:17). When it came time to start seriously thinking about the possibility of me getting out of prison, many friends offered to help, and two friends especially came to the fore— Jim Toms and Franklin Graham.

After my parole was denied and my appeal rejected, it became obvious that I was going to have to serve as much of my sentence as the government deemed possible. My sentence being reduced to eight years, the usual government procedure under the old laws passed prior to 1987 was to release a prisoner who had served with good behavior after five of the eight years. The last six months of such a sentence could often be served in a halfway house or sometimes even under house arrest with the person wearing an electronic monitor or otherwise making daily reports to the prison appointed officers. On that basis, my lawyers informed me that my actual release date was scheduled for December 1, 1994. Compared to my original forty-five-year sentence, that sounded like a blink of the eyes, but after over four years in prison, every day of confinement, lack of freedom, and absence from my family felt like an eternity.

Knowing that I was a candidate for a good-behavior release to a halfway house, my lawyer and friend, Jim Toms, studied the latest prison requirements regarding my case to ascertain how such a release might be expedited. He discovered there were some basic requirements that, while they did not guarantee my release to a halfway house, were necessary before the prison system would even consider allowing me out of Jesup. One, I had to have a place to live, preferably with a family member. Two, I needed to have a job waiting for me before I left the prison compound. Three, I needed to have the potential to get my driver's license and to have access to a car in order to get back and forth to work. If an inmate could prove that he had realistic opportunities outside of prison, the odds of receiving a release to a halfway house increased immensely. Jim Toms began working toward that end.

Around the same time, Franklin Graham came to visit and to conduct a chapel service at Jesup. During his visit, Franklin again invited me to go along with him to Africa once I got out of prison to see the hospital at Tenwek that *PTL* viewers had helped furnish by their generous contributions and to help oversee the construction of two more hospitals in Africa. I told him that I would consider going but that I would like for Jamie to be able to go along, partially because I felt Jamie would greatly enjoy the experience, but also because Jamie had been waiting for me to get out of prison for so long, I didn't want to run off on another building project soon after being released. Franklin expressed certainty that Jamie could accompany me to Africa, and that Tammy Sue could visit me and minister through her music as well.

In April 1994, Franklin wrote a series of letters formally extending the invitation to work with his organization in their medical relief efforts. In essence, Franklin guaranteed me employment, if the prison system saw fit to release me to a halfway house. Jim Toms checked into the halfway houses around Boone, North Carolina, where Franklin's ministry was headquartered. Although most halfway houses in the U.S. were full, there was space available at the Salvation Army in Asheville, about an hour-and-a-half drive from Boone.

Franklin offered to pay for a place for me to live along with Jamie, and to provide an automobile for me to use. He put his name on the line and sent all the necessary information to my lawyers, who presented it to the prison officials in charge of granting the halfway-house releases.

It was beginning to look as though I might be able to serve the last part of my sentence in the halfway house after all! Yet the more I thought about it, the more I was troubled by something. I did not want Franklin to feel obligated to pay me back for a small kindness I had extended to him years ago. Besides, he had paid me back bountifully by coming to see me in Rochester and at Jesup, and simply by being my friend. Moreover, I did not want to give the impression that I was trying to slip into the good graces of the public, and especially the Christian community, on the coat-tails of the Grahams' good name. I recognized that the Graham family name was one of the most respected in the country, and mine was one of the most disrespected.

During Franklin's next visit to Jesup to conduct a chapel service, I pulled him aside to a lawyer's room where we could talk about it. "Franklin, you don't need me," I told him. "More importantly, my baggage could hurt you. I could be a real detriment to you. If people find out that you are associating with me, it could hurt your reputation or that of your family. You don't want to identify with me—the world thinks I'm a felon. You don't need my baggage."

Franklin looked slightly offended. "Jim!" he said, "you're my *friend*." I will never forget the way Franklin Graham said that word: "friend."

"You were my friend before," Franklin said. "You helped me when very few people wanted to have anything to do with me at the beginning. The people who began supporting me at your encouragement are still the foundation of our ministry's support today. You were my friend then, and you're my friend now."

Then Franklin Graham flashed his trademark grin and with his eyes twinkling, he said, "Besides, if anyone doesn't like it, I'm ready for a fight!"

In late June, I began to hear rumors that most inmates in Jesup could serve the last six months of their sentences in halfway houses. I was thrilled to think that I might soon be released to a less-restrictive environment. The rumors were confirmed by an unusual source. A man whom I had never met, Terry Inman, a prominent Assemblies of God pastor from California, traveled all the way across the country with a special message he felt that God had laid upon his heart. Pastor Inman quoted Isaiah 40:1-2, "Comfort ye, comfort ye my people, saith your God. Speak ye comfortably to Jerusalem, and cry unto her, that her warfare is accomplished, that her iniquity is pardoned: for she hath received of the LORD's hand double for all her sins" (KJV).

Pastor Inman explained to me that God had sent him there to comfort me and to tell me that the work that God had wanted to do in me had been accomplished, that I had received double for my sins, and that I would be released.

I was humbled and awed by Pastor Inman's words. They resonated in my heart, but I had a hard time accepting his message.

I was cautiously excited, but I did not want to allow my hopes to get too high. I believed the message that Pastor Inman delivered, and I was overjoyed with the news, yet I had learned enough about God's timing in prison that I knew not everything happened overnight. Beyond that, I had learned well that what seemed a certainty one day in prison could vanish without a trace the next day. Nevertheless, I began to mentally and emotionally prepare for my exit.

I also prepared spiritually. God had taught me so many things in prison over the past four and a half years. My whole life had been revolutionized. I was now a different person. Indeed, when Bishop Earl Paulk came to preach in our chapel service and spoke on the subject of dying to ourselves, his message struck a chord in my heart. Bishop Paulk spoke on the words of Jesus in John 12:24, "Most assuredly, I say to you, unless a grain of wheat falls into the ground and dies, it remains alone; but if it dies, it produces much grain." Jesus went on to say, "He who loves his life shall lose it. . . ." I now fully realized that the only real cure to the awful loneliness I had experienced in prison was not by surrounding myself with activities or more people. It was by dying to myself and allowing Christ Jesus to abide in me. In a real way, God had brought me to prison to die, but not physically; He allowed me to be incarcerated so I could die to myself.

Around 3:00 A.M., on Friday, July 1, 1994, a guard awakened me in my cell. "Bakker, it's time," the guard said.

Those were some of the sweetest words I had ever heard.

A few days before, the prison officials had informed me that my release to a halfway house at the Salvation Army in Asheville, North Carolina, had been granted.

Finally, it was my turn to go on the merry-go-round!

You'll remember the "merry-go-round" was the term inmates used to describe the mandatory process by which prisoners are released. Before getting out of prison, the inmate must go around to each prison department head and have him or her sign off, saying that it was okay for the inmate to be released and that there were no outstanding responsibilities undone. It usually took most of a day to make the rounds, but I had never heard an inmate complain about it. This was the day every inmate longed for!

I had seen hundreds of other guys go on the merry-go-round. In the early days of my prison experience, facing a forty-five-year sentence, I dared not even think that one day I might be able to take that wonderful trip too. And now it was my turn to go on the merry-go-round. I couldn't believe it.

603

At last, I was done, and I went to my counselor who certified that I had a current social security card.

"Everything is in order, Bakker," she said, with a trace of kindness in her voice. "I wish you the best in the future."

I thanked her and left before she changed her mind. The prison adage, "You ain't got nothin' comin'," remained with me to the final hours of incarceration, echoing in my brain.

The media received word of my imminent release and began gathering a full day ahead of time. A slew of press people set up camp in front of the gates to the Jesup prison camp in anticipation of the first photographs and interviews I might grant in almost five years. Television remote trucks lined the road outside of the prison. Mr. Harris, the camp administrator, called me to his office late Thursday afternoon. Sitting there was one of the assistant wardens from across the street at the main prison. Mr. Harris expressed his concern about the circuslike atmosphere outside the prison compound. To avoid the media hassles, the prison officials at Jesup decided to process me out in the middle of the night. I didn't mind a bit.

Immediately I called Jim Toms and he began making preparations to fly me out of Savannah, about an hour's drive from Jesup.

At about 4:00 A.M., I walked out of Jesup prison camp, wearing the clothes my family had sent to me. I got in a car driven by a female prison official, and we drove out the back gate of the prison while the throng of media people snoozed out front. I sat in the front seat. I was not cuffed, shackled, or chained. Along the way to Savannah, the woman offered me a stick of gum. I accepted it as a first token of my freedom. Inmates are not permitted to have any gum at all in prison. I had been told that gum could be used to get impressions of keys and to stick to locks, causing them to not close tightly, thus creating the possibility of an escape. Consequently, when the woman offered the gum to me, I happily accepted it, popped it into my mouth, and chewed more vigorously than I had in years. The taste of freedom was in my mouth!

In Savannah, I was met by Jamie Charles and Jim Toms. Jamie could hardly believe that I was actually out of prison. Meeting in the airport in the middle of the night made for an extremely surreal reunion, but nonetheless special. Jamie was sporting a goatee and a mustache, a new look for him, and one I had never before seen. Before we caught the flight to Atlanta, however, he ran into the rest room and shaved it off. He seemed to sense that the images of this morning were going to be indelibly impressed upon our minds, not to mention newspapers and magazines all over the country, so he didn't wish to risk making a fashion statement he might regret in years to come. That's my boy, always cognizant of the big picture.

We hugged and hugged and did not want to let each other go. Despite our fatigue, we didn't want to miss the excitement of this moment. This was the day we had dreamed about, prayed for, and longed for. We kept saying, "I feel like I'm dreaming!"

Jamie, Jim, and I flew to Atlanta and quickly boarded an Atlantic Southwest Airlines flight that would take us directly to the small airport at Asheville. I took the window seat and Jamie sat in the aisle seat to shield me from other passengers. Fortunately, we had escaped relatively unnoticed. The only picture taken on the plane that morning was by Jim Toms, who took a picture of Jamie and me, a picture I treasure to this day and have titled "Escape to Freedom."

We arrived in Asheville at 10:35 A.M. We waited until everyone else got off before we exited the small aircraft. A white automobile, arranged by Jim Toms, was waiting for us on the tarmac. A few well-wishers who had somehow heard of our arrival were on the other side of the fence surrounding the tarmac, and I waved to them as I bounded toward the car. I was nervous, and I wasn't sure how they would respond to me, so I was elated when they waved back enthusiastically with warm smiles on their faces. I felt so good, I wanted to wave to everyone at that point!

We drove the short distance from the Asheville airport to the Salvation Army halfway house and arrived there shortly after 11:00 A.M. A larger crowd of well-wishers was there, as well as a throng of reporters and photographers. I knew we had only limited time, because I had to report to the halfway house by noon, but I wanted to take just a few minutes to greet the well-wishers and make a statement for the press. I felt great! I was fit and tanned from walking the track in the Georgia sunshine. I was dressed casually in a black shirt and trousers and a charcoal-gray sports jacket.

One of the reporters shouted, "Jim are you happy to be here?"

I smiled broadly and said, "I'm glad to be here." Then I added, "I'm excited to be anywhere!" *Anywhere outside of prison*, I could have added but didn't.

In a prepared statement, I said,

It is with joy and thanksgiving to God that I walk from prison today. I look forward to a time of rebonding with my son, Jamie Charles, and daughter, Tammy Sue, and my two delightful grandsons, James, my namesake, and Jonathan, who was born while I was in prison.

605

Also, I am anxious to spend time with my other family members, especially my mother and father, who both will celebrate their eighty-eighth birthdays in a few weeks and who have faithfully stood by me.

There are no words to express my gratitude to my friends and family who have fulfilled the great Proverb, "A friend loveth at all times, and a brother is born for adversity."

Most of all, I want to thank my Lord and Savior Jesus Christ, who walked with me through this valley of despair and loneliness and turned it into a time of healing solitude with Him, for truly in this valley "He restored my soul."

Once again, I want to humbly ask for forgiveness to those I have offended or hurt in any way by my sin and arrogant lifestyle. I also ask the family of God to forgive me for the pain and shame I brought on them and most of all on the name of our Lord.

After halfway house, I will make my home with my son, Jamie Charles. I leave you with the words of the apostle Paul, written from his prison cell: "The Lord stood with me and strengthened me."

At the close of my statement, I greeted a few members of the press and the small group of people who had gathered to welcome me home. Jim Toms answered a few more technical questions about my release, and then I went inside to report and be fingerprinted. A few minutes later, Jim brought me my first meal at the halfway house, a turkey club sandwich and a piece of key lime pie he purchased from one of his favorite restaurants.

The press swarmed around the halfway house all day long, poking cameras and tape recorders in the windows, trying to get scoops. Some photographers even hired "street people" who were staying at the Salvation Army at the time to sneak in and snap pictures of me inside the halfway house. For a while, members of the media made life miserable for the Salvation Army members who were trying to minister to the people most others passed by.

One of the residents, an older, mentally challenged woman with a towel draped around her head, felt compelled to protect me from the press. She crept near the windows, peeking out to spy where the cameras were hiding, and then reported back to me in covert tones. She took it upon herself to keep me apprised of the press's every move throughout my stay at the halfway house.

The Salvation Army halfway house was a split-level, brick building that accommodated anywhere from ten to sixteen men at one time. I was to be housed with five other men. There were no guards, bars, or razor-wire fences. During the days, I was permitted to leave early in the morning to go to work, then required to return each night to sleep at the halfway house. I could eat my meals at the Salvation Army house, or I could buy my own elsewhere. I was to do my own laundry, ironing, and keep my room orderly and clean. After over four and a half years of cleaning experience in prison, I did not anticipate that as being a problem. Although I was still considered a prisoner of the federal government, a percentage of my income went toward paying for my lodging at the halfway house until my full release date in December.

Lt. Colonel David Holtz and his staff of Salvation Army officers were some of the kindest, most compassionate people I could have hoped to meet at that juncture. They did not judge me in any way, they simply loved me and cared for me, and helped me make the transition back into the mainstream of community life.

In one of the multitude of ironies connected to my case, just two blocks down the street from the halfway house was the office of Jerry Miller, one of the federal prosecutors who had tried my case in court and had represented the government in all the subsequent hearings concerning the criminal charges.

In another ironic twist, the same week that one of the major national news magazines ran the story of my release from prison to the halfway house—on the same page, in the same story—the magazine ran the news of Norman Roy Grutman's death. Mr. Grutman had been the lawyer who had accompanied Jerry Falwell to Palm Springs in March 1987 to inform me that *The Charlotte Observer* was going to expose my adulterous encounter with Jessica Hahn. The Saturday before I was released to the halfway house, Norman Roy Grutman succumbed to liver cancer. He was sixty-three years of age.[1]

True to his word, Franklin Graham paid the rent on a home in the town of Etowah, a small mountain town about thirty minutes from Asheville, where I could stay with Jamie when I was not at the halfway house. Ruby and Roy Morgan literally moved out of their mountain home and lived in their motor home so we would have a place of privacy and tranquility. Franklin also gave me a car to use during my first six months out of prison—a nice station wagon too, not a jalopy. Everything that Franklin had said he would do, he did.

That first afternoon when Jamie and I rode up the mountain to the Etowah house, I could hardly believe my eyes. To be able to enjoy the natural beauty of God's creation, unfettered, unguarded, and without fear of getting in someone else's prison space was mind-boggling. But the best part was yet to come: When Jamie and I pulled in to the house Franklin had rented, there were Tammy Sue, Doug, and James and Jonathan. They were holding a large sign they had painted that read, "Welcome home Dad! We love you! July 1, 1994." What a joyous reunion we had!

Ruby and Roy showed us around their wonderful little house. Over the next few weeks, the couple would become like family to us.

On Saturday, one of Franklin Graham's assistants took me to a store so I could pick up some items I might need in order to go to church on Sunday morning. We went into a drugstore and I was struck by how bright and cheerful the store was. I had grown accustomed to shopping at the commissaries in prison, looking through a glass at a limited selection of products in a locked room on the other side of a window. Now, all the vibrant colors of packages danced before my eyes. I stepped tentatively down the aisles, taking in the wonder of it all. At one point I stopped and looked around to make sure nobody was listening. Franklin's assistant stopped with me and asked, "Is anything wrong, Jim?"

I whispered quietly as I pointed to the items on the shelf, "Man, somebody could steal this stuff!"

The assistant convulsed in laughter. "Yes, I guess they could," he said. When we left the store, he asked me where I would like to eat. I didn't have a clue.

I told him, "I'd really like some seafood. It's been a long time since I've had any of that."

He took me to a Red Lobster restaurant, and as soon as the waitress brought the menu, I knew I was in trouble. The menu was so big! And there were so many selections. I read the menu again and again and I simply could not make up my mind. There were just too many choices. Tears welled up in my eyes. I could not yet adjust to life outside of prison. Eventually, I ordered a seafood platter with a little bit of everything on it. Wow! Was it ever great to be out!

I rose early on Sunday morning to get ready for church. I felt somewhat nervous about attending a formal church service outside of prison. I had many concerns: How would people react to seeing *me* in their sanctuary? Would I be a distraction from the worship service? Would the pastor want me in the congregation? I did not want to cause any trouble to the pastor, create any disturbances for the congregation, or divert anyone's attention from the Lord.

Nevertheless, I had promised Franklin's mother, Ruth Graham, that I would attend the Sunday morning worship service with her and her family at the Montreat Presbyterian Church. Franklin was to be the guest speaker at the 10:45 A.M. service.

The beautiful stone church was already nearly full when I arrived. I was ushered back to the office of the pastor, Dr. Calvin Thielman, to meet with him and Franklin before the service. The pastor was extremely kind and gracious. He assured me that I was welcome in the church and told me that he had been a lifelong friend of the Graham family. We talked a while longer and Pastor Thielman told wonderful stories of Franklin's childhood and teen years as he grew up in the mountains of North Carolina. Before we knew it, the organ began to play, signaling it was time for the service to begin. One of Franklin's staff members ushered me to the row where they had saved a seat for me . . . with the Graham family. The Graham family, with all the children and grandchildren, filled up nearly two rows of the sanctuary.

By the time the organist finished playing the prelude on the stately pipe organ, the church was packed with people. Just before the invocation, Ruth Graham walked down the aisle and sat down right next to me.

The introductory hymn that morning was "Christ Has Set Us Free." When Franklin got up to preach, one of the first things he did was present me to the congregation. He told them the story of Tenwek Hospital and how he had come to know me. When he introduced me as his friend to his sophisticated home congregation, the audience applauded and I lost control of my emotions. Tears streamed down my face as I sat with the congregation and the members of one of the most respected families in America applauding all around me. I spent most of Franklin's sermon trying to regain my composure. I was experiencing total culture shock. Only forty-eight hours previously I was in prison, Inmate 07407-058, and now I was in the beautiful Montreat church with Ruth Graham and her family.

After the service, I climbed into Franklin Graham's pickup to drive up to his parents' home. Fortunately for me, he had removed the guns from his gun rack—federal felons are not allowed to be in the same vehicle with a gun.

By the time we arrived at "the cabin," as the Grahams refer to their lovely, old, log mountain home, Ruth and Franklin's wife, Jane Austin, and the children had already arrived. Ruth had prepared a full-course dinner for us. We enjoyed a wonderful, casual dinner together. I felt as though I was sitting in the midst of a family reunion. We talked and laughed just as any family might during the Sunday afternoon meal. We talked a great deal about one of Ruth's favorite subjects, as well—how we could better get Bibles to inmates and their families.

During the course of our conversation, Ruth asked me a question that required an address. I reached into my back pocket and pulled out a paper envelope in which I kept my addresses and cash. I had not owned a wallet for over four and a half years—prisoners are not allowed to have wallets.

As I fumbled through the envelope looking for the address, Ruth Graham watched me quizzically. "Don't you have a wallet, Jim?" she asked tenderly.

"This is my wallet," I replied pointing to the envelope. Right then it seemed natural to me to have a paper envelope as a wallet.

Ruth got up and left the room. In a few minutes she returned carrying one of Billy Graham's wallets. "Here is a brand-new wallet Billy has never used. I want you to have it," she said.

I still carry that wallet to this day.

Before I left that afternoon, Ruth Graham insisted upon sitting down and writing a thank you letter that she asked me to carry with me to Darlene Thompson, the woman who was in charge of the Salvation Army halfway house. In the letter, Ruth wrote thanking the directors of the halfway house for being good to me. She also thanked them for allowing me to come and spend the day with the Graham family.

Over the years, I have met literally thousands of wonderful Christian men and women and families. I have never met anyone more humble, gracious, and, in a word, "real," than Ruth Graham and the members of her marvelous family.

During my first few weeks out of prison, I went to several meetings with Franklin Graham and his staff members to get a better understanding of the work of Samaritan's Purse. I was amazed by what I saw. Many people ballyhoo about the good work they do. Franklin and his staff just do it.

I met with some of the staff and the doctors who were supplying medical help overseas. I met with the head of the overseas hospitals. I attended Samaritan's Purse planning meetings at "The Cove," the Billy Graham Conference Center. With every person I talked to, I came away impressed and convinced that it was truly Christianity in action.

Franklin and the staff of Samaritan's Purse have huge warehouses, filled with everything from medical supplies to hospital tools. The buildings were stocked with baby beds and anything else that might be necessary to meet the needs of diseased and dying people in Third World countries. As I toured the facilities in one location, I saw workers rebuilding X-ray machines and other technical medical equipment to be used on the mission field. On another floor, I saw their staff working on a worldwide communications system to create faster and better lines of communication with missions all over the world in times of need or crisis. Samaritan's Purse is an awesome ministry, a massive undertaking, and without a hint of ostentation, Franklin and his coworkers simply go about their work in a quiet but effective manner, saving and changing lives around the world.

It seems to me that wherever there is a crisis of human need, Franklin is there. On a moment's notice he hops in his small plane, which he enjoys flying himself, landing in the most war-torn, disease-ridden areas of the world, to see how he and his organization can help.

As impressed as I was with Franklin's work, I was not able to go to Africa with him at that time. The government was reluctant to let me leave the country, having just been released from prison. More importantly, I was not emotionally ready to help anyone yet. My composure often crumbled at the slightest memory of a negative prison experience. Tears came easily and frequently. I needed time for emotional healing. I needed to get acclimated to a semblance of normal living again. I had grown spiritually by leaps and bounds while in prison, but I needed time to recuperate from the prison environment and learn how to function in polite society again. Beyond that, my family needed me to be home; I had been gone for such a long time. As much as I enjoyed working with Franklin Graham and was disappointed that I could not help in Africa yet, I felt it was part of God's plan that I stay home for the time being.

So I worked part-time for my attorney, Jim Toms. I prepared lunches for Jim's clients, buying all the ingredients at the local grocery store, cooking the meals, and serving the clients. One of my favorite jobs was painting the front of Jim's law office, wearing old, paint-spattered clothes and a baseball cap as I worked. Besides getting to work outside in the fresh air, it was fun to watch the reaction of people as they went by on the street. Their facial expressions said, "Is that Jim Bakker covered with paint on that ladder? Naaahhhh!"

CHAPTER

54

Back From the Grave

MY DEAR FRIEND OWEN CARR HEARD THAT I HAD BEEN
released from prison and wrote to rejoice with me. As always, Owen
included some wise advice, "From now on the tempo will pick up. You
will discover that you will miss those extended periods for Bible study,
meditation, and prayer. You must be careful not to let other pressures
crowd out those important times." I knew Owen was absolutely right.
Within a few days of being out of prison I received several job offers,
dozens of interview requests, and a number of invitations for speaking
engagements. I accepted none at that time. I kept busy and out of the public eye. As much as possible, I stayed at the mountain house in Etowah,
which was a wonderful time of rest and refuge for me, but terribly boring
for Jamie.

Jamie slept on a pull-out couch in the den on the lower level of the
house. He loved his room with the pool table, a fifties jukebox, and the
walls covered with Coca Cola memorabilia, but he eventually tired of
doing little besides watching television and playing old fifties songs on the
jukebox. One day Jamie and I were coming out of the grocery store, and
there in the back seat of a car in the parking lot, Jamie spotted two beautiful white Samoyed dogs. They were gorgeous, huge creatures. We had
always had a houseful of pets when Jamie was growing up. When Jamie
saw these dogs, he exclaimed, "Dad, that's the kind of dog I wish I had."

When I returned home, I began calling all around the area to see if any pet shops carried the Samoyed puppies. A veterinarian gave me a lead. With Jamie driving, we were soon off to find a new friend. It felt good to be free and doing a father-and-son sort of thing. Jamie picked out a fluffy, little, white, female pup that which he named Elizabeth.

Even though Jamie enjoyed the companionship of his new pet, he soon told me the isolation of being out in the middle of nowhere was causing him to go stir-crazy. For several years, Jamie had lived for the day that I got out of prison. Especially since the parole board had refused to grant me parole, Jamie had spent much of his time and energy doing everything possible, talking to everyone and anyone that might help me be released. Now that I was actually out of prison, I wanted to live quietly in the mountains and rebond with my son and rebuild our lives. Jamie, on the other hand, wanted to visit his former friends in Charlotte, some of whom I feared were not a positive influence on him. I felt helpless to do anything for him.

Like Jamie, I too had dreamed of the day we could be together. When things did not automatically work out the way we had hoped, I felt that I was failing him as a father again. I knew I had failed him when he was a boy, and the last thing I wanted to do now was to fail him again when as a young man, he needed my love, acceptance, and guidance. I knew he needed more than just being around me. Jamie needed to be with friends his own age as well. He also needed desperately to catch up on the education he missed while I was in prison.

Furthermore, because the mountain house had only one actual bedroom, and that with French doors, we had little privacy for Tammy Sue and her family members when they came to visit. Besides, Jamie, Tammy Sue, and I had lived very separate lives for the past four and a half years, intersecting with each other only for a few days every so often in prison, in a stressful, artificial setting. We all had our own image of the family that we used be, back in the glory years of Heritage USA, and we all wanted that image of "family" to return. But the heart of our family, Tammy Faye, was missing. We all missed Tammy Faye's presence in our family.

Secondly, and tougher to admit, we were not functioning well as a family before the fall of PTL. Tammy Sue hit me with that truth one day when I was lamenting the good old days of family life. "Dad, get a grip," she said in her down-to-earth manner. "We *never* really were a family. We all were doing our own things. We came out of our rooms for meals and then went back to doing our own things."

When I stopped to think of it, Tammy Sue was right. If we were going to rebond as a family, it would have to be almost like starting from scratch.

Consequently, we did not know how to react to one another. Life was not like it once was. After praying so hard and so long, and having such lofty expectations of what it would be like if I could just get out of prison, we were all somewhat disappointed when reality poked holes in our illusions of perfection.

About that time, I heard from Dr. Raymond Meadors, a former professor at Heritage School of Evangelism. He told me about a wonderful program that his children were attending at the First Assemblies of God Church in Phoenix, a church pastored by my longtime friend Tommy Barnett. The group was known as "Master's Commission" and was having spectacular results, especially with the children of missionaries, pastors, and other teenagers who had grown up in the glass house of some ministry.

I immediately called Lloyd Zigler, the leader of Master's Commission, and explained to him that Jamie and I were having some difficulties. I explained that Jamie had had some drug problems as well as difficulties resulting from a learning disability. The leader assured me that Jamie would be welcome at Master's Commission.

Shortly after that, I talked with Tommy Barnett by phone. He too assured me that Jamie would be welcome there. He extended an invitation for Jamie to stay with his family or live in the school apartments if he decided to be a part of the group. I told Jamie about the idea. At first, Jamie recoiled at the thought of leaving me so soon after I had gotten out of prison. When I realized how Jamie felt, I suggested that he go visit for a week, "just to check it out."

Jamie agreed to go to Phoenix. When he arrived, he soon discovered a special branch ministry directed by Mike Wall, a former member of Master's Commission. Jamie wanted to do something to take the gospel to some of the fringe elements of the youth culture, for instance, the skateboard crowd with whom he identified and participated. Consequently, he easily related to Mike Wall, who dressed more like a rock musician than a youth pastor. Mike had a passion to minister to the youth of his generation, "alternative" kids, punk rockers, hippies, grungers, and other nonconformist youth. Mike told Jamie about a new youth ministry he was just forming. The group was to be called "Revolution." Jamie joined on the spot and moved in with Mike and his wife, Heather. Mike trained Jamie for five months, studying the Bible together and preparing to take the gospel to a new generation.

In addition, Jamie sat under the ministry of Tommy Barnett, who powerfully impacted him. The entire experience helped change and deepen

Jamie's spiritual life. He was able to move away from drugs, cigarettes, alcohol, and rebellion. During that time, my boy was transformed into a youth minister who began helping other kids solve their problems by introducing them to Christ. My little boy had become a man—a man of God.

Shortly after Jamie left for Phoenix, Jamie's dog and I moved to the Bennett Farm, a small, secluded farm outside Hendersonville, North Carolina, about forty minutes from Asheville. The farm, with its rolling hills, apple trees, old barn, and wonderful view of the mountains, was a perfect spot for gently easing back into normal society. It was quiet, peaceful, and restorative. The farm was located between a large cattle pasture on one side and a cemetery on the other, so my neighbors were no bother, except for those few times when the cattle got out.

The owners of the farm gave me a credit card from Lowe's, a building-supply company, to purchase items to use in fixing up the place. I threw myself into turning the stark white walls of the house—which reminded me of the blandness of prison—into a warm, cozy home. I painted my bedroom a deep forest green and decorated one of the guest rooms in a deep mauve motif. I called it the Tammy Sue Room. The other bedroom I painted dark navy blue and called it the Jamie Charles Room. I hung family photographs in each room; many of the photos came from the children's childhood bedrooms.

One day as I was working on the house, I realized that I had no bath towels or shower curtain in my guest bathroom. I decided to take some of the money I had earned from working and go shopping. I went to J. C. Penney's department store and found a wallpaper border, a shower curtain, and a set of mauve towels and facial cloths that matched. The woman who checked me out at the counter was extremely kind, but shortly thereafter, another clerk at the store did an interview on the local television station in which she expressed the sentiment that I should not even be allowed to buy towels! I realized then that not everyone was glad that I was out of prison and living in the area.

Most people, however, in the Hendersonville area were extremely kind to me. I often took my grandchildren to the old main-street drug-store, which has an old-fashioned soda fountain and a player piano. My grandsons loved hearing the old songs, many of which I hadn't heard since I was a little boy. We drank cherry-ice-cream sodas and plunked quarters into the old player piano and sang along with the songs. Nobody ever bothered us. On the contrary, most of the people of the town were almost always supportive and friendly. In fact, the day following the woman's protest on TV, as I was going into a Wal-Mart store, an elderly gentleman expressed to me, "I wish they would just leave you alone. You have already gone through enough."

A few days later, something happened that totally overshadowed the J.C. Penney clerk's judgment. I had looked everywhere in Hendersonville to find drapes within my price range that would match my living room. Finding nothing suitable, I decided to drive to the Asheville Montgomery Ward. Slightly nervous about being out of my small-town environment, I made my way to the "big city" store's drapery department, where I found what seemed like hundreds of drapes and curtains from which to choose. As I ambled from one aisle to the next, my eyes fell upon the exact pattern and fabric I was looking for. As I checked the price tag, out of the corner of my eye I saw a rotund black lady looking at me intently from the door-way leading to the stockroom. My heart began to race and I prayed, "Oh, God. Please don't let me have an unpleasant confrontation."

The woman was making a beeline right for me! When she was within an arm's length, she said, "Aren't you Jim Bakker?"

I looked down at the floor and said, "Yes."

She said, "I knew it! I knew it!" She turned her head back toward the stockroom doorway and exclaimed loudly, "I told you it was him!"

At that, an entire lineup of clerks rushed out of the stockroom as the first lady said, "Do you mind if I give you a hug? I have always loved your ministry so much!"

I was in no position to argue. Anyway, I was in need of a hug.

She threw her arms around me and squeezed tightly. One by one, each of the other salesclerks lined up to give me a hug. It was like God was expressing His love toward me through these people in the drapery department of Montgomery Ward.

I got the draperies, hooks, and a whole lot more!

When Tammy Faye and I divorced, we struck an extremely simple set-tlement. Through our lawyers, I told her to take whatever she wanted, and I'd take anything that she didn't want and have it placed in storage. Tammy Faye left behind quite a large amount of household items and pictures, as well as several roomfuls of our old furniture and odds and ends that we had bought over the years. When I first moved to the farm, I spent many of my early days there playing Mr. Fix-It, cleaning, painting, wallpapering, putting up light fixtures, and other things that I could do by myself. Finally, I was ready for the furniture and other items in storage.

To my delight, when everything was unloaded from the U-Haul truck,

I discovered that I had enough furniture to completely furnish the one-story house. It was as though God had provided for me in advance. Coming out of prison, I had nothing with me except my clothes and a few belongings, yet I had three beds in storage, a dining-room table and chairs, some living-room furniture, and perhaps best of all, my desk that Tammy had bought back for me at one of the PTL auctions. I had dishes, a full set of silverware, and some cooking utensils. The only problem was that I had several pans that I'm sure Tammy Faye had the lids for and several lids for which she probably had the pans.

Along with the furniture, I found box after box of old, family photographs. At first it hurt me that Tammy had left behind so many priceless memories of our life, but as I opened one box after another filled with framed photos and other trinkets from our past, I was grateful that Tammy had left them for me. In the boxes, I found photographs from every stage of our life and ministry, dating back to some of our childhood pictures, to the early days at CBN, TBN, and PTL, to pictures with Presidents Carter and Reagan. I found dozens of framed photos of Tammy and me with various celebrities who had graced our *PTL* sets. I also found a huge painting done by a Disney artist, depicting the existing Heritage USA and some of the ideas I had only dreamed about. The artist titled the work "The Dream Never Ends."

I found so many pictures that I decided to turn my living room, dining area, and hallway into a family gallery. Any area on the walls above the chair rail was open game for picture hanging. It took me days to hang all the pictures, but each one was a special memory. Tammy Faye was in many of the pictures along with our children, grandchildren, and me.

When I finished hanging all the photographs, it was as though my whole life was hanging there on the walls. I walked through each part of the house, gazing at the walls and remembering. Then I broke down and sobbed and sobbed and sobbed. Since then, several people have asked me, "Why would you put up pictures that include your former wife?" For me, it was good therapy. By not trying to hide the photos of the woman who had been such an important part of my life for so long, I was refusing to live in denial. I was facing the reality that she was gone. The pictures became part of my healing process.

A further help in my healing was simply doing the outdoor, day-to-day work on the farm that constantly cried out for attention. While I didn't raise livestock or grain or apples that Hendersonville is known for, I nonetheless had large fields to mow, fences to mend, and other usual maintenance matters. It was great therapy for me simply to be out puttering around in my flower and vegetable garden.

When my grandsons came to visit, we decided what the farm really needed was a tree house. We started with only one plank placed across several branches of a large mulberry tree near the farmhouse. When I was growing up, an old mulberry tree at my school produced big, black mulberries and I used to love to pick and eat them. Now, as an adult, I felt that God had given me another mulberry tree to enjoy, this time with my grandsons.

We kept adding boards to make the floor of the tree house. Before long, I was involved in another major building project, along with my two grandsons, ages four and six at the time. I put a window and door in the tree house. I shingled the roof. Soon we added a slide, which created a fun, quick exit from the structure. After that, we added a set of swings. In hardly any time at all, the tree house was almost bigger than the tree in which it was perched. When some of my friends and family members saw the project, they jokingly said, "Yep, that's a Jim Bakker tree house!"

On December 1, 1994, I was officially released from the halfway house. People who don't understand the American legal system and dichotomy between the way sentences are handed out compared to the amount of time served thought that I was getting out early. Not so. I had served the mandatory amount of time normally served by an inmate with an eight-year sentence, under old law. Granted, at any point, had I been a problem prisoner, the system could have kept me in prison and made me serve every day of the sentence I was given. That, however, would have been unusual treatment for an inmate who was not considered to be incorrigible. Under old law, it is extremely rare that someone's sentence and time served are identical. Basically, I was treated normally by the system, no better and no worse.

To be declared free at last meant an enormous amount to me. Practically speaking, however, it did not greatly change my day-to-day routine, other than the fact that I no longer had to pay the halfway house part of my earnings, and I no longer had to report to the Salvation Army. I could live in my own rented home, without having to check in with anyone except my parole officer, Glen Alexander. Technically, my prison sentence does not expire until April 18, 1997. Until that time, I was to be accountable to the parole officer, who checked in on me regularly and often unexpectedly at the farm. At that point in my life, I had few visitors, so I actually enjoyed Mr. Alexander's routine visits.

The parole officer's job required that he know my whereabouts at all times. Before leaving the western part of North Carolina, I had to get Mr. Alexander's permission. Because my case was considered high-profile, not only was I under the supervision of my parole officer, I was also accountable to the parole commission in Washington, D.C. Before engaging in any public speaking opportunities at churches or Christian events, I had to have permission from the government at least three weeks in advance. Two federal officers were assigned to attend all my early speaking engagements. Eventually, the agents stopped coming to hear me preach . . . as far as I knew!

At the Eighteenth Annual Pastors and Leaders Conference to be held at Phoenix First Assembly in early February, Pastor Tommy Barnett asked Jamie to give a testimony of what God had done in his life. Each year, at the pastor's conference, Tommy has what he calls a "Parade of Ministries," in which each of the church's more than 180 ministry groups parades across the platform and presents a brief review of their ministry and key testimonies. Jamie's testimony was to be part of the presentation by the alternative youth ministry, Revolution.

Tommy wrote to me, informing me of the special conference and the Parade of Ministries. He said he hadn't mentioned to Jamie that he was contacting me, but since this was going to be Jamie's first public testimony, the pastor thought I might like to attend. At first, I declined Pastor Barnett's kind invitation. I told him that the media had not ceased to be interested in me since my release from prison, plus I did not want to hurt his church by my being there. I truly felt that enough people hated me that for me to attend the conference would be detrimental to the church.

A few days after I sent my answer, Tommy called me by telephone to personally invite me to attend the service. "We won't tell anybody you are coming," he said. "Not even Jamie. It will be a great surprise, plus that way you won't have to deal with the press. I know Jamie would love for you to be here."

I appreciated his boldness in inviting me. "I don't know, Tommy," I replied, still hesitant.

"Jim, anybody has a right to hear his boy give his first testimony," he urged.

"Do you really think I could do it without causing a bunch of press attention and harm to your church?" I asked.

"I know we can do it," he assured me.

I wanted to see Jamie so I decided to go. Also, I felt it would give me a fresh feeling of freedom to drive across the country. I planned to go by car all the way from Asheville to Phoenix, but my friends Bob and Debby Gass were shocked when they learned that I was going to make the trip by myself.

"You'll have the media on your tail all the way!" Bob protested. Bob and Debby insisted that for my own good, I should fly to Phoenix. They were so concerned they bought an airline ticket for me. In the process of getting the ticket, Bob said to me, "Jim, I don't think it's wise for you to fly out there by yourself. You're too recognizable and too fragile yet to deal with the press and the public on your own. Would you mind if I came along with you?"

"Mind? I'd be delighted if you could go with me."

Bob bought another ticket, and he accompanied me to Phoenix. To assure privacy, Pastor Barnett arranged for us to stay with Craig and Melissa Smith and their two precious daughters, a family from his congregation. The Smith family not only opened their home and hearts to me during the conference, they invited Jamie and me to stay there for two weeks after the conference as well, just to relax, swim in their pool, and have a reunion together.

The night of the Parade of Ministries, I was as nervous as I had ever been at the opening of a new facility at Heritage USA or the launching of a new television program. And I didn't even have to do anything but sit in the audience, as inconspicuously as possible! Jamie was not aware that I was there. For an hour and a half, thousands of people marched, sang, and testified about Jesus. It was overwhelming. The church had ministries to everyone, from children to the aged, from AIDS patients to street people to nursing homes, and on and on. At one point, the "Bikers' Ministry" rode right across the platform on their motorcycles. Many of them reminded me of men with whom I had been incarcerated.

"And now for our last ministry," Tommy Barnett announced. My heart began to beat more rapidly, for I knew that Jamie Charles was about to come out on the platform. The pastor had saved my son's testimony to the very end. When the youth group Revolution was introduced by a wild music video featuring teenage skateboarders, my heart was in my throat. I could hardly breathe. I strained to see my son as the group bounded onto the stage. I almost did not recognize Jamie. His black hair was cut short and dyed blonde, and he had grown back his goatee.

Jamie's best friend and the director of Revolution, Mike Wall, spoke with deep concern and compassion for young people. After that, Pastor Barnett introduced Jamie as Jay Bakker, the name he had been using for some time, partly to establish his own identity, separate and distinct from being known as Jamie Bakker, son of Jim and Tammy Faye Bakker and PTL infamy. Most people in the auditorium and even in the local church and ministry group with which Jamie worked did not know Jamie was my son. Few in the auditorium would have guessed he was once the little boy they had watched growing up on Christian television.

Jamie took a deep breath and began slowly, "I want to tell you why Revolution is important to me. My dad got out of prison a few months ago. . . .

"Jim Bakker," Pastor Barnett whispered in Jamie's ear, encouraging him to tell the audience who his dad was.

"Jim Bakker is my dad. Jim and Tammy Faye Bakker are my parents. . . ."

The crowd erupted in applause and a standing ovation that never seemed to end. Surprised and shaken, Jamie broke down sobbing. Tommy Barnett put his arms around Jamie and comforted him. The crowd continued to applaud. When the people finally sat down, Jamie attempted to continue through his sobs, "You don't know how much that means to me. . . ."

Or me either. The entire crowd of more than seven thousand people continued applauding all around me. One man shouted out, "We love you, Jamie!" I was one of the few people in the room not on my feet. I was slumped forward in my chair, my face in my hands. I simply could not handle this marvelous outpouring of love expressed toward my son, and indirectly toward me. I had thought that people hated my family and me, but these people were applauding at the mention of our name! It was at the same time an overwhelmingly humbling and yet wonderfully relieving experience, just to know that God's people cared that much.

Jamie fought through his tears to give his testimony. "I was living right up until the time my dad got out of prison—well, I was living wrong a little before that—but then when dad was getting out, I figured I better take a summer off and party a little. I had had drug problems before, and I started getting into some stuff that I shouldn't have been. My dad and I began to have some problems."

Jamie continued, "My dad is the greatest person in the world and I love him to death. He said, 'I want you to go to Master's Commission.' That's where I met Mike Wall. God had given me a dream before, and Mike was living that dream and allowed me to be a part of that dream, a place where my generation can fit in, where we're not judged because of the color of our hair or because of an earring.

"I also would like to talk about some things I went through in my past," said Jamie. "When my dad lost Heritage USA and PTL, it hurt me . . . bad. There weren't a lot of people who stood by us, not a lot of ministers, not a lot of preachers. . . . There were a few great people who stood by . . . but it was hard.

"Then two years later, my dad went to prison. He was in prison for four and a half years. That's serious. Then my mom and dad got a divorce." The ache of Jamie's soul caused his face to contort.

"You all know this, I guess it's been in the media and everything, and everybody has been in our business." Jamie paused. "I found out there is a way to make it, people. . . . " The crowd broke into applause once again.

Jamie drew himself up and said, "You might remember a song from my parents. . . . They used to say on their show, 'you can make it.' We used to say that by faith, but now we say it by experience." The crowd erupted again.

Jamie went on to encourage the churches represented at the conference to care for their pastors. "People, there are hurting pastors out there—some of you are here and you don't have churches because your churches have been taken away from you. Church, we have got to start healing people. We've got to stop playing games with each other. It's important. It almost destroyed my life. It put my dad in prison for four and a half years. But the only way to do that is with a personal relationship with Jesus Christ. So if you know of a hurting pastor, show him the love of Jesus Christ. Have a love relationship with Jesus Christ. Thank you."

The crowd broke into another standing ovation that sounded like a crowd cheering at a professional sporting event. Loud whistles filled the air as well as applause, cheers, and praises to God. Standing as part of the audience, I could barely contain my own emotions.

Pastor Barnett brought the room to order and put his arm around Jamie. When the room was quiet, the pastor told Jamie and the congregation about his and my correspondence and my reluctance to come to Phoenix, for fear of being an embarrassment to the church or to Jamie. Tommy Barnett then told the congregation what he had told me, "Any man has a right to hear his son's testimony!"

Then Tommy Barnett announced, "Jim's here tonight!" Jamie's face expressed his surprise and elation. The audience burst into wild applause. "Come on, Jim!" Pastor Barnett encouraged me through the bedlam. "Come on down here and give your boy a hug!"

As I was moving toward the front of the auditorium, I could feel the thousands of eyes on me. I hurried to the platform, but I had only one sight in my focus—my son standing on the platform, tears streaming down his face.

Tommy Barnett was ecstatic. He said to Jamie and the crowd, "You didn't know he was going to be here!" The crowd was still on its feet, cheering louder than any audience I had ever heard. The people kept clapping and clapping!

When I reached the platform, I went straight to Jamie. I wrapped my arms around him and we wept on each other's shoulders while the congregation continued to praise God and cheer. It was truly one of the most moving moments of my entire life.

I couldn't stop weeping. This was my first public appearance since getting out of prison, which would have been emotionally wrenching regardless of the circumstances, but to add Jamie's poignant testimony to it, accompanied by the massive response of the crowd at Phoenix First Assembly that night, it was almost more than I could take.

As the audience continued to applaud, I whispered in Jamie's ear, "I'm scared to death!"

Jamie said in reply, "I am too!"

When I finally let go of Jamie, I went to Mike Wall, who was standing on the platform behind Tommy Barnett. I threw my arms around Mike and said, "Thank you for loving my son."

Again the room erupted in thunderous applause. Next I hugged Pastor Barnett and thanked him, weeping uncontrollably the entire time. The congregation cheered each step. For nearly four minutes, the only visible activity going on in that church was a recently released federal prisoner hugging his boy and some friends, and seven thousand people, including numerous pastors and associate pastors, standing and applauding.

As the noise subsided, a loud voice called out of the crowd, "We love you, Jim!" Someone else shouted, "We love you, Jay!" Others picked up the call and the crowd applauded even more. "Say a few words," Tommy Barnett said, nodding toward the microphone. The audience picked up on the pastor's words. "Say a few words, Jim!"

I honestly did not know what to say. Beyond that, as I looked out into the bright lights and the sea of faces, I was not certain that my mind could form real words into actual sentences, or that my mouth and tongue would cooperate in speaking them aloud. I was as nervous as could be!

At last, with my emotions running rampant, I mustered five of the most meaningful words I have ever spoken: "I'm proud of my boy," I said. Once again the audience responded with applause.

I took a breath, tried to maintain some sort of composure, and started to speak slowly, "This is my first . . . public . . . appearance . . . in six years."

The audience exploded. I looked around and saw some of the bikers, a rough-looking bunch still on stage.

"Boy, am I glad these bikers are up here," I said. "I feel right at home. This is my group!" One of the bikers burst out of the crowd on stage and hugged me, as the crowd went wild again.

I began to share from my heart with the people in that audience. "I have sat with the presidents of the United States of America. I have flown on Air Force One. I have sat with the most famous people in all the world. I built parks for the young people to enjoy. But I want to tell you people something. I want to tell you pastors something. I had to go to prison for this boy to spend the first day with me in his lifetime." I went on to tell the crowd about the day, shortly after Jamie's sixteenth birthday, when he came to prison by himself. "After we had spent the day together, he said, 'Dad, this is the best day of my whole life. I've spent my whole life trying to get your attention. I wanted just to spend one day with you and have you to myself.'" Knowing that there were many busy pastors in the audience, I felt compelled to tell the group, "Preachers, don't go around the world and win the world and lose your own kids." The crowd broke into another long round of applause.

Holding onto Jamie, I told the group, "This boy at four and five—I put his pictures up in prison—he was the cutest little boy that ever walked the face of the earth." Jamie looked embarrassed. The crowd crowed with delight at that image of Jamie. "But I was too busy," I confessed. "I missed it. Somebody sent me a picture of me building Heritage, and there in the background following me was this little boy. All he wanted was his dad."

I finished with: "Tonight . . . I have seen a church with the love of God in action. A church that says, 'We're not going to hurt the hurting anymore. We're going to love them!' Thank you for your love." The room thundered with applause once again. Pastor Barnett stepped quickly to the microphone and asked those who wanted to pray to come to the front of the auditorium. Hundreds did. Many pastors came and poured their hearts out to God. One pastor knelt down beside Jamie and me and told me through his tears, "Jim, it has been a long time since I have spent any time with my boy. I'm not even going to stay for the remainder of the conference. I'm going home right now to spend some time with my son."

It was well past midnight when I finally crawled into bed at Craig and Melissa Smith's home. I was tired and emotionally exhausted, but my heart was rejoicing in what God had done for Jamie . . . and for me.

The next morning, I relaxed and spent some time swimming at our hosts' pool before meeting Jamie at the old bar, located next to the church, which had been converted and now used by Revolution and the Bikers' Ministry as their meeting place. Jamie and Mike Wall were teaching a seminar for pastors and leaders on how to develop a ministry to nonconforming teens. Afterward I took Jamie and his friends out to eat, and Jamie proudly showed me the mobile home where he and the Walls lived out in the desert. He was particularly proud of a skateboarding ramp he and Mike and the teens in their ministry were building. I had planned to stay in Phoenix for about two weeks to enjoy some time with Jamie and to really have some good father-son time.

But then I got the phone call.

Uncle Henry Harrison, my longtime friend and sidekick on our *PTL* television programs, had died of complications caused by muscular dystrophy, and his wife, Aunt Susan, had contacted Tammy Sue to ask for me to come back to Heritage USA to preach the funeral. When Jamie heard the news of Henry's death, he was shocked and saddened. He was awfully disappointed that I would have to return east so soon, but he understood.

I grieved deeply at the loss of my friend Henry. We had worked together in Christian television for years, dating back to the fledgling days of the Christian Broadcasting Network. I had been Henry's best man when he and Susan married twenty-four years earlier. Pat Robertson was the presiding minister who performed the wedding ceremony. On *The Jim and Tammy Show*, the children's program we did at CBN, Henry and Susan Harrison became "Uncle Henry" and "Aunt Susan," who lived on a farm in the country and brought their vegetables and animals to show the children on our sets. Later, when I began hosting *The 700 Club*, Henry became my cohost and the name "Uncle Henry" stuck. When we moved to Charlotte to begin the *PTL Club*, Henry was by my side again. Throughout the years, Henry was right there with me, believing that God could and would do miracles to get His Word out over the airwaves. God often did.

Henry always had a kind, cheerful word, a jolly laugh, and a big hug for everyone he met. He spent his life demonstrating the love of Jesus Christ. As he grew older, he could no longer walk, but he still enjoyed being on the program every day. Sometimes, in the latter years, Uncle Henry fell asleep on the set, right in the middle of a show. Nobody seemed to mind. We had fifteen to twenty people on our sets during those shows, and we just made Uncle Henry comfortable and kept on going. Even when Henry was unable to get around without help, he still did his own ministry-centered program from The Upper Room. Although Henry's body was worn and uncooperative, Henry was a vital part of our ministry as long as I was at Heritage USA.

Henry had come to visit me on the farm in Hendersonville. shortly after my release from prison. He could barely move his body, except for his hands, but he wanted to make the trip anyhow. Despite his declining health, Henry was still so positive, so upbeat. Henry said, as he had so many times before, that he would see Jim Bakker preach again at Heritage USA. What a reunion we had down on the farm.

On January 21, 1995, I attended a party in Fort Mill in honor of Henry's sixty-seventh birthday. It was a festive gathering of close friends held in a restaurant not far from the entrance to Heritage USA, and I was glad I could help my friend celebrate. Once again, Henry reminded me that he would see me preach again at Heritage USA. Two weeks later, Henry went to be with the Lord.

Immediately after learning of Henry's death I placed a call to Aunt Susan. When she came on the line, she sounded very sad, but I could tell her faith in God was still strong. She told me that Henry had been bedridden almost since his birthday party two weeks earlier. He had been having dreams of heaven, that he was running through heaven. On his last day on earth, Aunt Susan related, he awakened and immediately started talking about Jesus. Later that day, Henry sat up in his bed and said, "Praise the Lord!" Then he said, "Jesus is my Rock!" Those were some of the last words he had spoken to Aunt Susan.

"I knew that he had either had a vision or he was going home to be with the Lord," said Aunt Susan. As we talked, Aunt Susan emphatically requested that I speak at Henry's memorial service that was to be held on Sunday. Although I recognized that my presence at Henry's funeral might be awkward, I couldn't refuse Aunt Susan. I told her that I would be there.

As soon as I disconnected with Aunt Susan, I was back on my phone calling Jim Toms. Agreeing to perform Henry's ceremony was difficult enough, but Aunt Susan had said that their plans were to have the service on the grounds of Heritage USA. I wanted Jim to check on whether the new owners would allow me to speak there. I would not have stepped foot on the property without the permission of the Malaysian businessmen who now owned and operated Heritage USA as the Radisson Grand Resort. I needn't have worried. The owners graciously consented to my preaching Henry's memorial service; they kindly offered to open any facilities we needed at no charge. Eventually it was decided that to facilitate the anticipated crowd, the service should be held in The Barn. . . . the place where I had regularly preached to our local congregation and guests on Sunday mornings all through my years at PTL.

Bob and Debby Gass accompanied me to Charlotte, and we arrived at the Radisson Grand Resort—the place I knew as Heritage USA—on Saturday afternoon, February 11. Ironically, at some point after PTL was sold, the new owners had put a facade sign over the old Heritage USA sign at the entrance way. A few days before Henry's memorial service, an automobile had crashed into the base of the structure, dislodging the facade that had been placed over the old Heritage USA sign. The Radisson Grand Resort facade had fallen down and had not yet been replaced. The original sign was showing plain as day. As I drove in, I could not help noticing the name on the sign: *Heritage USA*. I thought of Henry's words that were now sounding more and more prophetic, "I will see Jim Bakker preach at *Heritage USA*."

I checked in at the Heritage Grand Hotel, the place that held such wonderful memories for me, yet had also been the foundation of the case that put me in prison. The management arranged complimentary lodging for me in one of the most beautiful suites in the hotel, the Maude Aimee Humbard Suite, named after the wife of the famous preacher Rex Humbard. I had this suite decorated with special care due to my friendship with the Humbards. It was the only suite in the hotel in which I had installed pure-white carpet, because that suited Maude Aimee's tastes. I was surprised how beautiful the suite still looked. I took off my shoes and walked barefoot on the beautiful white carpet. It felt slightly damp; the management must have just recently cleaned it.

Later that evening, I dined with Mr. Kok Yin Khet, the president of the New Heritage USA. Mr. Khet was so kind, warm, and gracious to me. He took me to a Chinese restaurant, did all the ordering, and personally served the meal to me. I presented my host with a small gift, a copy of a book of poems, the same collection I planned to give to Aunt Susan after using it in the memorial service the next day. During the course of the evening, I thanked Mr. Khet again and again for maintaining Heritage USA so well, and especially for keeping it all together as I believed God had intended rather than selling off parcels of land, which would have been an easy and lucrative thing to do. It was a very pleasant evening for me, but the tension of speaking at Heritage USA the following day was weighing heavily upon me. When Mr. Khet dropped me off at the Heritage Grand, I thanked him sincerely and hastily went to my room, where I continued preparing my message for Henry's memorial service.

The service was held Sunday afternoon, February 12, 1995. I joined Aunt Susan ahead of time and, to avoid a media scene, we waited until most of the people attending the funeral had arrived. Because of the crowd and because so many people wanted to eulogize Uncle Henry, the funeral actually began thirty minutes or so before the scheduled starting time.

Aunt Susan and I arrived, riding in the funeral car to The Barn. No local news cameras or reporters with cameras were permitted inside where the ceremony was to take place, so we anticipated that there might be a group of media people outside. Although we wanted an atmosphere of celebration and praise to permeate the ceremony, we did not want the service to be a media event. This was Henry's day. I didn't want the attention to be diverted to me.

I was particularly concerned with how people in the audience might react to me. This was, after all, my first officially announced return to Heritage USA. Many people's jobs had been lost and lives had been uprooted when I toppled from the pinnacle of PTL. More than a few, especially those who had been among the higher ranks at PTL, could not find jobs in the area after the fall. Ostensibly they were overqualified, but most of those who later told me their stories probably had grounds for winnable job discrimination suits, not being hired simply because they had once been employed at PTL.

Now as I entered The Barn, supporting Aunt Susan on my arm, I tried not to look around too much, not really wanting to know who was there until I faced the full audience, but I could see in my peripheral vision that the building was packed. I walked in and sat down with Aunt Susan on the front row.

Stepping back into that auditorium was an emotional experience for me. I had preached here so many times before. This was the church I had pioneered, the pulpit behind which I had stood so many times before. What amazed me most, perhaps, was that the platform looked almost the same as it had the last time I had preached there in 1986. The stage looked just as I had left it, with royal-blue carpet and a white pulpit set against a deep- red, Austrian-pleated stage curtain. According to those who had seen it, the platform had not looked that way a mere twenty-four hours earlier. When the Inspirational Network had been sold off, the purchaser stripped from the building the state-of-the-art audio and video equipment, worth hundreds of thousands of dollars.

The announcement that Henry's memorial service was to be held in

The Barn drew our former crew members together like a magnet. Even our former ushers gathered to help. They reset the platform and the auditorium seating. The new owners of Heritage USA even had my former dressing room repainted. Lee Mowry and Don Kendrick brought in their own audio equipment and put together a professional sound system on the spot. Our former staff moved in plants and set up columns and all the things that people would have seen had they tuned in to one of our live programs broadcast from The Barn in the mideighties. The former crew members did it without anyone even asking, free of charge. They simply came together to make things right for Uncle Henry. When Tammy Sue walked into that building late Saturday night, she couldn't believe her eyes. As she looked around the huge Barn auditorium, everywhere she turned she saw former team members: Bernie Lempke, Lee Keels, Buddy Kelly, Mike Byrd, Mike Balbi, Jerry Carey, Dean Rhyne, Tom Holmes, and many others.

There was Eric Von Fange up in the rigging in the ceiling, setting the lights. Eric had been with us at PTL since our early days. He and his family had become involved with our ministry while we were still at CBN. He had since grown to be one of the most inventive television lighting designers and directors in the business. Tammy Sue was overwhelmed at seeing all these people with whom she had grown up on the set. It was like stepping back in time. She simply stood there and wept at the sight.

The memorial service itself was a celebration of Uncle Henry's homecoming. The service lasted well over two hours. Although everyone in the room would miss him dearly, we all had perfect confidence that Henry was in heaven with Jesus. Bob and Jeannie Johnson, two of my longtime singers and staff members at PTL, kept things moving. Bob introduced Tammy Sue to sing and without any fanfare—as I had asked him to do—he said simply, "After Tammy Sue sings, her father will bring the message."

The first song Tammy Sue sang was "When Jesus Passes By." I had never heard the song before, but to me, it was the perfect selection. It set the theme for the message I was about to preach. I had not heard my daughter sing in front of a large crowd since she had rededicated her life to Christ and had gone into full-time music ministry. It was also the first time I heard her sing since I had become a free man. Tammy Sue had come to Jesup and had sung for the inmates in the chapel program, but to hear her sing at Henry's funeral was the fulfillment of a dream for me. Many times while in prison, I had dreamed of a day when Tammy Sue might sing on the same program at which I was preaching.

Yet preaching seemed such a remote possibility for me. Feelings of total worthlessness often overwhelmed me. I was out of prison, but I couldn't get prison out of me. I just didn't know what I was supposed to do with the rest of my life. I had plenty of job offers, some of which were quite interesting and challenging, but I didn't sense God directing me to any of them. I thought at times that I should simply go try to find work in the secular world, make enough money to eke out a living, and spend the rest of my life in seclusion on the farm. Yet deep inside, I had a dream of one day preaching again, with Tammy Sue singing. Who could have guessed that it would have been Uncle Henry who pulled us all together?

When Tammy Sue concluded her second song, as planned, there was no introduction of me as the speaker. I stepped up to the pulpit in my home church for the first time in nearly a decade. The auditorium was full and the huge crowd rose to greet me with a thunderous ovation. I was shocked! I had never before seen a standing ovation at a funeral, but then, this was not just any funeral. This was homecoming day, for Henry . . . and for me.

The people wouldn't stop clapping. The applause went on for close to a minute. I felt dizzy from the waves of love that washed over me from the audience. I grabbed the edges of the pulpit to steady myself from swaying backwards. Gradually I felt more confident and stepped away from the pulpit to wave at friends. Dressed in a dark blue, double-breasted suit, I looked relaxed to the unknowing onlookers, but inside, my stomach was churning and I was scared to death. I figured I might as well level with the audience. "I'm scared to death and I'm going to tell you that. . . . This is my first time in the pulpit in many, many, many years."

"We love you, Jim!" someone shouted.

As I looked out into the audience, I saw so many friendly faces. I recognized many longtime Heritage USA residents and PTL Partners and old friends. A. T. Lawing, one of the PTL Board Members, sat near the front of the auditorium. Mr. Lawing had been one of my strongest supporters throughout the ministry of PTL. The last time I had seen him we were in the Charlotte federal courthouse at my trial.

Bill and Jeannie Garthwaite were there too. Bill was one of my first mentors at the Christian Broadcasting Network. Later Bill came to PTL to produce television shows and eventually directed our tape-duplication department.

One face I saw almost reduced me to tears. There was Frances, my angelic, childlike, mentally handicapped friend sitting right where she always sat during almost every service I had preached during my years at

PTL. She couldn't talk, but I could tell by the expression on her face that her heart was overflowing with love.

I looked over to one side and noticed my old friend Jim Moss. Jim had been a vice president at PTL, who managed our affiliate stations and helped put together the cable systems that comprised the foundations of The Inspirational Network. Dale Hill was there too. Dale had stood beside me since he was sixteen years old. I had hired him through his work program at high school, when I was at CBN doing *The Jim and Tammy Show*. Since then Dale had become one of the premier television directors ever to work in the field of Christian television. Eventually, the young man I had hired as a teenager became the vice president of our entire television department.

As I looked at the crowd, it was like looking at a high school yearbook, only the living pictures in front of me represented segments of my whole life. Sitting at the front of the auditorium were my mother and father. I had prayed so many times that my parents would live long enough to see me get out of prison. To have them hear me preach again at Heritage USA was more than I could even imagine! I said to the audience, "All these faces, I can hardly stand it." I told the crowd, "I've got my whole life in front of me."

Every face I saw evoked a memory. Charlie Tudor, one of the cameramen who worked with me on our children's programs twenty-five years earlier at CBN, was there. So was Don Hardister, my former head of security, and Charlotte Whiting along with her son David. Charlotte was a former PTL vice president who was in charge of the Heritage Grand. All across the room, I saw many of my associate pastors, including Russ and Sandy Hosey, who sang for so many of our services and programs; Derek Floyd, one of our *PTL* featured singers; and my beloved Phoebe Conway, the woman who hosted all the *PTL* guests in the backstage "greenroom." Wanda Carter, a member of my executive staff who was now serving Mr. Khet in the same capacity, was also in attendance. My eyes settled upon dear friends Vern and Mary McLellan. Vern had been the former missions director at PTL. Ray and Karen Tripp, faithful workers from our ministry days at Heritage Village, were there as well.

For a moment my heart ached for what once was, but as I continued to look around the room and saw so many friends who were still serving God after surviving all that had happened at PTL, I was reminded afresh of God's promise, "I will never leave you or forsake you." The promise was not for me alone; it was for these people too. The faith of many in this room had been severely tried, and they had come through the refining fire as pure gold. They had not gotten bitter; they had become more loving, more kind, more Christlike. PTL was not a group of buildings; it was the people of God, in whom God was working. They truly were the People That Love, the people who, no matter what, have continued to Praise the Lord.

Slowly, and with deep emotion, I began to read the Twenty-third Psalm: "The LORD is my shepherd; I shall not want. . . . Yea, though I walk through the valley of the shadow of death, I will fear no evil. . . . Thou preparest a table before me in the presence of mine enemies."

I had once thought that God had abandoned me. I thought that my days of ministering for the Lord were done. I thought that I would never preach again.

I was wrong.

Epilogue

ON JULY 22, 1996, SHORTLY AFTER JIM BAKKER HAD COMPLETED the writing of this book, a federal jury ruled that PTL was not selling securities by offering Lifetime Partnerships at Heritage USA. The jury's ruling thus affirms what Jim Bakker has contended from the first day he was indicted and throughout this volume.

The Publishers

Notes

Chapter 1
1. Karen Garloch and Nancy Webb, "A Sign in the Sky? Some People Saw It," *The Charlotte Observer*, Wednesday, 25 October 1989.

Chapter 2
1. *The Saturday Evening Post*, 1 September 1980.

Chapter 4
1. Richard Dortch, *Integrity* (Green Forest, AR: New Leaf Press, 1992), 15, 80-81.
2. Ibid., 87-89. Also Charles E. Shepard, *Forgiven* (New York: Atlantic Monthly Press, 1989), 284-86.
3. Shepard, *Forgiven*, 277, 284.
4. John Stewart, *Holy War* (Enid, OK: Fireside Publishing and Communications, 1987), 75.
5. Ibid.
6. Shepard, *Forgiven*, 306.
7. Dortch, *Integrity*, 139.
8. Stewart, *Holy War*, 75.
9. Dortch, *Integrity*, 139.
10. Ibid.
11. Swaggart's fax is reprinted in its entirety in Dortch, *Integrity*, 140-41 and Shepard, *Forgiven*, 495-96.
12. Dortch, *Integrity*, 142.
13. Ibid.
14. Ibid., 149.

Chapter 5
1. Shepard, *Forgiven*, 500-501.

Chapter 6
1. David Margolick, *The New York Times*, 28 June 1994; B, 15.
2. Dortch, *Integrity*, 155.
3. Ibid., 185, 188.
4. Ibid., 39.
5. Ibid., 159.
6. Ibid., 160.

Chapter 7
1. Jim Bakker files.
2. Shepard, *Forgiven*, 512.

3. Ibid., 514.
4. *Nightline*, ABC-TV, 20 March 1987.
5. Stewart, *Holy War*, 83; *Nightline*, 24 March 1987.
6. Jim Bakker's files. Also, Shepard, *Forgiven*.
7. Shepard, *Forgiven*, 536.
8. Bob Gray, audio transcript, 26 April 1987.
9. Jerry Falwell, news conference, Cocoa Beach, FL, 25 March 1987, broadcast by CNN.
10. Jerry Falwell, news conference, 28 April 1987, broadcast by CNN.
11. Jerry Falwell, news conference, 27 May 1987, broadcast by CNN.
12. Jerry Falwell, news conference, 8 October 1987, broadcast by CNN.

Chapter 8
1. Basil Jackson, *Headline News*, 31 August 1989, CNN.
2. Kevin M. Denny, "Jimmy, Where Were We?" *The Charlotte Observer*, 29 October 1989, B, 1, 4.

Chapter 9
1. Gary L. Wright, Charles E. Shepard, and Elizabeth Leland, "Jim Bakker May Be Back in Court Today," *The Charlotte Observer*, 6 September 1989; A, 1.
2. June Preston, "Bakker Ruled Competent; Trial Resumes," *United Press International*, 6 September 1989.

Chapter 14
1. Mike Murdock, "You Can Make It." Copyright 1979. Win-Way Products, Inc. P.O. Box 99, Dallas, TX 75221. All rights reserved. Used by permission.

Chapter 17
1. Tim Funk, "It's the PTL Movie," *The Charlotte Observer*, 11 March 1990, F, 7.
2. Mike Adkins, "Don't Give Up on the Brink of a Miracle." Copyright 1985. All rights reserved. Used by permission.

Chapter 19
1. June Preston, "One Thing's for Sure—Bakker's Alibi Is Solid," *United Press International*, 10 March 1990.

Chapter 22
1. As quoted in Tim Hansel, *Through the Wilderness of Loneliness* (Elgin, IL: David C. Cook Publishing Co., 1991), 14.
2. Ibid., 17.
3. Hansel, *Loneliness*, 23.
4. Ibid., 26.
5. Ibid., 85.
6. Ibid., 29.
7. Ibid., 141.

8. Ibid., 159.
9. Ibid., 151.
10. Ibid., 159.

Chapter 23
1. Gary L. Wright, "Bidders Lining Up for PTL Retreat, TV Ministry," *The Charlotte Observer*, 15 November 1989.

Chapter 25
1. Jamie Buckingham, "Praying for the Forgotten," *Charisma*, December 1990, 122.
2. *United States of America v. James O. Bakker*, United States Court of Appeals for the Fourth Circuit; Case No. 89-5687; 925 F2nd Series, 740.
3. Ibid.
4. Ibid.

Chapter 28
1. *United States of America v. James O. Bakker*, Court Document: 925 Federal Reporter, 2d Series, 740-41.
2. Linda Marx, "Jim and Tammy Faye Bakker Cry Hallelujah at the Chance His Prison Term Will Be Cut," *People*, 4 March 1991, 41.
3. George James, "Appeals Court Voids Jim Bakker's Jail Term," *New York Times News Service*, 13 February 1991.
4. Stephen Strang, ed., "Followers Elated by Bakker Decision," *Charisma*, April 1991, 26.
5. Ibid.
6. Court Document Number C-CR-88-205, filed March 6, 1991, U.S. District Court W. District of N.C.

Chapter 29
1. Malcolm Smith, *Spiritual Burnout* (Tulsa, OK; Honor Books, Harrison House, 1988), 11.
2. Ibid., 113.
3. Ibid., 141, 143.
4. Ibid., 145.
5. Ibid.
6. Ibid., 169.
7. Ibid., 174.
8. Ibid., 181.

Chapter 31
1. "PTL Materials Used as Textbook," *The Chicago Tribune*, 9 March 1991; D, 4.
2. Ibid.
3. Paul Harvey, "Did Bakker's Victims Have a Choice?" *Delaware County Sunday Times*, 15 October 1989, 24.

4. "PTL Materials Used as Textbook," *The Chicago Tribune*.
5. Ibid.

Chapter 34
1. R.T. Kendall, *God Meant It for Good* (Charlotte, NC: Morningstar Publications, 1988), 152-53.
2. Ibid., 63.
3. Ibid., 83.
4. Ibid., 85.
5. Ibid.
6. Ibid., 86.
7. Ibid., 87.
8. Ibid., 83-87, adapted.
9. Ibid., 192.
10. Ibid.
11. Ibid., 193.
12. Ibid.
13. Ibid., 194.
14. Ibid., 247, 249.
15. Ibid., 250.
16. Ibid.
17. Ibid., 251.
18. Ibid., 251-52.
19. Ibid., 252.

Chapter 35
1. *Lifetime Partners of PTL v. M. Joseph Allman*, Successor Trustee for the Debtor, Heritage Village Church and Missionary Fellowship, Inc. a/k/a PTL, Case No. 87-01956; United States Bankruptcy Court for the District of South Carolina, 6 November 1991, 17-18.
2. "Dortch Gets His Credentials Back," *Associated Press: The Times-News*, Hendersonville, NC; 22 November 1991.

Chapter 40
1. Mike Murdock, "God Is Not Through Blessing You." Copyright 1981. Win-Way Productions, Inc. All rights reserved. Used by permission.

Chapter 43
1. Mario E. Rivera, *Emotional Freedom* (Green Forest, AR: New Leaf Press, 1983), 47.

Chapter 44
1. Dietrich Bonhoeffer, *Life Together* (New York: Harper & Row Publishers, 1954), 26-29.

2. Ibid.

Chapter 45
1. Ken Garfield, "Graham's New Journey: Reflecting on His Part," *The Charlotte Observer*, 16 August 1992.
2. Kendall, *God Meant It for Good*, 86.
3. *United States v. James O. Bakker;* Docket No. 88-CR-00205-01, 6-9. Official court transcripts of Rule 35 Hearing, November 16, 1992; Barbara K. Peterson, Official Court Reporter, U.S. District Court, Charlotte, NC, 6-9.
4. Ibid.
5. Ibid., 52-53.
6. Ibid., 54, 61, 63-64.

Chapter 46
1. Hansel, *Through the Wilderness of Loneliness*, 103.
2. Ibid.

Chapter 47
1. Ben Malcolm's written presentation to the U.S. Parole Commission, Kansas City Regional Office, April 1993.
2. *PTL*, 24 June 1987.
3. *United States v. James O. Bakker;* 925 F2d Federal Reporter, 731.
4. Kendall, *God Meant It for Good*, 86.
5. Cal Thomas, "Let Jim Bakker Go," *Los Angeles Times Syndicate*, 27 July 1993.
6. Notice of Action of Appeal; U.S. Dept. of Justice; U.S. Parole Commission, Chevy Chase, MD 20815, 27 July 1993.
7. Ibid.
8. Ibid.

Chapter 53
1. David Margolick, "Obituaries," *The New York Times*, 28 June 1994, B, 15.

Index